MICROECONOMICS

CANADA IN THE GLOBAL ENVIRONMENT

MICROECONOMICS

CANADA IN THE GLOBAL ENVIRONMENT

SIXTH EDITION

MICHAEL PARKIN ◆ ROBIN BADE

University of Western Ontario

PEARSON

Addison
Wesley

Toronto

Library and Archives Canada Cataloguing in Publication

Parkin, Michael, 1939–
    Microeconomics : Canada in the global environment / Michael Parkin, Robin Bade. — 6th ed.

Includes index.
ISBN 0-321-41843-3

1. Microeconomics—Textbooks. 2. Canada—Economic conditions-1991–
—Textbooks. I. Bade, Robin II. Title.

HB172.P37 2006   338.5   C2005-905355-0

0-321-41843-3

Vice President, Editorial Director: Michael J. Young
Editor in Chief, Business and Economics: Gary Bennett
Director of Marketing, Business and Economics: Bill Todd
Associate Editor: Stephen Broadbent
Production Editor: Jennifer Handel
Copy Editor: Lu Cormier
Proofreader: Edie Franks
Production Coordinator: Deborah Starks
Page Layout: Carolyn E. Sebestyen
Technical Illustrator: Richard Parkin
Indexer: Belle Wong
Permissions and Photo Research: Lisa Brant
Art Director: Julia Hall
Interior and Cover Design: Anthony Leung
Cover Image: Background, Ron Stroud/Masterfile; Centre, Greg Stott/Masterfile

Statistics Canada information is used with the permission of the Minister of Industry, as Minister responsible
for Statistics Canada. Information on the availability of the wide range of data from Statistics Canada can be
obtained from Statistics Canada's Regional Offices, its World Wide Web site at http://www.statcan.ca, and its
toll-free access number 1-800-263-1136. The Statistics Canada CANSIM II database can be accessed at
http://cansim2.statcan.ca/cgi-win/CNSMCGI.EXE.

3 4 5   10 09 08 07

Printed and bound in the United States of America.

PEARSON

Addison
Wesley

The cover depicts a Canadian urban scene viewed through the lens of the Parkin–Bade icon. You can look at this cover in many different ways. Here is what we see.

First, we see a metaphor for what our text, Web site, and other supplements seek to be—a window that gives students a sharply focused view of the world based on a clear and compelling account of timeless principles.

Second, we see a symbol of what economics (and all scientific endeavour) is about. The Parkin–Bade icon is like an economic model. We use models to understand reality. The model is abstract, like the diamond shape and its hole or aperture. The model distorts our view of the world by omitting some details. But it permits us to see the focus of our interest in the brightest and clearest possible light.

To our students

ABOUT THE AUTHORS

Michael Parkin received his training as an economist at the Universities of Leicester and Essex in England. Currently in the Department of Economics at the University of Western Ontario, Professor Parkin has held faculty appointments at Brown University, the University of Manchester, the University of Essex, and Bond University. He is a past president of the Canadian Economics Association and has served on the editorial boards of the *American Economic Review* and the *Journal of Monetary Economics* and as managing editor of the *Canadian Journal of Economics*. Professor Parkin's research on macroeconomics, monetary economics, and international economics has resulted in over 160 publications in journals and edited volumes, including the *American Economic Review*, the *Journal of Political Economy*, the *Review of Economic Studies*, the *Journal of Monetary Economics*, and the *Journal of Money, Credit and Banking*. He became most visible to the public with his work on inflation that discredited the use of wage and price controls. Michael Parkin also spearheaded the movement towards European monetary union.

Robin Bade earned degrees in mathematics and economics at the University of Queensland and her Ph.D. at the Australian National University. She has held faculty appointments in the business schools at the University of Edinburgh and Bond University and in the economics departments at the University of Manitoba, the University of Toronto, and the University of Western Ontario. Her research on international capital flows appears in the *International Economic Review* and the *Economic Record*.

Professor Parkin and Dr. Bade are the joint authors of *Modern Macroeconomics* (Pearson Education Canada), an intermediate text, and *Foundations of Economics* (Pearson Education Canada), and have collaborated on many research and textbook writing projects. They are both experienced and dedicated teachers of introductory economics.

PREFACE

This book presents economics as a serious, lively, and evolving science. Its goal is to open students' eyes to the "economic way of thinking" and to help them gain insights into how the economy works and how it might be made to work better.

We provide a thorough and complete coverage of the subject, using a straightforward, precise, and clear writing style.

We are conscious that many students find economics hard, so we place the student at centre stage and write for the student. We use language that doesn't intimidate and that allows the student to concentrate on the substance.

We open each chapter with a clear statement of learning objectives, a real-world student-friendly vignette to grab attention, and a brief preview. We illustrate principles with examples that are selected to hold the student's interest and to make the subject lively. And we put principles to work by using them to illuminate current real-world problems and issues.

We present some advanced topics, such as game theory, the modern theory of the firm, public choice theory, rational expectations, and new growth theory. But we explain these topics with familiar core ideas and tools.

Today's course springs from today's issues—the information revolution, the Asian economic boom, the Kyoto debate, and the expansion of international trade and investment. But the principles that we use to understand these issues remain the core principles of our science.

Governments and international agencies place renewed emphasis on long-term fundamentals as they seek to sustain economic growth. This book reflects this emphasis.

To help promote a rich, active learning experience, we have developed MyEconLab, a comprehensive online learning environment that features tests, personalized study plans, a dynamic eText, interactive tutorials, frequent news updates, and more.

The Sixth Edition Revision

ECONOMICS, SIXTH EDITION, RETAINS ALL OF the improvements achieved in its predecessor with its thorough and detailed presentation of modern economics, emphasis on real-world examples and critical thinking skills, diagrams renowned for pedagogy and precision, and path-breaking technology.

We organize our description of what is new in the sixth edition in four sections:

- Refocused and revised introductory chapters
- Revised and updated microeconomics content
- Revised and updated macroeconomics content
- MyEconLab

Refocused and Revised Introductory Chapters

1. We have refocused Chapter 1 to place greater emphasis on the role of incentives in influencing people's choices and on the question: Can choices made in the pursuit of self-interest also serve the social interest? This central question of economics is introduced through eight pressing issues in today's world that are explored further at various later points in the text. They are central planning versus the market, globalization, the new economy, the post 9/11 economy, corporate scandals, HIV/AIDS, disappearing tropical rainforests, and water shortages.

   These issues grab the student's attention and provide an early signal that economics is not a narrow business oriented subject but one that addresses issues of major social concern.

2. We have heavily revised our explanation of the gains from trade (Chapter 2), which we now begin with a numerical example and follow with a graphical analysis. The example has absolute advantage built into it so that the role of comparative advantage is demonstrated more vividly.

Revised and Updated Microeconomics Content

In addition to thorough and extensive updating, the microeconomics chapters feature the following eight revisions, some of them major:

1. Efficiency and Equity (Chapter 5) has been extensively revised. We have deleted the short refresher on efficiency and now refer the reader back to Chapter 2, where this topic is introduced and explained.

   We have added a new section that describes the eight alternative methods that might be used to allocate scarce resources: market price, command, majority rule, contest, first-come-first-served, lottery, personal characteristics, and force. By laying out these alternatives, we are better able to evaluate the ability of the market to achieve an efficient outcome. We return to these alternatives later in the chapter and ask whether there are situations in which one of them might improve on the market allocation.

   The sections that show the equivalence of demand and marginal social benefit and supply and marginal social cost have been rewritten to place the emphasis on moving from the individual to society. Consequently, we now derive the market demand and supply curves in this chapter. We also explain the connections between individual and economy-wide consumer surplus and producer surplus.

   We have rewritten the case study on a water shortage in a natural disaster to review the fairness and efficiency of the market compared with its alternatives.

2. Markets in Action (Chapter 6) has an expanded discussion of the inequity of rent ceilings, which also examines the equity implications of the alternative allocation methods. We have added an explicit graphical analysis of the inefficiency of the minimum wage and added brief discussion of living wage laws. A new section explicitly (and graphically) analyzes taxes levied on the seller and the buyer to demonstrate their equivalence.

3. Utility and Demand (Chapter 7) now opens with an explanation of how a change in income or prices changes the budget line (similar to what is done in the parallel indifference curve chapter, Chapter 8, but less technically and without equations. The section on individual demand and market demand has been removed from this chapter because it is now covered in Chapter 5—see above).

4. A new appendix to Chapter 8 explains the connection between marginal utility theory and indifference

curve theory for those wishing to teach both approaches to consumer theory.

5. Perfect Competition (Chapter 11) has a new explanation of the efficiency of perfect competition illustrated graphically with a figure of both the market and the individual firm in long-run equilibrium.

6. Monopolistic Competition and Oligopoly (Chapter 13) has an expanded discussion of short-run loss (as well as profit) and exit (as well as entry). It also has an expanded comparison of monopolistic competition and perfect competition covering both the markup over marginal cost and the excess capacity result. We have expanded the discussions of the efficiency of monopolistic competition and advertising. We also explain advertising as a signal and the role of brand names.

   A new introduction to oligopoly explains the cost and demand conditions in which it arises and gives some examples. The game theory section now includes an R&D game of chicken, which we contrast with the prisoners' dilemma.

7. Competition Policy (Chapter 14) includes new material on price cap regulation, which shows that a price cap with monopoly can lower the price and increase output.

8. Public Goods and Common Resources (Chapter 16) has a new introduction on classifying goods and resources and identifies common resources—rival and nonexcludable resources. It also notes that nonrival and excludable goods and services are produced by natural monopoly. The chapter now explores the tragedy of the commons (along with the free-rider problem). We have removed the section on taxes from this chapter and now cover them only in Chapter 6.

Revised and Updated Macroeconomics Content

In addition to thorough and extensive updating, the macroeconomics chapters feature the following eight major revisions:

1. A First Look at Macroeconomics (Chapter 19) has new material on the Lucas wedge and Okun gap—the wedge created by growth slowdown and the gap created by recession. This description serves to emphasize the vital importance of economic growth and the ability of small changes to make a big difference.

2. Fiscal Policy (Chapter 24) has been revised to explain the government expenditures multiplier and autonomous tax/transfer payments multiplier more generally in terms of the slope of the aggregate expenditure curve rather than the marginal propensity to consume. We have also improved our explanation of the role of induced taxes and transfer payments in affecting the multipliers and of the distinction between cyclical and structural budget balance.

3. Money, Banking, and Interest Rates (Chapter 25) is now the first of three chapters that pave the way towards an explanation of how the Bank of Canada conducts its monetary policy. The section on the banking system is broader than in the previous editions. As before, it describes the functions of the depository institutions. But it now also provides a brief description of the role played in the banking system by the Bank of Canada. It describes and explains of the functions of the Large Value Transfer System (LVTS) and the Automated Clearing Settlement System (ACCS), which lay an institutional foundation for a later (new) description and analysis of the Bank of Canada's monetary policy.

   Substantially rewritten material on how banks create money now unifies two sections of the fifth edition to explain the money multiplier. (The separate deposits multiplier is gone.)

4. The Exchange Rate (Chapter 26) is now placed before the discussion of monetary policy. This placement serves to emphasize the role of a flexible exchange rate as a foundation for the conduct of monetary policy. The chapter has a new section on exchange rate policy that reviews the four options: flexible, fixed, crawling peg, and currency union, and explains that only a flexible exchange rate leaves monetary policy free to pursue domestic goals.

5. Monetary Policy (Chapter 28) is the most heavily revised chapter in the new edition. It begins with a new discussion of the Bank of Canada's monetary policy objective, its achievement, and its rationale. A new description and analysis of the conduct of monetary policy explains how the overnight rate target is set and how it is achieved using the operating band between

bank rate and the settlements balances rate and open market operations. This section includes an explanation of the crucial distinction between an instrument rule and a targeting rule for the conduct of monetary policy. We have written a new explanation of the monetary policy transmission mechanism (building on that of the fifth edition but in the context of the Bank's current operating procedures) that includes the explanation of the interest-sensitive expenditure curve from the fifth edition Chapter 25. We also provide a new discussion of alternative approaches to monetary policy including Taylor and McCallum rules, exchange rate targeting, and money stock targeting and we explain why a rule for monetary policy is necessary.

6. Fiscal and Monetary Interactions (Chapter 29) has a new section on "Policy Coordination, Conflict, and Risk" that explains the risks of using an interest rate instrument if the response of the interest rate is too little or too slow and the difficulty of determining the appropriate level for the interest rate when fiscal policy changes.

7. The fifth edition chapters on the Business Cycle, Policy Challenges, and the Stock Market have been removed. (Web-based versions of these chapters are available for those who want to cover them).

8. Trading with the World (Chapter 32) now has a section on the balance of payments (from Chapter 34 in the previous edition).

MyEconLab

MyEconLab is a turnkey, online solution for your economics course. Featuring a new and powerful graphing engine and testing bank, students are able to self-test and generate a study plan, and instructors are able to assign homework and capture grades. With a tight, everything-in-one-place organization around the new testing tool, questions include true and false, fill-in-the-blank, multiple-choice, numerical, and complete-the-graph. Because questions are generated algorithmically, there are about 40,000 questions per chapter!

Users of our previous Web site will find MyEconLab an exciting and powerful resource. Practice Tests for each section of the textbook enable students to test their ability and identify the areas in which they need further work. Based on a student's performance on a practice test, a personalized study plan shows where further study needs to focus. Once students have received their study plan, additional practice exercises, keyed to the textbook, provide extensive practice and link directly to the eText, with animated graphs and other resources.

Users of MyEconLab will revel in the powerful graphing tool integrated into both the practice tests and practice exercises. This tool enables students to manipulate graphs and see how the concepts, numbers, and graphs are connected. A new, powerful feature is that questions using the graphing tool (like all other questions) can be submitted and graded.

For review and self-assessment, MyEconLab provides tutorials launched directly from the practice exercises. Using the tutorial instruction, students can see a demonstration of step-by-step solutions to practice problems, or they can participate in guided, step-by-step tutorials that promote self-discovery.

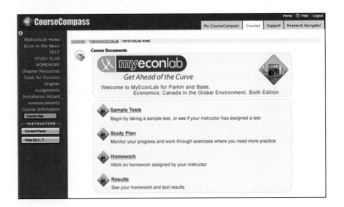

Features to Enhance Teaching and Learning

HERE, WE DESCRIBE THE CHAPTER FEATURES THAT are designed to enhance the learning process. Each chapter contains the following learning aids.

Chapter Opener

Each chapter opens with a one-page student-friendly, attention-grabbing vignette. The vignette raises questions that both motivate the student and focus the chapter. The sixth edition carries this story into the main body of the chapter, and relates it to the chapter-ending *Reading Between the Lines* feature.

Chapter Objectives

A list of learning objectives enables students to see exactly where the chapter is going and to set their goals before they begin the chapter. We link the objectives directly to the chapter's major headings.

> After studying this chapter,
> you will be able to
> - Describe a competitive market and think about a price as an opportunity cost
> - Explain the influences on demand
> - Explain the influences on supply
> - Explain how demand and supply determine prices and quantities bought and sold
> - Use demand and supply to make predictions about changes in prices and quantities

In-Text Review Quizzes

A review quiz at the end of most major sections enables students to determine whether a topic needs further study before moving on. The review quiz includes the corresponding Study Plan in MyEconLab.

> ### REVIEW QUIZ
>
> 1 What is the distinction between a money price and a relative price?
> 2 Why is a relative price an opportunity cost?
> 3 Can you think of an example of a good whose money price and relative price have risen?
> 4 Can you think of an example of a good whose money price and relative price have fallen?
>
> **Study Plan 3.1**

Key Terms

Highlighted terms within the text simplify the student's task of learning the vocabulary of economics. Each highlighted term appears in an end-of-chapter list and an end-of-book glossary with page numbers, boldfaced in the index, and on Flashcards on MyEconLab.

ffee by the price of a pack of gum and find
of one price to the other. The ratio of one
nother is called a **relative price**, and a *relative opportunity co*

> KEY TERMS
>
> Change in demand, 62
> Change in supply, 67
> demanded, 65

Above full-employment equilibrium A macroeconomic equilibrium in which real GDP exceeds potential GDP. (p. 519)

Absolute advantage A person has an absolute advantage if that person is more productive than another person. (p. 42)

Diagrams That Show the Action

This book has set new standards of clarity in its diagrams. Our goal has always been to show "where the economic action is." The diagrams in this book continue to generate an enormously positive response, which confirms our view that graphical analysis is the most powerful tool available for teaching and learning economics. But many students find graphs hard to work with. For this reason, we have developed the entire art program with the study and review needs of the student in mind. The diagrams feature

- Shifted curves, equilibrium points, and other important features highlighted in red
- Colour-blended arrows to suggest movement
- Graphs paired with data tables
- Diagrams labelled with boxed notes
- Extended captions that make each diagram and its caption a self-contained object for study and review

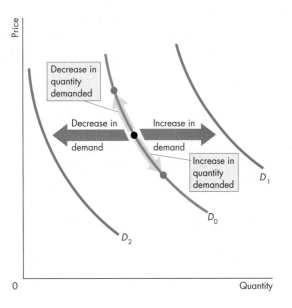

Reading Between the Lines

Each chapter ends with an economic analysis of a significant news article from the popular press together with a thorough economic analysis of the issues raised in the article. The sixth edition features 22 new *Reading Between the Lines* articles and analysis along with 8 classics from the fifth edition that remain relevant today. We chose each article because it sheds additional light on the questions first raised in the chapter opener.

Special "You're the Voter" sections in selected chapters invite students to analyze typical campaign topics and to probe their own stances on key public policy issues. Critical thinking questions about the article appear with the end-of-chapter questions and problems.

End-of-Chapter Study Material

Each chapter closes with a concise summary organized by major topics, lists of key figures, tables, and terms (all with page references), problems, critical thinking questions, and Web exercises. The problems are arranged in parallel pairs with solutions to the odd-numbered problems provided in MyEconLab.

Each problem also appears on MyEconLab, where it can be worked online in the chapter Test and Study Plan. We also provide the links needed for the Web exercises in MyEconLab.

SUMMARY

KEY POINTS

Production Possibilities and Opportunity Cost (pp. 34–36)

- The production possibilities frontier, *PPF*, is the boundary between production levels that are attainable and those that are not attainable when all the available resources are used to their limit.
- Production efficiency occurs at points on the *PPF*.
- Along the *PPF*, the opportunity cost of producing more of one good is the amount of the other good that must be given up.
- The opportunity cost of a good increases as production of the good increases.

Using Resources Efficiently (pp. 37–39)

- The marginal cost of a good is the opportunity cost of producing one more unit.
- The marginal benefit from a good is the maximum amount of another good that a person is willing to forgo to obtain more of the first good.
- The marginal benefit of a good decreases as the amount of the good available increases.
- Resources are used efficiently when the marginal cost of each good is equal to its marginal benefit.

Economic Growth (pp. 40–41)

- Economic growth, which is the expansion of production possibilities, results from capital accumulation and technological change.
- The opportunity cost of economic growth is forgone current consumption.

Gains from Trade (pp. 42–45)

- A person has a comparative advantage in producing a good if that person can produce the good at a lower opportunity cost than everyone else.
- People gain by specializing in the activity in which they have a comparative advantage and trading with others.
- Dynamic comparative advantage arises from learning-by-doing.

Economic Coordination (pp. 45–47)

- Firms coordinate a large amount of economic activity, but there is a limit to the efficient size of a firm.
- Markets coordinate the economic choices of people and firms.
- Markets can work efficiently only when property rights exist.
- Money makes trading in markets more efficient.

KEY FIGURES

Figure 2.1	Production Possibilities Frontier,	34
Figure 2.4	Efficient Use of Resources,	39
Figure 2.7	The Gains from Trade,	44
Figure 2.8	Circular Flows in the Market Economy,	47

KEY TERMS

Absolute advantage, 42
Allocative efficiency, 39
Capital accumulation, 40
Comparative advantage, 42
Dynamic comparative advantage, 45
Economic growth, 40
Firm, 45
Learning-by-doing, 45
Marginal benefit, 38
Marginal benefit curve, 38
Marginal cost, 37
Market, 46
Money, 46
Preferences, 45
Production efficiency, 35
Production possibilities frontier, 34
Property rights, 46
Technological change, 40

PROBLEMS

Go to **myeconlab** for solutions to odd-numbered problems and additional exercises.

1. Calculate Wendell's opportunity cost of one hour of tennis when he increases the time he plays tennis from
   a. 6 hours a week.
   b. 8 hours a week.

2. Calculate Tina's opportunity cost of a day of skiing when she increases her time spent skiing from
   a. 2 to 4 days a month.
   b. 4 to 6 days a month.

3. Wendell, in problem 1, has the following marginal benefit curve:

   a. If Wendell is efficient, what is his grade?
   b. Why would Wendell be worse off getting a higher grade?

4. Tina in problem 2, has the following marginal benefit curve:

   a. If Tina is efficient, how much does she ski?
   b. Why would Tina be worse off spending more days a month skiing?

5. Sunland's production possibilities are

Food (kilograms per month)		Sunscreen (litres per month)
300	and	0
200	and	50
100	and	100
0	and	150

   a. Draw a graph of Sunland's *PPF*

---

   b. What are Sunland's opportunity costs of producing food and sunscreen at each output?
6. Jane's Island's production possibilities are

Corn (kilograms per month)		Cloth (metres per month)
6	and	0
4	and	2
2	and	4
0	and	6

   a. Draw a graph of the *PPF* on Jane's Island.
   b. What are Jane's opportunity costs of producing corn and cloth at each output in the table?
7. In problem 5, to get a litre of sunscreen the people of Sunland are willing to give up 5 kilograms of food if they have 25 litres of sunscreen, 2 kilograms of food if they have 75 litres of sunscreen, and 1 kilogram of food if they have 125 litres of sunscreen.
   a. Draw a graph of Sunland's marginal benefit from sunscreen.
   b. What is the efficient quantity of sunscreen?
8. In problem 6, to get a metre of cloth Jane is willing to give up 1.5 kilograms of corn if she has 2 metres of cloth; 1.0 kilogram of corn if she has 4 metres of cloth; and 0.5 kilograms of corn if she has 6 metres of cloth.
   a. Draw a graph of Jane's marginal benefit from cloth.
   b. What is Jane's efficient quantity of cloth?
9. Busyland's production possibilities are

Food (kilograms per month)		Sunscreen (litres per month)
150	and	0
100	and	100
50	and	200
0	and	300

Calculate Busyland's opportunity costs of food and sunscreen at each output in the table.
10. Joe Island's production possibilities are

Corn (kilograms per month)		Cloth (metres per month)
12	and	0
8	and	1
4	and	2
0	and	3

What are Joe's opportunity costs of producing corn and cloth at each output in the table?

11. In problems 5 and 9, Sunland and Busyland each produce and consume 100 kilograms of food and 100 litres of sunscreen per month, and they do not trade. Now the countries begin to trade with each other.
    a. What good does Sunland sell to Busyland and what good does it buy from Busyland?
    b. If Sunland and Busyland divide the total output of food and sunscreen equally, what are the gains from trade?
12. In problems 6 and 10, Jane's Island and Joe's Island each produce and consume 4 kilograms of corn and 2 metres of cloth and they do not trade. Now the islands begin to trade.
    a. What good does Jane sell to Joe and what good does Jane buy from Joe?
    b. If Jane and Joe divide the total output of corn and cloth equally, what are the gains from trade?

CRITICAL THINKING

1. After you have studied *Reading Between the Lines* on pp. 48–49, answer the following questions:
   a. At what point on the blue *PPF* in Fig. 1 on p. 49 is the combination of education goods and services and consumption goods and services efficient? Explain your answer.
   b. Students are facing rising tuition. How does higher tuition change the opportunity cost of education and how does it change the *PPF*s in Fig. 1 and Fig. 2?
   c. Who receives the benefits from education? Is the marginal cost of education equal to the marginal benefit of education? Is resource use in the market for education efficient?

WEB EXERCISES

Use the links on **myeconlab** to work the following exercise.

1. Obtain data on the tuition and other costs of enrolling in the MBA program at a school that interests you.
   a. Draw a *PPF* that shows the tradeoff that you would face if you decided to enroll in the MBA program.
   b. Do you think the marginal benefit of an MBA exceeds the marginal cost?

For the Instructor

THIS BOOK ENABLES YOU TO ACHIEVE THREE objectives in your principles course:

- Focus on the economic way of thinking
- Explain the issues and problems of our time
- Choose your own course structure

Focus on the Economic Way of Thinking

You know how hard it is to encourage a student to think like an economist. But that is your goal. Consistent with this goal, the text focuses on and repeatedly uses the central ideas: choice; tradeoff; opportunity cost; the margin; incentives; the gains from voluntary exchange; the forces of demand, supply, and equilibrium; the pursuit of economic rent; and the effects of government actions on the economy.

Explain the Issues and Problems of Our Time

Students must use the central ideas and tools if they are to begin to *understand* them. There is no better way to motivate students than by using the tools of economics to explain the issues that confront today's world. Issues such as central planning versus the market; globalization and the emergence of China as a major economic force; the new economy with new near monopolies such as eBay and the widening income gap between rich and poor; the post-9/11 economy and the reallocation of resources towards counterterrorism and the defence that it entails; corporate scandals and the principal-agent problems and incentives faced by corporate managers; HIV/AIDS and the enormous cost of drugs for treating it; the disappearing tropical rainforests and the challenge that this tragedy of the commons creates; the challenge of managing the world's water resources.

Choose Your Own Course Structure

You want to teach your own course. We have organized this book to enable you to do so. We demonstrate the book's flexibility in the flexibility chart and alternative sequences table that appear on pp. xxii–xxiii. You can use this book to teach a traditional course that blends theory and policy or a current policy issues course. Your micro course can emphasize theory or policy. You can structure your macro course to emphasize long-term growth and supply-side fundamentals. Or you can follow a traditional macro sequence and emphasize short-term fluctuations. The choices are yours.

Instructor's Manual

The Instructor's Manual, written by Torben Drewes of Trent University, integrates the teaching and learning package and is a guide to all the supplements. Each chapter contains a chapter outline, what's new in the sixth edition, teaching suggestions, a look at where we have been and where we are going, descriptions of the electronic supplements, and additional discussion questions. The chapter outline and teaching suggestions sections are keyed to the PowerPoint lecture notes. Solutions to end-of-chapter problems are provided in a separate section.

New Lecture Notes This edition of the Instructor's Manual offers two new exciting features. Extensive lecture notes that incorporate alternative teaching examples— "Points of Interest"—enable a new user of Parkin and Bade to walk into the classroom well armed with engaging stories and explanations and a seasoned user to access a whole new set of fresh examples.

New Worksheets Another new and innovative feature is a set of worksheets. These Worksheets ask the student to contemplate real-world problems that illustrate economic principles. Examples include showing the effect of the catastropic events of 9/11 using a marginal cost/marginal benefit diagram and calculating the effects of funding social security for the huge number of baby-boomer retirees. Instructors can assign these as in-class group projects or as homework. There is a Worksheet for every chapter.

Two Test Banks

To provide lots of choice when preparing tests and exams, we offer two Test Banks in TestGen with a total of more than 8,700 questions. Test Bank 1, prepared by Morteza Haghiri of Mount Allison University and Wilson Wong of Champlain College, contains over 4,500 multiple-choice questions. Test Bank 2, prepared by Sigrid Ewender of Kwantlen University College and Ariel Lade of the University of Victoria, contains about 4,200 multiple-choice, true-false, and short-answer questions. Both testbanks are thoroughly revised, upgraded, and improved.

Personal Response System Questions

Gauge your students' course progress with clicker questions that enable instructors to pose questions, record results, and display those results instantly in the classroom. Questions are provided in PowerPoint® format.

Image Library

Nearly all of the tables and figures from the text are available for viewing in the Image Library included on the Instructor's Resource CD-ROM.

PowerPoint® Resources

We have developed a full-colour Microsoft PowerPoint Lecture Presentation for each chapter that includes all the figures from the text, animated graphs, and speaking notes. The slide outlines are based on the chapter outlines in the Instructor's Manual, and the speaking notes are based on the Instructor's Manual teaching suggestions. The presentations can be used electronically in the classroom or can be printed to create hard-copy transparency masters, and they can be accessed using Windows or Macintosh. We have also prepared a set of PowerPoint lecture notes for students. Students can download these from MyEconLab, print them, and bring them to class. The instructor's set contains the option to present full-screen-size graphs.

Instructor's Resource CD-ROM with Computerized Test Banks

This CD contains Computerized Test Bank files, Personal Response System questions, Instructor's Manual files in Microsoft Word, PowerPoint files, and an Image Library. Our two test banks are available in Test Generator Software (TestGen-EQ with QuizMaster-EQ). Fully networkable, they are available for Windows and Macintosh. TestGen-EQ's new graphical interface enables instructors to view, edit, and add questions; transfer questions to tests; and print different forms of tests. Tests can be formatted with varying fonts and styles, margins, and headers and footers, as in any word-processing document. Search and sort features let the instructor quickly locate questions and arrange them in a preferred order. QuizMaster-EQ, working with your school's computer network, automatically grades the exams, stores the results on disk, and allows the instructor to view or print a variety of reports.

Course Management Systems

We offer three alternative course management systems—CourseCompass, Blackboard, and WebCT. Each system provides a dynamic, interactive, content-rich, and flexible online course management tool that enables instructors to easily and effectively customize online course materials to suit their needs. Instructors can track and analyze student performance on an array of Internet activities. Please contact your Pearson Education Canada representative for more details.

MyEconLab

The Web site that accompanies *Economics*, Sixth Edition, breaks new ground by providing a structured environment in which students can practice what they learn and test their understanding and then pursue a study plan that is generated from their performance on practice tests. Every new copy of Parkin/Bade, *Economics: Canada in the Global Environment*, Sixth Edition, comes with a student code to access the power of MyEconLab.

MyEconLab provides rich content resources keyed to the eText as well as flexible tools that enable instructors to easily and effectively customize online course materials to suit their needs.

Instructors can create and assign tests, quizzes, or graded homework assignments that incorporate graphing questions and online versions of the end-of-chapter problems in the textbook. MyEconLab saves instructors time by automatically grading all questions and tracking results in an online grade book. Now available from within MyEconLab is the added testing capability of over 4,000 multiple-choice questions derived from the sixth edition of the Parkin/Bade Test Bank 1.

Once registered for MyEconLab, instructors have access to downloadable supplements such as Instructor's Manuals, PowerPoint lecture notes, and Test Banks. Instructors also have access to a "Consult the Author" feature that allows them to ask questions of and make suggestions to the author via e-mail and receive a response within 24 hours.

For more information about MyEconLab, or to request an Instructor Access Code, visit **http://www.myeconlab.com.**

For the Student

Study Guide

The sixth edition Study Guide by Avi Cohen of York University and Harvey King of the University of Regina is carefully coordinated with the main text. Each chapter of the Study Guide contains

- Key concepts
- Helpful hints
- True-false questions that ask students to explain their answers
- Multiple-choice questions
- Short-answer questions

Each part allows students to test their cumulative understanding with questions that go across chapters and work a sample midterm examination.

MyEconLab

MyEconLab—the online homework and tutorial system that is packaged with every new copy of *Economics*—puts students in control of their own learning through a suite of study and practice tools correlated with the online, interactive version of the textbook and other media tools. Every new copy of Parkin/Bade, *Economics: Canada in the Global Environment*, Sixth Edition, comes with a student code to access the power of MyEconLab.

Within MyEconLab's structured environment, students practice what they learn, test their understanding, and then pursue a Study Plan that MyEconLab generates for them based on their performance on practice tests.

At the core of MyEconLab are the following features:

- **Practice Tests**—Practice tests for every chapter section enable students to test their understanding and identify the areas in which they need to do further work. Practice Test questions based directly on the review quizzes and end-of-chapter problems ask students to work with graphs: interpreting them, manipulating them, and even drawing them. Instructors can let students use the supplied pre-built tests or create their own tests.
- **Personalized Study Plan**—Based on a student's performance on a practice test, MyEconLab generates a Personalized Study Plan that shows where further study is needed. The correlation between the text and MyEconLab is perfect and seamless.

- **Additional Practice Exercises**—The Personalized Study Plans direct students to additional exercises for each topic. Additional practice exercises are keyed to each section of the textbook and link students to the eText with animated graphs.

- **Tutorial Instruction**—Launched from the additional practice exercises, tutorial instruction is provided in the form of solutions to problems, step-by-step explanations, and other media-based explanations.

- **Powerful Graphing Tool**—Integrated into the practice tests and additional practice exercises, the graphing tool lets students manipulate and even draw graphs so that they grasp how the concepts, numbers, and graphs are connected.

- Three types of graphing problems:

1. Draw Graphs—MyEconLab's Draw Graph problems automatically grade the graphs students draw.

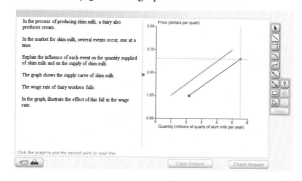

2. Model-based Graphs—Students can change data inputs and watch curves shift. Multiple-choice, true-false, and short-answer questions quiz students on their interpretations of the graph.

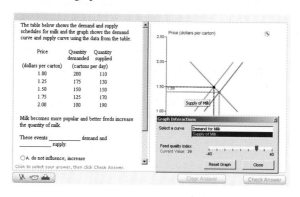

3. Data Graphs—Students can plot up to five variables against each other to give a clear picture of how economic indicators relate to each other.

MyEconLab Study Plan links to the following resources:

- **eText**—Quick reference to specific pages of the textbook that correspond to each Study Plan exercise.

- **Animated Figures**—Step-by-step animations of every figure from the textbook with audio explanations of the action.

- **Glossary**—A searchable version of the textbook glossary with additional examples and links to related terms.

Additional MyEconLab Resources

- **Ask the Authors**—Virtual office hours with Robin Bade and Michael Parkin.

- **Glossary Flashcards**—Every key term available as a flashcard, allowing students to quiz themselves on vocabulary from one or more chapters at a time.

- **Economics in the News**—Updated every week during the school year, news items with links to sources for further reading and discussion questions.

- **Links for Web Exercises**—All the links needed for answering the Web Exercises in the textbook—checked and updated regularly so that they don't disappear.

PowerPoints Lecture Notes

We have prepared a full set of PowerPoint lecture notes for students. These notes contain an outline of each chapter with the textbook figures animated. Students can downloaded these lecture notes from MyEconLab, print them, and bring them to class or use them in creating their own set of notes for use when preparing for tests and exams.

Acknowledgments

WE THANK OUR CURRENT AND FORMER COLLEAGUES AND friends at the University of Western Ontario who have taught us so much. They are Jim Davies, Jeremy Greenwood, Ig Horstmann, Peter Howitt, Greg Huffman, David Laidler, Phil Reny, Chris Robinson, John Whalley, and Ron Wonnacott. We also thank Doug McTaggart and Christopher Findlay, co-authors of the Australian edition, and Melanie Powell and Kent Matthews, co-authors of the European edition. Suggestions arising from their adaptations of earlier editions have been helpful to us in preparing this edition.

We thank the several thousand students whom we have been privileged to teach. The instant response that comes from the look of puzzlement or enlightenment has taught us how to teach economics.

It is an especial joy to thank the many outstanding managers, editors, and others at Pearson Education Canada who have contributed to the concerted publishing effort that brought this edition to completion. Allan Reynolds, President and CEO, and Steve O'Hern, President of Higher Education, have once again provided outstanding corporate direction. They have worked hard to build a corporate culture that brings the best out of its editors and authors. Michael Young, Vice President and Editorial Director for Higher Education, has been a devoted contributor through his appointment and management of the outstanding editors with whom we've worked. Gary Bennett, now Editor in Chief of Business and Economics, has played a major role in bringing this revision to completion and in finding and managing a team of outstanding supplements authors. Stephen Broadbent brought his experience and dedicated professionalism to the development effort. Matthew Christian and Laura Canning built MyEconLab. Bill Todd, Marketing Manager, provided inspired marketing direction. His brochures and, more important, his thoughtful questions and prodding for material had a significant impact on the shape of the text. Anthony Leung, Designer, designed the cover, text,

and package and surpassed the challenge of ensuring that we meet the highest design standards. Jennifer Handel, our Production Editor, worked miracles on a tight production schedule and coped calmly with late-changing content. Lu Cormier copyedited the text manuscript and Edie Franks proofread the final pages. We thank all of these wonderful people. It has been inspiring to work with them and to share in creating what we believe is a truly outstanding educational tool.

We thank our supplements authors, Avi Cohen, Harvey King, Torben Drewes, Sigrid Ewender, Morteza Haghiri, Ariel Lade, and Wilson Wong. And we thank Kit Pasula for the extraordinarily careful accuracy review of near-final pages. Kit caught many slips and even some errors of substance that we are relieved to have had the opportunity of correcting.

We thank the people who work directly with us. Jeannie Gillmore provided outstanding research assistance on many topics, including the *Reading Between the Lines* news articles and worked long and diligently to create the MyEconLab test questions and guided solutions. Jane McAndrew provided excellent library help. Richard Parkin created the electronic art files and offered many ideas that improved the figures in this book. And Laurel Davies managed an ever-growing and more complex coding of draw-graph objects, feedback, and many other features of the MyEconLab question database.

As with the previous editions, this one owes an enormous debt to our students. We dedicate this book to them and again thank them for their careful reading and critical comments on the previous edition.

Classroom experience will continue to test the value of this book. We would appreciate hearing from instructors and students about how we can continue to improve it in future editions.

Michael Parkin
Robin Bade
London, Ontario, Canada
michael.parkin@uwo.ca
robin@econ100.com

Reviewers

Ather H. Akbari, Saint Mary's University
Iris Au, University of Toronto
Bogdan Buduru, Concordia University
Beverly J. Cameron, University of Manitoba
Jason Childs, University of New Brunswick, Saint John
Marilyn Cottrell, Brock University
Livio Di Matteo, Lakehead University
Torben Drewes, Trent University
Oliver Franke, Athabasca University
Bruno Fullone, George Brown College
Philippe Ghayad, Dawson College and Concordia University
David Gray, University of Ottawa
Eric Kam, Ryerson University
Cevat Burc Kayahan, University of Guelph
Eva Lau, University of Waterloo
Anastasia M. Lintner, University of Guelph
Christian Marfels, Dalhousie University
Roberto Martínez-Espiñeira, St. Francis Xavier University
Rob Moir, University of New Brunswick Saint John
Saeed Moshiri, University of Manitoba
Derek Pyne, Memorial University of Newfoundland
Jim Sentance, University of Prince Edward Island
Lance Shandler, Kwantlen University College
Peter W. Sinclair, Wilfrid Laurier University
Glen Stirling, University of Western Ontario
Irene Trela, University of Western Ontario
Jane Waples, Memorial University of Newfoundland
Andrew Wong, Grant MacEwan College
Peter Wylie, University of British Colombia, Okanagan
Ayoub Yousefi, University of Western Ontario

Microeconomics Flexibility Chart

Core	Policy	Optional

Core

1. What Is Economics?

2. The Economic Problem

3. Demand and Supply

4. Elasticity

5. Efficiency and Equity
   A chapter that provides a description of the alternative methods of allocating resources and a non-technical explanation of efficiency and equity. The chapter unifies the micro chapters and permits early coverage of policy issues.

Policy

6. Markets in Action
   A unique chapter that gives extensive applications of demand and supply.

Optional

1. Appendix: Graphs in Economics
   A good appendix to assign to the student with a fear of graphs.

7. Utility and Demand
   Although this chapter is optional, it may be covered if desired *before* demand in Chapter 3.

8. Possibilities, Preferences, and Choices
   A full chapter on this strictly optional topic to ensure that it is covered clearly with intuitive explanations and illustrations.

9. Organizing Production
   This chapter may be skipped or assigned as a reading.

10. Output and Costs

11. Perfect Competition

12. Monopoly

13. Monopolistic Competition and Oligopoly

14. Competition Policy

15. Externalities
   Describes the full range of externalities, explains the Coase theorem, and the use of taxes, subsidies, and market solutions.

16. Public Goods and Common Resources
   Describes the four types of goods and explains the free-rider problem and the tragedy of the commons.

17. Demand and Supply in Factor Markets
   Enables you to cover all the factor market issues in a single chapter. Includes an explanation of present value.

18. Economic Inequality

17. Appendix: Labour Unions

32. Trading with the World

Four Alternative Micro Sequences

Traditional Theory and Policy Mix	Challenging Theory Emphasis	Public Choice Emphasis	Policy Emphasis (shorter)
1. What Is Economics?	1. What Is Economics?	1. What Is Economics?	1. What Is Economics?
2. The Economic Problem	2. The Economic Problem	2. The Economic Problem	2. The Economic Problem
3. Demand and Supply	3. Demand and Supply	3. Demand and Supply	3. Demand and Supply
4. Elasticity	4. Elasticity	4. Elasticity	4. Elasticity
5. Efficiency and Equity	5. Efficiency and Equity	5. Efficiency and Equity	5. Efficiency and Equity
6. Markets in Action	6. Markets in Action	6. Markets in Action	6. Markets in Action
7. Utility and Demand	8. Possibilities, Preferences, and Choices	7. Utility and Demand	15. Externalities
or	9. Organizing Production	9. Organizing Production	16. Public Goods and Common Resources
8. Possibilities, Preferences, and Choices	10. Output and Costs	10. Output and Costs	17. Demand and Supply in Factor Markets
9. Organizing Production	11. Perfect Competition	11. Perfect Competition	18. Economic Inequality
10. Output and Costs	12. Monopoly	12. Monopoly	32. Trading with the World
11. Perfect Competition	13. Monopolistic Competition and Oligopoly	13. Monopolistic Competition and Oligopoly	
12. Monopoly	14. Competition Policy	14. Competition Policy	
13. Monopolistic Competition and Oligopoly	17. Demand and Supply in Factor Markets	15. Externalities	
14. Competition Policy	32. Trading with the World	16. Public Goods and Common Resources	
17. Demand and Supply in Factor Markets			
18. Economic Inequality			
32. Trading with the World			

BRIEF CONTENTS

CONTENTS

Summary (Key Points, Key Figures and Tables, and Key Terms), Problems, Critical Thinking, and Web Exercises appear at the end of each chapter.

CREDITS

Photo Credits

Part 1: p. 54, Corbis-Bettmann; p. 55 (left), Culver Pictures; p. 55 (right), Bruce Ando/Tony Stone Images.

Part 2: p. 148, Stock Montage; p. 149 (left), Courtesy Stoddart Publishing Co. Limited, from *Canada: The Missing Years*; p. 149 (right), PhotoDisc, Inc.

Part 3: p. 192, Corbis-Bettmann; p. 193 (left), Keystone-Mass Collection (V22542) UCR/California Museum of Photography, University of California, Riverside; p. 193 (right), China Tourism Press/Getty Images.

Part 4: p. 207 (left), PhotoDisc, Inc.; p. 207 (left, inset), Dick Morton; p. 207 (right), Dick Morton; p. 207 (right, inset), © Reuters New Media; p. 215 (top), Jonathan Hayward/CP Photo Archive; p. 215 (bottom), Bloomberg News/Landov; p. 318, Stock Montage; p. 319 (left), Culver Pictures; p. 319 (right), Don Wilson/West Stock.

Part 5: p. 382, David Joel/David Joel Photography, Inc.; p. 383 (left), Jim Baron/The Image Finders; p. 383 (right), Patrick Mullen; p. 384, E. S. Lee.

Part 6: p. 440, Corbis-Bettmann; p. 441 (left), National Archives of Canada/PA-030176; p. 441 (right), Mark E. Gibson.

Part 7: p. 784, Corbis-Bettmann; p. 785 (left), North Wind Pictures Archives; p. 785 (right), © M. Timothy O'Keefe/ Weststock.

Additional Figure and Table Credits

p. 150, Photo and interview: Reprinted by permission of Professor Paul Beaudry.

p. 409, Figures 1–3: *Historical Statistics on the United States from Colonial Times to 1970*, U.S. Department of Energy Information, U.S. Bureau of Labour Statistics, University of Michigan Document Center, and Oilnergy at www.oilnergy.com/1obrent.htm.

What Is Economics?

Understanding Our Changing World

You are studying economics at a time of enormous change and uncertainty. Much of the change is for the better. The information age of laptop computers with wireless connection to the Internet, MP3 music, DVD movies, cell phones, Palm Pilots, iPods, and a host of other gadgets and toys have transformed the way we work and play.

But some change is for the worse. After the hype of the new millennium, the global economy slipped into recession. The September 11 terrorist attacks slashed business and vacation travel, shrank our airlines, and tightened security at the Canada-U.S. border and at airports and seaports. SARS, mad cow disease, and disputes with the United States about softwood lumber, all sent shockwaves through the Canadian economy.

◆ The information age, global recession, and the effects of terrorism are just some of the forces that are changing today's world. Your course in economics will help you to understand how these powerful forces shape our world. This chapter takes the first step. It describes the questions that economists try to answer, the way they think about those questions, and the methods they use in the search for answers. Economics makes extensive use of graphs, and an appendix provides a guide to these graphical methods.

After studying this chapter, you will be able to

- **Define economics and distinguish between microeconomics and macroeconomics**
- **Explain the big questions of economics**
- **Explain the key ideas that define the economic way of thinking**
- **Explain how economists go about their work as social scientists**

Definition of Economics

ALL ECONOMIC QUESTIONS ARISE BECAUSE WE want more than we can get. We want a peaceful and secure world. We want clean air, lakes, and rivers. We want long and healthy lives. We want good schools, colleges, and universities. We want spacious and comfortable homes. We want an enormous range of sports and recreational gear from running shoes to jet skis. We want the time to enjoy sports, games, novels, movies, music, travel, and hanging out with our friends.

What each one of us can get is limited by time, by the income we earn, and by the prices we must pay. Everyone ends up with some unsatisfied wants. What as a society we can get is limited by our productive resources. These resources include the gifts of nature, human labour and ingenuity, and tools and equipment that we have produced.

Our inability to satisfy all our wants is called **scarcity**. The poor and the rich alike face scarcity. A child wants a $1.00 can of pop and two 50¢ packs of gum but has only $1.00 in his pocket. He faces scarcity. A millionaire wants to spend the weekend playing golf *and* spend the same weekend at the office attending a business strategy meeting. She faces scarcity. A society wants to provide improved health care, install a computer in every classroom, explore space, clean polluted lakes and rivers, and so on. Society faces scarcity. Even parrots face scarcity!

Faced with scarcity, we must *choose* among the available alternatives. The child must *choose* the pop *or* the gum. The millionaire must *choose* the golf game *or* the meeting. As a society, we must *choose* among health care, national defence, and the environment.

The choices that we make depend on the incentives that we face. An **incentive** is a reward that encourages or a penalty that discourages an action. If the price of pop falls, the child has an *incentive* to choose more pop. If a profit of $10 million is at stake, the millionaire has an *incentive* to skip the golf game. As computer prices tumble, school boards have an *incentive* to connect more classrooms to the Internet.

Economics is the social science that studies the *choices* that individuals, businesses, governments, and entire societies make as they cope with *scarcity* and the *incentives* that influence and reconcile those choices. The subject divides into two main parts:

- Microeconomics
- Macroeconomics

Microeconomics

Microeconomics is the study of the choices that individuals and businesses make, the way these choices interact in markets, and the influence of governments. Some examples of microeconomic issues are: Why are people buying more SUVs and fewer minivans? How would a tax on e-commerce affect Amazon.com?

Macroeconomics

Macroeconomics is the study of the performance of the national economy and the global economy. Some examples of macroeconomic issues are: Why did production and jobs shrink in 2001? Why has Japan's economy stagnated? Can the government bring prosperity by cutting tax rates?

Not only do I want a cracker—we all want a cracker!

> ### REVIEW QUIZ
>
> 1 List some examples of choices being made in Canada today.
> 2 Use the headlines in today's news to provide some examples of scarcity around the world.
> 3 Use today's news to illustrate the distinction between microeconomics and macroeconomics.
>
> myeconlab   **Study Plan 1.1**

Two Big Economic Questions

TWO BIG QUESTIONS SUMMARIZE THE SCOPE OF economics:

- How do choices end up determining *what, how,* and *for whom* goods and services get produced?
- When do choices made in the pursuit of *self-interest* also promote the *social interest*?

What, How, and For Whom?

Goods and services are the objects that people value and produce to satisfy human wants. Goods are physical objects such as basketballs. Services are tasks performed for people such as haircuts. By far the largest part of what Canada produces today is services such as retail and wholesale trade, health care, and education. Goods are a small part of total production.

What? What we produce changes over time. Sixty years ago, almost 20 percent of Canadians worked on farms. That number has shrunk to less than 3 percent today. Over the same period, the number of people who produce goods—in mining, construction, and manufacturing—has shrunk from 60 percent to less than 25 percent. The decrease in farming and manufacturing is reflected in an increase in services. Sixty years ago, 20 percent of the population produced services. Today, more than 75 percent of working Canadians have service jobs. Figure 1.1 shows these trends.

What determines the quantities of corn, DVDs, and haircuts and all the other millions of items that we produce?

How? Goods and services are produced by using productive resources that economists call **factors of production.** Factors of production are grouped into four categories:

- Land
- Labour
- Capital
- Entrepreneurship

Land The "gifts of nature" that we use to produce goods and services are called **land.** In economics, land

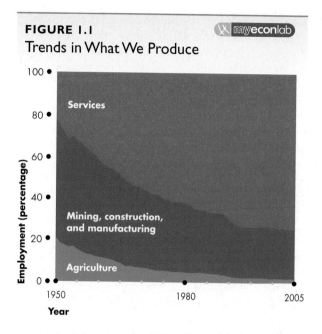

FIGURE 1.1 myeconlab
Trends in What We Produce

Services have expanded and agriculture, mining, construction, and manufacturing have shrunk.

Source of data: Statistics Canada.

is what in everyday language we call *natural resources.* It includes land in the everyday sense together with metal ores, oil, gas and coal, water, and air.

Our land surface and water resources are renewable and some of our mineral resources can be recycled. But the resources that we use to create energy are nonrenewable—they can be used only once.

Labour The work time and work effort that people devote to producing goods and services is called **labour.** Labour includes the physical and the mental efforts of all the people who work on farms and construction sites and in factories, shops, and offices.

The *quality* of labour depends on **human capital,** which is the knowledge and skill that people obtain from education, on-the-job training, and work experience. You are building your own human capital right now as you work on your economics course, and your human capital will continue to grow as you become better at your job.

Human capital expands over time. Today, more than 85 percent of the population of Canada has completed high school and more than 43 percent have a college or university degree. Figure 1.2 shows a measure of the growth of human capital in Canada over the past few decades.

Capital The tools, instruments, machines, buildings, and other items that businesses now use to produce goods and services are called **capital**.

In everyday language, we talk about money, stocks, and bonds as being capital. These items are financial capital. They play an important role in enabling people to lend to businesses and provide businesses with financial resources, but they are not used to produce goods and services. Because they are not productive resources, they are not capital.

Entrepreneurship The human resource that organizes labour, land, and capital is called **entrepreneurship**. Entrepreneurs come up with new ideas about what and how to produce, make business decisions, and bear the risks that arise from these decisions.

How do the quantities of factors of production that get used to produce the many different goods and services get determined?

For Whom? Who gets the goods and services that are produced depends on the incomes that people earn. A large income enables a person to buy large quantities of goods and services. A small income leaves a person with few options and small quantities of goods and services.

People earn their incomes by selling the services of the factors of production they own:

- Land earns **rent**.
- Labour earns **wages**.
- Capital earns **interest**.
- Entrepreneurship earns **profit**.

Which factor of production earns the most income? The answer is labour. Wages and fringe benefits are around 70 percent of total income. Land, capital, and entrepreneurship share the rest. These percentages have been remarkably constant over time.

Knowing how income is shared among the factors of production doesn't tell us how it is shared among individuals. You know of lots of people who earn very large incomes. The average baseball salary in 2005 was about $3 million, and some stars such as Roy Halladay of the Toronto Blue Jays get a bit more than $13 million.

You know of even more people who earn very small incomes. Servers at McDonald's average around $7 an hour; checkout clerks, gas station attendants, and textile and leather workers all earn less than $10 an hour.

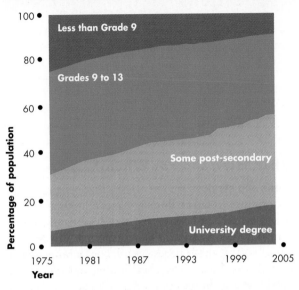

FIGURE 1.2
A Measure of Human Capital

Today, more than 43 percent of the Canadian population has post-secondary certificates, diplomas, or university degrees. A further 42 percent have completed high school.

Source of data: Statistics Canada.

You probably know about other persistent differences in incomes. Men, on the average, earn more than women; university and college graduates, on the average, earn more than high school graduates.

We can get a good sense of who consumes the goods and services produced by looking at the percentages of total income earned by different groups of people. The 20 percent of people with the lowest incomes receive 5 percent of total income, while the richest 20 percent receive 45 percent of total income. So on the average, people in the top 20 percent earn almost 9 times the incomes of those in the 20 percent who earn the least.

Why is the distribution of income so unequal? Why do women earn less than men?

Economics provides some answers to these questions about what, how, and for whom goods and services get produced.

The second big question of economics that we'll now examine is a harder question both to appreciate and to answer.

When Is the Pursuit of Self-Interest in the Social Interest?

Every day, you and 32 million other Canadians, along with 6.5 billion people in the rest of the world, make economic choices that result in "What," "How," and "For Whom" goods and services get produced.

Are the goods and services produced, and the quantities in which they are produced, the right ones? Do the factors of production employed get used in the best possible way? And do the goods and services that we produce go to the people who benefit most from them?

You know that your own choices are the best ones for you—or at least you think they're the best at the time that you make them. You use your time and other resources in the way that makes most sense to you. But you don't think much about how your choices affect other people. You order a home delivery pizza because you're hungry and want to eat. You don't order it thinking that the delivery person or the cook needs an income. You make choices that are in your self-interest. Choices made in **self-interest** are choices that are best for the person making them.

When you act on your economic decisions, you come into contact with thousands of other people who produce and deliver the goods and services that you decide to buy or who buy the things that you sell. These people have made their own decisions— what to produce and how to produce it, whom to hire or whom to work for, and so on. Like you, everyone else makes choices that they think are best for them. When the pizza delivery person shows up at your home, he's not doing you a favour. He's earning his income and hoping for a nice tip.

Could it be possible that when each one of us makes choices that are in our own best interest, it turns out that these choices are also the best for society as a whole? Choices that are the best for society as a whole are said to be in the **social interest**.

Economists have been trying to find the answer to this question since 1776, the year in which Adam Smith's monumental book, *An Inquiry into the Nature and the Causes of the Wealth of Nations*, was published. The question is a hard one to answer, but a lot of progress has been made. Much of the rest of this book helps you to learn what we know about this question and its answer. To help you start thinking about the question, we're going to illustrate it with eight topics that generate heated discus-

sion in today's world. You're already at least a little bit familiar with each one of them. They are

- Central planning versus the market
- Globalization
- The new economy
- The post 9/11 economy
- Corporate scandals
- HIV/AIDS
- Disappearing tropical rainforests
- Water shortages

Central Planning Versus the Market The Soviet Union was founded in 1924 and the People's Republic of China in 1948. These two nations operated the world's largest centrally planned economies.

The antithesis of central planning is the market economy in which resources are privately owned and people are free to trade in markets at prices that are determined by market forces.

From the 1920s until the 1980s, many people believed that self-interest and the social interest could be reconciled only by central economic planning and that the Soviet Union and China had adopted a superior economic system.

As it turned out these economies performed only modestly and China's decade-long so-called "Cultural Revolution" (1966–1976) was an economic disaster.

China began to transform its economy in 1978 when Deng Xiaoping succeeded Mao Zedong. Deng's dictum was to "seek truth from facts" and do what works. He could see Canada, the United States, Europe, Japan, Australia, and Taiwan and Hong Kong, the latter two of which he regarded as part of China, growing richer and richer while China stagnated. He had no time for poverty and said (he has many memorable sayings): "Poverty is not socialism. To be rich is glorious." And in line with his basic outlook: "It doesn't matter if a cat is black or white so long as it catches mice."

In the almost 30 years since China began developing markets and private enterprise, the Chinese economy has performed like no other. Output has grown at an average rate of around 8 percent a year, with living standards doubling every decade or so. All the expansion has occurred in the private market sector of the economy. The market economy continues to be a resounding success for China.

The experiment with central economic planning in the Soviet Union and Eastern Europe lasted a bit longer. But not much longer. On November 9, 1989, a date that will long be written about in economic history books, the Berlin Wall tumbled and with its destruction, two Germanys embarked on a path towards unity.

West Germany had a market economy and East Germany a centrally planned economy. The integration of the economies of the two Germanys took the form of converting the East German economy to capitalism. State-owned enterprises were sold and markets were freed. People previously completely banned from moving between East and West Germany became free to move to any part of Germany (and indeed to any part of the European Union).

Part of Germany's economic problem today stems from a heavy dose of socialism in the form of extraordinarily high wages and benefits as well as rigid employment regulations that make it hard for firms to fire workers (and so firms are cautious to hire them).

Soon after the collapse of the Berlin Wall, the Soviet Union collapsed. It splintered into a number of independent states, each of which embarked on a process of building free markets and the development of the ethics needed to operate an efficient capitalist economy.

Most Chinese and Eastern Europeans are in no doubt that despite a long and difficult adjustment process from central planning to a market economy, the move is worthwhile.

But are they correct? And if they are correct, how do markets manage to do a better job than central economic planning?

Globalization Whenever world leaders hold summit meetings, anti-globalization protests accompany them. Globalization—the expansion of international trade and investment—has been going on for centuries, but during the 1990s, advances in microchip, satellite, and fibre-optic technologies brought a dramatic fall in the cost of communication and accelerated the process. A phone call or even a video conference between people on different continents has become an everyday and easily affordable event. Every day, 20,000 people travel by air between North America and East Asia, and close to that number travel between North America and Europe.

The result of this explosion of communication is a globalization of production decisions. When Nike decides to increase the production of sports shoes, people who live in China, Indonesia, or Malaysia get

more work. As more and more people use credit cards, people in Barbados get hired to key in the data from sales slips. When Sony wants to create a new game for PlayStation 2, or when Steven Spielberg wants a movie animation sequence, programmers in India or New Zealand write the code. And when China Airlines wants some new regional jets, it is most likely that Canadians who work for Bombardier will build them.

As part of the process of globalization, Canada produces more services and fewer manufactured goods. And China and the small economies in East Asia produce an expanding volume of manufactures.

The economies of Asia are also growing more rapidly than are those of North America and Europe. China is already the world's second largest economy in terms of production and, on current trends, by 2013 it will be the world's largest economy. This rapid economic expansion in Asia will bring further changes to the global economy as the wealthier Chinese and other Asians begin to travel and buy more of the goods and services that Canada and other parts of the world produce. Globalization will proceed at an accelerated pace.

But globalization is leaving some behind. The nations of Africa and parts of South America are not sharing in the prosperity that globalization is bringing to other parts of the world.

Is globalization a good thing? Whom does it benefit? Globalization is pretty clearly in the interest of the owners of multinational firms that profit by producing in low-cost regions and selling in high-price regions. But is globalization in your interest and the interest of the young worker in Malaysia who sews your new running shoes? Is it in the social interest?

The New Economy The 1980s and 1990s were years of extraordinary economic change that have been called the *Information Revolution*. Economic revolutions don't happen very often. The previous one, the *Industrial Revolution*, occurred between 1760 and 1830 and saw the transformation from rural farm life to urban industrial life for most people. The revolution before that, the *Agricultural Revolution*, occurred around 10,000 years ago and saw the transformation from a life of hunting and gathering to a life of settled farming.

Placing the events of the last 20 years of the twentieth century on the status of those two previous revolutions might be a stretch. But the changes that occurred during those years were incredible. And they were based on one major technology: the microprocessor or computer chip. Moore's law predicted that the number of transistors that could be placed on one integrated chip would double every 18 months. This prediction turned out to be remarkably accurate. In 1980, a PC chip had 60,000 transistors. By 2000, chips with more than 40 million transistors were in machines like the one that sits on your lap.

The spinoffs from faster and cheaper computing were widespread. Telecommunications became much faster and cheaper, music and movie recording became more realistic and cheaper, millions of routine tasks that previously required human decision and action were automated. You encounter these automated tasks every day when you check out at the supermarket, call directory assistance, or call a government department or large business.

All the new products and processes and the low-cost computing power that made them possible were produced by people who made choices in the pursuit of self-interest. They did not result from any grand design or government economic plan.

When Gordon Moore set up Intel and started making chips, no one had told him to do so, and he wasn't thinking how much easier it would be for you to turn in your essay on time if you had a faster PC. When Bill Gates quit Harvard to set up Microsoft, he wasn't trying to create the best operating system and improve people's computing experience. Moore and Gates and thousands of other entrepreneurs were in hot pursuit of the big payoffs that many of them achieved. Yet their actions did make everyone else better off. They did advance the social interest.

But could more have been done? Were resources used in the best possible way during the information revolution? Did Intel make the best possible chips and sell them in the right quantities for the right prices? Or was the quality of the chips too low and the price too high? And what about Microsoft? Did Bill Gates have to be paid $US46 billion to produce the successive generations of Windows and Word? Were these programs developed in the social interest?

The Economic Response to 9/11 The awful events of September 11, 2001 created economic shockwaves that will last for some years and changed "What," "How," and "For Whom."

The biggest changes in production occurred in the travel, accommodation, and security industries. Much business travel was replaced by teleconferencing. Much vacation travel left the air and went onto the

highway. Foreign trips were cut back. Airlines lost business and cut back on their orders for new airplanes. Banks that had lent money to airlines wrote off millions of dollars in losses.

But sales of SUVs and RVs increased. And airports, although operating at lower capacity, beefed up their security services. Thousands of new security agents were hired and state-of-the-art scanners were installed.

Thousands of people made choices in pursuit of their self-interest that led to these changes in production. But were these changes also in the social interest?

Corporate Scandals In 2000, the names Enron and WorldCom meant corporate integrity and spectacular success. But today, they are tainted with scandal.

Founded in 1985, Enron expanded to become the seventh largest U.S. business by 2001. But its expansion was built on an elaborate web of lies, deceit, and fraud. In October 2001, after revelations by one of its former executives, Enron's directors acknowledged that by inflating reported income and hiding debts, they had made the firm appear to be worth considerably more than it actually was. One Enron executive, Michael Kopper, pleaded guilty to charges of money laundering and wire fraud and helped federal investigators uncover the fraud that made millions of dollars for the firm's executives and wiped out its stockholders' wealth.

Scott Sullivan, a highly respected financial officer, joined WorldCom in 1992 and helped turn it into one of the world's telecommunications giants. In his last year with the company, Sullivan's salary was $US700,000 and his bonus (in stock options) was $US10 million. But just ten years after joining the company, Sullivan was fired and arrested for allegedly falsifying the company's accounts, inflating its book profits by almost $US4 billion, and inflating his own bonus in the process. Shortly after these events, WorldCom filed for bankruptcy protection in the largest bankruptcy filing in U.S. history, laid off 17,000 workers, and, like Enron, wiped out its stockholders' wealth.

These cases illustrate the fact that sometimes, in the pursuit of self-interest, people break the law. Such behaviour is not in the social interest. Indeed, the law was established precisely to limit such behaviour.

But some corporate behaviour is legal yet regarded by some as inappropriate. For example, many people think that top executive salaries are out of control. In some cases, executives who have received huge incomes have brought ruin to the companies that they manage.

The people who hired the executives acted in their own self-interest and appointed the best people they could find. The executives acted in their own self-interest. But what became of the self-interest of the stockholders and the customers of these firms? Didn't they suffer? Aren't these glaring examples of conflict between self-interest and the social interest?

HIV/AIDS The World Health Organization and United Nations estimate that 42 million people were suffering from HIV/AIDS in 2002. During that year, 3 million died from the disease and there were 5 million new cases. Most of the HIV/AIDS cases—30 million of them in 2002—were in Africa, where incomes average around $7 a day. The most effective treatment for this disease is an antiretroviral drug made by the large multinational drug companies. The cost of this treatment is around $2,700 a year—more than $7 a day. For sales to poor countries, the cost has been lowered to around $1,200 a year—$3.30 a day.

Developing new drugs is a high-cost and high-risk activity. And if the activity were not in the self-interest of the drug companies, they would stop the effort. But once developed, the cost of producing a drug is just a few cents a dose. Would it be in the social interest for drugs to be made available at the low cost of producing them?

Disappearing Tropical Rainforests Tropical rainforests in South America, Africa, and Asia support the lives of 30 million species of plants, animals, and insects—approaching 50 percent of all species on the planet. These rainforests provide us with the ingredients for many goods including soaps, mouthwashes, shampoos, food preservatives, rubber, nuts, and fruits. The Amazon rainforest alone converts about 450 million tonnes of carbon dioxide into oxygen each year.

Yet tropical rainforests cover less than two percent of the Earth's surface and are heading for extinction. Logging, cattle ranching, mining, oil extraction, hydroelectric dams, and subsistence farming are destroying the equivalent of two football fields every second or an area larger than New York City every day. At the current rate of destruction, almost all the tropical rainforest ecosystems will be gone by 2030.

Each one of us makes economic choices that are in our self-interest to consume products, some of which are destroying this natural resource. Are our choices damaging the social interest? And if they are, what can be done to change the incentives we face and change our behaviour?

Water Shortages The world is awash with water—it is our most abundant resource. But 97 percent of it is seawater. Another 2 percent is frozen in glaciers and ice. The 1 percent of the earth's water that is available for human consumption would be sufficient if only it were in the right places. Canada, Finland, and a few other places have more water than they can use, but Australia, Africa, and California (and many other places) could use much more water than they can get. Some people pay less for water than others. California farmers, for example, pay less than California households. Some of the highest prices for water are faced by people in the poorest countries who must either buy from a water dealer's truck or carry water in buckets over long distances.

In the United Kingdom, water is provided by private water companies. In Canada, public enterprises deliver the water.

In India and Bangladesh, plenty of rain falls, but it falls during a short wet season and the rest of the year is dry. Dams could help to reduce the shortage in the dry season, but not enough have been built in those countries.

Are the nations' and the world's water resources being managed properly? Are the decisions that we each make in our self-interest to use, conserve, and transport water also in the social interest?

We've just looked at eight topics that illustrate the big question: Do choices made in the pursuit of self-interest also serve the social interest?

You'll discover, as you work through this book, that much of what we do in the pursuit of our self-interest does indeed further the social interest. But there are areas in which the social interest and self-interest come into conflict. You'll discover the principles that help economists to figure out when the social interest is being served, when it is not, and what might be done when it is not.

REVIEW QUIZ

1 Describe the broad facts about "What," "How," and "For Whom" goods and services get produced.

2 Use headlines from the recent news to illustrate the potential for conflict between self-interest and the social interest.

myeconlab **Study Plan 1.2**

The Economic Way of Thinking

THE DEFINITION OF ECONOMICS AND THE questions that you've just reviewed tell you about the *scope of economics*. But they don't tell you how economists *think* about these questions and go about seeking answers to them.

You're now going to begin to see how economists approach economic questions. First, in this section, we'll look at the ideas that define the *economic way of thinking*. This way of thinking needs practice, but it is powerful and as you become more familiar with it, you'll begin to see the world around you with a new and sharp focus.

Choices and Tradeoffs

Because we face scarcity, we must make choices. And when we make a choice, we select from the available alternatives. For example, you can spend the weekend studying for your next economics test and having fun with your friends, but you can't do both of these activities at the same time. You must choose how much time to devote to each. Whatever choice you make, you could have chosen something else instead.

You can think about your choice as a tradeoff. A **tradeoff** is an exchange—giving up one thing to get something else. When you choose how to spend your weekend, you face a tradeoff between studying and hanging out with your friends.

Guns Versus Butter   The classic tradeoff is between guns and butter. "Guns" and "butter" stand for any pair of goods. They might actually be guns and butter. Or they might be broader categories such as national defence and food. Or they might be any pair of specific goods or services such as cola and bottled water, baseball bats and tennis rackets, universities and hospitals, realtor services and career counselling.

Regardless of the specific objects that guns and butter represent, the guns-versus-butter tradeoff captures a hard fact of life: If we want more of one thing, we must trade something else in exchange for it.

The idea of a tradeoff is central to the whole of economics. We'll look at some examples, beginning with the big questions: What, How, and For Whom? We can view each of these questions about the goods and services that get produced in terms of tradeoffs.

What, How, and For Whom Tradeoffs

The questions what, how, and for whom goods and services are produced all involve tradeoffs that are similar to that between guns and butter.

"What" Tradeoffs   What goods and services get produced depends on choices made by each one of us, by our government, and by the businesses that produce the things we buy.

Each of these choices involves a tradeoff. Each one of us faces a tradeoff when we choose how to spend our income. You go to the movies this week, but you forgo a few cups of coffee to buy the ticket. You trade off coffee for a movie.

The federal government faces a tradeoff when it chooses how to spend our tax dollars. Parliament votes for more hospitals but cuts back on educational programs. The federal government trades off education for hospitals.

Businesses face a tradeoff when they decide what to produce. Nike hires Tiger Woods and allocates resources to designing and marketing a new golf ball but cuts back on its development of a new running shoe. Nike trades off running shoes for golf balls.

"How" Tradeoffs   How goods and services get produced depends on choices made by the businesses that produce the things we buy. These choices involve a tradeoff. For example, Tim Hortons opens a new doughnut store with an automated production line and closes an older store with a traditional kitchen— Tim Hortons trades off labour for capital.

"For Whom" Tradeoffs   For whom goods and services are produced depends on the distribution of buying power. Buying power can be redistributed —transferred from one person to another—in three ways: by voluntary payments, by theft, or through taxes and benefits organized by governments. Redistribution brings tradeoffs.

Each of us faces a "for whom" tradeoff when we choose how much to contribute to the United Nations' famine relief fund. You cut your spending and donate $50. You trade off your own spending for a small increase in economic equality.

We make choices that influence redistribution by theft when we vote to make theft illegal and devote resources to law enforcement. We trade off some goods and services for an increase in the security of our property.

We also vote for taxes and social programs that redistribute buying power from the rich to the poor. Government redistribution confronts society with what has been called the **big tradeoff**—the tradeoff between equality and efficiency. Taxing the rich and making transfers to the poor bring greater economic equality. But taxing productive activities such as running a business, working hard, and saving and investing in capital discourages these activities. So taxing productive activities means producing less. A more equal distribution means there is less to share.

You can think of the big tradeoff as being the problem of how to share a pie that everyone contributes to baking. If each person receives a share of the pie that reflects the size of her or his effort, everyone will work hard and the pie will be as large as possible. But if the pie is shared equally, regardless of contribution, some talented bakers will slacken off and the pie will shrink. The big tradeoff is one between the size of the pie and how equally it is shared. We trade off some production for increased equality.

Choices Bring Change

What, how, and for whom goods and services are produced changes over time. And choices bring change. The quantity and range of goods and services available today in Canada is much greater than that in Africa. And the economic condition of Canada today is much better than it was a generation ago. But the quality of economic life (and its rate of improvement) doesn't depend purely on nature and on luck. It depends on many of the choices made by each one of us, by governments, and by businesses. And these choices involve tradeoffs.

One choice is that of how much of our income to consume and how much to save. Our saving can be channelled through the financial system to finance businesses and to pay for new capital that increases production. The more we save and invest, the more goods and services we'll be able to produce in the future. When you decide to save an extra $1,000 and forgo a vacation, you trade off the vacation for a higher future income. If everyone saves an extra $1,000 and businesses invest in more equipment that increases production, the average consumption per person rises. As a society, we trade off current consumption for economic growth and higher future consumption.

A second choice is how much effort to devote to education and training. By becoming better educated and more highly skilled, we become more productive

and are able to produce more goods and services. When you decide to remain in school for another two years to complete a professional degree and forgo a huge chunk of leisure time, you trade off leisure today for a higher future income. If everyone becomes better educated, production increases and income per person rises. As a society, we trade off current consumption and leisure time for economic growth and higher future consumption.

A third choice, usually made by businesses, is how much effort to devote to research and the development of new products and production methods. Ford Motor Company can hire engineers to do research on a new robotic assembly line or to operate the existing plant and produce cars. More research brings greater productivity in the future but means smaller current production—a tradeoff of current production for greater future production.

Seeing choices as tradeoffs emphasizes the idea that to get something, we must give up something. What we give up is the cost of what we get. Economists call this cost the opportunity cost.

Opportunity Cost

The highest-valued alternative that we give up to get something is the **opportunity cost** of the activity chosen. "There's no such thing as a free lunch" is not just a clever throwaway line. It expresses the central idea of economics: that every choice involves a cost.

You can quit school, or you can remain in school. If you quit school and take a job at McDonald's, you earn enough to buy some CDs, go to the movies, and spend lots of free time with your friends. If you remain in school, you can't afford these things. You will be able to buy these things and more when you graduate, and that is one of the payoffs from being in school. But for now, when you've bought your books, you have nothing left for CDs and movies. And doing assignments leaves no time for hanging around with your friends. The opportunity cost of being in school is the highest-valued alternative that you would have done if you had quit school.

All the "what," "how," and "for whom" tradeoffs that we've just considered involve opportunity cost. The opportunity cost of some guns is the butter forgone; the opportunity cost of a movie ticket is the number of cups of coffee forgone.

And the choices that bring change also involve opportunity cost. The opportunity cost of more goods and services in the future is less consumption today.

Choosing at the Margin

You can allocate the next hour between studying and e-mailing your friends. But the choice is not all or nothing. You must decide how many minutes to allocate to each activity. To make this decision, you compare the benefit of a little bit more study time with its cost—you make your choice at the **margin**.

The benefit that arises from an increase in an activity is called **marginal benefit**. For example, suppose that you're spending four nights a week studying and your grade point average is 3.0. You decide that you want a higher grade and decide to study an extra night each week. Your grade now rises to 3.5. The marginal benefit from studying for one additional night a week is the 0.5 increase in your grade. It is *not* the 3.5 grade. The reason is that you already have the benefit from studying for four nights a week, so we don't count this benefit as resulting from the decision you are now making.

The cost of an increase in an activity is called **marginal cost**. For you, the marginal cost of increasing your study time by one night a week is the cost of the additional night not spent with your friends (if that is your best alternative use of the time). It does not include the cost of the four nights you are already studying.

To make your decision, you compare the marginal benefit from an extra night of study with its marginal cost. If the marginal benefit exceeds the marginal cost, you study the extra night. If the marginal cost exceeds the marginal benefit, you do not study the extra night.

By evaluating marginal benefits and marginal costs and choosing only those actions that bring greater benefit than cost, we use our scarce resources in the way that makes us as well off as possible.

Responding to Incentives

Our choices respond to incentives. A change in marginal cost or a change in marginal benefit changes the incentives that we face and leads us to change our choice.

For example, suppose your economics instructor gives you a problem set and tells you that all the problems will be on the next test. The marginal benefit from working these problems is large, so you diligently work them all. In contrast, if your math instructor gives you a problem set and tells you that none of the problems will be on the next test, the marginal benefit from working these problems is lower, so you skip most of them.

The central idea of economics is that we can predict how choices will change by looking at changes in incentives. More of an activity is undertaken when its marginal cost falls or marginal benefit rises; less of an activity is undertaken when its marginal cost rises or marginal benefit falls.

Incentives are also the key to reconciling self-interest and the social interest. When our choices are *not* in the social interest, it is because we face the wrong incentives. One of the central challenges for economists is to figure out the incentive systems that result in self-interested choices leading to the social interest.

Human Nature, Incentives, and Institutions

Economists take human nature as given and view people as acting in their self-interest. All people—consumers, producers, politicians, and public servants—pursue their self-interest.

Self-interested actions are not necessarily *selfish* actions. You might decide to use your resources in ways that bring pleasure to others as well as to yourself. But a self-interested act gets the most value for *you* based on *your* view about value.

If human nature is given and if people act in their self-interest, how can we take care of the social interest? Economists answer this question by emphasizing the crucial role that institutions play in influencing the incentives that people face as they pursue their self-interest.

The key institution is a legal system that protects personal security and private property and enables people to specialize and trade in markets. You will learn as you progress with your study of economics that where these institutions exist, self-interest can indeed promote the social interest.

REVIEW QUIZ

1 Provide three examples of a tradeoff and describe the opportunity cost involved in each.
2 Provide an everyday example to illustrate what we mean by choosing at the margin.
3 What is the main factor that influences choices?
4 What do economists say about the role of institutions in promoting the social interest?

X myeconlab **Study Plan 1.3**

Economics: A Social Science

ECONOMICS IS A SOCIAL SCIENCE (ALONG WITH political science, psychology, and sociology). Economists try to discover how the economic world works, and in pursuit of this goal (like all scientists), they distinguish between two types of statements:

- What *is*
- What *ought to be*

Statements about what *is* are called *positive* statements and they might be right or wrong. We can test a positive statement by checking it against the facts. When a chemist does an experiment in her laboratory, she is attempting to check a positive statement against the facts.

Statements about what *ought to be* are called *normative* statements. These statements depend on values and cannot be tested. When Parliament debates a motion, it is ultimately trying to decide what ought to be. It is making a normative statement.

To see the distinction between positive and normative statements, consider the controversy over global warming. Some scientists believe that centuries of the burning of coal and oil are increasing the carbon dioxide content of the earth's atmosphere and leading to higher temperatures that eventually will have devastating consequences for life on this planet. "Our planet is warming because of an increased carbon dioxide buildup in the atmosphere" is a positive statement. It can (in principle and with sufficient data) be tested. "We ought to cut back on our use of carbon-based fuels such as coal and oil" is a normative statement. You can agree with or disagree with this statement, but you can't test it. It is based on values. Health-care reform provides an economic example of the distinction. "Universal health care cuts the amount of work time lost to illness" is a positive statement. "All Canadians should have equal access to health care" is a normative statement.

The task of economic science is to discover positive statements that are consistent with what we observe and that help us to understand the economic world. This task can be broken into three steps:

- Observation and measurement
- Model building
- Testing models

Observation and Measurement

Economists observe and measure data on such things as the quantities of natural and human resources, wages and work hours, the prices and quantities of the different goods and services produced, taxes and government spending, and the quantities of goods and services bought from and sold to other countries.

Model Building

The second step towards understanding how the economic world works is to build a model. An **economic model** is a description of some aspect of the economic world that includes only those features of the world that are needed for the purpose at hand. A model is simpler than the reality it describes. What a model includes and what it leaves out result from assumptions about what is essential and what are inessential details.

You can see how ignoring details is useful—even essential—to our understanding by thinking about a model that you see every day: the TV weather map. The weather map is a model that helps to predict the temperature, wind speed and direction, and precipitation over a future period. The weather map shows lines called isobars—lines of equal barometric pressure. It doesn't show the highways. The reason is that our theory of the weather tells us that the pattern of air pressure, not the location of the highways, determines the weather.

An economic model is similar to a weather map. For example, an economic model of a cell phone network might tell us the effects of the development of a new low-cost technology on the number of cell phone subscribers and the volume of cell phone use. But the model would ignore such details as the colours of the covers on people's cell phones and the tunes they use for ring tones.

Testing Models

The third step is testing the model. A model's predictions might correspond to the facts or be in conflict with them. By comparing the model's predictions with the facts, we can test a model and develop an economic theory. An **economic theory** is a generalization that summarizes what we think we understand about the economic choices that people make and the performance of industries and entire economies. Economic theory is a bridge between an economic model and the real economy.

The process of building and testing models creates theories. For example, meteorologists have a theory that if the isobars form a particular pattern at a particular time of the year (a model), then it will snow (reality). They have developed this theory by repeated observation and by carefully recording the weather that follows specific pressure patterns.

Economics is a young science. It was born in 1776 with the publication of Adam Smith's *Wealth of Nations* (see p. 54). Over the years since then, economists have discovered many useful theories. But in many areas, economists are still looking for answers. The gradual accumulation of economic knowledge gives most economists some faith that their methods will, eventually, provide usable answers to the big economic questions.

But progress in economics comes slowly. Let's look at some of the obstacles to progress in economics.

Obstacles and Pitfalls in Economics

We cannot easily do economic experiments. And most economic behaviour has many simultaneous causes. For these two reasons, it is difficult in economics to unscramble cause and effect.

Unscrambling Cause and Effect By changing one factor at a time and holding all the other relevant factors constant, we isolate the factor of interest and are able to investigate its effects in the clearest possible way. This logical device, which all scientists use to identify cause and effect, is called *ceteris paribus*. **Ceteris paribus** is a Latin term that means "other things being equal" or "if all other relevant things remain the same." Ensuring that other things are equal is crucial in many activities, and all successful attempts to make scientific progress use this device.

Economic models (like the models in all other sciences) enable the influence of one factor at a time to be isolated in the imaginary world of the model. When we use a model, we are able to imagine what would happen if only one factor changed. But *ceteris paribus* can be a problem in economics when we try to test a model.

Laboratory scientists, such as chemists and physicists, perform experiments by actually holding all the relevant factors constant except for the one under investigation. In non-experimental sciences such as economics (and astronomy), we usually observe the outcomes of the simultaneous operation of many factors. Consequently, it is hard to sort out the effects of each individual factor and to compare them with what a model predicts. To cope with this problem, economists take three complementary approaches.

First, they look for pairs of events in which other things were equal (or similar). An example might be to study the effects of unemployment insurance on the unemployment rate by comparing the United States with Canada on the presumption that the people in the two economies are sufficiently similar. Second, economists use statistical tools—called econometrics. Third, when economists can, they perform experiments. This relatively new approach puts real subjects (usually students) in a decision-making situation and varies their incentives in some way to discover how they respond to a change in one factor at a time.

Economists try to avoid fallacies—errors of reasoning that lead to a wrong conclusion. But two fallacies are common, and you need to be on your guard to avoid them. They are the

- Fallacy of composition
- *Post hoc* fallacy

Fallacy of Composition The fallacy of composition is the (false) statement that what is true of the parts is true of the whole or that what is true of the whole is true of the parts. There are many everyday examples of this fallacy. Standing at a ball game to get a better view works for one person but not for all—what is true for a part of a crowd is not true for the whole crowd.

The fallacy of composition arises in many economic situations that stem from the fact that the parts interact with each other to produce an outcome for the whole that might differ from the intent of the parts.

For example, a firm fires some workers to cut costs and improve its profits. If all firms take similar actions, income falls and so does spending. The firm sells less, and its profits don't improve.

Or suppose that a firm thinks it can gain market share by cutting its price and mounting a large advertising campaign. Again, if the one firm takes these actions they work. But if all the firms in an industry take the same actions, they all end up with the same market share as before and lower profits.

Post Hoc Fallacy Another Latin phrase—*post hoc ergo propter hoc*—means "after this, therefore because of this." The *post hoc* fallacy is the error of reasoning that a first event *causes* a second event because the first occurred before the second. Suppose you are a visitor from a far-off world. You observe lots of people shopping in early December, and then you see them opening gifts and partying in the holiday season. "Does the shopping cause the holiday season?" you wonder. After a deeper study, you discover that the holiday season causes the shopping. A later event causes an earlier event.

Unravelling cause and effect is difficult in economics. And just looking at the timing of events often doesn't help. For example, the stock market booms, and some months later the economy expands—jobs and incomes grow. Did the stock market boom cause the economy to expand? Possibly, but perhaps businesses started to plan the expansion of production because a new technology that lowered costs had become available. As knowledge of the plans spread, the stock market reacted to *anticipate* the economic expansion. To disentangle cause and effect, economists use economic models and data and, to the extent that they can, perform experiments.

Economics is a challenging science. Does the difficulty of getting answers in economics mean that anything goes and that economists disagree on most questions? Perhaps you've heard the joke "If you laid all the economists in the world end to end, they still wouldn't reach a conclusion." Surprisingly, perhaps, the joke does not describe reality.

Agreement and Disagreement

Economists have reached conclusions and agree on a wide range of questions. And often the agreed-upon view of economists disagrees with the popular and sometimes politically correct view. When Bank of Canada Governor David Dodge testifies before Parliament, his words are rarely controversial among economists, even when they generate endless debate in the media and Parliament.

Here are 12 propositions with which at least 7 out of every 10 economists broadly agree:

- Tariffs and import restrictions make most people worse off.
- A large budget deficit has an adverse effect on the economy.
- A minimum wage increases unemployment among young workers and low-skilled workers.

- Cash payments to welfare recipients make them better off than do transfers-in-kind of equal cash value.
- A tax cut can help to lower unemployment when the unemployment rate is high.
- The distribution of income should be more equal.
- Inflation is primarily caused by a rapid rate of money creation.
- The government should restructure welfare along the lines of a "negative income tax."
- Rent ceilings cut the availability of housing.
- Pollution taxes are more effective than pollution limits.
- The redistribution of income is a legitimate role for the government.
- The federal budget should be balanced on the average over the business cycle but not every year.

Which of these propositions are positive and which are normative? Notice that economists are willing to offer their opinions on normative issues as well as their professional views on positive questions. Be on the lookout for normative propositions dressed up as positive propositions.

REVIEW QUIZ

1 What is the distinction between a positive statement and a normative statement? Provide an example (different from those in the chapter) of each type of statement.

2 What is a model? Can you think of a model that you might use (probably without thinking of it as a model) in your everyday life?

3 What is a theory? Why is the statement "It might work in theory, but it doesn't work in practice" a silly statement?

4 What is the *ceteris paribus* assumption and how is it used?

5 Try to think of some everyday examples of the fallacy of composition and the *post hoc* fallacy.

ⓧ myeconlab   **Study Plan 1.4**

SUMMARY

KEY POINTS

A Definition of Economics (p. 2)

- All economic questions arise from scarcity—from the fact that wants exceed the resources available to satisfy them.
- Economics is the social science that studies the choices that people make as they cope with scarcity.
- The subject divides into microeconomics and macroeconomics.

Two Big Economic Questions (pp. 3–8)

- Two big questions summarize the scope of economics:
  1. How do choices end up determining *what*, *how*, and *for whom* goods and services get produced?
  2. When do choices made in the pursuit of *self-interest* also promote the *social interest*?

The Economic Way of Thinking (pp. 9–11)

- Every choice is a tradeoff—exchanging more of something for less of something else.
- The classic guns-versus-butter tradeoff represents all tradeoffs.
- All economic questions involve tradeoffs.
- The big social tradeoff is that between equality and efficiency.
- The highest-valued alternative forgone is the opportunity cost of what is chosen.
- Choices are made at the margin and respond to incentives.

Economics: A Social Science (pp. 12–14)

- Economists distinguish between positive statements—what is—and normative statements—what ought to be.

- To explain the economic world, economists develop theories by building and testing economic models.
- Economists use the *ceteris paribus* assumption to try to disentangle cause and effect and are careful to avoid the fallacy of composition and the *post hoc* fallacy.
- Economists agree on a wide range of questions about how the economy works.

KEY TERMS

Big tradeoff, 10
Capital, 4
Ceteris paribus, 13
Economic model, 12
Economics, 2
Economic theory, 12
Entrepreneurship, 4
Factors of production, 3
Goods and services, 3
Human capital, 3
Incentive, 2
Interest, 4
Labour, 3
Land, 3
Macroeconomics, 2
Margin, 11
Marginal benefit, 11
Marginal cost, 11
Microeconomics, 2
Opportunity cost, 10
Profit, 4
Rent, 4
Scarcity, 2
Self-interest, 5
Social interest, 5
Tradeoff, 9
Wages, 4

PROBLEMS

Go to myeconlab **for solutions to odd-numbered problems and additional exercises.**

1. Your friends go the movies one evening and you decide to stay home and do your economics assignment and practice test. You get 80 percent on your next economics exam compared with the 70 percent that you normally score. What is the opportunity cost of your extra points?

2. You go to the movies one evening instead of studying for your economics test. You get 50 percent on your next economics test rather than the 70 percent that you usually get. What is the opportunity cost of going to the movies?

3. You plan to go to school this summer. If you do, you won't be able to take your usual job that pays $6,000 for the summer, and you won't be able to live at home for free. The cost of tuition is $2,000 and textbooks is $200, and living expenses are $1,400. What is the opportunity cost of going to summer school?

4. You plan to go skiing next weekend. If you do, you'll have to miss doing your usual weekend job that pays $100. You won't be able to study for 8 hours and you won't be able to use your prepaid college meal plan. The cost of travel and accommodations will be $350, the ski rental will cost $60, and your food will cost $40. What is the opportunity cost of the ski trip?

5. The local mall has free parking, but the mall is always very busy, and it usually takes 30 minutes to find a parking space. Today when you found a vacant spot, Harry also wanted it. Is parking really free at this mall? If not, what did it cost you to park today? When you parked your car today, did you impose any costs on Harry? Explain your answers.

6. The university has built a new movie house. Admission for students is free and there are always plenty of empty seats. But when the movie house screened *Lord of the Rings*, the lines were long. So the movie house decided to charge $4 per student. Cadbury Schweppes offered students a free soft drink. Compare the student's opportunity cost of seeing the movie *Lord of the Rings* with that of any other movie screened in the year. Which is less costly and by how much?

CRITICAL THINKING

1. Use the two big questions of economics and the economic way of thinking to organize a short essay about the economic life of a homeless man. Does he face scarcity? Does he make choices? Can you interpret his choices as being in his own best interest? Can either his own choices or the choices of others make him better off? If so, how?

WEB EXERCISES

Use the links on myeconlab **to work the following exercises.**

1. Visit the CBC.
   a. What is the top economic news story today?
   b. With which of the big questions does it deal? (It must deal with at least one of them and might deal with more than one.)
   c. What tradeoffs does the news item discuss?
   d. Write a brief summary of the news item in a few bulleted points using as much as possible of the economic vocabulary that you have learned in this chapter and that is in the key terms list on p. 15.

2. Visit *Resources for Economists on the Internet*. This site is a good place from which to search for economic information on the Internet.
   a. Scroll down the page and click on General Interest.
   b. Visit the "general interest" sites and become familiar with the types of information they contain.

3. Visit Statistics Canada.
   a. What is the number of people employed (nonfarm employment) in your area?
   b. Has employment increased or decreased?
   c. What is income per person (per capita income) in your area?

Graphs in Economics

After studying this appendix, you will be able to

- **Make and interpret a time-series graph, a cross-section graph, and a scatter diagram**

- **Distinguish between linear and nonlinear relationships and between relationships that have a maximum and a minimum**

- **Define and calculate the slope of a line**

- **Graph relationships among more than two variables**

Graphing Data

A GRAPH REPRESENTS A QUANTITY AS A DISTANCE on a line. Figure A1.1 shows two examples. Here, a distance on the horizontal line represents temperature, measured in degrees Celsius. A movement from left to right shows an increase in temperature. The point marked 0 represents zero degrees Celsius. To the right of 0, the temperature is positive. To the left of 0 (as indicated by the minus sign), the temperature is negative. A distance on the vertical line represents altitude or height, measured in thousands of metres above sea level. The point marked 0 represents sea level. Points above 0 represent metres above sea level. Points below 0 (indicated by a minus sign) represent metres below sea level.

By setting two scales perpendicular to each other, as in Fig. A1.1, we can visualize the relationship between two variables. The scale lines are called *axes*. The vertical line is the *y-axis*, and the horizontal line is the *x-axis*. Each axis has a zero point, which is shared by the two axes. This zero point, common to both axes, is called the *origin*.

To show something in a two-variable graph, we need two pieces of information: the value of the *x*-variable and the value of the *y*-variable. For example, off the coast of British Columbia on a winter's day, the temperature is 10 degrees—the value of *x*. A fishing boat is located at 0 metres above sea level—the value of *y*. These two bits of information appear as point *A* in Fig. A1.1. A climber at the top of Mt. McKinley on a cold day is 6,194 metres above sea level in a zero-degree gale. These two pieces of information appear as point *B*. The position of the

Making a Graph

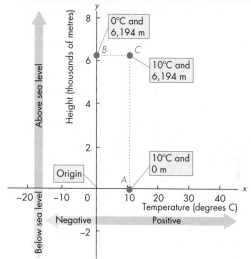

Graphs have axes that measure quantities as distances. Here, the horizontal axis (*x*-axis) measures temperature, and the vertical axis (*y*-axis) measures height. Point *A* represents a fishing boat at sea level (0 on the *y*-axis) on a day when the temperature is 10°C. Point *B* represents a climber on Mt. McKinley, 6,194 metres above sea level, at a temperature of 0°C. Point *C* represents a climber on Mt. McKinley, 6,194 metres above sea level, at a temperature of 10°C.

climber on a warmer day might be at the point marked *C*. This point represents the peak of Mt. McKinley at a temperature of 10 degrees.

We can draw two lines, called *coordinates*, from point *C*. One, called the *y*-coordinate, runs from *C* to the horizontal axis. Its length is the same as the value marked off on the *y*-axis. The other, called the *x*-coordinate, runs from *C* to the vertical axis. Its length is the same as the value marked off on the *x-axis*. We describe a point in a graph by the values of its *x*-coordinate and its *y*-coordinate.

Graphs like that in Fig. A1.1 can show any type of quantitative data on two variables. Economists use three types of graphs based on the principles in Fig. A1.1 to reveal and describe the relationships among variables. They are

- Time-series graphs
- Cross-section graphs
- Scatter diagrams

17

Time-Series Graphs

A **time-series graph** measures time (for example, months or years) on the *x*-axis and the variable or variables in which we are interested on the *y*-axis. Figure A1.2 is an example of a time-series graph. It provides some information on the average price of unleaded gasoline across Canada.

In Fig. A1.2, we measure time in years running from 1990 to 2005. We measure the price of gasoline (the variable that we are interested in) on the *y*-axis.

The point of a time-series graph is to enable us to visualize how a variable has changed over time and how its value in one period relates to its value in another period.

A time-series graph conveys an enormous amount of information quickly and easily, as this example illustrates. It shows

- The *level* of the price of gasoline—when it is *high* and *low*. When the line is a long way from the *x*-axis, the price is high. When the line is close to the *x*-axis, the price is low.
- How the price *changes*—whether it *rises* or *falls*. When the line slopes upward, as in 2000, the price is rising. When the line slopes downward, as in 1993, the price is falling.
- The *speed* with which the price changes—whether it rises or falls *quickly* or *slowly*. If the line is steep, then the price rises or falls quickly. If the line is not steep, the price rises or falls slowly. For example, the price rose quickly from 2003 to 2004 and slowly from 1995 to 1996. The price fell quickly from 2001 to 2002 and slowly from 1991 to 1994.

A time-series graph also reveals whether there is a trend. A trend is a general tendency for a variable to move in one direction. A **trend** might be upward or downward. In Fig. A1.2, you can see that the price of gasoline had a general tendency to rise from the mid-1990s to 2005. That is, although the price rose and fell, the general tendency was for it to rise—the price had an upward trend.

A time-series graph also helps us detect cycles in variables. You can see some peaks and troughs in the price of gasoline in Fig. A1.2. You can see a trough in 1998 and a peak in 2001.

Finally, a time-series graph also lets us compare the variable in different periods quickly. Figure A1.2 shows that the 1990s were different from the 2000s. The

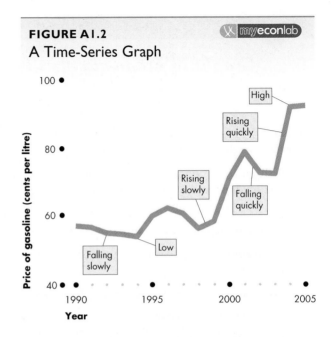

FIGURE A1.2
A Time-Series Graph

A time-series graph plots the level of a variable on the *y*-axis against time (day, week, month, or year) on the *x*-axis. This graph shows the average price of gasoline each year from 1990 to 2005. It shows us when the price of gasoline was *high* and when it was *low*, when the price *increased* and when it *decreased*, and when it changed *quickly* and when it changed *slowly*.

price of gasoline fluctuated more in the 2000s than it did in the 1990s.

You can see that a time-series graph conveys a wealth of information. And it does so in much less space than we have used to describe only some of its features. But you do have to "read" the graph to obtain all this information.

Cross-Section Graphs

A **cross-section graph** shows the values of an economic variable for different groups in a population at a point in time. Figure A1.3, called a *bar chart*, is an example of a cross-section graph.

The bar chart in Fig. A1.3 shows the number of visitors to each province in 2004. The length of each bar indicates the number of visitors. This figure enables you to compare the number of visitors across the provinces. And you can do so much more quickly and clearly than you could by looking at a list of numbers.

FIGURE A1.3
A Cross-Section Graph

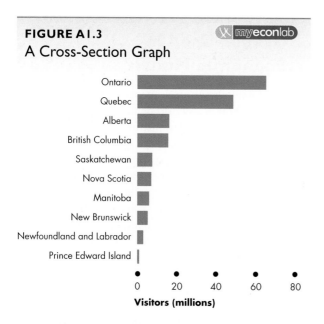

Visitors (millions)

A cross-section graph shows the level of a variable across the members of a population. This bar chart shows the number of visitors to each province in 2004.

Scatter Diagrams

A **scatter diagram** plots the value of one variable against the value of another variable. Such a graph reveals whether a relationship exists between two variables and describes their relationship. Figure A1.4(a) shows the relationship between expenditure and income. Each point shows expenditure per person and income per person in a given year from 1990 to 2004. The points are "scattered" within the graph. The point labelled *A* tells us that in 1999, income per person was $19,610 and expenditure per person was $18,448. The dots in this graph form a pattern, which reveals that as income increases, expenditure increases.

Figure A1.4(b) shows the relationship between the number of international phone calls and the price of a call. This graph shows that as the price per minute falls, the number of calls increases.

Figure A1.4(c) shows a scatter diagram of inflation and unemployment in Canada. Here, the dots show no clear relationship between these two variables. The dots in this graph reveal that there is no simple relationship between these variables.

FIGURE A1.4
Scatter Diagrams

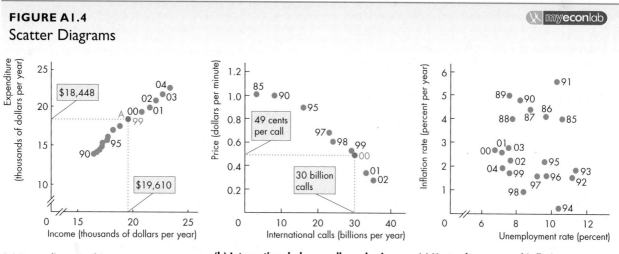

(a) Expenditure and income

(b) International phone calls and prices

(c) Unemployment and inflation

A scatter diagram reveals the relationship between two variables. Part (a) shows the relationship between expenditure and income. Each point shows the values of the two variables in a specific year. For example, point A shows that in 1999, average income was $19,610 and average expenditure was $18,448. The pattern formed by the points shows that as income increases, expenditure increases.

Part (b) shows the relationship between the price of an international phone call and the number of calls made. This graph shows that as the price of a phone call falls, the number of calls made increases. Part (c) shows the inflation rate and unemployment rate in Canada. This graph shows that the inflation rate and the unemployment rate are not closely related.

Breaks in the Axes Two of the graphs you've just looked at, Fig. A1.4(a) and Fig. A1.4(c), have breaks in their axes, as shown by the small gaps. The breaks indicate that there are jumps from the origin, 0, to the first values recorded.

In Fig. A1.4(a), the breaks are used because the lowest value of expenditure exceeds $13,000 and the lowest value of income exceeds $17,000. With no breaks in the axes of this graph, there would be a lot of empty space, all the points would be crowded into the top right corner, and we would not be able to see whether a relationship exists between these two variables. By breaking the axes, we are able to bring the relationship into view.

Putting a break in the axes is like using a zoom lens to bring the relationship into the centre of the graph and magnify it so that it fills the graph.

Misleading Graphs Breaks can be used to highlight a relationship. But they can also be used to mislead—to make a graph that lies. The most common way of making a graph lie is to use axis breaks either to stretch or to compress a scale. For example, suppose that in Fig. A1.4(a), the *y*-axis ran from zero to $45,000 while the *x*-axis was the same as the one shown. The graph would now create the impression that despite a huge increase in income, expenditure had barely changed.

To avoid being misled, it is a good idea to get into the habit of always looking closely at the values and the labels on the axes of a graph before you start to interpret it.

Correlation and Causation A scatter diagram that shows a clear relationship between two variables, such as Fig. A1.4(a) or Fig. A1.4(b), tells us that the two variables have a high correlation. When a high correlation is present, we can predict the value of one variable from the value of the other variable. But correlation does not imply causation.

Sometimes a high correlation is a coincidence, but sometimes it does arise from a causal relationship. It is likely, for example, that rising income causes rising expenditure (Fig. A1.4a) and that the falling price of a phone call causes more calls to be made (Fig. A1.4b).

You've now seen how we can use graphs in economics to show economic data and to reveal relationships between variables. Next, we'll learn how economists use graphs to construct and display economic models.

Graphs Used in Economic Models

THE GRAPHS USED IN ECONOMICS ARE NOT ALWAYS designed to show real-world data. Often they are used to show general relationships among the variables in an economic model.

An *economic model* is a stripped down, simplified description of an economy or of a component of an economy, such as a business or a household. It consists of statements about economic behaviour that can be expressed as equations or as curves in a graph. Economists use models to explore the effects of different policies or other influences on the economy in ways that are similar to the use of model airplanes in wind tunnels and models of the climate.

You will encounter many different kinds of graphs in economic models, but there are some repeating patterns. Once you've learned to recognize these patterns, you will instantly understand the meaning of a graph. Here, we'll look at the different types of curves that are used in economic models, and we'll see some everyday examples of each type of curve. The patterns to look for in graphs are the four cases:

- Variables that move in the same direction
- Variables that move in opposite directions
- Variables that have a maximum or a minimum
- Variables that are unrelated

Let's look at these four cases.

Variables That Move in the Same Direction

Figure A1.5 shows graphs of the relationships between two variables that move up and down together. A relationship between two variables that move in the same direction is called a **positive relationship** or a **direct relationship**. A line that slopes upward shows such a relationship.

Figure A1.5 shows three types of relationships: one that has a straight line and two that have curved lines. But all the lines in these three graphs are called curves. Any line on a graph—no matter whether it is straight or curved—is called a *curve*.

A relationship shown by a straight line is called a **linear relationship**. Figure A1.5(a) shows a linear rela-

FIGURE A1.5

Positive (Direct) Relationships

(a) Positive, linear relationship   **(b) Positive, becoming steeper**   **(c) Positive, becoming less steep**

Each part of this figure shows a positive (direct) relationship between two variables. That is, as the value of the variable measured on the *x*-axis increases, so does the value of the variable measured on the *y*-axis. Part (a) shows a linear relationship—as the two variables increase together, we move along a straight line. Part (b) shows a positive relationship such that as the two variables increase together, we move along a curve that becomes steeper. Part (c) shows a positive relationship such that as the two variables increase together, we move along a curve that becomes less steep.

tionship between the number of kilometres travelled in 5 hours and speed. For example, point *A* shows that we will travel 200 kilometres in 5 hours if our speed is 40 kilometres an hour. If we double our speed to 80 kilometres an hour, we will travel 400 kilometres in 5 hours.

Figure A1.5(b) shows the relationship between distance sprinted and recovery time (the time it takes the heart rate to return to its normal resting value). This relationship is an upward-sloping one that starts out quite flat but then becomes steeper as we move along the curve away from the origin. The reason this curve slopes upward and becomes steeper is because the additional recovery time needed from sprinting an additional 100 metres increases. It takes less than 5 minutes to recover from the first 100 metres, but it takes more than 10 minutes to recover from the second 100 metres.

Figure A1.5(c) shows the relationship between the number of problems worked by a student and the amount of study time. This relationship is an upward-sloping one that starts out quite steep and becomes flatter as we move away from the origin. Study time becomes less productive as the student spends more hours studying and becomes more tired.

Variables That Move in Opposite Directions

Figure A1.6 shows relationships between things that move in opposite directions. A relationship between variables that move in opposite directions is called a **negative relationship** or an **inverse relationship**.

Figure A1.6(a) shows the relationship between the number of hours available for playing squash and the number of hours for playing tennis when the total is 5 hours. One extra hour spent playing tennis means one hour less playing squash and vice versa. This relationship is negative and linear.

Figure A1.6(b) shows the relationship between the cost per kilometre travelled and the length of a journey. The longer the journey, the lower is the cost per kilometre. But as the journey length increases, the cost per kilometre decreases, and the fall in the cost is smaller, the longer the journey. This feature of the relationship is shown by the fact that the curve slopes downward, starting out steep at a short journey length and then becoming flatter as the journey length increases. This relationship arises because some of the costs are fixed (such as auto insurance), and the fixed cost is spread over a longer journey.

FIGURE A1.6
Negative (Inverse) Relationships

(a) Negative, linear relationship

(b) Negative, becoming less steep

(c) Negative, becoming steeper

Each part of this figure shows a negative (inverse) relationship between two variables. That is, as the value of the variable measured on the x-axis increases, the value of the variable measured on the y-axis decreases. Part (a) shows a linear relationship. The total time spent playing tennis and squash is 5 hours. As the time spent playing tennis increases, the time spent playing squash decreases, and we move along a straight line. Part (b) shows a negative relationship such that as the journey length increases, the curve becomes less steep. Part (c) shows a negative relationship such that as leisure time increases, the curve becomes steeper.

Figure A1.6(c) shows the relationship between the amount of leisure time and the number of problems worked by a student. Increasing leisure time produces an increasingly large reduction in the number of problems worked. This relationship is a negative one that starts out with a gentle slope at a small number of leisure hours and becomes steeper as the number of leisure hours increases. This relationship is a different view of the idea shown in Fig. A1.5(c).

Variables That Have a Maximum or a Minimum

Many relationships in economic models have a maximum or a minimum. For example, firms try to make the maximum possible profit and to produce at the lowest possible cost. Figure A1.7 shows relationships that have a maximum or a minimum.

Figure A1.7(a) shows the relationship between rainfall and wheat yield. When there is no rainfall, wheat will not grow, so the yield is zero. As the rainfall increases up to 10 days a month, the wheat yield increases. With 10 rainy days each month, the wheat

yield reaches its maximum at 2 tonnes per hectare (point *A*). Rain in excess of 10 days a month starts to lower the yield of wheat. If every day is rainy, the wheat suffers from a lack of sunshine and the yield decreases to zero. This relationship is one that starts out sloping upward, reaches a maximum, and then slopes downward.

Figure A1.7(b) shows the reverse case—a relationship that begins sloping downward, falls to a minimum, and then slopes upward. Most economic costs are like this relationship. An example is the relationship between the cost per kilometre and speed for a car trip. At low speeds, the car is creeping in a traffic jam. The number of kilometres per litre is low, so the cost per kilometre is high. At high speeds, the car is travelling faster than its efficient speed, using a large quantity of gasoline, and again the number of kilometres per litre is low and the cost per kilometre is high. At a speed of 100 kilometres an hour, the cost per kilometre is at its minimum (point *B*). This relationship is one that starts out sloping downward, reaches a minimum, and then slopes upward.

FIGURE A1.7
Maximum and Minimum Points

(a) Relationship with a maximum

(b) Relationship with a minimum

Part (a) shows a relationship that has a maximum point, A. The curve slopes upward as it rises to its maximum point, is flat at its maximum, and then slopes downward. Part (b) shows a relationship with a minimum point, B. The curve slopes downward as it falls to its minimum, is flat at its minimum, and then slopes upward.

Variables That Are Unrelated

There are many situations in which no matter what happens to the value of one variable, the other variable remains constant. Sometimes we want to show the independence between two variables in a graph, and Fig. A1.8 shows two ways of achieving this.

In describing the graphs in Figs. A1.5 through A1.7, we have talked about curves that slope upward and downward, and curves that become less steep or steeper. Let's spend a little time discussing exactly what we mean by slope and how we measure the slope of a curve.

FIGURE A1.8
Variables That Are Unrelated

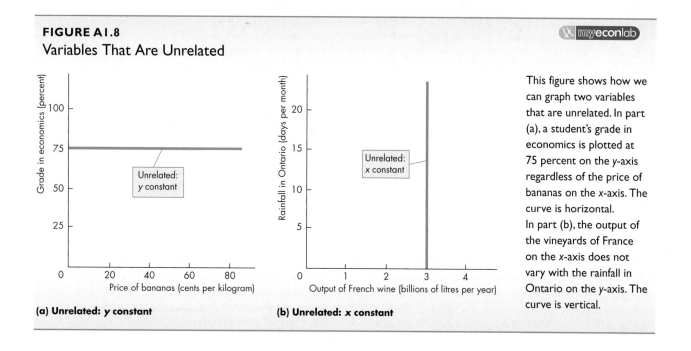

(a) Unrelated: *y* constant

(b) Unrelated: *x* constant

This figure shows how we can graph two variables that are unrelated. In part (a), a student's grade in economics is plotted at 75 percent on the *y*-axis regardless of the price of bananas on the *x*-axis. The curve is horizontal.
In part (b), the output of the vineyards of France on the *x*-axis does not vary with the rainfall in Ontario on the *y*-axis. The curve is vertical.

The Slope of a Relationship

WE CAN MEASURE THE INFLUENCE OF ONE variable on another by the slope of the relationship. The **slope** of a relationship is the change in the value of the variable measured on the *y*-axis divided by the change in the value of the variable measured on the *x*-axis. We use the Greek letter Δ (*delta*) to represent "change in." Thus Δ*y* means the change in the value of the variable measured on the *y*-axis, and Δ*x* means the change in the value of the variable measured on the *x*-axis. Therefore the slope of the relationship is

$$\Delta y/\Delta x$$

If a large change in the variable measured on the *y*-axis (Δ*y*) is associated with a small change in the variable measured on the *x*-axis (Δ*x*), the slope is large and the curve is steep. If a small change in the variable measured on the *y*-axis (Δ*y*) is associated with a large change in the variable measured on the *x*-axis (Δ*x*), the slope is small and the curve is flat.

We can make the idea of slope sharper by doing some calculations.

The Slope of a Straight Line

The slope of a straight line is the same regardless of where on the line you calculate it. The slope of a straight line is constant. Let's calculate the slopes of the lines in Fig. A1.9. In part (a), when *x* increases from 2 to 6, *y* increases from 3 to 6. The change in *x*

FIGURE A1.9
The Slope of a Straight Line

(a) Positive slope

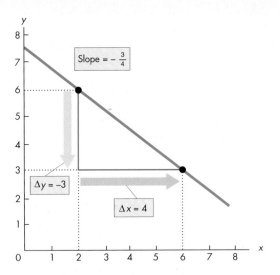

(b) Negative slope

To calculate the slope of a straight line, we divide the change in the value of the variable measured on the *y*-axis (Δ*y*) by the change in the value of the variable measured on the *x*-axis (Δ*x*), as we move along the curve. Part (a) shows the calculation of a positive slope. When *x* increases from 2 to 6, Δ*x* equals 4. That change in *x* brings about an increase in *y* from 3 to 6, so Δ*y* equals 3. The slope (Δ*y*/Δ*x*) equals 3/4. Part (b) shows the calculation of a negative slope. When *x* increases from 2 to 6, Δ*x* equals 4. That increase in *x* brings about a decrease in *y* from 6 to 3, so Δ*y* equals −3. The slope (Δ*y*/Δ*x*) equals −3/4.

is +4—that is, Δx is 4. The change in y is +3—that is, Δy is 3. The slope of that line is

$$\frac{\Delta y}{\Delta x} = \frac{3}{4}.$$

In part (b), when x increases from 2 to 6, y decreases from 6 to 3. The change in y is *minus* 3—that is, Δy is –3. The change in x is *plus* 4—that is, Δx is 4. The slope of the curve is

$$\frac{\Delta y}{\Delta x} = \frac{-3}{4}.$$

Notice that the two slopes have the same magnitude (3/4) but the slope of the line in part (a) is positive (+3/+4 = 3/4), while that in part (b) is negative (–3/+4 = –3/4). The slope of a positive relationship is positive; the slope of a negative relationship is negative.

The Slope of a Curved Line

The slope of a curved line is trickier. The slope of a curved line is not constant. Its slope depends on where on the line we calculate it. There are two ways to calculate the slope of a curved line: You can calculate the slope at a point, or you can calculate the slope across an arc of the curve. Let's look at the two alternatives.

Slope at a Point To calculate the slope at a point on a curve, you need to construct a straight line that has the same slope as the curve at the point in question. Figure A1.10 shows how this is done. Suppose you want to calculate the slope of the curve at point A. Place a ruler on the graph so that it touches point A and no other point on the curve, then draw a straight line along the edge of the ruler. The straight red line is this line, and it is the tangent to the curve at point A. If the ruler touches the curve only at point A, then the slope of the curve at point A must be the same as the slope of the edge of the ruler. If the curve and the ruler do not have the same slope, the line along the edge of the ruler will cut the curve instead of just touching it.

Now that you have found a straight line with the same slope as the curve at point A, you can calculate the slope of the curve at point A by calculating the slope of the straight line. Along the straight line, as x

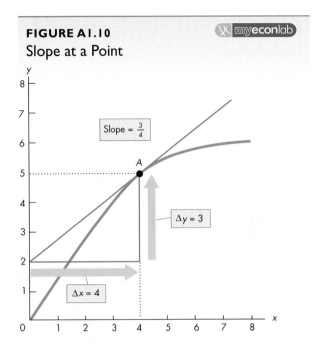

FIGURE A1.10
Slope at a Point

To calculate the slope of the curve at point A, draw the red line that just touches the curve at A—the tangent. The slope of this straight line is calculated by dividing the change in y by the change in x along the red line. When x increases from 0 to 4, Δx equals 4. That change in x is associated with an increase in y from 2 to 5, so Δy equals 3. The slope of the red line is 3/4. So the slope of the curve at point A is 3/4.

increases from 0 to 4 ($\Delta x = 4$) y increases from 2 to 5 ($\Delta y = 3$). Therefore the slope of the line is

$$\frac{\Delta y}{\Delta x} = \frac{3}{4}.$$

Thus the slope of the curve at point A is 3/4.

Slope Across an Arc An arc of a curve is a piece of a curve. In Fig. A1.11, you are looking at the same curve as in Fig. A1.10. But instead of calculating the slope at point A, we are going to calculate the slope across the arc from B to C. You can see that the slope at B is greater than the slope at C. When we calculate the slope across an arc, we are calculating the average slope between two points. As we move along the arc from B to C, x increases from 3 to 5 and y increases from 4 to 5.5. The change in x is 2 ($\Delta x = 2$), and the

FIGURE A1.11
Slope Across an Arc

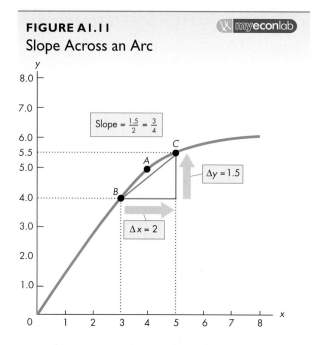

To calculate the average slope of the curve along the arc *BC*, draw a straight line from *B* to *C*. The slope of the line *BC* is calculated by dividing the change in *y* by the change in *x*. In moving from *B* to *C*, Δx equals 2 and Δy equals 1.5. The slope of the line *BC* is 1.5 divided by 2, or 3/4. So the slope of the curve across the arc *BC* is 3/4.

change in *y* is 1.5 ($\Delta y = 1.5$). Therefore the slope of the line is

$$\frac{\Delta y}{\Delta x} = \frac{1.5}{2} = \frac{3}{4}.$$

Thus the slope of the curve across the arc *BC* is 3/4.

This calculation gives us the slope of the curve between points *B* and *C*. The actual slope calculated is the slope of the straight line from *B* to *C*. This slope approximates the average slope of the curve along the arc *BC*. In this particular example, the slope across the arc *BC* is identical to the slope of the curve at point *A*. But the calculation of the slope of a curve does not always work out so neatly. You might have some fun constructing some more examples and some counter-examples.

You now know how to make and interpret a graph. But so far, we've limited our attention to graphs of two variables. We're now going to learn how to graph more than two variables.

Graphing Relationships Among More Than Two Variables

WE HAVE SEEN THAT WE CAN GRAPH THE relationship between two variables as a point formed by the *x*- and *y*-coordinates in a two-dimensional graph. You may be thinking that although a two-dimensional graph is informative, most of the things in which you are likely to be interested involve relationships among many variables, not just two. For example, the amount of ice cream consumed depends on the price of ice cream and the temperature. If ice cream is expensive and the temperature is low, people eat much less ice cream than when ice cream is inexpensive and the temperature is high. For any given price of ice cream, the quantity consumed varies with the temperature; and for any given temperature, the quantity of ice cream consumed varies with its price.

Figure A1.12 shows a relationship among three variables. The table shows the number of litres of ice cream consumed each day at various temperatures and ice cream prices. How can we graph these numbers?

To graph a relationship that involves more than two variables, we use the *ceteris paribus* assumption.

Ceteris Paribus We noted in the chapter (see p. 13) that every laboratory experiment is an attempt to create *ceteris paribus* and isolate the relationship of interest. We use the same method to make a graph when more than two variables are involved.

Figure A1.12(a) shows an example. There, you can see what happens to the quantity of ice cream consumed when the price of ice cream varies and the temperature is held constant. The line labelled 21°C shows the relationship between ice cream consumption and the price of ice cream if the temperature remains at 21°C. The numbers used to plot that line are those in the third column of the table in Fig. A1.12. For example, if the temperature is 21°C, 10 litres are consumed when the price is 60¢ a scoop and 18 litres are consumed when the price is 30¢ a scoop. The curve labelled 32°C shows consumption as the price varies if the temperature remains at 32°C.

We can also show the relationship between ice cream consumption and temperature when the price of ice cream remains constant, as shown

FIGURE A1.12
Graphing a Relationship Among Three Variables

(a) Price and consumption at a given temperature

(b) Temperature and consumption at a given price

(c) Temperature and price at a given consumption

	Ice cream consumption			
Price	**(litres per day)**			
(cents per scoop)	**–10°C**	**10°C**	**21°C**	**32°C**
15	12	18	25	50
30	10	12	18	37
45	7	10	13	27
60	5	7	10	20
75	3	5	7	14
90	2	3	5	10
105	1	2	3	6

The quantity of ice cream consumed depends on its price and the temperature. The table gives some hypothetical numbers that tell us how many litres of ice cream are consumed each day at different prices and different temperatures. For example, if the price is 60¢ a scoop and the temperature is 21°C, 10 litres of ice cream are consumed. This set of values is highlighted in the table and each part of the figure.

To graph a relationship among three variables, the value of one variable is held constant. Part (a) shows the relationship between price and consumption when temperature is held constant. One curve holds temperature at 32°C and the other at 21°C. Part (b) shows the relationship between temperature and consumption when price is held constant. One curve holds the price at 60¢ a scoop and the other at 15¢ a scoop. Part (c) shows the relationship between temperature and price when consumption is held constant. One curve holds consumption at 10 litres a day and the other at 7 litres a day.

in Fig. A1.12(b). The curve labelled 60¢ shows how the consumption of ice cream varies with the temperature when ice cream costs 60¢ a scoop, and a second curve shows the relationship when ice cream costs 15¢ a scoop. For example, at 60¢ a scoop, 10 litres are consumed when the temperature is 21°C and 20 litres when the temperature is 32°C.

Figure A1.12(c) shows the combinations of temperature and price that result in a constant consumption of ice cream. One curve shows the combination that results in 10 litres a day being consumed, and

the other shows the combination that results in 7 litres a day being consumed. A high price and a high temperature lead to the same consumption as a lower price and a lower temperature. For example, 10 litres of ice cream are consumed at 21°C and 60¢ a scoop, 32°C and 90¢ a scoop, and at 10°C and 45¢ a scoop.

With what you have learned about graphs, you can move forward with your study of economics. There are no graphs in this book that are more complicated than those that have been explained in this appendix.

Mathematical Note
Equations to Straight Lines

IF A STRAIGHT LINE IN A GRAPH DESCRIBES THE relationship between two variables, we call it a *linear relationship*. Figure 1 shows the linear relationship between a person's expenditure and income. This person spends $100 a week (by borrowing or spending previous savings) when income is zero. And out of each dollar earned, this person spends 50 cents (and saves 50 cents).

All linear relationships are described by the same general equation. We call the quantity that is measured on the horizontal (or *x*-axis) *x* and we call the quantity that is measured on the vertical (or *y*-axis) *y*. In the case of Fig. 1, *x* is income and *y* is expenditure.

A Linear Equation

The equation that describes a straight-line relationship between *x* and *y* is

$$y = a + bx.$$

In this equation, *a* and *b* are fixed numbers and they are called constants. The values of *x* and *y* vary so these numbers are called variables. Because the equation describes a straight line, it is called a *linear equation*.

The equation tells us that when the value of *x* is zero, the value of *y* is *a*. We call the constant *a* the *y*-axis intercept. The reason is that on the graph the straight line hits the *y*-axis at a value equal to *a*. Figure 1 illustrates the *y*-axis intercept.

For positive values of *x*, the value of *y* exceeds *a*. The constant *b* tells us by how much *y* increases above *a* as *x* increases. The constant *b* is the slope of the line.

Slope of Line

As we explain in the chapter, the *slope* of a relationship is the change in the value of *y* divided by the change in the value of *x* as we move along the line. We use the Greek letter Δ (*delta*) to represent "change in." Thus Δy means the change in the value of the variable measured on the *y*-axis, and Δx means the change in the value of the variable measured on the *x*-axis. Therefore the slope of the relationship is

$$\Delta y / \Delta x.$$

To see why the slope is *b*, suppose that initially the value of *x* is x_1, or $200 in Fig. 2. The corresponding value of *y* is y_1, also $200 in Fig. 2. The equation to the line tells us that

$$y_1 = a + bx_1. \qquad (1)$$

Now the value of *x* increases by Δx to $x_1 + \Delta x$ (or $400 in Fig. 2). And the value of *y* increases by Δy to $y_1 + \Delta y$ (or $300 in Fig. 2).

Figure 1 Linear relationship

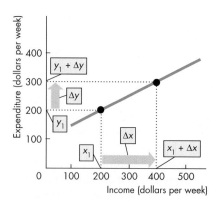

Figure 2 Calculating slope

The equation to the line now tells us that

$$y_1 + \Delta y = a + b(x_1 + \Delta x). \qquad (2)$$

To calculate the slope of the line, subtract equation (1) from equation (2) to obtain

$$\Delta y = b\Delta x \qquad (3)$$

and now divide equation (3) by Δx to obtain

$$\frac{\Delta y}{\Delta x} = b.$$

So, the slope of the line is b.

Position of Line

The y-axis intercept determines the position of the line on the graph. Figure 3 illustrates the relationship between the y-axis intercept and the position of the line on the graph. The y-axis measures saving and the x-axis measures income. When the y-axis intercept, a, is positive, the line hits the y-axis at a positive value of y—as the blue line does. When the y-axis intercept, a, is zero, the line hits the y-axis at the origin—as the purple line does. When the y-axis intercept, a, is negative, the line hits the y-axis at a negative value of y—as the red line does. As the equations to the three lines show, the value of the y-axis intercept does not influence the slope of the line.

Positive Relationships

Figure 1 shows a positive relationship—the two variables x and y move in the same direction. All positive relationships have a slope that is positive. In the equation to the line, the constant b is positive. In this example, the y-axis intercept, a, is 100. The slope b equals $\Delta y/\Delta x$, which is 100/200 or 0.5. The equation to the line is

$$y = 100 + 0.5x.$$

Negative Relationships

Figure 4 shows a negative relationship—the two variables x and y move in the opposite direction. All negative relationships have a slope that is negative. In the equation to the line, the constant b is negative. In the example in Fig. 4, the y-axis intercept, a, is 30. The slope, b, equals $\Delta y/\Delta x$, which is $-20/2$ or -10. The equation to the line is

$$y = 30 + (-10)x$$

or,

$$y = 30 - 10x.$$

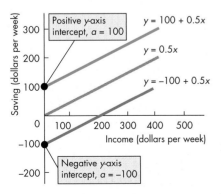

Figure 3 The *y*-axis intercept

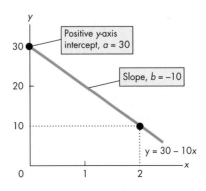

Figure 4 Negative relationship

SUMMARY

KEY POINTS

Graphing Data (pp. 17–20)

- A time-series graph shows the trend and fluctuations in a variable over time.
- A cross-section graph shows how variables change across the members of a population.
- A scatter diagram shows the relationship between two variables. It shows whether two variables are positively related, negatively related, or unrelated.

Graphs Used in Economic Models (pp. 20–23)

- Graphs are used to show relationships among variables in economic models.
- Relationships can be positive (an upward-sloping curve), negative (a downward-sloping curve), positive and then negative (have a maximum point), negative and then positive (have a minimum point), or unrelated (a horizontal or vertical curve).

The Slope of a Relationship (pp. 24–26)

- The slope of a relationship is calculated as the change in the value of the variable measured on the y-axis divided by the change in the value of the variable measured on the x-axis—that is, $\Delta y/\Delta x$.
- A straight line has a constant slope.
- A curved line has a varying slope. To calculate the slope of a curved line, we calculate the slope at a point or across an arc.

Graphing Relationships Among More Than Two Variables (pp. 26–27)

- To graph a relationship among more than two variables, we hold constant the values of all the variables except two.
- We then plot the value of one of the variables against the value of another.

KEY FIGURES

KEY TERMS

REVIEW QUIZ

1. What are the three types of graphs used to show economic data?
2. Give an example of a time-series graph.
3. List three things that a time-series graph shows quickly and easily.
4. Give examples, not those in the chapter, of scatter diagrams that show a positive relationship, a negative relationship, and no relationship.
5. Draw some graphs to show the relationships between two variables that
   a. Move in the same direction.
   b. Move in opposite directions.
   c. Have a maximum.
   d. Have a minimum.
6. Which relationship in question 5 is a positive relationship and which is a negative relationship?
7. What are the two ways of calculating the slope of a curved line?
8. How do we graph a relationship among more than two variables?

 myeconlab Study Plan 1.5

PROBLEMS

Go to myeconlab for solutions to odd-numbered problems and additional exercises.

The spreadsheet provides data on the Canadian economy: Column A is the year, column B is the inflation rate, column C is the interest rate, column D is the growth rate, and column E is the unemployment rate. Use this spreadsheet to answer problems 1, 2, 3, and 4.

	A	B	C	D	E
1	1995	2.2	7.2	2.9	9.6
2	1996	1.6	4.3	1.6	9.7
3	1997	1.6	3.6	4.2	9.2
4	1998	0.9	5.0	4.1	8.4
5	1999	1.7	4.9	5.6	7.6
6	2000	3.1	5.7	5.2	6.8
7	2001	2.1	3.9	1.8	7.2
8	2002	2.1	2.7	3.1	7.7
9	2003	3.0	2.9	2.1	7.6
10	2004	1.7	2.3	2.8	7.2

1. Draw a time-series graph of the inflation rate.
   a. In which year(s) (i) was inflation highest, (ii) was inflation lowest, (iii) did it increase, (iv) did it decrease most?
   b. What was the main trend in inflation?

2. Draw a time-series graph of the interest rate.
   a. In which year(s) (i) was the interest rate lowest, (ii) was it highest, (iii) did it increase, (iv) did it increase most?
   b. What was the main trend in the interest rate?

3. Draw a scatter diagram to show the relationship between the inflation rate and the interest rate. Describe the relationship.

4. Draw a scatter diagram to show the relationship between the growth rate and the unemployment rate. Describe the relationship.

5. Draw a graph to show the relationship between the two variables x and y:

x	0	1	2	3	4	5	6	7	8
y	0	1	4	9	16	25	36	49	64

   a. Is the relationship positive or negative?
   b. Does the slope of the relationship increase or decrease as the value of x increases?
   c. Think of some economic relationships that might be similar to this one.

6. Draw a graph that shows the relationship between the two variables x and y:

x	0	1	2	3	4	5
y	25	24	22	16	8	0

   a. Is the relationship positive or negative?
   b. Does the slope of the relationship increase or decrease as the value of x increases?
   c. Think of some economic relationships that might be similar to this one.

7. In problem 5, calculate the slope of the relationship between x and y when x equals 4.

8. In problem 6, calculate the slope of the relationship between x and y when x equals 3.

9. In problem 5, calculate the slope of the relationship across the arc when x increases from 3 to 4.

10. In problem 6, calculate the slope of the relationship across the arc when x increases from 4 to 5.

11. Calculate the slope of the relationship shown at point A in the following figure.

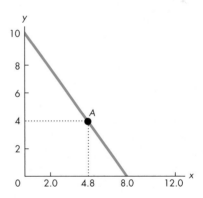

12. Calculate the slope of the relationship shown at point A in the following figure.

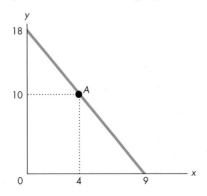

13. Calculate the slope of the relationship:

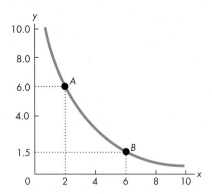

a. At points *A* and *B*.
b. Across the arc *AB*.

14. Calculate the slope of the relationship:

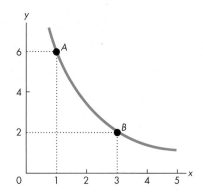

a. At points *A* and *B*.
b. Across the arc *AB*.

15. The table gives the price of a balloon ride, the temperature, and the number of rides a day.

| Price | Balloon rides (number per day) | | |
(dollars per ride)	10°C	20°C	30°C
5.00	32	40	50
10.00	27	32	40
15.00	18	27	32
20.00	10	18	27

Draw graphs to show the relationship between

a. The price and the number of rides, holding the temperature constant.
b. The number of rides and temperature, holding the price constant.
c. The temperature and price, holding the number of rides constant.

16. The table gives the price of an umbrella, the amount of rainfall, and the number of umbrellas purchased.

| Price | Umbrellas (number per day) | | |
| (dollars per umbrella) | 0 | 2 | 10 |
		(mm of rainfall)	
10	7	8	12
20	4	7	8
30	2	4	7
40	1	2	4

Draw graphs to show the relationship between

a. The price and the number of umbrellas purchased, holding the amount of rainfall constant.
b. The number of umbrellas purchased and the amount of rainfall, holding the price constant.
c. The amount of rainfall and the price, holding the number of umbrellas purchased constant.

WEB EXERCISES

Use the links on (X myeconlab) to work the following exercises.

1. Find the Consumer Price Index (CPI) for the latest 12 months. Make a graph of the CPI. During the most recent month, was the CPI rising or falling? Was the rate of rise or fall increasing or decreasing?

2. Find the unemployment rate for the latest 12 months. Graph the unemployment rate. During the most recent month, was it rising or falling? Was the rate of rise or fall increasing or decreasing?

3. Use the data that you obtained in exercises 1 and 2. Make a graph to show whether the CPI and the unemployment rate are related.

4. Use the data that you obtained in exercises 1 and 2. Calculate the percentage change in the CPI each month. Make a graph to show whether the percentage change in the CPI and the unemployment rate are related to each other.

The Economic Problem

Good, Better, Best!

We live in a style that surprises our grandparents and would have astonished our great-grandparents. MP3s, video games, cell phones, gene splicing, personal computers, and iPods, which did not exist even 25 years ago, have transformed our daily lives. For most of us, life is good and getting better. But we still make choices and face costs.

Perhaps the biggest choice that you will make is when to quit school and begin full-time work. When you've completed your current program, will you remain in school and work towards a post-graduate degree or a professional degree? What are the costs and consequences of this choice? We'll return to this question in *Reading Between the Lines* at the end of this chapter.

We see an incredible amount of specialization and trade in the world. Each one of us specializes in a particular job—as a lawyer, a journalist, a homemaker. Why? How do we benefit from specialization and trade?

Over many centuries, social institutions have evolved that we take for granted. They include firms, markets, and a political and legal system that protects private property. Why have these institutions evolved?

◆ These are the questions that we study in this chapter. We begin with the core economic problem—scarcity and choice—and the concept of the production possibilities frontier. We then learn about the central idea of economics: using resources efficiently. We also discover how we can expand production by accumulating capital, expanding our knowledge, and specializing and trading with each other. What you will learn in this chapter is the foundation on which all economics is built.

After studying this chapter, you will be able to

- **Define the production possibilities frontier and calculate opportunity cost**

- **Distinguish between production possibilities and preferences and describe an efficient allocation of resources**

- **Explain how current production choices expand future production possibilities**

- **Explain how specialization and trade expand our production possibilities**

- **Explain why property rights and markets have evolved**

Production Possibilities and Opportunity Cost

EVERY WORKING DAY, IN MINES, FACTORIES, SHOPS, and offices and on farms and construction sites across Canada, 16.5 million people produce a vast variety of goods and services valued at $4 billion. But the quantities of goods and services that we can produce are limited by both our available resources and by technology. And if we want to increase our production of one good, we must decrease our production of something else—we face tradeoffs. You are going to learn about the production possibilities frontier, which describes the limit to what we can produce and provides a neat way of thinking about and illustrating the idea of a tradeoff.

The **production possibilities frontier** *(PPF)* is the boundary between those combinations of goods and services that can be produced and those that cannot. To illustrate the *PPF*, we focus on two goods at a time and hold the quantities produced of all the other goods and services constant. That is, we look at a *model* economy in which everything remains the same (*ceteris paribus*) except for the production of the two goods we are considering.

Let's look at the production possibilities frontier for CDs and pizza, which stand for *any* pair of goods or services.

Production Possibilities Frontier

The *production possibilities frontier* for CDs and pizza shows the limits to the production of these two goods, given the total resources available to produce them. Figure 2.1 shows this production possibilities frontier. The table lists some combinations of the quantities of pizzas and CDs that can be produced in a month given the resources available. The figure graphs these combinations. The *x*-axis shows the quantity of pizzas produced, and the *y*-axis shows the quantity of CDs produced.

The *PPF* illustrates *scarcity* because we cannot attain the points outside the frontier. They are points that describe wants that can't be satisfied. We can produce at all the points *inside* the *PPF* and *on* the *PPF*. They are attainable points. Suppose that in a typical month, we produce 4 million pizzas and 5 million CDs. Figure 2.1 shows this combination as point *E* and as possibility *E* in the table. The figure also shows

FIGURE 2.1
Production Possibilities Frontier

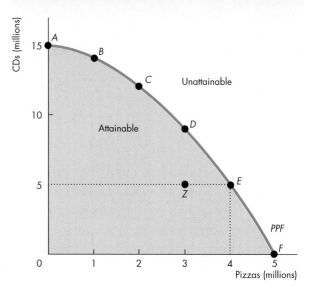

Possibility	Pizzas (millions)		CDs (millions)
A	0	and	15
B	1	and	14
C	2	and	12
D	3	and	9
E	4	and	5
F	5	and	0

The table lists six points on the production possibilities frontier for CDs and pizza. Row *A* tells us that if we produce no pizza, the maximum quantity of CDs we can produce is 15 million. Points *A, B, C, D, E,* and *F* in the figure represent the rows of the table. The line passing through these points is the production possibilities frontier (*PPF*). The *PPF* separates the attainable from the unattainable. Production is possible at any point *inside* the orange area or *on* the frontier. Points outside the frontier are unattainable. Points inside the frontier such as point *Z* are inefficient because resources are wasted or misallocated. At such points, it is possible to use the available resources to produce more of either or both goods.

other production possibilities. For example, we might stop producing pizza and move all the people who produce it into producing CDs. Point *A* in the figure and possibility *A* in the table show this case. The quantity of CDs produced increases to 15 million, and pizza production dries up. Alternatively, we might close the CD factories and switch all the resources into producing pizza. In this situation, we produce 5 million pizzas. Point *F* in the figure and possibility *F* in the table show this case.

Production Efficiency

We achieve **production efficiency** if we cannot produce more of one good without producing less of some other good. When production is efficient, we are at a point *on* the *PPF*. If we are at a point *inside* the *PPF*, such as point *Z*, production is *inefficient* because we have some *unused* resources or we have some *misallocated* resources or both.

Resources are unused when they are idle but could be working. For example, we might leave some of the factories idle or some workers unemployed.

Resources are *misallocated* when they are assigned to tasks for which they are not the best match. For example, we might assign skilled pizza makers to work in a CD factory and skilled CD makers to work in a pizza shop. We could get more pizza *and* more CDs from these same workers if we reassigned them to the tasks that more closely match their skills.

If we produce at a point inside the *PPF* such as *Z*, we can use our resources more efficiently to produce more pizzas, more CDs, or more of *both* pizzas and CDs. But if we produce at a point *on* the *PPF*, we are using our resources efficiently and we can produce more of one good only if we produce less of the other. That is, along the *PPF*, we face a *tradeoff*.

Tradeoff Along the *PPF*

Every choice *along* the *PPF* involves a *tradeoff*—we must give up something to get something else. On the *PPF* in Fig. 2.1, we must give up some CDs to get more pizza or give up some pizza to get more CDs.

Tradeoffs arise in every imaginable real-world situation, and you reviewed several of them in Chapter 1. At any given point in time, we have a fixed amount of labour, land, capital, and entrepreneurship. By using our available technologies, we can employ these resources to produce goods and services. But we are

limited in what we can produce. This limit defines a boundary between what we can attain and what we cannot attain. This boundary is the real-world's production possibilities frontier, and it defines the tradeoffs that we must make. On our real-world *PPF*, we can produce more of any one good or service only if we produce less of some other goods or services.

When doctors say that we must spend more on AIDS and cancer research, they are suggesting a tradeoff: more medical research for less of some other things. When the prime minister says that he wants to spend more on education and health care, he is suggesting a tradeoff: more education and health care for less national defence or less private spending (because of higher taxes). When an environmental group argues for less logging, it is suggesting a tradeoff: greater conservation of endangered wildlife for less paper. When your parents say that you should study more, they are suggesting a tradeoff: more study time for less leisure or sleep.

All tradeoffs involve a cost—an opportunity cost.

Opportunity Cost

The *opportunity cost* of an action is the highest-valued alternative forgone. The *PPF* helps us to make the concept of opportunity cost precise and enables us to calculate it. Along the *PPF*, there are only two goods, so there is only one alternative forgone: some quantity of the other good. Given our current resources and technology, we can produce more pizzas only if we produce fewer CDs. The opportunity cost of producing an additional pizza is the number of CDs we *must* forgo. Similarly, the opportunity cost of producing an additional CD is the quantity of pizzas we *must* forgo.

For example, at point *C* in Fig. 2.1, we produce fewer pizzas and more CDs than at point *D*. If we choose point *D* over point *C*, the additional 1 million pizzas *cost* 3 million CDs. One pizza costs 3 CDs.

We can also work out the opportunity cost of choosing point *C* over point *D* in Fig. 2.1. If we move from point *D* to point *C*, the quantity of CDs produced increases by 3 million and the quantity of pizzas produced decreases by 1 million. So if we choose point *C* over point *D*, the additional 3 million CDs *cost* 1 million pizzas. One CD costs 1/3 of a pizza.

Opportunity Cost Is a Ratio   Opportunity cost is a ratio. It is the decrease in the quantity produced of one good divided by the increase in the quantity produced of another good as we move along the production possibilities frontier.

Because opportunity cost is a ratio, the opportunity cost of producing an additional CD is equal to the *inverse* of the opportunity cost of producing an additional pizza. Check this proposition by returning to the calculations we've just worked through. When we move along the *PPF* from C to D, the opportunity cost of a pizza is 3 CDs. The inverse of 3 is 1/3, so if we decrease the production of pizza and increase the production of CDs by moving from D to C, the opportunity cost of a CD must be 1/3 of a pizza. You can check that this number is correct. If we move from D to C, we produce 3 million more CDs and 1 million fewer pizzas. Because 3 million CDs cost 1 million pizzas, the opportunity cost of 1 CD is 1/3 of a pizza.

Increasing Opportunity Cost The opportunity cost of a pizza increases as the quantity of pizzas produced increases. Also, the opportunity cost of a CD increases as the quantity of CDs produced increases. This phenomenon of increasing opportunity cost is reflected in the shape of the *PPF*—it is bowed outward.

When a large quantity of CDs and a small quantity of pizzas are produced—between points A and B in Fig. 2.1—the frontier has a gentle slope. A given increase in the quantity of pizzas *costs* a small decrease in the quantity of CDs, so the opportunity cost of a pizza is a small quantity of CDs.

When a large quantity of pizzas and a small quantity of CDs are produced—between points E and F in Fig. 2.1—the frontier is steep. A given increase in the quantity of pizzas *costs* a large decrease in the quantity of CDs, so the opportunity cost of a pizza is a large quantity of CDs.

The *PPF* is bowed outward because resources are not all equally productive in all activities. People with several years of experience working for Sony are good at producing CDs but not very good at making pizzas. So if we move some of these people from Sony to Domino's, we get a small increase in the quantity of pizzas but a large decrease in the quantity of CDs.

Similarly, people who have spent years working at Domino's are good at producing pizzas, but they have no idea how to produce CDs. So if we move some of these people from Domino's to Sony, we get a small increase in the quantity of CDs but a large decrease in the quantity of pizzas. The more of either good we try to produce, the less productive are the additional

resources we use to produce that good and the larger is the opportunity cost of a unit of that good.

Increasing Opportunity Costs Are Everywhere Just about every activity that you can think of is one with an increasing opportunity cost. We allocate the most skillful farmers and the most fertile land to the production of food. And we allocate the best doctors and the least fertile land to the production of health-care services. If we shift fertile land and tractors away from farming to hospitals and ambulances and ask farmers to become hospital porters, the production of food drops drastically and the increase in the production of health-care services is small. The opportunity cost of a unit of health-care services rises. Similarly, if we shift our resources away from health care towards farming, we must use more doctors and nurses as farmers and more hospitals as hydroponic tomato factories. The decrease in the production of health-care services is large, but the increase in food production is small. The opportunity cost of a unit of food rises.

This example is extreme and unlikely, but these same considerations apply to any pair of goods that you can imagine.

REVIEW QUIZ

1 How does the production possibilities frontier illustrate scarcity?
2 How does the production possibilities frontier illustrate production efficiency?
3 How does the production possibilities frontier show that every choice involves a tradeoff?
4 How does the production possibilities frontier illustrate opportunity cost?
5 Why is opportunity cost a ratio?
6 Why does the *PPF* for most goods bow outward so that opportunity cost increases as the quantity produced of a good increases?

myeconlab Study Plan 2.1

We've seen that what we can produce is limited by the production possibilities frontier. We've also seen that production on the *PPF* is efficient. But we can produce many different quantities on the *PPF*. How do we choose among them? How do we know which point on the *PPF* is the best one?

Using Resources Efficiently

YOU'VE SEEN THAT WE ACHIEVE PRODUCTION efficiency at every point on the *PPF*. But which point is best? What quantities of CDs and pizzas best serve the social interest?

This question is an example of real-world questions of enormous consequence such as: How much should we spend on treating AIDS and how much on cancer research? Should we expand education and health-care programs or cut taxes? Should we spend more on the preservation of rainforests and the conservation of endangered wildlife?

To answer these questions, we must find a way of measuring and comparing costs and benefits.

The *PPF* and Marginal Cost

The **marginal cost** of a good is the opportunity cost of producing *one more unit* of it. We calculate marginal cost from the *slope* of the *PPF*. As the quantity of pizza produced increases, the *PPF* gets steeper and marginal cost increases. Figure 2.2 illustrates the calculation of the marginal cost of a pizza.

Begin by finding the opportunity cost of pizza in blocks of 1 *million* pizzas. The first million pizzas cost 1 million CDs, the second million pizzas cost 2 million CDs, the third million pizzas cost 3 million CDs, and so on. The bars in part (a) illustrate these calculations.

The bars in part (b) show the cost of an average pizza in each of the 1 million pizza blocks. Focus on the 3rd million pizzas—the move from *C* to *D* in part (a). Over this range, because the 1 million pizzas cost 3 million CDs, one of these pizzas, on the average, costs 3 CDs—the height of the bar in part (b).

Next, find the opportunity cost of *each* additional pizza—the marginal cost of a pizza. The marginal cost of a pizza is increasing as the quantity of pizza produced increases. The marginal cost at point *C* is less than it is at point *D*. On the average over the range from *C* to *D*, the marginal cost of a pizza is 3 CDs. But it exactly equals 3 CDs only in the middle of the range between *C* and *D*. The red dot in part (b) indicates that the marginal cost of a pizza is 3 CDs when 2.5 million pizzas are produced. Each black dot in part (b) is interpreted in the same way. The orange curve that passes through these dots, labelled *MC*, is the marginal cost curve. It shows the marginal cost of a pizza at each quantity of pizza as we move along the *PPF*.

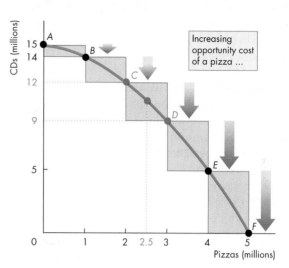

FIGURE 2.2

The *PPF* and Marginal Cost

(a) *PPF* and opportunity cost

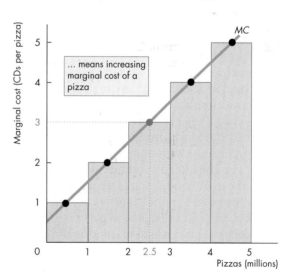

(b) Marginal cost

Marginal cost is calculated from the slope of the *PPF*. As the quantity of pizza produced increases, the *PPF* gets steeper and the marginal cost of a pizza increases. The bars in part (a) show the opportunity cost of pizza in blocks of 1 million pizzas. The bars in part (b) show the cost of an average pizza in each of these 1 million blocks. The orange curve, *MC*, shows the marginal cost of a pizza at each point along the *PPF*. This curve passes through the centre of each of the bars in part (b).

Preferences and Marginal Benefit

Look around your classroom and notice the wide variety of shirts, caps, pants, and shoes that you and your fellow students are wearing today. Why is there such a huge variety? Why don't you all wear the same styles and colours? The answer lies in what economists call preferences. **Preferences** are a description of a person's likes and dislikes.

You've seen that we have a concrete way of describing the limits to production: the *PPF*. We need a similarly concrete way of describing preferences. To describe preferences, economists use the concept of marginal benefit. The **marginal benefit** of a good or service is the benefit received from consuming one more unit of it.

We measure the marginal benefit of a good or service by the most that people are *willing to pay* for an additional unit of it. The idea is that you are not willing to pay more for a good than it is worth to you. But you are willing to pay an amount up to what it is worth. So the willingness to pay for something measures its marginal benefit.

Economists use the marginal benefit curve to illustrate preferences. The **marginal benefit curve** shows the relationship between the marginal benefit of a good and the quantity of that good consumed. It is a general principle that the more we have of any good or service, the smaller is its marginal benefit and the less we are willing to pay for an additional unit of it. This tendency is so widespread and strong that we call it a principle—the *principle of decreasing marginal benefit*.

The basic reason why marginal benefit of a good or service decreases as we consume more of it is that we like variety. The more we consume of any one good or service, the more of other things we see that we would like better.

Think about your willingness to pay for pizza (or any other item). If pizza is hard to come by and you can buy only a few slices a year, you might be willing to pay a high price to get an additional slice. But if pizza is all you've eaten for the past few days, you are willing to pay almost nothing for another slice.

In everyday life, we think of what we pay for goods and services as the money that we give up—dollars. But you've learned to think about cost as other goods or services forgone, not a dollar cost. You can think about willingness to pay in the same terms. The price you are willing to pay for something is the quantity of other goods and services that you are willing to forgo. Let's continue with the example of CDs and pizzas and illustrate preferences this way.

FIGURE 2.3

Preferences and the Marginal Benefit Curve

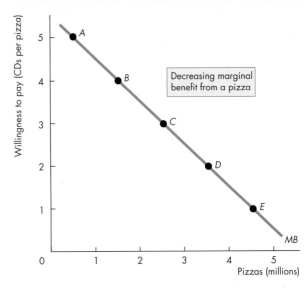

Possibility	Pizzas (millions)	Willingness to pay (CDs per pizza)
A	0.5	5
B	1.5	4
C	2.5	3
D	3.5	2
E	4.5	1

The smaller the quantity of pizzas produced, the more CDs people are willing to give up for an additional pizza. If pizza production is 0.5 million, people are willing to pay 5 CDs per pizza. But if pizza production is 4.5 million, people are willing to pay only 1 CD per pizza. Willingness to pay measures marginal benefit. And decreasing marginal benefit is a universal feature of people's preferences.

Figure 2.3 illustrates preferences as the willingness to pay for pizza in terms of CDs. In row *A*, pizza production is 0.5 million, and at that quantity, people are willing to pay 5 CDs per pizza. As the quantity of pizza produced increases, the amount that people are willing to pay for it falls. When pizza production is 4.5 million, people are willing to pay only 1 CD per pizza.

Let's now use the concepts of marginal cost and marginal benefit to describe the efficient quantity of pizzas to produce.

Efficient Use of Resources

When we cannot produce more of any one good without giving up some other good, we have achieved *production efficiency*, and we're producing at a point on the *PPF*. When we cannot produce more of any good without giving up some other good that we *value more highly*, we have achieved **allocative efficiency** and we are producing at the point on the *PPF* that we prefer above all other points.

Suppose in Fig. 2.4, we produce 1.5 million pizzas at point *A* on the *PPF*. The marginal cost of a pizza is 2 CDs and the marginal benefit from a pizza is 4 CDs. Because someone values an additional pizza more highly than it costs to produce, we can get more value from our resources by moving some of them out of producing CDs and into producing pizzas.

Now suppose we produce 3.5 million pizzas at point *C* on the *PPF*. The marginal cost of a pizza is now 4 CDs but the marginal benefit is only 2 CDs. Because the additional pizza costs more to produce than anyone thinks it is worth, we can get more value from our resources by moving some of them away from producing pizzas and into producing CDs.

But suppose we produce 2.5 million pizzas at point *B* on the *PPF*. Marginal cost and marginal benefit are now equal at 3 CDs. This allocation of resources is efficient. If more pizzas are produced, the forgone CDs are worth more than the additional pizzas. If fewer pizzas are produced, the forgone pizzas are worth more than the additional CDs.

REVIEW QUIZ

1 What is marginal cost? How is it measured?
2 What is marginal benefit? How is it measured?
3 How does the marginal benefit from a good change as the quantity of that good increases?
4 What is production efficiency and how does it relate to the production possibilities frontier?
5 What conditions must be satisfied if resources are used efficiently?

myeconlab Study Plan 2.2

You now understand the limits to production and the conditions under which resources are used efficiently. Your next task is to study the expansion of production possibilities.

FIGURE 2.4
Efficient Use of Resources

(a) On the PPF

(b) Marginal benefit equals marginal cost

The greater the quantity of pizzas produced, the smaller is the marginal benefit (*MB*) from pizza—the fewer CDs people are willing to give up to get an additional pizza. But the greater the quantity of pizzas produced, the greater is the marginal cost (*MC*) of pizza—the more CDs people must give up to get an additional pizza. When marginal benefit equals marginal cost, resources are being used efficiently.

Economic Growth

DURING THE PAST 30 YEARS, PRODUCTION PER person in the Canada has doubled. Such an expansion of production is called **economic growth**. Economic growth increases our *standard of living*, but it doesn't overcome scarcity and avoid opportunity cost. To make our economy grow, we face a trade-off—the faster we make production grow, the greater is the opportunity cost of economic growth.

The Cost of Economic Growth

Two key factors influence economic growth: technological change and capital accumulation. **Technological change** is the development of new goods and of better ways of producing goods and services. **Capital accumulation** is the growth of capital resources, which includes *human capital*.

As a consequence of technological change and capital accumulation, we have an enormous quantity of cars that enable us to produce more transportation than was available when we had only horses and carriages; we have satellites that make global communications possible on a scale that is much larger than that produced by the earlier cable technology. But new technologies and new capital have an opportunity cost. To use resources in research and development and to produce new capital, we must decrease our production of consumption goods and services. Let's look at this opportunity cost.

Instead of studying the *PPF* of pizzas and CDs, we'll hold the quantity of CDs produced constant and examine the *PPF* for pizzas and pizza ovens. Figure 2.5 shows this *PPF* as the blue curve *ABC*. If we devote no resources to producing pizza ovens, we produce at point *A*. If we produce 3 million pizzas, we can produce 6 pizza ovens at point *B*. If we produce no pizza, we can produce 10 ovens at point *C*.

The amount by which our production possibilities expand depends on the resources we devote to technological change and capital accumulation. If we devote no resources to this activity (point *A*), our *PPF* remains at *ABC*—the blue curve in Fig. 2.5. If we cut the current production of pizza and produce 6 ovens (point *B*), then in the future, we'll have more capital and our *PPF* will rotate outward to the position shown by the red curve. The fewer resources we devote to producing pizza and the more resources we

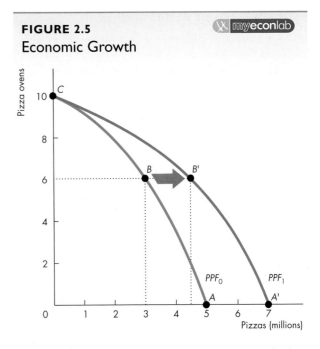

FIGURE 2.5
Economic Growth

PPF_0 shows the limits to the production of pizza and pizza ovens, with the production of all other goods and services remaining the same. If we devote no resources to producing pizza ovens and produce 5 million pizzas, we remain at point *A*. But if we decrease pizza production to 3 million and produce 6 ovens, at point *B*, our production possibilities expand. After one period, the *PPF* rotates outward to PPF_1 and we can produce at point *B'*, a point outside the original *PPF*. We can rotate the *PPF* outward, but we cannot avoid opportunity cost. The opportunity cost of producing more pizzas in the future is fewer pizzas today.

devote to producing ovens, the greater is the expansion of our production possibilities.

Economic growth is not free. To make it happen, we devote resources to producing new ovens and less to producing pizza. In Fig. 2.5, we move from *A* to *B*. There is no free lunch. The opportunity cost of more pizzas in the future is fewer pizzas today. Also, economic growth is no magic formula for abolishing scarcity. On the new production possibilities frontier, we continue to face a tradeoff and opportunity cost.

The ideas about economic growth that we have explored in the setting of the pizza industry also apply to nations. Let's look at two examples.

Economic Growth in Canada and Hong Kong

If as a nation we devote all our resources to producing consumption goods and none to research and capital accumulation, our production possibilities in the future will be the same as they are today. To expand our production possibilities in the future, we must devote fewer resources to producing consumption goods and some resources to accumulating capital and developing technologies so that we can produce more consumption goods in the future. The decrease in today's consumption is the opportunity cost of an increase in future consumption.

The experiences of Canada and Hong Kong make a striking example of the effects of our choices on the rate of economic growth. In 1965, the production possibilities per person in Canada were three times those in Hong Kong (see Fig. 2.6). Canada devoted one-fifth of its resources to accumulating capital and the other four-fifths to consumption. In 1965, Canada was at point *A* on its *PPF*. Hong Kong devoted one-third of its resources to accumulating capital and two-thirds to consumption. In 1965, Hong Kong was at point *A* on its *PPF*.

Since 1965, both countries have experienced economic growth, but growth in Hong Kong has been more rapid than that in Canada. Because Hong Kong devoted a bigger fraction of its resources to accumulating capital, its production possibilities have expanded more quickly.

By 2005, the production possibilities per person in Hong Kong and Canada were similar. If Hong Kong continues to devote more resources to accumulating capital than we do (at point *B* on its 2005 *PPF*), Hong Kong will continue to grow more rapidly than Canada. But if Hong Kong increases consumption and decreases capital accumulation (moving to point *D* on its 2005 *PPF*), then its rate of economic growth will slow.

Canada is typical of the rich industrial countries, which include the United States, Western Europe, and Japan. Hong Kong is typical of the fast-growing Asian economies, which include Taiwan, Thailand, South Korea, and China. Growth in these countries slowed during the Asia crisis of 1998 but quickly rebounded. Production possibilities expand in these countries by between 5 and almost 10 percent a year. If these high growth rates are maintained, these other Asian countries will eventually close the gap on Canada as Hong Kong has done.

FIGURE 2.6   myeconlab
Economic Growth in Canada and Hong Kong

In 1965, the production possibilities per person in Canada were much larger than those in Hong Kong. But Hong Kong devoted more of its resources to accumulating capital than did Canada, so Hong Kong's production possibilities frontier has shifted outward more quickly than has that of Canada. In 2005, Hong Kong's production possibilities per person were similar to those in Canada.

REVIEW QUIZ

1 What are the two key factors that generate economic growth?
2 How does economic growth influence the production possibilities frontier?
3 What is the opportunity cost of economic growth?
4 Why has Hong Kong experienced faster economic growth than Canada has?

myeconlab **Study Plan 2.3**

Next, we're going to study another way in which we expand our production possibilities—the amazing fact that *both* buyers and sellers gain from specialization and trade.

Gains from Trade

PEOPLE CAN PRODUCE FOR THEMSELVES ALL THE goods that they consume, or they can concentrate on producing one good (or perhaps a few goods) and then trade with others—exchange some of their own goods for those of others. Concentrating on the production of only one good or a few goods is called *specialization*. We are going to discover how people gain by specializing in the production of the good in which they have a *comparative advantage* and trading with each other.

Comparative Advantage and Absolute Advantage

A person has a **comparative advantage** in an activity if that person can perform the activity at a lower opportunity cost than anyone else. Differences in opportunity costs arise from differences in individual abilities and from differences in the characteristics of capital and land.

No one excels at everything. One person is an outstanding pitcher but a poor catcher; another person is a brilliant lawyer but a poor teacher. In almost all human endeavours, what one person does easily, someone else finds difficult. The same applies to land and capital. One plot of land is fertile but has no mineral deposits; another plot of land has outstanding views but is infertile. One machine has great precision but is difficult to operate; another is fast but often breaks down.

Although no one excels at everything, some people excel and can outperform others in a large number of activities—and perhaps even in all activities. A person who is more productive than others has an **absolute advantage**.

Absolute advantage involves comparing productivities—production per hour—while comparative advantage involves comparing opportunity costs.

Notice that a person who has an absolute advantage does not have a *comparative* advantage in every activity. John Grisham is a better lawyer and a better writer of fast-paced thrillers than most people. He has an absolute advantage in these two activities. But compared to others, he is a better writer than lawyer, so his *comparative* advantage is in writing.

Because people's abilities and the quality of their resources differ, they have different opportunity costs of producing various goods. These differences in opportunity cost are the source of comparative advantage.

Let's explore the idea of comparative advantage by looking at two smoothie bars: one operated by Liz and the other operated by Joe.

Liz's Smoothie Bar Liz produces smoothies and salads. In Liz's high-tech bar, she can turn out either a smoothie or a salad every 90 seconds. If she spends all her time making smoothies, she produces 40 an hour. And if she spends all her time making salads, she also produces 40 an hour. If she splits her time equally between the two, she can produce 20 smoothies and 20 salads an hour. For each additional smoothie Liz produces, she must decrease her production of salads by one and for each additional salad she produces, she must decrease her production of smoothies by one. So

Liz's opportunity cost of producing 1 smoothie is 1 salad,

and

Liz's opportunity cost of producing 1 salad is 1 smoothie.

Liz's customers buy smoothies and salads in equal quantities, so she splits her time equally between the two items and produces 20 smoothies and 20 salads an hour.

Joe's Smoothie Bar Joe also produces both smoothies and salads. But Joe's bar is smaller than Liz's. Also, Joe has only one blender and it's a slow old machine. Even if Joe uses all his resources to produce smoothies, he can produce only 6 an hour. But Joe is pretty good in the salad department so if he uses all his resources to make salads, he can produce 30 an hour.

TABLE 2.1	Liz's Production Possibilities	
Item	Minutes to produce 1	Quantity per hour
Smoothies	1.5	40
Salads	1.5	40

TABLE 2.2	Joe's Production Possibilities	
Item	Minutes to produce 1	Quantity per hour
Smoothies	10	6
Salads	2	30

Joe's ability to make smoothies and salads is the same regardless of how he splits an hour between the two tasks. He can make a salad in 2 minutes or a smoothie in 10 minutes. For each additional smoothie Joe produces, he must decrease his production of salads by 5. And for each additional salad he produces, he must decrease his production of smoothies by 1/5 of a smoothie. So

Joe's opportunity cost of producing 1 smoothie is 5 salads,

and

Joe's opportunity cost of producing 1 salad is 1/5 of a smoothie.

Joe's customers, like Liz's, buy smoothies and salads in equal quantities. So Joe spends 50 minutes of each hour making smoothies and 10 minutes of each hour making salads. With this division of his time, Joe produces 5 smoothies and 5 salads an hour.

Liz's Absolute Advantage You can see from the numbers that describe the two smoothie bars that Liz is four times as productive as Joe—her 20 smoothies and salads an hour are four times Joe's 5. Liz has an absolute advantage—she is more productive than Joe in producing both smoothies and salads. But Liz has a comparative advantage in only one of the activities.

Liz's Comparative Advantage In which of the two activities does Liz have a comparative advantage? Recall that comparative advantage is a situation in which one person's opportunity cost of producing a good is lower than another person's opportunity cost of producing that same good. Liz has a comparative advantage in producing smoothies. Her opportunity cost of a smoothie is 1 salad, whereas Joe's opportunity cost of a smoothie is 5 salads.

Joe's Comparative Advantage If Liz has a comparative advantage in producing smoothies, Joe must have a comparative advantage in producing salads. His opportunity cost of a salad is 1/5 of a smoothie, while Liz's opportunity cost of a salad is 1 smoothie.

Achieving the Gains from Trade

Liz and Joe run into each other one evening in a singles bar. After a few minutes of getting acquainted, Liz tells Joe about her amazingly profitable smoothie business that is selling 20 smoothies and 20 salads an hour. Her only problem, she tells Joe, is that she wishes she could produce more because potential customers leave when her lines get too long.

Joe isn't sure whether to risk spoiling his chances by telling Liz about his own struggling business. But he takes the risk. When he explains to Liz that he spends 50 minutes of every hour making 5 smoothies and 10 minutes making 5 salads, Liz's eyes pop. "Have I got a deal for you!" she exclaims.

Here's the deal that Liz sketches on a table napkin. Joe stops making smoothies and allocates all his time to producing salads. And Liz increases her production of smoothies to 35 an hour and cuts her production of salads to 5 an hour—see Table 2.3(a).

TABLE 2.3	Liz and Joe Gain from Trade	
(a) Production	**Liz**	**Joe**
Smoothies	35	0
Salads	5	30
(b) Trade	**Liz**	**Joe**
Smoothies	sell 10	buy 10
Salads	buy 20	sell 20
(c) After trade	**Liz**	**Joe**
Smoothies	25	10
Salads	25	10
(d) Gains from trade	**Liz**	**Joe**
Smoothies	+5	+5
Salads	+5	+5

They then trade. Liz sells Joe 10 smoothies and Joe sells Liz 20 salads—the price of a smoothie is 2 salads—see Table 2.3(b).

After the trade, Joe has 10 salads—the 30 he produces minus the 20 he sells to Liz. And he has the 10 smoothies that he buys from Liz. So Joe doubles the quantities of smoothies and salads he can sell—see Table 2.3(c).

Liz has 25 smoothies— the 35 she produces minus the 10 she sells to Joe. And she has 25 salads— the 5 she produces plus the 20 she buys from Joe—see Table 2.3(c). Both Liz and Joe gain 5 smoothies and 5 salads—see Table 2.3(d).

Liz draws a graph (Fig. 2.7) to illustrate her suggestion. The blue *PPF* in part (a) shows Joe's production possibilities. He is producing at 5 smoothies and 5 salads an hour at point *A*. The blue *PPF* in part (b)

shows Liz's production possibilities. She is producing at 20 smoothies and 20 salads an hour at point *A*.

Liz's proposal is that they each produce more of the good in which they have a comparative advantage. Joe produces 30 salads and no smoothies at point *B* on his *PPF*. Liz produces 35 smoothies and 5 salads at the point *B* on her *PPF*.

Liz and Joe then trade— exchange—smoothies and salads at a price of 2 salads per smoothie, or 1/2 of a smoothie per salad. Joe gets smoothies for 2 salads each, which is less than the 5 salads it costs him to produce a smoothie. And Liz gets salads for 1/2 a smoothie each, which is less than the 1 smoothie that it costs her to produce a salad.

With trade, Joe has 10 smoothies and 10 salads at point *C*—a gain of 5 smoothies and 5 salads. Joe moves to a point *outside* his *PPF*.

FIGURE 2.7
The Gains from Trade

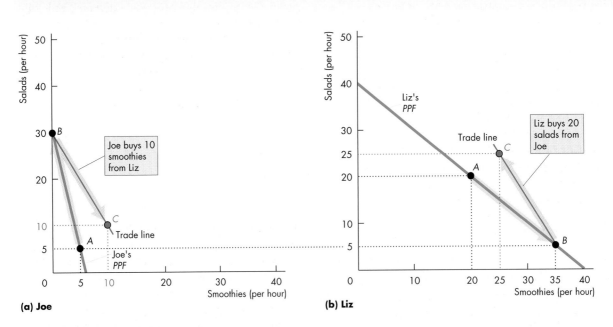

(a) Joe

(b) Liz

Joe initially produces at point *A* on his *PPF* in part (a), and Liz initially produces at point *A* on her *PPF* in part (b). Joe's opportunity cost of producing a salad is less than Liz's, so Joe has a comparative advantage in producing salad. Liz's opportunity cost of producing a smoothie is less than Joe's, so Liz has a comparative advantage in producing smoothies. If Joe specializes in salad, he produces 30 salads and no smoothies at point *B* on his *PPF*. If Liz produces 35 smoothies

and 5 salads, she produces at point *B* on her *PPF*. They exchange salads for smoothies along the red "Trade line." Liz buys salads from Joe for less than her opportunity cost of producing them, and Joe buys smoothies from Liz for less than his opportunity cost of producing them. Each goes to point *C*—a point outside his or her *PPF*. Both Joe and Liz increase production by 5 smoothies and 5 salads with no change in resources.

With trade, Liz has 25 smoothies and 25 salads at point *C*—a gain of 5 smoothies and 5 salads. Liz moves to a point *outside* her *PPF.*

Despite Liz's absolute advantage in producing smoothies and salads, both Liz and Joe gain from producing more of the good in which they have a comparative advantage and trading.

The gains that we achieve from international trade are similar to those achieved by Joe and Liz in this example. When Canadians buy T-shirts from China and when China buys regional jets from Canada, both countries gain. We get our shirts at a lower cost than that at which we can produce them, and China gets its regional jets at a lower cost than that at which it can produce them.

Dynamic Comparative Advantage

At any given point in time, the resources and technologies available determine the comparative advantages that individuals and nations have. But just by repeatedly producing a particular good or service, people become more productive in that activity, a phenomenon called **learning-by-doing**. Learning-by-doing is the basis of *dynamic* comparative advantage. **Dynamic comparative advantage** is a comparative advantage that a person (or country) possesses as a result of having specialized in a particular activity and, as a result of learning-by-doing, having become the producer with the lowest opportunity cost.

Singapore, for example, pursued dynamic comparative advantage vigorously when it decided to begin a bio-technology industry in which it initially didn't have a comparative advantage.

REVIEW QUIZ

1 What gives a person a comparative advantage?
2 Distinguish between comparative advantage and absolute advantage.
3 Is production still efficient when people specialize?
4 Why do people specialize and trade?
5 What are the gains from specialization and trade?
6 What is the source of the gains from trade?
7 How does dynamic comparative advantage arise?

myeconlab Study Plan 2.4

Economic Coordination

PEOPLE GAIN BY SPECIALIZING IN THE PRODUCTION of those goods and services in which they have a comparative advantage and then trading with each other. Liz and Joe, whose production of salads and smoothies we studied earlier in this chapter, can get together and make a deal that enables them to enjoy the gains from specialization and trade. But for billions of individuals to specialize and produce millions of different goods and services, their choices must somehow be coordinated.

Two competing economic coordination systems have been used—central economic planning and decentralized markets.

Central economic planning might appear to be the best system because it can express national priorities. But when this system was tried, as it was for 60 years in Russia, and for 30 years in China, it was a miserable failure. Today, these and most other previously planned economies are adopting a decentralized market system.

To make decentralized coordination work, four complementary social institutions that have evolved over many centuries are required. They are

- Firms
- Property rights
- Markets
- Money

Firms

A **firm** is an economic unit that hires factors of production and organizes those factors to produce and sell goods and services. Examples of firms are your local gas station, Wal-Mart, and Roots.

Firms coordinate a huge amount of economic activity. The coffee shop Second Cup, for example, might buy the machines and labour services of Liz and Joe and start to produce salads *and* smoothies at all its outlets.

But if a firm gets too big, it can't keep track of all the information that is needed to coordinate its activities. For this reason, firms themselves specialize and trade with each other. For example, Wal-Mart could produce all the things that it sells in its stores. And it could produce all the raw materials that are used to produce the things that it sells. But Sam Walton would not have become one of the wealthiest people in the world if he had followed that path. Instead, Wal-Mart buys from other firms that specialize in the production of a narrow range of items. And this trade takes place in markets.

Property Rights

The social arrangements that govern the ownership, use, and disposal of resources, goods, and services are called **property rights**. *Real property* includes land and buildings—the things we call property in ordinary speech—and durable goods such as plant and equipment. *Financial property* includes stocks and bonds and money in the bank. *Intellectual property* is the intangible product of creative effort. This type of property includes books, music, computer programs, and inventions of all kinds and is protected by copyrights and patents.

Where property rights are enforced, people have the incentive to specialize and produce the goods in which each person has a comparative advantage. Where people can easily steal the production of others, then time, energy, and resources are devoted not to production but to protecting possessions. If we had not developed property rights, we would still be hunting and gathering like our Stone Age ancestors.

Markets

In ordinary speech, the word *market* means a place where people buy and sell goods such as fish, meat, fruits, and vegetables. In economics, a *market* has a more general meaning. A **market** is any arrangement that enables buyers and sellers to get information and to do business with each other. An example is the market in which oil is bought and sold—the world oil market. The world oil market is not a place. It is the network of oil producers, oil users, wholesalers, and brokers who buy and sell oil. In the world oil market, decision makers do not meet physically. They make deals throughout the world by telephone, fax, and direct computer link.

Markets have evolved because they facilitate trade. Without organized markets, we would miss out on a substantial part of the potential gains from trade. Enterprising individuals and firms, each pursuing their own self-interest, have profited from making markets—standing ready to buy or sell the items in which they specialize. But markets can work only when property rights exist.

Money

Money is any commodity or token that is generally acceptable as a means of payment. Liz and Joe didn't use money in the example above. They exchanged salads and smoothies. In principle, trade in markets can exchange any item for any other item. But you can perhaps imagine how complicated life would be if we exchanged goods for other goods. The "invention" of money makes trading in markets much more efficient.

Circular Flows Through Markets

Figure 2.8 shows the flows that result from the choices that households and firms make. Households specialize and choose the quantities of labour, land, capital, and entrepreneurship to sell or rent to firms. Firms choose the quantities of factors of production to hire. These (red) flows go through the *factor markets*. Households choose the quantities of goods and services to buy, and firms choose the quantities to produce. These (red) flows go through the *goods markets*. Households receive incomes and make expenditures on goods and services (green flows). These green flows are payments for the corresponding real (red) flows.

How do markets coordinate all these decisions?

Coordinating Decisions

Markets coordinate individual decisions through price adjustments. To see how, think about your local market for hamburgers. Suppose that some people who want to buy hamburgers are not able to do so. To make the choices of buyers and sellers compatible, buyers must scale down their appetites or more hamburgers must be offered for sale (or both must happen). A rise in the price of a hamburger produces this outcome. A higher price encourages producers to offer more hamburgers for sale. It also encourages some people to change their lunch plans. Fewer people buy hamburgers, and more buy hot dogs. More hamburgers (and more hot dogs) are offered for sale.

Alternatively, suppose that more hamburgers are available than people want to buy. In this case, to make the choices of buyers and sellers compatible, more hamburgers must be bought or fewer hamburgers must be offered for sale (or both). A fall in the price of a hamburger achieves this outcome. A lower price encourages firms to produce fewer hamburgers. It also encourages people to buy more hamburgers.

FIGURE 2.8

Circular Flows in the Market Economy

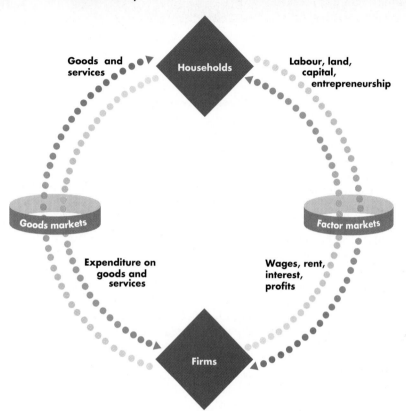

Households and firms make economic choices and markets coordinate these choices.

Households choose the quantities of labour, land, capital, and entrepreneurship to sell or rent to firms in exchange for wages, rent, interest, and profit. Households also choose how to spend their incomes on the various types of goods and services available.

Firms choose the quantities of factors of production to hire and the quantities of the goods and services to produce.

Goods markets and factor markets coordinate these choices of households and firms. The clockwise red flows are real flows—the flows of factors of production from households to firms and the flows of goods and services from firms to households. The counterclockwise green flows are the payments for the red flows—the flow of income for the factors of production and the flow of expenditure on goods and services.

REVIEW QUIZ

1 Why are social institutions such as markets and property rights necessary?

2 What are the main functions of markets?

3 What are the flows in the market economy that go from firms to households? Which of these flows is a money flow and which is a real flow?

myeconlab **Study Plan 2.5**

◆ You have now begun to see how economists approach economic questions. Scarcity, choice, and divergent opportunity costs explain why we specialize and trade and why firms, property rights, markets, and money have developed. You can see all around you the lessons you've learned in this chapter. *Reading Between the Lines* on pp. 48–49 gives an example. It explores the *PPF* of a student like you and the choices that students must make that influence their own economic growth—the growth of their incomes.

The Cost and Benefit of Education

GLOBE AND MAIL, AUGUST 28, 2002

Academics leap to defence of the MBA

They don't come with a guarantee, but business degrees offer students well-paying jobs with reputable companies, say many of Canada's top business schools, throwing coldwater on a new study questioning the value of an MBA. ...

After surveying decades of research, Jeffrey Pfeffer and Christina Fong of Stanford's graduate school of business have concluded that, with the possible exception of the most elite programs, master's degrees in business administration teach little that would be of real use in the business world. ...

The salaries for these graduates are a telling story. At Queen's University's School of Business, for example, the average starting salary is $95,000. Before joining the program, the average salary of students is $59,750. And at the Rotman School of Management at the University of Toronto, students entering the two-year program have salaries in the $50,000 [range] on average. But the average starting salary for this year's graduate was $89,000. ...

Brian Bemmels, associate dean for academic programs at the University of British Columbia's faculty of commerce, said the research article forces schools to evaluate their programs. He added that the article is based on a lot of opinion.

UBC's business school made a major change in 1995, restructuring its MBA program and reducing it to 15 months from two years to minimize losses of income to students. The average age of students in the program is 31.

Mr. Bemmels said the demand for an MBA degree speaks for itself. UBC had well over 700 applicants for 100 seats this year. Only 17 per cent of the incoming class has a business degree, he said. The rest are graduates of medicine, engineering and general arts.

"All these people wouldn't be doing it if they didn't think it was valuable," Mr. Bemmels said.

"I don't believe the notion that they have been fooled and tricked into something that's no good for them," he added.

Reprinted with permission from *The Globe and Mail.*

Essence of the Story

■ Jeffrey Pfeffer and Christina Fong of the Stanford Graduate School of Business say that MBA programs teach little of use in the business world.

■ The salaries earned by MBA graduates tell a different story.

■ The average starting salary for an MBA is $95,000, up from $59,750 before the MBA.

■ At the Rotman School of Management at the University of Toronto, students entering the two-year program have an average salary of $50,000 and an average starting salary of $89,000 after graduation.

■ Brian Bemmels said the UBC business school had over 700 applicants for 100 places and most were graduates of medicine, engineering, and general arts.

Economic Analysis

■ Education increases human capital and expands production possibilities.

■ The opportunity cost of a degree is forgone consumption. The payoff is an increase in lifetime production possibilities.

■ Figure 1 shows the choices facing a high school graduate who can consume education goods and services and consumption goods and services on the blue *PPF*.

■ Working full time, this person can consume at point *A* on the blue *PPF* in Fig. 1.

■ By attending university, the student moves from point *A* to point *B* along her *PPF*, forgoes current consumption (the opportunity cost of education), and increases the use of educational goods and services.

■ On graduating from university, earnings jump, so production possibilities expand to the red *PPF* in Fig. 1.

■ Figure 2 shows a university graduate's choices. The blue curve is the same *PPF* as the red *PPF* in Fig. 1.

■ Working full time, this person earns enough to consume at point *C* on the blue *PPF* in Fig. 2.

■ By pursuing an MBA, the student moves from point *C* to point *D* along her *PPF*, forgoes current consumption (the opportunity cost of an MBA), and increases the use of educational goods and services.

■ With an MBA, a person's earnings jump again, so production possibilities expand to the red *PPF* in Fig. 2.

■ For people who have the required ability, the benefits of post-secondary and post-graduate education exceed the costs.

You're the Voter

■ The Canada Millennium Scholarship Foundation, funded by the federal government, provides $4,000 a year to 900 young Canadians.

■ Do you think the Canada Millennium Scholarship Foundation should be expanded so that more students can benefit from it?

■ With the huge return from post-secondary and post-graduate education, why don't more people remain in school for longer?

■ Would you vote for or against a tax increase to provide greater funding for the Canada Millennium Scholarship Foundation? Why?

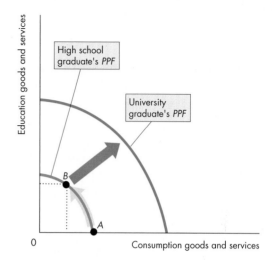

Figure 1 High school graduate's choices

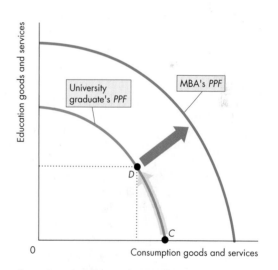

Figure 2 University graduate's choices

49

SUMMARY

KEY POINTS

Production Possibilities and Opportunity Cost (pp. 34–36)

- The production possibilities frontier, *PPF*, is the boundary between production levels that are attainable and those that are not attainable when all the available resources are used to their limit.
- Production efficiency occurs at points on the *PPF*.
- Along the *PPF*, the opportunity cost of producing more of one good is the amount of the other good that must be given up.
- The opportunity cost of a good increases as production of the good increases.

Using Resources Efficiently (pp. 37–39)

- The marginal cost of a good is the opportunity cost of producing one more unit.
- The marginal benefit from a good is the maximum amount of another good that a person is willing to forgo to obtain more of the first good.
- The marginal benefit of a good decreases as the amount of the good available increases.
- Resources are used efficiently when the marginal cost of each good is equal to its marginal benefit.

Economic Growth (pp. 40–41)

- Economic growth, which is the expansion of production possibilities, results from capital accumulation and technological change.
- The opportunity cost of economic growth is forgone current consumption.

Gains from Trade (pp. 42–45)

- A person has a comparative advantage in producing a good if that person can produce the good at a lower opportunity cost than everyone else.
- People gain by specializing in the activity in which they have a comparative advantage and trading with others.
- Dynamic comparative advantage arises from learning-by-doing.

Economic Coordination (pp. 45–47)

- Firms coordinate a large amount of economic activity, but there is a limit to the efficient size of a firm.
- Markets coordinate the economic choices of people and firms.
- Markets can work efficiently only when property rights exist.
- Money makes trading in markets more efficient.

KEY FIGURES

KEY TERMS

PROBLEMS

Go to myeconlab for solutions to odd-numbered problems and additional exercises.

1. Calculate Wendell's opportunity cost of one hour of tennis when he increases the time he plays tennis from
   a. 4 to 6 hours a week.
   b. 6 to 8 hours a week.

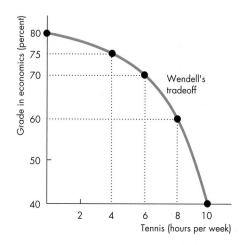

2. Calculate Tina's opportunity cost of a day of skiing when she increases her time spent skiing from
   a. 2 to 4 days a month.
   b. 4 to 6 days a month.

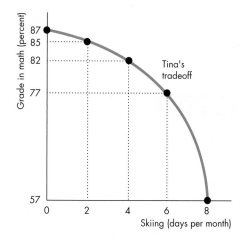

3. Wendell, in problem 1, has the following marginal benefit curve:

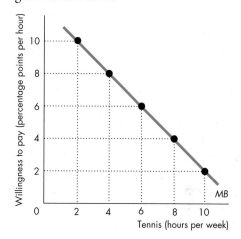

   a. If Wendell is efficient, what is his grade?
   b. Why would Wendell be worse off getting a higher grade?

4. Tina in problem 2, has the following marginal benefit curve:

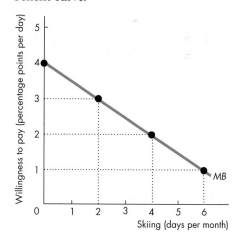

   a. If Tina is efficient, how much does she ski?
   b. Why would Tina be worse off spending more days a month skiing?

5. Sunland's production possibilities are

Food (kilograms per month)		Sunscreen (litres per month)
300	and	0
200	and	50
100	and	100
0	and	150

   a. Draw a graph of Sunland's *PPF.*

b. What are Sunland's opportunity costs of producing food and sunscreen at each output?

6. Jane's Island's production possibilities are

Corn (kilograms per month)		Cloth (metres per month)
6	and	0
4	and	2
2	and	4
0	and	6

a. Draw a graph of the *PPF* on Jane's Island.
b. What are Jane's opportunity costs of producing corn and cloth at each output in the table?

7. In problem 5, to get a litre of sunscreen the people of Sunland are willing to give up 5 kilograms of food if they have 25 litres of sunscreen, 2 kilograms of food if they have 75 litres of sunscreen, and 1 kilogram of food if they have 125 litres of sunscreen.
   a. Draw a graph of Sunland's marginal benefit from sunscreen.
   b. What is the efficient quantity of sunscreen?

8. In problem 6, to get a metre of cloth Jane is willing to give up 1.5 kilograms of corn if she has 2 metres of cloth; 1.0 kilogram of corn if she has 4 metres of cloth; and 0.5 kilograms of corn if she has 6 metres of cloth.
   a. Draw a graph of Jane's marginal benefit from cloth.
   b. What is Jane's efficient quantity of cloth?

9. Busyland's production possibilities are

Food (kilograms per month)		Sunscreen (litres per month)
150	and	0
100	and	100
50	and	200
0	and	300

Calculate Busyland's opportunity costs of food and sunscreen at each output in the table.

10. Joe Island's production possibilities are

Corn (kilograms per month)		Cloth (metres per month)
12	and	0
8	and	1
4	and	2
0	and	3

What are Joe's opportunity costs of producing corn and cloth at each output in the table?

11. In problems 5 and 9, Sunland and Busyland each produce and consume 100 kilograms of food and 100 litres of sunscreen per month, and they do not trade. Now the countries begin to trade with each other.
   a. What good does Sunland sell to Busyland and what good does it buy from Busyland?
   b. If Sunland and Busyland divide the total output of food and sunscreen equally, what are the gains from trade?

12. In problems 6 and 10, Jane's Island and Joe's Island each produce and consume 4 kilograms of corn and 2 metres of cloth and they do not trade. Now the islands begin to trade.
   a. What good does Jane sell to Joe and what good does Jane buy from Joe?
   b. If Jane and Joe divide the total output of corn and cloth equally, what are the gains from trade?

CRITICAL THINKING

1. After you have studied *Reading Between the Lines* on pp. 48–49, answer the following questions:
   a. At what point on the blue *PPF* in Fig. 1 on p. 49 is the combination of education goods and services and consumption goods and services efficient? Explain your answer.
   b. Students are facing rising tuition. How does higher tuition change the opportunity cost of education and how does it change the *PPF*s in Fig. 1 and Fig. 2?
   c. Who receives the benefits from education? Is the marginal cost of education equal to the marginal benefit of education? Is resource use in the market for education efficient?

WEB EXERCISES

Use the links on (X myeconlab) to work the following exercise.

1. Obtain data on the tuition and other costs of enrolling in the MBA program at a school that interests you.
   a. Draw a *PPF* that shows the tradeoff that you would face if you decided to enroll in the MBA program.
   b. Do you think the marginal benefit of an MBA exceeds the marginal cost?

Your Economic Revolution

Y ou are making progress in your study of economics. You've already encountered the big questions and big ideas of economics. And you've learned about the key insight that specialization and exchange create economic wealth.

You are studying economics at a time that future historians might call the *Information Revolution*. We reserve the word *Revolution* for big events that influence all future generations.

During the *Agricultural Revolution*, which occurred 10,000 years ago, people learned to domesticate animals and plant crops. They stopped roaming in search of food and settled in villages and eventually towns and cities, where they developed markets in which to exchange their products.

During the *Industrial Revolution*, which began 240 years ago, people used science to create new technologies. This revolution brought extraordinary wealth for some but created conditions in which others were left behind. It brought social and political tensions that we still face today.

During today's *Information Revolution*, people who embraced the new technologies prospered on an unimagined scale. But the incomes and living standards of the less educated are falling behind, and social and political tensions are increasing. Today's revolution has a global dimension. Some of the winners live in previously poor countries in Asia, and some of the losers live here in North America.

So you are studying economics at an interesting time. Whatever *your* motivation is for studying economics, *our* objective is to help you do well in your course, to enjoy it, and to develop a deeper understanding of the economic world around you.

Three reasons why we hope that we both succeed: First, a decent understanding of economics will help you to become a full participant in the Information Revolution. Second, an understanding of economics will help you play a more effective role as a citizen and voter and enable you to add your voice to those who are looking for solutions to our social and political problems. Third, you will enjoy the sheer fun of *understanding* the forces at play and how they are shaping our world.

If you are finding economics interesting, think seriously about majoring in the subject. A degree in economics gives the best training available in problem solving, offers lots of opportunities to develop conceptual skills, and opens doors to a wide range of graduate courses, including the MBA, and to a wide range of jobs. You can read more about the benefits of an economics degree in the essay by Robert Whaples and Harvey King in your *Study Guide*.

Economics was born during the Industrial Revolution. We'll look at its birth and meet its founder, Adam Smith. Then we'll talk about the progress that economists have made and some of the outstanding policy problems of today with one of today's most distinguished economists, Lawrence H. Summers, President of Harvard University.

The Sources of Economic Wealth

"It is not from the benevolence of the butcher, the brewer, or the baker that we expect our dinner, but from their regard to their own interest."

ADAM SMITH
The Wealth of Nations

THE FATHER OF ECONOMICS

Adam Smith *was a giant of a scholar who contributed to ethics and jurisprudence as well as economics. Born in 1723 in Kirkcaldy, a small fishing town near Edinburgh, Scotland, Smith was the only child of the town's customs officer (who died before Adam was born).*

His first academic appointment, at age 28, was as Professor of Logic at the University of Glasgow. He subsequently became tutor to a wealthy Scottish duke, whom he accompanied on a two-year grand European tour, following which he received a pension of £300 a year—ten times the average income at that time.

With the financial security of his pension, Smith devoted ten years to writing An Inquiry into the Nature and Causes of the Wealth of Nations, *which was published in 1776. Many people had written on economic issues before Adam Smith, but he made economics a science. Smith's account was so broad and authoritative that no subsequent writer on economics could advance ideas without tracing their connections to those of Adam Smith.*

THE ISSUES

Why are some nations wealthy while others are poor? This question lies at the heart of economics. And it leads directly to a second question: What can poor nations do to become wealthy?

Adam Smith, who is regarded by many scholars as the founder of economics, attempted to answer these questions in his book *The Wealth of Nations*, published in 1776. Smith was pondering these questions at the height of the Industrial Revolution. During these years, new technologies were invented and applied to the manufacture of cotton and wool cloth, iron, transportation, and agriculture.

Smith wanted to understand the sources of economic wealth, and he brought his acute powers of observation and abstraction to bear on the question. His answer:

- The division of labour
- Free markets

The division of labour—breaking tasks down into simple tasks and becoming skilled in those tasks—is the source of "the greatest improvement in the productive powers of labour," said Smith. The division of labour became even more productive when it was applied to creating new technologies. Scientists and engineers, trained in extremely narrow fields, became specialists at inventing. Their powerful skills accelerated the advance of technology, so by the 1820s, machines could make consumer goods faster and more accurately than any craftsman could. And by the 1850s, machines could make other machines that labour alone could never have made.

But, said Smith, the fruits of the division of labour are limited by the extent of the market. To make the market as large as possible, there must be no impediments to free trade both within a country and among countries. Smith argued that when each person makes the best possible economic choice, that choice leads as if by "an invisible hand" to the best outcome for society as a whole. The butcher, the brewer, and the baker each pursue their own interests but, in doing so, also serve the interests of everyone else.

THEN

Adam Smith speculated that one person, working hard, using the hand tools available in the 1770s, might possibly make 20 pins a day. Yet, he observed, by using those same hand tools but breaking the process into a number of individually small operations in which people specialize —by the *division of labour*—ten people could make a staggering 48,000 pins a day. One draws out the wire, another straightens it, a third cuts it, a fourth points it, a fifth grinds it. Three specialists make the head, and a fourth attaches it. Finally, the pin is polished and packaged. But a large market is needed to support the division of labour: one factory employing ten workers would need to sell more than 15 million pins a year to stay in business.

NOW

If Adam Smith were here today, the computer chip would fascinate him. He would see it as an extraordinary example of the productivity of the division of labour and of the use of machines to make machines that make other machines. From a design of a chip's intricate circuits, cameras transfer an image to glass plates that work like stencils. Workers prepare silicon wafers on which the circuits are printed. Some slice the wafers, others polish them, others bake them, and yet others coat them with a light-sensitive chemical. Machines transfer a copy of the circuit onto the wafer. Chemicals then etch the design onto the wafer. Further processes deposit atom-sized transistors and aluminum connectors. Finally, a laser separates the hundreds of chips on the wafer. Every stage in the process of creating a computer chip uses other computer chips. And like the pin of the 1770s, the computer chip of today benefits from a large market—a global market—to buy chips in the huge quantities in which they are produced efficiently.

Many economists have worked on the big themes that Adam Smith began. One of these is Lawrence H. Summers, President of Harvard University and a distinguished economist.

TALKING WITH

Lawrence H. Summers is President of Harvard University. Born in 1954 in New Haven, Connecticut, into a family of distinguished economists, he was an undergraduate at the Massachusetts Institute of Technology and a graduate student at Harvard University. While still in his 20s, he became one of the youngest tenured economics professors at Harvard University. In Washington, he has held a succession of public service jobs at the World Bank and in the U.S. government, culminating in 1999 with his appointment as Secretary of the Treasury—the chief financial officer of the United States and the president's highest-ranking advisor. Dr. Summers's research has covered an enormous range of macroeconomic and public policy issues that include capital taxation, unemployment, global financial crises, the transition to a market economy in Eastern Europe, and the problem of speeding progress in the developing countries.

Michael Parkin and Robin Bade talked with Lawrence Summers about his career and the progress that economists have made since the pioneering days of Adam Smith.

Lawrence H. Summers

How does Adam Smith's assessment of the "nature and causes of the wealth of nations" look today in light of the lessons that economists have learned over the past two centuries?

Adam Smith is looking very good today. I think one of the most important insights of the social sciences of the last several centuries is Smith's idea that good things can come from the invisible hand—from decentralization rather than from central planning and direction. But Smith is also prescient in recognizing the various qualifications to the argument for the invisible hand, whether involving fairness, externalities, or monopoly.

What do we know today that Adam Smith didn't know?

We know today much more than Smith did about economic fluctuations and about the role of money—about what we today call macroeconomics. We know more today about economic situations that involve bargaining, whether between two individuals or between small numbers of firms in an industry, or between a buyer and a seller. We know much more today about markets without perfect information. I know how good my used car is when I sell it—you don't when you buy it. I know whether I'm sick when I buy medical insurance, but the insurance company has to try to figure it out. The role of information in markets, which turns out to be quite profound, is something we understand much better today. And we also understand much better today the role of politics and governments in shaping the economy, which is far larger than it was in Smith's day.

Coincidentally, a few days before we're holding this conversation, a new nation was born—East Timor. What advice can economists offer a new and extremely poor nation as it takes its first steps?

Much of economic success involves strong rights to property. Has anyone ever washed a rented car or taken as good care of their hotel room as their home? When people own their farmlands, they're much more likely to farm them sustainably. When businesses own their machinery, they're much more likely to take care of it. When individuals own what they produce, they're much more likely to work hard.

Strong property rights and the framework of laws that support them are profoundly important to the market-based exchanges that are essential to economic success. So also is stable money that can be a basis for exchange. So also is an educated and capable population. But if there is a single lesson that is important for a starting economy, it is that strong property rights can motivate individuals.

One lesson that we've learned from your work at the World Bank is that the return to educating girls in developing countries is very high. What did you discover in that work?

Primary education, and especially for girls, may be the highest return investment available in the developing world. Those who read produce more and therefore earn more. Girls who are educated grow up to be better mothers who have smaller, happier, healthier families. Women who are educated are empowered with greater career options. They are less likely to fall into prostitution, and that reduces the spread of AIDS.

Women who are educated are much more likely to take care of the environment. So it is in many respects that primary education, and especially that of girls, generates very large returns.

Are there any other activities that yield comparable returns for developing countries?

Maybe some investments in health care that generate very large returns—it's a difficult evaluation to make. The really crucial lesson is that a country's most precious assets are its people, and investments in people are likely to be the most important investments of all.

Some of your earliest research was on taxing the income from capital. Why isn't the income from capital just like the income from labour?

Think about it this way: Two individuals both earn a hundred dollars. One spends it all this year; the other saves half of it and earns 10 percent interest next year. Who should pay more total taxes? Plausibly, for fairness, both should pay the same tax. A tax on income will lead to the same taxes in the first year for the two individuals; and higher taxes in the second year for the individual who saved.

In effect, taxes on capital income are taxes on future consumption, and it is far from clear why a society should want to tax future consumption more highly than present consumption.

On the other hand, very large fortunes often show up as capital income, and so designing a workable and fair tax system that doesn't tax investment income is something that is very difficult to do.

> " *The really crucial lesson is that a country's most precious assets are its people, and investments in people are likely to be the most important investments of all.* "

Would you say that we have not yet managed to figure this one out?

We'll all be working on finding the best tax systems for a long time to come. And it may mean that the income tax is, as Churchill said of democracy, terrible but the best alternative.

The United States has a large and persistent current account deficit, a low personal saving rate, and a projected deficit in the Social Security and Medicare trust funds. Are you concerned about these problems?

Herb Stein, who was a leading American policy economist, once said that the unsustainable cannot be sustained and must surely end!

This is a concern, given that U.S. national debt to foreigners is rising faster than U.S. income. And it's a concern in terms of the financing of Social Security and Medicare as our population ages. In a way, the solution to both these problems is more American saving, because that will put us in a stronger position as our population ages, and will allow us to have investment in the United States without incurring debts to foreigners.

Probably the most potent way of increasing a country's national savings is to improve the position of its budget. Whether to increase taxes or cut expenditures is a judgment for the congress to debate. My guess is that some combination would be appropriate. There are aspects of expenditures that are going to be hard to control. On the other hand, there are other aspects in terms of transfer payments and terms of various subsidies where economies probably are possible. And one virtue of a strong fiscal position is that it reduces interest expense down the road.

Did you always want to be an economist? How did you choose economics?

I thought I would be a mathematician or a physicist, but found myself very interested in questions of public policy. I was very involved in debate when I was in college. So I found myself wanting very much to combine an interest in public policy issues with an analytical approach, and economics gave me a way to do that. I also found that I had some aptitude, relative to my aptitude for pure mathematics or physics, so I gravitated to economics.

What led a brilliant academic economist to Washington? What did you want to achieve?

I hoped to put to use some of what I had learned in my studies in a direct way and to enhance my understanding of the way actual economies work by seeing how the policy process operated. I had a great time in Washington and feel that my economics training made a huge difference in everything I did. Whether it was thinking about how to respond to the Mexican and Asian financial crises or working on financial deregulation. Whether it was choosing optimal investments for the Customs Department in protecting our borders or designing tax incentives to promote saving. Whether it was supporting the protection of the Social Security trust fund or thinking about enforcement policies against corporate tax shelters. Principles of economics—in terms of maximizing benefits relative to costs, in terms of always thinking of the margin, in terms of always recognizing the opportunity cost of choices taken, in terms of always needing to see things add up—was quite valuable.

And what insights does economics bring to the task of running a major university?

I came to Harvard because I thought after my time in government the two most important resources that were going to shape the economies of the future were leaders and new ideas, and those are the two things that a university produces.

Successful leadership in a university is all about what economists think about all the time—incentives—whether it's for professors to do a good job teaching, attracting the best scholars in a particular area, or motivating concern and research about the most important problems.

Leadership and management for the university are very much about economics because they're very much about incentives. Some of them are pecuniary and involve money, but other incentives come from people's feelings of being appreciated; they come from the teams in which people have an opportunity to work; they come from the way in which the university is organized. If working at the treasury was heavily about applied macroeconomics, leadership in the university is heavily about applied microeconomics.

What is your advice to a student who is just setting out to become an economist? What other subjects work well with economics?

The best advice to students is, don't be a commodity that's available in a perfectly competitive market. Stand out by developing your own distinctive expertise in something you care deeply about. It matters much less what it is and much more that it be yours and it not be a hundred other people's.

I think there is enormous potential in almost every area of economics, but I think that the people who will contribute the most to economics over the next quarter century will be those who have some keen understanding of the context in which economics is playing out—the international context, the technological context, and the political context. So my hope would be that those interested in economics would understand that economics is very different from physics in that it is tracking a changing reality and that in order to do the best economics in a given period, you have to be able to track that changing reality, and that means understanding international, technological, and political contexts.

Demand and Supply

Slide, Rocket, and Roller Coaster

Slide, rocket, and roller coaster—Canada's Wonderland rides? No, they are commonly used descriptions of price changes.

The price of a personal computer took a dramatic slide from around $3,000 in 2000 to around $500 in 2005. The price of gasoline rocketed in the summer of 2005. The prices of coffee, bananas, and other agricultural products rise and fall like a roller coaster.

You've learned that economics is about the choices people make to cope with scarcity, and how those choices respond to incentives. Prices are one of the incentives to which people respond. You're now going to see how prices are determined by demand and supply.

The demand and supply model is the main tool of economics. It helps us to answer the big economic question: What, how, and for whom are goods and services produced. It also helps us to say when the pursuit of self-interest promotes the social interest.

◆ Your careful study of this topic will bring big rewards both in your further study of economics and in your everyday life. When you have completed your study of demand and supply, you will be able to explain how prices are determined and make predictions about price slides, rockets, and roller coasters. Once you understand demand and supply, you will view the world through new eyes.

After studying this chapter, you will be able to

- ■ **Describe a competitive market and think about a price as an opportunity cost**
- ■ **Explain the influences on demand**
- ■ **Explain the influences on supply**
- ■ **Explain how demand and supply determine prices and quantities bought and sold**
- ■ **Use demand and supply to make predictions about changes in prices and quantities**

Markets and Prices

WHEN YOU NEED A NEW PAIR OF RUNNING SHOES, want a bagel and a latte, plan to upgrade your stereo system, or need to fly home for Thanksgiving, you must find a place where people sell those items or offer those services. The place in which you find them is a *market*. You learned in Chapter 2 (p. 46) that a market is any arrangement that enables buyers and sellers to get information and to do business with each other.

A market has two sides: buyers and sellers. There are markets for *goods* such as apples and hiking boots, for *services* such as haircuts and tennis lessons, for *resources* such as computer programmers and earth-movers, and for other manufactured *inputs* such as memory chips and auto parts. There are also markets for money such as Japanese yen and for financial securities such as Yahoo! stock. Only our imagination limits what can be traded in markets.

Some markets are physical places where buyers and sellers meet and where an auctioneer or a broker helps to determine the prices. Examples of this type of market are the wholesale fish, meat, and produce markets and car auction markets.

Some markets are groups of people spread around the world who never meet and know little about each other but are connected through the Internet or by telephone and fax. Examples are the e-commerce markets and currency markets.

But most markets are unorganized collections of buyers and sellers. You do most of your trading in this type of market. An example is the market for basketball shoes. The buyers in this $3 billion-a-year market are the 45 million North Americans who play basketball (or who want to make a fashion statement). The sellers are the tens of thousands of retail sports equipment and footwear stores. Each buyer can visit several different stores, and each seller knows that the buyer has a choice of stores.

Markets vary in the intensity of competition that buyers and sellers face. In this chapter, we're going to study a **competitive market**—a market that has many buyers and many sellers, so no single buyer or seller can influence the price.

Producers offer items for sale only if the price is high enough to cover their opportunity cost. And consumers respond to changing opportunity cost by seeking cheaper alternatives to expensive items.

We are going to study the way people respond to *prices* and the forces that determine prices. But to pursue these tasks, we need to understand the relationship between a price and an opportunity cost.

In everyday life, the *price* of an object is the number of dollars that must be given up in exchange for it. Economists refer to this price as the **money price**.

The *opportunity cost* of an action is the highest-valued alternative forgone. If, when you buy a coffee, the highest-valued thing you forgo is some gum, then the opportunity cost of the coffee is the *quantity* of gum forgone. We can calculate the quantity of gum forgone from the money prices of coffee and gum.

If the money price of coffee is $1 a cup and the money price of gum is 50¢ a pack, then the opportunity cost of one cup of coffee is two packs of gum. To calculate this opportunity cost, we divide the price of a cup of coffee by the price of a pack of gum and find the *ratio* of one price to the other. The ratio of one price to another is called a **relative price**, and a *relative price is an opportunity cost.*

We can express the relative price of coffee in terms of gum or any other good. The normal way of expressing a relative price is in terms of a "basket" of all goods and services. To calculate this relative price, we divide the money price of a good by the money price of a "basket" of all goods (called a *price index*). The resulting relative price tells us the opportunity cost of the good in terms of how much of the "basket" we must give up to buy it.

The theory of demand and supply that we are about to study determines *relative prices,* and the word "price" means *relative* price. When we predict that a price will fall, we do not mean that its *money* price will fall—although it might. We mean that its *relative* price will fall. That is, its price will fall *relative* to the average price of other goods and services.

REVIEW QUIZ

1 What is the distinction between a money price and a relative price?
2 Why is a relative price an opportunity cost?
3 Can you think of an example of a good whose money price and relative price have risen?
4 Can you think of an example of a good whose money price and relative price have fallen?

myeconlab **Study Plan 3.1**

Let's begin our study of demand and supply, starting with demand.

Demand

IF YOU DEMAND SOMETHING, THEN YOU

1. Want it,
2. Can afford it, and
3. Plan to buy it.

Wants are the unlimited desires or wishes that people have for goods and services. How many times have you thought that you would like something "if only you could afford it" or "if it weren't so expensive"? Scarcity guarantees that many—perhaps most—of our wants will never be satisfied. Demand reflects a decision about which wants to satisfy.

The **quantity demanded** of a good or service is the amount that consumers plan to buy during a given time period at a particular price. The quantity demanded is not necessarily the same as the quantity actually bought. Sometimes the quantity demanded exceeds the amount of goods available, so the quantity bought is less than the quantity demanded.

The quantity demanded is measured as an amount per unit of time. For example, suppose that you buy one cup of coffee a day. The quantity of coffee that you demand can be expressed as 1 cup per day, 7 cups per week, or 365 cups per year. Many factors influence buying plans and one of them is price. We look first at the relationship between the quantity demanded of a good and its price. To study this relationship, we keep all other influences on buying plans the same and we ask: How, other things remaining the same, does the quantity demanded of a good change as its price changes?

The law of demand provides the answer.

The Law of Demand

The **law of demand** states

> Other things remaining the same, the higher the price of a good, the smaller is the quantity demanded; and the lower the price of a good, the greater is the quantity demanded.

Why does a higher price reduce the quantity demanded? For two reasons:

■ Substitution effect
■ Income effect

Substitution Effect When the price of a good rises, other things remaining the same, its *relative* price—its opportunity cost—rises. Although each good is unique, it has *substitutes*—other goods that can be used in its place. As the opportunity cost of a good rises, people buy less of that good and more of its substitutes.

Income Effect When a price rises and all other influences on buying plans remain unchanged, the price rises *relative* to people's incomes. So faced with a higher price and an unchanged income, people cannot afford to buy all the things they previously bought. They must decrease the quantities demanded of at least some goods and services, and normally, the good whose price has increased will be one of the goods that people buy less of.

To see the substitution effect and the income effect at work, think about the effects of a change in the price of a recordable compact disc—a CD-R. Several different goods are substitutes for a CD-R. For example, an audiotape and prerecorded CD provide services similar to those of a CD-R.

Suppose that a CD-R initially sells for $3.00 and then its price falls to $1.50. People now substitute CD-Rs for audiotapes and prerecorded CDs—the substitution effect. And with a budget that now has some slack from the lower price of a CD-R, people buy more CD-Rs—the income effect. The quantity of CD-Rs demanded increases for these two reasons.

Now suppose that a CD-R initially sells for $3.00 and then the price doubles to $6.00. People now substitute prerecorded CDs and audiotapes for CD-Rs—the substitution effect. And faced with a tighter budget, people buy fewer CD-Rs—the income effect. The quantity of CD-Rs demanded decreases for these two reasons.

Demand Curve and Demand Schedule

You are now about to study one of the two most used curves in economics: the demand curve. And you are going to encounter one of the most critical distinctions: the distinction between *demand* and *quantity demanded*.

The term **demand** refers to the entire relationship between the price of the good and the quantity demanded of the good. Demand is illustrated by the demand curve and the demand schedule. The term *quantity demanded* refers to a point on a demand curve—the quantity demanded at a particular price.

Figure 3.1 shows the demand curve for CD-Rs. A **demand curve** shows the relationship between the quantity demanded of a good and its price when all other influences on consumers' planned purchases remain the same.

The table in Fig. 3.1 is the demand schedule for CD-Rs. A *demand schedule* lists the quantities demanded at each price when all the other influences on consumers' planned purchases remain the same. For example, if the price of a CD-R is 50¢, the quantity demanded is 9 million a week. If the price is $2.50, the quantity demanded is 2 million a week. The other rows of the table show the quantities demanded at prices of $1.00, $1.50, and $2.00.

We graph the demand schedule as a demand curve with the quantity demanded of CD-Rs on the *x*-axis and the price of a CD-R on the *y*-axis. The points on the demand curve labelled *A* through *E* correspond to the rows of the demand schedule. For example, point *A* on the graph shows a quantity demanded of 9 million CD-Rs a week at a price of 50¢ a disc.

Willingness and Ability to Pay

Another way of looking at the demand curve is as a willingness-and-ability-to-pay curve. And the willingness and ability to pay is a measure of *marginal benefit.*

If a small quantity is available, the highest price that someone is willing and able to pay for one more unit is high. But as the quantity available increases, the marginal benefit of each additional unit falls and the highest price that someone is willing and able to pay also falls along the demand curve.

In Fig. 3.1, if only 2 million CD-Rs are available each week, the highest price that someone is willing to pay for the 2 millionth CD-R is $2.50. But if 9 million CD-Rs are available each week, someone is willing to pay 50¢ for the last CD-R bought.

A Change in Demand

When any factor that influences buying plans other than the price of the good changes, there is a **change in demand**. Figure 3.2 illustrates an increase in demand. When demand increases, the demand curve shifts rightward and the quantity demanded is greater at each and every price. For example, at a price of $2.50, on the original (blue) demand curve, the quantity demanded is 2 million discs a week. On the new (red) demand curve, the quantity demanded is 6 million discs a week. Look closely at the numbers in the table in Fig. 3.2 and check that the quantity demanded is greater at each price.

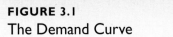

FIGURE 3.1

The Demand Curve

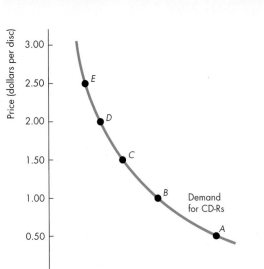

	Price (dollars per disc)	Quantity demanded (millions of discs per week)
A	0.50	9
B	1.00	6
C	1.50	4
D	2.00	3
E	2.50	2

The table shows a demand schedule for CD-Rs. At a price of 50¢ a disc, 9 million a week are demanded; at a price of $1.50 a disc, 4 million a week are demanded. The demand curve shows the relationship between quantity demanded and price, everything else remaining the same. The demand curve slopes downward: As price decreases, the quantity demanded increases.

The demand curve can be read in two ways. For a given price, the demand curve tells us the quantity that people plan to buy. For example, at a price of $1.50 a disc, the quantity demanded is 4 million discs a week. For a given quantity, the demand curve tells us the maximum price that consumers are willing and able to pay for the last disc available. For example, the maximum price that consumers will pay for the 6 millionth disc is $1.00.

Six main factors bring changes in demand. They are changes in

1. The prices of related goods
2. Expected future prices
3. Income
4. Expected future income
5. Population
6. Preferences

1. Prices of Related Goods The quantity of CD-Rs that consumers plan to buy depends in part on the prices of substitutes for CD-Rs. A **substitute** is a good that can be used in place of another good. For example, a bus ride is a substitute for a train ride; a prerecorded CD is a substitute for a CD-R, and a hamburger is a substitute for a hot dog. If the price of a substitute for a CD-R rises, people buy less of the substitute and more CD-Rs. For example, if the price of a prerecorded CD rises, people buy fewer CDs and more CD-Rs. The demand for CD-Rs increases.

The quantity of CD-Rs that people plan to buy also depends on the prices of complements with CD-Rs. A **complement** is a good that is used in conjunction with another good. Hamburgers and fries are complements. So are spaghetti and meat sauce, and so are CD-Rs and CD burners. If the price of a CD burner falls, people buy more CD burners *and more* CD-Rs. A fall in the price of a CD burner increases the demand for CD-Rs in Fig. 3.2.

2. Expected Future Prices If the price of a good is expected to rise in the future and if the good can be stored, the opportunity cost of obtaining the good for future use is lower today than it will be when the price has increased. So people retime their purchases—they substitute over time. They buy more of the good now before its price is expected to rise (and less after), so the current demand for the good increases. For example, suppose that Florida is hit by a frost that damages the season's orange crop. You expect the price of orange juice to rise in the future. So you fill your freezer with enough frozen juice to get you through the next six months. Your current demand for frozen orange juice has increased, and your future demand has decreased.

Similarly, if the price of a good is expected to fall in the future, the opportunity cost of buying the good today is high relative to what it is expected to be in the future. So again, people retime their purchases. They buy less of the good now before its price

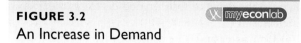

FIGURE 3.2
An Increase in Demand

Original demand schedule CD burner $300			New demand schedule CD burner $100		
	Price (dollars per disc)	Quantity demanded (millions of discs per week)		Price (dollars per disc)	Quantity demanded (millions of discs per week)
A	0.50	9	A'	0.50	13
B	1.00	6	B'	1.00	10
C	1.50	4	C'	1.50	8
D	2.00	3	D'	2.00	7
E	2.50	2	E'	2.50	6

A change in any influence on buyers' plans other than the price of the good itself results in a new demand schedule and a shift of the demand curve. A change in the price of a CD burner changes the demand for CD-Rs. At a price of $1.50 a disc, 4 million discs a week are demanded when a CD burner costs $300 (row C of the table) and 8 million CD-Rs a week are demanded when a CD burner costs $100. A *fall* in the price of a CD burner *increases* the demand for CD-Rs. The demand curve shifts *rightward*, as shown by the shift arrow and the resulting red curve.

falls, so the demand for the good decreases today and increases in the future.

Computer prices are constantly falling, and this fact poses a dilemma. Will you buy a new computer now, in time for the start of the school year, or will you wait until the price has fallen some more? Because people expect computer prices to keep falling, the current demand for computers is less (the future demand is greater) than it otherwise would be.

3. Income Consumers' income influences demand. When income increases, consumers buy more of most goods, and when income decreases, consumers buy less of most goods. Although an increase in income leads to an increase in the demand for *most* goods, it does not lead to an increase in the demand for *all* goods. A **normal good** is one for which demand increases as income increases. An **inferior good** is one for which demand decreases as income increases. Long-distance transportation has examples of both normal goods and inferior goods. As incomes increase, the demand for air travel (a normal good) increases and the demand for long-distance bus trips (an inferior good) decreases.

4. Expected future income When expected future income increases, demand might increase. For example, a sales person gets the news that she will receive a big bonus at the end of the year, so she decides to buy a new car right now.

5. Population Demand also depends on the size and the age structure of the population. The larger the population, the greater is the demand for all goods and services; the smaller the population, the smaller is the demand for all goods and services.

For example, the demand for parking spaces or movies or CD-Rs or just about anything that you can imagine is much greater in the Greater Toronto Area (population 4.6 million) than it is in North Bay (population 110,000).

Also, the larger the proportion of the population in a given age group, the greater is the demand for the goods and services used by that age group.

For example, in 2001, there were 2.1 million 20–24-year-olds in Canada compared with 2.5 million in 1981. As a result, the demand for university places decreased during those years. During those same years, the number of Canadians aged 85 years and over increased by 235,000. As a result, the demand for nursing home services increased.

TABLE 3.1 **The Demand for CD-Rs**	
The Law of Demand	
The quantity of CD-Rs demanded	
Decreases if:	*Increases if:*
■ The price of a CD-R rises	■ The price of a CD-R falls
Changes in Demand	
The demand for CD-Rs	
Decreases if:	*Increases if:*
■ The price of a substitute falls	■ The price of a substitute rises
■ The price of a complement rises	■ The price of a complement falls
■ The price of a CD-R is expected to fall in the future	■ The price of a CD-R is expected to rise in the future
■ Income falls*	■ Income rises*
■ Expected future income falls	■ Expected future income rises
■ The population decreases	■ The population increases
*A CD-R is a normal good.	

6. Preferences Demand depends on preferences. *Preferences* are an individual's attitudes towards goods and services. For example, a rock music fanatic has a much greater preference for CD-Rs than does a tone-deaf technophobe. As a consequence, even if they have the same incomes, their demands for CD-Rs will be very different.

Table 3.1 summarizes the influences on demand and the direction of those influences.

A Change in the Quantity Demanded Versus a Change in Demand

Changes in the factors that influence buyers' plans cause either a change in the quantity demanded or a change in demand. Equivalently, they cause either a movement along the demand curve or a shift of the demand curve. The distinction between a change in the quantity demanded and a change in demand is the same as that between a movement along the demand curve and a shift of the demand curve.

A point on the demand curve shows the quantity demanded at a given price. So a movement along the demand curve shows a **change in the quantity demanded**. The entire demand curve shows demand. So a shift of the demand curve shows a *change in demand*. Figure 3.3 summarizes these distinctions.

Movement Along the Demand Curve If the price of a good changes but everything else remains the same, there is a movement along the demand curve. Because the demand curve slopes downward, a fall in the price of a good increases the quantity demanded of it and a rise in the price of the good decreases the quantity demanded of it—the law of demand.

In Fig. 3.3, if the price of a good falls when everything else remains the same, the quantity demanded of that good increases and there is a movement down the demand curve D_0. If the price rises when everything else remains the same, the quantity demanded of that good decreases and there is a movement up the demand curve D_0.

A Shift of the Demand Curve If the price of a good remains constant but some other influence on buyers' plans changes, there is a change in demand for that good. We illustrate a change in demand as a shift of the demand curve. For example, if the price of a CD burner falls, consumers buy more CD-Rs regardless of the price of a CD-R. That is what a rightward shift of the demand curve shows—more CD-Rs are bought at each and every price.

In Fig. 3.3, when any factor that influences buying plans, other than the price of the good, changes, there is a *change in demand* and the demand curve shifts. Demand *increases* and the demand curve *shifts rightward* (to the red demand curve D_1) if the price of a substitute rises, the price of a complement falls, the expected future price of the good rises, income increases (for a normal good), expected future income increases, or the population increases. Demand *decreases* and the demand curve *shifts leftward* (to the red demand curve D_2) if the price of a substitute falls, the price of a complement rises, the expected future price of the good falls, income decreases (for a normal good), expected future income decreases, or the population decreases.(For an inferior good, the effects of changes in income are in the direction opposite to those described above.)

FIGURE 3.3

A Change in the Quantity Demanded Versus a Change in Demand

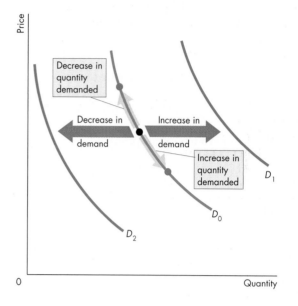

When the price of the good changes, there is a movement along the demand curve and *a change in the quantity demanded,* shown by the blue arrows on demand curve D_0. When any other influence on buyers' plans changes, there is a shift of the demand curve and a *change in demand.* An increase in demand shifts the demand curve rightward (from D_0 to D_1). A decrease in demand shifts the demand curve leftward (from D_0 to D_2).

REVIEW QUIZ

1 What is the law of demand and how do we illustrate it?
2 If a fixed amount of a good is available, what does the demand curve tell us about the price that consumers are willing to pay for that fixed quantity?
3 List all the influences on buying plans that change demand, and for each influence say whether it increases or decreases demand.
4 What happens to the quantity of Palm Pilots demanded and the demand for Palm Pilots if the price of a Palm Pilot falls and all other influences on buying plans remain the same?

 Study Plan 3.2

Supply

IF A FIRM SUPPLIES A GOOD OR SERVICE, THE FIRM

1. Has the resources and technology to produce it,
2. Can profit from producing it, and
3. Plans to produce it and sell it.

A supply is more than just having the *resources* and the *technology* to produce something. *Resources and technology* are the constraints that limit what is possible.

Many useful things can be produced, but they are not produced unless it is profitable to do so. Supply reflects a decision about which technologically feasible items to produce.

The **quantity supplied** of a good or service is the amount that producers plan to sell during a given time period at a particular price. The quantity supplied is not necessarily the same amount as the quantity actually sold. Sometimes the quantity supplied is greater than the quantity demanded, so the quantity bought is less than the quantity supplied.

Like the quantity demanded, the quantity supplied is measured as an amount per unit of time. For example, suppose that GM produces 1,000 cars a day. The quantity of cars supplied by GM can be expressed as 1,000 a day, 7,000 a week, or 365,000 a year. Without the time dimension, we cannot tell whether a particular number is large or small.

Many factors influence selling plans and again, one of them is price. We look first at the relationship between the quantity supplied of a good and its price. And again, as we did when we studied demand, to isolate this relationship, we keep all other influences on selling plans the same and we ask: How, other things remaining the same, does the quantity supplied of a good change as its price changes?

The law of supply provides the answer.

The Law of Supply

The **law of supply** states:

Other things remaining the same, the higher the price of a good, the greater is the quantity supplied; and the lower the price of a good, the smaller is the quantity supplied.

Why does a higher price increase the quantity supplied? It is because *marginal cost increases*. As the quantity produced of any good increases, the marginal cost of producing the good increases. (You can refresh your memory of increasing marginal cost in Chapter 2, p. 37.)

It is never worth producing a good if the price received for it does not at least cover the marginal cost of producing it. So when the price of a good rises, other things remaining the same, producers are willing to incur a higher marginal cost and increase production. The higher price brings forth an increase in the quantity supplied.

Let's now illustrate the law of supply with a supply curve and a supply schedule.

Supply Curve and Supply Schedule

You are now going to study the second of the two most used curves in economics: the supply curve. And you're going to learn about the critical distinction between *supply* and *quantity supplied*.

The term **supply** refers to the entire relationship between the quantity supplied and the price of a good. Supply is illustrated by the supply curve and the supply schedule. The term *quantity supplied* refers to a point on a supply curve—the quantity supplied at a particular price.

Figure 3.4 shows the supply curve of CD-Rs. A **supply curve** shows the relationship between the quantity supplied of a good and its price when all other influences on producers' planned sales remain the same. The supply curve is a graph of a supply schedule.

The table in Fig. 3.4 sets out the supply schedule for CD-Rs. A *supply schedule* lists the quantities supplied at each price when all the other influences on producers' planned sales remain the same. For example, if the price of a CD-R is 50¢, the quantity supplied is zero—in row *A* of the table. If the price of a CD-R is $1.00, the quantity supplied is 3 million CD-Rs a week—in row *B*. The other rows of the table show the quantities supplied at prices of $1.50, $2.00, and $2.50.

To make a supply curve, we graph the quantity supplied on the *x*-axis and the price on the *y*-axis, just as in the case of the demand curve. The points on the supply curve labelled *A* through *E* correspond to the rows of the supply schedule. For example, point *A* on the graph shows a quantity supplied of zero at a price of 50¢ a CD-R.

FIGURE 3.4

The Supply Curve

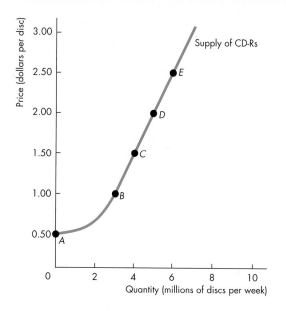

The table shows the supply schedule of CD-Rs. For example, at a price of $1.00, 3 million discs a week are supplied; at a price of $2.50, 6 million discs a week are supplied. The supply curve shows the relationship between the quantity supplied and price, everything else remaining the same. The supply curve usually slopes upward: As the price of a good increases, so does the quantity supplied.

A supply curve can be read in two ways. For a given price, it tells us the quantity that producers plan to sell at that price. And for a given quantity, it tells us the minimum price that producers are willing to accept for that quantity.

	Price (dollars per disc)	Quantity supplied (millions of discs per week)
A	0.50	0
B	1.00	3
C	1.50	4
D	2.00	5
E	2.50	6

Minimum Supply Price Just as the demand curve has two interpretations, so too does the supply curve. The demand curve can be interpreted as a willingness-and-ability-to-pay curve. The supply curve can be interpreted as a minimum-supply-price curve. It tells us the lowest price at which someone is willing to sell another unit.

If a small quantity is produced, the lowest price at which someone is willing to sell one more unit is low. But if a large quantity is produced, the lowest price at which someone is willing to sell one more unit is high.

In Fig. 3.4, if 6 million CD-Rs a week are produced, the lowest price that a producer is willing to accept for the 6 millionth disc is $2.50. But if only 4 million CD-Rs are produced each week, the lowest price that a producer is willing to accept for the 4 millionth disc is $1.50.

A Change in Supply

When any factor that influences selling plans other than the price of the good changes, there is a **change in supply**. Five main factors bring changes in supply. They are changes in

1. The prices of resources used to produce the good
2. The prices of related goods produced
3. Expected future prices
4. The number of suppliers
5. Technology

1. Prices of Productive Resources The prices of productive resources influence supply. The easiest way to see this influence is to think about the supply curve as a minimum-supply-price curve. If the price of a productive resource rises, the lowest price a producer of a good that uses that resource is willing to accept rises, so supply of the good decreases. For example, during 2005, the price of jet fuel increased and the supply of air transportation decreased. Similarly, a rise in the minimum wage decreases the supply of hamburgers. If the wages of disc producers rise, the supply of CD-Rs decreases.

2. Prices of Related Goods Produced The prices of related goods and services that firms produce influence supply. For example, if the price of a prerecorded CD rises, the supply of CD-Rs decreases. CD-Rs and prerecorded CDs are *substitutes in production*—goods that can be produced by using the same resources. If the price of beef rises, the supply of cowhide increases. Beef and cowhide are *complements in production*— goods that must be produced together.

3. Expected Future Prices If the price of a good is expected to rise, the return from selling the good in the future is higher than it is today. So supply of the good decreases today and increases in the future.

4. The Number of Suppliers The larger the number of firms that produce a good, the greater is the supply of the good. And as firms enter an industry, the supply in that industry increases. As firms leave an industry, the supply in that industry decreases.

5. Technology The term "technology" is used broadly to mean the way that factors of production are used to produce a good. Technology changes both positively and negatively. A positive technology change occurs when a new method is discovered that lowers the cost of producing a good. An example is new methods used in the factories that make CDs. A negative technology change occurs when an event such as extreme weather or natural disaster increases the cost of producing a good. A positive technology change increases supply, and a negative technology change decreases supply.

Figure 3.5 illustrates an increase in supply. When supply increases, the supply curve shifts rightward and the quantity supplied is larger at each and every price. For example, at a price of $1, on the original (blue) supply curve, the quantity supplied is 3 million discs a week. On the new (red) supply curve, the quantity supplied is 6 million discs a week. Look closely at the numbers in the table in Fig. 3.5 and check that the quantity supplied is larger at each price.

Table 3.2 summarizes the influences on supply and the directions of those influences.

A Change in the Quantity Supplied Versus a Change in Supply

Changes in the factors that influence sellers' plans cause either a change in the quantity supplied or a change in supply. Equivalently, they cause either a movement along the supply curve or a shift of the supply curve.

A point on the supply curve shows the quantity supplied at a given price. A movement along the supply curve shows a **change in the quantity supplied**. The entire supply curve shows supply. A shift of the supply curve shows a *change in supply*.

FIGURE 3.5
An Increase in Supply

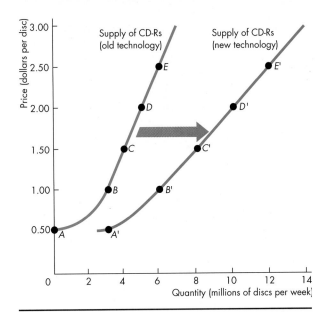

| Original supply schedule | | | New supply schedule | | |
Old technology			New technology		
	Price (dollars per disc)	**Quantity supplied** (millions of discs per week)		**Price** (dollars per disc)	**Quantity supplied** (millions of discs per week)
A	0.50	0	A'	0.50	3
B	1.00	3	B'	1.00	6
C	1.50	4	C'	1.50	8
D	2.00	5	D'	2.00	10
E	2.50	6	E'	2.50	12

A change in any influence on sellers' plans other than the price of the good itself results in a new supply schedule and a shift of the supply curve. For example, if Imation Enterprises invents a new, cost-saving technology for producing CD-Rs, the supply of CD-Rs changes. At a price of $1.50 a disc, 4 million discs a week are supplied when producers use the old technology (row *C* of the table) and 8 million CD-Rs a week are supplied when producers use the new technology. An advance in technology *increases* the supply of CD-Rs. The supply curve shifts *rightward*, as shown by the shift arrow and the resulting red curve.

Figure 3.6 illustrates and summarizes these distinctions. If the price of a good falls and everything else remains the same, the quantity supplied of that good decreases and there is a movement down the supply curve S_0. If the price of a good rises and everything else remains the same, the quantity supplied increases and there is a movement up the supply curve S_0. When any other influence on selling plans changes, the supply curve shifts and there is a *change in supply*. If the supply curve is S_0 and if production costs fall, supply increases and the supply curve shifts to the red supply curve S_1. If production costs rise, supply decreases and the supply curve shifts to the red supply curve S_2.

TABLE 3.2 The Supply of CD-Rs

The Law of Supply

The quantity of CD-Rs supplied

Decreases if:	Increases if:
■ The price of a CD-R falls	■ The price of a CD-R rises

Changes in Supply

The supply of CD-Rs

Decreases if:	Increases if:
■ The price of a resource used to produce CD-Rs rises	■ The price of a resource used to produce CD-Rs falls
■ The price of a substitute in production rises	■ The price of a substitute in production falls
■ The price of a complement in production falls	■ The price of a complement in production rises
■ The price of a CD-R is expected to rise in the future	■ The price of a CD-R is expected to fall in the future
■ The number of CD-R producers decreases	■ The number of CD-R producers increases
■ A less efficient technology for producing CD-Rs is used	■ A more efficient technology for producing CD-Rs is used

FIGURE 3.6
A Change in the Quantity Supplied Versus a Change in Supply

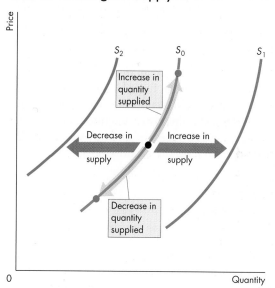

When the price of the good changes, there is a movement along the supply curve and *a change in the quantity supplied*, shown by the blue arrows on supply curve S_0. When any other influence on selling plans changes, there is a shift of the supply curve and a *change in supply*. An increase in supply shifts the supply curve rightward (from S_0 to S_1), and a decrease in supply shifts the supply curve leftward (from S_0 to S_2).

REVIEW QUIZ

1 What is the law of supply and how do we illustrate it?
2 What does the supply curve tell us about the price at which firms will supply a given quantity of a good?
3 List all the influences on selling plans, and for each influence say whether it changes supply.
4 What happens to the quantity of Palm Pilots supplied and the supply of Palm Pilots if the price of a Palm Pilot falls?

myeconlab Study Plan 3.3

Your next task is to use what you've learned about demand and supply and understand how prices and quantities are determined.

Market Equilibrium

WE HAVE SEEN THAT WHEN THE PRICE OF A GOOD rises, the quantity demanded *decreases* and the quantity supplied *increases*. We are now going to see how prices coordinate the plans of buyers and sellers and achieve an equilibrium.

An *equilibrium* is a situation in which opposing forces balance each other. Equilibrium in a market occurs when the price balances the plans of buyers and sellers. The **equilibrium price** is the price at which the quantity demanded equals the quantity supplied. The **equilibrium quantity** is the quantity bought and sold at the equilibrium price. A market moves towards its equilibrium because

- Price regulates buying and selling plans.
- Price adjusts when plans don't match.

Price as a Regulator

The price of a good regulates the quantities demanded and supplied. If the price is too high, the quantity supplied exceeds the quantity demanded. If the price is too low, the quantity demanded exceeds the quantity supplied. There is one price at which the quantity demanded equals the quantity supplied. Let's work out what that price is.

Figure 3.7 shows the market for CD-Rs. The table shows the demand schedule (from Fig. 3.1) and the supply schedule (from Fig. 3.4). If the price of a disc is 50¢, the quantity demanded is 9 million discs a week, but no discs are supplied. There is a shortage of 9 million discs a week. This shortage is shown in the final column of the table. At a price of $1.00 a disc, there is still a shortage, but only of 3 million discs a week. If the price of a disc is $2.50, the quantity supplied is 6 million discs a week, but the quantity demanded is only 2 million. There is a surplus of 4 million discs a week. The one price at which there is neither a shortage nor a surplus is $1.50 a disc. At that price, the quantity demanded is equal to the quantity supplied: 4 million discs a week. The equilibrium price is $1.50 a disc, and the equilibrium quantity is 4 million discs a week.

Figure 3.7 shows that the demand curve and the supply curve intersect at the equilibrium price of $1.50 a disc. At each price *above* $1.50 a disc, there is a surplus of discs. For example, at $2.00 a disc, the surplus

FIGURE 3.7
Equilibrium

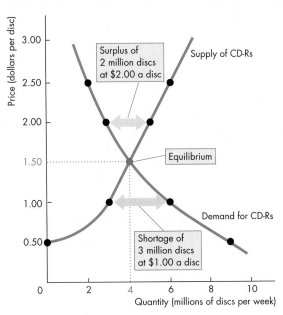

Price (dollars per disc)	Quantity demanded	Quantity supplied	Shortage (–) or surplus (+)
	(millions of discs per week)		
0.50	9	0	–9
1.00	6	3	–3
1.50	4	4	0
2.00	3	5	+2
2.50	2	6	+4

The table lists the quantities demanded and quantities supplied as well as the shortage or surplus of discs at each price. If the price is $1.00 a disc, 6 million discs a week are demanded and 3 million are supplied. There is a shortage of 3 million discs a week, and the price rises.

If the price is $2.00 a disc, 3 million discs a week are demanded and 5 million are supplied. There is a surplus of 2 million discs a week, and the price falls.

If the price is $1.50 a disc, 4 million discs a week are demanded and 4 million are supplied. There is neither a shortage nor a surplus. Neither buyers nor sellers have any incentive to change the price. The price at which the quantity demanded equals the quantity supplied is the equilibrium price.

is 2 million discs a week, as shown by the blue arrow. At each price *below* $1.50 a disc, there is a shortage of discs. For example, at $1.00 a disc, the shortage is 3 million discs a week, as shown by the red arrow.

Price Adjustments

You've seen that if the price is below equilibrium, there is a shortage and that if the price is above equilibrium, there is a surplus. But can we count on the price to change and eliminate a shortage or surplus? We can, because such price changes are beneficial to both buyers and sellers. Let's see why the price changes when there is a shortage or a surplus.

A Shortage Forces the Price Up Suppose the price of a CD-R is $1. Consumers plan to buy 6 million discs a week, and producers plan to sell 3 million discs a week. Consumers can't force producers to sell more than they plan, so the quantity that is actually offered for sale is 3 million discs a week. In this situation, powerful forces operate to increase the price and move it towards the equilibrium price. Some producers, noticing lines of unsatisfied consumers, raise the price. Some producers increase their output. As producers push the price up, the price rises towards its equilibrium. The rising price reduces the shortage because it decreases the quantity demanded and increases the quantity supplied. When the price has increased to the point at which there is no longer a shortage, the forces moving the price stop operating and the price comes to rest at its equilibrium.

A Surplus Forces the Price Down Suppose the price of a CD-R is $2. Producers plan to sell 5 million discs a week, and consumers plan to buy 3 million discs a week. Producers cannot force consumers to buy more than they plan, so the quantity that is actually bought is 3 million discs a week. In this situation, powerful forces operate to lower the price and move it towards the equilibrium price. Some producers, unable to sell the quantities of CD-Rs they planned to sell, cut their prices. In addition, some producers scale back production. As producers cut the price, the price falls towards its equilibrium. The falling price decreases the surplus because it increases the quantity demanded and decreases the quantity supplied. When the price has fallen to the point at which there is no longer a surplus, the forces moving the price stop operating and the price comes to rest at its equilibrium.

The Best Deal Available for Buyers and Sellers
When the price is below equilibrium, it is forced up towards the equilibrium. Why don't buyers resist the increase and refuse to buy at the higher price? Because they value the good more highly than the current price and they cannot satisfy all their demands at the current price. In some markets—for example, the auction markets that operate on eBay—the buyers might even be the ones who force the price up by offering to pay higher prices.

When the price is above equilibrium, it is bid down towards the equilibrium. Why don't sellers resist this decrease and refuse to sell at the lower price? Because their minimum supply price is below the current price and they cannot sell all they would like to at the current price. Normally, it is the sellers who force the price down by offering lower prices to gain market share from their competitors.

At the price at which the quantity demanded and the quantity supplied are equal, neither buyers nor sellers can do business at a better price. Buyers pay the highest price they are willing to pay for the last unit bought, and sellers receive the lowest price at which they are willing to supply the last unit sold.

When people freely make offers to buy and sell and when demanders try to buy at the lowest possible price and suppliers try to sell at the highest possible price, the price at which trade takes place is the equilibrium price—the price at which the quantity demanded equals the quantity supplied. The price coordinates the plans of buyers and sellers, and no one has an incentive to change it.

REVIEW QUIZ

1 What is the equilibrium price of a good or service?

2 Over what range of prices does a shortage arise?

3 Over what range of prices does a surplus arise?

4 What happens to the price when there is a shortage?

5 What happens to the price when there is a surplus?

6 Why is the price at which the quantity demanded equals the quantity supplied the equilibrium price?

Ⓧ myeconlab **Study Plan 3.4**

Predicting Changes in Price and Quantity

THE DEMAND AND SUPPLY THEORY THAT WE HAVE just studied provides us with a powerful way of analyzing influences on prices and the quantities bought and sold. According to the theory, a change in price stems from a change in demand, a change in supply, or a change in both demand and supply. Let's look first at the effects of a change in demand.

A Change in Demand

What happens to the price and quantity of CD-Rs if the demand for CD-Rs increases? We can answer this question with a specific example. Between 1998 and 2001, the price of a CD burner fell from $300 to $100. Because the CD burner and CD-R discs are complements, the demand for discs increased, as is shown in the table in Fig. 3.8. The original demand schedule and the new one are set out in the first three columns of the table. The table also shows the supply schedule for CD-Rs.

When demand increases, there is a shortage at the original equilibrium price of $1.50 a disc. To eliminate the shortage, the price must rise. The price that makes the quantity demanded and quantity supplied equal again is $2.50 a disc. At this price, 6 million discs are bought and sold each week. When demand increases, both the price and the quantity increase.

Figure 3.8 shows these changes. The figure shows the original demand for and supply of CD-Rs. The original equilibrium price is $1.50 a disc, and the quantity is 4 million discs a week. When demand increases, the demand curve shifts rightward. The equilibrium price rises to $2.50 a disc, and the quantity supplied increases to 6 million discs a week, as highlighted in the figure. There is an *increase in the quantity supplied* but *no change in supply*—a movement along, but no shift of, the supply curve.

We can reverse this change in demand. Start at a price of $2.50 a disc with 6 million discs a week being bought and sold, and then work out what happens if demand decreases to its original level. Such a decrease in demand might arise from a fall in the price of an MP3 player (a substitute for CD-R technology). The decrease in demand shifts the demand curve leftward. The equilibrium price falls to $1.50 a disc, and the equilibrium quantity decreases to 4 million discs a week.

FIGURE 3.8 myeconlab

The Effects of a Change in Demand

Price	Quantity demanded (millions of discs per week)		Quantity supplied (millions of discs per week)
(dollars per disc)	CD burner $300	CD burner $100	
0.50	9	13	0
1.00	6	10	3
1.50	**4**	**8**	**4**
2.00	3	7	5
2.50	2	6	6

With the price of a CD burner at $300, the demand for CD-Rs is the blue demand curve. The equilibrium price is $1.50 a disc, and the equilibrium quantity is 4 million discs a week. When the price of a CD burner falls from $300 to $100, the demand for CD-Rs increases and the demand curve shifts rightward to become the red curve.

At $1.50 a disc, there is now a shortage of 4 million discs a week. The price of a disc rises to a new equilibrium of $2.50. As the price rises to $2.50, the quantity supplied increases—shown by the blue arrow on the supply curve—to the new equilibrium quantity of 6 million discs a week. Following an increase in demand, the quantity supplied increases but supply does not change—the supply curve does not shift.

We can now make our first two predictions:

1. When demand increases, both the price and the quantity increase.
2. When demand decreases, both the price and the quantity decrease.

A Change in Supply

When Imation and other producers introduce new cost-saving technologies in their CD-R production plants, the supply of CD-Rs increases. The new supply schedule (the same one that was shown in Fig. 3.5) is presented in the table in Fig. 3.9. What are the new equilibrium price and quantity? The answer is highlighted in the table: The price falls to $1.00 a disc, and the quantity increases to 6 million a week. You can see why by looking at the quantities demanded and supplied at the old price of $1.50 a disc. The quantity supplied at that price is 8 million discs a week, and there is a surplus of discs. The price falls. Only when the price is $1.00 a disc does the quantity supplied equal the quantity demanded.

Figure 3.9 illustrates the effect of an increase in supply. It shows the demand curve for CD-Rs and the original and new supply curves. The initial equilibrium price is $1.50 a disc, and the quantity is 4 million discs a week. When the supply increases, the supply curve shifts rightward. The equilibrium price falls to $1.00 a disc, and the quantity demanded increases to 6 million discs a week, highlighted in the figure. There is an *increase in the quantity demanded* but *no change in demand*—a movement along, but no shift of, the demand curve.

We can reverse this change in supply. If we start out at a price of $1.00 a disc with 6 million discs a week being bought and sold, we can work out what happens if supply decreases to its original level. Such a decrease in supply might arise from an increase in the cost of labour or raw materials. The decrease in supply shifts the supply curve leftward. The equilibrium price rises to $1.50 a disc, and the equilibrium quantity decreases to 4 million discs a week.

We can now make two more predictions:

1. When supply increases, the quantity increases and the price falls.
2. When supply decreases, the quantity decreases and the price rises.

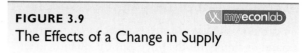

FIGURE 3.9
The Effects of a Change in Supply

Price (dollars per disc)	Quantity demanded (millions of discs per week)	Quantity supplied (millions of discs per week)	
		Old technology	New technology
0.50	9	0	3
1.00	6	3	6
1.50	4	4	8
2.00	3	5	10
2.50	2	6	12

With the old technology, the supply of CD-Rs is shown by the blue supply curve. The equilibrium price is $1.50 a disc, and the equilibrium quantity is 4 million discs a week. When the new technology is adopted, the supply of CD-Rs increases and the supply curve shifts rightward to become the red curve.

At $1.50 a disc, there is now a surplus of 4 million discs a week. The price of a CD-R falls to a new equilibrium of $1.00 a disc. As the price falls to $1.00, the quantity demanded increases—shown by the blue arrow on the demand curve—to the new equilibrium quantity of 6 million discs a week. Following an increase in supply, the quantity demanded increases but demand does not change—the demand curve does not shift.

A Change in Both Demand and Supply

You can now predict the effects of a change in either demand or supply on the price and the quantity. But what happens if *both* demand and supply change together? To answer this question, we look first at the case in which demand and supply move in the same direction—either both increase or both decrease. Then we look at the case in which they move in opposite directions—demand decreases and supply increases or demand increases and supply decreases.

Demand and Supply Change in the Same Direction We've seen that an increase in the demand for CD-Rs raises its price and increases the quantity bought and sold. And we've seen that an increase in the supply of CD-Rs lowers its price and increases the quantity bought and sold. Let's now examine what happens when both of these changes occur together.

The table in Fig. 3.10 brings together the numbers that describe the original quantities demanded and supplied and the new quantities demanded and supplied after the fall in the price of the CD burner and the improved CD-R production technology. These same numbers are illustrated in the graph. The original (blue) demand and supply curves intersect at a price of $1.50 a disc and a quantity of 4 million discs a week. The new (red) supply and demand curves also intersect at a price of $1.50 a disc but at a quantity of 8 million discs a week.

An increase in either demand or supply increases the quantity. So when both demand and supply increase, so does the equilibrium quantity.

An increase in demand raises the price, and an increase in supply lowers the price, so we can't say whether the price will rise or fall when demand and supply increase together. In this example, the price does not change. But notice that if demand increases by slightly more than the amount shown in the figure, the equilibrium price will rise. And if supply increases by slightly more than the amount shown in the figure, the equilibrium price will fall.

We can now make two more predictions:

1. When *both* demand and supply increase, the quantity increases and the price might increase, decrease, or remain the same.

2. When *both* demand and supply decrease, the quantity decreases and the price might increase, decrease, or remain the same.

FIGURE 3.10   Ⓧ myeconlab

The Effects of an Increase in Both Demand and Supply

	Original quantities (millions of discs per week)		New quantities (millions of discs per week)	
Price (dollars per disc)	**Quantity demanded** CD burner $300	**Quantity supplied** old technology	**Quantity demanded** CD burner $100	**Quantity supplied** new technology
0.50	9	0	13	3
1.00	6	3	10	6
1.50	4	4	8	8
2.00	3	5	7	10
2.50	2	6	6	12

When a CD burner costs $300 and firms use the old technology to produce discs, the price of a disc is $1.50 and the quantity is 4 million discs a week. A fall in the price of the CD burner increases the demand for CD-Rs, and improved technology increases the supply of CD-Rs. The new supply curve intersects the new demand curve at $1.50 a disc, the same price as before, but the equilibrium quantity increases to 8 million discs a week. These increases in demand and supply increase the quantity but leave the price unchanged.

Demand and Supply Change in Opposite Directions Let's now see what happens when demand and supply change together in *opposite* directions. A new production technology increases the supply of CD-Rs as before. But now the price of an MP3 download rises. An MP3 download is a *complement* of a CD-R. With more costly MP3 downloads, some people switch from buying CD-Rs to buying prerecorded CDs. The demand for CD-Rs decreases.

The table in Fig. 3.11 describes the original and new demand and supply schedules and the original (blue) and new (red) demand and supply curves. The original equilibrium price is $2.50 a disc, and the quantity is 6 million discs a week. The new supply and demand curves intersect at a price of $1.00 a disc and at the original quantity of 6 million discs a week.

A decrease in demand or an increase in supply lowers the price. So when a decrease in demand and an increase in supply occur together, the price falls.

A decrease in demand decreases the quantity, and an increase in supply increases the quantity, so we can't say for sure which way the quantity will change when demand decreases and supply increases at the same time. In this example, the quantity doesn't change. But notice that if demand had decreased by slightly more than is shown in the figure, the quantity would have decreased. And if supply had increased by slightly more than is shown in the figure, the quantity would have increased. So

1. When demand decreases and supply increases, the price falls and the quantity might increase, decrease, or remain the same.

2. When demand increases and supply decreases, the price rises and the quantity might increase, decrease, or remain the same.

REVIEW QUIZ

1   What is the effect on the price of a CD-R and the quantity of CD-Rs if (a) the price of a PC falls or (b) the price of an MP3 download rises or (c) more firms produce CD-Rs or (d) CD-R producers' wages rise or (e) any two of these events occur together? (Draw the diagrams!)

myeconlab   **Study Plan 3.5**

◆   To complete your study of demand and supply, take a look at *Reading Between the Lines* on pp. 76–77, which looks at the rocketing price of gasoline in the summer of 2005.

FIGURE 3.11   **myeconlab**

The Effects of a Decrease in Demand and an Increase in Supply

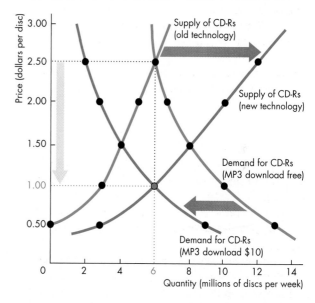

Price (dollars per disc)	Original quantities (millions of discs per week)		New quantities (millions of discs per week)	
	Quantity demanded MP3 download free	Quantity supplied old technology	Quantity demanded MP3 download $10	Quantity supplied new technology
0.50	13	0	9	3
1.00	10	3	6	6
1.50	8	4	4	8
2.00	7	5	3	10
2.50	6	6	2	12

When MP3 downloads are free and firms use the old technology to produce discs, the price is $2.50 a disc and the quantity is 6 million discs a week. A rise in the price of an MP3 download decreases the demand for CD-Rs, and improved technology increases the supply of CD-Rs. The new equilibrium price is $1.00 a disc, a lower price, but in this case the quantity remains constant at 6 million discs a week. This decrease in demand and increase in supply lower the price but leave the quantity unchanged.

Demand and Supply:
The Price of Oil

BLOOMBERG, AUGUST 23, 2005

Crude Oil Prices Rise on Concern Demand May Outstrip Supply

Crude oil rose above $66 a barrel in New York on concern that refiners will struggle to meet increased fuel demand during the Northern Hemisphere winter.

Kuwait Petroleum Corp. late yesterday said it shut its 85,000 barrel-a-day Europoort refinery near Rotterdam because of a failure in its steam boilers. More than 20 U.S. and European refineries have had unplanned unit shutdowns since early July.

"There is a perception that supply will be insufficient to meet demand later this year," said Steve Bellino, a trader at Fimat USA Inc. in New York. "The fact remains that there are no shortages, but the concern is there. Prices continue to be bid up just about every morning." ...

Essence of the Story

■ The price of crude oil reached $US66 a barrel in August 2005.

■ The reported reason for the price rise was an expected increase in demand for oil during the winter.

■ Another reported reason was a decrease in supply that resulted from shutdowns of refineries.

■ One trader said that there is a perception that supply will be insufficient to meet demand.

■ The trader also noted that there were no shortages.

Economic Analysis

■ The price of crude oil increased from an average of $US38 a barrel in 2004 to $66 a barrel in August 2005.

■ The quantity of oil produced increased from 83 million barrels a day in 2004 to 84 million barrels a day in 2005.

■ The most significant factor at work in the oil market in 2005 was an increasing awareness that the global demand for oil is going to increase at a much faster rate than previously thought.

■ The main source of the increase in demand is a rapid expansion in the economies of China and India, which is increasing the demand for oil in these countries. (China and India account for two-fifths of the world's population.)

■ The decrease in production by a refinery near Rotterdam reported in the news article is not significant. The production of this refinery is only one-tenth of one percent of world production and the shutdown is temporary.

■ Figure 1 illustrates the global market for oil in 2004 and 2005.

■ The supply of oil was constant and represented by the supply curve S.

■ In 2004, the demand for oil was D_{04}.

■ The equilibrium price was $US38 a barrel and the equilibrium quantity was 83 million barrels a day.

■ The demand for oil increased in 2005 and the demand curve shifted rightward to D_{05}.

■ The equilibrium price increased to $US66 a barrel and the equilibrium quantity increased to 84 million barrels a day.

■ There was no shortage of oil because the rise in the equilibrium price kept the quantity demanded equal to the quantity supplied.

Figure 1 The world oil market

Mathematical Note
Demand, Supply, and Equilibrium

Demand Curve

The law of demand says that as the price of a good or service falls, the quantity demanded of that good or service increases. We illustrate the law of demand by setting out a demand schedule, drawing a graph of the demand curve, or writing down an equation. When the demand curve is a straight line, the following linear equation describes it:

$$P = a - bQ_D$$

where P is the price and Q_D is the quantity demanded. The a and b are positive constants.

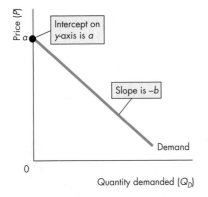

The demand equation tells us three things:

1. The price at which no one is willing to buy the good (Q_D is zero). That is, if the price is a, then the quantity demanded is zero. You can see the price a on the graph. It is the price at which the demand curve hits the y-axis—what we call the demand curve's "intercept on the y-axis."

2. As the price falls, the quantity demanded increases. If Q_D is a positive number, then the price P must be less than a. And as Q_D gets larger, the price P becomes smaller. That is, as the quantity increases, the maximum price that buyers are willing to pay for the good falls.

3. The constant b tells us how fast the maximum price that someone is willing to pay for the good falls as the quantity increases. That is, the constant b tells us about the steepness of the demand curve. The equation tells us that the slope of the demand curve is $-b$.

Supply Curve

The law of supply says that as the price of a good or service rises, the quantity supplied of that good or service increases. We illustrate the law of supply by setting out a supply schedule, drawing a graph of the supply curve, or writing down an equation. When the supply curve is a straight line, the following linear equation describes it:

$$P = c + dQ_S$$

where P is the price and Q_S is the quantity supplied. The c and d are positive constants.

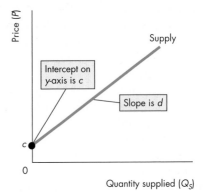

The supply equation tells us three things:

1. The price at which sellers are not willing to supply the good (Q_S is zero). That is, if the price is c, then no one is willing to sell the good. You can see the price c on the graph. It is the price at which the supply curve hits the y-axis—what we call the supply curve's "intercept on the y-axis."

2. As the price rises, the quantity supplied increases. If Q_S is a positive number, then the price P must be greater than c. And as Q_S increases, the price P gets larger. That is, as the quantity increases, the minimum price that sellers are willing to accept rises.

3. The constant d tells us how fast the minimum price at which someone is willing to sell the good rises as the quantity increases. That is, the constant d tells us about the steepness of the supply curve. The equation tells us that the slope of the supply curve is d.

Market Equilibrium

Demand and supply determine market equilibrium. The figure shows the equilibrium price (P^*) and equilibrium quantity (Q^*) at the intersection of the demand curve and the supply curve.

We can use the equations to find the equilibrium price and equilibrium quantity. The price of a good adjusts until the quantity demanded equals the quantity supplied. That is,

$$Q_D = Q_S.$$

So at the equilibrium price (P^*) and equilibrium quantity (Q^*),

$$Q_D = Q_S = Q^*.$$

To find the equilibrium price and equilibrium quantity, substitute Q^* for Q_D in the demand equation and Q^* for Q_S in the supply equation. Then the price is the equilibrium price (P^*), which gives

$$P^* = a - bQ^*$$

$$P^* = c + dQ^*.$$

Notice that

$$a - bQ^* = c + dQ^*.$$

Now solve for Q^*:

$$a - c = bQ^* + dQ^*$$

$$a - c = (b + d)Q^*$$

$$Q^* = \frac{a - c}{b + d}.$$

To find the equilibrium price, (P^*), substitute for Q^* in either the demand equation or the supply equation.

Using the demand equation, we have

$$P^* = a - b\left(\frac{a - c}{b + d}\right)$$

$$P^* = \frac{a(b + d) - b(a - c)}{b + d}$$

$$P^* = \frac{ad + bc}{b + d}.$$

Alternatively, using the supply equation, we have

$$P^* = c + d\left(\frac{a - c}{b + d}\right)$$

$$P^* = \frac{c(b + d) + d(a - c)}{b + d}$$

$$P^* = \frac{ad + bc}{b + d}.$$

An Example

The demand for ice cream cones is

$$P = 800 - 2Q_D.$$

The supply of ice cream cones is

$$P = 200 + 1Q_S.$$

The price of a cone is expressed in cents, and the quantities are expressed in cones per day.

To find the equilibrium price (P^*) and equilibrium quantity (Q^*), substitute Q^* for Q_D and Q_S and P^* for P. That is,

$$P^* = 800 - 2Q^*$$

$$P^* = 200 + 1Q^*.$$

Now solve for Q^*:

$$800 - 2Q^* = 200 + 1Q^*$$

$$600 = 3Q^*$$

$$Q^* = 200.$$

And

$$P^* = 800 - 2(200) = 400.$$

The equilibrium price is $4 a cone, and the equilibrium quantity is 200 cones per day.

SUMMARY

KEY POINTS

Markets and Prices (p. 60)

- A competitive market is one that has so many buyers and sellers that no one can influence the price.
- Opportunity cost is a relative price.
- Demand and supply determine relative prices.

Demand (pp. 61–65)

- Demand is the relationship between the quantity demanded of a good and its price when all other influences on buying plans remain the same.
- The higher the price of a good, other things remaining the same, the smaller is the quantity demanded—the law of demand.
- Demand depends on the prices of substitutes and complements, expected future prices, income, expected future income, population, and preferences.

Supply (pp. 66–69)

- Supply is the relationship between the quantity supplied of a good and its price when all other influences on selling plans remain the same.
- The higher the price of a good, other things remaining the same, the greater is the quantity supplied—the law of supply.
- Supply depends on the prices of resources used to produce a good, the prices of related goods produced, expected future prices, the number of suppliers, and technology.

Market Equilibrium (pp. 70–71)

- At the equilibrium price, the quantity demanded equals the quantity supplied.
- At prices above equilibrium, there is a surplus and the price falls.
- At prices below equilibrium, there is a shortage and the price rises.

Predicting Changes in Price and Quantity (pp. 72–75)

- An increase in demand brings a rise in the price and an increase in the quantity supplied. (A decrease in demand brings a fall in the price and a decrease in the quantity supplied.)

- An increase in supply brings a fall in the price and an increase in the quantity demanded. (A decrease in supply brings a rise in the price and a decrease in the quantity demanded.)
- An increase in demand and an increase in supply bring an increased quantity, but the price might rise, fall, or remain the same. An increase in demand and a decrease in supply bring a higher price, but the quantity might increase, decrease, or remain the same.

KEY FIGURES

Figure 3.1   The Demand Curve, 62
Figure 3.3   A Change in the Quantity Demanded Versus a Change in Demand, 65
Figure 3.4   The Supply Curve, 67
Figure 3.6   A Change in the Quantity Supplied Versus a Change in Supply, 69
Figure 3.7   Equilibrium, 70
Figure 3.8   The Effects of a Change in Demand, 72
Figure 3.9   The Effects of a Change in Supply, 73

KEY TERMS

Change in demand, 62
Change in supply, 67
Change in the quantity demanded, 65
Change in the quantity supplied, 68
Competitive market, 60
Complement, 63
Demand, 61
Demand curve, 62
Equilibrium price, 70
Equilibrium quantity, 70
Inferior good, 64
Law of demand, 61
Law of supply, 66
Money price, 60
Normal good, 64
Quantity demanded, 61
Quantity supplied, 66
Relative price, 60
Substitute, 63
Supply, 66
Supply curve, 66

PROBLEMS

Go to (myeconlab) for solutions to odd-numbered problems and additional exercises.

1. What is the effect on the price of an audiotape and the quantity of audiotapes sold if
   a. The price of a CD rises?
   b. The price of a Walkman rises?
   c. The supply of CD players increases?
   d. Consumers' incomes increase?
   e. Workers who make audiotapes get a pay raise?
   f. The price of a Walkman rises at the same time as the workers who make audiotapes get a pay raise?

2. What is the effect on the price of a DVD player and the quantity of DVD players sold if
   a. The price of a DVD rises?
   b. The price of a DVD falls?
   c. The supply of DVD players increases?
   d. Consumers' incomes decrease??
   e. The wage rate of workers who produce DVD players increases?
   f. The wage rate of workers who produce DVD players rises and at the same time the price of a DVD falls?

3. The following events occur one at a time:
   i.   The price of crude oil rises.
   ii. The price of a car rises.
   iii. All speed limits on highways are abolished.
   iv. Robot technology cuts the cost of producing a car.
   Which of these events will increase or decrease (state which)
   a. The demand for gasoline?
   b. The supply of gasoline?
   c. The quantity of gasoline demanded?
   d. The quantity of gasoline supplied?

4. The following events occur one at a time:
   i.   The price of airfares halve.
   ii. The price of beef falls.
   iii. A cheap new strong cloth, a close substitute for leather, is invented.
   iv. A new high-speed technology for cutting leather is invented.
   Which of these events will increase or decrease (state which)
   a. The demand for leather bags?
   b. The supply of leather bags?
   c. The quantity of leather bags demanded?
   d. The quantity of leather bags supplied?

5. The figure illustrates the market for pizza.
   a. Label the curves in the figure.
   b. What are the equilibrium price of a pizza and the equilibrium quantity of pizza?

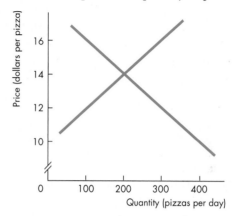

6. The figure illustrates the market for fish.
   a. Label the curves in the figure.
   b. What are the equilibrium price of a fish and the equilibrium quantity of fish?

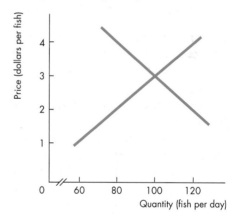

7. The demand and supply schedules for gum are

Price (cents per pack)	Quantity demanded	Quantity supplied
	(millions of packs per week)	
20	180	60
30	160	80
40	140	100
50	120	120
60	100	140
70	80	160
80	60	180

   a. Draw a graph of the gum market and mark in the equilibrium price and quantity.

b. Suppose that gum is 70¢ a pack. Describe the situation in the gum market and explain how the price of gum adjusts.

8. The demand and supply schedules for potato chips are

Price (cents per bag)	Quantity demanded	Quantity supplied
	(millions of bags per week)	
50	160	130
60	150	140
70	140	150
80	130	160
90	120	170
100	110	180

a. Draw a graph of the potato chip market and mark in the equilibrium price and quantity.

b. Suppose that chips are 60¢ a bag. Describe the situation in the market for chips and explain how the price adjusts.

9. In problem 7, suppose that a fire destroys some gum-producing factories and the supply of gum decreases by 40 million packs a week.

a. Has there been a shift of or a movement along the supply curve of gum?

b. Has there been a shift of or a movement along the demand curve for gum?

c. What are the new equilibrium price and equilibrium quantity of gum?

10. In problem 8, suppose a new dip comes onto the market, which is very popular and the demand for potato chips increases by 30 million bags per week.

a. Has there been a shift of or a movement along the supply curve of potato chips?

b. Has there been a shift of or a movement along the demand curve for gum?

c. What are the new equilibrium price and equilibrium quantity of potato chips?

11. In problem 9, suppose an increase in the teenage population increases the demand for gum by 40 million packs per week at the same time as the fire occurs. What are the new equilibrium price and quantity of gum?

12. In problem 10, suppose that a virus destroys several potato farms with the result that the supply of potato chips decreases by 40 million bags a week at the same time as the dip comes onto the market. What are the new equilibrium price and quantity of potato chips?

CRITICAL THINKING

1. After you have studied *Reading Between the Lines* on pp. 76–77, answer the following questions:

a. What happened to the price of oil between 2004 and 2005?

b. Why did the supply-side event reported in the news article have almost no effect on the supply of oil?

c. Why did the demand for oil increase in 2005?

d. Why did the equilibrium quantity of oil increase in 2005?

e. What might eventually decrease the demand for oil and lower its equilibrium price?

WEB EXERCISES

Use the links on (myeconlab) to work the following exercises.

1. Obtain data on the prices and quantities of wheat.

a. Make a figure similar to Fig. 3.7 on p. 70 to illustrate the market for wheat since 2001.

b. Show the changes in demand and supply and the changes in the quantity demanded and the quantity supplied that are consistent with the price and quantity data.

2. Obtain data on the price of oil.

a. Describe how the price of oil has changed over the past five years.

b. Draw a demand-supply graph to explain what happens to the price when there is an increase or a decrease in supply and no change in demand.

c. What do you predict would happen to the price of oil if a new drilling technology permitted deeper ocean sources to be used?

d. What do you predict would happen to the price of oil if a clean and safe nuclear technology were developed?

e. What do you predict would happen to the price of oil if automobiles were powered by batteries instead of by internal combustion engines?

Elasticity

Tough Times in the Recording Industry

The recording industry is operating in tough times. Faced with the alternatives of paying $12 for a CD or nothing for a download, more and more people are choosing to download. This activity is an example of a conflict between self-interest and the social interest. If artists and recording companies don't get rewarded for their work, the amount of recorded music available will dry up.

Some CD producers are trying to combat the problem by slashing the price of a CD. Will this strategy work? Can lower-priced CDs beat downloads, bring greater revenue to the CD producers and the artists whose work they sell, and help to promote the social interest?

◆ In this chapter, you will learn about a tool that helps us to answer this question. You will learn about the elasticities of demand and supply. At the end of the chapter, we'll return to the question confronting CD producers and see whether lower-priced CDs are the solution to the dilemma of the recorded music industry.

After studying this chapter, you will be able to

- ■ **Define, calculate, and explain the factors that influence the price elasticity of demand**

- ■ **Define, calculate, and explain the factors that influence the cross elasticity of demand and the income elasticity of demand**

- ■ **Define, calculate, and explain the factors that influence the elasticity of supply**

Price Elasticity of Demand

YOU KNOW THAT WHEN SUPPLY INCREASES, THE equilibrium price falls and the equilibrium quantity increases. But does the price fall by a large amount and the quantity increase by a little? Or does the price barely fall and the quantity increase by a large amount?

The answer depends on the responsiveness of the quantity demanded to a change in price. You can see why by studying Fig. 4.1, which shows two possible scenarios in a local pizza market. Figure 4.1(a) shows one scenario, and Fig. 4.1(b) shows the other.

In both cases, supply is initially S_0. In part (a), the demand for pizza is shown by the demand curve D_A. In part (b), the demand for pizza is shown by the demand curve D_B. Initially, in both cases, the price is $20 a pizza and the quantity of pizza produced and consumed is 10 pizzas an hour.

Now a large pizza franchise opens up, and the supply of pizza increases. The supply curve shifts rightward to S_1. In case (a), the price falls by an enormous $15 to $5 a pizza, and the quantity increases by only 3 to 13 pizzas an hour. In contrast, in case (b), the price falls by only $5 to $15 a pizza and the quantity increases by 7 to 17 pizzas an hour.

The different outcomes arise from differing degrees of responsiveness of the quantity demanded to a change in price. But what do we mean by responsiveness? One possible answer is slope. The slope of demand curve D_A is steeper than the slope of demand curve D_B.

In this example, we can compare the slopes of the two demand curves. But we can't always do so. The reason is that the slope of a demand curve depends on the units in which we measure the price and quantity. And we often must compare the demand curves for different goods and services that are measured in unrelated units. For example, a pizza producer might want to compare the demand for pizza with the demand for soft drinks. Which quantity demanded is more responsive to a price change? This question can't be answered by comparing the slopes of two demand curves. The units of measurement of pizza and soft drinks are unrelated. The question can be answered with a measure of responsiveness that is independent of units of measurement. Elasticity is such a measure.

The **price elasticity of demand** is a units-free measure of the responsiveness of the quantity demanded of a good to a change in its price when all other influences on buyers' plans remain the same.

FIGURE 4.1
How a Change in Supply Changes Price and Quantity

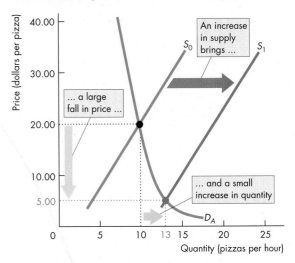

(a) Large price change and small quantity change

(b) Small price change and large quantity change

Initially the price is $20 a pizza and the quantity sold is 10 pizzas an hour. Then supply increases from S_0 to S_1. In part (a), the price falls by $15 to $5 a pizza, and the quantity increases by 3 to 13 pizzas an hour. In part (b), the price falls by only $5 to $15 a pizza, and the quantity increases by 7 to 17 pizzas an hour. The price change is smaller and the quantity change is larger in case (b) than in case (a). The quantity demanded is more responsive to a change in price in case (b) than in case (a).

Calculating Price Elasticity of Demand

We calculate the *price elasticity of demand* by using the formula:

$$\text{Price elasticity of demand} = \frac{\text{Percentage change in quantity demanded}}{\text{Percentage change in price}}.$$

To use this formula, we need to know the quantities demanded at different prices when all other influences on buyers' plans remain the same. Suppose we have the data on prices and quantities demanded of pizza and we calculate the price elasticity of demand for pizza.

Figure 4.2 zooms in on the demand curve for pizza and shows how the quantity demanded responds to a small change in price. Initially, the price is $20.50 a pizza and 9 pizzas an hour are sold—the original point in the figure. The price then falls to $19.50 a pizza, and the quantity demanded increases to 11 pizzas an hour—the new point in the figure. When the price falls by $1 a pizza, the quantity demanded increases by 2 pizzas an hour.

To calculate the price elasticity of demand, we express the changes in price and quantity demanded as percentages of the *average price* and the *average quantity*. By using the average price and average quantity, we calculate the elasticity at a point on the demand curve midway between the original point and the new point. The original price is $20.50 and the new price is $19.50, so the average price is $20. The $1 price decrease is 5 percent of the average price. That is,

$$\Delta P/P_{ave} = (\$1/\$20) \times 100 = 5\%.$$

The original quantity demanded is 9 pizzas and the new quantity demanded is 11 pizzas, so the average quantity demanded is 10 pizzas. The 2 pizza increase in the quantity demanded is 20 percent of the average quantity. That is,

$$\Delta Q/Q_{ave} = (2/10) \times 100 = 20\%.$$

So the price elasticity of demand, which is the percentage change in the quantity demanded (20 percent) divided by the percentage change in price (5 percent) is 4. That is,

$$\text{Price elasticity of demand} = \frac{\%\Delta Q}{\%\Delta P}$$

$$= \frac{20\%}{5\%} = 4.$$

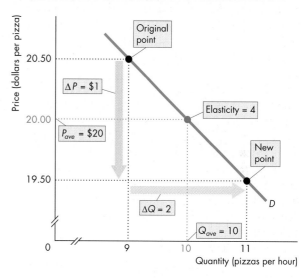

FIGURE 4.2

Calculating the Elasticity of Demand

The elasticity of demand is calculated by using the formula:*

$$\text{Price elasticity of demand} = \frac{\text{Percentage change in quantity demanded}}{\text{Percentage change in price}}$$

$$= \frac{\%\Delta Q}{\%\Delta P}$$

$$= \frac{\Delta Q/Q_{ave}}{\Delta P/P_{ave}}$$

$$= \frac{2/10}{1/20}$$

$$= 4.$$

This calculation measures the elasticity at an average price of $20 a pizza and an average quantity of 10 pizzas an hour.

*In the formula, the Greek letter delta (Δ) stands for "change in" and %Δ stands for "percentage change in."

Average Price and Quantity Notice that we use the *average* price and *average* quantity. We do this because it gives the most precise measurement of elasticity—at the midpoint between the original price and the new price. If the price falls from $20.50 to $19.50, the $1 price change is 4.9 percent of $20.50. The 2 pizza change in quantity is 22.2 percent of 9 pizzas, the original quantity. So if we use these numbers, the price elasticity of demand is 22.2 divided by 4.9, which equals 4.5. If the price rises from $19.50 to $20.50, the $1 price change is 5.1 percent of $19.50. The 2 pizza change in quantity is 18.2 percent of 11 pizzas, the original quantity. So if we use these numbers, the price elasticity of demand is 18.2 divided by 5.1, which equals 3.6. By using percentages of the *average* price and *average* quantity, we get the same value for the elasticity regardless of whether the price falls from $20.50 to $19.50 or rises from $19.50 to $20.50.

Percentages and Proportions Elasticity is the ratio of two percentage changes. So when we divide one percentage change by another, the 100s cancel. A percentage change is a *proportionate* change multiplied by 100. The proportionate change in price is $\Delta P / P_{ave}$, and the proportionate change in quantity demanded is $\Delta Q / Q_{ave}$. So if we divide $\Delta Q / Q_{ave}$ by $\Delta P / P_{ave}$ we get the same answer as we get by using percentage changes.

A Units-Free Measure Now that you've calculated a price elasticity of demand, you can see why it is a *units-free measure*. Elasticity is a units-free measure because the percentage change in each variable is independent of the units in which the variable is measured. And the ratio of the two percentages is a number without units.

Minus Sign and Elasticity When the price of a good *rises*, the quantity demanded *decreases* along the demand curve. Because a *positive* change in price brings a *negative* change in the quantity demanded, the price elasticity of demand is a negative number. But it is the magnitude, or *absolute value*, of the price elasticity of demand that tells us how responsive—how elastic—demand is. To compare price elasticities of demand, we use the magnitude of the elasticity and ignore the minus sign.

Inelastic and Elastic Demand

Figure 4.3 shows three demand curves that cover the entire range of possible elasticities of demand. In Fig. 4.3(a), the quantity demanded is constant regardless of the price. If the quantity demanded remains constant when the price changes, then the price elasticity of demand is zero and the good is said to have a **perfectly inelastic demand**. One good that has a very low price elasticity of demand (perhaps zero over some price range) is insulin. Insulin is of such importance to some diabetics that if the price rises or falls, they do not change the quantity they buy.

If the percentage change in the quantity demanded equals the percentage change in price, then the price elasticity equals 1 and the good is said to have a **unit elastic demand**. The demand in Fig. 4.3(b) is an example of unit elastic demand.

Between the cases shown in Fig. 4.3(a) and Fig. 4.3(b) is the general case in which the percentage change in the quantity demanded is less than the percentage change in price. In this case, the price

FIGURE 4.3
Inelastic and Elastic Demand

(a) **Perfectly inelastic demand**

(b) **Unit elastic demand**

(c) **Perfectly elastic demand**

Each demand illustrated here has a constant elasticity. The demand curve in part (a) illustrates the demand for a good that has a zero elasticity of demand. The demand curve in part (b) illustrates the demand for a good with a unit elasticity of demand. And the demand curve in part (c) illustrates the demand for a good with an infinite elasticity of demand.

elasticity of demand is between zero and 1 and the good is said to have an **inelastic demand**. Food and housing are examples of goods with inelastic demand.

If the quantity demanded changes by an infinitely large percentage in response to a tiny price change, then the price elasticity of demand is infinity and the good is said to have a **perfectly elastic demand**. Figure 4.3(c) shows a perfectly elastic demand. An example of a good that has a very high elasticity of demand (almost infinite) is a soft drink from two campus machines located side by side. If the two machines offer the same soft drinks for the same price, some people buy from one machine and some from the other. But if one machine's price is higher than the other's, by even a small amount, no one will buy from the machine with the higher price. Soft drinks from the two machines are perfect substitutes.

Between the cases in Fig. 4.3(b) and Fig. 4.3(c) is the general case in which the percentage change in the quantity demanded exceeds the percentage change in price. In this case, the price elasticity of demand is greater than 1 and the good is said to have an **elastic demand**. Automobiles and furniture are examples of goods that have elastic demand.

Elasticity Along a Straight-Line Demand Curve

Elasticity and slope are not the same, but they are related. To understand how they are related, let's look at elasticity along a straight-line demand curve—a demand curve that has a constant slope.

Figure 4.4 illustrates the calculation of elasticity along a straight-line demand curve. First, suppose the price falls from $25 to $15 a pizza. The quantity demanded increases from zero to 20 pizzas an hour. The average price is $20 a pizza, and the average quantity is 10 pizzas. So

$$\text{Price elasticity of demand} = \frac{\Delta Q/Q_{ave}}{\Delta P/P_{ave}}$$

$$= \frac{20/10}{10/20}$$

$$= 4.$$

That is, the price elasticity of demand at an average price of $20 is 4.

Next, suppose that the price falls from $15 to $10 a pizza. The quantity demanded increases from 20 to 30 pizzas an hour. The average price is now $12.50 a

pizza, and the average quantity is 25 pizzas an hour. So

$$\text{Price elasticity of demand} = \frac{10/25}{5/12.50}$$

$$= 1.$$

That is, the price elasticity of demand at an average price of $12.50 a pizza is 1.

Finally, suppose that the price falls from $10 to zero. The quantity demanded increases from 30 to 50 pizzas an hour. The average price is now $5 and the average quantity is 40 pizzas an hour. So

$$\text{Price elasticity of demand} = \frac{20/40}{10/5}$$

$$= 1/4.$$

That is, the price elasticity of demand at an average price of $5 a pizza is 1/4.

You've now seen how elasticity changes along a straight-line demand curve. At the midpoint of the curve, demand is unit elastic. Above the midpoint, demand is elastic. Below the midpoint, demand is inelastic.

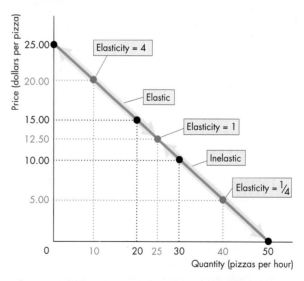

FIGURE 4.4   myeconlab

Elasticity Along a Straight-Line Demand Curve

On a straight-line demand curve, elasticity decreases as the price falls and the quantity demanded increases. Demand is unit elastic at the midpoint of the demand curve (elasticity is 1). Above the midpoint, demand is elastic; below the midpoint, demand is inelastic.

Total Revenue and Elasticity

The **total revenue** from the sale of a good equals the price of the good multiplied by the quantity sold. When a price changes, total revenue also changes. But a rise in price does not always increase total revenue. The change in total revenue depends on the elasticity of demand in the following way:

- If demand is elastic, a 1 percent price cut increases the quantity sold by more than 1 percent and total revenue increases.
- If demand is inelastic, a 1 percent price cut increases the quantity sold by less than 1 percent and total revenue decreases.
- If demand is unit elastic, a 1 percent price cut increases the quantity sold by 1 percent and so total revenue does not change.

Figure 4.5 shows how we can use this relationship between elasticity and total revenue to estimate elasticity using the total revenue test. The **total revenue test** is a method of estimating the price elasticity of demand by observing the change in total revenue that results from a change in the price, when all other influences on the quantity sold remain the same.

- If a price cut increases total revenue, demand is elastic.
- If a price cut decreases total revenue, demand is inelastic.
- If a price cut leaves total revenue unchanged, demand is unit elastic.

In Fig. 4.5(a), over the price range from $25 to $12.50, demand is elastic. Over the price range from $12.50 to zero, demand is inelastic. At a price of $12.50, demand is unit elastic.

Figure 4.5(b) shows total revenue. At a price of $25, the quantity sold is zero, so total revenue is zero. At a price of zero, the quantity demanded is 50 pizzas an hour and total revenue is again zero. A price cut in the elastic range brings an increase in total revenue—the percentage increase in the quantity demanded is greater than the percentage decrease in price. A price cut in the inelastic range brings a decrease in total revenue—the percentage increase in the quantity demanded is less than the percentage decrease in price. At unit elasticity, total revenue is at a maximum.

FIGURE 4.5
Elasticity and Total Revenue

(a) Demand

(b) Total revenue

When demand is elastic, in the price range from $25 to $12.50, a decrease in price (part a) brings an increase in total revenue (part b). When demand is inelastic, in the price range from $12.50 to zero, a decrease in price (part a) brings a decrease in total revenue (part b). When demand is unit elastic, at a price of $12.50 (part a), total revenue is at a maximum (part b).

Your Expenditure and Your Elasticity

When a price changes, the change in your expenditure on the good depends on *your* elasticity of demand.

- If your demand is elastic, a 1 percent price cut increases the quantity you buy by more than 1 percent and your expenditure on the item increases.
- If your demand is inelastic, a 1 percent price cut increases the quantity you buy by less than 1 percent and your expenditure on the item decreases.
- If your demand is unit elastic, a 1 percent price cut increases the quantity you buy by 1 percent and your expenditure on the item does not change.

So if you spend more on an item when its price falls, your demand for that item is elastic; if you spend the same amount, your demand is unit elastic; and if you spend less, your demand is inelastic.

The Factors That Influence the Elasticity of Demand

Table 4.1 lists some estimates of actual elasticities in the real world. You can see that these real-world elasticities of demand range from 1.52 for metals, the item with the most elastic demand in the table, to 0.05 for oil, the item with the most inelastic demand in the table. What makes the demand for some goods elastic and the demand for others inelastic?

The magnitude of the elasticity of demand depends on:

- The closeness of substitutes
- The proportion of income spent on the good
- The time elapsed since a price change

Closeness of Substitutes The closer the substitutes for a good or service, the more elastic is the demand for it. For example, oil from which we make gasoline has substitutes but none that are currently very close (imagine a steam-driven, coal-fuelled car). So the demand for oil is inelastic. Plastics are close substitutes for metals, so the demand for metals is elastic.

The degree of substitutability between two goods also depends on how narrowly (or broadly) we define them. For example, the elasticity of demand for meat is low, but the elasticity of demand for beef or pork is high. The elasticity of demand for personal computers is low, but the elasticity of demand for a Dell, IBM, or Hewlett-Packard computer is high.

In everyday language we call some goods, such as food and housing, *necessities* and other goods, such as exotic vacations, *luxuries*. A necessity is a good that

TABLE 4.1   Some Real-World Price Elasticities of Demand

Good or Service	Elasticity
Elastic Demand	
Metals	1.52
Electrical engineering products	1.39
Mechanical engineering products	1.30
Furniture	1.26
Motor vehicles	1.14
Instrument engineering products	1.10
Professional services	1.09
Transportation services	1.03
Inelastic Demand	
Gas, electricity, and water	0.92
Chemicals	0.89
Drinks (all types)	0.78
Clothing	0.64
Tobacco	0.61
Banking and insurance services	0.56
Housing services	0.55
Agricultural and fish products	0.42
Books, magazines, and newspapers	0.34
Food	0.12
Oil	0.05

Sources: Ahsan Mansur and John Whalley, "Numerical Specification of Applied General Equilibrium Models: Estimation, Calibration, and Data," in Applied General Equilibrium Analysis, eds. Herbert E. Scarf and John B. Shoven (New York: Cambridge University Press, 1984), 109; and Henri Theil, Ching-Fan Chung, and James L. Seale, Jr., Advances in Econometrics, Supplement I, 1989, International Evidence on Consumption Patterns (Greenwich, Conn.: JAI Press Inc., 1989), and Geoffrey Heal, Columbia University, Web site.

has poor substitutes and that is crucial for our well-being. So generally, a necessity has an inelastic demand. In Table 4.1, food and oil might be classified as necessities.

A luxury is a good that usually has many substitutes, one of which is not buying it. So a luxury generally has an elastic demand. In Table 4.1, furniture and motor vehicles might be classified as luxuries.

Proportion of Income Spent on the Good Other things remaining the same, the greater the proportion of income spent on a good, the more elastic is the demand for it.

Think about your own elasticity of demand for chewing gum and housing. If the price of chewing gum doubles, you consume almost as much gum as before. Your demand for gum is inelastic. If apartment rents double, you shriek and look for more students to share accommodation with you. Your demand for housing is more elastic than your demand for gum. Why the difference? Housing takes a large proportion of your budget, and gum takes only a tiny proportion. You don't like either price increase, but you hardly notice the higher price of gum, while the higher rent puts your budget under severe strain.

Figure 4.6 shows the proportion of income spent on food and the price elasticity of demand for food in 10 countries. This figure confirms the general tendency we have just described. The larger the proportion of income spent on food, the larger is the price elasticity of demand for food. For example, in Tanzania, a nation where 62 percent of income is spent on food, the price elasticity of demand for food is 0.77. In contrast, in Canada, where 14 percent of income is spent on food, the price elasticity of demand for food is 0.13.

Time Elapsed Since Price Change The longer the time that has elapsed since a price change, the more elastic is demand. When the price of oil increased by 400 percent during the 1970s, people barely changed the quantity of oil and gasoline they consumed. But gradually, as more efficient auto and airplane engines were developed, the quantity consumed decreased. The demand for oil has become more elastic as more time has elapsed since the huge price hike. Similarly, when the price of a PC fell, the quantity of PCs demanded increased only slightly at first. But as more people have become better informed about the variety of ways of using a PC, the quantity of PCs bought has increased sharply. The demand for PCs has become more elastic.

FIGURE 4.6
Price Elasticities in 10 Countries

As income increases and the proportion of income spent on food decreases, the demand for food becomes less elastic.

Source of data: Henri Theil, Ching-Fan Chung, and James L. Seale, Jr., Advances in Econometrics, Supplement 1, 1989, International Evidence on Consumption Patterns (Greenwich, Conn.: JAI Press, Inc., 1989).

REVIEW QUIZ

1 Why do we need a units-free measure of the responsiveness of the quantity demanded of a good or service to a change in its price?
2 Can you define and calculate the price elasticity of demand?
3 Why, when we calculate the price elasticity of demand, do we express the change in price as a percentage of the *average* price and the change in quantity as a percentage of the *average* quantity?
4 What is the total revenue test and why does it work?
5 What are the main influences on the elasticity of demand that make the demand for some goods elastic and the demand for other goods inelastic?
6 Why is the demand for a luxury generally more elastic than the demand for a necessity?

Study Plan 4.1

You've now completed your study of the *price* elasticity of demand. Two other elasticity concepts tell us about the effects of other influences on demand. Let's look at these other elasticities of demand.

More Elasticities of Demand

BACK AT THE PIZZERIA, YOU ARE TRYING TO WORK out how a price cut by the burger shop next door will affect the demand for your pizza. You know that pizzas and burgers are substitutes. And you know that when the price of a substitute for pizza falls, the demand for pizza decreases. But by how much?

You also know that pizza and soft drinks are complements. And you know that if the price of a complement of pizza falls, the demand for pizza increases. So you wonder whether you might keep your customers by cutting the price you charge for soft drinks. But again by how much?

To answer these questions, you need to calculate the cross elasticity of demand. Let's examine this elasticity measure.

Cross Elasticity of Demand

We measure the influence of a change in the price of a substitute or complement by using the concept of the cross elasticity of demand. The **cross elasticity of demand** is a measure of the responsiveness of the demand for a good to a change in the price of a substitute or complement, other things remaining the same. We calculate the *cross elasticity of demand* by using the formula:

$$\text{Cross elasticity of demand} = \frac{\text{Percentage change in quantity demanded}}{\text{Percentage change in price of a substitute or complement}}.$$

The cross elasticity of demand can be positive or negative. It is *positive* for a *substitute* and *negative* for a *complement*.

Substitutes Suppose that the price of pizza is constant and 9 pizzas an hour are sold. Then the price of a burger rises from $1.50 to $2.50. No other influence on buying plans changes and the quantity of pizzas sold increases to 11 an hour.

The change in the quantity demanded is +2 pizzas—the new quantity, 11 pizzas, minus the original quantity, 9 pizzas. The average quantity is 10 pizzas. So the quantity of pizzas demanded increases by 20 percent (+20). That is,

$$\Delta Q/Q_{ave} = (+2/10) \times 100 = +20\%.$$

The change in the price of a burger, a substitute for pizza, is +$1—the new price, $2.50, minus the original price, $1.50. The average price is $2 a burger. So the price of a burger rises by 50 percent (+50). That is,

$$\Delta P/P_{ave} = (+\$1/\$2) \times 100 = +50\%.$$

So the cross elasticity of demand for pizza with respect to the price of a burger is

$$\frac{+20\%}{+50\%} = 0.4.$$

Figure 4.7 illustrates the cross elasticity of demand. Pizza and burgers are substitutes. Because they are substitutes, when the price of a burger rises, the demand for pizza increases. The demand curve for pizza shifts rightward from D_0 to D_1. Because a *rise* in the price of a burger brings an *increase* in the demand for pizza, the cross elasticity of demand for pizza with respect to the price of a burger is *positive*. Both the price and the quantity change in the same direction.

FIGURE 4.7

myeconlab

Cross Elasticity of Demand

Price of a burger, a substitute, rises. Positive cross elasticity

Price of soft drink, a complement, rises. Negative cross elasticity

D_1

D_0

D_2

A burger is a *substitute* for pizza. When the price of a burger rises, the demand for pizza increases and the demand curve for pizza shifts rightward from D_0 to D_1. The cross elasticity of the demand is *positive*.

Soft drinks are a *complement* of pizza. When the price of soft drinks rises, the demand for pizza decreases and the demand curve for pizza shifts leftward from D_0 to D_2. The cross elasticity of the demand is *negative*.

Complements Now suppose that the price of pizza is constant and 11 pizzas an hour are sold. Then the price of a soft drink rises from $1.50 to $2.50. No other influence on buying plans changes and the quantity of pizzas sold falls to 9 an hour.

The change in the quantity demanded is the opposite of what we've just calculated: The quantity of pizzas demanded decreases by 20 percent (–20).

The change in the price of a soft drink, a complement of pizza, is the same as the percentage change in the price of a burger that we've just calculated: The price rises by 50 percent (+50). So the cross elasticity of demand for pizza with respect to the price of a soft drink is

$$\frac{-20\%}{+50\%} = -0.4.$$

Because pizza and soft drinks are complements, when the price of a soft drink rises, the demand for pizza decreases. The demand curve for pizza shifts leftward from D_0 to D_2. Because a *rise* in the price of a soft drink brings a *decrease* in the demand for pizza, the cross elasticity of demand for pizza with respect to the price of a soft drink is *negative*. The price and quantity change in *opposite* directions.

The magnitude of the cross elasticity of demand determines how far the demand curve shifts. The larger the cross elasticity (absolute value), the greater is the change in demand and the larger is the shift in the demand curve.

If two items are very close substitutes, such as two brands of spring water, the cross elasticity is large. If two items are close complements, such as movies and popcorn, the cross elasticity is large.

If two items are somewhat unrelated to each other, such as newspapers and orange juice, the cross elasticity is small—perhaps even zero.

Income Elasticity of Demand

Suppose the economy is expanding and people are enjoying rising incomes. This prosperity is bringing an increase in the demand for most types of goods and services. But by how much will the demand for pizza increase? The answer depends on the **income elasticity of demand**, which is a measure of the responsiveness of the demand for a good or service to a change in income, other things remaining the same.

The income elasticity of demand is calculated by using the formula:

$$\text{Income elasticity of demand} = \frac{\text{Percentage change in quantity demanded}}{\text{Percentage change in income}}.$$

Income elasticities of demand can be positive or negative and fall into three interesting ranges:

- Greater than 1 (*normal* good, income elastic)
- Positive and less than 1 (*normal* good, income inelastic)
- Negative (*inferior* good)

Income Elastic Demand Suppose that the price of pizza is constant and 9 pizzas an hour are sold. Then incomes rise from $975 to $1,025 a week. No other influence on buying plans changes and the quantity of pizzas sold increases to 11 an hour.

The change in the quantity demanded is +2 pizzas. The average quantity is 10 pizzas, so the quantity demanded increases by 20 percent. The change in income is +$50 and the average income is $1,000, so incomes increase by 5 percent. The income elasticity of demand for pizza is

$$\frac{20\%}{5\%} = 4.$$

As income increases, the quantity of pizza demanded increases faster than income. The demand for pizza is income elastic. Other goods in this category include ocean cruises, international travel, jewellery, and works of art.

Income Inelastic Demand If the percentage increase in the quantity demanded is less than the percentage increase in income, the income elasticity of demand is positive and less than 1. In this case, the quantity demanded increases as income increases, but the quantity demanded does not increase as quickly as income increases. The demand for the good is income inelastic. Goods in this category include food, clothing, newspapers, and magazines.

Inferior Goods If the quantity demanded of a good decreases when income increases, the income elasticity of demand is negative. Goods in this category include small motorcycles, potatoes, and rice. Low-income consumers buy most of these goods.

Real-World Income Elasticities of Demand

Table 4.2 shows estimates of some real-world income elasticities of demand. The demand for a necessity such as food or clothing is income inelastic, while the demand for a luxury such as transportation, which includes airline and foreign travel, is income elastic.

But what is a necessity and what is a luxury depends on the level of income. For people with a low income, food and clothing can be luxuries. So the *level* of income has a big effect on income elasticities of demand. Figure 4.8 shows this effect on the income elasticity of demand for food in 10 countries. In countries with low incomes, such as Tanzania and India, the income elasticity of demand for food is high. In countries with high incomes, such as Canada, the income elasticity of demand for food is low.

TABLE 4.2   Some Real-World Income Elasticities of Demand

Good or Service	Elasticity
Elastic Demand	
Airline travel	5.82
Movies	3.41
Foreign travel	3.08
Electricity	1.94
Restaurant meals	1.61
Local buses and trains	1.38
Haircuts	1.36
Automobiles	1.07
Inelastic Demand	
Tobacco	0.86
Alcoholic drinks	0.62
Furniture	0.53
Clothing	0.51
Newspapers and magazines	0.38
Telephone	0.32
Food	0.14

Sources: H.S. Houthakker and Lester D. Taylor, *Consumer Demand in the United States* (Cambridge, Mass.: Harvard University Press, 1970); and Henri Theil, Ching-Fan Chung, and James L. Seale, Jr., *Advances in Econometrics, Supplement 1, 1989, International Evidence on Consumption Patterns* (Greenwich, Conn.: JAI Press, Inc., 1989).

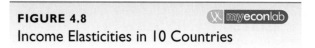

FIGURE 4.8
Income Elasticities in 10 Countries

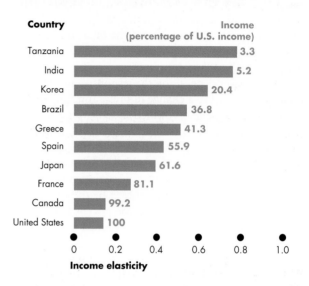

As income increases, the income elasticity of demand for food decreases. Low-income consumers spend a larger percentage of any increase in income on food than do high-income consumers.

Source of data: Henri Theil, Ching-Fan Chung, and James L. Seale, Jr., *Advances in Econometrics, Supplement 1, 1989, International Evidence on Consumption Patterns* (Greenwich, Conn.: JAI Press, Inc., 1989).

REVIEW QUIZ

1 What does the cross elasticity of demand measure?
2 What does the sign (positive versus negative) of the cross elasticity of demand tell us about the relationship between two goods?
3 What does the income elasticity of demand measure?
4 What does the sign (positive versus negative) of the income elasticity of demand tell us about a good?
5 Why does the level of income influence the magnitude of the income elasticity of demand?

 Study Plan 4.2

You've now completed your study of the *cross elasticity* of demand and the *income elasticity* of demand. Let's look at the other side of a market and examine the elasticity of supply.

Elasticity of Supply

YOU KNOW THAT WHEN DEMAND INCREASES, THE price rises and the quantity increases. But does the price rise by a large amount and the quantity increase by a little? Or does the price barely rise and the quantity increase by a large amount?

The answer depends on the responsiveness of the quantity supplied to a change in price. You can see why by studying Fig. 4.9, which shows two possible scenarios in a local pizza market. Figure 4.9(a) shows one scenario, and Fig. 4.9(b) shows the other.

In both cases, demand is initially D_0. In part (a), the supply of pizza is shown by the supply curve S_A. In part (b), the supply of pizza is shown by the supply curve S_B. Initially, in both cases, the price is $20 a pizza and the quantity produced and consumed is 10 pizzas an hour.

Now increases in incomes and population increase the demand for pizza. The demand curve shifts rightward to D_1. In case (a), the price rises by $10 to $30 a pizza, and the quantity increases by only 3 to 13 an hour. In contrast, in case (b), the price rises by only $1 to $21 a pizza, and the quantity increases by 10 to 20 pizzas an hour.

The different outcomes arise from differing degrees of responsiveness of the quantity supplied to a change in price. We measure the degree of responsiveness by using the concept of the elasticity of supply.

Calculating the Elasticity of Supply

The **elasticity of supply** measures the responsiveness of the quantity supplied to a change in the price of a good when all other influences on selling plans remain the same. It is calculated by using the formula:

$$\text{Elasticity of supply} = \frac{\text{Percentage change in quantity supplied}}{\text{Percentage change in price}}.$$

We use the same method that you learned when you studied the elasticity of demand. (Refer back to p. 85 to check this method.) Let's calculate the elasticity of supply along the supply curves in Fig. 4.9.

In Fig. 4.9(a), when the price rises from $20 to $30, the price rise is $10 and the average price is $25, so the price rises by 40 percent of the average price. The quantity increases from 10 to 13 pizzas an

FIGURE 4.9   myeconlab

How a Change in Demand Changes Price and Quantity

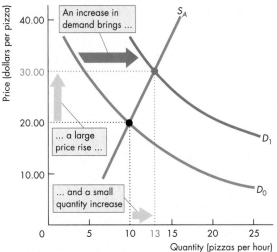

(a) Large price change and small quantity change

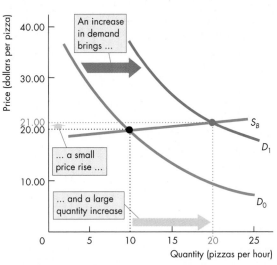

(b) Small price change and large quantity change

Initially, the price is $20 a pizza, and the quantity sold is 10 pizzas an hour. Then increases in incomes and population increase the demand for pizza. The demand curve shifts rightward to D_1. In part (a) the price rises by $10 to $30 a pizza, and the quantity increases by 3 to 13 pizzas an hour. In part (b), the price rises by only $1 to $21 a pizza, and the quantity increases by 10 to 20 pizzas an hour. The price change is smaller and the quantity change is larger in case (b) than in case (a). The quantity supplied is more responsive to a change in price in case (b) than in case (a).

hour, so the increase is 3 pizzas, the average quantity is 11.5 pizzas an hour, and the quantity increases by 26 percent. The elasticity of supply is equal to 26 percent divided by 40 percent, which equals 0.65.

In Fig. 4.9(b), when the price rises from $20 to $21, the price rise is $1 and the average price is $20.50, so the price rises by 4.9 percent of the average price. The quantity increases from 10 to 20 pizzas an hour, so the increase is 10 pizzas, the average quantity is 15 pizzas, and the quantity increases by 67 percent. The elasticity of supply is equal to 67 percent divided by 4.9 percent, which equals 13.67.

Figure 4.10 shows the range of elasticities of supply. If the quantity supplied is fixed regardless of the price, the supply curve is vertical and the elasticity of supply is zero. Supply is perfectly inelastic. This case is shown in Fig. 4.10(a). A special intermediate case is when the percentage change in price equals the percentage change in quantity. Supply is unit elastic. This case is shown in Fig. 4.10(b). No matter how steep the supply curve is, if it is linear and passes through the origin, supply is unit elastic. If there is a price at which sellers are willing to offer any quantity for sale, the supply curve is horizontal and the elasticity of supply is infinite. Supply is perfectly elastic. This case is shown in Fig. 4.10(c).

The Factors That Influence the Elasticity of Supply

The magnitude of the elasticity of supply depends on

- Resource substitution possibilities
- Time frame for the supply decision

Resource Substitution Possibilities Some goods and services can be produced only by using unique or rare productive resources. These items have a low, even perhaps a zero, elasticity of supply. Other goods and services can be produced by using commonly available resources that could be allocated to a wide variety of alternative tasks. Such items have a high elasticity of supply.

A Van Gogh painting is an example of a good with a vertical supply curve and a zero elasticity of supply. At the other extreme, wheat can be grown on land that is almost equally good for growing corn. So it is just as easy to grow wheat as corn, and the opportunity cost of wheat in terms of forgone corn is almost constant. As a result, the supply curve of wheat is almost horizontal and its elasticity of supply is very large. Similarly, when a good is produced in many different countries (for example, sugar and beef), the supply of the good is highly elastic.

FIGURE 4.10
Inelastic and Elastic Supply

(a) Perfectly inelastic supply

(b) Unit elastic supply

(c) Perfectly elastic supply

Each supply illustrated here has a constant elasticity. The supply curve in part (a) illustrates the supply of a good that has a zero elasticity of supply. The supply curve in part (b) illustrates the supply for a good with a unit elasticity of supply. All linear supply curves that pass through the origin illustrate supplies that are unit elastic. The supply curve in part (c) illustrates the supply for a good with an infinite elasticity of supply.

The supply of most goods and services lies between these two extremes. The quantity produced can be increased but only by incurring a higher cost. If a higher price is offered, the quantity supplied increases. Such goods and services have an elasticity of supply between zero and infinity.

Time Frame for Supply Decisions To study the influence of the length of time elapsed since a price change, we distinguish three time frames of supply:

1. Momentary supply
2. Long-run supply
3. Short-run supply

When the price of a good rises or falls, the *momentary supply curve* shows the response of the quantity supplied immediately following a price change.

Some goods, such as fruits and vegetables, have a perfectly inelastic momentary supply—a vertical supply curve. The quantities supplied depend on crop-planting decisions made earlier. In the case of oranges, for example, planting decisions have to be made many years in advance of the crop being available. The momentary supply curve is vertical because, on a given day, no matter what the price of oranges, producers cannot change their output. They have picked, packed, and shipped their crop to market, and the quantity available for that day is fixed.

In contrast, some goods have a perfectly elastic momentary supply. Long-distance phone calls are an example. When many people simultaneously make a call, there is a big surge in the demand for telephone cables, computer switching, and satellite time, and the quantity bought increases. But the price remains constant. Long-distance carriers monitor fluctuations in demand and reroute calls to ensure that the quantity supplied equals the quantity demanded without changing the price.

The *long-run supply curve* shows the response of the quantity supplied to a change in price after all the technologically possible ways of adjusting supply have been exploited. In the case of oranges, the long run is the time it takes new plantings to grow to full maturity—about 15 years. In some cases, the long-run adjustment occurs only after a completely new production plant has been built and workers have been trained to operate it—typically a process that might take several years.

The *short-run supply curve* shows how the quantity supplied responds to a price change when only *some* of the technologically possible adjustments to production have been made. The short-run response to a price change is a sequence of adjustments. The first adjustment that is usually made is in the amount of labour employed. To increase output in the short run, firms work their labour force overtime and perhaps hire additional workers. To decrease their output in the short run, firms either lay off workers or reduce their hours of work. With the passage of time, firms can make additional adjustments, perhaps training additional workers or buying additional tools and other equipment.

The short-run supply curve slopes upward because producers can take actions quite quickly to change the quantity supplied in response to a price change. For example, if the price of oranges falls, growers can stop picking and leave oranges to rot on the trees. Or if the price rises, they can use more fertilizer and improved irrigation to increase the yields of their existing trees. In the long run, they can plant more trees and increase the quantity supplied even more in response to a given price rise.

REVIEW QUIZ

1 Why do we need to measure the responsiveness of the quantity supplied of a good or service to a change in its price?
2 Can you define and calculate the elasticity of supply?
3 What are the main influences on the elasticity of supply that make the supply of some goods elastic and the supply of other goods inelastic?
4 Can you provide examples of goods or services whose elasticities of supply are (a) zero, (b) greater than zero but less than infinity, and (c) infinity?
5 How does the time frame over which a supply decision is made influence the elasticity of supply?

myeconlab   Study Plan 4.3

◆ You have now learned about the elasticities of demand and supply. Table 4.3 summarizes all the elasticities that you've met in this chapter. In the next chapter, we study the efficiency of competitive markets. But before doing that, *Reading Between the Lines* on pp. 98–99 puts the elasticity of demand to work and looks at the dilemma facing the recorded music industry that we described at the beginning of this chapter.

TABLE 4.3   A Compact Glossary of Elasticities

Price Elasticities of Demand

A relationship is described as	When its magnitude is	Which means that
Perfectly elastic or infinitely elastic	Infinity	The smallest possible increase in price causes an infinitely large decrease in the quantity demanded*
Elastic	Less than infinity but greater than 1	The percentage decrease in the quantity demanded exceeds the percentage increase in price
Unit elastic	1	The percentage decrease in the quantity demanded equals the percentage increase in price
Inelastic	Greater than zero but less than 1	The percentage decrease in the quantity demanded is less than the percentage increase in price
Perfectly inelastic or completely inelastic	Zero	The quantity demanded is the same at all prices

Cross Elasticities of Demand

A relationship is described as	When its value is	Which means that
Perfect substitutes	Infinity	The smallest possible increase in the price of one good causes an infinitely large increase in the quantity demanded of the other good
Substitutes	Positive, less than infinity	If the price of one good increases, the quantity demanded of the other good also increases
Independent	Zero	If the price of one good increases, the quantity demanded of the other good remains the same
Complements	Less than zero	If the price of one good increases, the quantity demanded of the other good decreases

Income Elasticities of Demand

A relationship is described as	When its value is	Which means that
Income elastic (normal good)	Greater than 1	The percentage increase in the quantity demanded is greater than the percentage increase in income
Income inelastic (normal good)	Less than 1 but greater than zero	The percentage increase in the quantity demanded is less than the percentage increase in income
Negative income elastic (inferior good)	Less than zero	When income increases, quantity demanded decreases

Elasticities of Supply

A relationship is described as	When its magnitude is	Which means that
Perfectly elastic	Infinity	The smallest possible increase in price causes an infinitely large increase in the quantity supplied
Elastic	Less than infinity but greater than 1	The percentage increase in the quantity supplied exceeds the percentage increase in the price
Inelastic	Greater than zero but less than 1	The percentage increase in the quantity supplied is less than the percentage increase in the price
Perfectly inelastic	Zero	The quantity supplied is the same at all prices

*In each description, the directions of change may be reversed. For example, in this case, the smallest possible *decrease* in price causes an infinitely large *increase* in the quantity demanded.

Elasticity of Demand for CDs

G L O B E   A N D   M A I L ,   S E P T E M B E R   4 ,   2 0 0 3

Music giant chops prices to combat downloads

North American record giant Universal Music is slashing prices on its compact discs in a desperate bid to get music fans back into stores and away from downloading music for free on their home computers.

Universal said yesterday it will chop prices starting in October, so that CDs that currently carry a suggested retail price in Canada of $19.98, $20.98 and $21.98 will sell for no more than $14.98.

Will consumers take the bait?

"Don't be too sure," said Josh Bernoff, an analyst at Forrester Research Inc. in Boston. "I think you'll see unit sales go up as prices go down, but this will not change the slide away from CDs towards downloading."

Jason Goorwah, a 17-year-old student in Toronto, agrees. "I've stopped buying a lot of CDs," he said, adding that he prefers to download music onto his MP3 player.

Mr. Goorwah said cheaper prices might persuade him to buy a few extra CDs, but a $5 saving isn't enough to lure him into record stores more often. ...

The new pricing policy will affect Universal's new releases, its top hits and the company's back catalogue. ...

Music sales have dropped 20 per cent in Canada in the past three years, a loss of about $250-million to the industry. ...

Universal Music Canada president Randy Lennox acknowledged that record companies must change their approach. "The industry needs to rethink its business model, and we at Universal are trying to lead that particular charge," he said.

He predicted that the price cut could boost CD sales by as much as 30 per cent.

Mr. Lennox wouldn't say how much the change will cost his company, but the hope is that increased volume will outweigh the decreased margins. ...

Reprinted with permission from *The Globe and Mail*.

Essence of the Story

■ The sale of music CDs has fallen 20 percent in Canada in the past three years and decreased industry total revenue by $250 million.

■ In a bid to combat lower revenue, Universal is slashing CD prices from around $21 to under $15.

■ An analyst says that more CDs will be sold at the lower price, but the move towards music downloading will not stop.

■ Universal Music Canada president Randy Lennox says that the price cut could increase the quantity of CDs sold by as much as 30 percent.

Economic Analysis

■ This news article is about the market for recorded music in Canada, but the problem that it describes applies everywhere.

■ The news article provides enough information for us to find the point on the demand curve for CDs before the price cut.

■ At an average price of $21 per CD, about 48 million CDs a year were demanded.

■ The price is in the news article. To find the quantity, first use the reported fact that $250 million of total revenue represents 20 percent of total revenue three years ago.

■ Total revenue three years ago must have been $250 million ÷ 0.2 = $1.25 billion, so total revenue in 2003 was $1 billion.

■ With total revenue of $1 billion and a price of $21 a CD, the number of CDs sold is a little less than 48 million. This is the quantity demanded at $21 a CD.

■ The news article also provides enough information for us to find what Universal Music thinks is a second point on the demand curve.

■ Randy Lennox says that the quantity of CDs sold will increase by 30 percent if the price is cut to $15 a CD.

■ If the quantity of CDs demanded increases by 30 percent, it becomes 62 million.

■ Figure 1 shows the demand curve for CDs based on the information that we've pulled from the news article.

■ We can calculate the elasticity of demand at the midpoint of the two points identified.

■ The quantity demanded increases by 14 million CDs and the average quantity is 55 million CDs, so the quantity demanded increases by 25.4 percent.

■ The price falls by $6 and the average price is $18 a CD, so the percentage fall in price is 33.3 percent.

■ The price elasticity of demand—percentage change in quantity demanded divided by percentage change in the price—is 25.4 ÷ 33.3 = 0.76.

■ So, according to the information provided in the news article, Universal Music believes that the demand for CDs is inelastic.

■ When a good has an inelastic demand, a price cut *decreases* total revenue.

■ With the price cut, Universal will sell more CDs but will suffer a loss of total revenue.

■ The total revenue test confirms this conclusion. At $21 a CD, total revenue is $21 × 48 million = $1 billion. At $15 a CD, total revenue is $15 × 62 million = $930 million.

■ Because downloads and CDs are substitutes, a rise in the price of a download increases the demand for CDs.

■ So if CD producers can find a way of increasing the price of a download, they can increase the demand for CDs.

■ The amount by which the demand for CDs would increase is determined by the cross elasticity of demand between CDs and downloads.

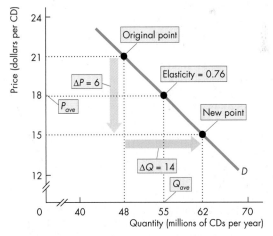

Figure 1 The market for music CDs in Canada

SUMMARY

KEY POINTS

Price Elasticity of Demand (pp. 84–90)

- Elasticity is a measure of the responsiveness of the quantity demanded of a good to a change in its price.
- Price elasticity of demand equals the percentage change in the quantity demanded divided by the percentage change in price.
- The larger the magnitude of the price elasticity of demand, the greater is the responsiveness of the quantity demanded to a given change in price.
- Price elasticity of demand depends on how easily one good serves as a substitute for another, the proportion of income spent on the good, and the length of time elapsed since the price change.
- If demand is elastic, a decrease in price leads to an increase in total revenue. If demand is unit elastic, a decrease in price leaves total revenue unchanged. And if demand is inelastic, a decrease in price leads to a decrease in total revenue.

More Elasticities of Demand (pp. 91–93)

- Cross elasticity of demand measures the responsiveness of demand for one good to a change in the price of a substitute or a complement.
- The cross elasticity of demand with respect to the price of a substitute is positive. The cross elasticity of demand with respect to the price of a complement is negative.
- Income elasticity of demand measures the responsiveness of demand to a change in income. For a normal good, the income elasticity of demand is positive. For an inferior good, the income elasticity of demand is negative.
- When the income elasticity of demand is greater than 1, the percentage of income spent on the good increases as income increases.
- When the income elasticity of demand is less than 1 but greater than zero, the percentage of income spent on the good decreases as income increases.

Elasticity of Supply (pp. 94–96)

- Elasticity of supply measures the responsiveness of the quantity supplied of a good to a change in its price.
- The elasticity of supply is usually positive and ranges between zero (vertical supply curve) and infinity (horizontal supply curve).
- Supply decisions have three time frames: momentary, long run, and short run.
- Momentary supply refers to the response of sellers to a price change at the instant that the price changes.
- Long-run supply refers to the response of sellers to a price change when all the technologically feasible adjustments in production have been made.
- Short-run supply refers to the response of sellers to a price change after some of the technologically feasible adjustments in production have been made.

KEY FIGURES AND TABLE

KEY TERMS

PROBLEMS

Go to **myeconlab** for solutions to odd-numbered problems and additional exercises.

1. Rain spoils the strawberry crop. As a result, the price rises from $4 to $6 a box and the quantity demanded decreases from 1,000 to 600 boxes a week. Over this price range,
   a. What is the price elasticity of demand?
   b. Describe the demand for strawberries.

2. Good weather brings a bumper tomato crop. The price falls from $7 to $5 a basket, and the quantity demanded increases from 300 to 500 baskets a day. Over this price range,
   a. What is the price elasticity of demand?
   b. Describe the demand for tomatoes.

3. The figure shows the demand for videotape rentals.

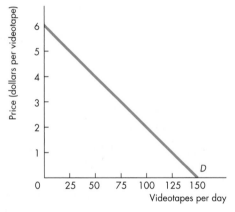

   a. Calculate the elasticity of demand for a rise in rental price from $3 to $5.
   b. At what price is the elasticity of demand equal to 1?

4. The figure shows the demand for pens.

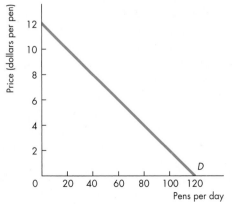

   a. Calculate the elasticity of demand for a rise in price from $6 to $10.
   b. At what prices is the elasticity of demand equal to 1, greater than 1, and less than 1?

5. If the quantity of dental services demanded increases by 10 percent when the price of dental services falls by 10 percent, is the demand for dental service inelastic, elastic, or unit elastic?

6. If the quantity of haircuts demanded decreases by 10 percent when the price of a haircut rises by 5 percent, is the demand for haircuts elastic, inelastic, or unit elastic? Explain your answer.

7. The demand schedule for computer chips is.

Price (dollars per chip)	Quantity demanded (millions of chips per year)
200	50
250	45
300	40
350	35
400	30

   a. What happens to total revenue if the price falls from $400 to $350 a chip?
   b. What happens to total revenue if the price falls from $350 to $300 a chip?
   c. At what price is total revenue at a maximum?
   d. At an average price of $350, is the demand for chips elastic or inelastic? Use the total revenue test to answer this question.

8. The demand schedule for sugar is

Price (dollars per kilogram)	Quantity demanded (millions of kilograms per year)
5	25
10	20
15	15
20	10
25	5

   a. What happens to total revenue if the price of sugar rises from $5 to $15 a kilogram?
   b. What happens to total revenue if the price rises from $15 to $25 a kilogram?
   c. At what price is total revenue at a maximum?
   d. At an average price of $20 a kilogram, is the demand for sugar elastic or inelastic? Use the total revenue test to answer this question.

9. In problem 7, at $250 a chip, is the demand for chips elastic or inelastic? Use the total revenue test to answer this question.

10. In problem 8, at $10 a kilogram, is the demand for sugar elastic or inelastic? Use the total revenue test to answer this question.

11. If a 2 percent rise in the price of orange juice decreases the quantity of orange juice demanded by 22 percent and increases the quantity of apple juice demanded by 14 percent, calculate the cross elasticity of demand between orange juice and apple juice.

12. If a 5 percent fall in the price of chicken decreases the quantity of beef demanded by 20 percent and increases the quantity of chicken demanded by 15 percent, calculate the cross elasticity of demand between chicken and beef.

13. Alex's income has increased from $3,000 to $5,000. Alex increased his consumption of bagels from 4 to 8 a month and decreased his consumption of doughnuts from 12 to 6 a month. Calculate Alex's income elasticity of demand for (a) bagels and (b) doughnuts.

14. Judy's income has increased from $13,000 to $17,000. Judy increased her demand for concert tickets by 15 percent and decreased her demand for bus rides by 10 percent. Calculate Judy's income elasticity of demand for (a) concert tickets and (b) bus rides.

15. The table gives the supply schedule for long-distance phone calls.

Price (cents per minute)	Quantity supplied (millions of minutes per day)
10	200
20	400
30	600
40	800

Calculate the elasticity of supply when
a. The price falls from 40¢ to 30¢.
b. The average price is 20¢ a minute.

16. The table gives the supply schedule for jeans.

Price (dollars per pair)	Quantity supplied (millions of pairs per year)
120	2,400
125	2,800
130	3,200
135	3,600

Calculate the elasticity of supply when
a. The price rises from $125 to $135 a pair.
b. The average price is $125 a pair.

CRITICAL THINKING

1. After you have studied *Reading Between the Lines* (pp. 98–99) on the elasticity of demand for CDs and then answer the following questions:
   a. Do you think that the demand for CDs is inelastic as implied by the numbers in the news article? Explain why or why not.
   b. If the demand for CDs is inelastic, how might the recording industry increase its total revenue?
   c. What elasticity information would you need to predict the change in the demand for CDs and music downloads over the next five years?

2. The demand for illegal drugs is estimated to be inelastic. Much of the expenditure on illegal drugs comes from crime. Assuming these statements to be correct:
   a. How will a successful campaign that decreases the supply of drugs influence the price of drugs and the amount spent on them?
   b. What will happen to the amount of crime?

WEB EXERCISES

Use the links on **myeconlab** to work the following exercise.

1. a. Find the price of gasoline in the summer of 2005.
   b. Use the concepts of demand, supply, and elasticity to explain recent changes in the price of gasoline.
   c. Find the price of crude oil.
   d. Use the concepts of demand, supply, and elasticity to explain recent changes in the price of crude oil.

2. a. Find the number of litres in a barrel and the cost of crude oil in a litre of gasoline.
   b. What are the other costs that make up the total cost of a litre of gasoline?
   c. If the price of crude oil falls by 10 percent, by what percentage would you expect the price of gasoline to change, other things remaining the same?
   d. Which demand do you think is more elastic: that for crude oil or gasoline? Why?

Efficiency and Equity

CHAPTER 5

Self-Interest and the Social Interest

Every time you buy a pair of sports shoes or a textbook, fill your gas tank, download some MP3 files and burn a CD, order a pizza, check in at the airport, or even just take a shower, you express *your* view about how scarce resources should be used. You try to spend your income and your time in ways that get the most out of *your* scarce resources—you make choices that further your *self-interest*. And markets coordinate your decisions along with those of everyone else. But do markets do a good job? Do they enable us to allocate resources *efficiently* when we buy shoes, books, gasoline, music, CD-Rs, pizza, airline services, water, and other things? Could we as a *society* be better off if we spent more on some things and less on others?

The market economy generates huge incomes for some people and miserable pickings for others. For example, software sales by Microsoft have generated enough profit over the past ten years to rocket Bill Gates, one of its founders, into the position of being one of the richest people in the world. Is it *fair* that Bill Gates is so incredibly rich while others live in miserable poverty?

The social interest has the two dimensions we've just discussed—efficiency and fairness (or equity). So our central question in this chapter is: Does the market achieve an efficient and fair use of resources?

◆ At the end of the chapter, in *Reading Between the Lines,* we return to the issue that we first raised in Chapter 1 about the use of the world's water resources. Do we use markets and other arrangements that allocate the world's scarce water in the social interest?

After studying this chapter, you will be able to

- Describe the alternative methods of allocating scarce resources
- Distinguish between value and price and define consumer surplus
- Distinguish between cost and price and define producer surplus
- Explain the conditions under which markets are efficient and describe the sources of inefficiency in our economy
- Explain the main ideas about fairness and evaluate claims that markets result in unfair outcomes

Resource Allocation Methods

THE GOAL OF THIS CHAPTER IS TO EVALUATE THE ability of markets to allocate resources *efficiently* and *fairly*. But to see whether the market does a good job, we must compare it with its alternatives. Resources are scarce, so they must be allocated *somehow*. And trading in markets is just one of several alternative methods.

Resources might be allocated by

- Market price
- Command
- Majority rule
- Contest
- First-come, first-served
- Lottery
- Personal characteristics
- Force

Let's briefly examine each method.

Market Price

When a market price allocates a scarce resource, the people who are willing and able to pay that price get the resource. Two kinds of people decide not to pay the market price: those who can afford to pay but choose not to buy and those who are too poor and simply can't afford to buy.

For many goods and services, distinguishing between those who choose not to buy and those who can't afford to buy doesn't matter. But for a few items, it does matter. For example, poor people can't afford to pay school fees and doctor's fees. Because poor people can't afford items that most people consider to be essential, these items are usually allocated by one of the other methods.

Command

A **command system** allocates resources by the order (command) of someone in authority. In the Canadian economy, the command system is used extensively inside firms and government departments. For example, if you have a job, most likely someone tells you what to do. Your labour is allocated to specific tasks by a command.

A command system works well in organizations in which the lines of authority and responsibility are clear and it is easy to monitor the activities being performed. But a command system works badly when the range of activities to be monitored is large and when it is easy for people to fool those in authority. The system works so badly in North Korea, where it is used extensively in place of markets, that it fails even to deliver an adequate supply of food.

Majority Rule

Majority rule allocates resources in the way that a majority of voters choose. Societies use majority rule to elect representative governments that make some of the biggest decisions. For example, majority rule decides the tax rates that end up allocating scarce resources between private use and public use. And majority rule decides how tax dollars are allocated among competing uses such as education and health care.

Majority rule works well when the decisions being made affect large numbers of people and self-interest must be suppressed to use resources most effectively.

Contest

A contest allocates resources to a winner (or a group of winners). Sporting events use this method. Mike Wier, Tiger Woods, and other golfers compete and the winner gets the biggest payoff.

But contests are more general than those in a sports arena, though we don't normally call them contests. For example, Bill Gates won a contest to provide the world's personal computer operating system.

Contests do a good job when the efforts of the "players" are hard to monitor and reward directly. By dangling the opportunity to win a big prize, people are motivated to work hard and try to become the "winner." Only a few people end up with a big prize, but many people work harder in the process of trying to win. So total production is much greater than it would be without the contest.

First-Come, First-Served

A first-come, first-served method allocates resources to those who are first in line. Many casual restaurants won't accept reservations. They use first-come, first-served to allocate their scarce tables. Highway space is allocated in this way too—the first to arrive at the on-ramp gets the road space. If too many vehicles enter the highway, the speed slows and people wait in line for some space to become available.

First-come, first-served works best when, as in the above examples, a scarce resource can serve just one user at a time in a sequence. By serving the user who arrives first, this method minimizes the time spent waiting for the resource to become free.

Lottery

Lotteries allocate resources to those who pick the winning number, draw the lucky cards, or come up lucky on some other gaming system. Provincial lotteries and casinos reallocate millions of dollars worth of goods and services every year.

But lotteries are more widespread than jackpots and roulette wheels in casinos. They are used to allocate landing slots to airlines at some airports and have been used to allocate fishing rights and the electromagnetic spectrum used by cell phones.

Lotteries work best when there is no effective way to distinguish among potential users of a scarce resource.

Personal Characteristics

When resources are allocated on the basis of personal characteristics, people with the "right" characteristics get the resources. Some of the resources that matter most to you are allocated in this way. For example, you will choose a marriage partner on the basis of personal characteristics. But this method also gets used in unacceptable ways. Allocating the best jobs to white, Anglo-Saxon males and discriminating against visible minorities and women is an example.

Force

Force plays a crucial role, for both good and ill, in allocating scarce resources. Let's start with the ill.

War, the use of military force by one nation against another, has played an enormous role historically in allocating resources. The economic supremacy of European settlers in the Americas and Australia owes much to the use of this method.

Theft, the taking of the property of others without their consent, also plays a large role. Both large-scale

organized crime and small-scale petty crime collectively allocate billions of dollars worth of resources annually.

But force plays a crucial positive role in allocating resources. It provides the state with an effective method of transferring wealth from the rich to the poor, and it provides the legal framework in which voluntary exchange in markets takes place.

A legal system is the foundation on which our market economy functions. Without courts to enforce contracts, it would not be possible to do business. But the courts could not enforce contracts without the ability to apply force if neccesary. The state provides the ultimate force that enables the courts to do their work.

More broadly, the force of the state is essential to uphold the principle of the rule of law. This principle is the bedrock of civilized economic (and social and political) life. With the rule of law upheld, people can go about their daily economic lives with the assurance that their property will be protected—that they can sue for violations of their property (and be sued if they violate the property of others).

Free from the burden of protecting their property and confident in the knowledge that those with whom they trade will honor their agreements, people can get on with focusing on the activity at which they have a comparative advantage and trading for mutual gain.

REVIEW QUIZ

1 Describe the alternative methods of allocating scarce resources.
2 Provide an example of each allocation method that illustrates when it works well.
3 Provide an example of each allocation method that illustrates when it works badly.

 Study Plan 5.1

In the next sections, we're going to see how a market can achieve an efficient use of resources, examine the obstacles to efficiency, and see how sometimes, an alternative method might improve on the market.

After looking at efficiency, we'll turn our attention to the more difficult issue of fairness.

Demand and Marginal Benefit

RESOURCES ARE ALLOCATED EFFICIENTLY WHEN they are used in the ways that people value most highly. This outcome occurs when marginal benefit equals marginal cost (pp. 37–39). So to determine whether a competitive market is efficient, we need to see whether, at the market equilibrium quantity, marginal benefit equals marginal cost. We begin by seeing how market demand reflects marginal benefit.

Demand, Willingness to Pay, and Value

In everyday life, we talk about "getting value for money." When we use this expression, we are distinguishing between *value* and *price*. Value is what we get, and the price is what we pay.

The value of one more unit of a good or service is its marginal benefit. And we measure marginal benefit by the maximum price that is willingly paid for another unit of the good or service. But willingness to pay determines demand. A *demand curve is a marginal benefit curve*.

In Fig. 5.1(a), Lisa is willing to pay $1 for the 30th slice and $1 is her marginal benefit from that slice. In Fig. 5.1(b), Nick is willing to pay $1 for the 10th slice and $1 is his marginal benefit from that slice. But for which slice is the economy willing to pay $1? The answer is provided by the *market demand curve*.

Individual Demand and Market Demand

The relationship between the price of a good and the quantity demanded by one person is called *individual demand*. And the relationship between the price of a good and the quantity demanded by all buyers is called *market demand*.

The market demand curve is the horizontal sum of the individual demand curves and is formed by adding the quantities demanded by all the individuals at each price.

Figure 5.1(c) illustrates the market demand if Lisa and Nick are the only people. Lisa's demand curve (part a) and Nick's demand curve (part b) sum horizontally to the market demand curve in part (c).

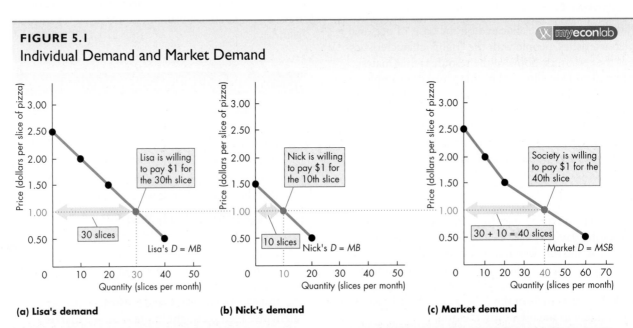

FIGURE 5.1
Individual Demand and Market Demand

(a) Lisa's demand   **(b) Nick's demand**   **(c) Market demand**

At a price of $1 a slice, the quantity demanded by Lisa is 30 slices and the quantity demanded by Nick is 10 slices, so the quantity demanded by the market is 40 slices. Lisa's demand curve in part (a) and Nick's demand curve in part (b) sum horizontally to the market demand curve in part (c). The market demand curve is the *marginal social benefit (MSB)* curve.

At a price of $1, Lisa demands 30 slices, Nick demands 10 slices, and the quantity demanded by the market is 40 slices.

So from the market demand curve, we see that the economy (or society) is willing to pay $1 for the 40th slice a month. The market demand curve is the economy's *marginal social benefit* (*MSB*) curve.

Although we're measuring price in dollars, think of it as telling us the number of *dollars' worth of other goods and services willingly forgone* to obtain one more slice of pizza (see Chapter 3, p. 60).

Consumer Surplus

We don't always have to pay what we are willing to pay—we get a bargain. When people buy something for less than it is worth to them, they receive a consumer surplus. A **consumer surplus** is the value (or marginal benefit) of a good minus the price paid for it, summed over the quantity bought.

Figure 5.2(a) shows Lisa's consumer surplus from pizza when the price is $1 a slice. At this price, she buys 30 slices a week because the 30th slice is worth $1 to her. But Lisa is willing to pay $2 for the 10th slice, so her marginal benefit from this slice is $1 more

than she pays for it—she receives a *consumer surplus* of $1 on the 10th slice.

Lisa's consumer surplus is the sum of the surpluses on *all of the slices* she buys. This sum is the area of the green triangle—the area below the demand curve and above the market price line. In Fig. 5.2(a), this area is equal to its base (30 slices) multiplied by its height ($1.50) divided by 2, which is $22.50. The area of the blue rectangle shows what Lisa pays for 30 slices of pizza.

Figure 5.2(b) shows Nick's consumer surplus and part (c) shows the consumer surplus for the economy. You can see that the consumer surplus for the economy is the sum of the consumer surpluses of Lisa and Nick.

All goods and services, like pizza, have decreasing marginal benefit. So people receive more benefit from their consumption than the amount they pay.

REVIEW QUIZ

1 How do we measure the value or marginal benefit of a good or service?
2 What is consumer surplus? How do we measure it?

myeconlab **Study Plan 5.2**

FIGURE 5.2
Demand and Consumer Surplus

myeconlab

(a) Lisa's consumer surplus   **(b) Nick's consumer surplus**   **(c) Market consumer surplus**

Lisa is willing to pay $2.00 for her 10th slice of pizza (part a). At a market price of $1 a slice, Lisa gets a consumer surplus of $1 on the 10th slice. The green triangle shows her consumer surplus on the 30 slices she buys at $1 a slice. The green triangle in part (b) shows Nick's consumer surplus on the 10 slices that he buys at $1 a slice. The green area in part (c) shows the consumer surplus for the economy. The blue rectangles show the amounts spent on pizza.

Supply and Marginal Cost

WE ARE NOW GOING TO SEE HOW MARKET SUPPLY reflects marginal cost. This section closely parallels the related ideas about market demand and marginal benefit that you've just studied. Firms are in business to make a profit. To do so, they must sell their output for a price that exceeds the cost of production. Let's investigate the relationship between cost and price.

Supply, Cost, and Minimum Supply-Price

Earning a profit means receiving more for the sale of a good or service than the cost of producing it. Just as consumers distinguish between *value* and *price*, so producers distinguish between *cost* and *price*. Cost is what a producer gives up, and the price is what a producer receives.

The cost of one more unit of a good or service is its marginal cost. And marginal cost is the minimum price that producers must receive to induce them to offer to sell another unit of the good or service. But the minimum supply-price determines supply. *A supply curve is a marginal cost curve.*

In Fig. 5.3(a), Max is willing to produce the 100th pizza for $15, his marginal cost of that pizza. In Fig. 5.3(b), Mario is willing to produce the 50th pizza for $15, his marginal cost of that pizza. But which pizza is the economy willing to produce for $15? The answer is provided by the *market supply curve*.

Individual Supply and Market Supply

The relationship between the price of a good and the quantity supplied by one producer is called *individual supply*. And the relationship between the price of a good and the quantity supplied by all producers is called *market supply*.

The market supply curve is the horizontal sum of the individual supply curves and is formed by adding the quantities supplied by all the producers at each price.

Figure 5.1(c) illustrates the market supply if Max and Mario are the only producers. Max's supply curve (part a) and Mario's supply curve (part b) sum horizontally to the market supply curve in part (c).

FIGURE 5.3
Individual Supply and Market Supply

(a) Max's supply   **(b) Mario's supply**   **(b) Market supply**

At a price of $15 a pizza, the quantity supplied by Max is 100 pizzas and the quantity supplied by Mario is 50 pizzas, so the quantity supplied by the market is 150 pizzas. Max's supply curve in part (a) and Mario's supply curve in part (b) sum horizontally to the market supply curve in part (c). The market supply curve is the marginal social cost (*MSC*) curve.

At a price of $15 a pizza, Max supplies 100 pizzas, Mario supplies 50 pizzas and the quantity supplied by the market is 150 pizzas.

So from the market supply curve, we see that the economy (or society) is willing to produce the 150th pizza a month for $15. The market supply curve is the economy's *marginal social cost* (*MSC*) curve.

Again, although we're measuring price in dollars, think of it as telling us the number of *dollars' worth of other goods and services that must be forgone* to obtain one more pizza.

Producer Surplus

When price exceeds marginal cost, the firm receives a producer surplus. A **producer surplus** is the price received for it minus minimum-supply price (or marginal cost) of a good, summed over the quantity sold.

Figure 5.4(a) shows Max's producer surplus from pizza when the price is $15 a pizza. At this price, he sells 100 pizzas a week because the 100th pizza costs him $15 to produce. But Max is willing to produce the 50th pizza for his marginal cost, which is $10. So he receives a *producer surplus* of $5 on this pizza.

Max's producer surplus is the sum of the surpluses on all the pizza he sells. This sum is the area of the blue triangle—the area below the market price and above the supply curve. In Fig. 5.4(a), this area is equal to its base (100) multiplied by its height ($10) divided by 2, which is $500. The red area below the supply curve shows what it costs Max to produce 100 pizzas.

Figure 5.4(b) shows Mario's producer surplus and part (c) shows the producer surplus for the economy. You can see that the producer surplus for the economy is the sum of the producer surpluses of Max and Mario.

Consumer surplus and producer surplus can be used to measure the efficiency of a market. Let's see how we can use these concepts to study the efficiency of a competitive market.

REVIEW QUIZ

1 What is the relationship between marginal cost, minimum supply-price, and supply?
2 What is producer surplus? How do we measure it?

myeconlab   Study Plan 5.3

FIGURE 5.4

Supply and Producer Surplus

(a) Max's producer surplus

(b) Mario's producer surplus

(c) Economy producer surplus

Max is willing to produce the 50th pizza for $10 (part a). At a market price of $15 a pizza, Max gets a producer surplus of $5 on the 50th pizza. The blue triangle shows his producer surplus on the 100 pizzas he sells at $15 each. The blue triangle in part (b) shows Mario's producer surplus on the 50 pizzas that he sells at $15 each. The blue area in part (c) shows producer surplus for the economy. The red areas show the cost of producing the pizzas sold.

Is the Competitive Market Efficient?

FIGURE 5.5(a) SHOWS THE MARKET FOR PIZZA. The market forces that you studied in Chapter 3 (pp. 70–71) pull the pizza market to its equilibrium price of $15 a pizza and equilibrium quantity of 10,000 pizzas a day. Buyers enjoy a consumer surplus (green area) and sellers enjoy a producer surplus (blue area). Is this competitive equilibrium efficient?

Efficiency of Competitive Equilibrium

You've seen that the market demand curve for pizza tells us the marginal social benefit from pizza. So in Fig. 5.5(b), we label the demand curve as the marginal social benefit curve, *MSB*.

You've also seen that the market supply curve of pizza tells us the marginal social cost of pizza. So in Fig 5.5(b), we label the supply curve as the marginal social cost curve, *MSC*. You can see that where the demand curve and the supply curve intersect in part (a), the marginal social benefit curve and the marginal social cost curve intersect in part (b). So at the equilibrium price and quantity, marginal social benefit equals marginal social cost. But when marginal social benefit equals marginal social cost, resources are allocated efficiently. So the competitive equilibrium is efficient and resources are allocated to their highest-value uses.

If production is less than 10,000 pizzas a day, the marginal social benefit from pizza exceeds its marginal social cost. If production exceeds 10,000 pizzas a day, the marginal social cost of pizza exceeds its marginal social benefit. Only when 10,000 pizzas a day are produced is the marginal social benefit of pizza equal to its marginal social cost.

The competitive market pushes the quantity of pizza produced to its efficient level of 10,000 a day. If production is less than 10,000 pizzas a day, a shortage raises the price, which increases production. If production exceeds 10,000 pizzas a day, a surplus lowers the price, which decreases production. So, a competitive pizza market is efficient.

Notice that when the efficient quantity is produced, *total surplus* (the sum of consumer surplus and producer surplus) is maximized. Buyers and sellers acting in their self-interest end up promoting the social interest.

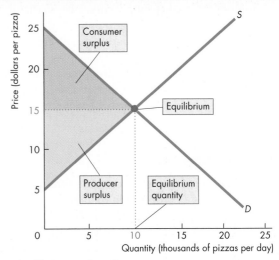

FIGURE 5.5
An Efficient Market for Pizza

(a) Equilibrium and surpluses

(b) Efficiency

Competitive equilibrium in part (a) occurs when the quantity demanded equals the quantity supplied. Consumer surplus is the area under the demand curve and above the price—the green triangle. Producer surplus is the area above the supply curve and below the price—the blue triangle.

Resources are used efficiently in part (b) when marginal social benefit, *MSB*, equals marginal social cost, *MSC*.

The efficient quantity in part (b) is the same as the equilibrium quantity in part (a). The competitive pizza market produces the efficient quantity of pizza.

The Invisible Hand

Writing in his *Wealth of Nations* in 1776, Adam Smith was the first to suggest that competitive markets send resources to the uses in which they have the highest value (see pp. 54–55). Smith believed that each participant in a competitive market is "led by an invisible hand to promote an end [the efficient use of resources] which was no part of his intention."

You can see the invisible hand at work in the cartoon. The cold drinks vendor has both cold drinks and shade. He has an opportunity cost of each and a minimum supply-price of each. The reader on the park bench has a marginal benefit from each and a willingness to pay for each. You can see from the transaction that occurs that the marginal benefit from shade exceeds the price of shade and the price of a cold drink exceeds its marginal benefit. The transaction creates a producer surplus and a consumer surplus. The vendor obtains a producer surplus from selling the shade for more than its opportunity cost, and the reader obtains a consumer surplus from buying the shade for less than its marginal benefit. In the third frame of the cartoon, both the consumer and the producer are better off than they were in the first frame. The umbrella has moved to its highest-valued use.

The Invisible Hand at Work Today

The market economy relentlessly performs the activity illustrated in the cartoon and in Fig. 5.5 to achieve an efficient allocation of resources. And rarely has the market been working as hard as it is today: Think about some changes taking place that the market is guiding towards an efficient use of resources.

New technologies have cut the cost of producing a computer. As these advances have occurred, the supply of computers has increased and the price has fallen. Lower prices have encouraged an increase in the quantity demanded of this now less costly tool. The marginal social benefit from computers is brought to equality with their marginal social cost.

A Florida frost cuts the supply of oranges. With fewer oranges available, the marginal social benefit from oranges increases. A shortage of oranges raises their price, so the market allocates the smaller quantity to the people who value them most highly.

Market forces persistently bring marginal social cost and marginal social benefit to equality and maximize total surplus (the sum of consumer surplus and producer surplus).

© The New Yorker Collection 1985,
Mike Twohy from cartoonbank.com. All Rights Reserved.

Underproduction and Overproduction

Inefficiency can occur because either too little of an item is produced—underproduction—or too much is produced—overproduction.

Underproduction In Fig. 5.6(a), the quantity of pizza produced is 5,000 a day. At this quantity, consumers are willing to pay $20 for a pizza that costs only $10 to produce. The quantity produced is inefficient—there is underproduction.

The scale of the inefficiency is measured by **deadweight loss**, which is the decrease in total surplus that results from inefficiency. The grey triangle in Fig. 5.6(a) shows the deadweight loss.

FIGURE 5.6
Underproduction and Overproduction

(a) Underproduction

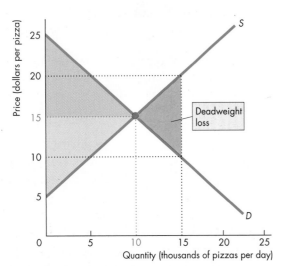

(b) Overproduction

In part (a), if pizza production is cut to 5,000 a day, the benefit of one more pizza exceeds its cost. Total surplus, the sum of the green and blue areas, is reduced and a deadweight loss (the grey triangle) arises.

In part (b), if pizza production increases to 15,000 a day, the cost of the 15,000th pizza exceeds its benefit. A deadweight loss (grey triangle) arises. Total surplus equals the sum of the green and blue areas minus the grey triangle.

Overproduction In Fig. 5.6(b), the quantity of pizza produced is 15,000 a day. At this quantity, consumers are willing to pay only $10 for a pizza that costs $20 to produce. By producing the 15,000th pizza, $10 of resources are wasted. Again, the grey triangle shows the deadweight loss. The total surplus (the sum of consumer surplus and producer surplus) is smaller than its maximum by the amount of the deadweight loss. The deadweight loss is borne by the entire society. It is not a loss for the consumers and a gain for the producer. It is a *social* loss.

Obstacles to Efficiency

The obstacles to efficiency that bring underproduction or overproduction are

- Price and quantity regulations
- Taxes and subsidies
- Externalities
- Public goods and common resources
- Monopoly
- High transactions costs

Price and Quantity Regulations *Price regulations* that put a cap on the rent that a landlord is permitted to charge and laws that require employers to pay a minimum wage sometimes block the price adjustments that balance the quantity demanded and the quantity supplied and lead to underproduction. *Quantity regulations* that limit the amount that a farm is permitted to produce also lead to underproduction.

Taxes and Subsidies *Taxes* increase the prices paid by buyers and lower the prices received by sellers. So taxes decrease the quantity produced and lead to underproduction. *Subsidies*, which are payments by the government to producers, decrease the prices paid by buyers and increase the prices received by sellers. So subsidies increase the quantity produced and lead to overproduction.

Externalities An *externality* is a cost or a benefit that affects someone other than the seller or the buyer of a good. An electric utility creates an *external cost* by burning coal that brings acid rain and crop damage. The utility doesn't consider the cost of pollution when it decides how much power to produce. The result is overproduction. An apartment owner would provide an *external benefit* if she installed a smoke detector. But she doesn't consider her neighbor's marginal benefit and decides not to install a smoke detector. There is underproduction.

Public Goods and Common Resources A *public good is* a good or service that is consumed simultaneously by everyone even if they don't pay for it. Examples are national defence and law enforcement. Competitive markets would underproduce a public good because of a *free-rider problem*—it is in each person's interest to free ride on everyone else and avoid paying for her or his share of a public good.

A common resource is owned by no one but used by everyone. Atlantic salmon is an example. It is in everyone's self-interest to ignore the costs of their own use of a common resource that fall on others (called *the tragedy of the commons*), which leads to overproduction.

Monopoly A *monopoly* is a firm that is the sole provider of a good or service. Local water supply and cable television are supplied by firms that are monopolies. The self-interest of a monopoly is to maximize its profit. And because the monopoly has no competitors, it can set the price to achieve its self-interested goal. To achieve its goal, a monopoly produces too little and charges too high a price. It leads to underproduction.

High Transactions Costs Stroll around a shopping mall and observe the retail markets in which you participate. You'll see that these markets employ enormous quantities of scarce labor and capital resources. It is costly to operate any market. Economists call the opportunity costs of making trades in a market **transactions costs**.

To use market price as the allocator of scarce resources, it must be worth bearing the opportunity cost of establishing a market. Some markets are just too costly to operate. For example, when you want to play tennis on your local "free" court, you don't pay a market price for your slot on the court. You hang around until the court becomes vacant, and you "pay" with your waiting time. When transactions costs are high, the market might underproduce.

You now know the conditions under which resource allocation is efficient. You've seen how a competitive market can be efficient, and you've seen some impediments to efficiency. But can alternative allocation methods improve on the market?

Alternatives to the Market

When a market is inefficient, can one of the alternative non-market methods that we described at the beginning of this chapter do a better job? Sometimes it can.

Often, majority rule might be used in a number of ways in an attempt to improve the allocation of resources. But majority rule has its own shortcomings. A group that pursues the self-interest of its members can become the majority. For example, a price or quantity regulation that creates a deadweight loss is almost always the result of a self-interested group becoming the majority and imposing costs on the minority. Also, with majority rule, votes must be translated into actions by bureaucrats who have their own agendas based on their self-interest.

Managers in firms issue commands and avoid the transactions costs that they would incur if they went to a market every time they needed a job done. First-come, first-served saves a lot of hassle in waiting lines. These lines could have markets in which people trade their place in the line—but someone would have to enforce the agreements. Can you imagine the hassle at a busy ATM if you had to buy your spot at the head of the line?

There is no one efficient mechanism for allocating resources efficiently. But supplemented by majority rule, bypassed inside firms by command systems, and by occasionally using first-come, first-served, markets do an amazingly good job.

REVIEW QUIZ

1 Do competitive markets use resources efficiently? Explain why or why not.
2 What is deadweight loss and under what conditions does it occur?
3 What are the obstacles to achieving an efficient allocation of resources in the market economy?

myeconlab Study Plan 5.4

Is an efficient allocation of resources also a fair allocation? Does the competitive market provide people with fair incomes for their work? Do people always pay a fair price for the things they buy? Don't we need the government to step into some competitive markets to prevent the price from rising too high or falling too low? Let's now study these questions.

Are Markets Fair?

WHEN A NATURAL DISASTER STRIKES, SUCH AS A severe winter storm, the prices of many essential items jump. The reason the prices jump is that some people have a greater demand and greater willingness to pay when the items are in limited supply. So the higher prices achieve an efficient allocation of scarce resources. News reports of these price hikes almost never talk about efficiency. Instead, they talk about equity or fairness. The claim often made is that it is unfair for profit-seeking dealers to cheat the victims of natural disaster.

Similarly, when low-skilled people work for a wage that is below what most would regard as a "living wage," the media and politicians talk of employers taking unfair advantage of their workers.

How do we decide whether something is fair or unfair? You know when *you* think something is unfair. But how do you know? What are the *principles* of fairness?

Philosophers have tried for centuries to answer this question. Economists have offered their answers too. But before we look at these answers, you should know that there is no universally agreed upon answer.

Economists agree about efficiency. That is, they agree that it makes sense to make the economic pie as large as possible and to bake it at the lowest possible cost. But they do not agree about equity. That is, they do not agree about what are fair shares of the economic pie for all the people who make it. The reason is that ideas about fairness are not exclusively economic ideas. They touch on politics, ethics, and religion. Nevertheless, economists have thought about these issues and have a contribution to make. So let's examine the views of economists on this topic.

To think about fairness, think of economic life as a game—a serious game. All ideas about fairness can be divided into two broad groups:. They are

- It's not fair if the *result* isn't fair.
- It's not fair if the *rules* aren't fair.

It's Not Fair If the *Result* Isn't Fair

The earliest efforts to establish a principle of fairness were based on the view that the result is what matters. And the general idea was that it is unfair if people's incomes are too unequal. It is unfair that a bank president earns millions of dollars a year while a bank teller

earns only thousands of dollars a year. It is unfair that a store owner enjoys a larger profit and her customers pay higher prices in the aftermath of a winter storm.

There was a lot of excitement during the nineteenth century when economists thought they had made the incredible discovery that equality, which they regarded as a fair result, was also efficient. They argued that to make the economic pie as large as possible, it must be cut into equal pieces, one for each person. This idea turns out to be wrong, but there is a lesson in the reason why it is wrong. So this nineteenth century idea is worth a closer look.

Utilitarianism The nineteenth century idea that only equality brings efficiency is called *utilitarianism*. **Utilitarianism** is a principle that states that we should strive to achieve "the greatest happiness for the greatest number." The people who developed this idea were known as utilitarians. They included the most eminent thinkers, such as Jeremy Bentham and John Stuart Mill.

Utilitarians argued that to achieve "the greatest happiness for the greatest number," income must be transferred from the rich to the poor up to the point of complete equality—to the point at which there are no rich and no poor.

They reasoned in the following way: First, everyone has the same basic wants and a similar capacity to enjoy life. Second, the greater a person's income, the smaller is the marginal benefit of a dollar. The millionth dollar spent by a rich person brings a smaller marginal benefit to that person than the marginal benefit of the thousandth dollar spent by a poorer person. So by transferring a dollar from the millionaire to the poorer person, more is gained than is lost and the two people added together are better off.

Figure 5.7 illustrates this utilitarian idea. Tom and Jerry have the same marginal benefit curve, *MB*. (Marginal benefit is measured on the same scale of 1 to 3 for both Tom and Jerry.) Tom earns $5,000 a year and his marginal benefit of a dollar of income is 3 at point *A*. Jerry earns $45,000 a year and his marginal benefit of a dollar of income is 1at point *B*. If a dollar is transferred from Jerry to Tom, Jerry loses 1 unit of marginal benefit and Tom gains 3 units. So together, Tom and Jerry are better off. They are sharing the economic pie more efficiently. If a second dollar is transferred, the same thing happens: Tom gains more than Jerry loses. And the same is true for every dollar transferred until they both reach point *C*. At point *C*,

FIGURE 5.7
Utilitarian Fairness

Tom earns $5,000 and has 3 units of marginal benefit at point A. Jerry earns $45,000 and has 1 unit of marginal benefit at point B. If income is transferred from Jerry to Tom, Jerry's loss is less than Tom's gain. Only when each of them has $25,000 and 2 units of marginal benefit (at point C) can the sum of their total benefit increase no further.

Tom and Jerry have $25,000 each and a marginal benefit of 2 units. Now they are sharing the economic pie in the most efficient way. It is bringing the greatest attainable happiness to Tom and Jerry.

The Big Tradeoff One big problem with the utilitarian ideal of complete equality is that it ignores the costs of making income transfers. Recognizing the cost of making income transfers leads to what is called the **big tradeoff**, which is a tradeoff between efficiency and fairness.

The big tradeoff is based on the following facts. Income can be transferred from people with high incomes to people with low incomes only by taxing the high incomes. Taxing people's income from employment makes them work less. It results in the quantity of labour being less than the efficient quantity. Taxing people's income from capital makes them save less. It results in the quantity of capital being less than the efficient quantity. With smaller quantities of both labour and capital, the quantity of goods and services produced is less than the efficient quantity. The economic pie shrinks.

The tradeoff is between the size of the economic pie and the degree of equality with which it is shared. The greater the amount of income redistribution through income taxes, the greater is the inefficiency—the smaller is the economic pie.

There is a second source of inefficiency. A dollar taken from a rich person does not end up as a dollar in the hands of a poorer person. Some of it is spent on administration of the tax and transfer system. The cost of tax-collecting agencies, such as Canada Revenue Agency, and welfare-administering agencies, such as Social Development Canada, must be paid with some of the taxes collected. Also, taxpayers hire accountants, auditors, and lawyers to help them ensure that they pay the correct amount of taxes. These activities use skilled labour and capital resources that could otherwise be used to produce goods and services that people value.

You can see that when all these costs are taken into account, taking a dollar from a rich person does not give a dollar to a poor person. It is even possible that with high taxes, the poor might end up being worse off. Suppose, for example, that highly taxed entrepreneurs decide to work less and close some of their businesses. Low-income workers get fired and must seek other, perhaps even lower-paid, work.

Because of the big tradeoff, those who say that fairness is equality of income propose a modified version of utilitarianism.

Make the Poorest as Well Off as Possible A Harvard philosopher, John Rawls, proposed a modified version of utilitarianism in a classic book entitled *A Theory of Justice*, published in 1971. Rawls says that, taking all the costs of income transfers into account, the fair distribution of the economic pie is the one that makes the poorest person as well off as possible. The incomes of rich people should be taxed, and after paying the costs of administering the tax and transfer system, what is left should be transferred to the poor. But the taxes must not be so high that they make the economic pie shrink to the point at which the poorest person ends up with a smaller piece. A bigger share of a smaller pie can be less than a smaller share of a bigger pie. The goal is to make the piece enjoyed by the poorest person as big as possible. Most likely, this piece will not be an equal share.

The "fair results" idea requires a change in the results after the game is over. Some economists say that these changes are themselves unfair and propose a different way of thinking about fairness.

It's Not Fair If the *Rules* Aren't Fair

The idea that it's not fair if the rules aren't fair is based on a fundamental principle that seems to be hard-wired into the human brain: the symmetry principle. The **symmetry principle** is the requirement that people in similar situations be treated similarly. It is the moral principle that lies at the centre of all the big religions and that says, in some form or other, "behave towards other people in the way you expect them to behave towards you."

In economic life, this principle translates into *equality of opportunity*. But equality of opportunity to do what? This question is answered by the late Harvard philosopher Robert Nozick, in a book entitled *Anarchy, State, and Utopia*, published in 1974.

Nozick argues that the idea of fairness as an outcome or result cannot work and that fairness must be based on the fairness of the rules. He suggests that fairness obeys two rules:

1. The state must enforce laws that establish and protect private property.
2. Private property may be transferred from one person to another only by voluntary exchange.

The first rule says that everything that is valuable must be owned by individuals and that the state must ensure that theft is prevented. The second rule says that the only legitimate way a person can acquire property is to buy it in exchange for something else that the person owns. If these rules, which are the only fair rules, are followed, then the result is fair. It doesn't matter how unequally the economic pie is shared, provided that the pie is baked by people, each one of whom voluntarily provides services in exchange for the share of the pie offered in compensation.

These rules satisfy the symmetry principle. And if these rules are not followed, the symmetry principle is broken. You can see these facts by imagining a world in which the laws are not followed.

First, suppose that some resources or goods are not owned. They are common property. Then everyone is free to participate in a grab to use them. The strongest will prevail. But when the strongest prevails, the strongest effectively *owns* the resources or goods in question and prevents others from enjoying them.

Second, suppose that we do not insist on voluntary exchange for transferring ownership of resources from one person to another. The alternative is *involuntary* transfer. In simple language, the alternative is theft.

Both of these situations violate the symmetry principle. Only the strong get to acquire what they want. The weak end up with only the resources and goods that the strong don't want.

In a majority rule political system, the strong are those in the majority or those with enough resources to influence opinion and achieve a majority.

In contrast, if the two rules of fairness are followed, everyone, strong and weak, is treated in a similar way. Everyone is free to use their resources and human skills to create things that are valued by themselves and others and to exchange the fruits of their efforts with each other. This is the only set of arrangements that obeys the symmetry principle.

Fairness and Efficiency If private property rights are enforced and if voluntary exchange takes place in a competitive market, resources will be allocated efficiently if there are no

1. Price and quantity regulations
2. Taxes and subsidies
3. Externalities
4. Public goods and common resources
5. Monopolies
6. High transactions costs

And according to the Nozick rules, the resulting distribution of income and wealth will be fair. Let's study a concrete example to examine the claim that if resources are allocated efficiently, they are also allocated fairly.

Case Study: A Water Shortage in a Natural Disaster

An earthquake has broken the pipes that deliver drinking water to a city. Bottled water is available but there is no tap water. What is the fair way to allocate the bottled water?

Market Price Suppose that if the water is allocated by market price, the price jumps to $8 a bottle—five times its normal price. At this price, the people who own water can make a large profit by selling it. People who are willing and able to pay $8 a bottle get the water. And because most people can't afford the $8 price, they end up either without water or consuming just a few drops a day.

You can see that the water is being used efficiently. There is a fixed amount available, some people are willing to pay $8 to get a bottle, and the water goes to those people. The people who own and sell water receive a large producer surplus and total surplus (the sum of consumer surplus and producer surplus) is maximized.

On the rules view, the outcome is also fair. No one is denied the water they are willing to pay for. But on the results view, the outcome would most likely be regarded as unfair. The lucky owners of water make a killing and the poorest end up being the thirstiest.

Non-Market Methods Suppose that by a majority vote, the citizens decide that the government will buy all the water, pay for it with a tax, and allocate it to the citizens using one of the non-market methods. The possibilities now are:

1. Command Someone decides who is the most deserving and needy. Perhaps everyone is given an equal share. Or perhaps government officials and their families end up with most of the water.

2. Contest Bottles of water are prizes that go to those who are best at the particular contest.

3. First-come-first-served Water goes to the first off the mark or to those who place the lowest value on their time and can afford to wait in line.

4. Lottery Water goes to those in luck.

5. Personal characteristics Water goes to those with the "right" characteristics. Perhaps the old, the young, or pregnant mothers get the water.

Except by chance, none of these methods delivers an allocation of water that is either fair or efficient. It is unfair on the rules view because the tax involves involuntary transfers of resources among citizens. And it is unfair on the results view because the poorest don't end up being made as well off as possible.

The allocation is inefficient for two reasons. First, resources have been used to operate the allocation scheme. Second, some people are willing to pay for more water than they have been allocated and others have been allocated more water than they are willing to pay for.

The second source of inefficiency can be overcome if, after the non-market allocation, the city allows water to be traded at its market price. People who value the water they received at less than the market price sell and people who are willing to pay the market price to obtain more water than they were allocated buy. Those who value the water most highly are the ones who consume it.

Market Price with Taxes Another approach is to allocate the scarce water using the market price but after redistributing buying power by taxing the sellers of water and providing benefits to the poor.

Suppose water owners are taxed on each bottle sold and the revenue from these taxes is given to the poorest people. People are then free, starting from this new distribution of buying power, to trade water at the market price.

Because the owners of water are taxed on what they sell, they have a weaker incentive to offer water for sale and the supply decreases. The equilibrium price rises to more than $8 a bottle. There is now a deadweight loss in the market for water—similar to the loss that arises from underproduction on p. 112. (We study the effects of a tax and show its inefficiency in Chapter 6 on pp. 132–136.)

So the tax is inefficient. On the rules view, the tax is also unfair because it forces the owners of water to make a transfer to others. On the results view, the outcome might be regarded as being fair.

This brief case study illustrates the complexity of ideas about fairness. Economists have a clear criterion of efficiency but no comparably clear criterion of fairness. Most economists regard Nozick as being too extreme and want a fair tax in the rules. But there is no consensus about what would be a fair tax.

REVIEW QUIZ

1 What are the two big approaches to thinking about fairness?
2 What is the utilitarian idea of fairness and what is wrong with it?
3 Explain the big tradeoff. What idea of fairness has been developed to deal with it?
4 What is the main idea of fairness based on fair rules?

 Study Plan 5.5

◆ You've now studied the two biggest issues that run right through the whole of economics: efficiency and fairness. In the next chapter, we study some sources of inefficiency and unfairness. And at many points throughout this book—and in your life—you will return to and use the ideas about efficiency and fairness that you've learned in this chapter. *Reading Between the Lines* on pp. 118–119 looks at an example of an inefficiency in our economy today.

Inefficiency in Global Water Use

THE WALL STREET JOURNAL, NOVEMBER 26, 2003

Ravaged by Famine, Ethiopia Finally Gets Help From the Nile

MERAWI, Ethiopia—A barefoot farmer named Takele Tarekegn emerged from his cornfields one day this summer and encountered engineers and bankers stumbling through the dense bush in front of his mud-brick shack.

The interlopers, wielding compasses and blueprints, were blazing a trail to the nearby Koga River. They were also charting what could be a historic turn in the turbulent water politics of the Nile River, which have kept millions of Ethiopians on the ragged edge of starvation.

A small dam is to be built on the Koga, Mr. Tarekegn's visitors told him, and a network of canals, too—the first irrigation project for peasant farmers ever constructed in the area. "If we can finally use our water, we'll be able to feed our families all year long," says the 46-year-old farmer. "I have been waiting for this all my life."

For now, he watches water that could be his salvation rush away to another man's fields in another country. ...

In all, rivers originating in Ethiopia's highlands contribute 85% of the Nile water flowing through Egypt—where a vast web of dams and canals first commissioned by the Pharaohs turn millions of desert acres into fertile fields. ...

Essence of the Story

■ The Koga River in Ethiopia's highlands flows into the Nile River, which in turn flows into Egypt.

■ A vast web of dams and canals first built by Egypt's ancient rulers, the Pharaohs, make fertile millions of acres of desert.

■ A small dam with a supporting network of canals is to be built on the Koga.

■ Ethiopian farmers will be able to increase production and feed their families.

Economic Analysis

■ Water is one of the world's most vital resources, and it is used inefficiently.

■ Markets in water are not competitive. They are controlled by governments or private producers, and they do not work like the competitive markets that deliver an efficient use of resources.

■ The major problem in achieving an efficient use of water is to get it from the places where it is most abundant to the places in which it has the most valuable uses.

■ Some places have too little water, and some have too much.

■ The news article highlights two such places—Ethiopia with too little water and Egypt with too much.

■ The figures illustrate what is happening to water use in these two countries.

■ In Fig. 1, the curve D shows the demand for water in Ethiopia and the curve MC shows the marginal cost of providing water through dams and irrigation canals.

■ The absence of dams and irrigation canals means that the quantity of water available in Ethiopia Q_A is less than the efficient quantity. Farmers are willing to pay W, which exceeds the marginal cost C and a deadweight loss arises from underproduction.

■ In Fig. 2, the curve D shows the demand for water in Egypt and the curve MC shows the marginal cost of providing water through dams and irrigation canals.

■ The flow of free water from Ethiopia and the presence of extensive dams and irrigation canals mean that the quantity of water available in Egypt Q_B is greater than the efficient quantity. Farmers are willing to pay W, which is less than the marginal cost C and a deadweight loss arises from overproduction.

■ The situation in Ethiopia and Egypt is replicated in thousands of places around the world.

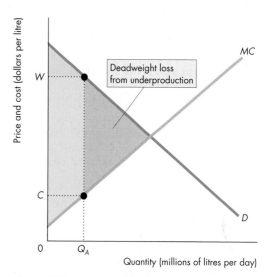

Figure 1 Water use in Ethiopia

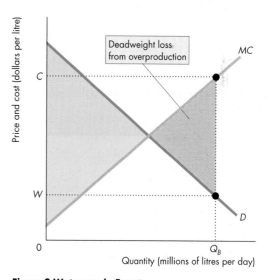

Figure 2 Water use in Egypt

You're the Voter

■ Do you think that water is too important to be left to the market to allocate?

■ Do you think that water should be shipped from Canada to Saudi Arabia?

119

SUMMARY

KEY POINTS

Resource Allocation Methods (pp. 104–105)

- Because resources are scarce, some mechanism must allocate them.
- The alternative allocation methods are: market price; command; majority rule; contest; first-come, first-served; lottery; personal characteristics; and force.

Demand and Marginal Benefit (pp. 106–107)

- Marginal benefit determines demand, and a demand curve is the marginal benefit curve.
- Market demand curve is the horizontal sum of the individual demand curves.
- Value is what people are *willing to* pay; price is what people *must* pay.
- Consumer surplus equals value minus price, summed over the quantity bought.

Supply and Marginal Cost (pp. 108–109)

- The minimum-supply price determines supply and the supply curve is the marginal cost curve.
- Market supply curve is the horizontal sum of the individual supply curves.
- Opportunity cost is what producers pay; price is what producers receive.
- Producer surplus equals price minus minimum supply-price, summed over the quantity sold.

Is the Competitive Market Efficient?
(pp. 110–113)

- In a competitive equilibrium, marginal social benefit equals marginal social cost and resource allocation is efficient.
- Buyers and sellers acting in their self-interest end up promoting the social interest.
- Total surplus, the sum of consumer surplus and producer surplus, is maximized.

- Producing less than or more than the efficient quantity creates deadweight loss.
- Price and quantity regulations, taxes and subsidies, externalities, public goods and common resources, monopoly, and high transactions costs create inefficiency and deadweight loss.

Are Markets Fair? (pp. 114–117)

- Ideas about fairness can be divided into two groups: fair *results* and fair *rules*.
- Fair-results ideas require income transfers from the rich to the poor.
- Fair-rules ideas require property rights and voluntary exchange.

KEY FIGURES

KEY TERMS

PROBLEMS

Go to **myeconlab** for solutions to odd-numbered problems and additional exercises.

1. The table gives the demand schedules for train travel for Ben, Beth, and Bo.

Price (cents per kilometre)	Quantity demanded (kilometres)		
	Ben	**Beth**	**Bo**
0	50	40	60
10	45	35	50
20	40	30	40
30	35	25	30
40	30	20	20
50	25	15	10
60	20	10	0

a. If the market price is 40 cents a kilometre
   i   What is each traveller's marginal benefit?
   ii Which traveller has the largest consumer surplus? Explain why.
   iii What is marginal social benefit? Why?
b. Construct the market demand schedule.

2. The table gives the supply schedules of jetski rides by three owners: Ann, Arthur, and Abby.

Price (dollars per ride)	Quantity supplied (rides per day)		
	Ann	**Arthur**	**Abby**
10.00	0	0	0
12.50	5	0	0
15.00	10	5	0
17.50	15	10	5
20.00	20	15	10
22.50	25	20	15

a. What is each owner's minimum supply-price of 10 rides a day?
b. Which owner has the largest producer surplus when the price of a ride is $17.50? Explain why.
c. What is marginal social cost of producing 45 rides a day?
d. Construct the market supply schedule.

3. The figure shows the market for floppy discs.

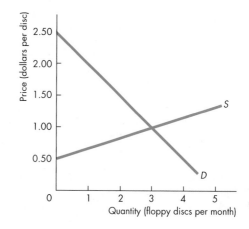

a. What are the equilibrium price and equilibrium quantity of floppy discs?
b. Calculate the consumer surplus.
c. Calculate the producer surplus.
d. Calculate the cost of producing the floppy discs sold.
e. What is the efficient quantity of floppy discs?

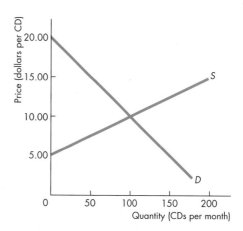

4. The figure illustrates the market for CDs.
a. What are the equilibrium price and equilibrium quantity of CDs?
b. Calculate the amount consumers paid for CDs.
c. Calculate the consumer surplus.
d. Calculate the producer surplus.
e. Calculate the cost of producing the CDs sold.
f. What is the efficient quantity of CDs?

5. The table gives the demand and supply schedules for sandwiches.

Price (dollars per sandwich)	Quantity demanded	Quantity supplied
	(sandwiches per day)	
0	300	0
1	250	50
3	200	100
4	150	150
5	100	200
6	50	250
7	0	300

a. What is the maximum price that consumers are willing to pay for the 200th sandwich?
b. What is the minimum price that producers are willing to accept for the 200th sandwich?
c. Are 200 sandwiches a day less than or greater than the efficient quantity?
d. Draw a graph of the sandwich market and mark in the efficient quantity, shade in the consumer surplus and the producer surplus.
e. On the graph of the sandwich market, shade in the deadweight loss created when 200 sandwiches a day are produced.

6. The table gives the demand and supply schedules for sunscreen.

Price (dollars per bottle)	Quantity demanded	Quantity supplied
	(bottles per day)	
0	600	0
1	500	100
2	400	200
3	300	300
4	200	400
5	100	500
6	0	600

a. What is the maximum price that consumers are willing to pay for the 200th bottle?
b. What is the minimum price that producers are willing to accept for the 200th bottle?
c. Are 200 bottles a day less than or greater than the efficient quantity? (Draw the graph.)
d. Draw a graph of the sunscreen market and mark in the efficient quantity, shade in the consumer surplus and the producer surplus.
e. On the graph of the sunscreen market, shade in the deadweight loss created when sunscreen bottlers produce 200 bottles a day.

CRITICAL THINKING

1. After you have studied *Reading Between the Lines* on pp. 118–119, answer the following questions:
   a. What is the major problem in achieving an efficient use of the world's water?
   b. If there were a global market in water, like there is in oil, how do you think the market would work?
   c. Would a free world market in water achieve an efficient use of the world's water resources? Explain why or why not.
   d. Would a free world market in water achieve a fair use of the world's water resources? Explain why or why not and be clear about the concept of fairness that you are using.

WEB EXERCISES

Use the links on (X myeconlab) **to work the following exercise.**

1. Visit the Web site of Health Action International and read the article by Catrin Schulte-Hillen entitled "Study concerning the availability and price of AZT." Then answer the following questions and explain your answers using the concepts of marginal benefit, marginal cost, price, consumer surplus, and producer surplus.
   a. What is the range of retail prices of AZT across the countries covered by the study?
   b. How do you think the range of prices influences the efficiency of the market for AZT?
   c. What, if anything, do you think could be done to increase the quantity of AZT and decrease its price?
   d. Canadian online pharmacies sell AZT to Americans for a price below the U.S. price. Does this practice increase or decrease consumer surplus in (i) Canada and (ii) the United States? Does it increase or decrease producer surplus in (i) Canada and (ii) the United States?
   e. What do you think must be done to make the market for AZT efficient?

Markets in Action

Turbulent Times

Apartment rents are skyrocketing in Toronto, and people are screaming for help. Do rent controls help renters live in affordable housing?

Almost every day, a new machine is invented that increases productivity and replaces some workers. Take a look at the machines in McDonald's that have replaced some low-skilled workers. Do minimum wage laws enable low-skilled people to earn a living wage?

Almost everything we buy is taxed. Beer is one heavily taxed item. How much of the beer tax gets paid by the buyer and how much by the seller? Do taxes help or hinder the market in its attempt to move resources to where they are valued most highly?

In 2003, ideal conditions brought record yields and global grain production increased. But in 2000 and 2001, yields were low and global grain production decreased. How do farm prices and revenues react to such output fluctuations and how do subsidies and production quotas affect farmers?

Trading in drugs is illegal. How do laws that make trading in a good or service illegal affect its price and the quantity bought and sold?

◆ In this chapter, we use the theory of demand and supply (Chapter 3) and the concepts of elasticity (Chapter 4) and efficiency (Chapter 5) to answer questions like those that we've just posed. In *Reading Between the Lines* at the end of the chapter, we explore the effects of an increase in Alberta's minimum wage in 2005.

After studying this chapter, you will be able to

- Explain how housing markets work and how price ceilings create housing shortages and inefficiency

- Explain how labour markets work and how minimum wage laws create unemployment and inefficiency

- Explain the effects of a tax

- Explain why farm prices and revenues fluctuate and how production subsidies and quotas influence farm production, costs, and prices

- Explain how markets for illegal goods work

Housing Markets and Rent Ceilings

TO SEE HOW A HOUSING MARKET WORKS, LET'S transport ourselves to San Francisco in April 1906, as the city is suffering from a massive earthquake and fire. You can sense the enormity of San Francisco's problems by reading a headline from the April 19, 1906, *New York Times* about the first days of the crisis:

Over 500 Dead, $200,000,000 Lost in San Francisco Earthquake
Nearly Half the City Is in Ruins and 50,000 Are Homeless

The commander of federal troops in charge of the emergency described the magnitude of the problem:

> Not a hotel of note or importance was left standing. The great apartment houses had vanished ... two hundred-and-twenty-five thousand people were ... homeless.[1]

Almost overnight, more than half the people in a city of 400,000 had lost their homes. Temporary shelters and camps alleviated some of the problem, but it was also necessary to utilize the apartment buildings and houses left standing. As a consequence, they had to accommodate 40 percent more people than they had before the earthquake.

The *San Francisco Chronicle* was not published for more than a month after the earthquake. When the newspaper reappeared on May 24, 1906, the city's housing shortage—what would seem to be a major news item that would still be of grave importance—was not mentioned. Milton Friedman and George Stigler describe the situation:

> There is not a single mention of a housing shortage! The classified advertisements listed sixty-four offers of flats and houses for rent, and nineteen of houses for sale, against five advertisements of flats or houses wanted. Then and thereafter a considerable number of all types of accommodation except hotel rooms were offered for rent.[2]

How did San Francisco cope with such a devastating reduction in the supply of housing?

---

[1] Reported in Milton Friedman and George J. Stigler, "Roofs or Ceilings? The Current Housing Problem," in *Popular Essays on Current Problems*, vol. 1, no. 2 (New York: Foundation for Economic Education, 1946), pp. 3–159.
[2] *Ibid.*, p. 3.

The Market Before and After the Earthquake

Figure 6.1 shows the market for housing in San Francisco. The demand curve for housing is *D*. There is a short-run supply curve, labelled *SS*, and a long-run supply curve, labelled *LS*.

Short-Run Supply The short-run supply curve shows the change in the quantity of housing supplied as the rent changes while the number of houses and apartment buildings remains constant. The short-run supply response arises from changes in the intensity with which existing buildings are used. The higher the rent, the greater is the incentive for families to rent out some of the rooms that they previously used themselves.

Long-Run Supply The long-run supply curve shows how the quantity of housing supplied responds to a change in price after enough time has elapsed for new apartment buildings and houses to be erected or for existing ones to be destroyed. In Fig. 6.1, the long-run supply curve is *perfectly elastic*. The marginal cost of building is the same regardless of the number of houses and apartments in existence. And so long as the rent exceeds the marginal cost of building, developers have an incentive to keep on building. So long-run supply is perfectly elastic at a rent equal to marginal cost.

Equilibrium The equilibrium rent and quantity are determined by demand and *short-run* supply. Before the earthquake, the equilibrium rent is $16 a month and the quantity is 100,000 units of housing.

Figure 6.1(a) shows the situation immediately after the earthquake. Few people died in the earthquake, so demand remains at *D*. But the devastation decreases supply and shifts the short-run supply curve *SS* leftward to SS_A. If the rent remains at $16 a month, only 44,000 units of housing are available. But with only 44,000 units of housing available, the maximum rent that someone is willing to pay for the last available apartment is $24 a month. So rents rise. In Fig. 6.1(a), the rent rises to $20 a month.

As the rent rises, the quantity of housing demanded decreases and the quantity supplied increases to 72,000 units. These changes occur because people economize on their use of space and make spare rooms, attics, and basements available to others. The higher rent allocates the scarce housing to the people who value it most highly and are willing to pay the most for it.

But the higher rent has other, long-run effects. Let's look at these long-run effects.

FIGURE 6.1
The San Francisco Housing Market in 1906

(a) After earthquake

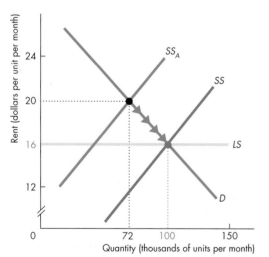

(b) Long-run adjustment

Part (a) shows that before the earthquake, 100,000 housing units were rented at $16 a month. After the earthquake, the short-run supply curve shifts from SS to SS$_A$. The rent rises to $20 a month, and the quantity of housing decreases to 72,000 units.

With rent at $20 a month, there is profit in building new apartments and houses. As the building proceeds, the short-run supply curve shifts rightward (part b). The rent gradually falls to $16 a month, and the quantity of housing increases to 100,000 units—as the arrowed line shows.

Long-Run Adjustments

With sufficient time for new apartments and houses to be constructed, supply increases. The long-run supply curve tells us that in the long run, housing is supplied at a rent of $16 a month. Because the rent of $20 a month exceeds the long-run supply price of $16 a month, there is a building boom. More apartments and houses are built, and the short-run supply curve shifts gradually rightward.

Figure 6.1(b) shows the long-run adjustment. As more housing is built, the short-run supply curve shifts gradually rightward and intersects the demand curve at lower rents and larger quantities. The market equilibrium follows the arrows down the demand curve. The building boom ends when there is no further profit in building new apartments and houses. The process ends when the rent is back at $16 a month, and 100,000 units of housing are available.

We've just seen how a housing market responds to a decrease in supply. And we've seen that a key part of the adjustment process is a rise in the rent. Suppose the government passes a law to stop the rent from rising. What happens then?

A Regulated Housing Market

We're now going to study the effects of a price ceiling in the housing market. A **price ceiling** is a regulation that makes it illegal to charge a price higher than a specified level. When a price ceiling is applied to housing markets, it is called a **rent ceiling**. How does a rent ceiling affect the housing market?

The effect of a price (rent) ceiling depends on whether it is imposed at a level that is above or below the equilibrium price (rent). A price ceiling set *above* the equilibrium price has no effect. The reason is that the price ceiling does not constrain the market forces. The force of the law and the market forces are not in conflict. But a price ceiling *below* the equilibrium price has powerful effects on a market. The reason is that the price ceiling attempts to prevent the price from regulating the quantities demanded and supplied. The force of the law and the market forces are in conflict, and one (or both) of these forces must yield to some degree.

Let's study the effects of a price ceiling that is set below the equilibrium price by returning to San Francisco. What would have happened in San Francisco if a rent ceiling of $16 a month—the rent before the earthquake—had been imposed?

FIGURE 6.2
A Rent Ceiling

A rent above $16 a month is illegal (in the grey-shaded illegal region). At a rent of $16 a month, the quantity of housing supplied after the earthquake is 44,000 units. Someone is willing to pay $24 a month for the 44,000th unit. Frustrated renters spend time searching for housing and they make deals with landlords in a black market.

Figure 6.2 enables us to answer this question. A rent that exceeds $16 a month is in the grey-shaded illegal region in the figure. At a rent of $16 a month, the quantity of housing supplied is 44,000 units and the quantity demanded is 100,000 units. So there is a shortage of 56,000 units of housing.

But the story does not end here. Somehow, the 44,000 units of available housing must be allocated among people who demand 100,000 units. How is this allocation achieved? When a rent ceiling creates a housing shortage, two developments occur. They are

■ Search activity
■ Black markets

Search Activity

The time spent looking for someone with whom to do business is called **search activity**. We spend some time in search activity almost every time we buy something. You want the latest hot CD, and you know four stores that stock it. But which store has the best deal? You

need to spend a few minutes on the Internet or calling your friends to find out. In some markets, we spend a lot of time searching. An example is the housing market in which we spend a lot of time checking the alternatives available before making a choice.

But when a price is regulated and there is a shortage, search activity increases. In the case of a rent-controlled housing market, frustrated would-be renters scan the newspapers, not only for housing ads but also for death notices! Any information about newly available housing is useful. And they race to be first on the scene when news of a possible supplier breaks.

The *opportunity cost* of a good is equal not only to its price but also to the value of the search time spent finding the good. So the opportunity cost of housing is equal to the rent (a regulated price) plus the time and other resources spent searching for the restricted quantity available. Search activity is costly. It uses time and other resources, such as telephones, cars, and gasoline that could have been used in other productive ways. A rent ceiling controls the rent portion of the cost of housing, but it does not control the opportunity cost, which might even be *higher* than the rent would be if the market were unregulated.

Black Markets

A **black market** is an illegal market in which the price exceeds the legally imposed price ceiling. Black markets occur in rent-controlled housing, the same way that scalpers run black markets in tickets for big sporting events and rock concerts.

When rent ceilings are in force, frustrated renters and landlords constantly seek ways of increasing rents. One common way is for a new tenant to pay a high price for worthless fittings, such as charging $2,000 for threadbare drapes. Another is for the tenant to pay an exorbitant price for new locks and keys—called "key money."

The level of a black market rent depends on how tightly the rent ceiling is enforced. With loose enforcement, the black market rent is close to the unregulated rent. But with strict enforcement, the black market rent is equal to the maximum price that renters are willing to pay.

With strict enforcement of the rent ceiling in the San Francisco example shown in Fig. 6.2, the quantity of housing available remains at 44,000 units. A small number of people offer housing for rent at $24 a month—the highest rent that someone is willing to pay—and the government detects and punishes some of these black market traders.

Inefficiency of Rent Ceilings

In an unregulated market, the market determines the rent at which the quantity demanded equals the quantity supplied. In this situation, scarce housing resources are allocated efficiently. *Marginal social benefit* equals *marginal social cost* (see Chapter 5, p. 105).

Figure 6.3 shows the inefficiency of a rent ceiling. If the rent is fixed at $16 per month, 44,000 units are supplied. Marginal benefit is $24 a month. The blue triangle above the supply curve and below the rent ceiling line shows producer surplus. Because the quantity of housing is less than the competitive quantity, there is a deadweight loss, shown by the grey triangle. This loss is borne by the consumers who can't find housing and by producers who can't supply housing at the new lower price. Consumers who do find housing at the controlled rent gain. If no one incurs search costs, consumer surplus is shown by the sum of the green triangle and the red rectangle. But search costs might eat up part of the consumer surplus, possibly as much as the amount shown by the red rectangle.

Are Rent Ceilings Fair?

Do rent ceilings achieve a fairer allocation of scarce housing? Chapter 5 (pp. 112–115) explores the complex ideas about fairness. According to the *fair rules* view, anything that blocks voluntary exchange is unfair, so rent ceilings are unfair. But according to the *fair result* view, a fair outcome is one that benefits the less well off. So according to this view, the fairest outcome is the one that allocates scarce housing to the poorest. To see whether rent ceilings help to achieve a fairer outcome in this sense, we need to consider how the market allocates scarce housing resources in the face of a rent ceiling.

Blocking rent adjustments doesn't eliminate scarcity. Rather, because it decreases the quantity of housing available, it creates an even bigger challenge for the housing market. So somehow, the market must ration a smaller quantity of housing and allocate that housing among the people who demand it.

When the rent is not permitted to allocate scarce housing, what other mechanisms are available? Some possibilities are

- A lottery
- A queue
- Discrimination

Are these mechanisms fair?

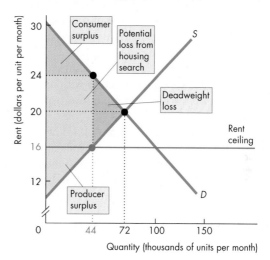

FIGURE 6.3

The Inefficiency of a Rent Ceiling

A rent ceiling of $16 a month decreases the quantity of housing supplied to 44,000 units. Producer surplus shrinks, and a deadweight loss (grey triangle) arises. If people use no resources in search activity, consumer surplus is the green triangle plus the red rectangle. But if people use resources in search activity equal to the amount shown by the red rectangle, the consumer surplus shrinks to the green triangle.

A lottery allocates housing to those who are lucky, not to those who are poor. A queue (a method used to allocate housing in England after World War II) allocates housing to those who have the greatest foresight and who get their names on a list first, not to the poorest. Discrimination allocates scarce housing based on the views and self-interest of the owner of the housing. In the case of public housing, it is the self-interest of the bureaucracy that administers the allocation that counts.

In principle, self-interested owners and bureaucrats could allocate housing to satisfy some criterion of fairness. But they are not likely to do so. Discrimination based on friendship, family ties, and criteria such as race, ethnicity, or sex is more likely to enter the equation. We might make such discrimination illegal, but we would not be able to prevent it from occurring.

It is hard, then, to make a case for rent ceilings on the basis of fairness. When rent adjustments are blocked, other methods of allocating scarce housing resources operate that do not produce a fair outcome.

Rent Ceilings in Practice

London, New York, Paris, and San Francisco, four of the world's great cities, have rent ceilings in some part of their housing markets. Winnipeg has rent ceilings and Toronto had them from 1975 until the late 1990s. Many Canadian cities including Calgary, Edmonton, and Vancouver do not have rent ceilings.

We can test for the effects of rent ceilings by comparing the housing markets in cities with and without ceilings. We learn two main lessons from such a comparison.

First, rent ceilings definitely create a housing shortage. Second, they do lower the rents for some but raise them for others. A survey[3] conducted in the United States in 1997 showed that the rents of housing units *actually available for rent* were 2.5 times the average of all rents in New York but equal to the average rent in Philadelphia where there is no rent ceiling. The winners from rent ceilings in New York City are the families that have lived there for a long time. These families include some rich and famous ones. The losers are mobile newcomers. It is the voting power of the winners that keeps New York's rent ceilings in place.

The bottom line is that in principle and in practice, rent ceilings are inefficient and unfair. They prevent the housing market from operating in the social interest.

REVIEW QUIZ

1 How does a decrease in the supply of housing change the equilibrium rent in the short run?
2 What are the effects of a rise in rent? And who gets the scarce housing resources?
3 What are the long-run effects of higher rents following a decrease in the supply of housing?
4 What is a rent ceiling and what are its effects if it is set above the equilibrium rent?
5 What are the effects of a rent ceiling that is set below the equilibrium rent?
6 How do scarce housing resources get allocated when a rent ceiling is in place?

myeconlab **Study Plan 6.1**

You now know how a price ceiling works. Next, we'll learn about the effects of a price floor by studying minimum wages in the labour market.

---

[3] William Tucker, "How Rent Control Drives Out Affordable Housing."

The Labour Market and the Minimum Wage

FOR EACH ONE OF US, THE LABOUR MARKET IS the market that influences the jobs we get and the wages we earn. Firms decide how much labour to demand, and the lower the wage rate, the greater is the quantity of labour demanded. Households decide how much labour to supply, and the higher the wage rate, the greater is the quantity of labour supplied. The wage rate adjusts to make the quantity of labour demanded equal to the quantity supplied.

Equilibrium wage rates give some people high incomes but leave many more people with low incomes. And the labour market is constantly hit by shocks that often hit the lowest paid the hardest. The most pervasive of these shocks is the arrival of new labour-saving technologies that decrease the demand for low-skilled workers and lower their wage rates. During the 1980s and 1990s, for example, the demand for telephone operators and television repair technicians decreased. Throughout the past 200 years, the demand for low-skilled farm labourers has steadily decreased.

How does the labour market cope with this continuous decrease in the demand for low-skilled labour? Doesn't it mean that the wage rate of low-skilled workers is constantly falling?

To answer these questions, we must study the market for low-skilled labour in both the short run and the long run.

In the short run, there are a given number of people who have a given skill, training, and experience. Short-run supply of labour describes how the number of hours of labour supplied by this given number of people changes as the wage rate changes. To get them to work more hours, they must be offered a higher wage rate.

In the long run, people can acquire new skills and find new types of jobs. The number of people in the low-skilled labour market depends on the wage rate in this market compared with other opportunities. If the wage rate of low-skilled labour is high enough, people will enter this market. If the wage rate is too low, people will leave it. Some will seek training to enter higher-skilled labour markets, and others will stop working.

The long-run supply of labour is the relationship between the quantity of labour supplied and the wage rate after enough time has passed for people to enter or leave the low-skilled labour market. If people can freely enter and leave the low-skilled labour market, the long-run supply of labour is *perfectly elastic*.

Figure 6.4 shows the market for low-skilled labour. Other things remaining the same, the lower the wage rate, the greater is the quantity of labour demanded by firms. The demand curve for labour, *D* in part (a), shows this relationship between the wage rate and the quantity of labour demanded. Other things remaining the same, the higher the wage rate, the greater is the quantity of labour supplied by households. But the longer the period of adjustment, the greater is the *elasticity of supply* of labour. The short-run supply curve is *SS*, and the long-run supply curve is *LS*. In the figure, long-run supply is assumed to be perfectly elastic (the *LS* curve is horizontal). This market is in equilibrium at a wage rate of $7 an hour and 22 million hours of labour employed.

What happens if a labour-saving invention decreases the demand for low-skilled labour? Figure 6.4(a) shows the short-run effects of such a change. Before the new technology is introduced, the demand curve is the curve labelled *D*. After the introduction of the new technology, the demand curve shifts leftward to D_A. The wage rate falls to $6 an hour, and the quantity of labour employed decreases to 21 million hours. But this short-run effect on the wage rate and employment is not the end of the story.

People who are now earning only $6 an hour look around for other opportunities. They see many other jobs (in markets for other types of skills) that pay more than $6 an hour. One by one, workers decide to go back to school or take jobs that pay less but offer on-the-job training. As a result, the short-run supply curve begins to shift leftward.

Figure 6.4(b) shows the long-run adjustment. As the short-run supply curve shifts leftward, it intersects the demand curve D_A at higher wage rates and fewer hours employed. The process ends when workers have no incentive to leave the low-skilled labour market and the short-run supply curve has shifted to SS_A. At this point, the wage rate has returned to $7 an hour and employment has decreased to 20 million hours a year.

Concerned about the incomes of low-paid workers, provincial governments have set minimum wage rates and many campaign for a living wage. Let's look at the effects of a minimum wage and a living wage.

FIGURE 6.4

A Market for Low-Skilled Labour

(a) After invention

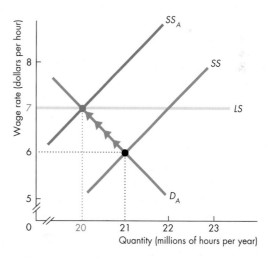

(b) Long-run adjustment

Part (a) shows the immediate effect of a labour-saving invention on the market for low-skilled labour. Initially, the wage rate is $7 an hour and 22 million hours are employed. A labour-saving invention shifts the demand curve from *D* to D_A. The wage rate falls to $6 an hour, and employment decreases to 21 million hours. With the lower wage rate, some workers leave this market and the short-run supply curve starts to shift gradually leftward to SS_A in part (b). The wage rate gradually increases, and employment decreases. In the long run, the wage rate returns to $7 an hour and employment decreases to 20 million hours a year.

A Minimum Wage

A **price floor** is a regulation that makes it illegal to trade at a price lower than a specified level. When a price floor is applied to labour markets, it is called a **minimum wage**. If a minimum wage is set *below* the equilibrium wage, the minimum wage has no effect. The minimum wage and market forces are not in conflict. But a minimum wage set *above* the equilibrium wage is in conflict with market forces, and it does have some effects on the labour market. Let's study these effects by returning to the market for low-skilled labour.

Suppose that with an equilibrium wage of $7 an hour (Fig. 6.4a), the government sets a minimum wage at $8 an hour. Figure 6.5 shows the minimum wage as the horizontal red line labelled "Minimum wage." A wage below this level is illegal, in the grey-shaded illegal region. At the minimum wage rate, 20 million hours of labour are demanded (point *A*) and 22 million hours of labour are supplied (point *B*), so 2 million hours of available labour are unemployed.

With only 20 million hours demanded, some workers are willing to supply that 20 millionth hour for $6. Frustrated unemployed workers spend time and other resources searching for hard-to-find jobs.

Inefficiency of a Minimum Wage

In an unregulated labour market, everyone who is willing to work for the going wage rate gets a job. And the market allocates the economy's scarce labour resources to the jobs in which they are valued most highly. The minimum wage frustrates the market mechanism and results in unemployment—wasted labour resources—and an inefficient amount of job search.

Figure 6.6 illustrates the inefficiency of the minimum wage. The deadweight loss arises because at the quantity of labour employed—20 million hours—the value to the firm of the marginal worker exceeds that wage rate for which that person is willing to work.

At this level of employment, unemployed people have a big incentive to spend time and effort looking for work. The red rectangle shows the potential loss from this extra job search. This loss arises because someone who finds a job earns $8 an hour (read off from the demand curve) but would have been willing to work for $6 an hour (read off from the supply curve). So everyone who is unemployed has an incentive to search hard and use resources that are worth the $2-an-hour surplus to find a job.

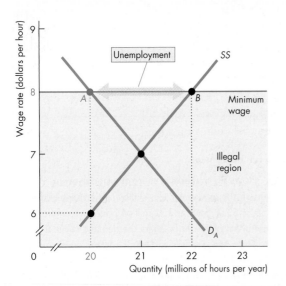

FIGURE 6.5   myeconlab
Minimum Wage and Unemployment

A wage below $8 an hour is illegal (in the grey-shaded illegal region). At the minimum wage of $8 an hour, 20 million hours are hired but 22 million hours are available. Unemployment—*AB*—of 2 million hours a year is created.

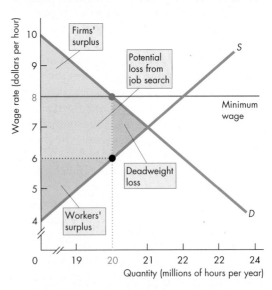

FIGURE 6.6   myeconlab
The Inefficiency of a Minimum Wage

A minimum wage shrinks the firms' surplus (blue) and workers' surplus (green) and creates a deadweight loss (grey). If people use resources in job search equal to the amount they are able to gain by finding a job, the red rectangle is also lost.

Provincial Minimum Wage Laws and Their Effects

Provincial governments in Canada set minimum wage rates. In 2005, minimum wage rates ranged from a low of $6.25 an hour in Newfoundland to highs of $8.00 an hour in British Columbia, $7.45 an hour in Ontario, $7.25 in Manitoba, $7.20 an hour in the Yukon, and $7.00 an hour in Alberta.

You saw in Fig. 6.5 that the minimum wage brings unemployment. But how much unemployment does it bring? Economists do not agree on the answer to this question. Until recently, most economists believed that the minimum wage was a big contributor to high unemployment among low-skilled young workers. But this view has recently been challenged and the challenge rebutted.

David Card of the University of California at Berkeley and Alan Krueger of Princeton University say that increases in the minimum wage have not decreased employment and created unemployment. From their study of minimum wages in California, New Jersey, and Texas, Card and Krueger say that the employment rate of low-income workers increased following an increase in the minimum wage. They suggest three reasons why higher minimum wages might increase employment. First, workers become more conscientious and productive. Second, workers are less likely to quit, so labour turnover, which is costly, is reduced. Third, managers make a firm's operations more efficient.

Most economists are skeptical about Card and Krueger's suggestions. They ask two questions. First, if higher wages make workers more productive and reduce labour turnover, why don't firms freely pay wage rates above the equilibrium wage to encourage more productive work habits? Second, are there other explanations for the employment responses that Card and Krueger have found?

Card and Krueger got the timing wrong according to Daniel Hamermesh of the University of Texas at Austin. He says that firms cut employment *before* the minimum wage is increased in anticipation of the increase. If he is correct, looking for the effects of an increase *after* it has occurred misses its main effects. Finis Welch of Texas A&M University and Kevin Murphy of the University of Chicago say the employment effects that Card and Krueger found are caused by regional differences in economic growth, not by changes in the minimum wage.

One effect of the minimum wage, according to Fig. 6.5, is an increase in the quantity of labour supplied. If this effect occurs, it might show up as an increase in the number of people who quit school before completing high school to look for work. Some economists say that this response does occur.

A Living Wage

You've seen that the provincial minimum wage rates probably cause unemployment and create a deadweight loss. Despite these effects of a price floor in the labour market, a popular movement is seeking to create a more pervasive and much higher floor at a living wage. A **living wage** has been defined as an hourly wage rate that enables a person who works a 40-hour work week to rent adequate housing for not more than 30 percent of the amount earned. For example, if the going market rent for a one-bedroom apartment is $180 a week, the living wage is $15 an hour. (Check: 40 hours at $15 an hour is $600, and $180 is 30 percent of $600.)

Living wage laws are being tried in Peterborough and Waterloo in Ontario and Kamloops in British Columbia. Campaigns to expand the use of living wages are being mounted in many cities and municipalities across the country. The effects of the living wage can be expected to be similar to those of the minimum wage.

REVIEW QUIZ

1. How does a decrease in the demand for low-skilled labour change the wage rate in the short run?
2. What are the long-run effects of a lower wage rate for low-skilled labour?
3. What is a minimum wage? What are the effects of a minimum wage set below the equilibrium wage?
4. What are the effects of a minimum wage or a living wage that is set above the equilibrium wage?

myeconlab   **Study Plan 6.2**

Next we're going to study a more widespread government action in markets: taxes. We'll see how taxes change prices and quantities. You will discover the surprising fact that while the government can impose a tax, it can't decide who will pay the tax! And you will see that a tax creates a deadweight loss.

Taxes

EVERYTHING YOU EARN AND ALMOST EVERYTHING you buy is taxed. Income taxes and social security taxes are deducted from your earnings and sales taxes and GST are added to the bill when you buy something. Employers also pay a social security tax for their workers, and producers of tobacco products, alcoholic drinks, and gasoline pay a tax every time they sell something.

Who *really* pays these taxes? Because the income tax and social security tax are deducted from your pay, and the sales tax is added to the prices that you pay, isn't it obvious that *you* pay these taxes? And isn't it equally obvious that your employer pays the employer's contribution to the social security tax and that tobacco producers pay the tax on cigarettes?

You're going to discover that it isn't obvious who *really* pays a tax and that lawmakers don't make that decision. We begin with a definition of tax incidence.

Tax Incidence

Tax incidence is the division of the burden of a tax between the buyer and the seller. When the government imposes a tax on the sale of a good,[4] the price paid by the buyer might rise by the full amount of the tax, by a lesser amount, or not at all. If the price paid by the buyer rises by the full amount of the tax, then the burden of the tax falls entirely on the buyer—the buyer pays the tax. If the price paid by the buyer rises by a lesser amount than the tax, then the burden of the tax falls partly on the buyer and partly on the seller. And if the price paid by the buyer doesn't change at all, then the burden of the tax falls entirely on the seller.

Tax incidence does not depend on the tax law. The law might impose a tax on sellers or on buyers, but the outcome is the same in either case. To see why, let's look at the tax on cigarettes.

A Tax on Sellers

In January 2005, the government of Ontario upped the tax on the sale of cigarettes for the third time since taking office in the fall 2003. To work out the effects

of a tax on the sellers of cigarettes, we begin by examining the effects on demand and supply in the cigarette market.

In Fig. 6.7, the demand curve is *D*, and the supply curve is *S*. With no tax, the equilibrium price is $6 per pack and 35 million packs a year are bought and sold.

A tax on sellers is like an increase in cost, so it decreases supply. To determine the position of the new supply curve, we add the tax to the minimum price that sellers are willing to accept for each quantity sold. You can see that without the tax, sellers are willing to offer 35 million packs a year for $6 a pack. So with a $2 tax, sellers will offer 35 million packs a year only if the price is $8 a pack. The supply curve shifts to the red curve labelled *S + tax on sellers*.

Equilibrium occurs where the new supply curve intersects the demand curve at 32 million packs a year. The price paid by buyers rises by $1.50 to $7.50 a pack. And the price received by sellers falls by 50¢ to $5.50 a pack. So buyers pay $1.50 of the tax and sellers pay the other 50¢.

FIGURE 6.7
A Tax on Sellers

With no tax, 35 million packs a year are bought and sold at $6 a pack. A tax on sellers of $2 a pack shifts the supply curve leftward to *S + tax on sellers*. The equilibrium quantity decreases to 32 million packs a year, the price paid by buyers rises to $7.50 a pack, and the price received by sellers falls to $5.50 a pack. The tax raises the price paid by buyers by less than the tax and lowers the price received by sellers, so buyers and sellers share the burden of the tax.

---

[4] These propositions also apply to services and factors of production (land, labour, capital).

A Tax on Buyers

Suppose that instead of taxing sellers, Ontario taxes cigarette buyers $2 a pack.

A tax on buyers lowers the amount they are willing to pay the seller, so it decreases demand and shifts the demand curve leftward. To determine the position of this new demand curve, we subtract the tax from the maximum price that buyers are willing to pay for each quantity bought. You can see that without the tax, buyers are willing to buy 35 million packs a year for $6 a pack. So with a $2 tax, they will buy 35 packs a year only if the price including the tax is $6 a pack, which means that they're willing to pay the seller only $4 a pack. The demand curve shifts to become the red curve labelled *D – tax on buyers*.

Equilibrium occurs where the new demand curve intersects the supply curve at a quantity of 32 million packs a year. The price received by sellers falls to $5.50 a pack, and the price paid by buyers rises to $7.50 a pack.

FIGURE 6.8
A Tax on Buyers

With no tax, 35 million packs a year are bought and sold at $6 a pack. A tax on buyers of $2 a pack shifts the demand curve leftward to *D – tax on buyers*. The equilibrium quantity decreases to 32 million packs a year, the price paid by buyers rises to $7.50 a pack, and the price received by sellers falls to $5.50 a pack. The tax raises the price paid by buyers by less than the tax and lowers the price received by sellers, so buyers and sellers share the burden of the tax.

Equivalence of Tax on Buyers and Sellers

You can see that the tax on buyers in Fig. 6.8 has the same effects as the tax on sellers in Fig. 6.7. In both cases, the equilibrium quantity decreases to 32 million packs a year, the price paid by buyers rises by $1.50 to $7.50 a pack, and the price received by sellers falls by 50¢ to $5.50 a pack. Buyers pay $1.50 of the $2.00 tax, and sellers pay the other 50¢ of the tax.

Can We Share the Burden Equally? Suppose that the government of Ontario wants the burden of the cigarette tax to fall equally on buyers and sellers and declares that a $1 tax be imposed on each. Is the burden of the tax then shared equally?

You can see that it is not. The tax is still $2 a pack. And you've seen that the tax has the same effect regardless of whether it is imposed on sellers or buyers. So imposing half the tax on one and half on the other is like an average of the two cases you've examined. (Draw the demand-supply graph and work out what happens in this case. The demand curve shifts downward by $1 and the supply curve shifts upward by $1. The new equilibrium quantity is still 32 million packs a year. Buyers pay $7.50 a pack, of which $1.50 is tax. Sellers receive from buyers $6.50, but must pay a $1 tax, so they net $5.50 a pack.)

The key point is that when a transaction is taxed, there are two prices: the price paid by buyers, which includes the tax; and the price received by sellers, which excludes the tax. Buyers respond only to the price that includes the tax, because that is the price they pay. Sellers respond only to the price that excludes the tax, because that is the price they receive.

A tax is like a wedge between the buying price and the selling price. It is the size of the wedge, not the side of the market on which the tax is imposed that determines the effects of the tax.

The Employment Insurance tax is an example of a tax that Parliament imposes on *both* buyers of labour (employers) and sellers of labour (employees). The principles you've just learned apply to this tax too. And the market for labour, not Parliament, decides how the burden of the Employment Insurance tax is divided between employers and employees.

In the Ontario cigarette tax example, the buyers bear three times the burden of the tax borne by sellers. But the division of the burden of a tax between buyers and sellers depends on the elasticities of demand and supply, as you will now see.

Tax Division and Elasticity of Demand

The division of the tax between buyers and sellers depends in part on the elasticity of demand. There are two extreme cases:

- Perfectly inelastic demand—buyers pay.
- Perfectly elastic demand—sellers pay.

Perfectly Inelastic Demand Figure 6.9(a) shows the market for insulin, a vital daily medication of diabetics. Demand is perfectly inelastic at 100,000 doses a day, regardless of the price, as shown by the vertical curve *D*. That is, a diabetic would sacrifice all other goods and services rather than not consume the insulin dose that provides good health. The supply curve of insulin is *S*. With no tax, the price is $2 a dose and the quantity is 100,000 doses a day.

If insulin is taxed at 20¢ a dose, we must add the tax to the minimum price at which drug companies are willing to sell insulin. The result is the new supply curve *S + tax*. The price rises to $2.20 a dose, but the quantity does not change. Buyers pay the entire sales tax of 20¢ a dose.

Perfectly Elastic Demand Figure 6.9(b) shows the market for pink marker pens. Demand is perfectly elastic at $1 a pen, as shown by the horizontal curve *D*. If pink pens are less expensive than the others, everyone uses pink. If pink pens are more expensive than the others, no one uses pink. The supply curve is *S*. With no tax, the price of a pink marker is $1, and the quantity is 4,000 pens a week.

If a tax of 10¢ a pen is imposed on pink marker pens but not on other colours, we add the tax to the minimum price at which sellers are willing to offer pink pens for sale, and the new supply curve is *S + tax*. The price remains at $1 a pen, and the quantity decreases to 1,000 a week. The 10¢ tax leaves the price paid by buyers unchanged but lowers the amount received by sellers by the full amount of the tax. Sellers pay the entire tax of 10¢ a pink pen.

We've seen that when demand is perfectly inelastic, buyers pay the entire tax and when demand is perfectly elastic, sellers pay the entire tax. In the usual case, demand is neither perfectly inelastic nor perfectly elastic and the tax is split between buyers and sellers. But the division depends on the elasticity of demand. The more inelastic the demand, the larger is the amount of the tax paid by buyers.

FIGURE 6.9   myeconlab
Tax and the Elasticity of Demand

(a) Perfectly inelastic demand

(b) Perfectly elastic demand

Part (a) shows the market for insulin, where demand is perfectly inelastic. With no tax, the price is $2 a dose and the quantity is 100,000 doses a day. A tax of 20¢ a dose shifts the supply curve to *S + tax*. The price rises to $2.20 a dose, but the quantity bought does not change. Buyers pay the entire tax.

Part (b) shows the market for pink pens, in which demand is perfectly elastic. With no tax, the price of a pen is $1 and the quantity is 4,000 pens a week. A tax of 10¢ a pink pen shifts the supply curve to *S + tax*. The price remains at $1 a pen, and the quantity of pink pens sold decreases to 1,000 a week. Sellers pay the entire tax.

Tax Division and Elasticity of Supply

The division of the tax between buyers and sellers also depends, in part, on the elasticity of supply. Again, there are two extreme cases:

- Perfectly inelastic supply—sellers pay.
- Perfectly elastic supply—buyers pay.

Perfectly Inelastic Supply Figure 6.10(a) shows the market for water from a mineral spring that flows at a constant rate that can't be controlled. Supply is perfectly inelastic at 100,000 bottles a week, as shown by the supply curve *S*. The demand curve for the water from this spring is *D*. With no tax, the price is 50¢ a bottle and the 100,000 bottles that flow from the spring are bought.

Suppose this spring water is taxed at 5¢ a bottle. The supply curve does not change because the spring owners still produce 100,000 bottles a week even though the price they receive falls. But buyers are willing to buy the 100,000 bottles only if the price is 50¢ a bottle. So the price remains at 50¢ a bottle. The tax reduces the price received by sellers to 45¢ a bottle, and sellers pay the entire tax.

Perfectly Elastic Supply Figure 6.10(b) shows the market for sand from which computer-chip makers extract silicon. Supply of this sand is perfectly elastic at a price of 10¢ a kilogram, as shown by the supply curve *S*. The demand curve for sand is *D*. With no tax, the price is 10¢ a kilogram and 5,000 kilograms a week are bought.

If this sand is taxed at 1¢ a kilogram, we must add the tax to the minimum supply-price. Sellers are now willing to offer any quantity at 11¢ a kilogram along the curve *S* + *tax*. A new equilibrium is determined where the new supply curve intersects the demand curve: at a price of 11¢ a kilogram and a quantity of 3,000 kilograms a week. The tax has increased the price buyers pay by the full amount of the tax—1¢ a kilogram—and has decreased the quantity sold. Buyers pay the entire tax.

We've seen that when supply is perfectly inelastic, sellers pay the entire tax and when supply is perfectly elastic, buyers pay the entire tax. In the usual case, supply is neither perfectly inelastic nor perfectly elastic and the tax is split between buyers and sellers. But how the tax is split depends on the elasticity of supply. The more elastic the supply, the larger is the amount of the tax paid by buyers.

FIGURE 6.10

Tax and the Elasticity of Supply

(a) Perfectly inelastic supply

(b) Perfectly elastic supply

Part (a) shows the market for water from a mineral spring. Supply is perfectly inelastic. With no tax, the price is 50¢ a bottle. With a tax of 5¢ a bottle, the price remains at 50¢ a bottle. The number of bottles bought remains the same, but the price received by sellers decreases to 45¢ a bottle. Sellers pay the entire tax.

Part (b) shows the market for sand. Supply is perfectly elastic. With no tax, the price is 10¢ a kilogram. A tax of 1¢ a kilogram increases the minimum supply-price to 11¢ a kilogram. The supply curve shifts to *S* + *tax*. The price increases to 11¢ a kilogram. Buyers pay the entire tax.

Taxes in Practice

Supply and demand are rarely perfectly elastic or perfectly inelastic. But some items tend towards one of the extremes. For example, alcohol, tobacco, and gasoline have low elasticities of demand and high elasticities of supply. So the burden of these taxes falls more heavily on buyers than on sellers. Labour has a low elasticity of supply and a high elasticity of demand. So despite Parliament's desire for employers to pay more of the Employment Insurance tax than do workers, the burden of this tax falls mainly on workers.

The most heavily taxed items are those that have either a low elasticity of demand or a low elasticity of supply. For these items, when a tax is imposed the equilibrium quantity doesn't decrease much. So the government collects a large tax revenue and the deadweight loss from the tax is small.

It is unusual to tax an item heavily if neither its demand nor its supply is inelastic. With an elastic supply *and* demand, a tax brings a large decrease in the equilibrium quantity and a small tax revenue.

Taxes and Efficiency

You've seen that a tax places a wedge between the price that buyers pay and the price that sellers receive. The price that buyers pay is also the buyers' willingness to pay, which measures marginal benefit. The price that sellers receive is also the sellers' minimum supply-price, which equals marginal cost.

So because a tax places a wedge between the buyers' price and the sellers' price, it also puts a wedge between marginal benefit and marginal cost and creates inefficiency. With a higher buyers' price and a lower sellers' price, the tax decreases the quantities produced and consumed and a deadweight loss arises. Figure 6.11 shows the inefficiency of a tax on CD players. With a tax, both consumer surplus and producer surplus shrink. Part of each surplus goes to the government in tax revenue (purple area) and part becomes a deadweight loss—the grey area.

In the extreme cases of perfectly inelastic demand and perfectly inelastic supply, a tax does not change the quantity bought and sold and there is no deadweight loss. The more inelastic is either demand or supply, the smaller is the decrease in quantity and the smaller is the deadweight loss. When demand or supply is perfectly inelastic, the quantity remains constant and no deadweight loss arises.

FIGURE 6.11
Taxes and Efficiency

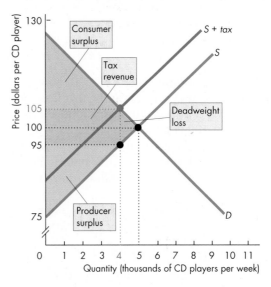

With no tax on CD players, 5,000 a week are bought and sold at $100 each. With a $10 tax on a CD player, the buyer's price rises to $105 a player, the seller's price falls to $95 a player, and the quantity decreases to 4,000 CD players a week. Consumer surplus shrinks to the green area, and the producer surplus shrinks to the blue area. Part of the loss of consumer surplus and producer surplus goes to the government as tax revenue, the purple area. A deadweight loss arises, which is shown by the grey area.

REVIEW QUIZ

1 How does the elasticity of demand influence the effect of a tax on the price paid by buyers, the price received by sellers, the quantity, the tax revenue, and the deadweight loss?

2 How does the elasticity of supply influence the effect of a tax on the price paid by buyers, the price received by sellers, the quantity, the tax revenue, and the deadweight loss?

3 Why does a tax create a deadweight loss?

myeconlab Study Plan 6.3

Your next task is to study intervention in the markets for farm products. These markets have special problems and provide examples of two additional ways of changing market outcomes: subsidies and quotas.

Subsidies and Quotas

AN EARLY OR LATE FROST, A HOT DRY SUMMER, and a wet autumn present just a few of the challenges that fill the lives of farmers with uncertainty and sometimes with economic hardship. Fluctuations in the weather bring big fluctuations in farm output. How do changes in farm output affect farm prices and farm revenues? And how might farmers be helped by intervention in the markets for farm products?

Let's look at some agricultural markets and see how they're affected by the weather and by government interventions.

Harvest Fluctuations

Figure 6.12 shows the market for wheat. In both parts, the demand curve for wheat is D. Once farmers have harvested their crop, they have no control over the quantity supplied and supply is perfectly inelastic along a *momentary supply curve*. With a normal harvest, the momentary supply curve is MS_0, the price is $200 a tonne, the quantity produced is 20 million tonnes, and farm revenue (price multiplied by quantity) is $4 billion.

Poor Harvest In Fig. 6.12(a), a poor harvest decreases the quantity supplied to 15 million tonnes. The momentary supply curve shifts leftward to MS_1, the price rises to $300 a tonne, and farm revenue increases to $4.5 billion. A *decrease* in supply brings a rise in price and an *increase* in farm revenue.

Bumper Harvest In Fig. 6.12(b) a bumper harvest increases the quantity supplied to 25 million tonnes. The momentary supply curve shifts rightward to MS_2, the price falls to $100 a tonne, and farm revenue decreases to $2.5 billion. An *increase* in supply brings a fall in price and a *decrease* in farm revenue.

Elasticity of Demand Farm revenue and the quantity produced fluctuate in opposite directions because the demand for wheat is *inelastic*. The percentage change in the quantity demanded is less than the percentage change in price. In Fig. 6.12(a), the increase in revenue from the higher price ($1.5 billion—the light blue area) exceeds the decrease in revenue from the smaller quantity ($1 billion—the red area). And in Fig. 6.12(b), the decrease in revenue from the lower price ($2 billion—the red area) exceeds the increase in revenue from the increase in the quantity sold ($0.5 billion—the light blue area).

FIGURE 6.12   ⓧ myeconlab
Harvests, Farm Prices, and Farm Revenue

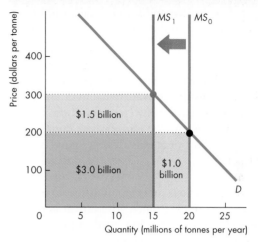

(a) Poor harvest: revenue increases

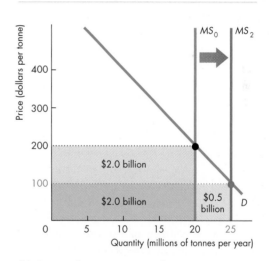

(b) Bumper harvest: revenue decreases

The demand curve for wheat is D. In normal times, the supply curve is MS_0 and 20 million tonnes are sold for $200 a tonne. Farm revenue is $4 billion a year.

In part (a), a poor harvest decreases supply to MS_1. The price rises to $300 a tonne, and farm revenue increases to $4.5 billion—the $1.5 billion increase from the higher price (light blue area) exceeds the $1 billion decrease from the smaller quantity sold (red area).

In part (b), a bumper harvest increases supply to MS_2. The price falls to $100 a tonne, and farm revenue decreases to $2.5 billion—the $2 billion decrease from the lower price (red area) exceeds the $0.5 billion increase from the increase in the quantity sold (light blue area).

If demand is *elastic*, farm revenue and the quantity produced fluctuate in the same direction. Bumper harvests increase revenue, and poor harvests decrease it. But the demand for most agricultural products is inelastic, so the case we've studied is the relevant one.

Avoiding a Fallacy of Composition Although *total* farm revenue increases when there is a poor harvest, the revenue of those *individual* farmers whose entire crop is wiped out decreases. Those whose crop is unaffected gain. So a poor harvest is not good news for all farmers.

Because the markets for farm products often confront farmers with low incomes, government intervention occurs in these markets. In Canada, there are more than 100 farm marketing boards, supported by federal and provincial governments. A **farm marketing board** is a regulatory agency that intervenes in an agricultural market to stabilize the price.

Farm marketing boards might use price floors that work a bit like the minimum wage to stabilize farm prices. You've already seen that a price floor creates a surplus and is inefficient. These same conclusions apply to markets for farm products. But farm marketing boards often use two other methods:

- Subsidies
- Production quotas

Subsidies

A **subsidy** is a payment made by the government to a producer. To see the effects of a subsidy, we'll look at a market for peanuts. Figure 6.13 shows this market. The demand for peanuts is *D* and the supply of peanuts is *S*. With no subsidy, the price is $40 a tonne and 40 million tonnes of peanuts are produced.

Suppose that the government introduces a subsidy of $20 a tonne. A subsidy is like a negative tax. You've seen that a tax is equivalent to an increase in cost. A subsidy is equivalent to a decrease in cost. And a decrease in cost brings an increase in supply.

To determine the position of the new supply curve, we subtract the subsidy from farmers' minimum supply-price. Without a subsidy, farmers are willing to offer 40 million tonnes a year for $40 a tonne. So with a subsidy of $20 a tonne, they will offer 40 million tonnes a year if the price is as low as

FIGURE 6.13   myeconlab

A Subsidy Increases Production

With no subsidy, 40 million tonnes a year are produced at $40 a tonne. A subsidy of $20 a tonne shifts the supply curve rightward to *S – subsidy*. The quantity produced increases to 60 million tonnes a year, the price falls to $30 a tonne, and farmers receive $50 a tonne (the price plus the subsidy). Because marginal cost ($50) exceeds marginal benefit ($30), a deadweight loss arises.

$20 a tonne. The supply curve shifts to the red curve labelled *S – subsidy*.

Equilibrium occurs where the new supply curve intersects the demand curve at 60 million tonnes a year. The price falls to $30 a tonne, but the price plus subsidy received by farmers rises to $50 a tonne.

Because the supply curve *S* is the marginal cost curve, and the demand curve is the marginal benefit curve, a subsidy raises marginal cost above marginal benefit and creates a deadweight loss from overproduction.

The effects of subsidies spill over to the rest of the world. Because they lower the price, subsidized farmers offer some of their output for sale on the world market, which lowers the price in the rest of the world. Faced with lower prices, farmers in other countries decrease production and receive smaller revenues.

Farm subsidies are a major obstacle to achieving an efficient use of resources in the global markets for farm products and are a source of tension between Europe, the United States, and developing nations.

Production Quotas

The markets for milk, eggs, and poultry (among others) have, from time to time, been regulated with production quotas. A **production quota** is an upper limit to the quantity of a good that may be produced in a specified period. To discover the effects of quotas, we'll look at a market for milk in Fig. 6.14. With no quota, the price is $3 a tonne and 16 million tonnes a year are produced.

Suppose that the dairy farmers want to limit total production to get a higher price. They persuade the marketing board to introduce a production quota that limits milk production to a maximum of 14 million tonnes a year.

The effect of a production quota depends on whether it is set below or above the equilibrium quantity. If the government introduced a quota above 16 million tonnes a year, the equilibrium quantity in Fig. 6.14, nothing would change because dairy farmers are already producing less than the quota. But a quota of 14 million is less than the equilibrium quantity. Figure 6.14 shows the effects of the production quota.

To implement the quota, each farmer is assigned a production limit and the total of the production limits equals 14 million tonnes. Production that in total exceeds 14 million tonnes is illegal, so we've shaded the illegal region above the quota. Farmers are no longer permitted to produce the equilibrium quantity because it is in the illegal region. As in the case of price ceilings and floors, market forces and political forces are in conflict.

When the marketing board sets a production quota, it does not regulate the price. Market forces determine it. In the example in Fig. 6.14, with production limited to 14 million tonnes a year, the market price rises to $5 a tonne.

The quota not only raises the price but also *lowers* the marginal cost of producing milk because the farmers slide down their supply (and marginal cost) curves.

A production quota is inefficient because it results in underproduction. At the quota quantity, marginal benefit is equal to the market price and marginal cost is less than the market price, so marginal benefit exceeds marginal cost.

Because of these effects of a quota, such arrangements are often popular with producers and in some cases, producers, not governments, attempt to implement them. But it is hard for quotas to work when they are voluntary. The reason is that each producer has an incentive to cheat and produce a little bit more than the allotted quota. You can see why by comparing the market price and marginal cost. If one producer

could get away with a tiny increase in production, her or his profit would increase. But if all producers cheat by producing above the quota, the market moves back towards the unregulated equilibrium and the gain for producers disappears.

FIGURE 6.14
A Quota Limits Production

With no quota, 16 million tonnes a year are produced at $3 a tonne. A quota of 14 million tonnes a year reduces the equilibrium quantity to 14 million tonnes a year, the price rises to $5 a tonne, and marginal cost falls to $2 a tonne. Because marginal cost ($2) is less than marginal benefit ($5), a deadweight loss arises from underproduction.

REVIEW QUIZ

1 How do poor harvests and bumper harvests influence farm prices and farm revenues?
2 Explain how a subsidy influences farm prices and output. How does a subsidy affect farm revenues?
3 Explain how a production quota influences farm prices and output. How does a production quota affect farm revenues?

myeconlab   **Study Plan 6.4**

Governments intervene in some markets by making it illegal to trade in a good. Let's now see how these markets work.

Markets for Illegal Goods

THE MARKETS FOR MANY GOODS AND SERVICES are regulated, and buying and selling some goods is illegal. The best-known examples of such goods are drugs, such as marijuana, cocaine, Ecstasy, and heroin.

Despite the fact that these drugs are illegal, trade in them is a multibillion-dollar business. This trade can be understood by using the same economic model and principles that explain trade in legal goods. To study the market for illegal goods, we're first going to examine the prices and quantities that would prevail if these goods were not illegal. Next, we'll see how prohibition works. Then we'll see how a tax might be used to limit the consumption of these goods.

A Free Market for Drugs

Figure 6.15 shows the market for drugs. The demand curve, *D,* shows that, other things remaining the same, the lower the price of drugs, the larger is the quantity of drugs demanded. The supply curve, *S,* shows that, other things remaining the same, the lower the price of drugs, the smaller is the quantity supplied. If drugs were not illegal, the quantity bought and sold would be Q_C and the price would be P_C.

A Market for Illegal Drugs

When a good is illegal, the cost of trading in the good increases. By how much the cost increases and who incurs the cost depend on the penalties for violating the law and the effectiveness with which the law is enforced. The larger the penalties and the more effective the policing, the higher are the costs. Penalties might be imposed on sellers, buyers, or both.

Penalties on Sellers Drug dealers in Canada face large penalties if their activities are detected. For example, a grower of marijuana with 50 plants could be fined and imprisoned for up to 14 years. A heroin trafficker could pay a fine and be imprisoned for life. These penalties are part of the cost of supplying illegal drugs, and they bring a decrease in supply—a leftward shift in the supply curve. To determine the new supply curve, we add the cost of breaking the law to the minimum price that drug dealers are willing to accept. In Fig. 6.15, the cost of breaking the law by selling drugs (*CBL*) is added to the minimum price that dealers will accept and the supply curve shifts

FIGURE 6.15
A Market for an Illegal Good

The demand curve for drugs is *D,* and the supply curve is *S.* If drugs are not illegal, the quantity bought and sold is Q_C at a price of P_C—point *E.* If selling drugs is illegal, the cost of breaking the law by selling drugs (*CBL*) is added to the minimum supply-price and supply decreases to *S + CBL.* The market moves to point *F.*

If buying drugs is illegal, the cost of breaking the law is subtracted from the maximum price that buyers are willing to pay, and demand decreases to *D – CBL.* The market moves to point *G.*

With both buying and selling illegal, the supply curve and the demand curve shift and the market moves to point *H.* The market price remains at P_C, but the market price plus the penalty for buying rises—point *J*—and the market price minus the penalty for selling falls—point *K.*

leftward to *S + CBL.* If penalties were imposed only on sellers, the market would move from point *E* to point *F.*

Penalties on Buyers In Canada, it is illegal to *possess* drugs such as marijuana, cocaine, Ecstasy, and heroin. For example, possession of 30 grams of marijuana can bring a one-year prison term and a $2,000 fine and possession of heroin can bring a seven-year prison term. Penalties fall on buyers, and the cost of breaking the law must be subtracted from the value of the good to determine the maximum price buyers are willing to pay for the drugs. Demand decreases, and the demand curve shifts leftward. In Fig. 6.15, the demand curve shifts to $D - CBL$. If penalties were imposed only on buyers, the market would move from point E to point G.

Penalties on Both Sellers and Buyers If penalties are imposed on both sellers *and* buyers, both supply and demand decrease. In Fig. 6.15, the costs of breaking the law are the same for both buyers and sellers, so both curves shift leftward by the same amount. The market moves to point H. The market price remains at the competitive market price P_C, but the quantity bought decreases to Q_P. The buyer pays P_C plus the cost of breaking the law, which is P_B. And the seller receives P_C minus the cost of breaking the law, which is P_S.

The larger the penalties and the greater the degree of law enforcement, the larger is the decrease in demand and/or supply. If the penalties are heavier on sellers, the supply curve shifts farther than the demand curve and the market price rises above P_C. If the penalties are heavier on buyers, the demand curve shifts farther than the supply curve and the market price falls below P_C. In Canada, the penalties on sellers are larger than those on buyers, so the quantity of drugs traded decreases and the market price increases compared with a free market.

With high enough penalties and effective law enforcement, it is possible to decrease demand and/or supply to the point at which the quantity bought is zero. But in reality, such an outcome is unusual. It does not happen in Canada in the case of illegal drugs. The key reason is the high cost of law enforcement and insufficient resources for the police to achieve effective enforcement. Because of this situation, some people suggest that drugs (and other illegal goods) should be legalized and sold openly but should also be taxed at a high rate in the same way that legal drugs such as alcohol are taxed. How would such an arrangement work?

Legalizing and Taxing Drugs

From your study of the effects of taxes, it is easy to see that the quantity of drugs bought could be decreased if drugs were legalized and taxed. A sufficiently high tax could be imposed to decrease supply, raise the price, and achieve the same decrease in the quantity bought as with a prohibition on drugs. The government would collect a large tax revenue.

Illegal Trading to Evade the Tax It is likely that an extremely high tax rate would be needed to cut the quantity of drugs bought to the level prevailing with a prohibition. It is also likely that many drug dealers and consumers would try to cover up their activities to evade the tax. If they did act in this way, they would face the cost of breaking the law—the tax law. If the penalty for tax law violation is as severe and as effectively policed as drug-dealing laws, the analysis we've already conducted applies also to this case. The quantity of drugs bought would depend on the penalties for law breaking and on the way in which the penalties are assigned to buyers and sellers.

Taxes Versus Prohibition: Some Pros and Cons Which is more effective: prohibition or taxes? In favour of taxes and against prohibition is the fact that the tax revenue can be used to make law enforcement more effective. It can also be used to run a more effective education campaign against illegal drug use. In favour of prohibition and against taxes is the fact that prohibition sends a signal that might influence preferences, decreasing the demand for illegal drugs. Also, some people intensely dislike the idea of the government profiting from trade in harmful substances.

REVIEW QUIZ

1 How does the imposition of a penalty for selling an illegal drug influence demand, supply, price, and the quantity of the drug consumed?
2 How does the imposition of a penalty for possessing an illegal drug influence demand, supply, price, and the quantity of the drug consumed?
3 How does the imposition of a penalty for selling *or* possessing an illegal drug influence demand, supply, price, and the quantity of the drug consumed?
4 Is there any case for legalizing drugs?

myeconlab **Study Plan 6.5**

◆ You now know how to use the demand and supply model to predict prices, to study government actions in markets, and to study the sources and costs of inefficiency. Before you leave this topic, take a look at *Reading Between the Lines* on pp. 142–143 about the rise in the minium wage in Alberta.

The Minimum Wage in Action

COCHRANE TIMES, AUGUST 24, 2005

Alberta's minimum wage finally gets boost

As the minimum wage increases in Alberta, consumers may be the ones paying the price.

On Sept. 1, the minimum wage in our province will increase from a measly $5.90 an hour to $7 an hour, putting the minimum wage on par with most other Canadian provinces, a move that unfortunately may mean menu increases at some local restaurants. ...

As a reaction to the minimum wage increase, Taylor last month raised starting wages at McDonald's from $6.50 (part time) and $8 (full time) to $7.50 (part time) and $9 (full time).

And the owner said there's no way the pay increase will not sting a little bit.

"I use about 1,200 hours of labour weekly, so a dollar raise across the board ... it's got to hurt," he said.

"I mean, I can't really see how it won't affect prices eventually."

Across town at Dairy Queen, however, the owner said prices aren't likely to increase. ...

While the wage increase may mean shelling out a few cents more for a Big Mac, 45,000 Albertans in entry-level jobs will benefit from the wage increase.

"Increasing the minimum wage is one way of ensuring Albertans get a better start in the workforce," said Human Resources and Employment Minister Mike Cardinal in a recent news release. "Most Albertans, including employers and employees, agree that the minimum wage should be raised." ...

Essence of the Story

■ The minimum wage in Alberta increased from $5.90 an hour to $7 an hour on September 1, 2005.

■ McDonald's increased its wage rates from $6.50 to $7.50 for part-time workers and from $8 to $9 for full-time workers in August.

■ McDonald's hires 1,200 hours of labour a week.

■ 45,000 Albertans will benefit from the wage increase.

■ Alberta's employment minister said "Increasing the minimum wage is one way of ensuring Albertans get a better start in the workforce."

Economic Analysis

■ Minimum wage rates in Canada range from $6.25 an hour in Newfoundland to $8.50 an hour in Nunavut. Figure 1 shows the data.

■ The minimum wage affects younger low-skilled workers more than older and more skilled workers.

■ A rise in the minimum wage rate in Alberta will decrease employment and increase the unemployment rate of young workers.

■ Figure 2 shows the Alberta labour market for young workers. The demand curve is *LD* and the supply curve is *LS*. (The assumed elasticity of demand is 0.5 and the assumed elasticity of supply is 0.25.)

■ Before September 1, 2005, when the minimum wage rate was $5.90 an hour, 45,000 young people were employed and approximately 5,000 were unemployed.

■ The rise in the minimum wage decreases the quantity of labour demanded, increases the quantity of labour supplied, and increases the unemployment of young workers.

■ With the assumed elasticities of demand and supply, unemployment approximately doubles.

■ If the elasticities are smaller than those assumed, unemployment will increase by a smaller amount.

■ The outcome in Fig. 2 assumes *ceteris paribus*—other things remaining the same.

■ Figure 3 shows that because other things are not the same across the provinces, many factors other than the minimum wage influence the unemployment rate of young workers.

■ The extent of unemployment among young workers, measured here by the ratio of the unemployment rates of the under 25s to the over 25s, is correlated with the minimum wage but the correlation is weak.

You're the Voter

■ Would you support or oppose a rise in the minimum wage in your own province?

■ Can you think of a better way of improving the incomes of young workers who have few skills?

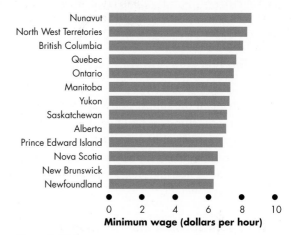

Figure 1 Minimum wage rates across Canada

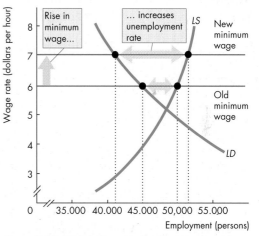

Figure 2 Alberta's labour market for young workers

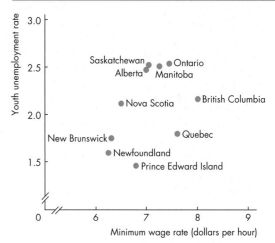

Figure 3 Minimum wage and youth unemployment rates

143

SUMMARY

KEY POINTS

Housing Markets and Rent Ceilings
(pp. 124–128)

- A decrease in the supply of housing raises rents.
- Higher rents stimulate building, and in the long run, the quantity of housing increases and rents fall.
- A rent ceiling that is set below the equilibrium rent creates a housing shortage, wasteful search, and a black market.

The Labour Market and the Minimum Wage
(pp. 128–131)

- A decrease in the demand for low-skilled labour lowers the wage rate and reduces employment.
- The lower wage rate encourages people with low skill to acquire more skill, which decreases the supply of low-skilled labour and, in the long run, raises their wage rate.
- A minimum wage set above the equilibrium wage rate creates unemployment and increases the amount of time people spend searching for a job.
- A minimum wage hits low-skilled young people hardest.

Taxes (pp. 132–136)

- A tax raises price but usually by less than the tax.
- The shares of a tax paid by buyers and by sellers depend on the elasticity of demand and the elasticity of supply.
- The less elastic the demand and the more elastic the supply, the greater is the price increase, the smaller is the quantity decrease, and the larger is the share of the tax paid by buyers.
- If demand is perfectly elastic or supply is perfectly inelastic, sellers pay the entire tax. And if demand is perfectly inelastic or supply is perfectly elastic, buyers pay the entire tax.

Subsidies and Quotas (pp. 137–139)

- Farm revenues fluctuate because supply fluctuates. Because the demand for most farm products is inelastic, a decrease in supply increases farm revenue, while an increase in supply decreases farm revenue.

- A subsidy is like a negative tax. It lowers the price and leads to inefficient overproduction.
- A quota leads to inefficient underproduction, which raises the price.

Markets for Illegal Goods (pp. 140–141)

- Penalties on sellers of an illegal good increase the cost of selling the good and decrease its supply. Penalties on buyers decrease their willingness to pay and decrease the demand for the good.
- The higher the penalties and the more effective the law enforcement, the smaller is the quantity bought.
- A tax that is set at a sufficiently high rate will decrease the quantity of drug consumed, but there will be a tendency for the tax to be evaded.

KEY FIGURES

KEY TERMS

PROBLEMS

Go to **myeconlab** for solutions to odd-numbered problems and additional exercises.

1. The figure shows the demand for and supply of rental housing in the Village.

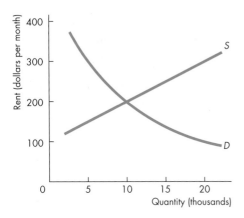

a. What is the market equilibrium?

If a rent ceiling is set at $150 a month, what is

b. The quantity of housing rented?
c. The shortage of housing?
d. The maximum price that someone is willing to pay for the last unit of housing available?

2. The figure shows the demand for and supply of rental housing in Townsville.

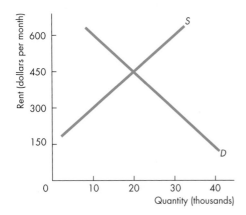

a. What is the market equilibrium?

If a rent ceiling is set at $300 a month, what is

b. The quantity of housing rented?
c. The shortage of housing?
d. The maximum price that someone is willing to pay for the last unit available?

3. The table gives the demand for and supply of teenage labour.

Wage rate (dollars per hour)	Quantity demanded	Quantity supplied
	(hours per month)	
4	3,000	1,000
5	2,500	1,500
6	2,000	2,000
7	1,500	2,500
8	1,000	3,000

a. What are the equilibrium wage rate and level of employment?
b. What is the quantity of unemployment?
c. If a minimum wage of $5 an hour is set for teenagers, how many hours do they work?
d. If a minimum wage of $5 an hour is set for teenagers, how many hours of their labour is unemployed?
e. If a minimum wage is set at $7 an hour for teenagers, what are quantities of employment and unemployment?
f. If a minimum wage is set at $7 an hour and demand increases by 500 hours a month, what is the wage rate paid to teenagers and how many hours of their labour are unemployed?

4. The table gives the demand for and supply of labour of high school graduates.

Wage rate (dollars per hour)	Quantity demanded	Quantity supplied
	(hours per month)	
8	10,000	4,000
9	8,000	6,000
10	6,000	8,000
11	4,000	10,000
12	2,000	12,000

a. On a graph, mark in the equilibrium wage rate and level of employment.
b. What is the level of unemployment?
c. If a minimum wage is set at $9 an hour, how many hours do high school graduates work?
d. If a minimum wage is set at $9 an hour, how many hours of labour are unemployed?
e. If a minimum wage is set at $10 an hour, what are employment and unemployment?
f. If the minimum wage is $10 an hour and demand decreases by 2,000 hours a month, what is the wage rate paid to high school graduates and how many hours of their labour are unemployed?

5. The table gives the demand and supply schedules for chocolate brownies:

Price (cents per brownie)	Quantity demanded	Quantity supplied
	(millions per day)	
50	5	3
60	4	4
70	3	5
80	2	6
90	1	7

a. If brownies are not taxed, what is the price of a brownie and how many are consumed?
b. If brownies are taxed at 20¢ each, what is the price and how many brownies are consumed? Who pays the tax?

6. Demand and supply schedules for roses are

Price (dollars per bunch)	Quantity demanded	Quantity supplied
	(bunches per week)	
10	100	40
12	90	60
14	80	80
16	70	100
18	60	120

a. If there is no tax on roses, what is the price and how many bunches are bought?
b. If a tax of $6 a bunch is introduced, what is the price and how many bunches are bought? Who pays the tax?

7. Demand and supply schedules for rice are

Price (dollars per box)	Quantity demanded	Quantity supplied
	(boxes per week)	
1.00	3,500	500
1.10	3,250	1,000
1.20	3,000	1,500
1.30	2,750	2,000
1.40	2,500	2,500
1.50	2,250	3,000
1.60	2,000	3,500

If the government introduces a subsidy of $0.30 a box on rice, what are the price of rice, the marginal cost of producing rice, and the quantity produced?

8. In problem 7, if instead of a subsidy, the government sets a quota of 2,000 boxes a week, what now are your answers?

CRITICAL THINKING

1. Study *Reading Between the Lines* (pp. 142–143) about the market for young workers in Alberta.
   a. If the minimum wage in Alberta were abolished, what do you predict would happen to the quantity of labour employed and the average wage rate?
   b. With the abolition of the minimum wage in Alberta, who would gain and who would lose? Would *society* gain or lose?
   c. Why do you think a large number of Albertans and the government of Alberta supported an increase in the minimum wage in 2005?

WEB EXERCISES

Use the links on myeconlab to work the following exercise.

1. Find information about living wage campaigns.
   a. What is the campaign for a living wage?
   b. How would you distinguish the minimum wage from a living wage?
   c. If the living wage campaign succeeds in getting wages increased above their equilibrium levels, how would you expect the living wage to affect (i) the quantity of labour demanded, (ii) the quantity of labour supplied and, (iii) the amount of unemployment?
   d. Would a living wage above the equilibrium wage be efficient?
   e. Who would stand to gain from a living wage above the equilibrium wage?
   f. Who would stand to lose from a living wage above the equilibrium wage?
   g. Would a living wage above the equilibrium wage be fair?
2. Find information about sugar quotas in Europe. Why do you think the European nations assign production quotas for sugar? If the European sugar quotas are less than the equilibrium quantities, who benefits from and who pays for the quotas?

The Amazing Market

The four chapters that you've just studied explain how markets work. The market is an amazing instrument. It enables people who have never met and who know nothing about each other to interact and do business. It also enables us to allocate our scarce resources to the uses that we value most highly. Markets can be very simple or highly organized.

A simple market is one that the American historian Daniel J. Boorstin describes in *The Discoverers* (p. 161). In the late fourteenth century,

> *The Muslim caravans that went southward from Morocco across the Atlas Mountains arrived after twenty days at the shores of the Senegal River. There the Moroccan traders laid out separate piles of salt, of beads from Ceutan coral, and cheap manufactured goods. Then they retreated out of sight. The local tribesmen, who lived in the strip mines where they dug their gold, came to the shore and put a heap of gold beside each pile of Moroccan goods. Then they, in turn, went out of view, leaving the Moroccan traders either to take the gold offered for a particular pile or to reduce the pile of their merchandise to suit the offered price in gold. Once again the Moroccan traders withdrew, and the process went on. By this system of commercial etiquette, the Moroccans collected their gold.*

An organized market is the Toronto Stock Exchange, which trades many millions of stocks each day. Another is an auction at which the government sells rights to broadcasters and cellular telephone companies for the use of the airwaves.

All of these markets determine the prices at which exchanges take place and enable both buyers and sellers to benefit.

Everything and anything that can be exchanged is traded in markets. There are markets for goods and services; for resources such as labour, capital, and raw materials; for dollars, pounds, and yen; for goods to be delivered now and for goods to be delivered in the future. Only the imagination places limits on what can be traded in markets.

You began your study of markets in Chapter 3 by learning about the laws of demand and supply. There, you discovered the forces that make prices adjust to coordinate buying plans and selling plans. In Chapter 4, you learned how to calculate and use the concept of elasticity to predict the responsiveness of prices and quantities to changes in supply and demand. In Chapter 5, you studied efficiency and discovered the conditions under which a competitive market sends resources to uses in which they are valued most highly. And finally, in Chapter 6, you studied markets in action. There, you learned how markets cope with change and discovered how they operate when governments intervene to fix prices, impose taxes or quotas, subsidize production, or make some goods illegal.

The laws of demand and supply that you've learned and used in these four chapters were discovered during the nineteenth century by some remarkable economists. We conclude our study of demand and supply and markets by looking at the lives and times of some of these economists and by talking to a leading Canadian economist who studies labour markets.

Discovering the Laws of Demand and Supply

THE ECONOMIST

Alfred Marshall *(1842–1924) grew up in an England that was being transformed by the railroad and by the expansion of manufacturing. Mary Paley was one of Marshall's students at Cambridge, and when Alfred and Mary married, in 1877, celibacy rules barred Alfred from continuing to teach at Cambridge. By 1884, with more liberal rules, the Marshalls returned to Cambridge, where Alfred became Professor of Political Economy.*

Many others had a hand in refining the theory of demand and supply, but the first thorough and complete statement of the theory as we know it today was set out by Alfred Marshall, with the acknowledged help of Mary Paley Marshall. Published in 1890, this monumental treatise, The Principles of Economics, *became the textbook on economics on both sides of the Atlantic for almost half a century. Marshall was an outstanding mathematician, but he kept mathematics and even diagrams in the background. His supply and demand diagram appears only in a footnote.*

THE ISSUES

The laws of demand and supply that you studied in Chapter 3 were discovered during the 1830s by Antoine-Augustin Cournot (1801–1877), a professor of mathematics at the University of Lyon, France. Although Cournot was the first to use demand and supply, it was the development and expansion of the railroads during the 1850s that gave the newly emerging theory its first practical applications. Railroads then were at the cutting edge of technology just as airlines are today. And as in the airline industry today, competition among the railroads was fierce.

Dionysius Lardner (1793–1859), an Irish professor of philosophy at the University of London, used demand and supply to show railroad companies how they could increase their profits by cutting rates on long-distance business on which competition was fiercest and by raising rates on short-haul business on which they had less to fear from other transportation suppliers.

Today, economists use the principles that Lardner worked out during the 1850s to calculate the freight rates and passenger fares that will give airlines the largest possible profit. And the rates calculated have a lot in common with the railroad rates of the nineteenth century. On local routes on which there is little competition, fares per kilometre are highest, and on long-distance routes on which the airlines compete fiercely, fares per kilometre are lowest.

Known satirically among scientists of the day as "Dionysius Diddler," Lardner worked on an amazing range of problems from astronomy to railway engineering to economics. A colourful character, he would have been a regular guest on late-night talk shows if they had been around in the 1850s. Lardner visited the École des Ponts et Chaussées (School of

Bridges and Roads) in Paris and must have learned a great deal from Jules Dupuit.

In France, Jules Dupuit (1804–1866), a French engineer/economist, used demand to calculate the benefits from building a bridge and, once the bridge was built, for calculating the toll to charge for its use. His work was the forerunner of what is today called *cost-benefit analysis*. Working with the principles invented by Dupuit, economists today calculate the costs and benefits of highways and airports, dams, and power stations.

NOW

Today, using the same principles that Dupuit devised, economists calculate whether the benefits of expanding airports and air-traffic control facilities are sufficient to cover their costs. Airline companies use the principles developed by Lardner to set their prices and to decide when to offer "seat sales." Like the railroads before them, the airlines charge a high price per kilometre on short flights, for which they face little competition, and a low price per kilometre on long flights, for which competition is fierce.

THEN

Dupuit used the law of demand to determine whether a bridge or canal would be valued enough by its users to justify the cost of building it. Lardner first worked out the relationship between the cost of production and supply and used demand and supply theory to explain the costs, prices, and profits of railroad operations. He also used the theory to discover ways of increasing revenue by raising rates on short-haul business and lowering them on long-distance freight.

Markets do an amazing job. The laws of demand and supply help us to understand how markets work. But in some situations, a market must be designed and institutions must be created to enable the market to function well. Also, the item traded often makes a crucial difference to how the market works. One market that has some special features is the labour market, as you will discover in the conversation on the following pages with Paul Beaudry, one of Canada's leading economists.

TALKING WITH

Paul Beaudry is a Professor of Economics at the University of British Columbia and currently holds the Canada Research Chair in Economics. He is also a Faculty Research Fellow at the National Bureau of Economic Research in the United States. He was born in Québec City in 1960. He obtained a bachelor's degree in Economics at the Université Laval, a master's degree at the University of British Columbia, and a doctoral degree at Princeton University. Professor Beaudry's research is concerned with the functioning of markets, particularly the labour market. Professor Beaudry was granted the Bank of Canada's Research Fellowship for 2005.

Paul Beaudry

Benoît Carmichael and Patrick González (co-authors of our French Canadian edition) talked with Paul Beaudry about his work and the progress economists have made since the time of Alfred Marshall in understanding how markets work.

Professor Beaudry, what attracted you to economics?

Several factors influenced my choice. During my secondary education and at the beginning of the CEGEP, I was mostly interested in mathematics and science. Then, at the university, I was introduced to philosophy and to philosophical questions. Philosophy classes deeply moved me. In fact, they changed my vision of the world. I became passionate about fundamental questions such as: Why do I exist? What is the notion of good and evil? What is a just society?

All these questions started to make me doubt. Initially, I thought that I would follow a career in science or engineering, but all these questions put me in a state of uncertainty. So I decided to stop my studies and travel. I worked in construction, so I could afford a big trip for myself. I travelled through all of Europe, North Africa, and Turkey. While on these trips, I talked a lot about philosophical and social questions with the people that I met. It was a fabulous experience!

During these talks economic questions were often raised: Why are certain countries rich and others poor? What should we do to reduce these inequalities? I quickly realized that the questions I understood the least were those related to the economics, and I thought that these question were important ones. Moreover, I was beginning to believe that several of the fundamental philosophical questions I was thinking about were impossible to solve. But this was not the case for economic questions. So I decided to get back to my studies and to study economics. I found that studies in economics allowed me both to address important social and human questions and to use formal mathematics tools that I liked.

What do we know today about the functioning of markets that Alfred Marshall ignored?

In the classical framework of Alfred Marshall, prices play an important role, but quite a simple one. When the price of a good rises, consumers want to consume less of it, and producers want to produce more of it. In Marshall's world, economic market participants do not try to extract information from prices, they react in a mechanical way.

On the other hand, in several markets, prices play a much more complex role than that envisioned by Marshall. Let's take the example of the stock market. The holder of a share listed on the stock exchange won't necessarily want to sell it when its price increases. Indeed, the increase in the share price can signify that the underlying company is in a good position to make profits; the holder will then want to wait for the share price to increase again. Let's take another example. When we buy a bottle of wine, we often think that its price is an indication of the quality of the wine. The information role of prices did not appear in Marshall's work.

In your research work, you are very interested in labour markets. What are the characteristics of labour markets that make them different from other markets?

When a company hires someone, it must ensure that the person is sufficiently motivated to perform the required tasks diligently and not shirk. In contrast, when a company buys a tonne of steel to build a bridge, it needn't wonder about the steel's motivation to do its work. A labour market is therefore very different from other markets because it is made up of individuals who have their own motivations and objectives. That is why one of the roles of a good employer is to find a way to reconcile the interests of an employee with those of the company.

For most goods, this kind of problem doesn't exist. Buying a good at the lowest possible price often proves to be the best strategy. However, an employer has to recognize that his employees want to be treated fairly and impartially. If he doesn't pay them enough, it is most probable that they won't put in much effort or show very much enthusiasm for their work.

> " *... when a company buys a tonne of steel to build a bridge, it needn't wonder about the steel's motivation to do its work. A labour market is ... different ... because it is made of individuals who have their own motivations and objectives.* "

Marshall believed that the market would direct young people towards the jobs they do best. But he believed that taxes should cover the cost of education. Today, some people see education as an investment in human capital that should be paid for by the families who benefit. What is your view on this issue?

Education has two aspects. It increases the skills of an individual in the labour market, and therefore also increases a person's earnings. Also, thanks to education, people are more informed, and that is important for the functioning of a democracy. In the first case, the gain is essentially private, so it seems reasonable to ask young people or their families to contribute to the costs of education. However, in the second case, the gain obtained through education is a social gain, so it seems fair that the state should cover a part of costs of education. This is, in fact, what we now observe. It remains very difficult to make decisions about what percentage of university fees students should pay? 75 percent? 50 percent? 25 percent? This question is open to debate.

Over the past 25 years in North America, we have observed a deterioration in the relative compensation of low-skilled workers. However, in European countries such as Germany, this decrease hasn't been as large. What explains this difference?

It is a very good question, and a topic that still raises lots of discussion. My own research puts forward the important role of demography. In North America, the baby boom of the 1950s and 1960s considerably increased the work force at the end of the 1970s and the beginning of the 1980s. On the other hand, during the same period, neither private savings nor investment in physical capital increased. Thus, the increase in labour supply and the absence of an increase in the supply of physical capital created a relative shortage of physical capital.

The economy reacted to this shortage in several ways. We have observed a strong tendency towards the adoption of new methods of production which use physical capital in an efficient way, as well as an increase in imports of goods that use physical capital in an intensive way. These two changes have resulted in a reduction of the demand for labour, in particular among less-qualified workers. This, in turn, has

> " What we have to remember is that the labour market is principally a market of long-term relations. "

resulted in an increase of the gap in income between qualified and less-qualified workers. In Germany, where the baby boom was not so importance, the problem of a relative shortage of physical capital did not occur. The structure of employment remained stable and the income of less-qualified workers did not decrease.

Through your work, you have demonstrated that people who enter the labour market during a time of recession have less interesting career prospects than those who enter it during a period of expansion. Why is this so?

In spite of the fact that the labour market does not function exactly as the apple market does, it still is a market which reflects the strengths of the supply and demand model. In times of recession, the demand for labour is weak and people who enter the labour market in such times receive less attractive job offers.

What we have to remember is that the labour market is principally a market of long-term relations. Thus, if a worker enters the labour market during a good period, he will generally manage to negotiate a job that will offer him promising career prospects. Conversely, a worker who enters the labour market during a time of recession will generally obtain a badly paid job which offers mediocre career prospects. This is in fact what the analytical frame-

152

work of supply and demand predicts in the case of a market based on long-term relations.

How should the government intervene in the labour market when it is undergoing profound structural change? Are the usual policies (such as employment insurance) still appropriate?

First, we have to understand that the labour market is in a state of continuous flux. It is very difficult for a government to make the distinction between a structural change and cyclical change (the latter being more temporary). Government intervention is therefore limited. At best, the state can help individuals absorb the many ups and downs of the labour market without having to determine whether the change is structural or not. This is precisely the role played by employment insurance.

Unfortunately, employment insurance programs are not perfect, and they often do not help people adapt to change. Employment insurance must be flexible and allow people to go back to university or to experiment with new types of jobs. Too often, employment insurance incites people to the status quo and in so doing does not fulfill its primary function: that of helping workers to adapt to a labour market in perpetual flux.

How do you recognize a good economics student? Are there any particular skills that you are looking for?

A good economics student is a student who likes history and politics and who is not afraid of mathematics. A good economic student is one who observes society and who asks why things are the way they are.

A characteristic that I always look for in an economics student is open-mindedness. A student must not have too many preconceived ideas or be too politically committed. If he or she is too involved in a social cause, he or she often loses some sense of objectivity. That said, the student must be passionate about social issues but shouldn't believe that he or she already knows all the answers and risks becoming the champion of a cause instead of an economics researcher.

Emotions and principles have their place, but facts and scientific methods are the very essence of the rigorous economic research that provides answers about the functioning of the economy.

Utility and Demand

Water, Water, Everywhere

We need water to live. We don't need diamonds for much besides decoration. If the benefits of water far outweigh the benefits of diamonds, why does water cost practically nothing while diamonds are expensive?

When a winter storm cuts off the power supply, the prices of alternative sources of heat and light, such as firewood and candles, rise dramatically. But people buy as much firewood and as many candles as they can get their hands on. Our demand for goods that provide heat and light is price inelastic. Why?

When the personal computer (PC) was introduced in 1980, it cost more than $5,000 and consumers didn't buy very many. Since then, the price has tumbled and people are buying PCs in enormous quantities. Our demand for PCs is price elastic. What makes the demand for some things price elastic while the demand for others is price inelastic?

When you buy a monthly transit pass, each additional ride you take is free. What limits the quantity bought when something is "free"?

◆ In the preceding four chapters, we saw that demand has an important effect on the price of a good. But we did not analyze what exactly shapes a person's demand. This chapter examines household behaviour and its influence on demand. It explains why demand for some goods is elastic and the demand for other goods is inelastic. It also explains the paradox that the prices of diamonds and water are so out of proportion to their benefits. And in *Reading Between the Lines* at the end of the chapter, we look at demand when you can buy a monthly pass so the price of an additional unit is zero.

After studying this chapter, you will be able to

■ **Explain what limits a household's consumption choices**

■ **Describe preferences using the concept of utility and distinguish between total utility and marginal utility**

■ **Explain the marginal utility theory of consumer choice**

■ **Use marginal utility theory to predict the effects of changing prices and incomes**

■ **Explain the paradox of value**

The Household's Budget

A HOUSEHOLD'S BUDGET PLACES A LIMIT ON ITS consumption choices. And a household's preferences determine which of all its possible choices a household makes. We begin by studying the factors that determine the household's budget and its consumption possibilities.[1]

Consumption Possibilities

A household's consumption choices are constrained by the household's income and by the prices of the goods and services it buys. The household has a given amount of income to spend and cannot influence the prices of the goods and services it buys.

A household's *budget line* describes the limits to its consumption choices. Let's consider Lisa's household. Lisa has an income of $30 a month, and she plans to buy only two goods: movies and pop. The price of a movie is $6; the price of pop is $3 a six-pack. If Lisa spends all her income, she will reach the limits to her consumption of movies and pop.

Figure 7.1 illustrates Lisa's possible consumption of movies and pop. Rows *A* through *F* in the table show six possible ways of allocating $30 to these two goods. For example, Lisa can see 2 movies for $12 and buy 6 six-packs of pop for $18 (row *C*). Points *A* through *F* in the graph illustrate the possibilities presented in the table. The line passing through these points is Lisa's budget line.

Lisa's budget line is a constraint on her choices. It marks the boundary between what she can afford and what she cannot afford. She can afford all the points on the line and those inside it. She cannot afford the points outside the line. Lisa's consumption possibilities depend on the price of a movie, the price of pop, and her income. Her consumption possibilities change when the price of a movie, the price of a six-pack of pop, or her income changes.

The budget line can be described by the relative price of the two goods and the consumer's real income.

---

[1] This chapter and Chapter 8 deal with the same topic but explain two different methods of representing a household's preferences. The chapters are written on the assumption that you will most likely study only one of them. If you do study both chapters, you will find that the first sections of each that discuss the household budget constraint are very similar.

FIGURE 7.1
Consumption Possibilities

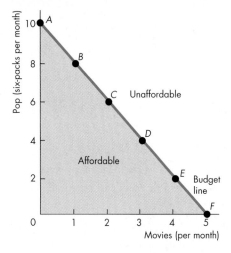

	Movies		Pop	
		Expenditure		Expenditure
Possibility	Quantity	(dollars)	Six-packs	(dollars)
A	0	0	10	30
B	1	6	8	24
C	2	12	6	18
D	3	18	4	12
E	4	24	2	6
F	5	30	0	0

Rows *A* through *F* in the table show six possible ways in which Lisa can allocate $30 to movies and pop. For example, Lisa can buy 2 movies and 6 six-packs of pop (row *C*). The combination in each row costs $30. These possibilities are points *A* through *F* in the graph. The line through those points is a boundary between what Lisa can afford and what she cannot afford. Her choices must lie along the line *AF* or inside the orange area.

Relative Price

A **relative price** is the price of one good divided by the price of another good. The price of a movie is $6 and the price of pop is $3 a six-pack, so the relative price of a movie in terms of pop is $6 per movie divided by $3 per six-pack, which equals 2 six-packs per movie. That is, to see one more movie, Lisa must

FIGURE 7.2

Changes in Prices and Income

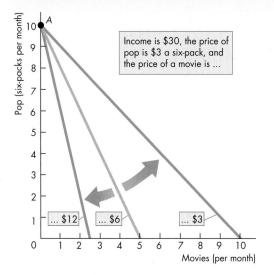

Income is $30, the price of pop is $3 a six-pack, and the price of a movie is ...

... $12   ... $6   ... $3

(a) A change in price

The price of pop is $3 a six-pack, the price of a movie is $6, and income is ...

... $18   ... $30   ... $42

(b) A change in income

In part (a), the price of a movie changes. A fall in the price from $6 to $3 rotates the budget line outward and makes it flatter. A rise in the price from $6 to $12 rotates the budget line inward and makes it steeper.

In part (b), income changes. A rise in income shifts the budget line outward and a fall in income shifts the budget line inward. But its slope does not change.

give up 2 six-packs. The opportunity cost of a movie is 2 six-packs.

A Price Change The relative price is the slope of the budget line. And when a price changes, the relative price changes, so the slope of the budget line changes. Figure 7.2(a) illustrates two changes. When the price of a movie falls from $6 to $3, Lisa's budget line rotates outward and she can afford to consume more of both goods. When the price of a movie rises from $6 to $12, Lisa's budget line rotates inward and she cannot afford as much of either good.

Real Income

A household's **real income** is the household's income expressed as the quantity of goods that the household can afford to buy. Expressed in terms of pop, Lisa's real income is 10 six-packs. This quantity is the maximum number of six-packs that she can buy. It is equal to her money income, $30, divided by the price of pop, $3 a six-pack.

A Change in Income Real income in terms of pop is the point at which the budget line intersects the *y*-axis. And when money income changes, real income changes, so the budget line shifts. But the slope of the budget line doesn't change. Figure 7.2(b) illustrates two changes in money income. When Lisa's money income rises from $30 to $42, her budget line shifts outward and she can afford to consume more of both goods. When Lisa's money income falls to $18, her budget line shifts inward and she cannot afford as much of either good.

REVIEW QUIZ

1 What does a household's budget line show?
2 How do real income and the relative price influence the budget line?
3 If the price of one good changes, what happens to the relative price and to the slope of the household's budget line?
4 If a household's money income changes and prices do not change, what happens to the household's real income

myeconlab Study Plan 7.1

Preferences and Utility

HOW DOES LISA DIVIDE HER AVAILABLE BUDGET between movies and pop? The answer depends on her likes and dislikes—her *preferences*. Economists use the concept of utility to describe preferences. The benefit or satisfaction that a person gets from the consumption of a good or service is called **utility**. Let's now see how we can use the concept of utility to describe preferences.

Total Utility

Total utility is the total benefit that a person gets from the consumption of goods and services. Total utility depends on the level of consumption—more consumption generally gives more total utility. The units of utility are arbitrary. Suppose we tell Lisa that we want to measure her utility. We're going to call the utility from no consumption zero. And we are going to call the utility she gets from 1 movie a month 50 units. We then ask her to tell us, on the same scale, how much she would like 2, 3, and more movies up to 14 a month. We also ask her to tell us, on the same scale, how much she would like 1 six-pack of pop a month, 2 six-packs, and more up to 14 six-packs a month. Table 7.1 shows Lisa's answers.

Marginal Utility

Marginal utility is the change in total utility that results from a one-unit increase in the quantity of a good consumed. When the number of six-packs Lisa buys increases from 4 to 5 a month, her total utility from pop increases from 181 units to 206 units. So for Lisa, the marginal utility of consuming a fifth six-pack each month is 25 units. The table in Fig. 7.3 shows Lisa's marginal utility from pop. Notice that marginal utility appears midway between the quantities of pop. It does so because it is the change in consumption from 4 to 5 six-packs that produces the marginal utility of 25 units. The table displays calculations of marginal utility for each number of six-packs that Lisa buys from 1 to 5.

Figure 7.3(a) illustrates the total utility that Lisa gets from pop. The more pop Lisa drinks in a month, the more total utility she gets. Figure 7.3(b) illustrates her marginal utility. This graph tells us that as Lisa drinks more pop, the marginal utility that she gets from pop decreases. For example, her marginal utility

decreases from 75 units for the first six-pack to 42 units from the second six-pack and to 36 units from the third.

Diminishing Marginal Utility

We call this decrease in marginal utility as the quantity of the good consumed increases the principle of **diminishing marginal utility**.

Marginal utility is positive but diminishes as consumption of a good increases. Why does marginal utility have these two features? In Lisa's case, she likes pop, and the more she drinks the better. That's why marginal utility is positive. The benefit that Lisa gets from the last six-pack consumed is its marginal utility. To see why marginal utility diminishes, think about the following two situations: In one, you've just been studying all through the day and evening and you've been too busy finishing an assignment to go shopping. A friend drops by with a six-pack of pop.

TABLE 7.1   Lisa's Total Utility from Movies and Pop

Movies		Pop	
Quantity per month	Total utility	Six-packs per month	Total utility
0	0	0	0
1	50	1	75
2	88	2	117
3	121	3	153
4	150	4	181
5	175	5	206
6	196	6	225
7	214	7	243
8	229	8	260
9	241	9	276
10	250	10	291
11	256	11	305
12	259	12	318
13	261	13	330
14	262	14	341

FIGURE 7.3

Total Utility and Marginal Utility

Quantity	Total utility	Marginal utility
0	0	
		75
1	75	
		42
2	117	
		36
3	153	
		28
4	181	
		25
5	206	

(a) Total utility

(b) Marginal utility

The table shows that as Lisa consumes more pop, her total utility from pop increases. The table also shows her marginal utility—the change in total utility resulting from the last six-pack she consumes. Marginal utility declines as consumption increases. The figure graphs Lisa's total utility and marginal

utility from pop. Part (a) shows her total utility. It also shows as a bar the extra total utility she gains from each additional six-pack—her marginal utility. Part (b) shows how Lisa's marginal utility from pop diminishes by placing the bars shown in part (a) side by side as a series of declining steps.

The utility you get from that pop is the marginal utility from one six-pack. In the second situation, you've been on a pop binge. You've been working on an assignment all day but you've guzzled three six-packs while doing so. You are up to your eyeballs in pop. You are happy enough to have one more can. But the thrill that you get from it is not very large. It is the marginal utility of the nineteenth can in a day.

We've now described Lisa's budget and preferences. Our next task is to combine these two elements and see how she chooses what to consume.

Maximizing Utility

⌐ A HOUSEHOLD'S INCOME AND THE PRICES THAT IT faces limit the household's consumption choices, and the household's preferences determine the utility that it can obtain from each consumption possibility. The key assumption of marginal utility theory is that the household chooses the consumption possibility that maximizes its total utility. This assumption of utility maximization is a way of expressing the fundamental economic problem: scarcity. People's wants exceed the resources available to satisfy those wants, so they must make hard choices. In making choices, they try to get the maximum attainable benefit—that is, to maximize total utility.

Let's see how Lisa allocates $30 a month between movies and pop to maximize her total utility when the price of a movie is $6 and pop is $3 a six-pack.

The Utility-Maximizing Choice

The most direct way of calculating how Lisa spends her income to maximize her total utility is by making a table like Table 7.2. The rows of this table show the affordable combinations of movies and pop that lie along Lisa's budget line in Fig. 7.1. The table records three things: first, the number of movies seen and the total utility derived from them (the left side of the table); second, the number of six-packs consumed and the total utility derived from them (the right side of the table); and third, the total utility derived from both movies and pop (the centre column).

The first row of Table 7.2 records the situation when Lisa watches no movies and buys 10 six-packs. In this case, Lisa gets no utility from movies and 291 units of total utility from pop. Her total utility from movies and pop (the centre column) is 291 units. The rest of the table is constructed in the same way.

The combination of movies and pop that maximizes Lisa's total utility is highlighted in the table. When Lisa sees 2 movies and buys 6 six-packs of pop, she gets 313 units of total utility. This is the best Lisa can do, given that she has only $30 to spend and given the prices of movies and six-packs. If she buys 8 six-packs of pop, she can see only 1 movie. She gets 310 units of total utility, 3 less than the maximum attainable. If she sees 3 movies, she can drink only 4 six-packs. She gets 302 units of total utility, 11 less than the maximum attainable.

TABLE 7.2   Lisa's Utility-Maximizing Combinations

	Movies		Total utility from movies and pop	Pop	
	Quantity per month	Total utility		Total utility	Six-packs per month
A	0	0	291	291	10
B	1	50	310	260	8
C	2	88	313	225	6
D	3	121	302	181	4
E	4	150	267	117	2
F	5	175	175	0	0

We've just described Lisa's consumer equilibrium. A **consumer equilibrium** is a situation in which a consumer has allocated all his or her available income in the way that, given the prices of goods and services, maximizes his or her total utility. Lisa's consumer equilibrium is 2 movies and 6 six-packs.

In finding Lisa's consumer equilibrium, we measured her *total* utility from all the affordable combinations of movies and pop. But there is a better way of determining her consumer equilibrium. It uses the idea that choices are made at the margin—an idea that you first met in Chapter 1. Let's look at this alternative.

Equalizing Marginal Utility per Dollar

A consumer's total utility is maximized by following the rule:

Spend all the available income and equalize the marginal utility per dollar for all goods.

The **marginal utility per dollar** is the marginal utility from a good divided by its price. For example, Lisa's marginal utility from seeing 1 movie a month, MU_M, is 50 units of utility. The price of a movie, P_M, is $6, which means that the marginal utility per dollar from 1 movie a month, MU_M/P_M, is 50 units divided by $6, or 8.33 units of utility per dollar.

You can see why following this rule maximizes total utility by thinking about a situation in which

Lisa has spent all her income but the marginal utilities per dollar is not equal for all goods. Suppose that Lisa's marginal utility per dollar for pop, MU_P/P_P exceeds that for movies. By spending a dollar more on pop and a dollar less on movies, her total utility from pop rises and her total utility from movies falls. But her utility gain from pop exceeds her utility loss from movies, so her total utility increases. Because she consumes more pop, her marginal utility from pop has fallen. And because she sees fewer movies, her marginal utility from movies has risen. Lisa keeps increasing her consumption of pop and decreasing the movies she sees until the two marginal utilities per dollar are equal, or when

$$\frac{MU_M}{P_M} = \frac{MU_P}{P_P} .$$

Table 7.3 calculates Lisa's marginal utility per dollar for each good. Each row exhausts Lisa's income of $30. In row B, Lisa's marginal utility from movies is 50 units (use Table 7.1 to calculate the marginal utilities). Because the price of a movie is $6, Lisa's marginal utility per dollar for movies is 50 units divided by $6, which is 8.33. Marginal utility per dollar for each good, like marginal utility, decreases as more of the good is consumed.

Lisa maximizes her total utility when the marginal utility per dollar for movies is equal to the marginal utility per dollar for pop—possibility C. Lisa consumes 2 movies and 6 six-packs.

Figure 7.4 shows why the rule "equalize marginal utility per dollar for all goods" works. Suppose that instead of seeing 2 movies and consuming 6 six-packs (possibility C), Lisa sees 1 movie and consumes 8 six-packs (possibility B). She then gets 8.33 units of utility per dollar for movies and 5.67 units per dollar for pop. Lisa can increase her total utility by buying less pop and seeing more movies. If she sees one additional movie and spends less on pop, her total utility from movies increases by 8.33 units per dollar and her total utility from pop decreases by 5.67 units per dollar. Her total utility increases by 2.66 units per dollar, as shown by the blue area.

Or suppose that Lisa sees 3 movies and consumes 4 six-packs (possibility D). In this situation, her

---

TABLE 7.3   Equalizing Marginal Utilities per Dollar

		Movies ($6 each)			Pop ($3 per six-pack)	
	Quantity	Marginal utility	Marginal utility per dollar	Six-packs	Marginal utility	Marginal utility per dollar
A	0	0		10	15	5.00
B	1	50	8.33	8	17	5.67
C	2	38	6.33	6	19	6.33
D	3	33	5.50	4	28	9.33
E	4	29	4.83	2	42	14.00
F	5	25	4.17	0	0	

FIGURE 7.4   myeconlab

Equalizing Marginal Utilities per Dollar

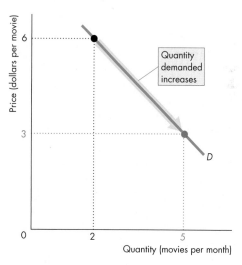

(a) Demand for movies

If Lisa sees 1 movie and consumes 8 six-packs (possibility B), her marginal utility per dollar for movies exceeds that for pop. She can get more total utility by seeing one more movie. If she consumes 4 six-packs and sees 3 movies (possibility D), her marginal utility per dollar for pop exceeds that for movies. She can get more total utility by seeing one less movie and consuming more pop. When Lisa's marginal utility per dollar for both goods is equal, her total utility is maximized.

marginal utility per dollar for movies (5.50) is less than her marginal utility per dollar for pop (9.33). Lisa can now increase her total utility by seeing one less movie and consuming more pop, as the green area shows.

The Power of Marginal Analysis   The method we've just used to find Lisa's utility-maximizing choice of movies and pop is an example of the power of marginal analysis. By comparing the marginal gain from having more of one good with the marginal loss from having less of another good, Lisa is able to ensure that she gets the maximum attainable utility.

The rule to follow is simple: If the marginal utility per dollar for movies exceeds the marginal utility per dollar for pop, see more movies and buy less pop; if the marginal utility per dollar for pop exceeds the marginal utility per dollar for movies, buy more pop and see fewer movies.

More generally, if the marginal gain from an action exceeds the marginal loss, take the action. You will meet this principle time and again in your study of economics. And you will find yourself using it when you make your own economic choices, especially when you must make a big decision.

Units of Utility   In maximizing total utility by making the marginal utility per dollar equal for both goods, the units in which utility is measured do not matter. Any arbitrary units will work. It is in this respect that utility is like temperature. Predictions about the freezing point of water don't depend on the temperature scale; and predictions about a household's consumption choice don't depend on the units of utility.

REVIEW QUIZ

1   What is Lisa's goal when she chooses the quantities of movies and pop to consume?

2   What are the two conditions that are met if a consumer is maximizing utility?

3   Explain why equalizing the marginal utility of each good does *not* maximize utility.

4   Explain why equalizing the marginal utility per dollar for all goods *does* maximize utility.

ⓧ myeconlab   **Study Plan 7.3**

Predictions of Marginal Utility Theory

WE'RE NOW GOING TO USE MARGINAL UTILITY theory to make some predictions. In Chapter 3, we assumed that a fall in the price of a good, other things remaining the same, brings an increase in the quantity demanded of that good—the law of demand. We also assumed that a fall in the price of a substitute of a good decreases demand for that good and a rise in income increases the demand for a normal good. We're now going to see that these assumptions are predictions of marginal utility theory.

A Fall in the Price of a Movie

A fall in the price of a movie, other things remaining the same, changes the quantity of movies demanded and brings a movement along the demand curve for movies. We've already found one point on Lisa's demand curve for movies. Figure 7.5 shows this point on Lisa's demand curve for movies.

To find another point on her demand curve for movies, we need to work out what Lisa buys when the price of a movie changes. Suppose that the price of a movie falls from $6 to $3 and nothing else changes.

To work out the effect of this change in the price of a movie on Lisa's buying plans, we must first determine the combinations of movies and pop that she can afford at the new prices. Then we calculate the new marginal utilities per dollar. Finally, we determine the combination that makes the marginal utilities per dollar for movies and pop equal.

The rows of Table 7.4 show the combinations of movies and pop that exhaust Lisa's $30 of income when the price of a movie is $3 and the price of a six-pack is $3. Lisa's preferences do not change when prices change, so her marginal utility schedule remains the same as that in Table 7.3. Divide her marginal utility from movies by $3 to get the marginal utility per dollar for movies.

Lisa now sees 5 movies and drinks 5 six-packs. She *substitutes* movies for pop. Figure 7.4 shows both of these effects. In part (a), we've found another point on Lisa's demand curve for movies. And we've discovered that her demand curve obeys the law of demand. In part (b), we see that a fall in the price of a movie decreases the demand for pop. The demand curve for pop shifts leftward. For Lisa, pop and movies are substitutes.

TABLE 7.4	How a Change in Price of a Movie Affects Lisa's Choices			
Movies ($3 each)			**Pop ($3 per six-pack)**	
Quantity	Marginal utility per dollar	Six-packs	Marginal utility per dollar	
0		10	5.00	
1	16.67	9	5.33	
2	**12.67**	8	5.67	
3	11.00	7	6.00	
4	9.67	**6**	**6.33**	
5	8.33	5	8.33	
6	7.00	4	9.33	
7	6.00	3	12.00	
8	5.00	2	14.00	
9	4.00	1	25.00	
10	3.00	0		

A Rise in the Price of Pop

In Fig. 7.5(b), we know only one point on Lisa's demand curve for pop when the price of a movie is $3. To find Lisa's demand curve for pop, we must see how she responds to a change in the price of pop. Suppose that the price of pop rises from $3 to $6 a six-pack. The rows of Table 7.5 show the combinations of movies and pop that exhaust Lisa's $30 of income when the price of a movie is $3 and the price of a six-pack is $6. Again, Lisa's preferences don't change when the price changes. Divide Lisa's marginal utility from pop by $6 to get her marginal utility per dollar for pop.

Lisa now drinks 2 six-packs a month and sees 6 movies a month. Lisa *substitutes* movies for pop. Figure 7.6 shows both of these effects. In part (a), we've found another point on Lisa's demand curve for pop. And we've confirmed that this demand curve obeys the law of demand. In part (b), we see that a rise in the price of pop increases the demand for movies. The demand curve for movies shifts rightward. This change again tells us that for Lisa, pop and movies are substitutes.

FIGURE 7.5   myeconlab

A Fall in the Price of a Movie

(a) Demand for movies

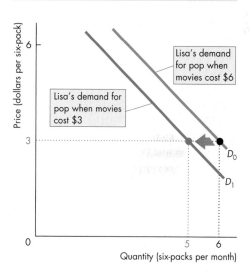

When the price of a movie falls and the price of pop remains the same, the quantity of movies demanded by Lisa increases, and in part (a), Lisa moves along her demand curve for movies. Also, when the price of a movie falls, Lisa's demand for pop decreases, and in part (b), her demand curve for pop shifts leftward. For Lisa, pop and movies are substitutes.

TABLE 7.5   How a Change in Price of Pop Affects Lisa's Choices

Movies ($3 each)		Pop ($6 per six-pack)	
Quantity	Marginal utility per dollar	Six-packs	Marginal utility per dollar
0		5	4.17
2	12.67	4	4.67
4	9.67	3	6.00
6	7.00	2	7.00
8	5.00	1	12.50
10	3.00	0	

Marginal utility theory predicts these two results:

1. When the price of a good rises, the quantity demanded of that good decreases.
2. When price of one good rises, the demand for another good that can serve as a substitute increases.

These predictions of marginal utility theory sound familiar because they correspond to the assumptions that we made about demand in Chapter 3. There, we assumed that the demand curve for a good slopes downward and that a rise in the price of a substitute for that good increases the demand for the good.

We have now seen that marginal utility theory predicts how the quantities of goods and services that people demand respond to price changes. The theory enables us to derive the consumer's demand curve and predict how the demand curve for one good shifts when the price of another good changes.

Marginal utility theory also helps us to predict how demand changes when income changes. Let's study the effects of a change in income on demand.

FIGURE 7.6
A Rise in the Price of Pop

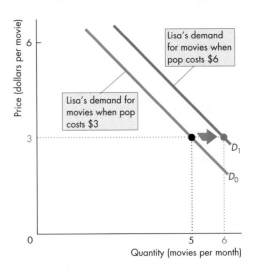

(a) Demand for pop

(b) Demand for movies

When the price of pop rises and the price of a movie remains the same, the quantity of pop demanded by Lisa decreases, and in part (a), Lisa moves along her demand

curve for pop. Also, when the price of pop rises, Lisa's demand for movies increases, and in part (b), her demand curve for movies shifts rightward.

A Rise in Income

Let's suppose that Lisa's income increases from $30 to $42 a month and that the price of a movie is $3 and the price of a six-pack is $3. We saw in Table 7.4 that with these prices and with an income of $30 a month, Lisa sees 5 movies and drinks 5 six-packs a month. We want to compare this choice of movies and pop with Lisa's choice when her income is $42.

Table 7.6 shows the calculations needed to make the comparison. With $42, Lisa can see 14 movies a month and buy no pop or buy 14 six-packs a month and see no movies or choose any combination of the two goods in the rows of the table. We calculate the marginal utility per dollar in exactly the same way as we did before and find the quantities at which the marginal utility per dollar for movies and the marginal utility per dollar for pop are equal. When Lisa's income

is $42, the marginal utility per dollar is equal for both goods when she sees 7 movies and drinks 7 six-packs of pop a month.

By comparing this situation with that in Table 7.4, we see that with an additional $12 a month, Lisa buys 2 more six-packs and sees 2 more movies a month. Lisa's response arises from her preferences, as described by her marginal utilities. Different preferences would produce different quantitative responses. With a larger income, the consumer always buys more of a *normal* good and less of an *inferior* good. For Lisa, pop and movies are normal goods. When her income increases, Lisa buys more of both goods.

You have now completed your study of the marginal utility theory of a household's consumption choices. Table 7.7 summarizes the key assumptions, implications, and predictions of the theory.

TABLE 7.6 Lisa's Choices with an Income of $42 a Month

Movies ($3 each)		Pop ($3 per six-pack)	
Quantity	Marginal utility per dollar	Six-packs	Marginal utility per dollar
0		14	3.67
1	16.67	13	4.00
2	12.67	12	4.33
3	11.00	11	4.67
4	9.67	10	5.00
5	**8.33**	9	5.33
6	7.00	8	5.67
7	6.00	7	6.00
8	5.00	6	6.33
9	4.00	**5**	**8.33**
10	3.00	4	9.33
11	2.00	3	12.00
12	1.00	2	14.00
13	0.67	1	25.00
14	0.33	0	

TABLE 7.7 Marginal Utility Theory

Assumptions

- A consumer derives utility from the goods consumed.
- Each additional unit of consumption yields additional total utility—marginal utility is positive.
- As the quantity of a good consumed increases, marginal utility decreases.
- A consumer's aim is to maximize total utility.

Implication

- Total utility is maximized when all the available income is spent and when the marginal utility per dollar is equal for all goods.

Predictions

- Other things remaining the same, the higher the price of a good, the smaller is the quantity bought (the law of demand).
- The higher the price of a good, the greater is the quantity bought of substitutes for that good.
- The larger the consumer's income, the greater is the quantity demanded of normal goods.

Temperature: An Analogy

Utility is similar to temperature. Both are abstract concepts, and both have units of measurement that are arbitrary. You can't *observe* temperature. You can observe water turning to steam if it is hot enough or turning to ice if it is cold enough. And you can construct an instrument—a thermometer—that can help you to predict when such changes will occur. We call the scale on the thermometer *temperature* and we call the units of temperature *degrees*. But these degree units are arbitrary. We can use Celsius units or the Fahrenheit units or some other.

The concept of utility helps us make predictions about consumption choices in much the same way that the concept of temperature helps us make predictions about physical phenomena.

Admittedly, marginal utility theory does not enable us to predict how buying plans change with the same precision that a thermometer enables us to predict when water will turn to ice or steam. But the theory provides important insights into buying plans and has some powerful implications, as you are about to discover. It helps us to understand why people buy more of a good or service when its price falls, why people buy more of most goods when their incomes increase. It also resolves the paradox of value, as you are about to see.

REVIEW QUIZ

1 When the price of a good falls and the prices of other goods and a consumer's income remain the same, what happens to the consumption of the good whose price has fallen and to the consumption of other goods?
2 Elaborate on your answer to the previous question by using demand curves. For which good is there a change in demand and for which is there a change in the quantity demanded?
3 If a consumer's income increases and if all goods are normal goods, how does the quantity bought of each good change?

myeconlab Study Plan 7.4

We're going to end this chapter by returning to a recurring theme throughout your study of economics: the concept of efficiency and the distinction between price and value.

Efficiency, Price, and Value

MARGINAL UTILITY THEORY HELPS US TO DEEPEN our understanding of the concept of efficiency and also helps us to see more clearly the distinction between value and price. Let's find out how.

Consumer Efficiency and Consumer Surplus

When Lisa allocates her limited budget to maximize utility, she is using her resources efficiently. Any other allocation of her budget wastes some resources.

But when Lisa has allocated her limited budget to maximize utility, she is *on* her demand curve for each good. A demand curve is a description of the quantity demanded at each price when utility is maximized. When we studied efficiency in Chapter 5, we learned that value equals marginal benefit and that a demand curve is also a willingness-to-pay curve. It tells us a consumer's *marginal benefit*—the benefit from consuming an additional unit of a good. You can now give the idea of marginal benefit a deeper meaning:

Marginal benefit is the maximum price a consumer is willing to pay for an extra unit of a good or service when utility is maximized.

The Paradox of Value

For centuries, philosophers have been puzzled by a paradox that we raised at the start of this chapter. Water, which is essential to life itself, costs little, but diamonds, which are useless in comparison to water, are expensive. Why? Adam Smith tried to solve this paradox. But not until the theory of marginal utility had been developed could anyone give a satisfactory answer.

You can solve this puzzle by distinguishing between *total* utility and *marginal* utility. The total utility that we get from water is enormous. But remember, the more we consume of something, the smaller is its marginal utility. We use so much water that its marginal utility—the benefit we get from one more glass of water—diminishes to a small value. Diamonds, on the other hand, have a small total utility relative to the total utility from water, but because we buy few diamonds, they have a high marginal utility. When a household has maximized its total utility, it has allocated its budget in the way that makes the

FIGURE 7.7

myeconlab

The Paradox of Value

(a) Water

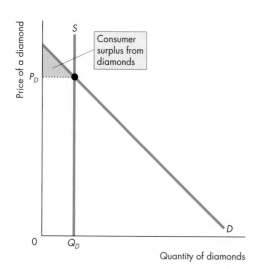

(b) Diamonds

Part (a) shows the demand for water, D, and the supply of water, S. The supply is assumed to be perfectly elastic at the price P_W. At this price, the quantity of water consumed is Q_W and the consumer surplus from water is the large green triangle. Part (b) shows the demand for diamonds, D, and the supply of diamonds, S. The supply is assumed to be perfectly inelastic at the quantity Q_D. At this quantity, the price of a diamond is P_D and the consumer surplus from diamonds is the small green triangle. Water is valuable—has a large consumer surplus—but cheap. Diamonds are less valuable than water—have a smaller consumer surplus—but are expensive.

marginal utility per dollar equal for all goods. That is, the marginal utility from a good divided by the price of the good is equal for all goods.

This equality of marginal utilities per dollar holds true for diamonds and water: Diamonds have a high price and a high marginal utility. Water has a low price and a low marginal utility. When the high marginal utility of diamonds is divided by the high price of diamonds, the result is a number that equals the low marginal utility of water divided by the low price of water. The marginal utility per dollar is the same for diamonds as for water.

Another way to think about the paradox of value uses *consumer surplus*. Figure 7.7 explains the paradox of value by using this idea. The supply of water (part a) is perfectly elastic at price P_W, so the quantity of water consumed is Q_W and the consumer surplus from water is the large green area. The supply of diamonds (part b) is perfectly inelastic at price Q_D, so the price of diamonds is P_D and the consumer surplus from diamonds is the small green area. Water is cheap but brings a large consumer surplus, while diamonds are expensive but bring a small consumer surplus.

REVIEW QUIZ

1   Can you explain why, along a demand curve, a consumer's choices are efficient?
2   Can you explain the paradox of value?
3   Is the marginal utility from water or from diamonds greater? Is the total utility from water or from diamonds greater? Is the consumer surplus from water or from diamonds greater?

myeconlab   **Study Plan 7.5**

◆ You have now completed your study of the marginal utility theory. And you've seen how the theory can be used to explain our real-world consumption choices. You can see the theory in action once again in *Reading Between the Lines* on pp. 166–167, where it is used to interpret how commuters in Winnipeg use the network of water buses along the Assiniboine and Red Rivers.

The next chapter presents an alternative theory of household behaviour. To help you see the connection between the two theories of consumer behaviour, we'll continue with the same example. We'll meet Lisa again and discover another way of understanding how she gets the most out of her $30 a month.

What's the Marginal Utility of a Boat Ride?

WINNIPEG FREE PRESS, JULY 25, 2001

New network of transit boats invite all aboard

With the city skyline behind him, Mayor Glen Murray rode to work yesterday morning, one of the first passengers in the city's new water transit boat.

"This is a fast, hassle-free and affordable way to travel that avoids traffic congestion," Murray said as the system's inaugural ride was filmed and photographed by the media.

The water bus shuttle links six public docks along the Assiniboine and Red Rivers.

Murray boarded the shuttle near his home, a new dock at the foot of Hugo Street, off Wellington Crescent. A 14-minute ride took Murray to the newly constructed dock in Stephen Juba Park at the end of Bannatyne Avenue, where he then walked to city hall.

The new service links the east Exchange area with the Corydon Avenue strip from the Hugo Street dock, with stops in between at The Forks, Tache, the Midtown bridge, and docks at the Legislature and the Osborne Street bridge.

...

For a $2 fee, riders can travel from dock to dock. Passengers are not given life jackets but they will be offered to children. Monthly commuter passes for rush-hour service costs $100. Day passes are $7; $6 for seniors and youths.

The shuttle will operate seven days a week; weekday service has rush-hour departures at eight-minute intervals from 7–9:30 a.m. and 4–6 p.m., with regular 15-minute departures until 11 p.m. On weekends, the service will have departures at 15-minute intervals from 10 a.m.–11 p.m.

The 12-passenger boats travel fully loaded at a maximum speed of about 40 kilometres per hour. ...

© *Winnipeg Free Press*, July 25, 2001. Reprinted with permission.

Essence of the Story

■ A water bus shuttle links six public docks along the Assiniboine and Red Rivers in Winnipeg.

■ The price of a one-way trip is $2. The price of a one-day pass is $7 ($6 for seniors and youths). The price of a one-month rush-hour pass is $100.

■ The shuttle operates seven days a week. On weekdays boats depart at 15-minute intervals and at eight-minute intervals during rush hours.

■ A boat carries 12 passengers at a maximum speed of 40 kilometres per hour.

Economic Analysis

■ The people who live in the region served by the Winnipeg water bus shuttle choose the method of transportation and number of trips that maximize utility.

■ The price of each trip is $2 (no special passes), so each person takes the number of trips that makes the marginal utility per dollar for boat trips equal to the marginal utility per dollar for other goods.

■ The table illustrates a person's choice if the amount available is $160, the price of a boat ride is $2, and the price of a unit of other goods is $10.

■ The person maximizes utility in this example by taking 20 boat trips and consuming 12 units of other goods.

■ But a Winnipeg commuter must make a more complicated choice because the boat company offers special passes. We'll consider just the $100 monthly pass.

■ Figure 1 shows the consumption possibilities that face the commuter. The commuter can pay $2 a trip or $100 for a month of "free" trips.

■ You can see that the person who takes fewer than 50 trips a month can buy more other goods by paying $2 a trip. The person who takes more than 50 trips a month can buy more other goods by paying $100 for the trips.

■ To decide whether to buy a monthly commuter pass for $100 or pay $2 per trip, the commuter must make two calculations, each similar to the one you've just seen, but with a twist.

■ If the utility-maximizing number of trips at $2 a trip turns out to be greater than 50 a month, the choice is easy: buy a commuter pass and save some money that can be spent on other goods.

■ If the utility-maximizing number of trips at $2 a trip turns out to be less than 50 a month, the commuter needs to reason as follows.

■ If I buy a commuter pass for $100, I can take any number of trips I choose and the cost of one marginal trip is zero. So I will take a trip if its marginal utility is positive.

■ The total utility that I get from these trips is the marginal utility from a commuter pass—it is the change in total utility that results from the decision to buy the pass.

■ So I will buy a commuter pass when the change in total utility that results from the decision to buy the pass divided by $100 is greater than or equal to the marginal utility per dollar for other goods.

■ In this case, I will take boat rides until the marginal utility of a ride is zero.

Winnipeg Traveller's Choices at $2 a Trip

	Boat trips ($2 each)			Other goods ($10 each)		
	Quantity	Marginal utility	Marginal utility per dollar	Quantity	Marginal utility	Marginal utility per dollar
A	0			16	10	1.00
B	10	10	5.00	14	20	2.00
C	**20**	**8**	**4.00**	**12**	**40**	**4.00**
D	30	6	3.00	10	60	6.00
E	40	4	2.00	8	80	8.00
F	50	3	1.50	6	100	10.00
G	60	2	1.00	4	120	12.00
H	70	1	0.50	2	140	14.00
I	80	0	0	0		

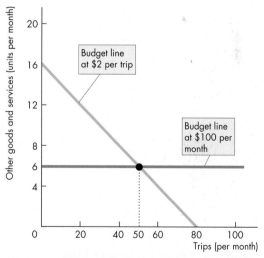

Figure 1 Budget lines for boat trips and other goods

SUMMARY

KEY POINTS

The Household's Budget (pp. 154–155)

- A household's budget limits its consumption choices.
- A household's consumption possibilities are constrained by its income and by the prices of goods and services. Some combinations of goods and services are affordable, and some are not affordable.

Preferences and Utility (pp. 156–157)

- A household's preferences can be described by marginal utility.
- The key assumption of marginal utility theory is that the marginal utility of a good or service decreases as consumption of the good or service increases.
- Marginal utility theory assumes that people buy the affordable combination of goods and services that maximizes their total utility.

Maximizing Utility (pp. 158–160)

- Total utility is maximized when all the available income is spent and when the marginal utility per dollar is equal for all goods.
- If the marginal utility per dollar for good *A* exceeds that for good *B*, total utility increases if the quantity purchased of good *A* increases and the quantity purchased of good *B* decreases.

Predictions of Marginal Utility Theory (pp. 160–164)

- Marginal utility theory predicts the law of demand. That is, other things remaining the same, the higher the price of a good, the smaller is the quantity demanded of that good.
- Marginal utility theory also predicts that other things remaining the same, the larger the consumer's income, the larger is the quantity demanded of a normal good.
- The market demand curve is found by summing horizontally all the individual demand curves.

Efficiency, Price, and Value (pp. 164–165)

- When a consumer maximizes utility, he or she is using resources efficiently.
- Marginal utility theory resolves the paradox of value.
- When we talk loosely about value, we are thinking of *total* utility or consumer surplus. But price is related to *marginal* utility.
- Water, which we consume in large amounts, has a high total utility and a large consumer surplus, but the price of water is low and the marginal utility from water is low.
- Diamonds, which we consume in small amounts, have a low total utility and a small consumer surplus, but the price of a diamond is high and the marginal utility from diamonds is high.

KEY FIGURES AND TABLE

KEY TERMS

PROBLEMS

Go to (X)myeconlab for solutions to odd-numbered problems and additional exercises.

1. Shirley spends all her income on movies and popcorn and the table shows her consumption possibilities.

Movies (number per week)	Popcorn (cartons per week)
0	20
1	15
2	10
3	5
4	0

If Shirley spends $40 a week:
a. What is the price of a carton of popcorn?
b. What is the price of a movie ticket?
c. What is the opportunity cost of a movie in terms of popcorn?
d. What is the Shirley's real income in terms of popcorn?

2. Lou spends all his income on CDs and spy novels. The price of a CD is $10 and the price of a spy novel is $15. Lou's income is $75 a month. Make a graph of Lou's budget to illustrate his consumption possibilities.

3. Jason enjoys rock CDs and spy novels and spends $60 a month on them. The table shows the utility he gets from each good.

Quantity per month	Utility from rock CDs	Utility from spy novels
1	60	20
2	110	38
3	150	53
4	180	64
5	200	70

a. Draw graphs showing Jason's utility from rock CDs and from spy novels and compare the two utility graphs. Can you say anything about Jason's preferences?
b. Draw graphs that show Jason's marginal utility from rock CDs and from spy novels.
c. What do the two marginal utility graphs tell you about Jason's preferences?

d. If the price of a rock CD is $10 and the price of a spy novel is $10, how does Jason spend the $60?

4. Martha enjoys classical CDs and travel books and spends $75 a month on them. The table shows the utility she gets from each good.

Quantity per month	Utility from classical CDs	Utility from travel books
1	90	120
2	110	136
3	126	148
4	138	152
5	146	154

a. Draw graphs showing Martha's utility from classical CDs and from travel books and compare the two utility graphs. Can you say anything about Martha's preferences?
b. Draw graphs that show Martha's marginal utility from classical CDs and from travel books.
c. What do the two marginal utility graphs tell you about Martha's preferences?
d. If the price of a classical CD is $15 and the price of a travel book is $15, how does Martha spend the $75 a month?

5. Max enjoys windsurfing and snorkelling. The table shows the marginal utility he gets from each activity.

Hours per day	Marginal utility from windsurfing	Marginal utility from snorkelling
1	120	40
2	100	36
3	80	30
4	60	22
5	40	12
6	12	10
7	10	8

Max has $35 to spend, and he can spend as much time as he likes on his leisure pursuits. Windsurfing equipment rents for $10 an hour, and snorkelling equipment rents for $5 an hour. How long does Max spend windsurfing and how long does he spend snorkelling?

6. Pete enjoys rock concerts and the opera. The table shows the marginal utility he gets from each activity.

Number per month	Marginal utility from rock concerts	Marginal utility from operas
1	120	200
2	100	160
3	80	120
4	60	80
5	40	40
6	20	0

Pete has $200 a month to spend on concerts. The price of a rock concert ticket is $20, and the price of an opera ticket is $40. How many rock concerts and how many operas does Pete attend?

7. In problem 5, Max's sister gives him $20 to spend on his leisure pursuits, so he now has $55.
   a. Draw a graph that shows Max's consumption possibilities.
   b. How many hours does Max choose to wind-surf and how many hours does he choose to snorkel now that he has $55 to spend?

8. In problem 6, Pete's uncle gives him $60 to spend on concert tickets, so he now has $260.
   a. Draw a graph that shows Pete's consumption possibilities.
   b. How many rock concerts and how many operas does Pete now attend?

9. In problem 7, if the rent on windsurfing equipment decreases to $5 an hour, how many hours does Max now windsurf and how many hours does he snorkel?

10. In problem 6, if the price of an opera ticket decreases to $20, how many rock concerts and operas will Pete attend?

11. Max, in problem 5, takes a Club Med vacation, the cost of which includes unlimited sports activities. There is no extra charge for equipment. If Max windsurfs and snorkels for 6 hours a day, how many hours does he windsurf and how many hours does he snorkel?

12. Pete, in problem 6, wins a prize and has more than enough money to satisfy his desires for rock concerts and opera. He decides that he would like to buy a total of 7 tickets each month. How many rock concerts and how many operas does he now attend?

CRITICAL THINKING

1. Study *Reading Between the Lines* (pp. 166–167) on the Winnipeg water transit boats and then answer the following questions:
   a. If price of a ride is $2 and the price of a day pass is $6, how does a person decide whether to buy the pass or pay for each ride?
   b. List the components of the opportunity cost of a ride other than the cost of the ticket.
   c. What does marginal utility theory predict will happen to the demand for public transit as incomes rise?

2. Smoking is banned on most airline flights. Use marginal utility theory to explain
   a. The effect of the ban on the utility of smokers.
   b. How the ban influences the decisions of smokers.
   c. The effects of the ban on the utility of non-smokers.
   d. How the ban influences the decisions of nonsmokers.

WEB EXERCISES

Use the links on [myeconlab] to work the following exercises.

1. Read what Henry Schimberg, former CEO of Coca-Cola, said about the market for bottled water. Use marginal utility theory to explain and interpret his remarks.

2. Obtain information about the prices on the Toronto Transit Commission system.
   a. Show the effects of the different ticket options on the consumer's budget line.
   b. How would a person decide whether to pay for each trip, to buy a day pass, or to buy a pass for a longer period? Use marginal utility theory to answer this question.
   c. How do you think the number of riders would change if the price of a single trip fell and the price of a day pass increased?

Possibilities, Preferences, and Choices

Subterranean Movements

Like the continents floating on the earth's mantle,
our spending patterns change steadily over time. On such subterranean
movements, business empires rise and fall. We can now choose whether
to buy our music on a CD or download it and play it on an iPod or
burn our own CD. As the prices of a music download, an iPod, and a
CD burner have tumbled, people are increasingly buying downloads
and music CD sales have taken a hit.

The prices of electronic textbooks—e-books—have also fallen and
these books are now cheaper than printed textbooks. Yet most students
continue to buy printed textbooks. Why, when e-books are cheaper than
printed books, have e-books not caught on and replaced printed books
in the same way that the new music technologies have replaced CDs?

Subterranean movements also govern the way we spend our time.
The average workweek has fallen steadily from 70 hours a week in the
nineteenth century to 35 hours a week today. While the average
workweek is now much shorter than it once was, far more people
now have jobs. Why has the average workweek declined?

◆ In this chapter, we're going to study a model of choice that predicts the effects of changes in prices and incomes on what people buy
and the effects of changes in wage rates on how people allocate time
between leisure and work. At the end of the chapter, in *Reading Between
the Lines*, we'll use the model to explain why students buy more printed
textbooks than e-books, even though e-books are cheaper.

After studying this chapter, you will be able to

- **Describe a household's budget line and show how it changes when income or prices change**

- **Make a map of preferences by using indifference curves and explain the principle of diminishing marginal rate of substitution**

- **Predict the effects of changes in prices and income on consumption choices**

- **Predict the effects of changes in wage rates on work–leisure choices**

Consumption Possibilities

CONSUMPTION CHOICES ARE LIMITED BY INCOME and by prices. A household has a given amount of income to spend and cannot influence the prices of the goods and services it buys. A household's **budget line** describes the limits to its consumption choices.

Let's look at Lisa's budget line.[1] Lisa has an income of $30 a month to spend. She buys two goods: movies and pop. The price of a movie is $6, and the price of pop is $3 a six-pack. Figure 8.1 shows alternative affordable ways for Lisa to consume movies and pop. Row *A* says that she can buy 10 six-packs of pop and see no movies, a combination of movies and pop that exhausts her monthly income of $30. Row *F* says that Lisa can watch 5 movies and drink no pop—another combination that exhausts the $30 available. Each of the other rows in the table also exhausts Lisa's income. (Check that each of the other rows costs exactly $30.) The numbers in the table define Lisa's consumption possibilities. We can graph Lisa's consumption possibilities as points *A* through *F* in Fig. 8.1.

Divisible and Indivisible Goods Some goods— called divisible goods—can be bought in any quantity desired. Examples are gasoline and electricity. We can best understand household choice if we suppose that all goods and services are divisible. For example, Lisa can consume a half a movie a month on the average by seeing one movie every two months. When we think of goods as being divisible, the consumption possibilities are not just the points *A* through *F* shown in Fig. 8.1, but those points plus all the intermediate points that form the line running from *A* to *F*. Such a line is a budget line.

Lisa's budget line is a constraint on her choices. It marks the boundary between what is affordable and what is unaffordable. She can afford any point on the line and inside it. She cannot afford any point outside the line. The constraint on her consumption depends on prices and her income, and the constraint changes when the price of a good or her income changes. Let's see how by studying the budget equation.

---

[1] If you have studied Chapter 7 on marginal utility theory, you have already met Lisa. This tale of her thirst for pop and zeal for movies will sound familiar to you—up to a point. But in this chapter, we're going to use a different method for representing preferences—one that does not require us to resort to the idea of utility.

FIGURE 8.1
The Budget Line

Consumption possibility	Movies (per month)	Pop (six-packs per month)
A	0	10
B	1	8
C	2	6
D	3	4
E	4	2
F	5	0

Lisa's budget line shows the boundary between what she can and cannot afford. The rows of the table list Lisa's affordable combinations of movies and pop when her income is $30, the price of pop is $3 a six-pack, and the price of a movie is $6. For example, row A tells us that Lisa spends all of her $30 income when she buys 10 six-packs and sees no movies. The figure graphs Lisa's budget line. Points A through F on the graph represent the rows of the table. For divisible goods, the budget line is the continuous line AF. To calculate the equation for Lisa's budget line, start with expenditure equal to income:

$$\$3Q_P + \$6Q_M = \$30.$$

Divide by $3 to obtain

$$Q_P + 2Q_M = \$10.$$

Subtract $2Q_M$ from both sides to obtain

$$Q_P = 10 - 2Q_M.$$

The Budget Equation

We can describe the budget line by using a *budget equation*. The budget equation starts with the fact that

$$\text{Expenditure} = \text{Income}.$$

Expenditure is equal to the sum of the price of each good multiplied by the quantity bought. For Lisa,

$$\text{Expenditure} = (\text{Price of pop} \times \text{Quantity of pop}) \\ + (\text{Price of a movie} \times \text{Quantity of a movie})$$

Call the price of pop P_P, the quantity of pop Q_P, the price of a movie P_M, the quantity of movies Q_M, and income Y. We can now write Lisa's budget equation as

$$P_P Q_P + P_M Q_M = Y.$$

Or, using the prices Lisa faces, $3 for a six-pack and $6 for a movie, and Lisa's income, $30, we get

$$\$3 Q_P + \$6 Q_M = \$30.$$

Lisa can choose any quantities of pop (Q_P) and movies (Q_M) that satisfy this equation. To find the relationship between these quantities, divide both sides of the equation by the price of pop (P_P) to get

$$Q_P + \frac{P_M}{P_P} \times Q_M = \frac{Y}{P_P}.$$

Now subtract the term $P_M/P_P \times Q_M$ from both sides of this equation to get

$$Q_P = \frac{Y}{P_P} - \frac{P_M}{P_P} \times Q_M.$$

For Lisa, income (Y) is $30, the price of a movie (P_M) is $6, and the price of pop (P_P) is $3 a six-pack. So Lisa must choose the quantities of movies and pop to satisfy the equation

$$Q_P = \frac{\$30}{\$3} - \frac{\$6}{\$3} \times Q_M,$$

or

$$Q_P = 10 - 2Q_M.$$

To interpret the equation, look at the budget line in Fig. 8.1 and check that the equation delivers that budget line. First, set Q_M equal to zero. The budget equation tells us that Q_P, the quantity of pop, is Y/P_P, which is 10 six-packs. This combination of Q_M and Q_P is the one shown in row *A* of the table in Fig. 8.1. Next set Q_M equal to 5. Q_P now equals zero (row *F* of the table). Check that you can derive the other rows.

The budget equation contains two variables (Q_M and Q_P) that the household chooses and two variables (Y/P_P and P_M/P_P) that the household takes as given. Let's look more closely at these variables.

Real Income A household's **real income** is the household's income expressed as a quantity of goods the household can afford to buy. Expressed in terms of pop, Lisa's real income is Y/P_P. This quantity is the maximum number of six-packs that she can buy. It is equal to her money income divided by the price of pop. Lisa's income is $30 and the price of pop is $3 a six-pack, so her real income in terms of pop is 10 six-packs, which is shown in Fig. 8.1 as the point at which the budget line intersects the *y*-axis.

Relative Price A **relative price** is the price of one good divided by the price of another good. In Lisa's budget equation, the variable P_M/P_P is the relative price of a movie in terms of pop. For Lisa, P_M is $6 a movie and P_P is $3 a six-pack, so P_M/P_P is equal to 2 six-packs per movie. That is, to see one more movie, Lisa must give up 2 six-packs.

You've just calculated Lisa's opportunity cost of a movie. Recall that the opportunity cost of an action is the best alternative forgone. For Lisa to see 1 more movie a month, she must forgo 2 six-packs. You've also calculated Lisa's opportunity cost of pop. For Lisa to consume 2 more six-packs a month, she must forgo seeing 1 movie. So her opportunity cost of 2 six-packs is 1 movie.

The relative price of a movie in terms of pop is the magnitude of the slope of Lisa's budget line. To calculate the slope of the budget line, recall the formula for slope (see the Chapter 1 Appendix): Slope equals the change in the variable measured on the *y*-axis divided by the change in the variable measured on the *x*-axis as we move along the line. In Lisa's case (Fig. 8.1), the variable measured on the *y*-axis is the quantity of pop and the variable measured on the *x*-axis is the quantity of movies. Along Lisa's budget line, as pop decreases from 10 to 0 six-packs, movies increase from 0 to 5. So the magnitude of the slope of the budget line is 10 six-packs divided by 5 movies, or 2 six-packs per movie. The magnitude of this slope is exactly the same as the relative price we've just calculated. It is also the opportunity cost of a movie.

A Change in Prices When prices change, so does the budget line. The lower the price of the good measured on the horizontal axis, other things remaining the same, the flatter is the budget line. For example, if the price of a movie falls from $6 to $3, real

FIGURE 8.2
Changes in Prices and Income

(a) A change in price

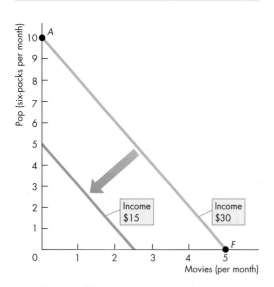

(b) A change in income

In part (a), the price of a movie changes. A fall in the price from $6 to $3 rotates the budget line outward and makes it flatter. A rise in the price from $6 to $12 rotates the budget line inward and makes it steeper.

In part (b), income falls from $30 to $15 while the prices of movies and pop remain constant. The budget line shifts leftward, but its slope does not change.

income in terms of pop does not change but the relative price of a movie falls. The budget line rotates outward and becomes flatter, as Fig. 8.2(a) illustrates. The higher the price of the good measured on the horizontal axis, other things remaining the same, the steeper is the budget line. For example, if the price of a movie rises from $6 to $12, the relative price of a movie increases. The budget line rotates inward and becomes steeper, as Fig. 8.2(a) illustrates.

A Change in Income A change in money income changes real income but does not change the relative price. The budget line shifts, but its slope does not change. The bigger a household's money income, the bigger is real income and the farther to the right is the budget line. The smaller a household's money income, the smaller is real income and the farther to the left is the budget line. Figure 8.2(b) shows the effect of a change in money income on Lisa's budget line. The initial budget line when Lisa's income is $30 is the same one that we began with in Fig. 8.1. The new budget line shows how much Lisa can consume if her income falls to $15 a month. The two budget lines have the same slope because the relative price is the same. The new budget line is closer to the origin because Lisa's real income has decreased.

REVIEW QUIZ

1 What does a household's budget line show?
2 How does the relative price and a household's real income influence its budget line?
3 If a household has an income of $40 and buys only bus rides at $4 each and magazines at $2 each, what is the equation of the household's budget line?
4 If the price of one good changes, what happens to the relative price and to the slope of the household's budget line?
5 If a household's money income changes and prices do not change, what happens to the household's real income and budget line?

myeconlab Study Plan 8.1

We've studied the limits to what a household can consume. Let's now learn how we can describe preferences and make a map that contains a lot of information about a household's preferences.

Preferences and Indifference Curves

YOU ARE GOING TO DISCOVER A VERY NEAT IDEA: that of drawing a map of a person's preferences. A preference map is based on the intuitively appealing idea that people can sort all the possible combinations of goods into three groups: preferred, not preferred, and indifferent. To make this idea more concrete, let's ask Lisa to tell us how she ranks various combinations of movies and pop.

Figure 8.3 shows part of Lisa's answer. She tells us that she currently sees 2 movies and drinks 6 six-packs a month at point C. She then lists all the combinations of movies and pop that she says are just as acceptable to her as her current consumption. When we plot these combinations of movies and pop, we get the green curve in Fig. 8.3(a). This curve is the key element in a map of preferences and is called an indifference curve.

An **indifference curve** is a line that shows combinations of goods among which a consumer is *indifferent*. The indifference curve in Fig. 8.3(a) tells us that Lisa is just as happy to see 2 movies and drink 6 six-packs a month at point C as she is to consume the combination of movies and pop at point G or at any other point along the curve.

Lisa also says that she prefers all the combinations of movies and pop above the indifference curve in Fig. 8.3(a)—the yellow area—to those on the indifference curve. And she prefers any combination on the indifference curve to any combination in the grey area below the indifference curve.

The indifference curve in Fig. 8.3(a) is just one of a whole family of such curves. This indifference curve appears again in Fig. 8.3(b) labelled I_1. The curves labelled I_0 and I_2 are two other indifference curves. Lisa prefers any point on indifference curve I_2 to any point on indifference curve I_1, and she prefers any point on I_1 to any point on I_0. We refer to I_2 as being a higher indifference curve than I_1 and I_1 as being higher than I_0.

A preference map is a series of indifference curves that resemble the contour lines on a map. By looking at the shape of the contour lines on a map, we can draw conclusions about the terrain. Similarly, by looking at the shape of indifference curves, we can draw conclusions about a person's preferences.

Let's learn how to "read" a preference map.

FIGURE 8.3

A Preference Map

myeconlab

(a) An indifference curve

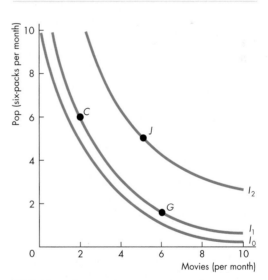

(b) Lisa's preference map

In part (a), Lisa drinks 6 six-packs of pop and sees 2 movies a month at point C. She is indifferent between all the points on the green indifference curve such as C and G. She prefers any point above the indifference curve (the yellow area) to any point on it, and she prefers any point on the indifference curve to any point below it (the grey area). A preference map is a number of indifference curves. Part (b) shows three indifference curves—I_0, I_1, and I_2—that are part of Lisa's preference map. She prefers point J to point C or G, so she prefers any point on I_2 to any point on I_1.

Marginal Rate of Substitution

The **marginal rate of substitution** (*MRS*) is the rate at which a person will give up good *y* (the good measured on the *y*-axis) to get an additional unit of good *x* (the good measured on the *x*-axis) and at the same time remain indifferent (remain on the same indifference curve). The magnitude of the slope of an indifference curve measures the marginal rate of substitution.

- If the indifference curve is *steep*, the marginal rate of substitution is *high*. The person is willing to give up a large quantity of good *y* to get an additional unit of good *x* while remaining indifferent.

- If the indifference curve is *flat*, the marginal rate of substitution is *low*. The person is willing to give up a small amount of good *y* to get an additional unit of good *x* while remaining indifferent.

Figure 8.4 shows you how to calculate the marginal rate of substitution. Suppose that Lisa drinks 6 six-packs and sees 2 movies at point *C* on indifference curve I_1. To calculate her marginal rate of substitution we measure the magnitude of the slope of the indifference curve at point *C*. To measure this magnitude, place a straight line against, or tangent to, the indifference curve at point *C*. Along that line, as the quantity of pop decreases by 10 six-packs, the number of movies increases by 5—an average of 2 six-packs per movie. So at point *C*, Lisa is willing to give up pop for movies at the rate of 2 six-packs per movie—a marginal rate of substitution of 2.

Now suppose that Lisa drinks 1.5 six-packs and sees 6 movies at point *G* in Fig. 8.4. Her marginal rate of substitution is now measured by the slope of the indifference curve at point *G*. That slope is the same as the slope of the tangent to the indifference curve at point *G*. Here, as the quantity of pop decreases by 4.5 six-packs, the number of movies increases by 9—an average of 1/2 six-pack per movie. So at point *G*, Lisa is willing to give up pop for movies at the rate of 1/2 six-pack per movie—a marginal rate of substitution of 1/2.

As Lisa sees more movies and drinks less pop, her marginal rate of substitution diminishes. Diminishing marginal rate of substitution is the key assumption of consumer theory. A **diminishing marginal rate of substitution** is a general tendency for a person to be willing to give up less of good *y* to get one more unit of good *x*, and at the same time remain indifferent, as the quantity of *x* increases. In Lisa's case, she is less willing to give up less pop to see one more movie, as the number of movies she sees increases.

FIGURE 8.4
The Marginal Rate of Substitution

The magnitude of the slope of an indifference curve is called the marginal rate of substitution (*MRS*). The red line at point *C* tells us that Lisa is willing to give up 10 six-packs to see 5 movies. Her marginal rate of substitution at point *C* is 10 divided by 5, which equals 2. The red line at point *G* tells us that Lisa is willing to give up 4.5 six-packs to see 9 movies. Her marginal rate of substitution at point *G* is 4.5 divided by 9, which equals 1/2.

Your Own Diminishing Marginal Rate of Substitution Think about your own diminishing marginal rate of substitution. Imagine that in a week, you drink 10 six-packs of pop and see no movies. Most likely, you are willing to give up a lot of pop so that you can see just 1 movie. But now imagine that in a week, you drink 1 six-pack and see 6 movies. Most likely, you will now not be willing to give up much pop to see a seventh movie. As a general rule, the greater the number of movies you see, the smaller is the quantity of pop you are willing to give up to see one additional movie.

The shape of a person's indifference curves incorporates the principle of the diminishing marginal rate of substitution because the curves are bowed towards the origin. The tightness of the bend of an indifference curve tells us how willing a person is to substitute one good for another while remaining indifferent. Let's look at some examples that make this point clear.

Degree of Substitutability

Most of us would not regard movies and pop as being close substitutes. We probably have some fairly clear ideas about how many movies we want to see each month and how many cans of pop we want to drink. But to some degree, we are willing to substitute between these two goods. No matter how big a pop freak you are, there is surely some increase in the number of movies you can see that will compensate you for being deprived of a can of pop. Similarly, no matter how addicted you are to the movies, surely some number of cans of pop will compensate you for being deprived of seeing one movie. A person's indifference curves for movies and pop might look something like those shown in Fig. 8.5(a).

Close Substitutes Some goods substitute so easily for each other that most of us do not even notice which we are consuming. The different brands of personal computers are an example. As long as it has an "Intel inside" and runs Windows, most of us don't care whether our PC is a Dell, a Sony, or any other brand. The same holds true for marker pens. Most of

us don't care whether we use a marker pen from the campus bookstore or one from the local supermarket. When two goods are perfect substitutes, their indifference curves are straight lines that slope downward, as Fig. 8.5(b) illustrates. The marginal rate of substitution is constant.

Complements Some goods cannot substitute for each other at all. Instead, they are complements. The complements in Fig. 8.5(c) are left and right running shoes.Indifference curves of perfect complements are L-shaped. One left running shoe and one right running shoe are as good as one left shoe and two right ones. Having two of each is preferred to having one of each, but having two of one and one of the other is no better than having one of each.

The extreme cases of perfect substitutes and perfect complements shown here don't often happen in reality. But they do illustrate that the shape of the indifference curve shows the degree of substitutability between two goods. The more perfectly substitutable the two goods, the more nearly are their

FIGURE 8.5
The Degree of Substitutability

(a) Ordinary goods

(b) Perfect substitutes

(c) Perfect complements

The shape of the indifference curves reveals the degree of substitutability between two goods. Part (a) shows the indifference curves for two ordinary goods: movies and pop. To drink less pop and remain indifferent, one must see more movies. The number of movies that compensates for a reduction in pop increases as less pop is consumed. Part (b) shows the indifference curves for two perfect substitutes. For the consumer to remain indifferent, one fewer marker pen from the local supermarket must be replaced by one extra marker pen from the campus bookstore. Part (c) shows two perfect complements—goods that cannot be substituted for each other at all. Having two left running shoes with one right running shoe is no better than having one of each. But having two of each is preferred to having one of each.

*"With the pork I'd recommend an
Alsatian white or a Coke."*

© The New Yorker Collection 1988, Robert Weber from
cartoonbank.com. All Rights Reserved.

indifference curves straight lines and the less quickly
does the marginal rate of substitution diminish. Poor
substitutes for each other have tightly curved indifference curves, approaching the shape of those
shown in Fig. 8.5(c).

As you can see in the cartoon, according to the
waiter's preferences, Coke and Alsatian white wine are
perfect substitutes and each is a complement of pork.
We hope the customers agree with him.

REVIEW QUIZ

1 What is an indifference curve and how does an
   indifference map show preferences?
2 Why does an indifference curve slope downward and why is it bowed towards the origin?
3 What do we call the magnitude of the slope of
   an indifference curve?
4 What is the key assumption about a consumer's
   marginal rate of substitution?

myeconlab   Study Plan 8.2

The two components of the model of household
choice are now in place: the budget line and the preference map. We will now use these components to
work out the household's choice and to predict how
choices change when prices and income change.

Predicting Consumer Behaviour

WE ARE NOW GOING TO PREDICT THE QUANTITIES
of movies and pop that Lisa chooses to buy. Figure
8.6 shows Lisa's budget line from Fig. 8.1 and her
indifference curves from Fig. 8.3(b). We assume that
Lisa consumes at her best affordable point, which is 2
movies and 6 six-packs—at point C. Here, Lisa

■ Is on her budget line.
■ Is on her highest attainable indifference curve.
■ Has a marginal rate of substitution between
   movies and pop equal to the relative price of
   movies and pop.

For every point inside the budget line, such as
point I, there are points *on* the budget line that Lisa
prefers. For example, she prefers all the points on the

FIGURE 8.6   myeconlab
The Best Affordable Point

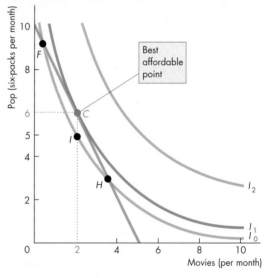

Lisa's best affordable point is C. At that point, she is on her
budget line and also on the highest attainable indifference
curve. At a point such as H, Lisa is willing to give up more
movies in exchange for pop than she has to. She can move
to point I, which is just as good as point H, and have some
unspent income. She can spend that income and move to
C, a point that she prefers to point I.

budget line between *F* and *H* to point *I*. So she chooses a point on the budget line.

Every point on the budget line lies on an indifference curve. For example, point *H* lies on the indifference curve I_0. At point *H*, Lisa's marginal rate of substitution is less than the relative price. Lisa is willing to give up more movies in exchange for pop than the budget line says she must. So she moves along her budget line from *H* towards *C*. As she does so, she passes through a number of indifference curves (not shown in the figure) located between indifference curves I_0 and I_1. All of these indifference curves are higher than I_0, and therefore Lisa prefers any point on them to point *H*. But when Lisa gets to point *C*, she is on the highest attainable indifference curve. If she keeps moving along the budget line, she starts to encounter indifference curves that are lower than I_1. So Lisa chooses point *C*.

At the chosen point, the marginal rate of substitution (the magnitude of the slope of the indifference curve) equals the relative price (the magnitude of the slope of the budget line).

Let's use this model of household choice to predict the effects on consumption of changes in prices and income. We'll begin by studying the effect of a change in price.

A Change in Price

The effect of a change in the price on the quantity of a good consumed is called the **price effect**. We will use Fig. 8.7(a) to work out the price effect of a fall in the price of a movie. We start with the price of a movie at $6, the price of pop at $3 a six-pack, and Lisa's income at $30 a month. In this situation, she drinks 6 six-packs and sees 2 movies a month at point *C*.

Now suppose that the price of a movie falls to $3. With a lower price of a movie, the budget line rotates outward and becomes flatter. (Check back to Fig. 8.2(a) for a refresher on how a price change affects the budget line.) The new budget line is the dark orange one in Fig. 8.7(a).

Lisa's best affordable point is now point *J*, where she sees 5 movies and drinks 5 six-packs of pop. Lisa drinks less pop and watches more movies now that movies are cheaper. She cuts her pop consumption from 6 to 5 six-packs and increases the number of movies she sees from 2 to 5 a month. Lisa substitutes movies for pop when the price of a movie falls and the price of pop and her income remain constant.

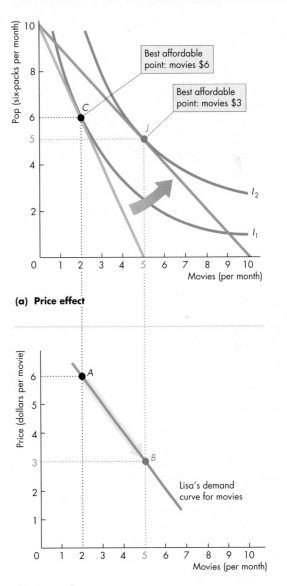

FIGURE 8.7
Price Effect and Demand Curve

(a) Price effect

(b) Demand curve

Initially, Lisa consumes at point *C* (part a). If the price of a movie falls from $6 to $3, Lisa consumes at point *J*. The move from *C* to *J* is the price effect.

At a price of $6 a movie, Lisa sees 2 movies a month, at point *A* in part (b). At a price of $3 a movie, she sees 5 movies a month, at point *B*. Lisa's demand curve traces out her best affordable quantity of movies as the price of a movie varies, other things remaining the same.

The Demand Curve In Chapter 3, we asserted that the demand curve slopes downward. We can now derive a demand curve from a consumer's budget line and indifference curves. By doing so, we can see that the law of demand and the downward-sloping demand curve are consequences of the consumer's choosing his or her best affordable combination of goods.

To derive Lisa's demand curve for movies, lower the price of a movie and find her best affordable point at different prices. We've just done this for two movie prices in Fig. 8.7(a). Figure 8.7(b) highlights these two prices and two points that lie on Lisa's demand curve for movies. When the price of a movie is $6, Lisa sees 2 movies a month at point A. When the price falls to $3, she increases the number of movies she sees to 5 a month at point B. The demand curve is made up of these two points plus all the other points that tell us Lisa's best affordable consumption of movies at each movie price, given the price of pop and Lisa's income. As you can see, Lisa's demand curve for movies slopes downward—the lower the price of a movie, the more movies she watches each month. This is the law of demand.

Next, let's see how Lisa changes her consumption of movies and pop when her income changes.

A Change in Income

The effect of a change in income on consumption is called the **income effect**. Let's work out the income effect by examining how consumption changes when income changes and prices remain constant. Figure 8.8 shows the income effect when Lisa's income falls. With an income of $30 and with the price of a movie at $3 and the price of pop at $3 a six-pack, she consumes at point *J*—5 movies and 5 six-packs. If her income falls to $21, she consumes at point *K*—she sees 4 movies and drinks 3 six-packs. When Lisa's income falls, she consumes less of both goods. Movies and pop are normal goods.

The Demand Curve and the Income Effect A change in income leads to a shift in the demand curve, as shown in Fig. 8.8(b). With an income of $30, Lisa's demand curve is D_0, the same as in Fig. 8.7(b). But when her income falls to $21, she plans to see fewer movies at each price, so her demand curve shifts leftward to D_1.

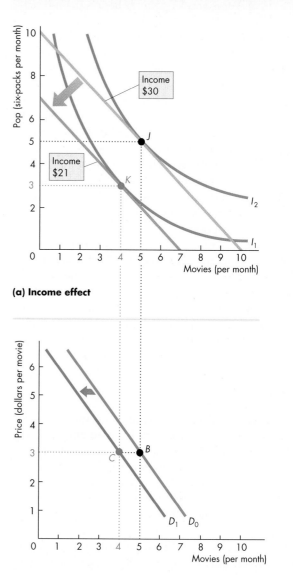

FIGURE 8.8   myeconlab
Income Effect and Change in Demand

(a) Income effect

(b) Demand curve

A change in income shifts the budget line, changes the best affordable point, and changes consumption.

In part (a), when Lisa's income decreases from $30 to $21, she consumes less of both movies and pop.

In part (b), Lisa's demand curve for movies when her income is $30 is D_0. When Lisa's income decreases to $21, her demand curve for movies shifts leftward to D_1. Lisa's demand for movies decreases because she now sees fewer movies at each price.

Substitution Effect and Income Effect

For a normal good, a fall in price *always* increases the quantity bought. We can prove this assertion by dividing the price effect into two parts:

- Substitution effect
- Income effect

Figure 8.9 shows the price effect, and Fig. 8.9(b) divides the price effect into its two parts.

Substitution Effect The **substitution effect** is the effect of a change in price on the quantity bought when the consumer (hypothetically) remains indifferent between the original situation and the new one. To work out Lisa's substitution effect, when the price of a movie falls, we cut her income by enough to leave her on the same indifference curve as before.

When the price of a movie falls from $6 to $3, suppose (hypothetically) that we cut Lisa's income to $21. What's special about $21? It is the income that is just enough, at the new price of a movie, to keep Lisa's best affordable point on the same indifference curve as her original consumption point C. Lisa's budget line is now the light orange line in Fig. 8.9(b). With the lower price of a movie and a smaller income, Lisa's best affordable point is K on indifference curve I_1. The move from C to K is the substitution effect of the price change. The substitution effect of the fall in the price of a movie is an increase in the consumption of movies from 2 to 4. The direction of the substitution effect never varies: When the relative price of a good falls, the consumer substitutes more of that good for the other good.

Income Effect To calculate the substitution effect, we gave Lisa a $9 pay cut. To calculate the income effect, we give Lisa her $9 back. The $9 increase in income shifts Lisa's budget line outward, as shown in Fig. 8.9(b). The slope of the budget line does not change because both prices remain constant. This change in Lisa's budget line is similar to the one illustrated in Fig. 8.8. As Lisa's budget line shifts outward, her consumption possibilities expand and her best affordable point becomes J on indifference curve I_2. The move from K to J is the income effect of the price change. In this example, as Lisa's income increases, she increases the number of movies she sees. For Lisa, a movie is a normal good. For a normal good, the income effect reinforces the substitution effect.

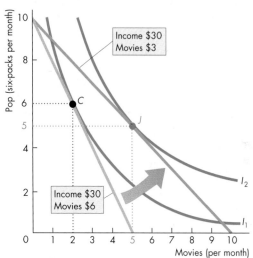

FIGURE 8.9 myeconlab

Substitution Effect and Income Effect

(a) Price effect

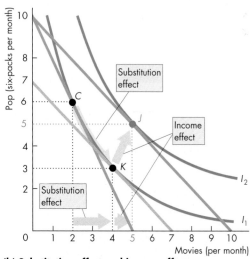

(b) Substitution effect and income effect

The price effect in part (a) can be separated into a substitution effect and an income effect in part (b).

To isolate the substitution effect, we confront Lisa with the new price but keep her on her original indifference curve, I_1. The substitution effect is the move from C to K.

To isolate the income effect, we confront Lisa with the new price of movies but increase her income so that she can move from the original indifference curve, I_1, to the new one, I_2. The income effect is the move from K to J.

Inferior Goods The example that we have just studied is that of a change in the price of a normal good. The effect of a change in the price of an inferior good is different. Recall that an inferior good is one whose consumption decreases as income increases. For an inferior good, the income effect is negative. Thus for an inferior good, a lower price does not always lead to an increase in the quantity demanded. The lower price has a substitution effect that increases the quantity demanded. But the lower price also has a negative income effect that reduces the demand for the inferior good. So the income effect offsets the substitution effect to some degree. If the negative income effect exceeded the positive substitution effect, the demand curve would slope upward. This case does not appear to occur in the real world.

Back to the Facts

We started this chapter by observing how consumer spending has changed over the years. The indifference curve model explains those changes. The best affordable choices determine spending patterns. Changes in prices and income change the best affordable choice and change consumption patterns.

REVIEW QUIZ

1 When a consumer chooses the combination of goods and services to buy, what is she or he trying to achieve?
2 Can you explain the conditions that are met when a consumer has found the best affordable combination of goods to buy? (Use the terms budget line, marginal rate of substitution, and relative price in your explanation.)
3 The price of a normal good falls, what happens to the quantity demanded of that good?
4 Into what two effects can we divide the effect of a price change?
5 For a normal good, does the income effect reinforce the substitution effect or does it partly offset the substitution effect?

myeconlab Study Plan 8.3

The model of household choice can explain many other household choices. Let's look at one of them.

Work–Leisure Choices

HOUSEHOLDS MAKE MANY CHOICES OTHER THAN those about how to spend their income on the various goods and services available. We can use the model of consumer choice to understand many other household choices. Some of these choices are discussed on pp. 192–196. Here we'll study a key choice: how much labour to supply.

Labour Supply

Every week, we allocate our 168 hours between working—called *labour*—and all other activities—called *leisure.* How do we decide how to allocate our time between labour and leisure? We can answer this question by using the theory of household choice.

The more hours we spend on *leisure,* the smaller is our income. The relationship between leisure and income is described by an *income-time budget line.* Figure 8.10(a) shows Lisa's income-time budget line. If Lisa devotes the entire week to leisure—168 hours—she has no income and is at point Z. By supplying labour in exchange for a wage, she can convert hours into income along the income-time budget line. The slope of that line is determined by the hourly wage rate. If the wage rate is $5 an hour, Lisa faces the flattest budget line. If the wage rate is $10 an hour, she faces the middle budget line. And if the wage rate is $15 an hour, she faces the steepest budget line.

Lisa buys leisure by not supplying labour and by forgoing income. The opportunity cost of an hour of leisure is the hourly wage rate forgone.

Figure 8.10(a) also shows Lisa's indifference curves for income and leisure. Lisa chooses her best attainable point. This choice of income and time allocation is just like her choice of movies and pop. She gets onto the highest possible indifference curve by making her marginal rate of substitution between income and leisure equal to her wage rate. Lisa's choice depends on the wage rate she can earn. At a wage rate of $5 an hour, Lisa chooses point A and works 20 hours a week (168 minus 148) for an income of $100 a week. At a wage rate of $10 an hour, she chooses point B and works 35 hours a week (168 minus 133) for an income of $350 a week. And at a wage rate of $15 an hour, she chooses point C and works 30 hours a week (168 minus 138) for an income of $450 a week.

FIGURE 8.10

myeconlab

The Supply of Labour

(a) Time allocation decision

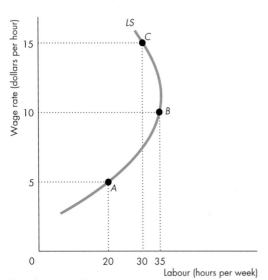

(b) Labour supply curve

In part (a), at a wage rate of $5 an hour, Lisa takes 148 hours of leisure and works 20 hours a week at point A. If the wage rate increases from $5 to $10, she decreases her leisure to 133 hours and increases her work to 35 hours a week at point B. But if the wage rate increases from $10 to $15, Lisa *increases* her leisure to 138 hours and *decreases* her work to 30 hours a week at point C. Part (b) shows Lisa's labour supply curve. Points A, B, and C on the supply curve correspond to Lisa's choices on her income-time budget line in part (a).

The Labour Supply Curve

Figure 8.10(b) shows Lisa's labour supply curve. This curve shows that as the wage rate increases from $5 an hour to $10 an hour, Lisa increases the quantity of labour supplied from 20 hours a week to 35 hours a week. But when the wage rate increases to $15 an hour, she decreases her quantity of labour supplied to 30 hours a week.

Lisa's supply of labour is similar to that described for the economy as a whole at the beginning of this chapter. As wage rates have increased, work hours have decreased. At first, this pattern seems puzzling. We've seen that the hourly wage rate is the opportunity cost of leisure. So a higher wage rate means a higher opportunity cost of leisure. This fact on its own leads to a decrease in leisure and an increase in work hours. But instead, we've cut our work hours. Why? Because our incomes have increased. As the wage rate increases, incomes increase, so people demand more of all normal goods. Leisure is a normal good, so as incomes increase, people demand more leisure.

The higher wage rate has both a *substitution effect* and an *income effect*. The higher wage rate increases the opportunity cost of leisure and so leads to a substitution effect away from leisure. And the higher wage rate increases income and so leads to an income effect towards more leisure. This outcome of rational household choice explains why the average workweek has fallen steadily as wage rates have increased. With higher wage rates, people have decided to use their higher incomes in part to consume more leisure.

REVIEW QUIZ

1 What is the opportunity cost of leisure?
2 Why might a rise in the wage rate lead to an increase in leisure and a decrease in work hours?

myeconlab Study Plan 8.4

◆ *Reading Between the Lines* on pp. 184–185 shows you how the theory of household choice explains why, even though e-books are cheaper than print books, students continue to buy more print books than e-books.

In the chapters that follow, we study firms' choices. We'll see how, in the pursuit of profit, firms make choices that determine the supply of goods and services and the demand for productive resources.

The Marginal Rate of Substitution Between Printed Books and E-Books

THE TORONTO STAR, AUGUST 15, 2005

E-books' latest bid to send paper packing

Move over hardcopies. Starting today, there's a new item on bookstore shelves.

Ten U.S. university bookstores are stocking digital versions of popular textbooks alongside the paper products. The digital version will sell for approximately 33 per cent less than a new, paper copy.

The pilot project will include approximately 200 titles from McGraw-Hill Higher Education, Thomson Learning, Sage Publications and Houghton Mifflin Company.

"We're interested in measuring student demand for digital content," said David Serbun, director of partnerships for Houghton Mifflin's college division. "We're also interested in offering students a choice."

Once a digital textbook has been downloaded to a student's computer, sections can be highlighted and pages can be printed. Students can also search their digital book for keywords.

Downloadable books have been available online for years, but according to Jeff Cohen, advertising and promotions manager for MBS Textbook Exchange Inc., this is the first time that digital books will be featured on stores shelves, right beside the traditional, bound versions.

It was essential to get the digital products into brick and mortar stores, Cohen said, because "the majority of textbook purchases still take place in a physical bookstore."

...

Reprinted with permission—Torstar Syndication Services. From an article originally appearing in the *Toronto Star*, August 2005.

Essence of the Story

■ Ten U.S. university bookstores are stocking electronic versions of textbooks—e-books—alongside the paper products.

■ The price of a digital textbook will be approximately 33 percent less than a new paper copy. One of the publishers says it wants to measure student demand for digital content.

■ E-books have been available online for years but this is the first time that they can be bought alongside print books in a bookstore. The majority of textbook purchases still take place in a physical bookstore.

Economic Analysis

■ Print books and e-books are good substitutes, but not perfect substitutes for most students.

■ When two goods are close substitutes, the marginal rate of substitution doesn't change much as the quantities consumed change, so the indifference curves are relatively straight and a small change in the relative price brings a large change in the quantities bought.

■ Figure 1 shows an example of what a student's indifference curves for print books and e-books might look like.

■ These indifference curves imply that although both print books and e-books have their own unique advantages, on balance, the traditional print book still does a better job than the e-book. It is more convenient and easier to use.

■ The figure also shows two budget lines, the line *AB* and the line *AC*.

■ On these budget lines, the student has a budget for books that enables her to buy 9 print books a year and no e-books.

■ Along the budget line *AB*, the price of a print book is the same as the price of an e-book.

■ Along the budget line *AC*, the price of an e-book is 33 percent lower than the price of a print book.

■ If the two types of book have the same price, the student's best affordable point, where her budget line just touches her indifference curve I_0, is where she buys 9 print books and no e-books.

■ With the price of an e-book 33 percent lower than the price of a print book, the student's best affordable point, where her budget line just touches her indifference curve I_1, is where she buys 7 print books and 3 e-books.

■ If the price of an e-book falls further, relative to the price of a print book, students will substitute more e-books for print books.

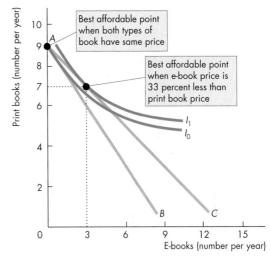

Best affordable point when both types of book have same price

Best affordable point when e-book price is 33 percent less than print book price

Figure 1 A student's choices

185

SUMMARY

KEY POINTS

Consumption Possibilities (pp. 172–174)

- The budget line is the boundary between what the household can and cannot afford given its income and the prices of goods.
- The point at which the budget line intersects the *y*-axis is the household's real income in terms of the good measured on that axis.
- The magnitude of the slope of the budget line is the relative price of the good measured on the *x*-axis in terms of the good measured on the *y*-axis.
- A change in price changes the slope of the budget line. A change in income shifts the budget line but does not change its slope.

Preferences and Indifference Curves (pp. 175–178)

- A consumer's preferences can be represented by indifference curves. An indifference curve joins all the combinations of goods among which the consumer is indifferent.
- A consumer prefers any point above an indifference curve to any point on it and any point on an indifference curve to any point below it.
- The magnitude of the slope of an indifference curve is called the marginal rate of substitution.
- The marginal rate of substitution diminishes as consumption of the good measured on the *y*-axis decreases and consumption of the good measured on the *x*-axis increases.

Predicting Consumer Behaviour (pp. 178–182)

- A household consumes at its best affordable point. This point is on the budget line and on the highest attainable indifference curve and has a marginal rate of substitution equal to relative price.
- The effect of a price change (the price effect) can be divided into a substitution effect and an income effect.
- The substitution effect is the effect of a change in price on the quantity bought when the consumer

(hypothetically) remains indifferent between the original situation and the new situation.

- The substitution effect always results in an increase in consumption of the good whose relative price has fallen.
- The income effect is the effect of a change in income on consumption.
- For a normal good, the income effect reinforces the substitution effect. For an inferior good, the income effect works in the opposite direction to the substitution effect.

Work–Leisure Choices (pp. 182–183)

- The indifference curve model of household choice enables us to understand how a household allocates its time between work and leisure.
- Work hours have decreased and leisure hours have increased because the income effect on the demand for leisure has been greater than the substitution effect.

KEY FIGURES

Figure 8.1   The Budget Line, 172
Figure 8.2   Changes in Prices and Income, 174
Figure 8.3   A Preference Map, 175
Figure 8.4   The Marginal Rate of Substitution, 176
Figure 8.6   The Best Affordable Point, 178
Figure 8.7   Price Effect and Demand Curve, 179
Figure 8.8   Income Effect and Change in Demand, 180
Figure 8.9   Substitution Effect and Income Effect, 181

KEY TERMS

Budget line, 172
Diminishing marginal rate of substitution, 176
Income effect, 180
Indifference curve, 175
Marginal rate of substitution, 176
Price effect, 179
Real income, 173
Relative price, 173
Substitution effect, 181

PROBLEMS

Go to 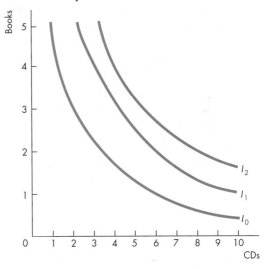 myeconlab **for solutions to odd-numbered problems and additional exercises.**

1. Sara's income is $12 a week, popcorn is $3 a bag, and cola is $3 a can.
   a. What is Sara's real income in terms of cola?
   b. What is her real income in terms of popcorn?
   c. What is the relative price of cola in terms of popcorn?
   d. What is the opportunity cost of a can of cola?
   e. What is the equation for Sara's budget line (with popcorn on the left side).
   f. Draw a graph of Sara's budget line with cola on the *x*-axis.
   g. In (f), what is the slope of Sara's budget line? What determines its value?

2. Rashid's income is $100 per week. The price of a CD is $10, and the price of a book is $20.
   a. What is Rashid's real income in terms of CDs?
   b. What is his real income in terms of books?
   c. What is the relative price of a CD in terms of books?
   d. What is the opportunity cost of a book?
   e. What is the equation for Rashid's budget line (with books on the left side).
   f. Draw a graph of Rashid's budget line with CDs on the *x*-axis.
   g. In (f), what is the slope of Rashid's budget line? What determines its value?

3. Sara's income and the prices of popcorn and cola are the same as those in problem 1. The figure illustrates Sara's preferences.

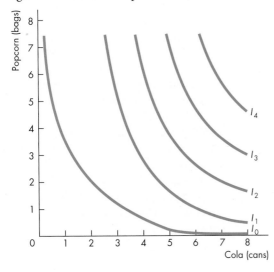

a. What quantities of popcorn and cola does Sara buy?
b. What is Sara's marginal rate of substitution at the point at which she consumes?

4. Rashid's income and the prices of CDs and books are the same as those in problem 2. The figure illustrates his preferences.

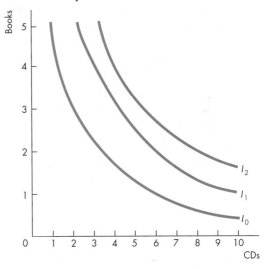

a. What quantities of CDs and books does Rashid buy?
b. What is Rashid's marginal rate of substitution at the point at which he consumes?

5. Now suppose that in problem 3, the price of cola falls to $1.50 a can and the price of popcorn and Sara's income remain the same.
   a. What quantities of cola and popcorn does Sara now buy?
   b. Find two points on Sara's demand curve for cola.
   c. Find the substitution effect of the price change.
   d. Find the income effect of the price change.
   e. Is cola a normal good or an inferior good for Sara?

6. Now suppose that in problem 4, the price of a CD rises to $20 and the price of a book and Rashid's income remain the same.
   a. What quantities of CDs and books does Rashid now buy?
   b. Find two points on Rashid's demand curve for CDs.
   c. Find the substitution effect of the price change.

d. Find the income effect of the price change.

e. Is a CD a normal good or an inferior good for Rashid?

7. Pam buys cookies and comic books. The price of a cookie is $1, and the price of a comic book is $2. Each month, Pam spends all of her income and buys 30 cookies and 5 comic books. Next month, the price of a cookie will fall to 50¢ and the price of a comic book will rise to $5. Assume that Pam's preference map is similar to that in Fig. 8.3(b). Use a graph to answer the following questions.

a. Will Pam be able to buy 30 cookies and 5 comic books next month?

b. Will Pam want to buy 30 cookies and 5 comic books?

c. Which situation does Pam prefer: cookies at $1 and comic books at $2 or cookies at 50¢ and comic books at $5?

d. If Pam changes the quantities that she buys, which good will she buy more of and which will she buy less of?

e. When the prices change next month, will there be an income effect and a substitution effect at work or just one of them?

8. Yangjie buys smoothies and sushi. The price of a smoothie is $5, and the price of sushi is $1 a piece. Each month, Yangjie spends all of her income and buys 10 smoothies and 20 pieces of sushi. Next month, the price of a smoothie will fall to $3 and the price of sushi will rise to $2 a piece. Assume that Yangjie's preference map is similar to that in Fig. 8.3(b). Use a graph to answer the following questions.

a. Will Yangjie be able to buy 10 smoothies and 20 pieces of sushi next month?

b. Will Yangjie want to buy 10 smoothies and 20 pieces of sushi? Explain why.

c. Which situation does Yangjie prefer: smoothies at $5 each and sushi at $1 a piece or smoothies at $3 each and sushi at $2 a piece?

d. If Yangjie changes the quantities that she buys, which good will she buy more of and which will she buy less of?

e. When the prices change next month, will there be an income effect and a substitution effect at work or just one of them? Explain.

CRITICAL THINKING

1. Study *Reading Between the Lines* about print books and e-books on pp. 184–185, and then answer the following questions.

a. Do you buy print books only, or do you buy some e-books as well?

b. Sketch your budget constraint for textbooks and other items.

c. Sketch your indifference curves for textbooks and other goods.

d. What do you predict would happen to the way that you allocate your budget between textbooks and other goods and services if the price of an e-book fell to 10 percent of the price of a current print book?

2. A sales tax is a tax on goods and the GST is a tax on both goods and services. Canadians hate the GST but is a federal sales tax better than the GST? When Canada replaced the federal sales tax with the GST:

a. What happened to the relative price of CD-Rs and haircuts and to a consumer's budget line of CD-Rs and haircuts?

b. How did purchases of CD-Rs and haircuts change?

c. Which tax is better for the consumer? Why?

Use a graph to illustrate your answers and to show the substitution effect and the income effect of the price change.

WEB EXERCISES

Use the links on (myeconlab) **to work the following exercise.**

1. Obtain information about the prices of cell phone service and first-class mail.

a. Sketch the budget constraint for a consumer who spent $50 a month on these two goods in 2002 and 2003.

b. Can you say whether the consumer was better off or worse off in 2002 than in 2003?

c. Sketch some indifference curves for cell phone calls and first-class letters mailed and show the income effect and the substitution effect of the changes in prices that occurred between 2002 and 2003.

APPENDIX

Marginal Utility and Indifference Curves

After studying Chapters 7 and 8 and this appendix, you will be able to

■ Explain the connection between utility and indifference curves

■ Explain why maximizing utility is the same as choosing the best affordable point

■ Explain why utility exists

Two Ways of Describing Preferences

THE MARGINAL UTILITY MODEL DESCRIBES preferences by using the concept of utility. An increase in the quantity consumed of a good brings an increase in the total utility derived from that good and a decrease in its marginal utility (see Table 7.1, p. 155, and Figure 7.2, p. 156).

The indifference curve model describes preferences by using the concepts of preference and indifference to define a map of indifference curves. A higher indifference curve is preferred to a lower one. And along an indifference curve, the marginal rate of substitution diminishes (see Figure 8.3, p. 175, and Figure 8.4, p. 176).

The indifference curve model doesn't need the concept of utility. In fact, it was developed precisely because economists wanted a more objective way of describing preferences. But we can interpret the indifference curve model by using the concept of utility.

Because a consumer is indifferent among the combinations of goods at all the points on an indifference curve, these combinations provide the same amount of total utility. An indifference curve is a constant utility curve.

You can see the connection between utility and an indifference map by looking at Fig. A8.1. Part (a) provides information about the total utility from movies and pop. It is based on Table 7.1, (p. 155), but instead of listing the quantities of the two goods and the total utility arising from each quantity consumed, the numbers are arranged with movies across the bottom and pop down the side. With no pop, the total utility from

FIGURE A8.1

Total Utility and the Indifference Map

(a) Total utility

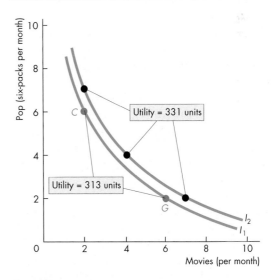

(b) Indifference curves

We can represent preferences by using the concept of utility or indifference curves. In the table, Lisa's total utility depends on the quantities of movies and pop that she consumes. Different combinations yield the same total utility. These combinations lie on an indifference curve. The figure shows two indifference curves: one for 313 units of utility and one for 331 units of utility.

6 movies is 196 units. And with no movies, the total utility from 2 six-packs is 117 units.

Figure A8.1(a) also shows the total utility from some other combinations of movies and pop. For example, the total utility from 6 movies and 2 six-packs is 313 units (196 plus 117). Part (a) shows another combination that delivers 313 units and three combinations that deliver 331 units of utility.

The figure shows the indifference curves associated with these two levels of total utility.

Maximizing Utility Is Choosing the Best Affordable Point

IN THE MARGINAL UTILITY MODEL, LISA maximizes total utility by spending all of her income on the combination of movies and pop that makes the marginal utility per dollar on movies equal to the marginal utility per dollar on pop. That is,

$$MU_M/P_M = MU_P/P_P,   (1)$$

where MU_M is the marginal utility of a movie, P_M is the price of a movie, MU_P is the marginal utility of pop, and P_P is the price of pop.

In the indifference curve model, Lisa chooses the best affordable point by spending all of her income on the combination of movies and pop that makes the marginal rate of substitution (MRS) equal to the relative price of the two goods.

That is,

$$MRS = P_M/P_P.   (2)$$

Maximizing total utility and choosing the best affordable point are the same. To see why, first multiply both sides of equation (1) above by P_M and divide both sides by MU_P to obtain

$$MU_M/MU_P = P_M/P_P.   (3)$$

This equation states that the ratio of the marginal utilities of the two goods is equal to the relative price of the two goods.

Inspect equations (2) and (3) and you can see that if the two ways of describing a consumer's choice are the same, then the marginal rate of substitution must equal the ratio of the marginal utilities of the two goods.

That is,

$$MRS = MU_M/MU_P.   (4)$$

To establish that this proposition is true, note that total utility changes when the quantities consumed change in the following way:

$$\Delta U = MU_M \times \Delta Q_M + MU_P \times \Delta Q_P,   (5)$$

where Δ means "change in," U is utility, Q_M is the quantity of movies consumed, and Q_P is the quantity of pop consumed.

Recall that along an indifference curve, total utility is constant so the change in total utility is zero. Then, along an indifference curve, it must be the case that

$$0 = MU_M \times \Delta Q_M + MU_P \times \Delta Q_P,   (6)$$

or

$$MU_M \times \Delta Q_M = -MU_P \times \Delta Q_P.   (7)$$

Divide both sides of equation (7) by MU_P and by ΔQ_M to obtain

$$MU_M/MU_P = -\Delta Q_P/\Delta Q_M.   (8)$$

This equation tells us that along an indifference curve, the change in the quantity of pop consumed divided by the change in the quantity of movies consumed equals the ratio of the marginal utilities of movies and pop.

But $-\Delta Q_P/\Delta Q_M$ (rise over run) is the slope of the indifference curve. And, removing the minus sign, $\Delta Q_P/\Delta Q_M$ is the marginal rate of substitution of movies for pop. So,

$$MRS = \Delta Q_P/\Delta Q_M = MU_M/MU_P.   (9)$$

You've now seen that the two models of consumer choice make identical predictions about the quantities that a consumer chooses. Spending the available budget with the marginal utility per dollar the same for both goods is the same as spending the available budget with the marginal rate of substitution between the two goods equal to their relative price.

Utility Exists!

THE INDIFFERENCE CURVE MODEL IS POWERFUL because its only assumptions are that people can rank alternative combinations of goods as preferred or indifferent and that the marginal rate of substitution diminishes. From these assumptions, we can derive the downward-sloping demand curve. We can also easily visualize the effects of changes in prices and income on a consumer's choice.

The indifference curve model is also powerful because its assumptions imply the existence of utility and of (generally) diminishing marginal utility.

By observing the prices of goods and the quantities consumed, we can infer a consumer's marginal utilities at each quantity.

UNDERSTANDING HOUSEHOLDS' CHOICES

Making the Most of Life

The powerful forces of demand and supply shape the fortunes of families, businesses, nations, and empires in the same unrelenting way that the tides and winds shape rocks and coastlines. You saw in Chapters 3 through 6 how these forces raise and lower prices, increase and decrease quantities bought and sold, cause revenues to fluctuate, and send resources to their most valuable uses.

These powerful forces begin quietly and privately with the choices that each one of us makes.

Chapters 7 and 8 probe these individual choices. Chapter 7 explores the marginal utility theory of human decisions. This theory explains people's consumption plans. It also explains people's consumption of leisure time and its flip side, the supply of work time. Marginal utility theory can even be used to explain "non-economic" choices, such as whether to marry and how many children to have. In a sense, there are no non-economic choices. If there is scarcity, there must be choice. And economics studies all such choices.

Chapter 8 describes a tool that enables us to make a map of people's likes and dislikes, a tool called an *indifference curve*. Indifference curves are considered an advanced topic, so this chapter is *strictly optional*. But the presentation of indifference curves in Chapter 8 is the clearest and most straightforward available, so if you want to learn about this tool, this chapter is the place to do so.

The earliest economists (Adam Smith and his contemporaries) did not have a very deep understanding of households' choices. It was not until the nineteenth century that progress was made in this area. On the following pages, you can spend some time with Jeremy Bentham, the person who pioneered the use of the concept of utility to the study of human choices, and with Steven Levitt of the University of Chicago, who is one of today's most influential students of human behaviour.

PROBING THE IDEAS

People as Rational Decision Makers

THE ECONOMIST

Jeremy Bentham *(1748–1832), who lived in London, was the son and grandson of a lawyer and was himself trained as a barrister. But he rejected the opportunity to maintain the family tradition and, instead, spent his life as a writer, activist, and Member of Parliament in the pursuit of rational laws that would bring the greatest happiness to the greatest number of people.*

Bentham, whose embalmed body is preserved to this day in a glass cabinet in the University of London, was the first person to use the concept of utility to explain human choices. But in Bentham's day, the distinction between explaining and prescribing was not a sharp one, and Bentham was ready to use his ideas to tell people how they ought to behave. He was one of the first to propose pensions for the retired, guaranteed employment, minimum wages, and social benefits such as free education and free medical care.

"... It is the greatest happiness of the greatest number that is the measure of right and wrong."

JEREMY
BENTHAM
*Fragment on
Government*

THE ISSUES

The economic analysis of human behaviour in the family, the workplace, the markets for goods and services, the markets for labour services, and financial markets is based on the idea that our behaviour can be understood as a response to scarcity. Everything we do can be understood as a choice that maximizes total benefit subject to the constraints imposed by our limited resources and technology. If people's preferences are stable in the face of changing constraints, then we have a chance of predicting how they will respond to an evolving environment.

The economic approach explains the incredible change that has occurred during the past 100 years in the way women allocate their time as the consequence of changing constraints, not of changing attitudes. Technological advances have equipped the nation's farms and factories with machines that have increased the productivity of both women and men, thereby raising the wages they can earn. The increasingly technological world has increased the return to education for both women and men and has led to a large increase in high school and university graduates of both sexes. And equipped with an ever-widening array of gadgets and appliances that cut the time taken to do household jobs, an increasing proportion of women have joined the labour force.

The economic explanation might not be correct, but it is a powerful one. And if it is correct, the changing attitudes are a consequence, not a cause, of the economic advancement of women.

NOW

By 2002, more than 60 percent of women were in the labour force, and although many had low-paying jobs, women were increasingly found in the professions and in executive positions. What brought about this dramatic change compared with 100 years earlier? Was it a change in preferences or a change in the constraints that women face?

THEN

Economists explain people's actions as the consequences of choices that maximize total utility subject to constraints. In the 1890s, fewer than 20 percent of women chose market employment, and most of those who did had low-paying and unattractive jobs. The other 80 percent of women chose nonmarket work in the home. What constraints led to these choices?

Steven Levitt, whom you can meet on the following pages, shows us how economic reasoning combined with the data generated by natural experiments deepens our understanding of an astonishing range of human choices.

TALKING WITH

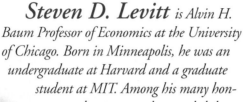

Steven D. Levitt *is Alvin H. Baum Professor of Economics at the University of Chicago. Born in Minneapolis, he was an undergraduate at Harvard and a graduate student at MIT. Among his many honours, he was recently awarded the John Bates Clark Medal given to the best economist under 40.*

Professor Levitt has studied an astonishingly wide range of human choices and their outcomes. He has examined the effects of policing on crime, shown that realtors get a higher price when they sell their own homes than when they sell other people's, devised a test to detect teachers who cheat, and studied the choices of drug dealers and gang members.

Steven D. Levitt

The use of natural experiments unifies this apparently diverse body of research. Professor Levitt has an incredible ability to find just the right set of events and the data the events have generated to enable him to isolate the effect he's looking for.

Steven Levitt's research has been made accessible to a wide audience in Freakonomics *(with Stephen J. Dubner), which in August 2005 outsold the new Harry Potter story on Amazon.ca!*

Michael Parkin and Robin Bade talked with Steven Levitt about his career and the progress that economists have made in understanding how people respond to incentives in all aspects of life.

Why did you become an economist?

As a freshman in college, I took introductory economics. All the ideas made perfect sense to me – it was the way I naturally thought. My friends were befuddled. I thought, "This is the field for me!"

The idea of rational choice made at the margin lies at the heart of economics. Would you say that your work generally supports that idea or challenges it? Can you provide some examples?

I don't like the word "rational" in this context. I think economists model agents as being rational just for convenience. What really matters is whether people respond to incentives. My work very much supports the idea that humans in all types of circumstances respond strongly to incentives. I've seen it with drug dealers, auto thieves, sumo wrestlers, real estate agents, and elementary school teachers, just to name a few examples.

Can you elaborate? What are the incentives to which drug dealers respond? And does an understanding of these responses tell us anything about how public policy might influence drug use?

The incentives people face differ depending on their particular circumstances. Drug dealers, for instance, want to make money, but they also want to avoid being arrested or even killed. In the data we have on drug sellers, we see that when the drug trade is more lucrative, dealers are willing to take greater risks of arrest to carve out a share of the market. On the other hand, they also do their best to minimize their risks. For example, crack sellers used to carry the crack with them. When laws were passed imposing stiff penalties on anyone caught with anything more than a minimal amount of crack, drug dealers responded by storing the crack somewhere else, and retrieving only the amount being

194

sold to the current client. Sumo wrestlers, on the other hand, care mostly about their official ranking. Sometimes matches occur where one wrestler has more to lose or gain than the other wrestler. We find that sumo wrestlers make corrupt deals to make sure the wrestler who needs the win is the one who actually wins.

> " *I think of economics as being primarily about a way of looking at the world and a set of tools for thinking clearly.* "

Why is an economist interested in crime and cheating?

I think of economics as being primarily about a way of looking at the world and a set of tools for thinking clearly. The topics you apply these tools to are unlimited. That is why I think economics has been so powerful. If you understand economics and use the tools wisely, you will be a better business person, doctor, public servant, parent.

What is the economic model of crime? And how does it help to design better ways of dealing with criminal activity? Can you illustrate by talking a bit about your work on the behaviour of auto thieves?

The economic model of crime argues that people have a choice of either working for a wage in the legal sector or earning money from illegal activity. The model carefully lays out the set of costs associated with being a criminal (e.g., forgone wages and being punished) and benefits (e.g., the loot) associated with crime and analyzes how a maximizing individual will choose whether to commit crimes and how much crime to commit. One reason the model is useful is because it lays out the various ways in which public policy might influence crime rates. For instance, we can increase the probability of a criminal getting caught, or make the prison sentence longer for those who are caught. The government might also try to intervene in the labour market to make legal work more attractive—for instance, with a minimum wage.

> " *If you just look at different cities, the places with the most police also have the most crime, but it is not because police cause crime, it is because crime causes police to be hired.* "

What is the problem in figuring out whether more police leads to less crime? How did you find the answer?

We think that when you add more police, crime will fall because the cost of being a criminal goes up because of increased detection. From a public policy perspective, understanding how much crime falls in response to police is an important question. In practice, it is hard to answer this question because we don't randomly hire police. Rather, where crime is bad, there is greater demand for police and thus more police. If you just look at different cities, the places with the most police also have the most crime, but it is not because police cause crime, it is because crime causes police to be hired.

To figure out a causal impact of police on crime, you would like to do a randomized experiment where you added a lot of police at random to some cities and took them away in other cities. That is something you cannot really do in real life. So instead, the economist has to look for "natural experiments" to answer the question.

I used the timing of mayoral elections. It turns out that mayors hire a lot of police before elections to "look tough on crime." If elections do not otherwise affect crime, then the election is kind of like a randomizing device that puts more police in some cities every once in a while. Indeed, I found that crime goes down in the year following elections once the police hired are up and running. It is indirect evidence, but it is an example of how economists use their toolbox to handle difficult questions.

Your work shows that legalized abortion leads to less crime. Can you explain how you reach that conclusion? Can you also explain its implications for the pro-life pro-choice debate?

The theory is simple: unwanted children have hard lives (including being much more likely to be criminals); after legalized abortion, there are fewer unwanted children. Therefore, there should be less crime (with a 15–20 year lag while the babies grow up and reach high crime ages).

We looked at what happened to crime 15–20 years after Roe v. Wade, in states with high and low abortion rates, and in states that legalized abortion a few years earlier than the rest of the country. We could even look at people born immediately before or after abortion became legal.

All the evidence pointed the same way: crime fell a lot because abortion was legalized.

Our results, however, don't have large implications for the abortion debate. If abortion is murder, as pro-life advocates argue, then the changes in crime we see are trivial in comparison. If a woman simply has the right to control her body, as pro-choice advocates argue, then our estimates about crime are likewise irrelevant.

Our results have more to say about unwantedness: There are big benefits to making sure that children who are brought into the world are wanted and well cared for, either through birth control, adoption, abortion, or parental education.

Terrorism is on everyone's minds these days. And presumably, terrorists respond to incentives. Have you thought about how we might be able to use the insights of economics to better understand and perhaps even combat terrorism?

Terrorism is an unusually difficult question to tackle through incentives. The religious terrorists we are

most worried about are willing to give up their lives to carry out terrorist acts. So the only punishment we can really offer is preventing them from committing the act by catching them before hand, or maybe minimizing the damage they can do. Unlike typical criminals, the threat of punishing them after the fact will not help deter the crime. Luckily, even among extremists, there are not many people willing to give their lives for a cause.

> *...every time I observed anything in the world I asked myself, "Is that a natural experiment?"*

Can a student learn how to use natural experiments or do you have a gift that is hard to teach?

I don't think I have such a gift. Most people who are good at something are good because they have worked hard and practised. That is certainly true with me.

For a while, I just walked around and every time I observed anything in the world I asked myself, "Is that a natural experiment?" Every once in a while I stumbled onto one because I was on the lookout.

What else can a student who wants to become a natural experimenting economist or broader social scientist do to better prepare for that career?

I would say that the best thing students can do is to try to really apply what they are learning to their lives, rather than just memorizing for an exam and quickly forgetting. If you are passionate about economics (or anything else for that matter), you are way ahead of others who are just trying to get by.

Organizing Production

Spinning a Web

In the fall of 1990, a British scientist named Tim Berners-Lee invented the World Wide Web. This remarkable idea paved the way for the creation and growth of thousands of profitable businesses. One of these businesses is McCain Foods Limited, a privately owned multinational frozen food manufacturer with global revenues of almost $6 billion a year. How do McCain Foods and the other 2 million firms in Canada make their business decisions? How do they operate efficiently?

One way in which firms seek to operate efficiently is by establishing incentives for their top executives, managers, and workers. Most of the time, these incentives work well. But sometimes, the people who run big firms spin another web—a web of deceit—and operate outside the law. When this happens, as it did at Enron and WorldCom, spectacular business failures can result. What are the incentive schemes that firms use and why do they sometimes result in catastrophic business failure?

Most of the firms that you know the names of don't make things. They buy and sell things. For example, most of the components of a Dell personal computer are made by other firms. Microsoft creates the operating system, and Intel makes the processor chip. Other firms make the hard drive and modem, and yet others make the CD drive, sound card, and so on. Why doesn't Dell make its own computer components? Why does it leave these activities to other firms and buy from them in markets? How do firms decide what to make themselves and what to buy in the marketplace from other firms?

◆ In this chapter, we are going to learn about firms and the choices they make to cope with scarcity. We begin by studying the economic problems and choices that are common to all firms.

After studying this chapter, you will be able to

- Explain what a firm is and describe the economic problems that *all* firms face

- Distinguish between technological efficiency and economic efficiency

- Define and explain the principal–agent problem and describe how different types of business organizations cope with this problem

- Describe and distinguish between different types of markets in which firms operate

- Explain why markets coordinate some economic activities and firms coordinate others

The Firm and Its Economic Problem

THE 2 MILLION FIRMS IN CANADA DIFFER IN SIZE and in the scope of what they do. But they all perform the same basic economic functions. Each **firm** is an institution that hires and organizes factors of production to produce and sell goods and services.

Our goal is to predict firms' behaviour. To do so, we need to know a firm's goals and the constraints it faces. We begin with the goals.

The Firm's Goal

If you asked a group of entrepreneurs what they are trying to achieve, you would get many different answers. Some would talk about making a high-quality product, others about business growth, others about market share, and others about the job satisfaction of their work force. All of these goals might be pursued, but they are not the fundamental goal. They are means to a deeper goal.

A firm's goal is to maximize profit. A firm that does not seek to maximize profit is either eliminated or bought out by firms that do seek to maximize profit.

What exactly is the profit that a firm seeks to maximize? To answer this question, let's look at Sidney's Sweaters.

Measuring the Firm's Profit

Sidney runs a successful business that makes sweaters. Sidney's Sweaters receives $400,000 a year for the sweaters it sells. Its expenses are $80,000 a year for wool, $20,000 for utilities, $120,000 for wages, and $10,000 in interest on a bank loan. With receipts of $400,000 and expenses of $230,000, Sidney's Sweaters' annual surplus is $170,000.

Sidney's accountant lowers this number by $20,000, which he says is the depreciation (fall in value) of the firm's buildings and knitting machines during the year. (Accountants use Canada Revenue Agency rules based on standards established by the accounting profession to calculate the depreciation.) So the accountant reports that the profit of Sidney's Sweaters is $150,000 a year.

Sidney's accountant measures cost and profit to ensure that the firm pays the correct amount of income tax and to show the bank how its loan has been used. But economists want to predict the decisions that a firm makes. These decisions respond to *opportunity cost* and *economic profit*.

Opportunity Cost

The *opportunity cost* of any action is the highest-valued alternative forgone. The action that you choose not to take—the highest-valued alternative forgone—is the cost of the action that you choose to take. For a firm, the opportunity cost of production is the value of the firm's best alternative use of its resources.

Opportunity cost is a real alternative forgone. But so that we can compare the cost of one action with that of another action, we express opportunity cost in money units. A firm's opportunity cost includes both

- Explicit costs
- Implicit costs

Explicit Costs Explicit costs are paid in money. The amount paid for a resource could have been spent on something else, so it is the opportunity cost of using the resource. For Sidney's Sweaters' expenditures on wool, utilities, wages, and bank interest are explicit costs.

Implicit Costs A firm incurs implicit costs when it forgoes an alternative action but does not make a payment. A firm incurs implicit costs when it

1. Uses its own capital.
2. Uses its owner's time or financial resources.

The cost of using its own capital is an implicit cost—and an opportunity cost—because the firm could rent the capital to another firm. The rental income forgone is the firm's opportunity cost of using its own capital. This opportunity cost is called the **implicit rental rate** of capital.

Firms rent photocopiers, computers, earth-moving equipment, satellite-launching services, and so on. If a firm rents capital, it incurs an explicit cost. If a firm buys the capital it uses, it incurs an implicit cost. The implicit rental rate of capital is made up of

1. Economic depreciation
2. Interest forgone

Economic depreciation is the change in the *market* value of capital over a given period. It is calculated as the market price of the capital at the beginning of the period minus its market price at the end of the period. For example, suppose that Sidney's Sweaters could have sold its buildings and knitting machines on December 31, 2005, for $400,000. If it can sell the same capital on December 31, 2006, for $375,000, its economic depreciation during 2006 is $25,000—the fall in the market value of the capital. This $25,000 is an implicit cost of using the capital during 2006.

The funds used to buy capital could have been used for some other purpose. And in their next best use, they would have yielded a return—an interest income. This forgone interest is part of the opportunity cost of using the capital. For example, Sidney's Sweaters could have bought bonds instead of knitting machines. The interest forgone on the bonds is an implicit cost of using the capital.

Cost of Owner's Resources A firm's owner often supplies entrepreneurial ability—the factor of production that organizes the business, makes business decisions, innovates, and bears the risk of running the business. The return to entrepreneurship is profit, and the return that an entrepreneur can expect to receive on the average is called **normal profit**. Normal profit is part of a firm's opportunity cost because it is the cost of a forgone alternative—running another firm. If normal profit in the textile business is $50,000 a year, this amount is part of the opportunity costs of operating Sidney's Sweaters.

The owner of a firm also can supply labour (in addition to entrepreneurship). The return to labour is a wage. And the opportunity cost of the owner's time spent working for the firm is the wage income forgone by not working in the best alternative job. Suppose that Sidney continues to supply entrepreneurial services to his sweater firm but could at the same time takes another job that pays $40,000 a year. By working for his knitting business, he forgoes $40,000 a year. The amount is part of the opportunity costs of operating Sidney's Sweaters.

Economic Profit

What is the bottom line—the firm's profit or loss? A firm's **economic profit** is equal to its total revenue minus its opportunity cost. The firm's opportunity cost is the sum of its explicit costs and implicit costs. Implicit costs, remember, include *normal profit*. The return to entrepreneurial ability is greater than normal in a firm that makes a positive economic profit. And the return to entrepreneurial ability is less than

normal in a firm that makes a negative economic profit—a firm that incurs an economic loss.

Economic Accounting: A Summary

Table 9.1 summarizes the economic accounting concepts that you've just studied. Sidney's Sweaters has total revenue of $400,000 and opportunity cost (explicit costs plus implicit costs) of $365,000. So its economic profit is $35,000.

To achieve the goal of maximum economic profit a firm must make five basic decisions:

1. What goods and services to produce and in what quantities
2. How to produce—the techniques of production to use
3. How to organize and compensate its managers and workers
4. How to market and price its products
5. What to produce itself and what to buy from other firms

In all these decisions, a firm's actions are limited by the constraints that it faces. Our next task is to learn about these constraints.

TABLE 9.1   Economic Accounting

Item		Amount
Total Revenue		**$400,000**
Opportunity Costs		
Wool	$80,000	
Utilities	20,000	
Wages paid	120,000	
Bank interest paid	10,000	
Total Explicit Costs		$230,000
Sidney's wages forgone	40,000	
Sidney's interest forgone	20,000	
Economic depreciation	25,000	
Normal profit	50,000	
Total Implicit Costs		$135,000
Total Cost		**$365,000**
Economic Profit		**$35,000**

The Firm's Constraints

The maximum profit a firm can make is limited by three features of its environment:

- Technology constraints
- Information constraints
- Market constraints

Technology Constraints Economists define technology broadly. A **technology** is any method of producing a good or service. Technology includes the detailed designs of machines. It also includes the layout of the workplace. And it includes the organization of the firm. For example, the shopping mall is a technology for producing retail services. It is a different technology from the catalogue store, which in turn is different from the downtown store.

It might seem surprising that a firm's profits are limited by technology, for it seems that technological advances are constantly increasing profit opportunities. Almost every day, we learn about some new technological advance that amazes us. With computers that speak and recognize our own speech and cars that can find the address we need in a city we've never visited before, we are able to accomplish ever more.

Technology advances over time. But at each point in time, to produce more output and gain more revenue, a firm must hire more resources and incur greater costs. The increase in profit that the firm can achieve is limited by the technology available. For example, by using its current plant and work force, Ford can produce some maximum number of cars per day. To produce more cars per day, Ford must hire more resources, which increases Ford's costs and limits the increase in profit that Ford can make by selling the additional cars.

Information Constraints We never possess all the information we would like to have to make decisions. We lack information about both the future and the present. For example, suppose you plan to buy a new computer. When should you buy it? The answer depends on how the price is going to change in the future. Where should you buy it? The answer depends on the prices at hundreds of different computer shops. To get the best deal, you must compare the quality and prices in every shop. But the opportunity cost of this comparison exceeds the cost of the computer!

Similarly, a firm is constrained by limited information about the quality and effort of its work force, the current and future buying plans of its customers, and the plans of its competitors. Workers might slacken off when the manager believes they are working hard. Customers might switch to competing suppliers. Firms must compete against competition from a new firm.

Firms try to create incentive systems for workers to ensure that they work hard even when no one is monitoring their efforts. And firms spend millions of dollars on market research. But none of these efforts and expenditures eliminates the problems of incomplete information and uncertainty. And the cost of coping with limited information itself limits profit.

Market Constraints What each firm can sell and the price it can obtain are constrained by its customers' willingness to pay and by the prices and marketing efforts of other firms. Similarly, the resources that a firm can buy and the prices it must pay for them are limited by the willingness of people to work for and invest in the firm. Firms spend billions of dollars a year marketing and selling their products. Some of the most creative minds strive to find the right message that will produce a knockout television advertisement. Market constraints and the expenditures firms make to overcome them limit the profit a firm can make.

REVIEW QUIZ

1 Why do firms seek to maximize profit? What happens to firms that don't pursue this goal?
2 Why do accountants and economists calculate a firm's cost and profit in different ways?
3 What are the items that make opportunity cost differ from the accountant's cost measure?
4 Why is normal profit part of the opportunity cost of operating a firm?
5 What are the constraints that firms face? How does each constraint limit the firm's profit?

 Study Plan 9.1

In the rest of this chapter and in Chapters 10 through 13, we study the decisions that firms make. We're going to learn how we can predict a firm's behaviour as the response to the constraints that it faces and to changes in those constraints. We begin by taking a closer look at the technology constraints, information constraints, and market constraints that firms face.

Technological and Economic Efficiency

MICROSOFT EMPLOYS A LARGE WORK FORCE, AND most Microsoft workers possess a large amount of human capital. But the firm uses a small amount of physical capital. In contrast, a coal-mining company employs a huge amount of mining equipment (physical capital) and almost no labour. Why? The answer lies in the concept of efficiency. There are two concepts of production efficiency: technological efficiency and economic efficiency. **Technological efficiency** occurs when the firm produces a given output by using the least amount of inputs. **Economic efficiency** occurs when the firm produces a given output at the least cost. Let's explore the two concepts of efficiency by studying an example.

Suppose that there are four alternative techniques for making TV sets:

A. *Robot production.* One person monitors the entire computer-driven process.
B. *Production line.* Workers specialize in a small part of the job as the emerging TV set passes them on a production line.
C. *Bench production.* Workers specialize in a small part of the job but walk from bench to bench to perform their tasks.
D. *Hand-tool production.* A single worker uses a few hand tools to make a TV set.

Table 9.2 sets out the amounts of labour and capital required by each of these four methods to make 10 TV sets a day.

Which of these alternative methods are technologically efficient?

Technological Efficiency

Recall that technological efficiency occurs when the firm produces a given output by using the least inputs. Inspect the numbers in the table and notice that method *A* uses the most capital but the least labour. Method *D* uses the most labour but the least capital. Method *B* and method *C* lie between the two extremes. They use less capital but more labour than method *A* and less labour but more capital than method *D*. Compare methods *B* and *C*. Method *C* requires 100 workers and 10 units of capital to produce 10 TV sets. Those same 10 TV

sets can be produced by method *B* with 10 workers and the same 10 units of capital. Because method *C* uses the same amount of capital and more labour than method *B*, method *C* is not technologically efficient.

Are any of the other methods not technologically efficient? The answer is no. Each of the other three methods is technologically efficient. Method *A* uses more capital but less labour than method *B*, and method *D* uses more labour but less capital than method *B*.

Which of the methods are economically efficient?

Economic Efficiency

Recall that economic efficiency occurs when the firm produces a given output at the least cost. Suppose that labour costs $75 per person-day and that capital costs $250 per machine-day. Table 9.3(a) calculates the costs of using the different methods to make a TV set. By inspecting the table, you can see that method *B* has the lowest cost. Although method *A* uses less labour, it uses too much expensive capital. And although method *D* uses less capital, it uses too much expensive labour.

Method *C*, which is technologically inefficient, is also economically inefficient. It uses the same amount of capital as method *B* but 10 times as much labour. So it costs more. A technologically inefficient method is never economically efficient.

Although *B* is the economically efficient method in this example, method *A* or *D* could be economically efficient with different input prices.

Suppose that labour costs $150 a person-day and capital costs only $1 a machine-day. Table 9.3(b) now shows the costs of making a TV set. In this case,

---

TABLE 9.2   Four Ways of Making 10 TV Sets a Day

Method		Quantities of inputs	
		Labour	Capital
A	Robot production	1	1,000
B	Production line	10	10
C	Bench production	100	10
D	Hand-tool production	1,000	1

TABLE 9.3   The Costs of Different Ways of Making 10 TV Sets a Day

(a) Four ways of making TVs

Method	Labour cost ($75 per day)		Capital cost ($250 per day)		Total cost	Cost per TV set
A	$75	+	$250,000	=	$250,075	$25,007.50
B	750	+	2,500	=	3,250	325.00
C	7,500	+	2,500	=	10,000	1,000.00
D	75,000	+	250	=	75,250	7,525.00

(b) Three ways of making TVs: High labour costs

Method	Labour cost ($150 per day)		Capital cost ($1 per day)		Total cost	Cost per TV set
A	$150	+	$1,000	=	$1,150	$115.00
B	1,500	+	10	=	1,510	151.00
D	150,000	+	1	=	150,001	15,000.10

(c) Three ways of making TVs: High capital costs

Method	Labour cost ($1 per day)		Capital cost ($1,000 per day)		Total cost	Cost per TV set
A	$1	+	$1,000,000	=	$1,000,001	$100,000.10
B	10	+	10,000	=	10,010	1,001.00
D	1,000	+	1,000	=	2,000	200.00

---

method *A* is economically efficient. Capital is now so cheap relative to labour that the method that uses the most capital is the economically efficient method.

Next, suppose that labour costs only $1 a person-day while capital costs $1,000 a machine-day. Table 9.3(c) shows the costs in this case. Method *D*, which uses a lot of labour and little capital, is now the least-cost method and the economically efficient method.

From these examples, you can see that while technological efficiency depends only on what is feasible, economic efficiency depends on the relative costs of resources. The economically efficient method is the one that uses less of a more expensive resource and more of a less expensive resource.

A firm that is not economically efficient does not maximize profit. Natural selection favours efficient firms and opposes inefficient firms. Inefficient firms go out of business or are taken over by firms with lower costs.

REVIEW QUIZ

1 How do we define technological efficiency? Is a firm technologically efficient if it uses the latest technology? Why or why not?

2 How do we define economic efficiency? Is a firm economically inefficient if it can cut costs by producing less? Why or why not?

3 Explain the key distinction between technological efficiency and economic efficiency.

4 Why do some firms use a lot of capital and not much labour, while others use not much capital and lots of labour?

⟨X⟩ **myeconlab   Study Plan 9.2**

Next we study information constraints that firms face and the diversity of organization structures they generate.

Information and Organization

EACH FIRM ORGANIZES THE PRODUCTION OF goods and services by combining and coordinating the productive resources it hires. But there is variety across firms in how they organize production. Firms use a mixture of two systems:

- Command systems
- Incentive systems

Command Systems

A **command system** is a method of organizing production that uses a managerial hierarchy. Commands pass downward through the managerial hierarchy, and information passes upward. Managers spend most of their time collecting and processing information about the performance of the people under their control and making decisions about commands to issue and how best to get those commands implemented.

The military uses the purest form of command system. A commander-in-chief makes the big decisions about strategic objectives. Beneath this highest level, generals organize their military resources. Beneath the generals, successively lower ranks organize smaller and smaller units but pay attention to ever-increasing degrees of detail. At the bottom of the managerial hierarchy are the people who operate weapons systems.

Command systems in firms are not as rigid as those in the military, but they share some similar features. A chief executive officer (CEO) sits at the top of a firm's command system. Senior executives who report to and receive commands from the CEO specialize in managing production, marketing, finance, personnel, and perhaps other aspects of the firm's operations. Beneath these senior managers might be several tiers of middle management ranks that stretch downward to the managers who supervise the day-to-day operations of the business. Beneath these managers are the people who operate the firm's machines and who make and sell the firm's goods and services.

Small firms have one or two layers of managers, while large firms have several layers. As production processes have become ever more complex, management ranks have swollen. Today, more people have management jobs than ever before. But the information revolution of the 1990s slowed the growth of management, and in some industries, it reduced the number of layers of managers and brought a shakeout of middle managers.

Managers make enormous efforts to be well informed. And they try hard to make good decisions and issue commands that end up using resources efficiently. But managers always have incomplete information about what is happening in the divisions of the firm for which they are responsible. It is for this reason that firms use incentive systems as well as command systems to organize production.

Incentive Systems

An **incentive system** is a method of organizing production that uses a market-like mechanism inside the firm. Instead of issuing commands, senior managers create compensation schemes that will induce workers to perform in ways that maximize the firm's profit.

Selling organizations use incentive systems most extensively. Sales representatives who spend most of their working time alone and unsupervised are induced to work hard by being paid a small salary and a large performance-related bonus.

But incentive systems operate at all levels in a firm. CEOs' compensation plans include a share in the firm's profit, and factory floor workers sometimes receive compensation based on the quantity they produce.

Mixing the Systems

Firms use a mixture of commands and incentives. And they choose the mixture that maximizes profit. They use commands when it is easy to monitor performance or when a small deviation from an ideal performance is very costly. They use incentives when monitoring performance is either not possible or too costly to be worth doing.

For example, it is easy to monitor the performance of workers on a production line. If one person works too slowly, the entire line slows. So a production line is organized with a command system.

In contrast, it is costly to monitor a CEO. For example, what did John Roth (former CEO of Nortel) contribute to the initial success and subsequent problems of Nortel? This question can't be answered with certainty, yet Nortel's stockholders had to put someone in charge of the business and provide that person with an incentive to maximize their returns. The performance of Nortel illustrates the nature of this problem, known as the principal–agent problem.

The Principal–Agent Problem

The **principal–agent problem** is the problem of devising compensation rules that induce an *agent* to act in the best interest of a *principal.* For example, the stockholders of Nortel are *principals,* and the firm's managers are *agents.* The stockholders (the principals) must induce the managers (agents) to act in the stockholders' best interest. Similarly, Bill Gates (a principal) must induce the programmers who are working on the next generation of Windows (agents) to work efficiently.

Agents, whether they are managers or workers, pursue their own goals and often impose costs on a principal. For example, the goal of stockholders of CIBC (principals) is to maximize the firm's profit. But the firm's profit depends on the actions of its managers (agents) who have their own goals. Perhaps a manager takes a customer to a ball game on the pretense that she is building customer loyalty, when in fact she is simply enjoying on-the-job leisure. This same manager is also a principal, and her tellers are agents. The manager wants the tellers to work hard and attract new customers so that she can meet her operating targets. But the workers enjoy conversations with each other and take on-the-job leisure. Nonetheless, the firm constantly strives to find ways of improving performance and increasing profits.

Coping with the Principal–Agent Problem

Issuing commands does not address the principal–agent problem. In most firms, the shareholders can't monitor the managers and often the managers can't monitor the workers. Each principal must create incentives that induce each agent to work in the interests of the principal. Three ways of attempting to cope with the principal–agent problem are

- Ownership
- Incentive pay
- Long-term contracts

Ownership By assigning to a manager or worker ownership (or part-ownership) of a business, it is sometimes possible to induce a job performance that increases a firm's profits. Part-ownership schemes for senior managers are quite common, but they are less

common but not unknown for workers. For example, in 1995 Canadian Pacific Ltd. sold off CP Express and Transport, a coast-to-coast trucking operation, to its 3,500 employees.

Incentive Pay Incentive pay schemes—pay related to performance—are very common. They are based on a variety of performance criteria such as profits, production, or sales targets. Promoting an employee for good performance is another example of an incentive pay scheme.

Long-Term Contracts Long-term contracts tie the long-term fortunes of managers and workers (agents) to the success of the principal(s)—the owner(s) of the firm. For example, a multiyear employment contract for a CEO encourages that person to take a long-term view and devise strategies that achieve maximum profit over a sustained period.

These three ways of coping with the principal–agent problem give rise to different types of business organization. Each type of business organization is a different response to the principal–agent problem. Each type uses ownership, incentives, and long-term contracts in different ways. Let's look at the main types of business organization.

Types of Business Organization

The three main types of business organization are

- Sole proprietorship
- Partnership
- Corporation

Sole Proprietorship A *sole proprietorship* is a firm with a single owner—a proprietor—who has unlimited liability. *Unlimited liability* is the legal responsibility for all the debts of a firm up to an amount equal to the entire wealth of the owner. If a sole proprietorship cannot pay its debts, those to whom the firm owes money can claim the personal property of the owner. Some farmers, computer programmers, and artists are examples of sole proprietorships.

The proprietor makes management decisions, receives the firm's profits, and is responsible for its losses. The profits are taxed at the same rate as other sources of the proprietor's personal income.

Partnership A *partnership* is a firm with two or more owners who have unlimited liability. Partners must agree on an appropriate management structure and on how to divide the firm's profits among themselves. The profits of a partnership are taxed as the personal income of the owners. But each partner is legally liable for all the debts of the partnership (limited only by the wealth of that individual partner). Liability for the full debts of the partnership is called *joint unlimited liability*. Most law firms are partnerships.

Corporation A *corporation* is a firm owned by one or more limited liability stockholders. *Limited liability* means that the owners have legal liability only for the value of their initial investment. This limitation of liability means that if the corporation becomes bankrupt, its owners are not required to use their personal wealth to pay the corporation's debts.

Corporations' profits are taxed independently of stockholders' incomes. The stockholders pay tax on dividends and a capital gains tax on the profit they earn when they sell a stock for a higher price than they paid for it. Corporate stocks generate capital gains when a corporation retains some of its profit and reinvests it in profitable activities.

Pros and Cons of Different Types of Firms

The different types of business organization arise as different ways of trying to cope with the principal–agent problem. Each has advantages in particular situations. And because of its special advantages, each type continues to exist. Each type also has its disadvantages, which explains why it has not driven out the other two.

Table 9.4 summarizes these pros and cons of the different types of firms.

TABLE 9.4   The Pros and Cons of Different Types of Firms

Type of Firm	Pros	Cons
Sole proprietorship	■ Easy to set up ■ Simple decision making ■ Profits taxed only once as owner's income	■ Bad decisions not checked by need for consensus ■ Owner's entire wealth at risk ■ Firm dies with owner ■ Capital is expensive ■ Labour is expensive
Partnership	■ Easy to set up ■ Diversified decision making ■ Can survive withdrawal of partner ■ Profits taxed only once as owners' incomes	■ Achieving consensus may be slow and expensive ■ Owners' entire wealth at risk ■ Withdrawal of partner may create capital shortage ■ Capital is expensive
Corporation	■ Owners have limited liability ■ Large-scale, low-cost capital available ■ Professional management not restricted by ability of owners ■ Perpetual life ■ Long-term labour contracts cut labour costs	■ Complex management structure can make decisions slow and expensive ■ Profits taxed twice as company profit and as stockholders' income

FIGURE 9.1

myeconlab

Relative Importance of the
Three Types of Firms

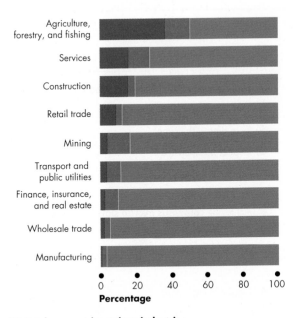

(a) Number of firms and total revenue

(b) Total revenue in various industries

Three-quarters of all U.S. firms are sole proprietorships, almost one-fifth are corporations, and only a twentieth are partnerships. Corporations account for **86** percent of business revenue (part a). But sole proprietorships and partnerships account for a significant percentage of business revenue in some industries (part b). (We don't have Canadian data on firm types.)

Source of data: U.S. Bureau of the Census, *Statistical Abstract of the United States: 2001.*

The Relative Importance of Different Types of Firms

Figure 9.1(a) shows the relative importance of the three main types of firms in the U.S. economy. The figure also shows that the revenue of corporations is much larger than that of the other types of firms. Although only 18 percent of all firms are corporations, they generate 86 percent of revenue.

Figure 9.1(b) shows the percentage of revenue generated by the different types of firms in various industries. Sole proprietorships in agriculture, forestry, and fishing generate about 40 percent of the total revenue in those sectors. Sole proprietorships in the service sector, construction, and retail trades also generate a large percentage of total revenue. Partnerships in agriculture, forestry, and fishing generate about 15 percent of total revenue. Partnerships are more prominent in services; mining; and finance, insurance, and real estate than in other sectors. Corporations are important in all sectors and have the manufacturing field almost to themselves.

Why do corporations dominate the business scene? Why do the other types of business survive? And why are sole proprietorships and partnerships more prominent in some sectors? The answers to these questions lie in the pros and cons of the different types of business organization that are summarized in Table 9.4. Corporations dominate where a large amount of capital is used. But sole proprietorships dominate where flexibility in decision making is critical.

REVIEW QUIZ

1 Explain the distinction between a command system and an incentive system.
2 What is the principal–agent problem? What are the three ways in which firms try to cope with it?
3 What are the three types of firms? Explain the major advantages and disadvantages of each.
4 Why do all three types of firms survive and in which sectors is each type most prominent?

 Study Plan 9.3

You've now seen how technology constraints influence a firm's use of capital and labour and how information constraints influence a firm's organization. We'll now look at market constraints and see how they influence the environment in which firms compete for business.

Markets and the Competitive Environment

THE MARKETS IN WHICH FIRMS OPERATE VARY A great deal. Some are highly competitive, and profits in these markets are hard to come by. Some appear to be almost free from competition, and firms in these markets earn large profits. Some markets are dominated by fierce advertising campaigns in which each firm seeks to persuade buyers that it has the best products. And some markets display a warlike character.

Economists identify four market types:

1. Perfect competition
2. Monopolistic competition
3. Oligopoly
4. Monopoly

Perfect competition arises when there are many firms, each selling an identical product, many buyers, and no restrictions on the entry of new firms into the industry. The many firms and buyers are all well informed about the prices of the products of each firm in the industry. The worldwide markets for corn, rice, and other grain crops are examples of perfect competition.

Monopolistic competition is a market structure in which a large number of firms compete by making similar but slightly different products. Making a product slightly different from the product of a competing firm is called **product differentiation**. Product differentiation gives the firm in monopolistic competition an element of market power. The firm is the sole producer of the particular version of the good in question. For example, in the market for running shoes, Nike, Reebok, Fila, New Balance, and Asics all make their own version of the perfect shoe. Each of these firms is the sole producer of a particular brand of shoe. Differentiated products are not necessarily different products. What matters is that consumers perceive them to be different. For example, different brands of aspirin are chemically identical (salicylic acid) and differ only in their packaging.

Oligopoly is a market structure in which a small number of firms compete. Computer software, airplane manufacture, and international air transportation are examples of oligopolistic industries. Oligopolies might produce almost identical products, such as the colas produced by Coke and Pepsi. Or they might produce differentiated products such as Chevrolet's Lumina and Ford's Taurus.

Monopoly arises when there is only one firm and it produces a good or service that has no close substitutes and is protected by a barrier preventing the entry of new firms. In some places, the phone, gas, electricity, and water suppliers are local monopolies—monopolies restricted to a given location. Microsoft Corporation, the software developer that created Windows, the operating system used by most PCs, is an example of a global monopoly.

Perfect competition is the most extreme form of competition. Monopoly is the most extreme absence of competition. The other two market types fall between these extremes.

Many factors must be taken into account to determine which market structure describes a particular real-world market. One of these factors is the extent to which the market is dominated by a small number of firms. To measure this feature of markets, economists use indexes called measures of concentration. Let's look at these measures.

Measures of Concentration

Economists use two measures of concentration:

■ The four-firm concentration ratio
■ The Herfindahl–Hirschman Index

The Four-Firm Concentration Ratio The **four-firm concentration ratio** is the percentage of the value of sales accounted for by the four largest firms in an industry. The range of the concentration ratio is from almost zero for perfect competition to 100 percent for monopoly. This ratio is the main measure used to assess market structure.

Table 9.5 shows two calculations of the four-firm concentration ratio: one for tiremakers and one for printers. In the tiremaking industry with14 firms, the largest four have 80 percent of the sales, so the four-firm concentration ratio is 80 percent. In the printing industry, with 1,004 firms, the largest four firms have only 0.5 percent of the sales, so the four-firm concentration ratio is 0.5 percent.

A low concentration ratio indicates a high degree of competition, and a high concentration ratio indicates an absence of competition. A monopoly has a concentration ratio of 100 percent—the largest (and only) firm has 100 percent of the sales. A four-firm concentration ratio that exceeds 40 percent is regarded as an indication of a market that is highly concentrated and dominated by a few firms in an oligopoly. A ratio of less than 40 percent is regarded as an indication of a competitive market.

The Herfindahl–Hirschman Index The **Herfindahl–Hirschman Index**—also called the HHI—is the square of the percentage market share of each firm summed over the largest 50 firms (or summed over all the firms if there are fewer than 50) in a market. For example, if there are four firms in a market and the market shares of the firms are 50 percent, 25 percent, 15 percent, and 10 percent, the Herfindahl–Hirschman Index is

$$HHI = 50^2 + 25^2 + 15^2 + 10^2 = 3,450.$$

TABLE 9.5   Concentration Ratio Calculations

Tiremakers		Printers	
Firm	**Sales** (millions of dollars)	**Firm**	**Sales** (millions of dollars)
Top, Inc.	200	Fran's	2.5
ABC, Inc.	250	Ned's	2.0
Big, Inc.	150	Tom's	1.8
XYZ, Inc.	100	Jill's	1.7
Largest 4 firms	700	Largest 4 firms	8.0
Other 10 firms	175	Other 1,000 firms	1,592.0
Industry	875	Industry	**1,600.0**

Four-firm concentration ratios:

Tiremakers: $\dfrac{700}{875} \times 100 = 80\%$ Printers: $\dfrac{8}{1,600} \times 100 = 0.5\%$

In perfect competition, the HHI is small. For example, if each of the largest 50 firms in an industry has a market share of 0.1 percent, then the HHI is $0.1^2 \times 50 = 0.5$. In a monopoly, the HHI is 10,000—the firm has 100 percent of the market: $100^2 = 10,000$.

The HHI can be used to classify markets across the spectrum of types. A market in which the HHI is less than 1,000 is regarded as being competitive and the smaller the number, the greater is the degree of competition. A market in which the HHI lies between 1,000 and 1,800 is regarded as being moderately competitive—a form of monopolistic competition. Although the HHI of 10,000 is needed for pure monopoly, a market in which the HHI exceeds 1,800 is regarded as being uncompetitive and a potential matter for concern by competition regulators.

Concentration Measures for the Canadian Economy

Figure 9.2 shows a selection of concentration ratios for Canada that Statistics Canada has calculated.

Industries that produce sugar, tobacco products, beer, tires, and soft drinks and ice have a high degree of concentration and are oligopolies. Industries that produce clothing, bakery items, textiles, and fabrics have low concentration measures and are highly competitive. Industries that produce women's and girl's shirts, pharmaceutical products, and wooden windows and doors are moderately concentrated. These industries are examples of monopolistic competition.

Concentration measures are a useful indicator of the degree of competition in a market. But they must be supplemented by other information to determine a market's structure. Table 9.6 summarizes the range of other information, along with the measures of concentration, that determine which market structure describes a particular real-world market.

Limitations of Concentration Measures

The three main limitations of concentration measures alone as determinants of market structure are their failure to take proper account of

- The geographical scope of the market
- Barriers to entry and firm turnover
- The correspondence between a market and an industry

FIGURE 9.2
Concentration Measures in Canada

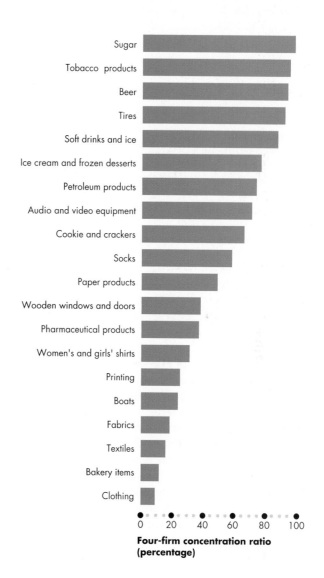

The industries that produce sugar, tobacco products, beer, tires, and soft drinks and ice are highly concentrated, while those that produce clothing, bakery items, textiles, and fabrics are highly competitive. The industries that produce women's and girl's shirts and pharmaceutical products have an intermediate degree of concentration.

Source of data: Adapted from the Statistics Canada publication CANSIM DISC. 10F0007, March 1999.

TABLE 9.6   Market Structure

Characteristics	Perfect competition	Monopolistic competition	Oligopoly	Monopoly
Number of firms in industry	Many	Many	Few	One
Product	Identical	Differentiated	Either identical or differentiated	No close substitutes
Barriers to entry	None	None	Moderate	High
Firm's control over price	None	Some	Considerable	Considerable or regulated
Concentration ratio	0	Low	High	100
HHI (approx. ranges)	Less than 100	101 to 999	More than 1,000	10,000
Examples	Wheat, corn	Food, clothing	Automobiles, cereals	Local water supply

Geographical Scope of Market   Concentration measures take a national view of the market. Many goods are sold in a *national* market, but some are sold in a *regional* market and some in a *global* one. The newspaper industry consists of local markets. The concentration measures for newspapers are low, but there is a high degree of concentration in the newspaper industry in most cities. The auto industry has a global market. The three biggest North American car producers don't have much domestic competition, either in Canada or in the United States. But they face tough competition from foreign producers both here and more especially in foreign markets.

Barriers to Entry and Firm Turnover
Concentration measures don't measure barriers to entry. Some industries are highly concentrated but have easy entry and an enormous amount of turnover of firms. For example, many small towns have few restaurants, but there are no restrictions on opening a restaurant and many firms attempt to do so.

Also, an industry might be competitive because of *potential entry*—because a few firms in a market face competition from many firms that can easily enter the market and will do so if economic profits are available.

Market and Industry Correspondence   To calculate concentration ratios, Statistics Canada classifies each firm as being in a particular industry. But markets do not always correspond closely to industries for three reasons.

First, markets are often narrower than industries. For example, the pharmaceutical industry, which has a moderate concentration ratio, operates in many separate markets for individual products—for example, measles vaccines and AIDS-fighting drugs. These drugs do not compete with each other, so this industry, which looks competitive, includes firms that are monopolies (or near monopolies) in markets for individual drugs.

Second, most firms make several products. For example, Nortel produces telecommunication equipment and Internet database services, among other things. So this one firm operates in several separate markets. But Statistics Canada classifies Nortel as being in the telecommunication equipment industry. The fact that Nortel competes with other providers of e-commerce database services does not show up in the concentration data for that market.

Third, firms switch from one market to another depending on profit opportunities. For example, Canadian Pacific Ltd., which today produces hotel services, forest products, coal and petroleum products, as well as rail services, has diversified from being just a railroad company. Publishers of newspapers, magazines, and textbooks are today rapidly diversifying into Internet and multimedia products. These switches among industries show that there is much scope for entering and exiting an industry, and so measures of concentration have limited usefulness.

Despite their limitations, concentration measures do provide a basis for determining the degree of competition in an industry when they are combined with information about the geographical scope of the market, barriers to entry, and the extent to which large, multiproduct firms straddle a variety of markets.

Market Structures in the North American Economy

How competitive are the markets of North America? Do most firms operate in competitive markets or in non-competitive markets?

Figure 9.3 provides part of the answer to these questions. It shows the market structure of the U.S. economy and the trends in market structure between 1939 and 1980. (Unfortunately, comparable data for Canada alone and data for the 1980s and 1990s are not available.)

In 1980, three-quarters of the value of goods and services bought and sold in the United States were traded in markets that are essentially competitive—markets that have almost perfect competition or monopolistic competition. Monopoly and the dominance of a single firm accounted for about 5 percent of sales. Oligopoly, which is found mainly in manufacturing, accounted for about 18 percent of sales.

Over the period shown in Fig. 9.3, the U.S. economy became increasingly competitive. You can see that competitive markets have expanded most (blue bars) and oligopoly markets have shrunk most (red bars).

But also during the past decades, the U.S. economy has become much more exposed to competition from the rest of the world. Figure 9.3 does not capture this international competition.

FIGURE 9.3

The Market Structure in North America

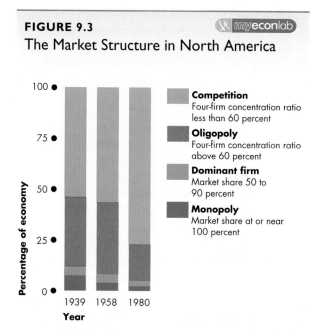

Competition
Four-firm concentration ratio less than 60 percent

Oligopoly
Four-firm concentration ratio above 60 percent

Dominant firm
Market share 50 to 90 percent

Monopoly
Market share at or near 100 percent

Three-quarters of the North American economy is effectively competitive (perfect competition or monopolistic competition), one-fifth is oligopoly, and the rest is monopoly. The economy became more competitive between 1939 and 1980. (Professor Shepherd, whose 1982 study remains the latest word on this topic, suspects that although some industries have become more concentrated, others have become less concentrated, so the net picture has probably not changed much since 1980.)

Source of data: William G. Shepherd, "Causes of Increased Competition in the U.S. Economy, 1939–1980," *Review of Economics and Statistics*, November 1982, pp. 613–626.

REVIEW QUIZ

1. What are the four market types? Explain the distinguishing characteristics of each.
2. What are the two measures of concentration? Explain how each measure is calculated.
3. Under what conditions do the measures of concentration give a good indication of the degree of competition in a market?
4. Is the North American economy competitive? Is it becoming more competitive or less competitive?

myeconlab **Study Plan 9.4**

You now know the variety of market types and the way we classify firms and industries into the different market types. Our final question in this chapter is: What determines the things that firms decide to buy from other firms rather than produce for themselves?

Markets and Firms

AT THE BEGINNING OF THIS CHAPTER, WE defined a firm as an institution that hires productive resources and organizes them to produce and sell goods and services. To organize production, firms coordinate the economic decisions and activities of many individuals. But firms are not the only coordinators of economic decisions. You learned in Chapter 3 that markets coordinate decisions. They do so by adjusting prices and making the decisions of buyers and sellers consistent—making the quantity demanded equal to the quantity supplied for each good and service.

Market Coordination

Markets can coordinate production. For example, markets might coordinate the production of a rock concert. A promoter hires a stadium, some stage equipment, audio and video recording engineers and technicians, some rock groups, a superstar, a publicity agent, and a ticket agent—all market transactions—and sells tickets to thousands of rock fans, audio rights to a recording company, and video and broadcasting rights to a television network—another set of market transactions. Alternatively, if rock concerts were produced like cornflakes, the firm producing them would own all the capital used (stadiums, stage, sound and video equipment) and would employ all the labour needed (singers, engineers, salespeople, and so on).

Outsourcing—buying parts or products from other firms—is another example of market coordination. Dell uses outsourcing for all the components of the computers it produces. The major auto makers use outsourcing for windshields and windows, gearboxes, tires, and many other car parts.

What determines whether a firm or a market coordinates a particular set of activities? How does a firm decide whether to buy from another firm or manufacture an item itself? The answer is cost. Taking account of the opportunity cost of time as well as the costs of the other inputs, a firm uses the method that costs least. In other words, it uses the economically efficient method.

Firms coordinate economic activity when they can perform a task more efficiently than markets can. In such a situation, it is profitable to set up a firm. If markets can perform a task more efficiently than a firm can, people will use markets, and any attempt to set up a firm to replace such market coordination will be doomed to failure.

Why Firms?

There are four key reasons why, in many instances, firms are more efficient than markets as coordinators of economic activity. Firms can achieve

- Lower transactions costs
- Economies of scale
- Economies of scope
- Economies of team production

Transactions Costs The idea that firms exist because there are activities in which they are more efficient than markets was first suggested by University of Chicago economist and Nobel Laureate Ronald Coase. Coase focused on the firm's ability to reduce or eliminate transactions costs. **Transactions costs** are the costs that arise from finding someone with whom to do business, of reaching an agreement about the price and other aspects of the exchange, and of ensuring that the terms of the agreement are fulfilled. Market transactions require buyers and sellers to get together and to negotiate the terms and conditions of their trading. Sometimes lawyers have to be hired to draw up contracts. A broken contract leads to still more expenses. A firm can lower such transactions costs by reducing the number of individual transactions undertaken.

Consider, for example, two ways of getting your creaking car fixed.

1. *Firm coordination:* You take the car to the garage. The garage owner coordinates parts and tools as well as the mechanic's time, and your car gets fixed. You pay one bill for the entire job.
2. *Market coordination:* You hire a mechanic, who diagnoses the problems and makes a list of the parts and tools needed to fix them. You buy the parts from the local wrecker's yard and rent the tools from ABC Rentals. You hire the mechanic again to fix the problems. You return the tools and pay your bills—wages to the mechanic, rental to ABC, and the cost of the parts used to the wrecker.

What determines the method that you use? The answer is cost. Taking account of the opportunity cost of your own time as well as the costs of the other inputs that you would have to buy, you will use the method that costs least. In other words, you will use the economically efficient method.

The first method requires that you undertake only one transaction with one firm. It's true that the firm has to undertake several transactions—hiring the labour and buying the parts and tools required to do the job. But the firm doesn't have to undertake those transactions simply to fix your car. One set of such transactions enables the firm to fix hundreds of cars. Thus there is an enormous reduction in the number of individual transactions that take place if people get their cars fixed at the garage rather than going through an elaborate sequence of market transactions.

Economies of Scale When the cost of producing a unit of a good falls as its output rate increases, **economies of scale** exist. Auto makers, for example, experience economies of scale because as the scale of production increases, the firm can use cost-saving equipment and highly specialized labour. An auto maker that produces only a few cars a year must use hand-tool methods that are costly. Economies of scale arise from specialization and the division of labour that can be reaped more effectively by firm coordination rather than by market coordination.

Economies of Scope A firm experiences **economies of scope** when it uses specialized (and often expensive) resources to produce a *range of goods and services*. For example, Microsoft hires specialist programmers, designers, and marketing experts and uses their skills across a range of software products. As a result, Microsoft coordinates the resources that produce software at a lower cost than can an individual who buys all these services in markets.

Economies of Team Production A production process in which the individuals in a group specialize in mutually supportive tasks is team production. Sport provides the best example of team activity. Some baseball team members specialize in pitching and some in batting, some basketball team members specialize in defence and some in offence. The production of goods and services offers many examples of team activity. For example, production lines in automobile and TV manufacturing plants work most efficiently when individual activity is organized in teams, each specializing in a small task. You can also think of an entire firm as being a team. The team has buyers of raw material and other inputs, production workers, and salespeople. There are even specialists within these various groups. Each individual member of the team specializes, but the value of the output of the team and the profit that it earns depend on the coordinated activities of all the team's members. The idea that firms arise as a consequence of the economies of team production was first suggested by Armen Alchian and Harold Demsetz of the University of California at Los Angeles.

Because firms can economize on transactions costs, reap economies of scale and economies of scope, and organize efficient team production, it is firms rather than markets that coordinate most of our economic activity. But there are limits to the economic efficiency of firms. If a firm becomes too big or too diversified in the things that it seeks to do, the cost of management and monitoring per unit of output begins to rise, and at some point, the market becomes more efficient at coordinating the use of resources.

Nortel Networks, for example, decided that its corporate business and its wireless business would be handled more efficiently if it split itself into two distinct product divisions.

Sometimes firms enter into long-term relationships with each other that effectively cut out ordinary market transactions and make it difficult to see where one firm ends and another begins. For example, GM has long-term relationships with suppliers of windows, tires, and other parts. Wal-Mart has long-term relationships with suppliers of the goods it sells in its stores. Such relationships make transactions costs lower than they would be if GM or Wal-Mart went shopping on the open market each time it wanted new supplies.

REVIEW QUIZ

1 What are the two ways in which economic activity can be coordinated?
2 What determines whether a firm or a market coordinates production?
3 Why can firms often coordinate production at a lower cost than markets can?

myeconlab Study Plan 9.5

◆ *Reading Between the Lines* on pp. 214–215 explores the challenges and opportunities faced by Nortel Networks. We continue to study firms and their decisions in the next four chapters. In Chapter 10, we learn about the relationships between cost and output at different output levels. These cost–output relationships are common to all types of firms in all types of markets. We then turn to problems that are specific to firms in different types of markets.

Nortel's Challenges and Opportunities

OTTAWASUN.COM SEPTEMBER 7, 2005

Nortel scores major Korean contract

Nortel Networks Corp. and LG Electronics have been chosen by Korea's KTF Corp. cell phone giant to provide equipment for an ultra-high-speed broadband wireless service throughout the country's major metropolitan areas.

Nortel said Wednesday it will provide its high speed downlink packet access wireless equipment, while LGE will provide the core network solution.

"This is the first collaborative win for LGE and Nortel since announcement of the LG-Nortel joint venture in August 2005," Nortel said in a release.

The service will allow KTF subscribers to access new wireless multimedia services such as high-speed music transfers, real-time DVD-quality video, gaming applications, videoconferencing and multimedia collaboration.

The network will be rolled out to 17 cities by December and extended to an additional 45 cities by June 2006.

"We chose the Nortel solution because we believe it will enable us to bring KTF subscribers new and unprecedented levels of wireless speed and functionality and help us to maintain our position as a global leader in mobile broadband," KTF executive vice-president Won-Jin Park said in a statement.

Korea's LGE and Toronto-based Nortel signed a joint venture agreement on Aug. 17 to establish a telecommunication infrastructure company. The company is expected to be established this year.

...

Reprinted by permission of Canadian Press.

Essence of the Story

■ Nortel Networks Corp. and LG Electronics will provide equipment for an ultra-high-speed broadband wireless service in Korea.

■ Nortel will provide high-speed wireless equipment while LGE will provide the core network.

■ The service will allow subscribers to access a wide range of wireless multimedia services including high-speed music transfers and real-time DVD-quality video.

■ Nortel was chosen for its ability to deliver "unprecedented levels of wireless speed and functionality."

Economic Analysis

■ Nortel Networks is a very old Canadian corporation that was in business (under a different name) at the birth of the telephone.

■ Nortel produces a wide range of telecommunications equipment and services to customers in more than 150 countries. During the 1990s, Nortel grew to become the world's second largest telecommunications equipment producer (second to Lucent).

■ Nortel's main customers are telecommunications companies such as Bell, AT&T, Global Crossing, and 360network.

■ Nortel faced a major problem in 2001 as the global market for telecommunications equipment and services collapsed.

■ The collapse came partly from an over expansion as firms scrambled to dominate the $1 trillion global telecommunications market during the 1990s expansion.

■ Faced with a collapse in revenues, Nortel cut back its scale partly by selling assets in businesses outside its core activities and partly by cutting its work force.

■ Nortel also changed its CEO. This move was a change in its entrepreneurial resources.

■ Nortel's goal is to maximize profit, and the news article illustrates one way in which the firm is pursuing this goal.

■ By partnering with other firms, LG in the story, Nortel is able to exploit its own comparative advantage in provideng high-speed wireless technologies.

■ In a world of ever more complex technologies, there is an increasing opportunity for profitable specialization and cooperation between firms.

215

SUMMARY

KEY POINTS

The Firm and Its Economic Problem
(pp. 198–200)

- Firms hire factors of production and organize them to produce and sell goods and services.
- Firms seek to maximize economic profit, which is total revenue minus opportunity cost.
- Technology, information, and market constraints limit a firm's profit.

Technological and Economic Efficiency
(pp. 201–202)

- A method of production is technologically efficient when the firm produces a given output by using the least amount of inputs.
- A method of production is economically efficient when the cost of producing a given output is as low as possible.

Information and Organization (pp. 203–206)

- Firms use a combination of command systems and incentive systems to organize production.
- Faced with incomplete information and uncertainty, firms induce managers and workers to perform in ways that are consistent with the firm's goals.
- Sole proprietorships, partnerships, and corporations use ownership, incentives, and long-term contracts to cope with the principal–agent problem.

Markets and the Competitive Environment
(pp. 207–211)

- Perfect competition occurs when there are many buyers and sellers of an identical product and when new firms can easily enter a market.
- Monopolistic competition occurs when a large number of firms compete with each other by making slightly different products.
- Oligopoly occurs when a small number of producers compete with each other.

- Monopoly occurs when one firm produces a good or service for which there are no close substitutes and the firm is protected by a barrier that prevents the entry of competitors.

Markets and Firms (pp. 212–213)

- Firms coordinate economic activities when they can perform a task more efficiently—at lower cost—than markets can.
- Firms economize on transactions costs and achieve the benefits of economies of scale, economies of scope, and economies of team production.

KEY FIGURE AND TABLES

KEY TERMS

PROBLEMS

Go to [myeconlab] for solutions to odd-numbered problems and additional exercises.

1. One year ago, Jack and Jill set up a vinegar-bottling firm (called JJVB). Use the following information to calculate JJVB's explicit costs and implicit costs during its first year:
   a. Jack and Jill put $50,000 of their own money into the firm.
   b. They bought equipment for $30,000.
   c. They hired one employee to help them for an annual wage of $20,000.
   d. Jack gave up his previous job, at which he earned $30,000, and spent all his time working for JJVB.
   e. Jill kept her old job, which paid $30 an hour, but gave up 10 hours of leisure each week (for 50 weeks) to work for JJVB.
   f. JJVB bought $10,000 of goods and services from other firms.
   g. The market value of the equipment at the end of the year was $28,000.

2. One year ago, Ms. Moffat and Mr. Spieder opened a cheese firm (called MSCF). Use the following information to calculate MSCF's explicit costs and implicit costs during its first year of operation:
   a. Moffat and Spieder put $70,000 of their own money into the firm.
   b. They bought equipment for $40,000.
   c. They hired one employee to help them for an annual wage of $18,000.
   d. Moffat gave up her previous job, at which she earned $22,000, and spent all her time working for MSCF.
   e. Spieder kept his old job, which paid $20 an hour, but gave up 20 hours of leisure each week (for 50 weeks) to work for MSCF.
   f. MSCF bought $5,000 of goods from other firms.
   g. The market value of the equipment at the end of the year was $37,000.

3. Four methods for doing a tax return are with a personal computer, a pocket calculator, a pocket calculator with pencil and paper, and a pencil and paper. With a PC, the job takes an hour; with a pocket calculator, it takes 12 hours; with a pocket calculator and paper and pencil, it takes 12 hours; and with a pencil and paper, it takes 16 hours. The PC and its software cost $1,000, the pocket calculator costs $10, and the pencil and paper cost $1.
   a. Which methods are technologically efficient?
   b. Which method is economically efficient if the wage rate is
      i. $5 an hour?
      ii. $50 an hour?
      iii. $500 an hour?

4. Shawn is a part-time student and he can do his engineering assignment by using a personal computer, a pocket calculator, a pocket calculator and a pencil and paper, or a pencil and paper. With a PC, Shawn completes the job in 1 hour; with a pocket calculator, it takes 15 hours; with a pocket calculator and paper and pencil, it takes 7 hours; and with a pencil and paper, it takes 30 hours. The PC and its software cost $1,000, the pocket calculator costs $20, and the pencil and paper cost $5.
   a. Which methods are technologically efficient?
   b. Which method is economically efficient if the wage rate is
      i. $10 an hour?
      ii. $20 an hour?
      iii. $250 an hour?

5. Alternative ways of laundering 100 shirts are

Method	Labour (hours)	Capital (machines)
A	1	10
B	5	8
C	20	4
D	50	1

   a. Which methods are technologically efficient?
   b. Which method is economically efficient if the hourly wage rate and implicit rental rate of capital are
      i.   Wage rate: $1; rental rate: $100?
      ii. Wage rate: $5; rental rate: $50?
      iii. Wage rate: $50; rental rate: $5?

6. Four ways of making 10 surfboards a day are

Method	Labour (hours)	Capital (machines)
A	40	10
B	40	20
C	20	30
D	10	40

   a. Which methods are technologically efficient?

b. Which method is economically efficient if the hourly wage rate and implicit rental rate of capital are
  iv. Wage rate: $1; rental rate: $100?
  v. Wage rate: $5; rental rate: $50?
  vi. Wage rate: $50; rental rate: $5?

7. Sales of the firms in the tattoo industry are

Firm	Sales (dollars)
Bright Spots	4,500
Freckles	3,250
Love Galore	2,500
Native Birds	2,000
Other 15 firms	8,000

a. Calculate the four-firm concentration ratio.
b. What is the structure of the tattoo industry?

8. Sales of the firms in the dry cleaning industry are

Firm	Sales (thousands of dollars)
SqueakyClean, Inc.	15
Village Cleaners, Inc.	25
Plaza Cleaners, Inc.	30
The Cleanery, Inc.	40
Other 20 firms	300

a. Calculate the four-firm concentration ratio.
b. What is the structure of the industry?

9. Market shares of chocolate makers are

Firm	Market Share (percent)
Mayfair, Inc.	15
Bond, Inc.	10
Magic, Inc.	20
All Natural, Inc.	15
Truffles, Inc.	25
Gold, Inc.	15

a. Calculate the Herfindahl–Hirschman Index.
b. What is the structure of the industry?

10. Market shares of orange juice suppliers are

Firm	Market Share (percent)
Natural Fresh, Inc.	75
Fresh Squeezed, Inc.	10
Juice-to-Go, Inc.	8
Juiced-Out, Inc.	7

a. Calculate the Herfindahl–Hirschman Index.
b. What is the structure of the industry?

CRITICAL THINKING

1. Study *Reading Between the Lines* about Nortel Network's challenges and opportunities on pp. 214–215, and then answer the following questions.
   a. What is the deal that Nortel struck with LG Electronics in 2005?
   b. Why did Nortel win this business deal?
   c. Why do you think LG Electronics wanted to enter into a joint venture agreement with Nortel rather than just buying Nortel products?
   d. Why do you think Nortel wanted to enter into a joint venture agreement with LG Electronics rather than just selling its products to LG?
   e. What fundamental economic principle is illustrated and exploited by Nortel's deal with LG?

2. What is the principal–agent problem? Do you think Nortel and LG have such a problem? Describe the problem and explain how Nortel and LG might cope with it.

3. Why are Nortel and LG cooperating to deliver new wireless services in Korea? Why doesn't one of the firms deliver the entire package?

WEB EXERCISES

Use the links on ⓧ myeconlab **to work the following exercise.**

1. Read James D. Miller's views on providing airport security services.
   a. What does Mr. Miller argue concerning the best way to organize airport security?
   b. Explain Mr. Miller's views using the principal–agent analysis. Who is the principal and who is the agent?
   c. What exactly is the principal–agent problem in providing airport security services?
   d. Why might a private provider offer better security than a public provider?
   e. Do you think that a private provider would operate at a lower cost than a public provider? Why or why not?

Output and Costs

Technologies Converging

Have you noticed how the traditional phone companies and the cable television companies, as well as Internet portals such as AOL, Yahoo! and MSN, are all getting into each other's lines of business? More and more options become available for everyone and ever more complex plans are on offer that combine cell and fixed phone service with high-speed Internet, cable TV, and other services. Why do we see this proliferation of communication services?

Firms differ in lots of ways—from mom-and-pop convenience stores to multinational giants producing high-tech goods. But regardless of their size or what they produce, all firms must decide how much to produce and how to produce it. How do firms make these decisions?

Most automakers could produce more cars than they can sell. Why do automakers have expensive equipment lying around that isn't fully used? Many electric utilities don't have enough production equipment on hand to meet demand on the coldest and hottest days and must buy power from other producers. Why don't these firms install more equipment so that they can supply the market themselves?

◆ We are going to answer these questions in this chapter. To do so, we are going to study the economic decisions of a small, imaginary firm: Cindy's Sweaters, Inc., a producer of knitted sweaters, which Cindy owns and operates. By studying the economic problems of Cindy's Sweaters and the way Cindy copes with them, we will be able to get a clear view of the problems that face all firms. We're going to begin by setting the scene and describing the time frames in which Cindy makes her business decisions. At the end of the chapter, in *Reading Between the Lines*, we'll return to the telecommunication industry and look at a key feature of its costs.

After studying this chapter, you will be able to

- ■ **Distinguish between the short run and the long run**

- ■ **Explain the relationship between a firm's output and labour employed in the short run**

- ■ **Explain the relationship between a firm's output and costs in the short run and derive a firm's short-run cost curves**

- ■ **Explain the relationship between a firm's output and costs in the long run and derive a firm's long-run average cost curve**

Decision Time Frames

PEOPLE WHO OPERATE FIRMS MAKE MANY decisions. And all of the decisions are aimed at one overriding objective: maximum attainable profit. But the decisions are not all equally critical. Some of the decisions are big ones. Once made, they are costly (or impossible) to reverse. If such a decision turns out to be incorrect, it might lead to the failure of the firm. Some of the decisions are small ones. They are easily changed. If one of these decisions turns out to be incorrect, the firm can change its actions and survive.

The biggest decision that any firm makes is what industry to enter. For most entrepreneurs, their background knowledge and interests drive this decision. But the decision also depends on profit prospects. No one sets up a firm without believing that it will be profitable—that total revenue will exceed opportunity cost (see Chapter 9, pp. 198–199).

The firm that we'll study has already chosen the industry in which to operate. It has also chosen its most effective method of organization, but it has not decided the quantity to produce, the quantities of resources to hire, or the price at which to sell its output.

Decisions about the quantity to produce and the price to charge depend on the type of market in which the firm operates. Perfect competition, monopolistic competition, oligopoly, and monopoly all confront the firm with their own special problems.

But decisions about how to produce a given output do not depend on the type of market in which the firm operates. These decisions are similar for *all* types of firms in *all* types of markets.

The actions that a firm can take to influence the relationship between output and cost depend on how soon the firm wants to act. A firm that plans to change its output rate tomorrow has fewer options than one that plans to change its output rate six months from now.

To study the relationship between a firm's output decision and its costs, we distinguish between two decision time frames:

- The short run
- The long run

The Short Run

The **short run** is a time frame in which the quantities of some resources are fixed. For most firms, the fixed resources are the firm's technology, buildings, and capital. The management organization is also fixed in the short run. We call the collection of fixed resources the firm's *plant*. So in the short run, a firm's plant is fixed.

For Cindy's Sweaters, the fixed plant is its factory building and its knitting machines. For an electric power utility, the fixed plant is its buildings, generators, computers, and control systems.

To increase output in the short run, a firm must increase the quantity of variable inputs it uses. Labour is usually the variable input. So to produce more output, Cindy's Sweaters must hire more labour and operate its knitting machines for more hours per day. Similarly, an electric power utility must hire more labour and operate its generators for more hours per day.

Short-run decisions are easily reversed. The firm can increase or decrease its output in the short run by increasing or decreasing the amount of labour it hires.

The Long Run

The **long run** is a time frame in which the quantities of *all* resources can be varied. That is, the long run is a period in which the firm can change its *plant*.

To increase output in the long run, a firm can choose to change its plant as well as increase the quantity of labour it hires. Cindy's Sweaters can decide to install some additional knitting machines, use a new type of machine, and hire more labour. An electric power utility can decide to install more generators.

Long-run decisions are *not* easily reversed. Once a plant decision is made, the firm usually must live with it for some time. To emphasize this fact, we call the past cost of buying a plant that has no resale value a **sunk cost**. A sunk cost is irrelevant to the firm's decisions. The only costs that influence its decisions are the short-run cost of changing its labour inputs and the long-run cost of changing its plant.

REVIEW QUIZ

1 Explain the short run and the long run.
2 Why is a sunk cost irrelevant to the decision that the firm is making today?

 Study Plan 10.1

We're going to study costs in the short run and the long run. We begin with the short run and describe the technology constraint the firm faces.

Short-Run Technology Constraint

TO INCREASE OUTPUT IN THE SHORT RUN, A FIRM must increase the quantity of labour employed. We describe the relationship between output and the quantity of labour employed by using three related concepts:

1. Total product
2. Marginal product
3. Average product

These product concepts can be illustrated either by product schedules or by product curves. Let's look first at the product schedules.

TABLE 10.1 Total Product, Marginal Product, and Average Product

Labour (workers per day)	Total product (sweaters per day)	Marginal product (sweaters per additional worker)	Average product (sweaters per worker)
A 0	0		
		 4	
B 1	4		4.00
		 6	
C 2	10		5.00
		 3	
D 3	13		4.33
		 2	
E 4	15		3.75
		 1	
F 5	16		3.20

Total product is the total amount produced. Marginal product is the change in total product that results from a one-unit increase in labour. For example, when labour increases from 2 to 3 workers a day (row C to row D), total product increases from 10 to 13 sweaters. The marginal product of going from 2 to 3 workers is 3 sweaters. Average product is total product divided by the quantity of labour employed. For example, the average product of 3 workers is 4.33 sweaters per worker (13 sweaters a day divided by 3 workers).

Product Schedules

Table 10.1 shows some data that describe Cindy's Sweaters' total product, marginal product, and average product. The numbers tell us how Cindy's Sweaters' production increases as more workers are employed. They also tell us about the productivity of Cindy's Sweaters' workers.

Focus first on the columns headed "Labour" and "Total product." **Total product** is the total output produced. You can see from the numbers in these columns that as Cindy's employs more labour, total product increases. For example, when Cindy's employs 1 worker, total product is 4 sweaters a day, and when Cindy's employs 2 workers, total product is 10 sweaters a day. Each increase in employment brings an increase in total product.

The **marginal product** of labour is the increase in total product that results from a one-unit increase in the quantity of labour employed with all other inputs remaining the same. For example, in Table 10.1, when Cindy's increases the number of workers from 2 to 3 and keeps its capital the same, the marginal product of the third worker is 3 sweaters—total product goes from 10 to 13 sweaters.

Average product tells how productive workers are on the average. The **average product** of labour is equal to total product divided by the quantity of labour employed. For example, in Table 10.1, the average product of 3 workers is 4.33 sweaters per worker—13 sweaters a day divided by 3 workers.

If you look closely at the numbers in Table 10.1, you can see some patterns. As the number of workers increases, marginal product at first increases and then begins to decrease. For example, marginal product increases from 4 sweaters a day for the first worker to 6 sweaters a day for the second worker and then decreases to 3 sweaters a day for the third worker. Average product also increases at first and then decreases. You can see the relationships between employment and the three product concepts more clearly by looking at the product curves.

Product Curves

The product curves are graphs of the relationships between employment and the three product concepts you've just studied. They show how total product, marginal product, and average product change as employment changes. They also show the relationships among the three concepts. Let's look at the product curves.

Total Product Curve

Figure 10.1 shows Cindy's Sweaters' total product curve, *TP*. As employment increases, so does the number of sweaters knitted. Points *A* through *F* on the curve correspond to the same rows in Table 10.1.

The total product curve is similar to the *production possibilities frontier* (explained in Chapter 2). It separates the attainable output levels from those that are unattainable. All the points that lie above the curve are unattainable. Points that lie below the curve, in the orange area, are attainable. But they are inefficient—they use more labour than is necessary to produce a given output. Only the points *on* the total product curve are technologically efficient.

Notice especially the shape of the total product curve. As employment increases from zero to 1 to 2 workers per day, the curve becomes steeper. Then, as employment increases to 3, 4, and 5 workers a day, the curve becomes less steep. The steeper the slope of the total product curve, the greater is marginal product, as you are about to see.

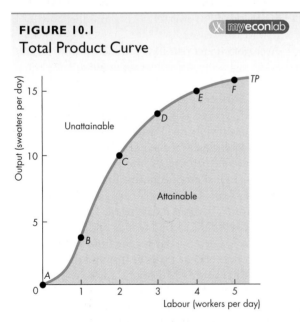

FIGURE 10.1
Total Product Curve
myeconlab

The total product curve, *TP*, is based on the data in Table 10.1. The total product curve shows how the quantity of sweaters changes as the quantity of labour employed changes. For example, 2 workers can produce 10 sweaters a day (point *C*). Points *A* through *F* on the curve correspond to the rows of Table 10.1. The total product curve separates attainable outputs from unattainable outputs. Points below the *TP* curve are inefficient.

Marginal Product Curve

Figure 10.2 shows Cindy's Sweaters' marginal product of labour. Part (a) reproduces the total product curve from Fig. 10.1. Part (b) shows the marginal product curve, *MP*.

In part (a), the orange bars illustrate the marginal product of labour. The height of each bar measures marginal product. Marginal product is also measured by the slope of the total product curve. Recall that the slope of a curve is the change in the value of the variable measured on the *y*-axis—output—divided by the change in the variable measured on the *x*-axis—labour input—as we move along the curve. A one-unit increase in labour input, from 2 to 3 workers, increases output from 10 to 13 sweaters, so the slope from point *C* to point *D* is 3, the same as the marginal product that we've just calculated.

We've calculated the marginal product of labour for a series of unit increases in the quantity of labour. But labour is divisible into smaller units than one person. It is divisible into hours and even minutes. By varying the amount of labour in the smallest units imaginable, we can draw the marginal product curve shown in Fig. 10.2(b). The *height* of this curve measures the *slope* of the total product curve at a point. Part (a) shows that an increase in employment from 2 to 3 workers increases output from 10 to 13 sweaters (an increase of 3). The increase in output of 3 sweaters appears on the vertical axis of part (b) as the marginal product of going from 2 to 3 workers. We plot that marginal product at the midpoint between 2 and 3 workers. Notice that marginal product shown in Fig. 10.2(b) reaches a peak at 1.5 workers, and at that point, marginal product is 6. The peak occurs at 1.5 workers because the total product curve is steepest when employment increases from 1 worker to 2 workers.

The total product and marginal product curves are different for different firms and different types of goods. Ford Motor Company's product curves are different from those of Jim's Burger Stand, which in turn are different from those of Cindy's Sweaters. But the shapes of the product curves are similar because almost every production process has two features:

- Increasing marginal returns initially
- Diminishing marginal returns eventually

Increasing Marginal Returns Increasing marginal returns occur when the marginal product of an additional worker exceeds the marginal product of the

FIGURE 10.2
Marginal Product

(a) Total product

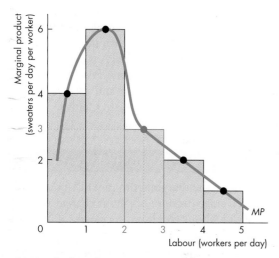

(b) Marginal product

Marginal product is illustrated by the orange bars. For example, when labour increases from 2 to 3, marginal product is the orange bar whose height is 3 sweaters. (Marginal product is shown midway between the labour inputs to emphasize that it is the result of *changing* inputs.) The steeper the slope of the total product curve (*TP*) in part (a), the larger is marginal product (*MP*) in part (b). Marginal product increases to a maximum (in this example when the second worker is employed) and then declines—diminishing marginal product.

previous worker. Increasing marginal returns arise from increased specialization and division of labour in the production process.

For example, if Cindy employs just one worker, that person must learn all the aspects of sweater production: running the knitting machines, fixing breakdowns, packaging and mailing sweaters, buying and checking the type and colour of the wool. All these tasks must be performed by that one person.

If Cindy hires a second person, the two workers can specialize in different parts of the production process. As a result, two workers produce more than twice as much as one. The marginal product of the second worker is greater than the marginal product of the first worker. Marginal returns are increasing.

Diminishing Marginal Returns Most production processes experience increasing marginal returns initially. But all production processes eventually reach a point of *diminishing* marginal returns. **Diminishing marginal returns** occur when the marginal product of an additional worker is less than the marginal product of the previous worker.

Diminishing marginal returns arise from the fact that more and more workers are using the same capital and working in the same space. As more workers are added, there is less and less for the additional workers to do that is productive. For example, if Cindy hires a third worker, output increases but not by as much as it did when she hired the second worker. In this case, after two workers are hired, all the gains from specialization and the division of labour have been exhausted. By hiring a third worker, the factory produces more sweaters, but the equipment is being operated at a rate closer to its limits. There are even times when the third worker has nothing to do because the machines are running without the need for further attention. Hiring more and more workers continues to increase output but by successively smaller amounts. Marginal returns are diminishing. This phenomenon is such a pervasive one that it is called a "law"—the law of diminishing returns. The **law of diminishing returns** states that

As a firm uses more of a variable input, with a given quantity of fixed inputs, the marginal product of the variable input eventually diminishes.

You are going to return to the law of diminishing returns when we study a firm's costs. But before we do that, let's look at the average product of labour and the average product curve.

Average Product Curve

Figure 10.3 illustrates Cindy's Sweaters' average product of labour, *AP*. It also shows the relationship between average product and marginal product. Points *B* through *F* on the average product curve correspond to those same rows in Table 10.1. Average product increases from 1 to 2 workers (its maximum value at point *C*) but then decreases as yet more workers are employed. Notice also that average product is largest when average product and marginal product are equal. That is, the marginal product curve cuts the average product curve at the point of maximum average product. For the numbers of workers at which marginal product exceeds average product, average product is increasing. For the numbers of workers at which marginal product is less than average product, average product is decreasing.

The relationship between the average and marginal product curves is a general feature of the relationship between the average and marginal values of any variable. Let's look at a familiar example.

FIGURE 10.3
Average Product
myeconlab

The figure shows the average product of labour and the connection between the average product and marginal product. With 1 worker per day, marginal product exceeds average product, so average product is increasing. With 2 workers per day, marginal product equals average product, so average product is at its maximum. With more than 2 workers per day, marginal product is less than average product, so average product is decreasing.

Marginal Grade and Grade Point Average

To see the relationship between average product and marginal product, think about the similar relationship between Cindy's average grade and marginal grade over five semesters. (Suppose Cindy is a part-time student who takes just one course each semester.) In the first semester, Cindy takes calculus and her grade is a C (2). This grade is her marginal grade. It is also her average grade—her GPA. In the next semester, Cindy takes French and gets a B (3). French is Cindy's marginal course, and her marginal grade is 3. Her GPA rises to 2.5. Because her marginal grade exceeds her average grade, it pulls her average up. In the third semester, Cindy takes economics and gets an A (4)— her new marginal grade. Because her marginal grade exceeds her GPA, it again pulls her average up. Cindy's GPA is now 3, the average of 2, 3, and 4. The fourth semester, she takes history and gets a B (3). Because her marginal grade is equal to her average, her GPA does not change. In the fifth semester, Cindy takes English and gets a D (1). Because her marginal grade, a 1, is below her GPA of 3, her GPA falls.

Cindy's GPA increases when her marginal grade exceeds her GPA. Her GPA falls when her marginal grade is below her GPA. And her GPA is constant when her marginal grade equals her GPA. The relationship between marginal product and average product is exactly the same as that between Cindy's marginal grade and average grade.

REVIEW QUIZ

1   Explain how the marginal product of labour and the average product of labour change as the quantity of labour employed increases (a) initially and (b) eventually.
2   Why does marginal product eventually diminish?
3   Explain the relationship between marginal and average product. How does average product change when marginal product (a) exceeds average product and (b) is less than average product?

myeconlab   Study Plan 10.2

Cindy's Sweaters cares about its product curves because they influence its costs. Let's now look at Cindy's Sweaters' costs.

Short-Run Cost

TO PRODUCE MORE OUTPUT IN THE SHORT RUN, a firm must employ more labour, which means that it must increase its costs. We describe the relationship between output and cost by using three cost concepts:

- Total cost
- Marginal cost
- Average cost

Total Cost

A firm's **total cost** (*TC*) is the cost of the productive resources it uses. Total cost includes the cost of land, capital, and labour. It also includes the cost of entrepreneurship, which is *normal profit* (see Chapter 9, p. 199). We divide total cost into total fixed cost and total variable cost.

Total fixed cost (*TFC*) is the cost of the firm's fixed inputs. Because the quantity of a fixed input does not change as output changes, total fixed cost does not change as output changes.

Total variable cost (*TVC*) is the cost of the firm's variable inputs. Because to change its output a firm must change the quantity of variable inputs, total variable cost changes as output changes.

Total cost is the sum of total fixed cost and total variable cost. That is,

$$TC = TFC + TVC.$$

The table in Fig. 10.4 shows Cindy's total costs. With one knitting machine that Cindy rents for $25 a day, *TFC* is $25. To produce sweaters, Cindy hires labour, which costs $25 a day. *TVC* is the number of workers multiplied by $25. For example, to produce 13 sweaters a day, Cindy hires 3 workers and *TVC* is $75. *TC* is the sum of *TFC* and *TVC*, so to produce 13 sweaters a day, Cindy's total cost, *TC*, is $100. Check the calculation in each row of the table.

Figure 10.4 shows Cindy's total cost curves, which graph total cost against total product. The green total fixed cost curve (*TFC*) is horizontal because total fixed cost does not change when output changes. It is a constant at $25. The purple total variable cost curve (*TVC*) and the blue total cost curve (*TC*) both slope upward because total variable cost increases as output increases. The arrows highlight total fixed cost as the vertical distance between the *TVC* and *TC* curves.

Let's now look at Cindy's marginal cost.

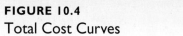

FIGURE 10.4
Total Cost Curves

$TC = TFC + TVC$

Labour (workers per day)	Output (sweaters per day)	Total fixed cost (TFC)	Total variable cost (TVC)	Total cost (TC)
		(dollars per day)		
A 0	0	25	0	25
B 1	4	25	25	50
C 2	10	25	50	75
D 3	13	25	75	100
E 4	15	25	100	125
F 5	16	25	125	150

Cindy rents a knitting machine for $25 a day. This amount is Cindy's total fixed cost. Cindy hires workers at a wage rate of $25 a day, and this cost is Cindy's total variable cost. For example, if Cindy employs 3 workers, total variable cost is 3 × $25, which equals $75. Total cost is the sum of total fixed cost and total variable cost. For example, when Cindy employs 3 workers, total cost is $100—total fixed cost of $25 plus total variable cost of $75. The graph shows Cindy's Sweaters' total cost curves. Total fixed cost (*TFC*) is constant—it graphs as a horizontal line—and total variable cost (*TVC*) increases as output increases. Total cost (*TC*) increases as output increases. The vertical distance between the total cost curve and the total variable cost curve is total fixed cost, as illustrated by the two arrows.

Marginal Cost

Figure 10.4 shows that total variable cost and total cost increase at a decreasing rate at small outputs and then begin to increase at an increasing rate as output increases. To understand these patterns in the changes in total cost, we need to use the concept of *marginal cost*.

A firm's **marginal cost** is the increase in total cost that results from a one-unit increase in output. We calculate marginal cost as the increase in total cost divided by the increase in output. The table in Fig. 10.5 shows this calculation. When, for example, output increases from 10 sweaters to 13 sweaters (row *C* to row *D*), total cost increases from $75 to $100. The change in output is 3 sweaters, and the change in total cost is $25. The marginal cost of one of those 3 sweaters is ($25 ÷ 3), which equals $8.33.

Figure 10.5 graphs the marginal cost data in the table as the red marginal cost curve, *MC*. This curve is U-shaped because when Cindy hires a second worker, marginal cost decreases, but when she hires a third, a fourth, and a fifth worker, marginal cost successively increases.

Marginal cost decreases at small outputs because of economies from greater specialization. Marginal cost eventually increases because of *the law of diminishing returns*. The law of diminishing returns means that each additional worker produces a successively smaller addition to output. So to get an additional unit of output, ever more workers are required. Because more workers are required to produce one additional unit of output, the cost of the additional output—marginal cost—must eventually increase.

Marginal cost tells us how total cost changes as output changes. The final cost concept tells us what it costs, on the average, to produce a unit of output. Let's now look at Cindy's Sweaters' average costs.

Average Cost

There are three average costs:

1. Average fixed cost
2. Average variable cost
3. Average total cost

Average fixed cost (*AFC*) is total fixed cost per unit of output. **Average variable cost** (*AVC*) is total variable cost per unit of output. **Average total cost** (*ATC*) is total cost per unit of output. The average

cost concepts are calculated from the total cost concepts as follows:

$$TC = TFC + TVC.$$

Divide each total cost term by the quantity produced, *Q*, to get,

$$\frac{TC}{Q} = \frac{TFC}{Q} + \frac{TVC}{Q}$$

or

$$ATC = AFC + AVC.$$

The table in Fig. 10.5 shows the calculation of average total cost. For example, when output is 10 sweaters (row *C*), average fixed cost is ($25 ÷ 10), which equals $2.50, average variable cost is ($50 ÷ 10), which equals $5.00, and average total cost is ($75 ÷ 10), which equals $7.50. Note that average total cost is equal to average fixed cost ($2.50) plus average variable cost ($5.00).

Figure 10.5 shows the average cost curves. The green average fixed cost curve (*AFC*) slopes downward. As output increases, the same constant fixed cost is spread over a larger output. The blue average total cost curve (*ATC*) and the purple average variable cost curve (*AVC*) are U-shaped. The vertical distance between the average total cost and average variable cost curves is equal to average fixed cost—as indicated by the two arrows. That distance shrinks as output increases because average fixed cost declines with increasing output.

The marginal cost curve (*MC*) intersects the average variable cost curve and the average total cost curve at their minimum points. That is, when marginal cost is less than average cost, average cost is decreasing, and when marginal cost exceeds average cost, average cost is increasing. This relationship holds for both the *ATC* curve and the *AVC* curve and is another example of the relationship you saw in Fig. 10.3 for average product and marginal product and in Cindy's course grades.

Why the Average Total Cost Curve Is U-Shaped

Average total cost, *ATC*, is the sum of average fixed cost, *AFC*, and average variable cost, *AVC*. So the shape of the *ATC* curve combines the shapes of the *AFC* and *AVC* curves. The U shape of the average

FIGURE 10.5
Marginal Cost and Average Costs

Marginal cost is calculated as the change in total cost divided by the change in output. When output increases from 4 to 10, an increase of 6, total cost increases by $25 and marginal cost is $25 ÷ 6, which equals $4.17. Each average cost concept is calculated by dividing the related total cost by output. When 10 sweaters are produced, AFC is $2.50 ($25 ÷ 10), AVC is $5 ($50 ÷ 10), and ATC is $7.50 ($75 ÷ 10).

The graph shows that the marginal cost curve (MC) is U-shaped and intersects the average variable cost curve and the average total cost curve at their minimum points. Average fixed cost (AFC) decreases as output increases. The average total cost curve (ATC) and average variable cost curve (AVC) are U-shaped. The vertical distance between these two curves is equal to average fixed cost, as illustrated by the two arrows.

	Labour (workers per day)	Output (sweaters per day)	Total fixed cost (TFC)	Total variable cost (TVC)	Total cost (TC)	Marginal cost (MC) (dollars per additional sweater)	Average fixed cost (AFC)	Average variable cost (AVC)	Average total cost (ATC)
			(dollars per day)				(dollars per sweater)		
A	0	0	25	0	25		—	—	—
						.... 6.25			
B	1	4	25	25	50		6.25	6.25	12.50
						.... 4.17			
C	2	10	25	50	75		2.50	5.00	7.50
						.... 8.33			
D	3	13	25	75	100		1.92	5.77	7.69
						.........12.50			
E	4	15	25	100	125		1.67	6.67	8.33
						.........25.00			
F	5	16	25	125	150		1.56	7.81	9.38

total cost curve arises from the influence of two opposing forces:

1. Spreading total fixed cost over a larger output
2. Eventually diminishing returns

When output increases, the firm spreads its total fixed cost over a larger output and so its average fixed cost decreases—its average fixed cost curve slopes downward.

Diminishing returns means that as output increases, ever-larger amounts of labour are needed to produce an additional unit of output. So average vari-

able cost eventually increases, and the *AVC* curve eventually slopes upward.

The shape of the average total cost curve combines these two effects. Initially, as output increases, both average fixed cost and average variable cost decrease, so average total cost decreases and the *ATC* curve slopes downward. But as output increases further and diminishing returns set in, average variable cost begins to increase. Eventually, average variable cost increases more quickly than average fixed cost decreases, so average total cost increases and the *ATC* curve slopes upward.

Cost Curves and Product Curves

The technology that a firm uses determines its costs. Figure 10.6 shows the links between the firm's technology constraint (its product curves) and its cost curves. The upper part of the figure shows the average product curve and the marginal product curve—like those in Fig. 10.3. The lower part of the figure shows the average variable cost curve and the marginal cost curve—like those in Fig. 10.5.

The figure highlights the links between technology and costs. As labour increases initially, marginal product and average product rise and marginal cost and average variable cost fall. Then, at the point of maximum marginal product, marginal cost is a minimum. As labour increases further, marginal product diminishes and marginal cost increases. But average product continues to rise, and average variable cost continues to fall. Then, at the point of maximum average product, average variable cost is a minimum. As labour increases further, average product diminishes and average variable cost increases.

Shifts in the Cost Curves

The position of a firm's short-run cost curves depend on two factors:

- Technology
- Prices of productive resources

Technology A technological change that increases productivity shifts the total product curve upward. It also shifts the marginal product curve and the average product curve upward. With a better technology, the same inputs can produce more output, so technological change lowers costs and shifts the cost curves downward. For example, advances in robot production techniques have increased productivity in the automobile industry. As a result, the product curves of DaimlerChrysler, Ford, and GM have shifted upward, and their cost curves have shifted downward. But the relationships between their product curves and cost curves have not changed. These curves are still linked in the way shown in Fig. 10.6.

Often, a technological advance results in a firm using more capital (a fixed input) and less labour (a variable input). For example, today the telephone companies use computers to provide directory assistance in place of the human operators they used in

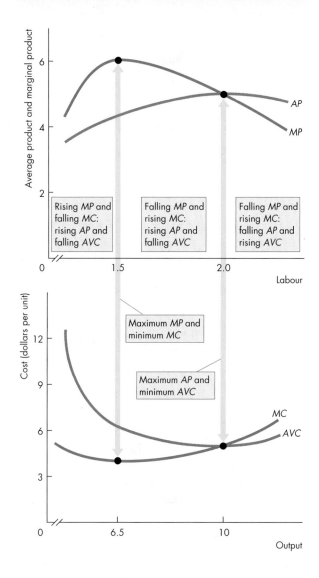

FIGURE 10.6

Product Curves and Cost Curves

A firm's marginal product curve is linked to its marginal cost curve. If marginal product rises, marginal cost falls. If marginal product is a maximum, marginal cost is a minimum. If marginal product diminishes, marginal cost rises. A firm's average product curve is linked to its average variable cost curve. If average product rises, average variable cost falls. If average product is a maximum, average variable cost is a minimum. If average product diminishes, average variable cost rises.

TABLE 10.2   A Compact Glossary of Costs

Term	Symbol	Definition	Equation
Fixed cost		Cost that is independent of the output level; cost of a fixed input	
Variable cost		Cost that varies with the output level; cost of a variable input	
Total fixed cost	TFC	Cost of the fixed inputs	
Total variable cost	TVC	Cost of the variable inputs	
Total cost	TC	Cost of all inputs	$TC = TFC + TVC$
Output (total product)	TP	Total quantity produced (output Q)	
Marginal cost	MC	Change in total cost resulting from a one-unit increase in total product	$MC = \Delta TC \div \Delta Q$
Average fixed cost	AFC	Total fixed cost per unit of output	$AFC = TFC \div Q$
Average variable cost	AVC	Total variable cost per unit of output	$AVC = TVC \div Q$
Average total cost	ATC	Total cost per unit of output	$ATC = AFC + AVC$

the 1980s. When such a technological change occurs, total cost decreases, but fixed costs increase and variable costs decrease. This change in the mix of fixed cost and variable cost means that at small output levels, average total cost might increase, while at large output levels, average total cost decreases.

Prices of Productive Resources An increase in the price of a productive resource increases costs and shifts the cost curves. But how the curves shift depends on which resource price changes. An increase in rent or some other component of *fixed* cost shifts the fixed cost curves (*TFC* and *AFC*) upward and shifts the total cost curve (*TC*) upward but leaves the variable cost curves (*AVC* and *TVC*) and the marginal cost curve (*MC*) unchanged. An increase in wages or some other component of *variable* cost shifts the variable cost curves (*TVC* and *AVC*) upward and shifts the marginal cost curve (*MC*) upward but leaves the fixed cost curves (*AFC* and *TFC*) unchanged. So, for example, if truck drivers' wages increase, the variable cost and marginal

cost of transportation services increase. If the interest expense paid by a trucking company increases, the fixed cost of transportation services increases.

You've now completed your study of short-run costs. All the concepts that you've met are summarized in a compact glossary in Table 10.2.

REVIEW QUIZ

1 What does a firm's short-run cost curves show?
2 How does marginal cost change as output increases (a) initially and (b) eventually?
3 What does the law of diminishing returns imply for the shape of the marginal cost curve?
4 What is the shape of the average fixed cost curve and why?
5 What are the shapes of the average variable cost curve and the average total cost curve and why?

 myeconlab **Study Plan 10.3**

Long-Run Cost

IN THE SHORT RUN, A FIRM CAN VARY THE quantity of labour but the quantity of capital is fixed. So the firm has variable costs of labour and fixed costs of capital. In the long run, a firm can vary both the quantity of labour and the quantity of capital. So in the long run, all the firm's costs are variable. We are now going to study the firm's costs in the long run, when all costs are variable costs and when the quantities of labour and capital vary.

The behaviour of long-run cost depends on the firm's *production function*, which is the relationship between the maximum output attainable and the quantities of both labour and capital.

The Production Function

Table 10.3 shows Cindy's Sweaters' production function. The table lists total product schedules for four different quantities of capital. We identify the quantity of capital by the plant size. The numbers for Plant 1 are for a factory with 1 knitting machine—the case we've just studied. The other three plants have 2, 3, and 4 machines. If Cindy's Sweaters doubles its capital to 2 knitting machines, the various amounts of labour can produce the outputs shown in the second column of the table. The other two columns show the outputs of yet larger quantities of capital. Each column of the table could be graphed as a total product curve for each plant.

Diminishing Returns

Diminishing returns occur at all four quantities of capital as the quantity of labour increases. You can check that fact by calculating the marginal product of labour in plants with 2, 3, and 4 machines. At each plant size, as the quantity of labour increases, the marginal product of labour (eventually) diminishes.

Diminishing Marginal Product of Capital

Diminishing returns also occur as the quantity of capital increases. You can check that fact by calculating the marginal product of capital at a given quantity of labour. The *marginal product of capital* is the change in total product divided by the change in capital when the quantity of labour is constant—equivalently, the change in output resulting from a one-unit increase in the quantity of capital. For example, if Cindy's has 3 workers and increases its capital from

TABLE 10.3   The Production Function

Labour (workers per day)	Output (sweaters per day)			
	Plant 1	Plant 2	Plant 3	Plant 4
1	4	10	13	15
2	10	15	18	20
3	13	18	22	24
4	15	20	24	26
5	16	21	25	27
Knitting machines (number)	1	2	3	4

The table shows the total product data for four quantities of capital. The greater the plant size, the larger is the total product for any given quantity of labour. But for a given plant size, the marginal product of labour diminishes. And for a given quantity of labour, the marginal product of capital diminishes.

1 machine to 2 machines, output increases from 13 to 18 sweaters a day. The marginal product of capital is 5 sweaters per day. If Cindy increases the number of machines from 2 to 3, output increases from 18 to 22 sweaters per day. The marginal product of the third machine is 4 sweaters per day, down from 5 sweaters per day for the second machine.

Let's now see what the production function implies for long-run costs.

Short-Run Cost and Long-Run Cost

Continue to assume that Cindy can hire a worker for $25 per day and rent a knitting machine for $25 per machine per day. Using these input prices and the data in Table 10.3, we can calculate and graph the average total cost curves for factories with 1, 2, 3, and 4 knitting machines. We've already studied the costs of a factory with 1 machine in Figs. 10.4 and 10.5. In Fig. 10.7, the average total cost curve for that case is ATC_1. Figure 10.7 also shows the average total cost curve for a factory with 2 machines, ATC_2, with 3 machines, ATC_3, and with 4 machines, ATC_4.

FIGURE 10.7

Short-Run Costs of Four Different Plants

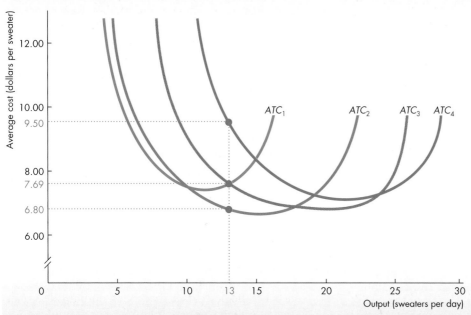

The figure shows short-run average total cost curves for four different quantities of capital. Cindy's can produce 13 sweaters a day with 1 knitting machine on ATC_1 or with 3 knitting machines on ATC_3 for an average cost of $7.69 per sweater. Cindy's can produce the same number of sweaters by using 2 knitting machines on ATC_2 for $6.80 per sweater or by using 4 machines on ATC_4 for $9.50 per sweater. If Cindy's produces 13 sweaters a day, the least-cost method of production—the long-run method—is with 2 machines on ATC_2.

Plant size has a big effect on the firm's average total cost. Two things stand out in Fig. 10.7:

1. Each short-run ATC curve is U-shaped.
2. For each short-run ATC curve, the larger the plant, the greater is the output at which average total cost is a minimum.

Each short-run average total cost curve is U-shaped because, as the quantity of labour increases, its marginal product at first increases and then diminishes. And these patterns in the marginal product of labour, which we examined in some detail for the plant with 1 knitting machine on pp. 222–223, occur at all plant sizes.

The minimum average total cost for a larger plant occurs at a greater output than it does for a smaller plant because the larger plant has a higher total fixed cost and therefore, for any given output level, a higher average fixed cost.

Which short-run average cost curve Cindy's Sweaters operates on depends on its plant size. But in the long run, Cindy chooses the plant size. And which plant size she chooses depends on the output she plans to produce. The reason is that the average total cost of producing a given output depends on the plant size.

To see why, suppose that Cindy plans to produce 13 sweaters a day. With 1 machine, the average total cost curve is ATC_1 (in Fig. 10.7) and the average total cost of 13 sweaters a day is $7.69 per sweater. With 2 machines, on ATC_2, average total cost is $6.80 per sweater. With 3 machines, on ATC_3, average total cost is $7.69 per sweater, the same as with 1 machine. Finally, with 4 machines, on ATC_4, average total cost is $9.50 per sweater.

The economically efficient plant size for producing a given output is the one that has the lowest average total cost. For Cindy's Sweaters, the economically efficient plant to use to produce 13 sweaters a day is the one with 2 machines.

In the long run, Cindy's chooses the plant size that minimizes average total cost. When a firm is producing a given output at the least possible cost, it is operating on its *long-run average cost curve*.

The **long-run average cost curve** is the relationship between the lowest attainable average total cost and output when both plant size and labour change.

The long-run average cost curve is a planning curve. It tells the firm the plant size and the quantity of labour to use at each output to minimize cost. Once the plant size is chosen, the firm operates on the short-run cost curves that apply to that plant size.

The Long-Run Average Cost Curve

Figure 10.8 shows Cindy's Sweaters' long-run average cost curve, *LRAC*. This long-run average cost curve is derived from the short-run average total cost curves in Fig. 10.7. For output rates up to 10 sweaters a day, average total cost is the lowest on ATC_1. For output rates between 10 and 18 sweaters a day, average total cost is the lowest on ATC_2. For output rates between 18 and 24 sweaters a day, average total cost is the lowest on ATC_3. And for output rates in excess of 24 sweaters a day, average total cost is the lowest on ATC_4. The segment of each of the four average total cost curves for which that quantity of capital has the lowest average total cost is highlighted in dark blue in Fig. 10.8. The scallop-shaped curve made up of these four segments is the long-run average cost curve.

Economies and Diseconomies of Scale

Economies of scale are features of a firm's technology that lead to falling long-run average cost as output increases. When economies of scale are present, the *LRAC* curve slopes downward. The *LRAC* curve in Fig. 10.8 shows that Cindy's Sweaters experiences economies of scale for outputs up to 15 sweaters a day.

With given input prices, economies of scale occur if the percentage increase in output exceeds the percentage increase in all inputs. For example, if when a firm increases its labour and capital by 10 percent, output increases by more than 10 percent, its average total cost falls. Economies of scale are present.

The main source of economies of scale is greater specialization of both labour and capital. For example, if GM produces 100 cars a week, each worker must perform many different tasks and the capital must be general-purpose machines and tools. But if GM produces 10,000 cars a week, each worker specializes and becomes highly proficient in a small number of tasks. Also, the capital is specialized and productive.

Diseconomies of scale are features of a firm's technology that lead to rising long-run average cost as output increases. When diseconomies of scale are present, the *LRAC* curve slopes upward. In Fig. 10.8, Cindy's Sweaters experiences diseconomies of scale at outputs greater than 15 sweaters a day.

With given input prices, diseconomies of scale occur if the percentage increase in output is less than the percentage increase in inputs. For example, if when a firm increases its labour and capital by 10 percent, output increases by less than 10 percent,

---

FIGURE 10.8
Long-Run Average Cost Curve

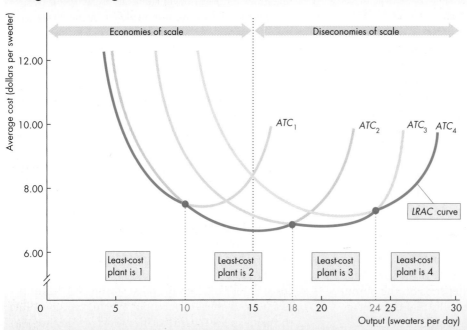

The long-run average cost curve traces the lowest attainable average total cost of production as both the plant size and labour change. Cindy's produces on its long-run average cost curve if it uses 1 machine to produce up to 10 sweaters a day, 2 machines to produce between 10 and 18 sweaters a day, 3 machines to produce between 18 and 24 sweaters a day, and 4 machines to produce more than 24 sweaters a day. Within these ranges, Cindy's varies its output by varying its labour input.

its average total cost rises. Diseconomies of scale are present.

The main source of diseconomies of scale is the difficulty of managing a very large enterprise. The larger the firm, the greater is the challenge of organizing it and the greater is the cost of communicating both up and down the management hierarchy and among managers. Eventually, management complexity brings rising average cost.

Diseconomies of scale occur in all production processes but perhaps only at a very large output rate.

Constant returns to scale are features of a firm's technology that lead to constant long-run average cost as output increases. When constant returns to scale are present, the *LRAC* curve is horizontal.

Constant returns to scale occur if the percentage increase in output equals the percentage increase in inputs. For example, if when a firm increases its labour and capital by 10 percent, output increases by 10 percent, then constant returns to scale are present.

For example, General Motors can double its production of Cavaliers by doubling its production facility for those cars. It can build an identical production line and hire an identical number of workers. With the two identical production lines, GM produces exactly twice as many cars.

Minimum Efficient Scale A firm experiences economies of scale up to some output level. Beyond that level, it moves into constant returns to scale or diseconomies of scale. A firm's **minimum efficient scale** is the smallest quantity of output at which long-run average cost reaches its lowest level.

The minimum efficient scale plays a role in determining market structure, as you will learn in the next three chapters. The minimum efficient scale also helps to answer some questions about real businesses.

Economies of Scale at Cindy's Sweaters The production technology that Cindy's Sweaters uses, shown in Table 10.3 on p. 230, illustrates economies of scale and diseconomies of scale. If Cindy's Sweaters increases its inputs from 1 machine and 1 worker to 2 of each, a 100 percent increase in all inputs, output increases by more than 100 percent, from 4 sweaters to 15 sweaters a day. Cindy's Sweaters experiences economies of scale, and its long-run average cost decreases. But if Cindy's Sweaters increases its inputs to 3 machines and 3 workers, a 50 percent increase, output increases by less than 50 percent, from 15 sweaters to 22 sweaters a day. Now Cindy's Sweaters experiences diseconomies of scale, and its long-run average cost increases. Its minimum efficient scale is at 15 sweaters a day.

Producing Cars and Generating Electric Power
Why do automakers have expensive equipment lying around that isn't fully used? You can now answer this question. An automaker uses the plant that minimizes the average total cost of producing the output that it can sell. But it operates below the minimum efficient scale. Its short-run average total cost curve looks like ATC_1 in Fig. 10.8. If it could sell more cars, it would produce more cars and its average total cost would fall.

Why do many electric utilities have too little production equipment to meet demand on the coldest and hottest days and have to buy power from other producers? You can now see why this happens and why an electric utility doesn't build more generating capacity. A power producer uses the plant size that minimizes the average total cost of producing the output that it can sell on a normal day. But it produces above the minimum efficient scale and experiences diseconomies of scale. Its short-run average total cost curve looks like ATC_3 in Fig. 10.8. With a larger plant size, its average total costs of producing its normal output would be higher.

REVIEW QUIZ

1 What does a firm's production function show and how is it related to a total product curve?
2 Explain why the law of diminishing returns applies to capital as well as to labour.
3 What does a firm's long-run average cost curve show? How is it related to the firm's short-run average cost curves?
4 What are economies of scale and diseconomies of scale? How do they arise? What do they imply for the the long-run average cost curve?
5 How is a firm's minimum efficient scale determined?

myeconlab   **Study Plan 10.4**

◆ *Reading Between the Lines* on pp. 234–235 applies what you've learned about a firm's cost curves. It looks at the key features of the cost curves of firms in the telecommunicatioins industry.

Traditional Phone Versus VoIP

THE GLOBE AND MAIL, AUGUST 22, 2005

Bell targets big business in IP challenge

Talk about a tough sales pitch: Try telling cost-conscious businesses their expensive existing telecommunication networks won't cut it in future, and they should switch to Internet protocol technology because it will lead to productivity improvements and cost savings.

But that's exactly what Bell Canada needs to do. It has a target to develop plans by year-end to move its 1,000 big-business customers to IP-based networks.

The conversion is a key part of Bell's strategy to cut its own expenses and uncover new sources of revenue growth at its business and consumer units amid rising competition from existing and new rivals.

Of course, the transition won't happen overnight. Many clients have poured significant money into their so-called legacy networks, so Bell must consider those investments as it develops timelines for a customer's transition to IP, according to William Bangert, senior vice-president of enterprise business development at Bell.

"If you go in and say I'm going to convert you entirely to IP tomorrow, come what may, without taking into account the investments that they've already made, you may ultimately cost them more money, not less money certainly in the short term," Mr. Bangert said in an interview in his Toronto office.

But when clients make the move to IP, which eliminates the need for separate voice-and-data networks, Bell says it will lower their costs and offer them new applications.

So far, Montreal-based Bell says 111 of its biggest customers have made the move to IP, including Bank of Montreal and Toronto-based Manulife Financial Corp.

It's a big investment. BMO, for example, is paying $84 million over four years to convert 1,100 branches to IP. The bill for Manulife is $140 million over seven years for IP-based voice and data services set up and managed by Bell.

Reprinted with permission from *The Globe and Mail*.

Essence of the Story

■ Bell is trying to get its 1,000 biggest customers to switch to Internet protocol (IP) technology.

■ The conversion is a key part of Bell's strategy to cut its own costs.

■ When Bell customers switch to IP, they too will face lower costs.

■ Bell says that so far 111 of its biggest customers have moved to IP.

■ The Bank of Montreal is spending $84 million and Manulife is spending $140 million to convert to IP.

Economic Analysis

■ Phone companies can choose between two main technologies: traditional telephone or Internet protocol (called VoIP or Voice over the Internet protocol when applied to voice communication).

■ IP technology uses more capital and less labour than does the traditional technology. The cost of the capital is a fixed cost, and the cost of the labour is a variable cost.

■ The total fixed cost of a VoIP system exceeds the total fixed cost of a traditional phone system.

■ The average variable cost of a traditional phone call exceeds the average variable cost of a VoIPcall.

■ Average total cost (ATC) is the sum of average fixed cost and average variable cost. The figure shows the ATC curves for the two technologies.

■ ATC_O is the average total cost curve for a traditional telephone system, and ATC_N is the average total cost curve for a VoIP system.

■ Small firms that make fewer than Q calls a year minimize average total cost by using traditional phone service and avoiding the large cost of installing a VoIP system.

■ Larger firms (like the Bank of Montreal, Manulife, the others of the 111 customers of Bell) that make more than Q calls a year minimize average total cost by using VoIP.

■ The figure shows the long-run average cost curve, $LRAC$, for voice conversations. Up to Q, the $LRAC$ curve is the highlighted section of ATC_O, and above Q, the $LRAC$ curve is the highlighted section of ATC_N.

■ The large fixed costs of using Internet and more broadly, digital technologies explains why phone companies, cable TV companies, and Internet portal companies are all offering the same array of services. By so doing, they are able to spread this large fixed cost over a greater number of products and services.

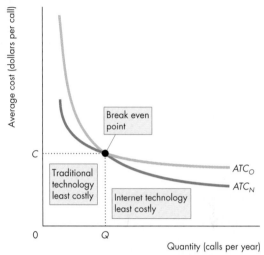

Figure 1 The cost of a phone call with two technologies

235

SUMMARY

KEY POINTS

Decision Time Frames (p. 220)

- In the short run, the quantity of some resources are fixed and the quantities of the other resources can be varied.
- In the long run, the quantities of all resources can be varied.

Short-Run Technology Constraint (pp. 221–224)

- A total product curve shows the quantity a firm can produce with a given quantity of capital and different quantities of labour.
- Initially, the marginal product of labour increases as the quantity of labour increases, but eventually, marginal product diminishes—the law of diminishing returns.
- Average product increases initially and eventually diminishes.

Short-Run Cost (pp. 225–229)

- As output increases, total fixed cost is constant, and total variable cost and total cost increase.
- As output increases, average fixed cost decreases and average variable cost, average total cost, and marginal cost decrease at small outputs and increase at large outputs. These cost curves are U-shaped.

Long-Run Cost (pp. 230–233)

- Long-run cost is the cost of production when all inputs—labour and capital—have been adjusted to their economically efficient levels.
- There is a set of short-run cost curves for each different plant size. There is one least-cost plant size for each output. The larger the output, the larger is the plant size that will minimize average total cost.

- The long-run average cost curve traces out the lowest attainable average total cost at each output when both capital and labour inputs can be varied.
- With economies of scale, the long-run average cost curve slopes downward. With diseconomies of scale, the long-run average cost curve slopes upward.

KEY FIGURES AND TABLE

KEY TERMS

PROBLEMS

Go to **myeconlab** for solutions to odd-numbered problems and additional exercises.

1. Rubber Dinghies' total product schedule is

Labour (workers per week)	Output (dinghies per week)
1	1
2	3
3	6
4	10
5	15
6	21
7	26
8	30
9	33
10	35

   a. Draw the total product curve.
   b. Calculate the average product of labour and draw the average product curve.
   c. Calculate the marginal product of labour and draw the marginal product curve.
   d. What is the relationship between average product and marginal product when Rubber Dinghies produces (i) fewer than 30 dinghies a week and (ii) more than 30 dinghies a week?

2. Sue's SurfBoards' total product schedule is

Labour (workers per week)	Output (surfboards per week)
1	40
2	100
3	140
4	170
5	190
6	200

   a. Draw the total product curve.
   b. Calculate the average product of labour and draw the average product curve.
   c. Calculate the marginal product of labour and draw the marginal product curve.
   d. What is the relationship between the average product and marginal product when Sue's SurfBoards produces (i) fewer than 100 surfboards a week and (ii) more than 100 surfboards a week?

3. In problem 1, the price of labour is $400 a week and total fixed cost is $1,000 a week.
   a. Calculate total cost, total variable cost, and total fixed cost for each output and draw the short-run total cost curves.
   b. Calculate average total cost, average fixed cost, average variable cost, and marginal cost at each output and draw the short-run average and marginal cost curves.

4. In problem 2, the price of labour is $100 per week and total fixed costs are $200 per week.
   a. Calculate total cost, total variable cost, and total fixed costs for each level of output and draw the short-run total cost curves.
   b. Calculate average total cost, average fixed cost, average variable cost, and marginal cost at each level of output and draw the short-run average and marginal cost curves.

5. In problem 3, suppose that Rubber Dinghies' total fixed cost increases to $1,100 a week. Explain what changes occur in the short-run average and marginal cost curves.

6. In problem 4, suppose that the price of labour increases to $150 per week. Explain what changes occur in the short-run average and marginal cost curves.

7. In problem 3, Rubber Dinghies buys a second plant and the total product of each quantity of labour doubles. The total fixed cost of operating each plant is $1,000 a week. The wage rate is $400 a week.
   a. Set out the average total cost schedule when Rubber Dinghies operates two plants.
   b. Draw the long-run average cost curve.
   c. Over what output ranges is it efficient to operate one plant and two plants?

8. In problem 4, Sue's SurfBoards buys a second plant and the total product of each quantity of labour increases by 50 percent. The total fixed cost of operating each plant is $200 a week. The wage rate is $100 a week.
   a. Set out the average total cost curve when Sue's SurfBoards operates two plants.
   b. Draw the long-run average cost curve.
   c. Over what output ranges is it efficient to operate one plant and two plants?

9. The table shows the production function of Bonnie's Balloon Rides.

Labour (workers per day)	Output (rides per day)			
	Plant 1	Plant 2	Plant 3	Plant 4
10	4	10	13	15
20	10	15	18	20
30	13	18	22	24
40	15	20	24	26
50	16	21	25	27
Balloons (number)	1	2	3	4

Bonnie pays $500 a day for each balloon she rents and $25 a day for each worker she hires.

a. Find and graph the average total cost curve for each plant size.
b. Draw Bonnie's long-run average cost curve.
c. What is Bonnie's minimum efficient scale?
d. Explain how Bonnie uses her long-run average cost curve to decide how many balloons to rent.

10. The table shows the production function of Cathy's Cakes.

Labour (workers per day)	Output (cakes per day)			
	Plant 1	Plant 2	Plant 3	Plant 4
1	20	40	55	65
2	40	60	75	85
3	65	75	90	100
4	65	85	100	110
Ovens (number)	1	2	3	4

Cathy pays $100 a day for each oven she rents and $50 a day for each kitchen worker she hires.

a. Find and graph the average total cost curve for each plant size.
b. Draw Cathy's long-run average cost curve.
c. Over what output range does Cathy experience economies of scale?
d. Explain how Cathy uses her long-run average cost curve to decide how many ovens to rent.

CRITICAL THINKING

1. Study *Reading Between the Lines* on pp. 234–235 and then answer the following questions:
   a. What is the main difference, from a cost point of view, between traditional telephone service and VoIP?
   b. Why do you think VoIP is becoming more popular?
   c. Would it ever make sense for a firm to use traditional phone service rather than VoIP?
   d. Do you think that VoIP is as common in Africa as it is in Canada? Explain why or why not.
   e. Suppppose the government put a tax on VoIP calls but did not put a similar tax on traditional phone calls. How would the tax affect the cost curves of the Bank of Montreal and Manulife? Might these firms want to switch back to traditional phone service?

WEB EXERCISES

Use the links on ⓧ myeconlab to work the following exercises.

1. Obtain information about the cost of producing pumpkins.
   a. List all the costs referred to on the Web page.
   b. For each item, say whether it is a fixed cost or a variable cost.
   c. Make some assumptions and sketch the average cost curves and the marginal cost curve for producing pumpkins.
2. Obtain information about the cost of producing vegetables. For one of the vegetables (your choice):
   a. List all the costs referred to on the Web page.
   b. For each item, say whether it is a fixed cost or a variable cost.
   c. Sketch the average cost curves and the marginal cost curve for producing the vegetable you've chosen.

Perfect Competition

Sweet Competition

Maple syrup is sweet, but producing it and selling it is a tough competitive business. Around 12,000 firms in Canada and the United States produce syrup. In the early 2000s, bumper crops sent the price of maple syrup tumbling. How did producers react to this drop in price? *Reading Between the Lines* at the end of the chapter answers this question. In recent years, new firms have entered the maple syrup business, while others have been squeezed out. Why do some firms enter an industry and others leave it? What are the effects on profits and prices of new firms entering and old firms leaving an industry?

In September 2005, around 150,000 people were unemployed because they had been laid off by the firms that previously employed them. Why do firms lay off workers? Why do firms temporarily shut down?

Over the past few years, there has been a dramatic fall in the prices of personal computers. For example, a slow computer cost almost $4,000 a few years ago, and a fast one costs less than $500 today. What goes on in an industry when the price of its output falls sharply? What happens to the profits of the firms producing such goods? Maple syrup, computers, and most other goods are produced by more than one firm, and these firms compete with each other for sales.

◆ To study competitive markets, we are going to build a model of a market in which competition is as fierce and extreme as possible—more extreme than in the examples we've just considered. We call this situation "perfect competition."

After studying this chapter, you will be able to

- ■ **Define perfect competition**
- ■ **Explain how firms make their supply decisions and why they sometimes shut down temporarily and lay off workers**
- ■ **Explain how price and output are determined and why firms enter and leave an industry**
- ■ **Predict the effects of a change in demand and of a technological advance**
- ■ **Explain why perfect competition is efficient**

Competition

THE FIRMS THAT YOU STUDY IN THIS CHAPTER face the force of raw competition. We call this extreme form of competition perfect competition. **Perfect competition** is an industry in which

■ Many firms sell identical products to many buyers.
■ There are no restrictions on entry into the industry.
■ Established firms have no advantage over new ones.
■ Sellers and buyers are well informed about prices.

Farming, fishing, wood pulping and paper milling, the manufacture of paper cups and plastic shopping bags, grocery retailing, photo finishing, lawn service, plumbing, painting, dry cleaning, and the provision of laundry services are all examples of highly competitive industries.

How Perfect Competition Arises

Perfect competition arises if the minimum efficient scale of a single producer is small relative to the demand for the good or service. A firm's *minimum efficient scale* is the smallest quantity of output at which long-run average cost reaches is lowest level. (See Chapter 10, p. 233.) Where the minimum efficient scale of a firm is small relative to demand, there is room for many firms in an industry.

Second, perfect competition arises if each firm is perceived to produce a good or service that has no unique characteristics so that consumers don't care which firm they buy from.

Price Takers

Firms in perfect competition must make many decisions. But one thing they do *not* decide is the price at which to sell their output. Firms in perfect competition are said to be price takers. A **price taker** is a firm that cannot influence the price of a good or service.

The key reason why a perfectly competitive firm is a price taker is that it produces a tiny proportion of the total output of a particular good and buyers are well informed about the prices of other firms.

Imagine that you are a wheat farmer in Saskatchewan. You have 500 hectares under cultivation—which sounds like a lot. But compared to the thousands of hectares across the Canadian prairies and in the Dakotas, Nebraska, Colorado, Oklahoma, and Texas, as well as the thousands more in Argentina,

Australia, and Ukraine, your 500 hectares is a drop in the ocean. Nothing makes your wheat any better than any other farmer's, and all the buyers of wheat know the price at which they can do business.

If everybody else sells their wheat for $300 a tonne and you want $310, why would people buy from you? They can go to the next farmer and the next and the one after that and buy all they need for $300 a tonne. This price is determined in the market for wheat, and you are a *price taker*.

A price taker faces a perfectly elastic demand. One farm's wheat is a *perfect substitute* for wheat from the farm next door or from any other farm. Note, though, that the *market* demand for wheat is not perfectly elastic. The market demand curve is downward sloping, and its elasticity depends on the substitutability of wheat for other grains such as barley, rye, corn, and rice.

Economic Profit and Revenue

A firm's goal is to maximize *economic profit*, which is equal to total revenue minus total cost. Total cost is the *opportunity cost* of production, which includes *normal profit*, the return that the entrepreneur can expect to receive on the average in an alternative business. (See Chapter 9, p. 199.)

A firm's **total revenue** equals the price of its output multiplied by the number of units of output sold (price × quantity). **Marginal revenue** is the change in total revenue that results from a one-unit increase in the quantity sold. Marginal revenue is calculated by dividing the change in total revenue by the change in the quantity sold.

Figure 11.1 illustrates these revenue concepts. Cindy's Sweaters is one of a thousand such small firms. Demand and supply in the sweater market determine the price of a sweater. Cindy must take this price. Cindy's Sweaters cannot influence the price by its own actions, so the price remains constant when Cindy changes the quantity of sweaters produced.

The table shows three different quantities of sweaters produced. As the quantity varies, the price remains constant—in this example, at $25 a sweater. Total revenue is equal to the price multiplied by the quantity sold. For example, if Cindy sells 8 sweaters, total revenue is 8 × $25, which equals $200.

Marginal revenue is the change in total revenue resulting from a one-unit change in quantity. For example, when the quantity sold increases from 8 to 9, total revenue increases from $200 to $225, so marginal

FIGURE 11.1

Demand, Price, and Revenue in Perfect Competition

(a) Sweater market

(b) Cindy's marginal revenue

(c) Cindy's total revenue

Quantity sold (Q) (sweaters per day)	Price (P) (dollars per sweater)	Total revenue (TR = P × Q) (dollars)	Marginal revenue (MR = ΔTR/ΔQ) (dollars per additional sweater)
8	25	200	
			25
9	25	225	
			25
10	25	250	

Market demand and supply determine the market price. In part (a), the market price is $25 a sweater and 9,000 sweaters are bought and sold. The demand for Cindy's Sweaters is perfectly elastic at the market price of $25 a sweater. The table calculates total revenue and marginal revenue. Part (b) shows Cindy's Sweaters' marginal revenue curve (MR). This curve is also the demand curve for Cindy's sweaters. Part (c) shows Cindy's total revenue curve (TR). Point A corresponds to the second row of the table.

revenue is $25 a sweater. (Notice that in the table, marginal revenue appears *between* the lines for the quantities sold to remind you that marginal revenue results from the *change* in the quantity sold.)

Because the price remains constant when the quantity sold changes, the change in total revenue resulting from a one-unit increase in the quantity sold equals price. Therefore in perfect competition, marginal revenue equals price.

Figure 11.1(b) shows Cindy's marginal revenue curve (MR). This curve tells us the change in total revenue that results from selling one more sweater. This curve is also the demand curve for Cindy's sweaters. The firm, being a price taker, can sell any quantity it chooses at the market price. The firm faces a perfectly elastic demand for its output.

The total revenue curve (TR) in Fig. 11.1(c) shows the total revenue at each quantity sold. For example, if Cindy sells 9 sweaters, total revenue is $225 (point A).

Because each additional sweater sold brings in a constant amount—$25—the total revenue curve is an upward-sloping straight line.

REVIEW QUIZ

1 Why is a firm in perfect competition a price taker?
2 In perfect competition, what is the relationship between the demand for the firm's output and the market demand?
3 In perfect competition, why is a firm's marginal revenue curve also the demand curve for the firm's output?
4 Why is the total revenue curve in perfect competition an upward-sloping straight line?

myeconlab Study Plan 11.1

The Firm's Decisions in Perfect Competition

FIRMS IN A PERFECTLY COMPETITIVE INDUSTRY face a given market price and have the revenue curves that you've studied. These revenue curves summarize the market constraint faced by a perfectly competitive firm.

Firms also face a technology constraint, which is described by the product curves (total product, average product, and marginal product) that you studied in Chapter 10. The technology available to the firm determines its costs, which are described by the cost curves (total cost, average cost, and marginal cost) that you also studied in Chapter 10.

The task of the competitive firm is to make the maximum economic profit possible, given the constraints it faces. To achieve this objective, a firm must make four key decisions: two in the short run and two in the long run.

Short-Run Decisions The *short run* is a time frame in which each firm has a given plant and the number of firms in the industry is fixed. But many things can change in the short run, and the firm must react to these changes. For example, the price for which the firm can sell its output might have a seasonal fluctuation, or it might fluctuate with general business conditions. The firm must react to such short-run price fluctuations and decide

1. Whether to produce or to shut down
2. If the decision is to produce, what quantity to produce

Long-Run Decisions The *long run* is a time frame in which each firm can change the size of its plant and decide whether to leave the industry. Other firms can decide whether to enter the industry. So in the long run, both the plant size of each firm and the number of firms in the industry can change. Also in the long run, the constraints that firms face can change. For example, the demand for the good can permanently fall, or a technological advance can change the industry's costs. The firm must react to such long-run changes and decide

1. Whether to increase or decrease its plant size
2. Whether to stay in an industry or leave it

The Firm and the Industry in the Short Run and the Long Run To study a competitive industry, we begin by looking at an individual firm's short-run decisions. We then see how the short-run decisions of all firms in a competitive industry combine to determine the industry price, output, and economic profit. We then turn to the long run and study the effects of long-run decisions on the industry price, output, and economic profit. All the decisions we study are driven by the pursuit of a single objective: maximization of economic profit.

Profit-Maximizing Output

A perfectly competitive firm maximizes economic profit by choosing its output level. One way of finding the profit-maximizing output is to study a firm's total revenue and total cost curves and find the output level at which total revenue exceeds total cost by the largest amount. Figure 11.2 shows how to do this for Cindy's Sweaters. The table lists Cindy's total revenue and total cost at different outputs, and part (a) of the figure shows Cindy's total revenue and total cost curves. These curves are graphs of the numbers shown in the first three columns of the table. The total revenue curve (*TR*) is the same as that in Fig. 11.1(c). The total cost curve (*TC*) is similar to the one that you met in Chapter 10: As output increases, so does total cost.

Economic profit equals total revenue minus total cost. The fourth column of the table in Fig. 11.2 shows Cindy's economic profit, and part (b) of the figure illustrates these numbers as Cindy's profit curve. This curve shows that Cindy makes an economic profit at outputs between 4 and 12 sweaters a day. At outputs less than 4 sweaters a day, Cindy incurs an economic loss. She also incurs an economic loss if output exceeds 12 sweaters a day. At outputs of 4 sweaters and 12 sweaters a day, total cost equals total revenue and Cindy's economic profit is zero. An output at which total cost equals total revenue is called a *break-even point*. The firm's economic profit at a break-even point is zero. But because normal profit is part of total cost, a firm makes normal profit at a break-even point. That is, at the break-even point, the entrepreneur makes an income equal to the best alternative return forgone.

Notice the relationship between the total revenue, total cost, and profit curves. Economic profit is measured by the vertical distance between the total

FIGURE 11.2

Total Revenue, Total Cost, and Economic Profit

(a) Revenue and cost

(b) Economic profit and loss

Quantity (Q) (sweaters per day)	Total revenue (TR) (dollars)	Total cost (TC) (dollars)	Economic profit (TR − TC) (dollars)
0	0	22	−22
1	25	45	−20
2	50	66	−16
3	75	85	−10
4	100	100	0
5	125	114	11
6	150	126	24
7	175	141	34
8	200	160	40
9	225	183	42
10	250	210	40
11	275	245	30
12	300	300	0
13	325	360	−35

The table lists Cindy's total revenue, total cost, and economic profit. Part (a) graphs the total revenue and total cost curves. The height of the blue area between the total cost and total revenue curves in part (a) is economic profit. Cindy's Sweaters makes maximum economic profit, $42 a day ($225 − $183), when it produces 9 sweaters. At outputs of 4 and 12 sweaters a day, Cindy makes zero economic profit—these are break-even points. At outputs less than 4 and greater than 12 sweaters a day, Cindy incurs an economic loss. In part (b), Cindy's profit curve is at its highest when economic profit is at a maximum and cuts the horizontal axis at the break-even points.

revenue and total cost curves. When the total revenue curve in part (a) is above the total cost curve, between 4 and 12 sweaters, the firm is making an economic profit and the profit curve in Fig. 11.2(b) is above the horizontal axis. At the break-even points, where the total cost and total revenue curves intersect, the profit curve intersects the horizontal axis. The profit curve is at its highest when the distance between *TR* and *TC* is greatest. In this example, profit maximization occurs at an output of 9 sweaters a day. At this output, Cindy's economic profit is $42 a day.

Marginal Analysis

Another way of finding the profit-maximizing output is to use *marginal analysis* and compare marginal revenue, *MR,* with marginal cost, *MC.* As output increases, marginal revenue remains constant but marginal cost changes. At small output levels, marginal cost decreases, but it eventually increases. So where the marginal cost curve intersects the marginal revenue curve, marginal cost is rising.

If marginal revenue exceeds marginal cost (if *MR* > *MC*), the extra revenue from selling one more unit exceeds the extra cost incurred to produce it. The firm makes an economic profit on the marginal unit, so economic profit increases if output *increases*. If marginal revenue is less than marginal cost (if *MR* < *MC*), the extra revenue from selling one more unit is less than the extra cost incurred to produce it. The firm incurs an economic loss on the marginal unit, so its economic profit decreases if output increases and its economic profit increases if output *decreases*.

If marginal revenue equals marginal cost (if *MR* = *MC*), economic profit is maximized. The rule *MR* = *MC* is an example of marginal analysis. Let's check that this rule works to find the profit-maximizing output by returning to Cindy's Sweaters.

Look at Fig. 11.3. The table records Cindy's marginal revenue and marginal cost. Marginal revenue is a constant $25 a sweater. Over the range of outputs shown in the table, marginal cost increases from $19 a sweater to $35 a sweater.

Focus on the highlighted rows of the table. If Cindy increases output from 8 sweaters to 9 sweaters, marginal revenue is $25 and marginal cost is $23. Because marginal revenue exceeds marginal cost, economic profit increases. The last column of the table shows that economic profit increases from $40 to $42, an increase of $2. This economic profit from the ninth sweater is shown as the blue area in the figure.

If Cindy increases output from 9 sweaters to 10 sweaters, marginal revenue is still $25 but marginal cost is $27. Because marginal revenue is less than marginal cost, economic profit decreases. The last column of the table shows that economic profit decreases from $42 to $40. This loss from the tenth sweater is shown as the red area in the figure.

Cindy maximizes economic profit by producing 9 sweaters a day, the quantity at which marginal revenue equals marginal cost.

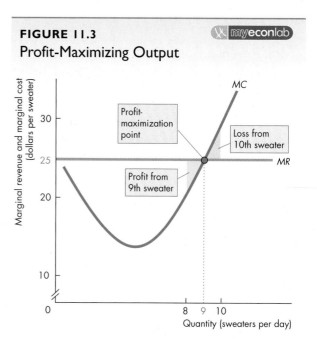

FIGURE 11.3
Profit-Maximizing Output

Quantity (Q) (sweaters per day)	Total revenue (TR) (dollars)	Marginal revenue (MR) (dollars per additional sweater)	Total cost (TC) (dollars)	Marginal cost (MC) (dollars per additional sweater)	Economic profit (TR – TC) (dollars)
7	175		141		34
		25		19	
8	200		160		40
		25		23	
9	225		183		42
		25		27	
10	250		210		40
		25		35	
11	275		245		30

Profit is maximized if marginal revenue equals marginal cost. If output increases from 8 to 9 sweaters, marginal cost is $23, which is less than the marginal revenue of $25. If output increases from 9 to 10 sweaters, marginal cost is $27, which exceeds the marginal revenue of $25. Marginal cost and marginal revenue are equal when Cindy produces 9 sweaters a day. If marginal revenue exceeds marginal cost, an increase in output increases economic profit. If marginal revenue is less than marginal cost, an increase in output decreases economic profit. If marginal revenue equals marginal cost, economic profit is maximized.

Profits and Losses in the Short Run

In short-run equilibrium, although the firm produces the profit-maximizing output, it does not necessarily end up making an economic profit. It might do so, but it might alternatively break even (earn a normal profit) or incur an economic loss. To determine which of these outcomes occurs, we compare the firm's total revenue and total cost or, equivalently, we compare price with average total cost. If price equals average total cost, a firm breaks even—makes normal profit. If price exceeds average total cost, a firm makes an economic profit. If price is less than average total cost, a firm incurs an economic loss. Figure 11.4 shows these three possible short-run profit outcomes.

Three Possible Profit Outcomes In Fig. 11.4(a), the price of a sweater is $20. Cindy's profit-maximizing output is 8 sweaters a day. Average total cost is $20 a sweater, so Cindy breaks even and makes normal profit (zero economic profit).

In Fig. 11.4(b), the price of a sweater is $25. Profit is maximized when output is 9 sweaters a day. The average total cost of a sweater is $20.33. Price

exceeds average total cost (*ATC*), so Cindy makes an economic profit. This economic profit is $42 a day. It is made up of $4.67 per sweater ($25.00 – $20.33) multiplied by the number of sweaters produced ($4.67 × 9 = $42). The blue rectangle shows this economic profit. The height of that rectangle is profit per sweater, $4.67, and the length is the quantity of sweaters produced, 9 a day, so the area of the rectangle is Cindy's economic profit of $42 a day.

In Fig. 11.4(c), the price of a sweater is $17. The average total cost of a sweater is $20.14. Price is less than average total cost, so Cindy incurs an economic loss. Price and marginal revenue are $17 a sweater, and the profit-maximizing (in this case, loss-minimizing) output is 7 sweaters a day. Cindy's total revenue is $119 a day (7 × $17). The economic loss is $3.14 per sweater ($20.14 – $17.00). This loss per sweater multiplied by the number of sweaters produced is $22 ($3.14 × 7 = $22). The red rectangle shows this economic loss. The height of that rectangle is economic loss per sweater, $3.14, and the length is the quantity of sweaters produced, 7 a day, so the area of the rectangle is Cindy's economic loss of $22 a day.

FIGURE 11.4

Three Possible Profit Outcomes in the Short Run

(a) Normal profit   **(b) Economic profit**   **(c) Economic loss**

In the short run, the firm might break even (make a normal profit), make an economic profit, or incur an economic loss. If the price equals minimum average total cost, the firm breaks even and makes a normal profit (part a). If the price exceeds the average total cost of producing the profit-

maximizing output, the firm makes an economic profit—the blue rectangle in part (b). If the price is below minimum average total cost, the firm incurs an economic loss—the red rectangle in part (c).

The Firm's Short-Run Supply Curve

A perfectly competitive firm's short-run supply curve shows how the firm's profit-maximizing output varies as the market price varies, other things remaining the same. Figure 11.5 shows how to derive Cindy's supply curve. Part (a) shows Cindy's Sweaters' marginal cost and average variable cost curves, and part (b) shows its supply curve. There is a direct link between the marginal cost and average variable cost curves and the supply curve. Let's see what that link is.

Temporary Plant Shutdown In the short run, a firm cannot avoid incurring its fixed cost. But the firm can avoid variable costs by temporarily laying off its workers and shutting down. If a firm shuts down, it produces no output and it incurs a loss equal to total fixed cost. This loss is the largest that a firm needs to incur. A firm shuts down if the price falls below minimum average variable cost. The **shutdown point** is the output and price at which the firm just covers its total variable cost—point T in Fig. 11.5(a). If the price is $17, the marginal revenue curve is MR_0 and the profit-maximizing output is 7 sweaters a day at point T. But both price and average variable cost equal $17, so Cindy's total revenue equals total variable cost. Cindy incurs an economic loss equal to total fixed cost. At a price below $17, no matter what quantity Cindy produces, average *variable* cost exceeds price and the firm's loss exceeds total fixed cost. At a price below $17, the firm shuts down temporarily.

The Short-Run Supply Curve If the price is above minimum average variable cost, Cindy maximizes profit by producing the output at which marginal cost equals price. We can determine the quantity produced at each price from the marginal cost curve. At a price of $25, the marginal revenue curve is MR_1 and Cindy maximizes profit by producing 9 sweaters. At a price of $31, the marginal revenue curve is MR_2 and Cindy produces 10 sweaters.

Cindy's short-run supply curve, shown in Fig. 11.5(b), has two separate parts: First, at prices that exceed minimum average variable cost, the supply curve is the same as the marginal cost curve above the shutdown point (T). Second, at prices below minimum average variable cost, Cindy shuts down and produces nothing. Its supply curve runs along the vertical axis. At a price of $17, Cindy is indifferent between shutting down and producing 7 sweaters a day. Either way, her loss is the same.

FIGURE 11.5
A Firm's Supply Curve

(a) Marginal cost and average variable cost

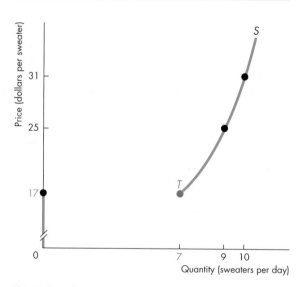

(b) Cindy's short-run supply curve

Part (a) shows Cindy's profit-maximizing output at various market prices. For example, at $25 a sweater, Cindy produces 9 sweaters. Point T is Cindy's shutdown point. At prices below $17, Cindy produces nothing. Part (b) shows Cindy's supply curve. It is made up of the marginal cost curve (part a) at all points above minimum average variable cost and the vertical axis at all prices below minimum average variable cost.

Short-Run Industry Supply Curve

The **short-run industry supply curve** shows the quantity supplied by the industry at each price when the plant size of each firm and the number of firms remain constant. The quantity supplied by the industry at a given price is the sum of the quantities supplied by all firms in the industry at that price.

Figure 11.6 shows the supply curve for the competitive sweater industry. In this example, the industry consists of 1,000 firms exactly like Cindy's Sweaters. At each price, the quantity supplied by the industry is 1,000 times the quantity supplied by a single firm.

The table in Fig. 11.6 shows the firm's and the industry's supply schedule and how the industry supply curve is constructed. At prices below $17, every firm in the industry shuts down; the quantity supplied by the industry is zero. At a price of $17, each firm is indifferent between shutting down and producing nothing or operating and producing 7 sweaters a day. Some firms will shut down, and others will supply 7 sweaters a day. The quantity supplied by each firm is *either* 0 or 7 sweaters, but the quantity supplied by the industry is *between* 0 (all firms shut down) and 7,000 (all firms produce 7 sweaters a day each).

To construct the industry supply curve, we sum the quantities supplied by the individual firms. Each of the 1,000 firms in the industry has a supply schedule like Cindy's. At prices below $17, the industry supply curve runs along the price axis. At a price of $17, the industry supply curve is horizontal—supply is perfectly elastic. As the price rises above $17, each firm increases its quantity supplied and the quantity supplied by the industry increases by 1,000 times that of each firm.

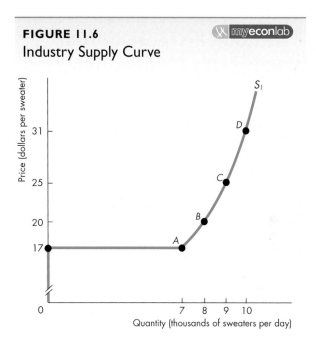

FIGURE 11.6

Industry Supply Curve

	Price (dollars per sweater)	Quantity supplied by Cindy's Sweaters (sweaters per day)	Quantity supplied by industry (sweaters per day)
A	17	0 or 7	0 to 7,000
B	20	8	8,000
C	25	9	9,000
D	31	10	10,000

The industry supply schedule is the sum of the supply schedules of all individual firms. An industry that consists of 1,000 identical firms has a supply schedule similar to that of the individual firm, but the quantity supplied by the industry is 1,000 times as large as that of the individual firm (see the table). The industry supply curve is S_I. Points A, B, C, and D correspond to the rows of the table. At the shutdown price of $17, each firm produces either 0 or 7 sweaters per day. The industry supply is perfectly elastic at the shutdown price.

So far, we have studied a single firm in isolation. We have seen that the firm's actions depend on the market price, which the firm takes as given. But how is the market price determined? Let's find out.

Output, Price, and Profit in Perfect Competition

TO DETERMINE THE MARKET PRICE AND THE quantity bought and sold in a perfectly competitive market, we need to study how market demand and market supply interact. We begin this process by studying a perfectly competitive market in the short run when the number of firms is fixed and each firm has a given plant size.

Short-Run Equilibrium

Industry demand and supply determine the market price and industry output. Figure 11.7(a) shows a short-run equilibrium. The supply curve S is the same as S_I in Fig. 11.6. If demand is shown by the demand curve D_1, the equilibrium price is $20. Each firm takes this price as given and produces its profit-maximizing output, which is 8 sweaters a day. Because the industry has 1,000 firms, industry output is 8,000 sweaters a day.

A Change in Demand

Changes in demand bring changes to short-run industry equilibrium. Figure 11.7(b) shows these changes.

If demand increases, the demand curve shifts rightward to D_2. The price rises to $25. At this price, each firm maximizes profit by increasing output. The new output is 9 sweaters a day for each firm and 9,000 sweaters a day for the industry.

If demand decreases, the demand curve shifts leftward to D_3. The price now falls to $17. At this price, each firm maximizes profit by decreasing its output. The new output is 7 sweaters a day for each firm and 7,000 sweaters a day for the industry.

If the demand curve shifts farther leftward than D_3, the price remains constant at $17 because the industry supply curve is horizontal at that price. Some firms continue to produce 7 sweaters a day, and others temporarily shut down. Firms are indifferent between these two activities, and whichever they choose, they incur an economic loss equal to total fixed cost. The number of firms continuing to produce is just enough to satisfy the market demand at a price of $17.

FIGURE 11.7
Short-Run Equilibrium

(a) Equilibrium

(b) Change in equilibrium

In part (a), the industry supply curve is S. Demand is D_1, and the price is $20. At this price, each firm produces 8 sweaters a day and the industry produces 8,000 sweaters a day. In part (b), when demand increases to D_2, the price rises to $25 and

each firm increases its output to 9 sweaters a day. Industry output is 9,000 sweaters a day. When demand decreases to D_3, the price falls to $17 and each firm decreases its output to 7 sweaters a day. Industry output is 7,000 sweaters a day.

Long-Run Adjustments

In short-run equilibrium, a firm might make an economic profit, incur an economic loss, or break even (make normal profit). Although each of these three situations is a short-run equilibrium, only one of them is a long-run equilibrium. To see why, we need to examine the forces at work in a competitive industry in the long run.

In the long run, an industry adjusts in two ways:

■ Entry and exit
■ Changes in plant size

Let's look first at entry and exit.

Entry and Exit

In the long run, firms respond to economic profit and economic loss by either entering or exiting an industry. Firms enter an industry in which firms are making an economic profit, and firms exit an industry in which firms are incurring an economic loss. Temporary economic profit and temporary economic loss do not trigger entry and exit. But the prospect of persistent economic profit or loss does.

Entry and exit influence price, the quantity produced, and economic profit. The immediate effect of these decisions is to shift the industry supply curve. If more firms enter an industry, supply increases and the industry supply curve shifts rightward. If firms exit an industry, supply decreases and the industry supply curve shifts leftward.

Let's see what happens when new firms enter an industry.

The Effects of Entry Figure 11.8 shows the effects of entry. Suppose that all the firms in this industry have cost curves like those in Fig. 11.4. At any price greater than $20, firms make an economic profit. At any price less than $20, firms incur an economic loss. And at a price of $20, firms make zero economic profit. Also suppose that the demand curve for sweaters is D. If the industry supply curve is S_1, the market price is $23, and 7,000 sweaters a day are produced. Firms in the industry make an economic profit. This economic profit is a signal for new firms to enter the industry.

As these events unfold, supply increases and the industry supply curve shifts rightward to S_0. With the greater supply and unchanged demand, the market price falls from $23 to $20 a sweater and the quantity

produced by the industry increases from 7,000 to 8,000 sweaters a day.

Industry output increases, but Cindy's Sweaters, like each other firm in the industry, moves down its supply curve and *decreases* output! Because the price falls, each firm produces less. But because the number of firms in the industry increases, the industry as a whole produces more.

Because price falls, each firm's economic profit decreases. When the price falls to $20, economic profit disappears and each firm makes a normal profit.

You have just discovered a key proposition:

As new firms enter an industry, the price falls and the economic profit of each existing firm decreases.

An example of this process occurred during the 1980s in the personal computer industry. When IBM introduced its first PC, there was little competition

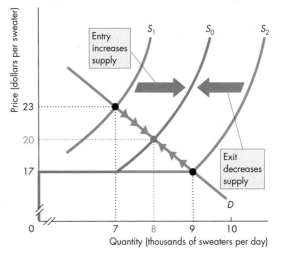

FIGURE 11.8
Entry and Exit

When new firms enter the sweater industry, the industry supply curve shifts rightward, from S_1 to S_0. The equilibrium price falls from $23 to $20, and the quantity produced increases from 7,000 to 8,000 sweaters.

When firms exit the sweater industry, the industry supply curve shifts leftward, from S_2 to S_0. The equilibrium price rises from $17 to $20, and the quantity produced decreases from 9,000 to 8,000 sweaters.

and the price of a PC gave IBM a big profit. But new firms such as Compaq, NEC, Dell, and a host of others entered the industry with machines that were technologically identical to IBM's. In fact, they were so similar that they came to be called "clones." The massive wave of entry into the personal computer industry shifted the supply curve rightward and lowered the price and the economic profit.

Let's now look at the effects of exit.

The Effects of Exit Figure 11.8 also shows the effects of exit. Suppose that firm's costs and market demand are the same as before. But now suppose the supply curve is S_2. The market price is $17, and 9,000 sweaters a day are produced. Firms in the industry now incur an economic loss. This economic loss is a signal for some firms to exit the industry. As firms exit, the industry supply curve shifts leftward to S_0. With the decrease in supply, industry output decreases from 9,000 to 8,000 sweaters and the price rises from $17 to $20.

As the price rises, Cindy's Sweaters, like each other firm in the industry, moves up along its supply curve and increases output. That is, for each firm that remains in the industry, the profit-maximizing output increases. Because the price rises and each firm sells more, economic loss decreases. When the price rises to $20, each firm makes a normal profit.

You've now discovered a second key proposition:

As firms leave an industry, the price rises and the economic loss of each remaining firm decreases.

The same PC industry that saw a large amount of entry during the 1980s and 1990s is now beginning to see some exit. In 2001, IBM, the firm that first launched the PC, announced that it would no longer produce PCs. The intense competition from Compaq, NEC, Dell, and many others that entered the industry following IBM's lead has lowered the price and eliminated the economic profit on PCs. So IBM will now concentrate on servers and other parts of the computer market.

IBM exited the PC market because it was incurring losses on that line of business. Its exit decreased supply and made it possible for the remaining firms in the industry to earn normal profit.

You've now seen how economic profits induce entry, which in turn lowers profits. And you've seen how economic losses induce exit, which in turn eliminates losses. Let's now look at changes in plant size.

Changes in Plant Size

A firm changes its plant size if, by doing so, it can lower its costs and increase its economic profit. You can probably think of lots of examples of firms that have changed their plant size.

One example that has almost certainly happened near your campus in recent years is a change in the plant size of Kinko's or similar copy shops. Another is the number of FedEx vans that you see on the streets and highways. And another is the number of square metres of retail space devoted to selling computers and video games. These are examples of firms increasing their plant size to seek larger profits.

There are also many examples of firms that have decreased their plant size to avoid economic losses. One of these is Country Style Donuts. As competition from other coffee shops became tougher, Country Style Donuts closed 45 shops across Canada in late 2002. Many firms have scaled back in a process called *downsizing* in recent years.

Figure 11.9 shows a situation in which Cindy's Sweaters can increase its profit by increasing its plant size. With its current plant, Cindy's marginal cost curve is MC_0, and its short-run average total cost curve is $SRAC_0$. The market price is $25 a sweater, so Cindy's marginal revenue curve is MR_0, and Cindy maximizes profit by producing 6 sweaters a day.

Cindy's Sweaters' long-run average cost curve is *LRAC*. By increasing its plant size—installing more knitting machines—Cindy's Sweaters can move along its long-run average cost curve. As Cindy's Sweaters increases its plant size, its short-run marginal cost curve shifts rightward.

Recall that a firm's short-run supply curve is linked to its marginal cost curve. As Cindy's marginal cost curve shifts rightward, so does its supply curve. If Cindy's Sweaters and the other firms in the industry increase their plants, the short-run industry supply curve shifts rightward. With a given market demand for sweaters, the market price falls. The fall in the market price limits the extent to which Cindy's can profit from increasing its plant size.

Figure 11.9 also shows Cindy's Sweaters in a long-run competitive equilibrium. This situation arises when the market price has fallen to $20 a sweater. Marginal revenue is MR_1, and Cindy maximizes profit by producing 8 sweaters a day. In this situation, Cindy cannot increase her profit by changing the plant size. Cindy is producing at minimum long-run average cost (point *M* on *LRAC*).

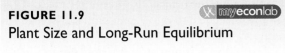

FIGURE 11.9
Plant Size and Long-Run Equilibrium

Initially, Cindy's plant has marginal cost curve MC_0 and short-run average total cost curve $SRAC_0$. The market price is $25 a sweater, and Cindy's marginal revenue is MR_0. The short-run profit-maximizing quantity is 6 sweaters a day. Cindy can increase profit by increasing the plant size.

If all firms in the sweater industry increase their plant sizes, the short-run industry supply increases and the market price falls. In long-run equilibrium, a firm operates with the plant size that minimizes its average cost. Here, Cindy's Sweaters operates the plant with short-run marginal cost MC_1 and short-run average cost $SRAC_1$. Cindy's is also on its long-run average cost curve $LRAC$ and produces at point M. Its output is 8 sweaters a day, and its average total cost equals the price of a sweater: $20.

Because Cindy's Sweaters is producing at minimum long-run average cost, it has no incentive to change its plant size. Either a bigger plant or a smaller plant has a higher long-run average cost. If Fig. 11.9 describes the situation of all firms in the sweater industry, the industry is in long-run equilibrium. No firm has an incentive to change its plant size. Also, because each firm is making zero economic profit (normal profit), no firm has an incentive to enter the industry or to leave it.

Long-Run Equilibrium

Long-run equilibrium occurs in a competitive industry when economic profit is zero (when firms earn normal profit). If the firms in a competitive industry are making an economic profit, new firms enter the industry.

If firms can lower their costs by increasing their plant size, they expand. Each of these actions increases the industry supply, shifts the industry supply curve rightward, lowers the price, and decreases economic profit.

Firms continue to enter and profit decreases as long as firms in the industry are making economic profits. When economic profit has been eliminated, firms stop entering the industry. And when firms are operating with the least-cost plant size, they stop expanding.

If the firms in a competitive industry are incurring an economic loss, some firms exit the industry. If firms can lower their costs by decreasing their plant size, they downsize. Each of these actions decreases industry supply, shifts the industry supply curve leftward, raises the price, and decreases economic loss.

Firms continue to exit and economic loss continues to decrease as long as firms in the industry are incurring economic losses. When economic loss has been eliminated, firms stop exiting the industry. And when firms are operating with the least-cost plant size, they stop downsizing.

So in long-run equilibrium in a competitive industry, firms neither enter nor exit the industry and old firms neither expand nor downsize. Each firm earns normal profit.

REVIEW QUIZ

1 When the market demand for the good decreases, explain how the price of the good and the output of each firm in perfect competition changes in the short run.

2 If the firms in a competitive industry earn an economic profit, what happens to supply, price, output, and economic profit in the long run?

3 If the firms in a competitive industry incur an economic loss, what happens to supply, price, output, and economic profit in the long run?

myeconlab Study Plan 11.3

You've seen how a competitive industry adjusts towards its long-run equilibrium. But a competitive industry is rarely *in* a state of long-run equilibrium. A competitive industry is constantly and restlessly evolving towards such an equilibrium. But the constraints that firms in an industry face are constantly changing. The two most persistent sources of change are in tastes and technology. Let's see how a competitive industry reacts to such changes.

Changing Tastes and Advancing Technology

INCREASED AWARENESS OF THE HEALTH HAZARDS of smoking has caused a decrease in the demand for tobacco and cigarettes. The development of inexpensive car and air transportation has caused a huge decrease in the demand for long-distance trains and buses. Solid-state electronics have caused a large decrease in the demand for TV and radio repair. The development of good-quality inexpensive clothing has decreased the demand for sewing machines. What happens in a competitive industry when there is a permanent decrease in the demand for its products?

The development of the microwave oven has produced an enormous increase in demand for paper, glass, and plastic cooking utensils and for plastic wrap. The widespread use of the personal computer has brought a huge increase in the demand for CD-Rs. What happens in a competitive industry when the demand for its output increases?

Advances in technology are constantly lowering the costs of production. New bio-technologies have dramatically lowered the costs of producing many food and pharmaceutical products. New electronic technologies have lowered the cost of producing just about every good and service. What happens in a competitive industry when technological change lowers its production costs?

Let's use the theory of perfect competition to answer these questions.

A Permanent Change in Demand

Figure 11.10(a) shows a competitive industry that initially is in long-run equilibrium. The industry demand curve is D_0, the industry supply curve is S_0, the market price is P_0, and industry output is Q_0. Figure 11.10(b) shows a single firm in this initial long-run equilibrium. The firm produces q_0 and makes a normal profit—zero economic profit.

Now suppose that demand decreases and the demand curve shifts leftward to D_1, as shown in Fig. 11.10(a). The price falls to P_1, and the quantity supplied by the industry decreases from Q_0 to Q_1 as the industry slides down its short-run supply curve S_0. Figure 11.10(b) shows the situation facing a firm. Price is now below the firm's minimum average total cost, so the firm incurs an economic loss. But to keep its loss

to a minimum, the firm adjusts its output to keep marginal cost equal to price. At a price of P_1, each firm produces an output of q_1.

The industry is now in short-run equilibrium but not long-run equilibrium. It is in short-run equilibrium because each firm is maximizing profit. But it is not in long-run equilibrium because each firm is incurring an economic loss—its average total cost exceeds the market price.

The economic loss is a signal for some firms to leave the industry. As they do so, short-run industry supply decreases and the supply curve gradually shifts leftward. As industry supply decreases, the price rises. At each higher price, a firm's profit-maximizing output is greater, so the firms remaining in the industry increase their output as the price rises. Each firm slides up its marginal cost or supply curve in Fig. 11.10(b). That is, as firms exit the industry, industry output decreases but the output of the firms that remain in the industry increases.

Eventually, enough firms leave the industry for the industry supply curve to have shifted leftward to S_1 in Fig. 11.10(a). At this time, the price has returned to its original level, P_0. At this price, the firms remaining in the industry produce q_0, the same quantity that they produced before the decrease in demand. Because firms are now making normal profit (zero economic profit), no firm wants to enter or exit the industry. The industry supply curve remains at S_1, and industry output is Q_2. The industry is again in long-run equilibrium.

The difference between the initial long-run equilibrium and the final long-run equilibrium is the number of firms in the industry. A permanent decrease in demand has decreased the number of firms. Each remaining firm produces the same output in the new long-run equilibrium as it did initially and earns a normal profit. In the process of moving from the initial equilibrium to the new one, firms incur economic losses.

We've just worked out how a competitive industry responds to a permanent *decrease* in demand. A permanent increase in demand triggers a similar response, except in the opposite direction. The increase in demand brings a higher price, economic profit, and entry. Entry increases industry supply and eventually the price falls to its original level and economic profit returns to normal profit.

The demand for Internet service increased permanently during the 1990s and huge profit opportunities arose in this industry. The result was

FIGURE 11.10
A Decrease in Demand

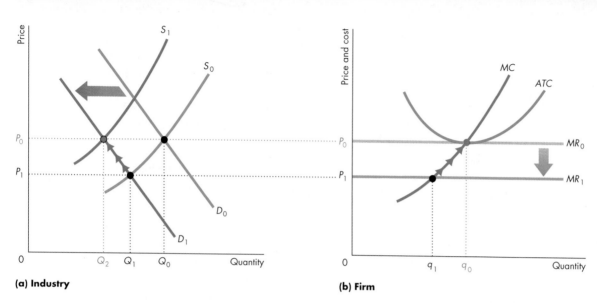

(a) Industry

(b) Firm

An industry starts out in long-run competitive equilibrium. Part (a) shows the industry demand curve D_0, the industry supply curve S_0, the equilibrium quantity Q_0, and the market price P_0. Each firm sells its output at price P_0, so its marginal revenue curve is MR_0 in part (b). Each firm produces q_0 and makes a normal profit. Demand decreases permanently from D_0 to D_1 (part a). The equilibrium price falls to P_1, each firm decreases its output to q_1 (part b), and industry output

decreases to Q_1 (part a).

In this new situation, firms incur economic losses and some firms leave the industry. As they do so, the industry supply curve gradually shifts leftward, from S_0 to S_1. This shift gradually raises the market price from P_1 back to P_0. Once the price has returned to P_0, each firm makes a normal profit. Firms have no further incentive to leave the industry. Each firm produces q_0, and industry output is Q_2.

a massive rate of entry of Internet service providers. The process of competition and change in the Internet service industry is similar to what we have just studied (but with an increase in demand rather than a decrease in demand).

We've now studied the effects of a permanent change in demand for a good. To study these effects, we began and ended in a long-run equilibrium and examined the process that takes a market from one equilibrium to another. It is this process, not the equilibrium points, that describes the real world.

One feature of the predictions that we have just generated seems odd: In the long run, regardless of whether demand increases or decreases, the price returns to its original level. Is this outcome inevitable? In fact, it is not. It is possible for the long-run equilibrium price to remain the same, rise, or fall.

External Economies and Diseconomies

The change in the long-run equilibrium price depends on external economies and external diseconomies. **External economies** are factors beyond the control of an individual firm that lower the firm's costs as the *industry* output increases. **External diseconomies** are factors outside the control of a firm that raise the firm's costs as industry output increases. With no external economies or external diseconomies, a firm's costs remain constant as the industry output changes.

Figure 11.11 illustrates these three cases and introduces a new supply concept: the long-run industry supply curve.

A **long-run industry supply curve** shows how the quantity supplied by an industry varies as the market price varies after all the possible adjustments have been made, including changes in plant size and the number of firms in the industry.

Figure 11.11(a) shows the case we have just studied—no external economies or diseconomies. The long-run industry supply curve (LS_A) is horizontal. In this case, a permanent increase in demand from D_0 to D_1 has no effect on the price in the long run. The increase in demand brings a temporary increase in price to P_S and in the short run, the quantity increases from Q_0 to Q_S. Entry increases short-run supply from S_0 to S_1, which lowers the price to its original level, P_0, and increases the quantity to Q_1.

Figure 11.11(b) shows the case of external diseconomies. The long-run supply industry curve (LS_B) slopes upward. A permanent increase in demand from D_0 to D_1 increases the price in both the short run and the long run. As in the previous case, the increase in demand brings a temporary increase in price to P_S and in the short run, the quantity increases from Q_0 to Q_S. Entry increases short-run supply from S_0 to S_2, which lowers the price to P_2 and increases the quantity to Q_2.

One source of external diseconomies is congestion. The airline industry provides a good example. With bigger airline industry output, congestion of airports and airspace increases and results in longer delays and extra waiting time for passengers and airplanes. These external diseconomies mean that as the output of air transportation services increases (in the absence of technological advances), average cost increases. As a result, the long-run supply curve is upward sloping. So a permanent increase in demand brings an increase in quantity and a rise in the price. (Industries with external diseconomies might nonetheless have a falling price because technological advances shift the long-run supply curve downward.)

Figure 11.11(c) shows the case of external economies. In this case, the long-run industry supply curve (LS_C) slopes downward. A permanent increase in demand from D_0 to D_1 increases the price in the short run and lowers it in the long run. Again, the increases in demand brings a temporary increase in price to P_S, and in the short run, the quantity increases from Q_0 to Q_S. Entry increases short-run supply from S_0 to S_3, which lowers the price to P_3 and increases the quantity to Q_3.

FIGURE 11.11
Long-Run Changes in Price and Quantity

(a) Constant-cost industry

(b) Increasing-cost industry

(c) Decreasing-cost industry

When demand increases from D_0 to D_1, entry occurs and the industry supply curve gradually shifts rightward from S_0 to S_1. In part (a), the long-run supply curve, LS_A, is horizontal. The quantity increases from Q_0 to Q_1, and the price remains constant at P_0. In part (b), the long-run supply curve is LS_B; the price rises to P_2, and the quantity increases to Q_2. This case occurs in industries with external diseconomies. In part (c), the long-run supply curve is LS_C; the price falls to P_3, and the quantity increases to Q_3. This case occurs in an industry with external economies.

An example of external economies is the growth of specialist support services for an industry as it expands. As farm output increased in the nineteenth and early twentieth centuries, the services available to farmers expanded. New firms specialized in the development and marketing of farm machinery and fertilizers. As a result, average farm costs decreased. Farms enjoyed the benefits of external economies. As a consequence, as the demand for farm products increased, the output increased but the price fell.

Over the long term, the prices of many goods and services have fallen, not because of external economies but because of technological change. Let's now study this influence on a competitive market.

Technological Change

Industries are constantly discovering lower-cost techniques of production. Most cost-saving production techniques cannot be implemented, however, without investing in a new plant and equipment. As a consequence, it takes time for a technological advance to spread through an industry. Some firms whose plants are on the verge of being replaced will be quick to adopt the new technology, while other firms whose plants have recently been replaced will continue to operate with an old technology until they can no longer cover their average variable cost. Once average variable cost cannot be covered, a firm will scrap even a relatively new plant (embodying an old technology) in favour of a plant with a new technology.

New technology allows firms to produce at a lower cost. As a result, as firms adopt a new technology, their cost curves shift downward. With lower costs, firms are willing to supply a given quantity at a lower price or, equivalently, they are willing to supply a larger quantity at a given price. In other words, industry supply increases, and the industry supply curve shifts rightward. With a given demand, the quantity produced increases and the price falls.

Two forces are at work in an industry undergoing technological change. Firms that adopt the new technology make an economic profit. So there is entry by new-technology firms. Firms that stick with the old technology incur economic losses. They either exit the industry or switch to the new technology.

As old-technology firms exit and new-technology firms enter, the price falls and the quantity produced increases. Eventually, the industry arrives at a long-run

equilibrium in which all the firms use the new technology and make a zero economic profit (a normal profit). Because in the long run competition eliminates economic profit, technological change brings only temporary gains to producers. But the lower prices and better products that technological advances bring are permanent gains for consumers.

The process that we've just described is one in which some firms experience economic profits and others experience economic losses. It is a period of dynamic change for an industry. Some firms do well, and others do badly. Often, the process has a geographical dimension—the expanding new-technology firms bring prosperity to what was once the boondocks, and traditional industrial regions decline. Sometimes the new-technology firms are in a foreign country, while the old-technology firms are in the domestic economy. The information revolution of the 1990s produced many examples of changes like these. The computer programming industry, traditionally concentrated in the United States, now flourishes in Canada, the United Kingdom, and India. Television shows and movies, traditionally made in Los Angeles and New York, are now made in large numbers in Toronto and Vancouver.

Technological advances are not confined to the information and entertainment industries. Even milk production is undergoing a major technological change because of genetic engineering.

REVIEW QUIZ

1 Describe the course of events in a competitive industry following a permanent decrease in demand. What happens to output, price, and economic profit in the short run and in the long run?

2 Describe the course of events in a competitive industry following a permanent increase in demand. What happens to output, price, and economic profit in the short run and in the long run?

3 Describe the course of events in a competitive industry following the adoption of a new technology. What happens to output, price, and economic profit in the short run and in the long run?

myeconlab   **Study Plan 11.4**

Competition and Efficiency

A COMPETITIVE INDUSTRY CAN ACHIEVE AN efficient use of resources. You studied efficiency in Chapter 5 using only the concepts of demand, supply, consumer surplus, and producer surplus. But now that you have learned what lies behind the demand and supply curves of a competitive market, you can gain a deeper understanding of how the competitive market achieves efficiency.

Efficient Use of Resources

Recall that resource use is efficient when we produce the goods and services that people value most highly (see Chapter 5, pp. 104–105). If someone can become better off without anyone else becoming worse off, resources are *not* being used efficiently. For example, suppose we produce a computer that no one wants and no one will ever use and at the same time some people are clamouring for more video games. If we produce one computer less and reallocate the unused resources to produce more video games, some people will become better off and no one will be worse off. So the initial resource allocation was inefficient.

In the more technical language that you have learned, resource use is efficient when marginal social benefit equals marginal social cost. In the computer and video games example, the marginal social benefit of video games exceeds the marginal social cost. And the marginal social cost of a computer exceeds its marginal social benefit. So by producing fewer computers and more video games, we move resources towards a higher-valued use.

Choices, Equilibrium, and Efficiency

We can use what you have learned about the decisions made by consumers and competitive firms and market equilibrium to describe an efficient use of resources.

Choices Consumers allocate their budgets to get the most value possible out of them. And we derive a consumer's demand curve by finding how the best budget allocation changes as the price of a good changes. So consumers get the most value out of their resources at all points along the market demand curve, which is also the marginal social benefit curve.

Competitive firms produce the quantity that maximizes profit. And we derive the firm's supply curve by finding the profit-maximizing quantity at each price. So firms get the most value out of their resources at all points along the market supply curve, which is also the marginal social cost curve. (On their supply curves, firms are *technologically efficient*—they get the maximum possible output from given inputs—and *economically efficient*—they combine resources to minimize cost. See Chapter 9, pp. 201–202.)

Equilibrium In competitive equilibrium, the quantity demanded equals the quantity supplied. So the price equals marginal social benefit and marginal social cost. In this situation, the gains from trade between consumers and producers are maximized.

The gains from trade for consumers are measured by *consumer surplus*, which is the area below the demand curve and above the price paid. (See Chapter 5, p. 107.) The gains from trade for producers are measured by *producer surplus*, which is the area above the marginal cost curve and below the price received. (See Chapter 5, p. 109.) The total gains from trade are the sum of consumer surplus and producer surplus.

Efficiency In the absence of external benefits and external costs (see Chapter 5, p. 112 and Chapter 15), when the market for the good or service is in equilibrium resources are being used efficiently. They cannot be reallocated to increase their value.

An Efficient Allocation Figure 11.12 shows an efficient allocation in perfect competition in long-run equilibrium. Part (a) shows the situation of an individual firm and part (b) shows the market. The equilibrium market price is P^*. At that price, each firm earns normal profit (zero economic profit). Each firm has a plant size that enables it to produce at the lowest possible average total cost. In this situation, consumers are as well off as possible because the good cannot be produced at a lower cost and the price equals that least possible cost.

In part (b), consumers are efficient at all points on the market demand curve, $D = MSB$. Producers are efficient at all points on the market supply curve, $S = MSC$. Resources are used efficiently at the quantity Q^* and price P^*. At this point, marginal social benefit equals marginal social cost, and the sum of

FIGURE 11.12
Efficiency of Perfect Competition

(a) A single firm

(b) A market

In part (a), a firm in perfect competition produces at the lowest possible long-run average total cost at the quantity q^*. In part (b), consumers have made the best available choices and are on the market demand curve and firms are

producing at least cost and are on the market supply curve. With no external benefits or external costs, resources are used efficiently at the quantity Q^* and the price P^*. Perfect competition achieves an efficient use of resources.

producer surplus (blue area) and consumer surplus (green area) is maximized.

When firms in perfect competition are away from long-run equilibrium, either entry or exit is taking place and the market is moving towards the situation depicted in Fig. 11.12. But the market is still efficient.

As long as marginal social benefit (on the market demand curve) equals marginal social cost (on the market supply curve), the equilibrium in perfect competition is efficient. But it is only in long-run equilibrium that consumers pay the lowest possible price.

◆ You've now completed your study of perfect competition. And *Reading Between the Lines* on pp. 258–259 gives you an opportunity to use what you have learned to understand recent events in the highly competitive maple syrup market.

Although many markets approximate the model of perfect competition, many do not. In Chapter 12, we study markets at the opposite extreme of market power: monopoly. Then, in Chapter 13, we'll study markets that lie between perfect competition and monopoly: monopolistic competition (competition with monopoly elements) and oligopoly (competition among a few producers). When you have completed this study, you'll have a tool kit that will enable you to understand the variety of real-world markets.

REVIEW QUIZ

1 State the conditions that must be met for resources to be used efficiently.
2 Describe the choices that consumers make and explain why along the market demand curve, consumers are efficient.
3 Describe the choices that producers make and explain why along the market supply curve, producers are efficient.
4 Explain why resources are used efficiently in competitive equilibrium.

Ⓧ myeconlab **Study Plan 11.5**

Perfect Competition in Maple Syrup

MONTREAL GAZETTE, MARCH 14, 2001

Maple syrup sits unsold in warehouses

A sticky turf war has boiled over in Canada's sugar patch, with farmers and processors feuding over what to do with a glut of maple syrup. . . .

. . . after two bumper crops in a row, producers wonder if it's worth the effort to tap all their trees.

"People naturally aren't encouraged by the prices," said Stanley Holmes, a farmer and maple-syrup producer from Ayer's Cliff who also buys syrup in bulk from neighbouring producers on behalf of Ontario-based processor Delta Foods International.

"Really what they need is less production to get rid of some of this surplus that's hanging over the industry."

Prices alone won't dictate supply, though. Operating conditions, particularly the deep snow still lying in the woods across the province, could also influence the number of trees farmers tap this spring, Holmes said.

"With the snow it's very difficult to get around, and when your prices aren't good, if you have hard conditions like that to overcome, that's another reason not to tackle the job."

Holmes's own sugarbush has a production capacity of 10,000 taps with three-quarters of his trees connected to a pipeline and the rest on buckets. He said he may forego bringing into production those trees that are difficult to reach, especially those not already hooked to a pipeline. . . .

The average floor price for syrup has tumbled from a high of around $2.50 per pound in 1997 and 1998 to $1.56 in 2000 and is not expected to be any higher in 2001.

Reprinted by permission of Dwane Wilkin.

Essence of the Story

■ Two back-to-back bumper maple syrup crops have lowered the price of syrup from $2.50 per pound to $1.56.

■ At this low price, producers are decreasing the number of trees they tap.

■ Supply is influenced by snow, which makes it difficult for producers to tap some of their trees.

■ Stanley Holmes has a production capacity of 10,000 taps. 7,500 of these are connected to a pipeline and the rest on buckets.

■ At today's low price, Stanley Holmes says he may forgo the production on those trees that are difficult to reach and not already hooked to a pipeline.

Economic Analysis

■ Maple syrup—the real kind, not the synthetic syrup such as Aunt Jemima—is produced in Canada and the United States by about 12,000 firms.

■ The market for maple syrup is close to perfectly competitive.

■ Before the bumper crop, the price of maple syrup (in the news article) was $2.50 a pound.

■ After the bumper crop, the price fell to $1.56 a pound.

■ Figure 1 shows why the price fell. The demand curve for maple syrup is D, and before the bumper harvest, the supply curve was S_0. The equilibrium price was $2.50 a pound.

■ The bumper harvest shifted the supply curve rightward to S_1. At the price of $2.50 a pound, there was a surplus of syrup, so the price fell. The new equilibrium price is $1.56 a pound.

■ Figure 2 shows the situation facing Stanley Holmes. Stanley is a price taker and maximizes his profit by producing the quantity at which marginal cost (MC) equals marginal revenue (MR).

■ The figure shows Stanley Holmes' cost curves: average total cost curve, ATC, average variable cost curve, AVC, and marginal cost curve, MC.

■ We don't know the exact position of these curves, and those in the figure are assumed. But we do know from Stanley's description of his supply conditions that his marginal cost curve slopes upward.

■ When Stanley says, "With the snow it's very difficult to get around, and when your prices aren't good, if you have hard conditions like that to overcome, that's another reason not to tackle the job," it means that the marginal cost of tapping all his trees is greater than the market price.

■ Figure 2 also shows Stanley's marginal revenue curves before, MR_0, and after, MR_1, the bumper harvest.

■ At $2.50 a pound, Stanley would tap all his trees (10,000 taps according to the news article). At $1.56 a pound, Stanley doesn't bother to tap the distant trees that are not connected to the pipeline.

■ Although the price is low, Stanley says that he

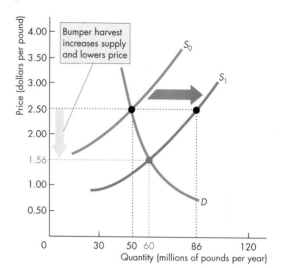

Figure 1 **The maple syrup market**

Figure 2 **Stanley Holmes' maple farm**

will produce from his 7,500 taps that are connected to the pipeline. This fact implies, as Fig. 2 shows, that the price of $1.56 exceeds average variable cost. If it didn't, Stanley would temporarily shut down.

SUMMARY

KEY POINTS

Competition (pp. 240–241)

- A perfectly competitive firm is a price taker.

The Firm's Decisions in Perfect Competition (pp. 242–247)

- The firm produces the output at which marginal revenue (price) equals marginal cost.
- In short-run equilibrium, a firm can make an economic profit, incur an economic loss, or make normal profit.
- If price is less than minimum average variable cost, the firm temporarily shuts down.
- A firm's supply curve is the upward-sloping part of its marginal cost curve above minimum average variable cost.
- An industry supply curve shows the sum of the quantities supplied by each firm at each price.

Output, Price, and Profit in Perfect Competition (pp. 248–251)

- Market demand and market supply determine price.
- Persistent economic profit induces entry. Persistent economic loss induces exit.
- Entry and plant expansion increase supply, lower the price, and reduce economic profit. Exit and downsizing decrease supply, raise the price, and reduce economic loss.
- In long-run equilibrium, economic profit is zero (firms earn normal profit). There is no entry, exit, plant expansion, or downsizing.

Changing Tastes and Advancing Technology (pp. 252–255)

- A permanent decrease in demand leads to a smaller industry output and a smaller number of firms.
- A permanent increase in demand leads to a larger industry output and a larger number of firms.

- The long-run effect of a change in demand on price depends on whether there are external economies (the price falls) or external diseconomies (the price rises) or neither (the price remains constant).
- New technologies increase supply and in the long run lower the price and increase the quantity.

Competition and Efficiency (pp. 256–257)

- Resources are used efficiently when we produce goods and services in the quantities that people value most highly.
- When there are no external benefits and external costs, perfect competition achieves an efficient allocation. Marginal social benefit equals marginal social cost, and the sum of consumer surplus and producer surplus is maximized.

KEY FIGURES

KEY TERMS

PROBLEMS

Go to **myeconlab** for solutions to odd-numbered problems and additional exercises.

1. The figure shows the cost curves of Quick Copy, one of many copy shops near campus.

a. If the market price of copying one page is 10 cents, what is Quick Copy's profit-maximizing output?
b. Calculate Quick Copy's profit.
c. With no change in demand or technology, how will the price change in the long run?

2. Jerry's is one of many ice cream stands along the beach. The figure shows Jerry's cost curves.

a. If the market price of an ice cream cone is $3, what is Jerry's profit-maximizing output?
b. Calculate Jerry's profit.
c. With no change in demand or technology, how will the price change in the long run?

3. Pat's Pizza Kitchen is a price taker. Its costs are

Output (pizzas per hour)	Total cost (dollars per hour)
0	10
1	21
2	30
3	41
4	54
5	69

a. What is Pat's profit-maximizing output and how much economic profit does Pat make if the market price is (i) $14, (ii) $12, and (iii) $10?
b. What is Pat's shutdown point?
c. Derive Pat's supply curve.
d. At what price will Pat exit the pizza industry?

4. Luigi's Lasagna is a price taker. Its costs are

Output (plates per day)	Total cost (dollars per day)
0	14
1	38
2	48
3	62
4	80
5	102
6	128

a. What is Luigi's profit-maximizing output and how much profit does Luigi make if the market price is (i) $24 a plate, (ii) $20 a plate, and (iii) $12 a plate?
b. What is Luigi's shutdown point?
c. What is Luigi's profit at the shutdown point?
d. At what prices will firms with costs the same as Luigi's enter the lasagna market?

5. The market demand schedule for cassettes is

Price (dollars per cassette)	Quantity demanded (thousands of cassettes per week)
3.65	500
5.20	450
6.80	400
8.40	350
10.00	300
11.60	250
13.20	200
14.80	150

The market is perfectly competitive, and each firm has the following cost structure:

Output (cassettes per week)	Marginal cost (dollars per additional cassette)	Average variable cost	Average total cost
		(dollars per cassette)	
150	6.00	8.80	15.47
200	6.40	7.80	12.80
250	7.00	7.00	11.00
300	7.65	7.10	10.43
350	8.40	7.20	10.06
400	10.00	7.50	10.00
450	12.40	8.00	10.22
500	20.70	9.00	11.00

There are 1,000 firms in the industry.

a. What is the market price?
b. What is the industry's output?
c. What is the output produced by each firm?
d. What is each firm's economic profit?
e. Do firms enter or exit the industry?
f. What is the number of firms in the long run?

6. The same demand conditions as those in problem 5 prevail and there are 1,000 firms in the industry. Firms use the same plant size, but fixed costs increase by $980. What now are your answers to the questions in problem 5?

7. In problem 5, a fall in the price of a compact disc permanently decreases the demand for cassettes and the demand schedule becomes

Price (dollars per cassette)	Quantity demanded (thousands of cassettes per week)
2.95	500
4.13	450
5.30	400
6.48	350
7.65	300
8.83	250
10.00	200
11.18	150

What now are your answers to the questions in problem 5?

8. In problem 6, the fall in the price of a compact disc permanently decreases the demand for cassettes and the demand schedule becomes that given in problem 7. What now are your answers to the questions in problem 6?

CRITICAL THINKING

1. After you have studied *Reading Between the Lines* on pp. 258–259, answer the following questions.
   a. What are the features of the market for maple syrup that make it an example of perfect competition?
   b. During the 1980s, the technology for extracting sap advanced. What effect do you predict that this development had on the price of syrup and the number of firms that produce it?
   c. Suppose that Aunt Jemima invents a syrup that no one can distinguish (in a blind test) from the real thing and can produce it for half the price of real maple syrup. What effect would you expect this development to have on the market for real maple syrup?

2. Why have the prices of pocket calculators and VCRs fallen? What do you think has happened to the costs and economic profits of the firms that make these products?

3. What has been the effect of an increase in world population on the wheat market and the individual wheat farmer?

4. How has the diaper service industry been affected by the decrease in the Canadian birth rate and the development of disposable diapers?

WEB EXERCISES

Use the links on (X myeconlab) to work the following exercises.

1. Study the *Web Reading Between the Lines* "Dumping Steel." Then answer the following questions:
   a. What is the argument in the news article about limiting steel imports?
   b. Do you agree with the argument? Why or why not?
   c. Why do Canada and the United States claim that foreign steel is being dumped in North America? (Use the links in the *Web Reading Between the Lines* to answer this question.)

Monopoly

Dominating the Internet

eBay and Google are dominant players in the markets they serve. Because most buyers use eBay, most sellers do too. And because most sellers use eBay, so do most buyers. This phenomenon, called a network externality, makes it hard for any other firm to break into the Internet auction business. Because Google is such a good search engine, most people use it to find what they're seeking on the Internet. And because most people use it, most Web site operators advertise with Google.

eBay and Google are obviously not like firms in perfect competition. They don't face a market-determined price. They can choose their own prices. How do firms like these behave? How do they choose the quantity to produce and the price at which to sell it? How does their behaviour compare with that of firms in perfectly competitive industries? Do they charge prices that are too high and that damage the interests of consumers? What benefits do they bring?

As a student, you get lots of discounts: when you get your hair cut, go to a museum, or go to a movie. When you take a trip by air, you almost never pay the full fare. Instead, you buy a discounted ticket. Are the people who operate barbershops, museums, movie theatres, and airlines simply generous folks who don't maximize profit? Aren't they throwing profit away by offering discounts?

◆ In this chapter, we study markets in which the firm can influence the price. We also compare the performance of the firm in such a market with that of a competitive market and examine whether monopoly is as efficient as competition. In *Reading Between the Lines* at the end of the chapter, we'll return to eBay and Google and discover an interesting difference between the market power they enjoy.

After studying this chapter, you will be able to

- **Explain how monopoly arises and distinguish between single-price monopoly and price-discriminating monopoly**

- **Explain how a single-price monopoly determines its output and price**

- **Compare the performance and efficiency of single-price monopoly and competition**

- **Explain how price discrimination increases profit**

- **Explain how monopoly regulation influences output, price, economic profit, and efficiency**

Market Power

MARKET POWER AND COMPETITION ARE THE TWO forces that operate in most markets. **Market power** is the ability to influence the market, and in particular the market price, by influencing the total quantity offered for sale.

The firms in perfect competition that you studied in Chapter 11 have no market power. They face the force of raw competition and are price takers. The firms that we study in this chapter operate at the opposite extreme. They face no competition and exercise raw market power. We call this extreme monopoly. A **monopoly** is an industry that produces a good or service for which no close substitute exists and in which there is one supplier that is protected from competition by a barrier preventing the entry of new firms.

Examples of monopoly include your gas, electricity, and water distributors, as well as De Beers, the South African diamond producer, and Microsoft Corporation, the software developer that created the Windows operating system.

How Monopoly Arises

Monopoly has two key features:

■ No close substitutes
■ Barriers to entry

No Close Substitutes If a good has a close substitute, even though only one firm produces it, that firm effectively faces competition from the producers of substitutes. Water supplied by a local public utility is an example of a good that does not have close substitutes. While it does have a close substitute for drinking—bottled spring water—it has no effective substitutes for showering or washing a car.

Monopolies are constantly under attack from new products and ideas that substitute for products produced by monopolies. For example, FedEx, Purolator, the fax machine, and e-mail have weakened the monopoly of Canada Post. Similarly, the satellite dish has weakened the monopoly of cable television companies.

But new products also are constantly creating monopolies. An example is Microsoft's monopoly in the DOS operating system during the 1980s and in the Windows operating system today.

Barriers to Entry Legal or natural constraints that protect a firm from potential competitors are called **barriers to entry**. A firm can sometimes create its own barrier to entry by acquiring a significant portion of a key resource. For example, De Beers controls more than 80 percent of the world's supply of natural diamonds. But most monopolies arise from two other types of barriers: legal barriers and natural barriers.

Legal Barriers to Entry Legal barriers to entry create legal monopoly. A **legal monopoly** is a market in which competition and entry are restricted by the granting of a public franchise, government licence, patent, or copyright.

A *public franchise* is an exclusive right granted to a firm to supply a good or service. An example is Canada Post, which has the exclusive right to carry first-class mail. A *government licence* controls entry into particular occupations, professions, and industries. Examples of this type of barrier to entry occur in medicine, law, dentistry, schoolteaching, architecture, and many other professional services. Licensing does not always create monopoly, but it does restrict competition.

A *patent* is an exclusive right granted to the inventor of a product or service. A *copyright* is an exclusive right granted to the author or composer of a literary, musical, dramatic, or artistic work. Patents and copyrights are valid for a limited time period that varies from country to country. In Canada, a patent is valid for 20 years. Patents encourage the *invention* of new products and production methods. They also stimulate *innovation*—the use of new inventions—by encouraging inventors to publicize their discoveries and offer them for use under licence. Patents have stimulated innovations in areas as diverse as soybean seeds, pharmaceuticals, computer memory chips, and video games.

Natural Barriers to Entry Natural barriers to entry create **natural monopoly**, which is an industry in which one firm can supply the entire market at a lower average total cost than two or more firms can.

Figure 12.1 shows a natural monopoly in the distribution of electric power. Here, the market demand curve for electric power is D, and the average total cost curve is ATC. Because average total cost decreases as output increases, economies of scale prevail over the entire length of the ATC curve. One firm can produce 4 million kilowatt-hours at 5 cents a kilowatt-hour. At this price, the quantity demanded is 4 million kilowatt-hours. So if the price were 5 cents, one firm could

855justified.

supply the entire market. If two firms shared the market, it would cost each of them 10 cents a kilowatt-hour to produce a total of 4 million kilowatt-hours. If four firms shared the market, it would cost each of them 15 cents a kilowatt-hour to produce a total of 4 million kilowatt-hours. So in conditions like those shown in Fig. 12.1, one firm can supply the entire market at a lower cost than two or more firms can. The distribution of electric power is an example of natural monopoly. So is the distribution of water and gas.

Most monopolies are regulated in some way by government agencies. We will study such regulation at the end of this chapter. But for two reasons, we'll first study unregulated monopoly. First, we can better understand why governments regulate monopolies and the effects of regulation if we also know how an unregulated monopoly behaves. Second, even in industries with more than one producer, firms often have a degree of monopoly power, and the theory of monopoly sheds light on the behaviour of such firms and industries.

A major difference between monopoly and competition is that a monopoly sets its own price. But in doing so, it faces a market constraint. Let's see how the market limits a monopoly's pricing choices.

FIGURE 12.1
Natural Monopoly

myeconlab

The market demand curve for electric power is *D*, and the average total cost curve is *ATC*. Economies of scale exist over the entire *ATC* curve. One firm can distribute 4 million kilowatt-hours at a cost of 5 cents a kilowatt-hour. This same total output costs 10 cents a kilowatt-hour with two firms and 15 cents a kilowatt-hour with four firms. So one firm can meet the market demand at a lower cost than two or more firms can, and the market is a natural monopoly.

Monopoly Price-Setting Strategies

All monopolies face a tradeoff between price and the quantity sold. To sell a larger quantity, the monopoly must charge a lower price. But there are two broad monopoly situations that create different tradeoffs. They are

- Price discrimination
- Single price

Price Discrimination Airlines offer a dizzying array of different prices for the same trip. Pizza producers charge one price for a single pizza and almost give away a second pizza. These are examples of *price discrimination*. **Price discrimination** is the practice of selling different units of a good or service for different prices.

When a firm price discriminates, it looks as though it is doing its customers a favour. In fact, it is charging the highest possible price for each unit sold and making the largest possible profit.

Single Price De Beers sells diamonds (of a given size and quality) for the same price to all its customers. If it tried to sell at a low price to some customers and at a higher price to others, only the low-price customers would buy from De Beers. Others would buy from De Beers' low-price customers. De Beers is a *single-price* monopoly. A **single-price monopoly** is a firm that must sell each unit of its output for the same price to all its customers.

REVIEW QUIZ

1. How does monopoly arise?
2. How does a natural monopoly differ from a legal monopoly?
3. Distinguish between a price-discriminating and a single-price monopoly.

myeconlab **Study Plan 12.1**

A Single-Price Monopoly's Output and Price Decision

TO UNDERSTAND HOW A SINGLE-PRICE MONOPOLY makes its output and price decision, we must first study the link between price and marginal revenue.

Price and Marginal Revenue

Because in a monopoly there is only one firm, the demand curve facing the firm is the market demand curve. Let's look at Bobbie's Barbershop, the sole supplier of haircuts in Trout River, Newfoundland. The table in Fig. 12.2 shows the market demand schedule. At a price of $20, Bobbie sells no haircuts. The lower the price, the more haircuts per hour Bobbie can sell. For example, at $12, consumers demand 4 haircuts per hour (row E).

Total revenue (*TR*) is the price (*P*) multiplied by the quantity sold (*Q*). For example, in row *D*, Bobbie sells 3 haircuts at $14 each, so total revenue is $42. *Marginal revenue* (*MR*) is the change in total revenue (ΔTR) resulting from a one-unit increase in the quantity sold. For example, if the price falls from $16 (row *C*) to $14 (row *D*), the quantity sold increases from 2 to 3 haircuts. Total revenue rises from $32 to $42, so the change in total revenue is $10. Because the quantity sold increases by 1 haircut, marginal revenue equals the change in total revenue and is $10. Marginal revenue is placed between the two rows to emphasize that marginal revenue relates to the *change* in the quantity sold.

Figure 12.2 shows the market demand curve and marginal revenue curve (*MR*) and also illustrates the calculation we've just made. Notice that at each quantity of output, marginal revenue is *less* than price—the marginal revenue curve lies below the demand curve. Why is marginal revenue less than price? It is because when the price is lowered to sell one more unit, two opposing forces affect total revenue. The lower price results in a revenue loss, and the increased quantity sold results in a revenue gain. For example, at a price of $16, Bobbie sells 2 haircuts (point *C*). If she lowers the price to $14, she sells 3 haircuts and has a revenue gain of $14 on the third haircut. But she now receives only $14 on the first two—$2 less than before. As a result, she loses $4 of revenue on the first 2 haircuts. To calculate marginal revenue, she must deduct this amount from the revenue gain of $14. So her marginal revenue is $10, which is less than the price.

FIGURE 12.2
Demand and Marginal Revenue   myeconlab

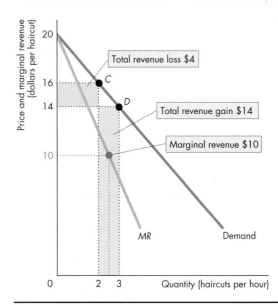

	Price (P) (dollars per haircut)	Quantity demanded (Q) (haircuts per hour)	Total revenue (TR = P × Q) (dollars)	Marginal revenue (MR = ΔTR/ΔQ) (dollars per haircut)
A	20	0	0	
				18
B	18	1	18	
				14
C	16	2	32	
				10
D	14	3	42	
				6
E	12	4	48	
				2
F	10	5	50	

The table shows the demand schedule. Total revenue (*TR*) is price multiplied by quantity sold. For example, in row *C*, the price is $16 a haircut, Bobbie sells 2 haircuts and total revenue is $32. Marginal revenue (*MR*) is the change in total revenue that results from a one-unit increase in the quantity sold. For example, when the price falls from $16 to $14 a haircut, the quantity sold increases by 1 haircut and total revenue increases by $10. Marginal revenue is $10. The demand curve and the marginal revenue curve, *MR*, are based on the numbers in the table and illustrate the calculation of marginal revenue when the price of a haircut falls from $16 to $14.

Marginal Revenue and Elasticity

A single-price monopoly's marginal revenue is related to the *elasticity of demand* for its good. The demand for a good can be *elastic* (the elasticity of demand is greater than 1), *inelastic* (the elasticity of demand is less than 1), or *unit elastic* (the elasticity of demand is equal to 1). Demand is *elastic* if a 1 percent fall in price brings a greater than 1 percent increase in the quantity demanded. Demand is *inelastic* if a 1 percent fall in price brings a less than 1 percent increase in the quantity demanded. And demand is *unit elastic* if a 1 percent fall in price brings a 1 percent increase in the quantity demanded. (See Chapter 4, pp. 86–87.)

If demand is elastic, a fall in price brings an increase in total revenue—the increase in revenue from the increase in quantity sold outweighs the decrease in revenue from the lower price—and marginal revenue is positive. If demand is inelastic, a fall in price brings a decrease in total revenue—the increase in revenue from the increase in quantity sold is outweighed by the decrease in revenue from the lower price—and marginal revenue is negative. If demand is unit elastic, total revenue does not change—the increase in revenue from the increase in quantity sold offsets the decrease in revenue from the lower price—and marginal revenue is zero. (The relationship between total revenue and elasticity is explained in Chapter 4, on p. 88.)

Figure 12.3 illustrates the relationship between marginal revenue, total revenue, and elasticity. As the price of a haircut gradually falls from $20 to $10, the quantity of haircuts demanded increases from 0 to 5 an hour. Over this output range, marginal revenue is positive (part a), total revenue increases (part b), and the demand for haircuts is elastic. As the price falls from $10 to $0 a haircut, the quantity of haircuts demanded increases from 5 to 10 an hour. Over this output range, marginal revenue is negative (part a), total revenue decreases (part b), and the demand for haircuts is inelastic. When the price is $10 a haircut, marginal revenue is zero, total revenue is a maximum, and the demand for haircuts is unit elastic.

In Monopoly, Demand Is Always Elastic The relationship between marginal revenue and elasticity that you've just discovered implies that a profit-maximizing monopoly never produces an output in the inelastic range of its demand curve. If it did so, it could charge a higher price, produce a smaller quantity, and increase its profit. Let's now look more closely at a monopoly's output and price decision.

FIGURE 12.3 ⓧ myeconlab
Marginal Revenue and Elasticity

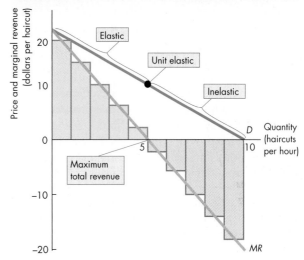

(a) Demand and marginal revenue curves

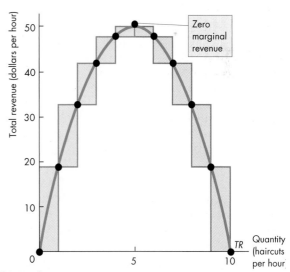

(b) Total revenue curve

In part (a), the demand curve is *D* and the marginal revenue curve is *MR*. In part (b), the total revenue curve is *TR*. Over the range from 0 to 5 haircuts an hour, a price cut increases total revenue, so marginal revenue is positive—as shown by the blue bars. Demand is elastic. Over the range 5 to 10 haircuts an hour, a price cut decreases total revenue, so marginal revenue is negative—as shown by the red bars. Demand is inelastic. At 5 haircuts an hour, total revenue is maximized and marginal revenue is zero. Demand is unit elastic.

Output and Price Decision

A monopoly sets its price and output at the levels that maximize economic profit. To determine this price and output level, we need to study the behaviour of both cost and revenue as output varies. A monopoly faces the same types of technology and cost constraints as a competitive firm. So a monopoly's costs (total cost, average cost, and marginal cost) behave just like those of a firm in perfect competition. And a monopoly's revenues (total revenue, price, and marginal revenue) behave in the way we've just described.

Table 12.1 provides information about Bobbie's costs, revenues, and economic profit and Figure 12.4 shows the same information graphically.

Maximizing Economic Profit You can see in the table and part (a) of the figure that total cost (TC) and total revenue (TR) both increase as output increases, but TC increases at an increasing rate and TR increases at a decreasing rate. Economic profit, which equals TR minus TC, increases at small output levels, reaches a maximum, and then decreases. The maximum profit ($12) occurs when Bobbie sells 3 haircuts for $14 each. If she sells 2 haircuts for $16 each or 4 haircuts for $12 each, her economic profit will be only $8.

Marginal Revenue Equals Marginal Cost You can see in the table and part (b) of the figure Bobbie's marginal revenue (MR) and marginal cost (MC). When Bobbie increases output from 2 to 3 haircuts, MR is $10 and MC is $6. MR exceeds MC by $4 and Bobbie's profit increases by that amount. If Bobbie increases output yet further, from 3 to 4 haircuts, MR is $6 and MC is $10. In this case, MC exceeds MR by $4, so profit decreases by that amount.

When MR exceeds MC, profit increases if output increases. When MC exceeds MR, profit increases if output *decreases*. When MC equals MR, profit is maximized.

Figure 12.4(b) shows the maximum profit as price (on the demand curve D) minus average total cost (on the ATC curve) multiplied by the quantity produced—the blue rectangle.

Maximum Price the Market Will Bear Unlike a firm in perfect competition, a monopoly influences the price of what it sells. But a monopoly doesn't set the price at the maximum *possible* price. At the maximum *possible* price, the firm would be able to sell only one unit of output, which in general is less than the profit-maximizing quantity. Rather, a monopoly produces the profit-maximizing quantity and sells that quantity for the highest price it can get.

TABLE 12.1   A Monopoly's Output and Price Decision

Price (P) (dollars per haircut)	Quantity demanded (Q) (haircuts per hour)	Total revenue (TR = P × Q) (dollars)	Marginal revenue (MR =ΔTR/ΔQ) (dollars per haircut)	Total cost (TC) (dollars)	Marginal cost (MC = ΔTC/ΔQ) (dollars per haircut)	Economic profit (TR − TC) (dollars)
20	0	0		20		−20
			18		1	
18	1	18		21		−3
			14		3	
16	2	32		24		+8
			10		6	
14	3	42		30		+12
			6		10	
12	4	48		40		+8
			2		15	
10	5	50		55		−5

This table gives the information needed to find the profit-maximizing output and price. Total revenue (TR) equals price multiplied by the quantity sold. Profit equals total revenue minus total cost (TC). Profit is maximized when 3 haircuts are sold at $14 a haircut. Total revenue is $42, total cost is $30, and economic profit is $12 ($42 − $30).

FIGURE 12.4

A Monopoly's Output and Price

(a) Total revenue and total cost curves

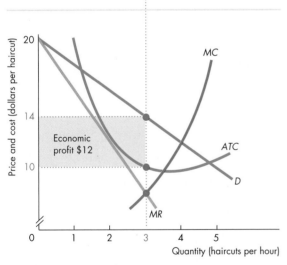

(b) Demand and marginal revenue and cost curves

In part (a), economic profit is the vertical distance equal to total revenue (*TR*) minus total cost (*TC*) and economic profit is maximized at 3 haircuts an hour. In part (b), economic profit is maximized when marginal cost (*MC*) equals marginal revenue (*MR*). The profit-maximizing output is 3 haircuts an hour. The price, determined by the demand curve (*D*), is $14 a haircut. Average total cost is $10 a haircut, so economic profit, the blue rectangle, is $12—the profit per haircut ($4) multiplied by 3 haircuts.

All firms maximize profit by producing the output at which marginal revenue equals marginal cost. For a competitive firm, price equals marginal revenue, so price also equals marginal cost. For a monopoly, price exceeds marginal revenue, so price also exceeds marginal cost.

A monopoly charges a price that exceeds marginal cost, but does it always make an economic profit? In Bobbie's case, when she produces 3 haircuts an hour, her average total cost is $10 (read from the *ATC* curve) and her price is $14 (read from the *D* curve). Her profit per haircut is $4 ($14 minus $10). Bobbie's economic profit is shown by the blue rectangle, which equals the profit per haircut ($4) multiplied by the number of haircuts (3), for a total of $12.

If firms in a perfectly competitive industry make a positive economic profit, new firms enter. That does not happen in monopoly. Barriers to entry prevent new firms from entering an industry in which there is a monopoly. So a monopoly can make a positive economic profit and continue to do so indefinitely. Sometimes that profit is large, as in the international diamond business.

Bobbie makes a positive economic profit. But suppose that the owner of the shop that Bobbie rents increases Bobbie's rent. If Bobbie pays an additional $12 an hour for rent, her fixed cost increases by $12 an hour. Her marginal cost and marginal revenue don't change, so her profit-maximizing output remains at 3 haircuts an hour. Her profit decreases by $12 an hour to zero. If Bobbie pays more than an additional $12 an hour for her shop rent, she incurs an economic loss. If this situation were permanent, Bobbie would go out of business. But entrepreneurs are a hardy lot, and Bobbie might find another shop where the rent is less.

REVIEW QUIZ

1 What is the relationship between marginal cost and marginal revenue when a single-price monopoly maximizes profit?

2 How does a single-price monopoly determine the price it will charge its customers?

3 What is the relationship between price, marginal revenue, and marginal cost when a single-price monopoly is maximizing profit?

4 Why can a monopoly make a positive economic profit even in the long run?

✃ myeconlab   **Study Plan 12.2**

Single-Price Monopoly and Competition Compared

IMAGINE AN INDUSTRY THAT IS MADE UP OF MANY small firms operating in perfect competition. Then imagine that a single firm buys out all these small firms and creates a monopoly.

What will happen in this industry? Will the price rise or fall? Will the quantity produced increase or decrease? Will economic profit increase or decrease? Will either the original competitive situation or the new monopoly situation be efficient?

These are the questions we're now going to answer. First, we look at the effects of monopoly on the price and quantity produced. Then we turn to the questions about efficiency.

Comparing Output and Price

Figure 12.5 shows the market we'll study. The market demand curve is D. The demand curve is the same regardless of how the industry is organized. But the supply side and the equilibrium are different in monopoly and competition. First, let's look at the case of perfect competition.

Perfect Competition Initially, with many small perfectly competitive firms in the market, the market supply curve is S. This supply curve is obtained by summing the supply curves of all the individual firms in the market.

In perfect competition, equilibrium occurs where the supply curve and the demand curve intersect. The quantity produced by the industry is Q_C, and the price is P_C. Each firm takes the price P_C and maximizes its profit by producing the output at which its own marginal cost equals the price. Because each firm is a small part of the total industry, there is no incentive for any firm to try to manipulate the price by varying its output.

Monopoly Now suppose that this industry is taken over by a single firm. Consumers do not change, so the demand curve remains the same as in the case of perfect competition. But now the monopoly recognizes this demand curve as a constraint on its sales. The monopoly's marginal revenue curve is MR.

The monopoly maximizes profit by producing the quantity at which marginal revenue equals marginal cost. To find the monopoly's marginal cost curve, first

recall that in perfect competition, the industry supply curve is the sum of the supply curves of the firms in the industry. Also recall that each firm's supply curve is its marginal cost curve (see Chapter 11, pp. 246–247). So when the industry is taken over by a single firm, the competitive industry's supply curve becomes the monopoly's marginal cost curve. To remind you of this fact, the supply curve is also labelled MC.

The output at which marginal revenue equals marginal cost is Q_M. This output is smaller than the competitive output Q_C. And the monopoly charges the price P_M, which is higher than P_C. We have established that

Compared to a perfectly competitive industry, a single-price monopoly restricts its output and charges a higher price.

We've seen how the output and price of a monopoly compare with those in a competitive industry. Let's now compare the efficiency of the two types of markets.

FIGURE 12.5
Monopoly's Smaller Output and Higher Price

A competitive industry produces the quantity Q_C at price P_C. A single-price monopoly produces the quantity Q_M at which marginal revenue equals marginal cost and sells that quantity for the price P_M. Compared to perfect competition, a single-price monopoly restricts output and raises the price.

Efficiency Comparison

You saw in Chapter 11 (pp. 256–257) that (with no external costs and benefits) perfect competition is efficient. Figure 12.6(a), illustrates the efficiency of perfect competition and serves as a benchmark against which to measure the inefficiency of monopoly.

Along the market demand curve ($D = MSB$), consumers are efficient. Along the market supply curve ($S = MSC$), producers are efficient. In competitive equilibrium, the price is P_C, the quantity is Q_C, and marginal social benefit equals marginal social cost.

Consumer surplus is the green triangle under the demand curve and above the equilibrium price (see Chapter 5, p. 107). *Producer surplus* is the blue area above the supply curve and below the equilibrium price (see Chapter 5, p. 109). The sum of the consumer surplus and producer surplus is maximized.

Also, in long-run competitive equilibrium, entry and exit ensure that each firm produces its output at the minimum possible long-run average cost.

To summarize: At the competitive equilibrium, marginal social benefit equals marginal social cost; the sum of consumer surplus and producer surplus is maximized; firms produce at the lowest possible long-run average cost; and resource use is efficient.

Figure 12.6(b) illustrates the inefficiency of monopoly and the sources of that inefficiency. A monopoly restricts output to Q_M and sells its output for P_M. With no external costs ($MC = MSC$) and no external benefits, the smaller output and higher price drive a wedge between marginal social benefit and marginal social cost and create a *deadweight loss*. The grey area shows the deadweight loss and its magnitude is a measure of the inefficiency of monopoly.

Consumer surplus shrinks for two reasons. First, consumers lose by having to pay more for the good. This loss to consumers is a gain for the producer and increases the producer surplus. Second, consumers lose by getting less of the good, and this loss is part of the deadweight loss.

Although the monopoly gains from a higher price, it loses some of the original producer surplus because of the smaller monopoly output. That loss is another part of the deadweight loss.

Because a monopoly produces less than the efficient quantity and faces no competitive threat, it does not produce at the minimum possible long-run average cost. As a result, monopoly damages the social interest in three ways: it produces less, it increases the cost of production, and it increases the price above the increased cost of production.

FIGURE 12.6
Inefficiency of Monopoly

(a) Perfect competition

(b) Monopoly

In perfect competition (part a), output is Q_C and the price is P_C. Marginal social benefit (*MSB*) equals marginal social cost (*MSC*); consumer surplus (the green triangle) plus producer surplus (the blue area) is maximized; and in the long-run, firms produce at the lowest possible average cost. A monopoly (part b) restricts output to Q_M and raises the price to P_M. Consumer surplus shrinks, the monopoly gains, and a deadweight loss (the grey area) arises.

Redistribution of Surpluses

You've seen that monopoly is inefficient because marginal social benefit exceeds marginal social cost and there is deadweight loss—a social loss. But monopoly also brings a *redistribution* of surpluses.

Some of the lost consumer surplus goes to the monopoly. In Fig. 12.6, the monopoly gets the difference between the higher price, P_M, and the competitive price, P_C, on the quantity sold, Q_M. So the monopoly takes the part of the consumer surplus shown by the darker blue rectangle. This portion of the loss of consumer surplus is not a loss to society. It is redistribution from consumers to the monopoly producer.

Rent Seeking

You've seen that monopoly creates a deadweight loss and so is inefficient. But the social cost of monopoly exceeds the deadweight loss because of an activity called rent seeking. **Rent seeking** is any attempt to capture a consumer surplus, a producer surplus, or an economic profit. The activity is not confined to monopoly. But attempting to capture the economic profit of a monopoly is a major form of rent seeking.

You've seen that a monopoly makes its economic profit by diverting part of consumer surplus to itself. Thus the pursuit of an economic profit by a monopoly is rent seeking. It is the attempt to capture consumer surplus.

Rent seekers pursue their goals in two main ways. They might

- Buy a monopoly
- Create a monopoly

Buy a Monopoly To rent seek by buying a monopoly, a person searches for a monopoly that is for sale at a lower price than the monopoly's economic profit. Trading of taxicab licences is an example of this type of rent seeking. In some cities, taxicabs are regulated. The city restricts both the fares and the number of taxis that can operate so operating a taxi results in economic profit, or rent. A person who wants to operate a taxi must buy a licence from someone who already has one. People rationally devote their time and effort to seeking out profitable monopoly businesses to buy. In the process, they use scarce resources that could otherwise have been employed to produce goods and services. The value of this lost production is part of the social cost of monopoly. The amount paid for a monopoly is not a social cost because the payment is just a transfer of an existing producer surplus from the buyer to the seller.

Create a Monopoly Rent seeking by creating monopoly is mainly a political activity. It takes the form of lobbying and trying to influence the political process. Such influence might be sought by making campaign contributions in exchange for legislative support or by seeking to influence political outcomes indirectly through publicity in the media or more direct contacts with politicians and bureaucrats. An example of a monopoly right created in this way is the cable television monopoly created and regulated by the Canadian Radio-Television and Telecommunications Commission (CRTC). Another is a regulation that restricts "split-run" magazines. These regulations restrict output and increase price.

This type of rent seeking is a costly activity that uses up scarce resources. Taken together, firms spend billions of dollars lobbying MPs, MPPs, and bureaucrats in the pursuit of licences and laws that create barriers to entry and establish a monopoly right. Everyone has an incentive to rent seek, and because there are no barriers to entry into the rent-seeking activity, there is a great deal of competition for new monopoly rights.

Rent-Seeking Equilibrium

Barriers to entry create monopoly. But there is no barrier to entry into rent seeking. Rent seeking is like perfect competition. If an economic profit is available, a new rent seeker will try to get some of it. And competition among rent seekers pushes up the price that must be paid for a monopoly right to the point at which only a normal profit can be made by operating the monopoly. For example, competition for the right to operate a taxi in Toronto leads to a price of more than $80,000 for a taxi licence, which is sufficiently high to eliminate economic profit for taxi operators and leave them with normal profit.

Figure 12.7 shows a rent-seeking equilibrium. The cost of rent seeking is a fixed cost that must be added to a monopoly's other costs. Rent seeking and rent-seeking costs increase to the point at which no economic profit is made. The average total cost curve, which includes the fixed cost of rent seeking, shifts upward until it just touches the demand curve. Economic profit is zero. It has been lost in rent seeking. Consumer surplus is unaffected. But the dead-

FIGURE 12.7

Rent-Seeking Equilibrium

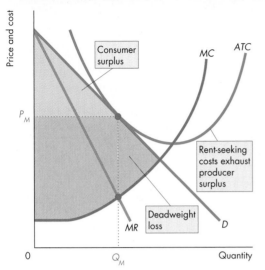

With competitive rent seeking, a monopoly uses all its economic profit to prevent another firm from taking its economic rent. The firm's rent-seeking costs are fixed costs. They shift the *ATC* curve upward until, at the profit-maximizing price, the firm breaks even.

weight loss of monopoly now includes the original deadweight loss triangle plus the lost producer surplus, shown by the enlarged grey area in the figure.

REVIEW QUIZ

1 Why does a single-price monopoly produce a smaller output and charge a higher price than what would prevail if the industry were perfectly competitive?

2 How does a monopoly transfer consumer surplus to itself?

3 Why is a single-price monopoly inefficient?

4 What is rent seeking and how does it influence the inefficiency of monopoly?

 Study Plan 12.3

So far, we've considered only a single-price monopoly. But many monopolies do not operate with a single price. Instead, they price discriminate. Let's now see how a price-discriminating monopoly works.

Price Discrimination

PRICE DISCRIMINATION—SELLING A GOOD OR service at a number of different prices—is widespread. You encounter it when you travel, go to the movies, get your hair cut, buy pizza, or visit an art museum. Most price discriminators are not monopolies, but monopolies price discriminate when they can do so.

To be able to price discriminate, a monopoly must

1. Identify and separate different buyer types.
2. Sell a product that cannot be resold.

Price discrimination is charging different prices for a single good or service because of differences in buyers' willingness to pay and not because of differences in production costs. So not all price *differences* are price *discrimination*. Some goods that are similar but not identical have different prices because they have different production costs. For example, the cost of producing electricity depends on the time of day. If an electric power company charges a higher price during the peak consumption periods from 7:00 to 9:00 in the morning and from 4:00 to 7:00 in the evening than it does at other times of the day, it is not price discriminating.

At first sight, it appears that price discrimination contradicts the assumption of profit maximization. Why would a movie theatre allow children to see movies at half price? Why would a hairdresser charge students and senior citizens less? Aren't these firms losing profit by being nice to their customers?

Deeper investigation shows that far from losing profit, price discriminators make a bigger profit than they would otherwise. So a monopoly has an incentive to find ways of discriminating and charging each buyer the highest possible price. Some people pay less with price discrimination, but others pay more.

Price Discrimination and Consumer Surplus

The key idea behind price discrimination is to convert consumer surplus into economic profit. Demand curves slope downward because the value that people place on any good decreases as the quantity consumed of that good increases. When all the units consumed are sold for a single price, consumers benefit. The benefit is the value the consumers get from each unit of the good minus the price actually paid for it. This benefit is *consumer surplus.* Price discrimination is an attempt by a monopoly to capture as much of the consumer surplus as possible for itself.

To extract every dollar of consumer surplus from every buyer, the monopoly would have to offer each individual customer a separate price schedule based on that customer's own willingness to pay. Clearly, such price discrimination cannot be carried out in practice because a firm does not have enough information about each consumer's demand curve.

But firms try to extract as much consumer surplus as possible, and to do so, they discriminate in two broad ways:

- Among units of a good
- Among groups of buyers

Discriminating Among Units of a Good One method of price discrimination charges each buyer a different price on each unit of a good bought. A discount for bulk buying is an example of this type of discrimination. The larger the quantity bought, the larger is the discount—and the lower is the price. (Note that some discounts for bulk arise from lower costs of production for greater bulk. In these cases, such discounts are not price discrimination.)

Discriminating Among Groups of Buyers Price discrimination often takes the form of discriminating between different groups of consumers on the basis of age, employment status, or some other easily distinguished characteristic. This type of price discrimination works when each group has a different average willingness to pay for the good or service.

For example, a face-to-face sales meeting with a customer might bring a large and profitable order. For salespeople and other business travellers, the marginal benefit from a trip is large and the price that such a traveller will pay for a trip is high. In contrast, for a vacation traveller, any of several different trips and even no vacation trip are options. So for vacation travellers, the marginal benefit of a trip is small and the price that such a traveller will pay for a trip is low. Because business travellers are willing to pay more than vacation travellers are, it is possible for an airline to profit by price discriminating between these two groups. Similarly, because students have a lower willingness to pay for a haircut than a working person does, it is possible for a hairdresser to profit by price discriminating between these two groups.

Let's see how an airline exploits the differences in demand by business and vacation travellers and increases its profit by price discriminating.

Profiting by Price Discriminating

Global Air has a monopoly on an exotic route. Figure 12.8 shows the demand curve (*D*) and the marginal revenue curve (*MR*) for travel on this route. It also shows Global Air's marginal cost curve (*MC*) and average total cost curve (*ATC*).

Initially, Global is a single-price monopoly and maximizes its profit by producing 8,000 trips a year (the quantity at which *MR* equals *MC*). The price is $1,200 per trip. The average total cost of producing a trip is $600, so economic profit is $600 a trip. On 8,000 trips, Global's economic profit is $4.8 million a year, shown by the blue rectangle. Global's customers enjoy a consumer surplus shown by the green triangle.

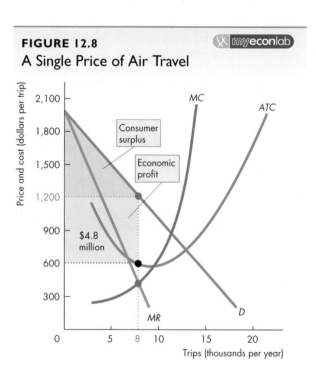

FIGURE 12.8
A Single Price of Air Travel

Global Airlines has a monopoly on an air route. The market demand curve is *D* and marginal revenue curve is *MR*. Global Air's marginal cost curve is *MC*, and its average total cost curve is *ATC*. As a single-price monopoly, Global maximizes profit by selling 8,000 trips a year at $1,200 a trip. Its profit is $4.8 million a year—the blue rectangle. Global's customers enjoy a consumer surplus—the green triangle.

Global is struck by the fact that many of its customers are business travellers, and Global suspects that they are willing to pay more than $1,200 a trip. So Global does some market research, which tells Global that some business travellers are willing to pay as much as $1,800 a trip. Also, these customers frequently change their travel plans at the last moment. Another group of business travellers is willing to pay $1,600. These customers know one week ahead when they will travel, and they never want to stay over a weekend. Yet another group would pay up to $1,400. These travellers know two weeks ahead when they will travel and don't want to stay over a weekend.

So Global announces a new fare schedule: no restrictions, $1,800; 7-day advance purchase, non-refundable, $1,600; 14-day advance purchase, non-refundable, $1,400; 14-day advance purchase, must stay over a weekend, $1,200.

Figure 12.9 shows the outcome with this new fare structure and also shows why Global is pleased with

its new fare structure. Global sells 2,000 seats at each of its four new fares. Its economic profit increases by the dark blue steps in Fig. 12.9. Its economic profit is now its original $4.8 million a year plus an additional $2.4 million from its new higher fares. Consumer surplus has shrunk to the smaller green area.

Perfect Price Discrimination

But Global reckons that it can do even better. It plans to achieve **perfect price discrimination**, which extracts the entire consumer surplus. To do so, Global must get creative and come up with a host of additional fares—ranging between $2,000 and $1,200, each of which appeals to a small segment of the business market—that will extract the entire consumer surplus from the business travellers.

With perfect price discrimination, something special happens to marginal revenue. For the perfect price discriminator, the market demand curve becomes the marginal revenue curve. The reason is that when the price is cut to sell a larger quantity, the firm sells only the marginal unit at the lower price. All the other units continue to be sold for the highest price that each buyer is willing to pay. So for the perfect price discriminator, marginal revenue *equals* price and the demand curve becomes the marginal revenue curve.

With marginal revenue equal to price, Global can obtain yet greater profit by increasing output up to the point at which price (and marginal revenue) is equal to marginal cost.

So Global now seeks additional travellers who will not pay as much as $1,200 a trip but who will pay more than marginal cost. More creative pricing comes up with vacation specials and other fares that have combinations of advance reservation, minimum stay, and other restrictions that make these fares unattractive to its existing customers but attractive to a further group of travellers. With all these fares and specials, Global increases sales, extracts the entire consumer surplus, and maximizes economic profit. Figure 12.10 shows the outcome with perfect price discrimination. The dozens of fares paid by the original travellers who are willing to pay between $1,200 and $2,000 have extracted the entire consumer surplus from this group and converted it into economic profit for Global.

The new fares between $900 and $1,200 have attracted 3,000 additional travellers but taken their entire consumer surplus also. Global is earning an economic profit of more than $9 million a year.

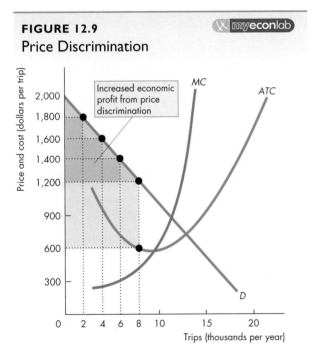

FIGURE 12.9
Price Discrimination

Global revises its fare structure: no restrictions at $1,800, 7-day advance purchase at $1,600, 14-day advance purchase at $1,400, and must stay over a weekend at $1,200. Global sells 2,000 trips at each of its four new fares. Its economic profit increases by $2.4 million a year to $7.2 million a year, which is shown by the original blue rectangle plus the dark blue steps. Global's customers' consumer surplus shrinks.

FIGURE 12.10
Perfect Price Discrimination

With perfect price discrimination, Global's demand curve becomes its marginal revenue curve. Economic profit is maximized when the lowest price equals marginal cost. Here, Global sells 11,000 trips and makes an economic profit of $9.35 million a year.

Real-world airlines are just as creative as Global, as you can see in the cartoon!

Would it bother you to hear how little I paid for this flight?

From William Hamilton, "Voodoo Economics," © 1992 by Chronicle Books. Published by Chronicle Books LLC, San Francisco. Used with permission. Visit http://www.chroniclebooks.com.

Efficiency and Rent Seeking with Price Discrimination

With perfect price discrimination, output increases to the point at which price equals marginal cost—where the marginal cost curve intersects the demand curve. This output is identical to that of perfect competition. Perfect price discrimination pushes consumer surplus to zero but increases producer surplus to equal the sum of consumer surplus and producer surplus in perfect competition. Deadweight loss with perfect price discrimination is zero. So perfect price discrimination achieves efficiency.

The more perfectly the monopoly can price discriminate, the closer its output gets to the competitive output and the more efficient is the outcome.

But there are two differences between perfect competition and perfect price discrimination. First, the distribution of the total surplus is different. It is shared by consumers and producers in perfect competition, while the producer gets it all with perfect price discrimination. Second, because the producer grabs the surplus, rent seeking becomes profitable.

People use resources in pursuit of rents, and the bigger the rents, the more resources get used in pursuing them. With free entry into rent seeking, the long-run equilibrium outcome is that rent seekers use up the entire producer surplus.

REVIEW QUIZ

1 What is price discrimination and how is it used to increase a monopoly's profit?
2 Explain how consumer surplus changes when a monopoly price discriminates.
3 Explain how consumer surplus, economic profit, and output change when a monopoly perfectly price discriminates.
4 What are some of the ways in which real-world airlines price discriminate?

myeconlab Study Plan 12.4

You've seen that monopoly is profitable for the monopolist but costly for other people. It results in inefficiency. Because of these features of monopoly, it is subject to policy debate and regulation. We'll now study the key monopoly policy issues.

Monopoly Policy Issues

MONOPOLY LOOKS BAD WHEN WE COMPARE IT with competition. Monopoly is inefficient, and it captures consumer surplus and converts it into producer surplus or pure waste in the form of rent-seeking costs. If monopoly is so bad, why do we put up with it? Why don't we have laws that crack down on monopoly so hard that it never rears its head? We do indeed have laws that limit monopoly power and regulate the prices that monopolies are permitted to charge. But monopoly also brings some benefits. We begin this review of monopoly policy issues by looking at the benefits of monopoly. We then look at monopoly regulation.

Gains from Monopoly

The main reason why monopoly exists is that it has potential advantages over a competitive alternative. These advantages arise from

- Incentives to innovation
- Economies of scale and economies of scope

Incentives to Innovation Invention leads to a wave of innovation as new knowledge is applied to the production process. Innovation may take the form of developing a new product or a lower-cost way of making an existing product. Controversy has raged over whether large firms with market power or small competitive firms lacking such market power are the most innovative. It is clear that some temporary market power arises from innovation. A firm that develops a new product or process and patents it obtains an exclusive right to that product or process for the term of the patent.

But does the granting of a monopoly, even a temporary one, to an innovator increase the pace of innovation? One line of reasoning suggests that it does. Without protection, an innovator is not able to enjoy the profits from innovation for very long. Thus the incentive to innovate is weakened. A contrary argument is that monopolies can afford to be lazy while competitive firms cannot. Competitive firms must strive to innovate and cut costs even though they know that they cannot hang onto the benefits of their innovation for long. But that knowledge spurs them on to greater and faster innovation.

The evidence on whether monopoly leads to greater innovation than competition is mixed. Large firms do more research and development than do small firms. But research and development are inputs into the process of innovation. What matters is not input but output. Two measures of the output of research and development are the number of patents and the rate of productivity growth. On these measures, it is not clear that bigger is better. But as a new process or product spreads through an industry, the large firms adopt the new process or product more quickly than do small firms. So large firms help to speed the process of diffusion of technological change.

Economies of Scale and Scope Economies of scale and economies of scope can lead to natural monopoly. As you saw at the beginning of this chapter, in a natural monopoly, a single firm can produce at a lower average total cost than can a number of firms.

A firm experiences *economies of scale* when an increase in its output of a good or service brings a decrease in the average total cost of producing it (see Chapter 10, p. 232). A firm experiences *economies of scope* when an increase in the *range of the goods produced* brings a decrease in average total cost (see Chapter 9, p. 213). Economies of scope occur when different goods can share specialized (and usually costly) capital resources. For example, McDonald's can produce both hamburgers and french fries at a lower average total cost than can two separate firms—a burger firm and a french fry firm—because at McDonald's, hamburgers and french fries share the use of specialized food storage and preparation facilities. A firm that produces a wide range of products can hire specialist designers and marketing experts whose skills can be used across the product range, thereby spreading the costs and lowering the average total cost of production of each of the goods.

There are many examples in which a combination of economies of scale and economies of scope arises, but not all of them lead to monopoly. Some examples are the brewing of beer, the manufacture of refrigerators and other household appliances, the manufacture of pharmaceuticals, and the refining of petroleum.

Examples of industries in which economies of scale are so significant that they lead to a natural monopoly are becoming rare. Public utilities such as gas, electric power, local telephone service, and garbage collection once were natural monopolies. But technological advances now enable us to separate the *production* of electric power or natural gas from its *distribution*. The provision of water, though, remains a natural monopoly.

A large-scale firm that has control over supply and can influence price—and therefore behaves like the monopoly firm that you've studied in this chapter—can reap these economies of scale and scope. Small, competitive firms cannot. Consequently, there are situations in which the comparison of monopoly and competition that we made earlier in this chapter is not valid. Recall that we imagined the takeover of a large number of competitive firms by a monopoly firm. But we also assumed that the monopoly would use exactly the same technology as the small firms and have the same costs. If one large firm can reap economies of scale and economies of scope, its marginal cost curve will lie below the supply curve of a competitive industry made up of many small firms. It is possible for such economies of scale and economies of scope to be so large as to result in a larger output and lower price under monopoly than a competitive industry would achieve.

Where significant economies of scale and economies of scope exist, it is usually worth putting up with monopoly and regulating its price.

Regulating Natural Monopoly

Where demand and cost conditions create a natural monopoly, a federal, provincial, or local government agency usually steps in to regulate the prices of the monopoly. By regulating a monopoly, some of the worst aspects of monopoly can be avoided or at least moderated. Let's look at monopoly price regulation.

Figure 12.11 shows the market demand curve *D*, the marginal revenue curve *MR*, the average total cost curve *ATC*, and the marginal cost curve *MC* for a natural gas distribution company that is a natural monopoly.

The firm's marginal cost is constant at 10 cents per cubic metre. But average total cost decreases as output increases. The reason is that the natural gas company has a large investment in pipelines and so has high fixed costs. These fixed costs are part of the company's average total cost and so appear in the *ATC* curve. The average total cost curve slopes downward because as the number of cubic metres sold increases, the fixed cost is spread over a larger number of units. (If you need to refresh your memory on how the average total cost curve is calculated, look back at Chapter 10, pp. 226–227.)

This one firm can supply the entire market at a lower cost than two firms can because average total cost is falling even when the entire market is supplied. (Refer back to pp. 264–265 if you need a quick refresher on natural monopoly.)

Profit Maximization Suppose the natural gas company is not regulated and instead maximizes profit. Figure 12.11 shows the outcome. The company produces 2 million cubic metres a day, the quantity at which marginal cost equals marginal revenue. It prices the gas at 20 cents a cubic metre and makes an economic profit of 2 cents a cubic metre, or $40,000 a day.

This outcome is fine for the gas company, but it is inefficient. The price of gas is 20 cents a cubic metre when its marginal cost is only 10 cents a cubic metre. Also, the gas company is making a big profit. What can regulation do to improve this outcome?

The Efficient Regulation If the monopoly regulator wants to achieve an efficient use of resources, it must require the gas monopoly to produce the quantity of gas that brings marginal benefit into equality with marginal cost. Marginal benefit is what the consumer is willing to pay and is shown by the demand curve. Marginal cost is shown by the firm's marginal cost curve. You can see in Fig. 12.11 that this outcome occurs if the price is regulated at 10 cents per cubic metre and if 4 million cubic metres per day are produced. The regulation that produces this outcome is called a marginal cost pricing rule. A **marginal cost pricing rule** sets price equal to marginal cost. It maximizes total surplus in the regulated industry. In this example, that surplus is all consumer surplus and it equals the area of the triangle beneath the demand curve and above the marginal cost curve.

The marginal cost pricing rule is efficient. But it leaves the natural monopoly incurring an economic loss. Because average total cost is falling as output increases, marginal cost is below average total cost. And because price equals marginal cost, price is below average total cost. Average total cost minus price is the loss per unit produced. It's pretty obvious that a natural gas company that is required to use a marginal cost pricing rule will not stay in business for long. How can a company cover its costs and, at the same time, obey a marginal cost pricing rule?

One possibility is price discrimination. The company might charge a higher price to some customers but marginal cost to the customers who pay least. Another possibility is to use a two-part price (called a

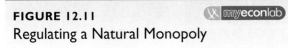

FIGURE 12.11

Regulating a Natural Monopoly

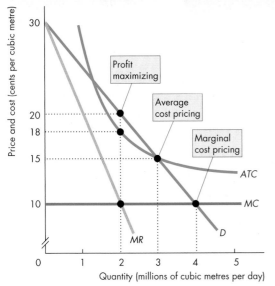

A natural monopoly is an industry in which average total cost is falling even when the entire market demand is satisfied. A natural gas producer faces the demand curve D. The firm's marginal cost is constant at 10 cents per cubic metre, as shown by the curve labelled MC. Fixed costs are large, and the average total cost curve, which includes average fixed cost, is shown as ATC. A marginal cost pricing rule sets the price at 10 cents per cubic metre. The monopoly produces 4 million cubic metres per day and incurs an economic loss. An average cost pricing rule sets the price at 15 cents per cubic metre. The monopoly produces 3 million cubic metres per day and makes normal profit.

two-part tariff). For example, the gas company might charge a monthly fixed fee that covers its fixed cost and then charge for gas consumed at marginal cost.

But a natural monopoly cannot always cover its costs in these ways. If a natural monopoly cannot cover its total cost from its customers and if the government wants it to follow a marginal cost pricing rule, then the government must give the firm a subsidy. In such a case, the government raises the revenue for the subsidy by taxing some other activity. But as we saw in Chapter 6, taxes themselves generate deadweight loss. Thus the deadweight loss resulting from additional taxes must be subtracted from the efficiency gained by forcing the natural monopoly to adopt a marginal cost pricing rule.

Average Cost Pricing Regulators almost never impose efficient pricing because of its consequences for the firm's profit. Instead, they compromise by permitting the firm to cover its costs and to earn a normal profit. Recall that normal profit is a cost of production and we include it along with the firm's other fixed costs in the average total cost curve. So pricing to cover cost including normal profit means setting price equal to average total cost—called an **average cost pricing rule**.

Figure 12.11 shows the average cost pricing outcome. The natural gas company charges 15 cents a cubic metre and sells 3 million cubic metres per day. This outcome is better for consumers than the unregulated profit-maximizing outcome. The price is 5 cents a cubic metre lower, and the quantity consumed is 1 million cubic metres per day more. And the outcome is better for the producer than the marginal cost pricing rule outcome. The firm earns normal profit. The outcome is inefficient but less so than the unregulated profit-maximizing outcome.

REVIEW QUIZ

1 What are the two main reasons why monopoly is worth tolerating?
2 Can you provide some examples of economies of scale and economies of scope?
3 Why might the incentive to innovate be greater for a monopoly than for a small competitive firm?
4 What is the price that achieves an efficient outcome for a regulated monopoly? And what is the problem with this price?
5 Compare the consumer surplus, producer surplus, and deadweight loss that arise from average cost pricing with those that arise from profit-maximization and marginal cost pricing.

myeconlab **Study Plan 12.5**

◆ You've now studied perfect competition and monopoly. *Reading Between the Lines* on pp. 280–281 looks at market power in the markets for Internet auctions and search. In the next chapter, we study markets that lie between the extremes of perfect competition and monopoly and that blend elements of the two.

READING BETWEEN THE LINES

POLICY WATCH

eBay Is a Monopoly But Google Isn't!

THE ECONOMIST, OCTOBER 30, 2002

How Good is Google

... As search engines go... Google has clearly been a runaway success. Not only is its own site the most popular for search on the web, but it also powers the search engines of major portals, such as Yahoo! and AOL. All told, 75% of referrals to websites now originate from Google's algorithms. That is power.

For some time now, Google's board... has been deliberating how to translate that power into money. They appear to have decided to bring Google to the stock market next spring. Bankers have been overheard estimating Google's value at $15 billion or more. That could make Google Silicon Valley's first hot IPO since the dotcom bust, and perhaps its biggest ever.

...To be worth the rumoured $15 billion for longer than it takes a bubble to burst, it will need to raise its profitability substantially. That means matching such internet stars as eBay (market capitalisation $37 billion), but without the natural-monopoly advantages that have made eBay so dominant—the classic network effect of buyers and sellers knowing they do best by all trading in one place. For Google to stay permanently ahead of other search-engine technologies is almost impossible, since it takes so little—only a bright idea by another set of geeks—to lose the lead. In contrast to a portal such as Yahoo!, which also offers customers free e-mail and other services, a pure search engine is always but a click away from losing users.

Essence of the Story

■ Google is the most popular search engine, and 75 percent of referrals to Web sites originate from its searches.

■ Some bankers estimate Google's value at $15 billion or more.

■ It is almost impossible for Google to stay permanently ahead of other search-engine technologies because it takes only a bright idea by another set of programmers to lose its lead.

■ Google does not have the natural-monopoly advantages that have made eBay dominant—network effect of buyers and sellers who know they do best by all trading in one place.

Economic Analysis

■ Almost all the costs of eBay or Google are fixed costs.

■ When all costs are fixed, average fixed cost equals average total cost, and marginal cost is zero. Figure 1 shows eBay's cost curves. (Google's cost curves look just like these.)

■ A natural monopoly has two features:

1) Economies of scale at the output that meets the market demand

2) No close substitutes

■ Both eBay and Google have the first feature but only eBay has the second.

■ If another firm developed a better search engine than Google—a close but better substitute for Google—that firm would take the market for Internet search.

■ Constant vigilance in improving its search engine and keeping it the best available can prevent this outcome for Google.

■ Because eBay enjoys the benefit of a network externality, eBay has no close substitute and is unlikely to be confronted with one.

■ The demand for eBay's services is D in Fig. 1. The firm maximizes profit by setting a price, P, that generates a quantity

demanded, Q, where marginal revenue is equal to the zero marginal cost.

■ eBay users enjoy a consumer surplus, eBay earns a large economic profit (capital value at an estimated $37 billion), but there is a deadweight loss.

■ Although as a monopoly eBay is inefficient and creates a deadweight loss, the world is better off with eBay than it would be without it. Figure 2 shows why.

■ In the market for a rarely traded item such as carved bone fishes, the supply including the cost of finding a buyer was S_0 before eBay began to operate. The cost of finding a buyer was so large that this item was not traded.

■ Supply increases to S_1 when eBay lowers the cost of finding a buyer. Now the item is traded. The buyer pays PB and receives a consumer surplus, the seller receives PS and a seller's surplus, and eBay earns an economic profit.

■ A deadweight loss arises because eBay doesn't set price equal to marginal cost. So the market is inefficient. But compared to the situation before eBay existed, a huge consumer surplus and a surplus for the seller arise.

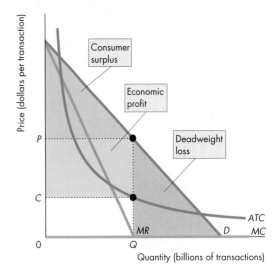

Figure 1 eBay's market for auction services

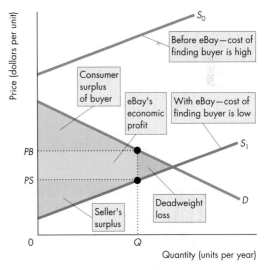

Figure 2 The view from the market for carved bone fishes

You're the Voter

■ Do you think eBay should be regulated and required to set its price equal to its marginal cost? Explain why or why not.

SUMMARY

KEY POINTS

Market Power (pp. 264–265)

- A monopoly is an industry in which there is a single supplier of a good or service that has no close substitutes and in which barriers to entry prevent competition.
- Barriers to entry may be legal (public franchise, licence, patent, copyright) or natural (created by economies of scale) or the firm owns control of a resource.
- A monopoly might be able to price discriminate when there is no resale possibility.
- Where resale is possible, a firm charges one price.

A Single-Price Monopoly's Output and Price Decision (pp. 266–269)

- A monopoly's demand curve is the market demand curve, and a single-price monopoly's marginal revenue is less than price.
- A monopoly maximizes profit by producing the output at which marginal revenue equals marginal cost and by charging the maximum price that consumers are willing to pay for that output.

Single-Price Monopoly and Competition Compared (pp. 270–273)

- A single-price monopoly charges a higher price and produces a smaller quantity than a perfectly competitive industry.
- A single-price monopoly restricts output and creates a deadweight loss.
- The cost of monopoly is the sum of deadweight loss and the resources devoted to rent seeking.

Price Discrimination (pp. 273–276)

- Price discrimination is an attempt by the monopoly to convert consumer surplus into economic profit.
- Perfect price discrimination extracts the entire consumer surplus. Such a monopoly charges a different price for each unit sold and obtains the maximum price that each consumer is willing to pay for each unit bought.

- With perfect price discrimination, the monopoly produces the same output as would a perfectly competitive industry.
- Rent seeking with perfect price discrimination might eliminate the entire consumer surplus and producer surplus.

Monopoly Policy Issues (pp. 277–279)

- A monopoly with large economies of scale and economies of scope can produce a larger quantity at a lower price than a competitive industry can achieve, and a monopoly might be more innovative than small competitive firms.
- Efficient regulation requires a monopoly to charge a price equal to marginal cost, but for a natural monopoly, such a price is less than average total cost.
- Average cost pricing is a compromise pricing rule that covers a firm's costs and provides a normal profit but is not efficient. It is more efficient than unregulated profit maximization.

KEY FIGURES AND TABLE

KEY TERMS

PROBLEMS

Go to **myeconlab** for solutions to odd-numbered problems and additional exercises.

1. Minnie's Mineral Springs, a single-price monopoly, faces the demand schedule.

Price (dollars per bottle)	Quantity demanded (bottles per hour)
10	0
8	1
6	2
4	3
2	4
0	5

   a. Calculate Minnie's total revenue schedule.
   b. Calculate its marginal revenue schedule.

2. Burma Ruby Mines, a single-price monopoly, faces the demand schedule.

Price (dollars per ruby)	Quantity demanded (rubies per day)
1,100	0
900	1
700	2
500	3
300	4

   a. Calculate Burma's total revenue schedule.
   b. Calculate its marginal revenue schedule.

3. Minnie's Mineral Springs in problem 1 has the following total cost:

Quantity produced (bottles per hour)	Total cost (dollars)
0	1
1	3
2	7
3	13
4	21
5	31

   a. Calculate the marginal cost of producing each output in the table.
   b. Calculate the profit-maximizing output and price.
   c. Calculate the economic profit.

   d. Does Minnie's use resources efficiently? Explain your answer.

4. Burma Ruby Mines in problem 2 has the following total cost:

Quantity produced (rubies per day)	Total cost (dollars)
1	1,220
2	1,300
3	1,400
4	1,520

   a. Calculate the marginal cost of producing each quantity listed in the table.
   b. Calculate the profit-maximizing output and price.
   c. Calculate the economic profit.
   d. Does Burma Ruby Mines use its resources efficiently? Explain your answer.

5. The figure illustrates the situation facing the publisher of the only newspaper containing local news in an isolated community.

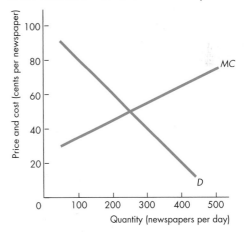

   a. On the graph, draw the publisher's marginal revenue curve.
   b. What are the profit-maximizing quantity and price?
   c. What is the publisher's daily total revenue?
   d. At the price charged, is the demand for newspapers elastic or inelastic? Why?
   e. On the graph, mark in the consumer surplus and deadweight loss.
   f. Might the newspaper try to price discriminate? Explain why or why not.

6. The figure illustrates the situation facing the only coffee shop in an isolated community.

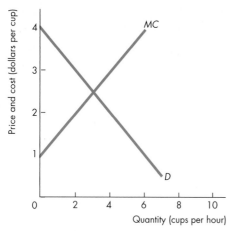

a. What are the profit-maximizing quantity and price of coffee?
b. On the graph, mark the coffee shop's profit.
c. What are consumer surplus and deadweight loss?
d. What is the efficient quantity? Explain your answer.
e. Might the coffee shop try to price discriminate? Explain why or why not.

7. The figure shows the situation facing a natural monopoly that cannot price discriminate.

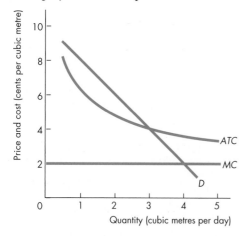

What quantity will be produced and what will be the deadweight loss if the firm is

a. An unregulated profit maximizer?
b. Regulated to earn only normal profit?
c. Regulated to be efficient?

8. In problem 7, marginal cost doubles, what now are your answers?

CRITICAL THINKING

1. After you have studied *Reading Between the Lines* on pp. 280–281, answer the following questions:
   a. Why is eBay a monopoly but Google not a monopoly?
   b. How would you regulate the Internet search engine business to ensure that resources are used efficiently?
   c. How would you regulate the Internet auction business to ensure that resources are used efficiently?
   "Anyone is free to buy stock in eBay, so everyone is free to share in eBay's economic profit, and the bigger that economic profit, the better for all." Evaluate this statement.

WEB EXERCISES

Use the links on ⓧ myeconlab to work the following exercises.

1. Read the statement by Ralph Nader about Microsoft.
   a. What are Ralph Nader's main claims about Microsoft?
   b. Do you agree with Ralph Nader? Why or why not?
   c. If some other operating systems are better than Windows, why don't they take off?
   d. Does Ralph Nader identify the main costs to the consumer of Microsoft's practices? Explain why or why not.

2. Study the market for computer chips.
   a. Is it correct to call Intel a monopoly? Why or why not?
   b. How does Intel try to raise barriers to entry in this market?

3. Learn about developments in the Canadian railroad industry of the 1880s.
   a. Was Canadian Pacific a monopoly? Why or why not?
   b. What other elements of market power are discussed on this Web page?
   c. Do you think monopoly was a bigger problem in the 1880s than it is today? Why or why not?

Monopolistic Competition and Oligopoly

Searching the Globe for a Niche

Globalization brings an enormous diversity of products. Canadians enjoy hundreds of varieties of products from around the world. And our entrepreneurs along with others from Europe and the United States search the globe for niche markets in which to sell their products and earn a profit. Paul Rasch, whom you will meet in *Reading Between the Lines* at the end of this chapter, is one of these entrepreneurs. Mr. Rasch sells fruit juice in a fiercely competitive Chinese market. How does he set his price, pick his product line, and choose the quantity to produce? How is Mr. Rasch's profit affected by the actions of other firms in the market?

Two firms make the chips that drive most PCs: Advanced Micro Devices and Intel. How does competition between just two chip makers work? Do they operate in the social interest, like firms in perfect competition? Or do they restrict output to increase profit, like a monopoly?

◆ The theories of perfect competition and monopoly don't predict the behaviour of the firms we've just described. To understand the search for a market niche and the way markets work when only a handful of firms compete, we need the richer models that are explained in this chapter.

After studying this chapter, you will be able to

■ **Define and identify monopolistic competition**

■ **Explain how price and output are determined in a monopolistically competitive industry**

■ **Explain why advertising costs are high in a monopolistically competitive industry**

■ **Define and identify oligopoly**

■ **Explain two traditional oligopoly models**

■ **Use game theory to explain how price and output are determined in oligopoly**

■ **Use game theory to explain other strategic decisions**

What Is Monopolistic Competition?

YOU HAVE STUDIED PERFECT COMPETITION, IN which a large number of firms produce at the lowest possible cost, earn no economic profit, and are efficient. And you've studied monopoly, in which a single firm restricts output, produces at a higher cost and price than in perfect competition, and is inefficient.

Most real-world markets are competitive but not perfectly competitive because firms in these markets possess some power to set their prices as monopolies do. We call this type of market *monopolistic competition*.

Monopolistic competition is a market structure in which

- A large number of firms compete.
- Each firm produces a differentiated product.
- Firms compete on product quality, price, and marketing.
- Firms are free to enter and exit.

Large Number of Firms

In monopolistic competition, as in perfect competition, the industry consists of a large number of firms. The presence of a large number of firms has three implications for the firms in the industry.

Small Market Share In monopolistic competition, each firm supplies a small part of the total industry output. Consequently, each firm has only limited power to influence the price of its product. Each firm's price can deviate from the average price of other firms by a relatively small amount.

Ignore Other Firms A firm in monopolistic competition must be sensitive to the average market price of the product. But it does not pay attention to any one individual competitor. Because all the firms are relatively small, no one firm can dictate market conditions, and so no one firm's actions directly affect the actions of the other firms.

Collusion Impossible Firms in monopolistic competition would like to be able to conspire to fix a higher price—called *collusion*. But because there are many firms, collusion is not possible.

Product Differentiation

A firm practises **product differentiation** if it makes a product that is slightly different from the products of competing firms. A differentiated product is one that is a close substitute but not a perfect substitute for the products of the other firms. Some people will pay more for one variety of the product, so when its price rises, the quantity demanded falls but it does not (necessarily) fall to zero. For example, Adidas, Asics, Diadora, Etonic, Fila, New Balance, Nike, Puma, and Reebok all make differentiated running shoes. Other things remaining the same, if the price of Adidas running shoes rises and the prices of the other shoes remain constant, Adidas sells fewer shoes and the other producers sell more. But Adidas shoes don't disappear unless the price rises by a large enough amount.

Competing on Quality, Price, and Marketing

Product differentiation enables a firm to compete with other firms in three areas: product quality, price, and marketing.

Quality The quality of a product is the physical attributes that make it different from the products of other firms. Quality includes design, reliability, the service provided to the buyer, and the buyer's ease of access to the product. Quality lies on a spectrum that runs from high to low. Some firms—such as Dell Computer Corp.—offer high-quality products. They are well designed and reliable, and the customer receives quick and efficient service. Other firms offer a lower-quality product that is less well designed, that might not work perfectly, and that the buyer must travel some distance to obtain.

Price Because of product differentiation, a firm in monopolistic competition faces a downward-sloping demand curve. So, like a monopoly, the firm can set both its price and its output. But there is a tradeoff between the product's quality and price. A firm that makes a high-quality product can charge a higher price than a firm that makes a low-quality product.

Marketing Because of product differentiation, a firm in monopolistic competition must market its product. Marketing takes two main forms: advertising and packaging. A firm that produces a high-quality product wants to sell it for a suitably high price. To be able to do so, it must advertise and package its product in a way that convinces buyers that they are getting the higher quality for which they are paying a higher price. For example, pharmaceutical companies advertise and package their brand-name drugs to persuade buyers that these items are superior to the lower-priced generic alternatives. Similarly, a low-quality producer uses advertising and packaging to persuade buyers that although the quality is low, the low price more than compensates for this fact.

Entry and Exit

In monopolistic competition, there is free entry and free exit. Consequently, a firm cannot make an economic profit in the long run. When firms make an economic profit, new firms enter the industry. This entry lowers prices and eventually eliminates economic profit. When firms incur economic losses, some firms leave the industry. This exit increases prices and profits and eventually eliminates the economic loss. In long-run equilibrium, firms neither enter nor leave the industry and the firms in the industry make zero economic profit.

Examples of Monopolistic Competition

Figure 13.1 shows ten industries that are good examples of monopolistic competition. These industries have a large number of firms (shown in parentheses after the name of the industry). In the most concentrated of these industries, upholstered household furniture, the 4 largest firms produce 30 percent of the industry's total sales and the 20 largest firms produce 69 percent of total sales. The number on the right is the Herfindahl-Hirschman Index. Producers of clothing, bakery items, plastic bags, and boat building operate in monopolistic competition.

FIGURE 13.1
Examples of Monopolistic Competition

myeconlab

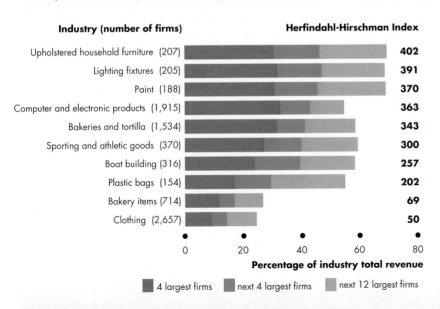

Industry (number of firms)	Herfindahl-Hirschman Index
Upholstered household furniture (207)	402
Lighting fixtures (205)	391
Paint (188)	370
Computer and electronic products (1,915)	363
Bakeries and tortilla (1,534)	343
Sporting and athletic goods (370)	300
Boat building (316)	257
Plastic bags (154)	202
Bakery items (714)	69
Clothing (2,657)	50

Percentage of industry total revenue
■ 4 largest firms ■ next 4 largest firms ■ next 12 largest firms

These industries operate in monopolistic competition. The number of firms in the industry is shown in parentheses after the name of the industry. The red bars show the percentage of industry sales by the 4 largest firms. The blue bars show the percentage of industry sales by the next 4 largest firms, and the orange bars show the percentage of industry sales by the next 12 largest firms. So the entire length of the combined red, blue, and orange bars shows the percentage of industry sales by the 20 largest firms. The Herfindahl-Hirschman Index is shown on the right.

Source of data: Adapted from Statistics Canada, Manufacturing, Construction, and Energy Division.

Price and Output in Monopolistic Competition

SUPPOSE YOU'VE BEEN HIRED BY VF CORPORATION, the firm that owns Nautica Clothing Corporation, to manage the production and marketing of Nautica jackets. Think about the decisions that you must make at Nautica. First, you must decide on the design and quality of jackets and on your marketing program. Second, you must decide on the quantity of jackets to produce and the price at which to sell them.

We'll suppose that Nautica has already made its decisions about design, quality, and marketing and now we'll concentrate on the output and pricing decisions. We'll study quality and marketing decisions in the next section.

For a given quality of jackets and marketing activity, Nautica faces given costs and market conditions. How, given its costs and the demand for its jackets, does Nautica decide the quantity of jackets to produce and the price at which to sell them?

The Firm's Short-Run Output and Price Decision

In the short run, a firm in monopolistic competition makes its output and price decision just like a monopoly firm does. Figure 13.2 illustrates this decision for Nautica jackets.

The demand curve for Nautica jackets is *D*. This demand curve tells us the quantity of Nautica jackets demanded at each price, given the prices of other jackets. It is not the demand curve for jackets in general.

The *MR* curve shows the marginal revenue curve associated with the demand curve for Nautica jackets. It is derived just like the marginal revenue curve of a single-price monopoly that you studied in Chapter 12.

The *ATC* curve and the *MC* curve show the average total cost and the marginal cost of producing Nautica jackets.

Nautica's goal is to maximize its economic profit. To do so, it will produce the output at which marginal revenue equals marginal cost. In Fig. 13.2, this output is 125 jackets a day. Nautica charges the highest price that buyers are willing to pay for this quantity, which is determined by the demand curve. This price is $75 per jacket. When Nautica produces 125 jackets a day, its average total cost is $25 per jacket and it makes an economic profit of $6,250 a day ($50 per jacket

FIGURE 13.2
Economic Profit in the Short Run

Profit is maximized where marginal revenue equals marginal cost. The profit-maximizing quantity is 125 jackets a day. The price of $75 a jacket exceeds the average total cost of $25 a jacket, so the firm makes an economic profit of $50 a jacket. The blue rectangle illustrates economic profit, which equals $6,250 a day ($50 a jacket multiplied by 125 jackets a day).

multiplied by 125 jackets a day). The blue rectangle shows Nautica's economic profit.

Profit Maximizing Might Be Loss Minimizing

Figure 13.2 shows that Nautica is earning a healthy economic profit. But such an outcome is not inevitable. A firm might face a level of demand for its product that is too low for it to earn an economic profit.

Excite@Home was such a firm. Offering high-speed Internet service over the same cable that provides television, Excite@Home hoped to capture a large share of the Internet portal market in competition with AOL, MSN, and a host of other providers.

Figure 13.3 illustrates the situation facing Excite@Home in 2001. The demand curve for its portal service is *D*, the marginal revenue curve is *MR*, the average total cost curve is *ATC*, and the marginal cost curve is *MC*. Excite@Home maximized profit—

FIGURE 13.3

Economic Loss in the Short Run

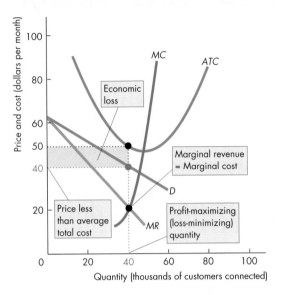

Profit is maximized where marginal revenue equals marginal cost. The loss-minimizing quantity is 40,000 customers. The price of $40 a month is less than the average total cost of $50 a month, so the firm incurs an economic loss of $10 a customer. The red rectangle illustrates the economic loss, which equals $400,000 a month ($10 a customer multiplied by 40,000 customers).

equivalently, it minimized its loss—by producing the output at which marginal revenue equals marginal cost. In Fig. 13.3, this output is 40,000 customers. Excite@Home charged the price that buyers were willing to pay for this quantity, which was determined by the demand curve and which was $40 a month. With 40,000 customers, Excite@Home's average total cost was $50 per customer, so it incurred an economic loss of $400,000 a month ($10 a customer multiplied by 40,000 customers). The red rectangle shows Excite@Home's economic loss.

So far, the firm in monopolistic competition looks like a single-price monopoly. It produces the quantity at which marginal revenue equals marginal cost and then charges the highest price that buyers are willing to pay for that quantity, determined by the demand curve. The key difference between monopoly and monopolistic competition lies in what happens next when firms either make economic profits or incur economic losses.

Long Run: Zero Economic Profit

A firm like Excite@Home is not going to incur an economic loss for long. Eventually, it goes out of business. Also, there is no restriction on entry into monopolistic competition, so if firms in an industry are making economic profits, other firms have an incentive to enter that industry.

As the Gap and other firms start to make jackets similar to jackets made by Nautica, the demand for Nautica jackets decreases. The demand curve for Nautica jackets and the marginal revenue curve shift leftward. And as these curves shift leftward, the profit-maximizing quantity and price fall.

Figure 13.4 shows the long-run equilibrium. The demand curve for Nautica jackets and the marginal revenue curve have shifted leftward. The firm produces 75 jackets a day and sells them for $50 each. At this output level, average total cost is also $50 per jacket.

FIGURE 13.4

Output and Price in the Long Run

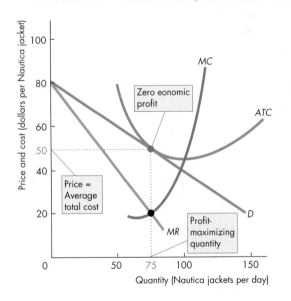

Economic profit encourages entry, which decreases the demand for each firm's product. When the demand curve touches the ATC curve at the quantity at which MR equals MC, the market is in long-run equilibrium. The output that maximizes profit is 75 jackets a day, and the price is $50 per jacket. Average total cost is also $50 per jacket, so economic profit is zero.

So Nautica is making zero economic profit on its jackets. When all the firms in the industry are making zero economic profit, there is no incentive for new firms to enter.

If demand is so low relative to costs that firms incur economic losses, exit will occur. As firms leave an industry, the demand for the products of the remaining firms increases and their demand curves shift rightward. The exit process ends when all the firms in the industry are making zero economic profit.

Monopolistic Competition and Perfect Competition

Figure 13.5 compares monopolistic competition and perfect competition and highlights two key differences between them:

- Excess capacity
- Markup

Excess Capacity A firm has excess capacity if it produces below its efficient scale, which is the quantity at which average total cost is a minimum—the quantity at the bottom of the U-shaped *ATC* curve. In Fig. 13.5, the efficient scale is 100 jackets a day. Nautica (part a) produces 75 Nautica jackets a day and has *excess capacity* of 25 jackets a day. But if all jackets are alike and are produced by firms in perfect competition (part b) each firm produces 100 jackets a day, which is the efficient scale. Average total cost is the lowest possible only in *perfect* competition.

You can see the excess capacity in monopolistic competition all around you. Family restaurants (except for the truly outstanding ones) almost always have some empty tables. You can always get a pizza delivered in less than 30 minutes. It is rare that every pump at a gas station is in use with customers waiting in line. There is always an abundance of realtors ready to help find or sell a home. These industries are examples of monopolistic competition. The firms

---

FIGURE 13.5
Excess Capacity and Markup

(a) Monopolistic competition

(b) Perfect competition

The efficient scale is 100 jackets a day. In monopolistic competition in the long run, because the firm faces a downward-sloping demand curve for its product, the quantity produced is less than the efficient scale and the firm has excess capacity. Price exceeds marginal cost by the amount of the markup.

In contrast, because in perfect competition the demand for each firm's product is perfectly elastic, the quantity produced equals the efficient scale and price equals marginal cost. The firm produces at the least possible cost and there is no markup.

have excess capacity. They could sell more by cutting their prices, but they would then incur losses.

Markup A firm's markup is the amount by which price exceeds marginal cost. Figure 13.5(a) shows Nautica's markup. In perfect competition, price always equals marginal cost and there is no markup. Figure 13.5(b) shows this case. In monopolistic competition, buyers pay a higher price than in perfect competition and also pay more than marginal cost.

Is Monopolistic Competition Efficient?

You've learned that resources are used efficiently when marginal benefit equals marginal cost. You've also learned that price measures marginal benefit. So if the price of a Nautica jacket exceeds the marginal cost of producing it, the quantity of Nautica jackets produced is less than the efficient quantity. And you've just seen that in long-run equilibrium in monopolistic competition, price *does* exceed marginal cost. So is the quantity produced in monopolistic competition less than the efficient quantity?

Making the Relevant Comparison Two economists meet in the street, and one asks the other how her husband is. "Compared to what?" is the quick reply. This bit of economic wit illustrates a key point: Before we can conclude that something needs fixing, we must check out the available alternatives.

The markup that drives a gap between price and marginal cost in monopolistic competition arises from product differentiation. It is because Nautica jackets are not quite the same as jackets from Banana Republic, CK, Diesel, DKNY, Earl Jackets, Gap, Levi, Ralph Lauren, or any of the other dozens of producers of jackets that the demand for Nautica jackets is not perfectly elastic. The only way in which the demand for jackets from Nautica might be perfectly elastic is if there is only one kind of jacket and all firms make it. In this situation, Nautica jackets are indistinguishable from all other jackets. They don't even have identifying labels.

If there was only one kind of jacket, the marginal benefit of jackets would almost certainly be less than it is with variety. People value variety. And people value variety not only because it enables each person to select what he or she likes best but also because it provides an external benefit. Most of us enjoy seeing variety in the choices of others. Contrast a scene from the China of the 1960s, when everyone wore a Mao tunic, with the China of today, where everyone wears the clothes of their own choosing. Or contrast a scene from the Germany of the 1930s, when almost everyone who could afford a car owned a first-generation Volkswagen Beetle, with the world of today with its enormous variety of styles and types of automobiles.

If people value variety, why don't we see infinite variety? The answer is that variety is costly. Each different variety of any product must be designed, and then customers must be informed about it. These initial costs of design and marketing—called setup costs—mean that some varieties that are too close to others already available are just not worth creating.

The Bottom Line Product variety is both valued and costly. The efficient degree of product variety is the one for which the marginal benefit of product variety equals its marginal cost. The loss that arises because the marginal benefit of one more unit of a given variety exceeds marginal cost is offset by a gain that arises from having an efficient degree of product variety. So compared to the alternative—complete product uniformity—monopolistic competition is probably efficient.

REVIEW QUIZ

1 How does a firm in monopolistic competition decide how much to produce and at what price to offer its product for sale?
2 Why can a firm in monopolistic competition earn an economic profit only in the short run?
3 Why do firms in monopolistic competition operate with excess capacity?
4 Why is there a price markup over marginal cost in monopolistic competition?
5 Is monopolistic competition efficient?

myeconlab Study Plan 13.2

You've seen how the firm in monopolistic competition determines its output and price in both the short run and the long run when the firm produces a given product and undertakes a given marketing effort. But how does the firm *choose* its product quality and marketing effort? We'll now study these decisions.

Product Development and Marketing

WHEN WE STUDIED NAUTICA'S OUTPUT AND price decisions, we assumed that it had already made its product quality and marketing decisions. We're now going to study these decisions and the impact they have on the firm's output, price, and economic profit.

Innovation and Product Development

The prospect of new firms entering the industry keeps firms in monopolistic competition on their toes!

To enjoy economic profits, firms in monopolistic competition must be continually seeking ways of keeping one step ahead of imitators—other firms who imitate the success of the economically profitable firms.

One major way of trying to maintain economic profit is for a firm to seek out new products that will provide it with a competitive edge, even if only temporarily. A firm that introduces a new and differentiated product faces a less elastic demand curve and is able to increase its price and earn an economic profit. Eventually, imitators will make close substitutes for the innovative product and compete away the economic profit arising from an initial advantage. So to restore economic profit, the firm must again innovate.

Cost Versus Benefit of Product Innovation The decision to innovate is based on the same type of profit-maximizing calculation that you've already studied. Innovation and product development are costly activities, but they also bring in additional revenues. The firm must balance the cost and benefit at the margin. At a low level of product development, the marginal revenue from a better product exceeds the marginal cost. When the marginal dollar of product development expenditure (the marginal cost of product development) brings in a dollar of additional revenue (the marginal benefit of product development), the firm is spending the profit-maximizing amount on product development.

For example, when Eidos Interactive released "Lara Croft Tomb Raider: The Angel of Darkness," it was probably not the best game that Eidos could have created. But it was a game with features whose marginal benefit—and consumers' willingness to pay—equalled the marginal cost of those features.

Efficiency and Product Innovation Is product innovation an efficient activity? Does it benefit the consumer? There are two views about the answers to these questions. One view is that monopolistic competition brings to market many improved products that give great benefits to the consumer. Clothing, kitchen and other household appliances, computers, computer programs, cars, and many other products keep getting better every year, and the consumer benefits from these improved products.

But many so-called improvements amount to little more than changing the appearance of a product or giving a different look to the packaging. In these cases, there is little objective benefit to the consumer.

But regardless of whether a product improvement is real or imagined, its value to the consumer is its marginal benefit, which equals the amount the consumer is willing to pay. In other words, the value of product improvements is the increase in price that the consumer is willing to pay. The marginal benefit to the producer is marginal revenue, which in equilibrium equals marginal cost. Because price exceeds marginal cost in monopolistic competition, product improvement is not pushed to its efficient level.

Advertising

Designing and developing products that are actually different from those of its competitors helps a firm achieve some product differentiation. But firms also attempt to create a consumer perception of product differentiation even when actual differences are small. Advertising and packaging are the principal means firms use to achieve this end. An American Express card is a different product from a Visa card. But the actual differences are not the main ones that American Express emphasizes in its marketing. The deeper message is that if you use an American Express card, you can be like Tiger Woods (or some other high-profile successful person).

Advertising Expenditures Firms in monopolistic competition incur huge costs to ensure that buyers appreciate and value the differences between their own products and those of their competitors. So a large proportion of the price we pay for a good covers the cost of selling it. And this proportion is increasing. Advertising in newspapers and magazines and on radio, television, and the Internet is the main selling cost. But it is not the only one. Selling costs include the cost of shopping malls that look like movie sets, glossy catalogues and brochures, and the salaries, air-fares, and hotel bills of salespeople.

The total scale of advertising costs is hard to estimate, but some components can be measured. A survey conducted by a commercial agency suggests that for cleaning supplies and toys, around 15 percent of the price of one of these items is spent on advertising. Figure 13.6 shows estimates for some industries.

For the North American economy as a whole, some 20,000 advertising agencies employ more than 200,000 people and have sales of $45 billion. But these numbers are only part of the total cost of advertising because firms have their own internal advertising departments, the costs of which we can only guess.

Advertising expenditures and other selling costs affect the profits of firms in two ways. They increase costs, and they change demand. Let's look at these effects.

Selling Costs and Total Cost Selling costs such as advertising expenditures increase the costs of a monopolistically competitive firm above those of a

perfectly competitive firm or a monopoly. Advertising costs and other selling costs are fixed costs. They do not vary as total output varies. So, just like fixed production costs, advertising costs per unit decrease as production increases.

Figure 13.7 shows how selling costs and advertising expenditures change a firm's average total cost. The blue curve shows the average total cost of production. The red curve shows the firm's average total cost of production plus advertising. The height of the red area between the two curves shows the average fixed cost of advertising. The *total* cost of advertising is fixed. But the *average* cost of advertising decreases as output increases.

The figure shows that if advertising increases the quantity sold by a large enough amount, it can lower average total cost. For example, if the quantity sold increases from 25 jackets a day with no advertising to 100 jackets a day with advertising, average total cost falls from $60 to $40 a jacket. The reason is that although the *total* fixed cost has increased, the greater fixed cost is spread over a greater output, so average total cost decreases.

FIGURE 13.6
Advertising Expenditures

Advertising expenditures are a large part of the total price of cleaning supplies, toys, confectionery, and cosmetics.

Source of data: From Schoenfeld & Associates, Lincolnwood, IL. Reported at www.toolkit.cch.com/text/p03_7006.asp.

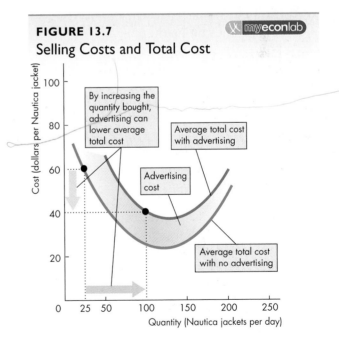

FIGURE 13.7
Selling Costs and Total Cost

Selling costs such as the cost of advertising are fixed costs. When added to the average total cost of production, selling costs increase average total cost by a greater amount at small outputs than at large outputs. If advertising enables sales to increase from 25 jackets a day to 100 jackets a day, average total cost *falls* from $60 to $40 a jacket.

Selling Costs and Demand Advertising and other selling efforts change the demand for a firm's product. But how? Does demand increase or does it decrease? The most natural answer is that advertising increases demand. By informing people about the quality of its products or by persuading people to switch from the products of other firms, a firm might expect to increase the demand for its own products.

But all firms in monopolistic competition advertise. And all seek to persuade customers that they have the best deal. If advertising enables a firm to survive, it might increase the number of firms in the market. And to the extent that it increases the number of firms, it *decreases* the demand for any one firm's product. It also makes the demand for any one firm's product more elastic. So advertising can end up not only lowering average total cost but also lowering the markup and the price.

Figure 13.8 illustrates this possible effect of advertising. In part (a), with no advertising, the demand for Nautica jackets is not very elastic. Profit is maximized at 75 jackets per day, and the markup is large. In part

(b), advertising, which is a fixed cost, increases average total cost from ATC_0 to ATC_1 but leaves marginal cost unchanged at MC. Demand becomes much more elastic, the profit-maximizing quantity increases, and the markup shrinks.

Using Advertising to Signal Quality

Some advertising, such as the Tiger Woods American Express card ads on television and in glossy magazines or the expensive Coke and Pepsi ads, seems hard to understand. There doesn't seem to be any concrete information about a credit card in the glistening smile of a golfer. And surely everyone knows about Coke and Pepsi. What is the gain from pouring millions of dollars a month into advertising these well-known colas?

One answer is that advertising is a signal to the consumer of a high-quality product. A **signal** is an action taken by an informed person (or firm) to send a message to uninformed people. Think about two colas:

FIGURE 13.8
Advertising and the Markup

(a) No firms advertise

With no firms advertising, demand is low and not very elastic. The profit-maximizing output is small, the markup is large, and the price is high.

(b) All firms advertise

Advertising increases average total cost and shifts the *ATC* curve upward from ATC_0 to ATC_1. With all firms advertising, the demand for each firm's product becomes more elastic. Output increases, the price falls, and the markup shrinks.

Coke and Oke. Oke knows that its cola is not very good and that its taste varies a lot depending on which cheap batch of unsold cola it happens to buy each week. So Oke knows that while it could get a lot of people to try Oke by advertising, they would all quickly discover what a poor product it is and switch back to the cola they bought before. Coke, in contrast, knows that its product has a high-quality consistent taste and that once consumers have tried it, there is a good chance they'll never drink anything else. On the basis of this reasoning, Oke doesn't advertise but Coke does. And Coke spends a lot of money to make a big splash.

Cola drinkers who see Coke's splashy ads know that the firm would not spend so much money advertising if its product were not truly good. So consumers reason that Coke is indeed a really good product. The flashy expensive ad has signalled that Coke is really good without saying anything about Coke.

Notice that if advertising is a signal, it doesn't need any specific product information. It just needs to be expensive and hard to miss. That's what a lot of advertising looks like. So the signalling theory of advertising predicts much of the advertising that we see.

Brand Names

Many firms create and spend a lot of money promoting a brand name. Why? What benefit does a brand name bring to justify the sometimes high cost of establishing it?

The basic answer is that a brand name provides information about the quality of a product to consumers and an incentive to the producer to achieve a high and consistent quality standard.

To see how a brand name helps the consumer, think about how you use brand names to get information about quality. You're on a road trip, and it is time to find a place to spend the night. You see roadside advertisements for Holiday Inn and Embassy Suites and for Joe's Motel and Annie's Driver Stop. You know about Holiday Inn and Embassy Suites because you've stayed in them before. And you've seen their advertisements. You know what to expect from them. You have no information at all about Joe's and Annie's. They might be better than the lodging you do know about, but without that knowledge, you're not going to chance them. You use the brand name as information and stay at Holiday Inn.

This same story explains why a brand name provides an incentive to achieve high and consistent quality. Because no one would know whether they were

offering a high standard of service, Joe's and Annie's have no incentive to do so. But equally, because everyone expects a given standard of service from Holiday Inn, a failure to meet a customer's expectation would almost surely lose that customer to a competitor. So Holiday Inn has a strong incentive to deliver what it promises in the advertising that creates its brand name.

Efficiency of Advertising and Brand Names

To the extent that advertising and brand names provide consumers with information about the precise nature of product differences and about product quality, they benefit the consumer and enable a better product choice to be made. But the opportunity cost of the additional information must be weighed against the gain to the consumer.

The final verdict on the efficiency of monopolistic competition is ambiguous. In some cases, the gains from extra product variety unquestionably offset the selling costs and the extra cost arising from excess capacity. The tremendous varieties of books and magazines, clothing, food, and drinks are examples of such gains. It is less easy to see the gains from being able to buy a brand-name drug that has a chemical composition identical to that of a cheaper generic alternative. But many people do willingly pay more for the brand-name alternative.

REVIEW QUIZ

1 What are the two main ways, other than by adjusting price, in which a firm in monopolistic competition competes with other firms?

2 Why might product innovation and development be efficient and why might it be inefficient?

3 How does a firm's advertising expenditure influence its cost curves? Does average total cost increase or decrease?

4 How does a firm's advertising expenditure influence the demand for its product? Does demand increase or decrease?

5 Why is it difficult to determine whether monopolistic competition is efficient or inefficient? What is your opinion about the bottom line and why?

X myeconlab **Study Plan 13.3**

What Is Oligopoly?

OLIGOPOLY, LIKE MONOPOLISTIC COMPETITION, lies between perfect competition and monopoly. The firms in oligopoly might produce an identical product and compete only on price, or they might produce a differentiated product and compete on price, product quality, and marketing. **Oligopoly** is a market structure in which

- Natural or legal barriers prevent the entry of new firms.
- A small number of firms compete.

Barriers to Entry

Either natural or legal barriers to entry can create oligopoly. You saw in Chapter 12 how economies of scale and market demand form a natural barrier to entry that can create a *natural monopoly*. These same factors can create a natural oligopoly.

Figure 13.9 illustrates two natural oligopolies. The demand curve, D (in both parts of the figure), shows the demand for taxi rides in a town. If the average total cost curve of a taxi company is ATC_1 in part (a), the market is a natural **duopoly**—an oligopoly market with two firms. You can probably see some examples of duopoly where you live. Some cities have only two taxi companies, two car rental firms, two copy centres, or two bookstores.

The lowest price at which the firm would remain in business is $10 a ride. At that price, the quantity of rides demanded is 60 a day, the quantity that can be provided by just two firms. There is no room in this market for three firms. But if there were only one firm, it would earn an economic profit and a second firm would enter to take some of the business and economic profit.

If the average total cost curve of a taxi company is ATC_2 in part (b), the efficient scale of one firm is 20 rides a day. This market is large enough for three firms.

A legal oligopoly arises when a legal barrier to entry protects the small number of firms in a market. A city might license two taxi firms or two bus companies, for example, even though the combination of market demand and economies of scale leaves room for more than two firms.

FIGURE 13.9
Natural Oligopoly

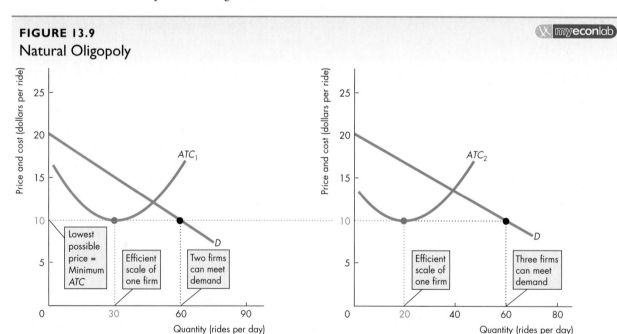

(a) Natural duopoly

The lowest possible price is $10 a ride, which is the minimum average total cost. When a firm produces 30 rides a day, the efficient scale, two firms can satisfy the market demand. This natural oligopoly has two firms—a natural duopoly.

(b) Natural oligopoly with three firms

When the efficient scale of one firm is 20 rides per day, three firms can satisfy the market demand at the lowest possible price. This natural oligopoly has three firms.

Small Number of Firms

Because barriers to entry exist, oligopoly consists of a small number of firms each of which has a large share of the market. Such firms are interdependent and they face a temptation to collude to increase their joint economic profit.

Interdependence With a small number of firms in a market, each firm's actions influence the profits of the other firms. To see how, suppose you run one of the three gas stations in a small town. If you cut your price, your market share increases, and your profits might increase too. But the market share and profits of the other two firms fall, so they most likely cut their prices too. If they do cut their prices, your market share and profit take a tumble. So before deciding to cut your price, you must predict how the other firms will react and take into account the effects of those reactions on your own profit. You are interdependent.

Temptation to Collude When a small number of firms share a market, they can increase their profits by forming a cartel and acting like a monopoly. A **cartel** is a group of firms acting together—colluding—to limit output, raise price, and increase economic profit. Cartels are illegal, but they do operate in some markets. But for reasons that you'll discover in this chapter, cartels tend to break down.

Examples of Oligopoly

Figure 13.10 shows some examples of oligopoly. Identifying oligopoly is the flip side of identifying monopolistic competition. But the borderline between the two market types is hard to pin down. As a practical matter, we try to identify oligopoly by looking at the four-firm concentration ratio and the Herfindahl-Hirschman Index, qualified with other information about the geographical scope of the market and barriers to entry. The HHI that divides oligopoly from monopolistic competition is generally taken to be 1,800. An HHI below 1,800 is usually an example of monopolistic competition, and a market in which the HHI exceeds 1,800 is usually an example of oligopoly.

REVIEW QUIZ

1 What are the two distinguishing features of oligopoly?
2 Why are firms in oligopoly interdependent?
3 Why do firms in oligopoly face a temptation to collude?
4 Think of some examples of oligopolies that you buy from.

myeconlab **Study Plan 13.4**

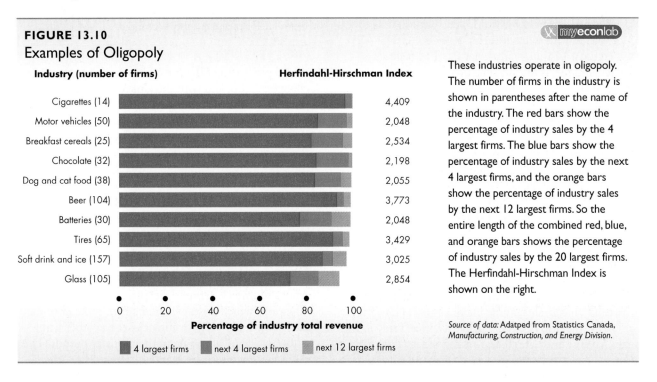

FIGURE 13.10
Examples of Oligopoly

myeconlab

Industry (number of firms)	Herfindahl-Hirschman Index
Cigarettes (14)	4,409
Motor vehicles (50)	2,048
Breakfast cereals (25)	2,534
Chocolate (32)	2,198
Dog and cat food (38)	2,055
Beer (104)	3,773
Batteries (30)	2,048
Tires (65)	3,429
Soft drink and ice (157)	3,025
Glass (105)	2,854

Percentage of industry total revenue: 0   20   40   60   80   100

■ 4 largest firms   ■ next 4 largest firms   ■ next 12 largest firms

These industries operate in oligopoly. The number of firms in the industry is shown in parentheses after the name of the industry. The red bars show the percentage of industry sales by the 4 largest firms. The blue bars show the percentage of industry sales by the next 4 largest firms, and the orange bars show the percentage of industry sales by the next 12 largest firms. So the entire length of the combined red, blue, and orange bars shows the percentage of industry sales by the 20 largest firms. The Herfindahl-Hirschman Index is shown on the right.

Source of data: Adatped from Statistics Canada, *Manufacturing, Construction, and Energy Division.*

Two Traditional Oligopoly Models

IN OLIGOPOLY, THE QUANTITY SOLD BY ANY ONE firm depends on that firm's price *and* on the other firms' prices and quantities sold. If you run one of the three gas stations in a small town, you know that you can't ignore the response of your competitor's to your price decisions. But how will your competitors respond? If you cut your price, will they cut their price too? And if you raise your price, will they follow you with their own price rise? Or will they hold their price and leave you to lose market share? Before deciding to raise or lower your price, you must predict how the other firms will react and attempt to calculate the effects of those reactions on your own profit.

Several models have been developed to explain the prices and quantities in oligopoly markets. But no one theory has been found that can explain all the different types of behaviour that we observe in such markets. The models fall into two broad groups: traditional models and game theory models. We'll look at examples of both, starting with two traditional models.

The Kinked Demand Curve Model

The kinked demand curve model of oligopoly is based on the assumption that each firm believes that if it raises its price, others will not follow, but if it cuts its price, other firms will cut theirs.

Figure 13.11 illustrates what the firm believes is the demand for its output. The demand curve (D) has a kink at the current price, P, and quantity, Q. At prices above P, a small price rise brings a big decrease in the quantity sold because other firms do not raise their prices and the firm believes that it loses market share. At prices below P, even a large price cut brings only a small increase in the quantity sold because other firms match the price cut and the firm gets no price advantage over its competitors.

The kink in the demand curve creates a break in the marginal revenue curve (MR). To maximize profit, the firm produces the quantity at which marginal cost equals marginal revenue. That quantity, Q, is where the marginal cost curve passes through the gap AB in the marginal revenue curve. If marginal cost fluctuates between A and B, such as the marginal cost curves MC_0 and MC_1, the firm does not change its price. Only if marginal cost fluctuates outside the range AB does the firm change its price. So the kinked demand curve

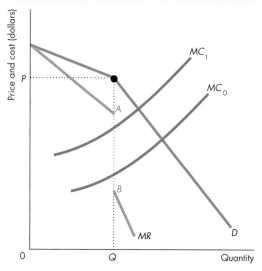

FIGURE 13.11   myeconlab
The Kinked Demand Curve Model

The price in an oligopoly market is P. Each firm believes that the demand for its output is the demand curve D. At prices above P, a small price rise brings a big decrease in the quantity sold because other firms do not raise their prices. At prices below P, even a big price cut brings only a small increase in the quantity sold because other firms cut their prices. Because the demand curve is kinked, the marginal revenue curve, MR, has a gap AB. Profit is maximized by producing Q. Marginal cost changes inside the range AB leave the price and quantity unchanged.

model predicts that the price is insensitive to small cost changes. A problem with the kinked demand curve model is that the firm's beliefs about the demand for its output are not always correct and the firm can figure that out. If marginal cost increases by enough to cause the firm to increase its price and if all firms experience the same increase in marginal cost, all firms will increase their prices together. The firm's belief that others will not join it in a price rise is incorrect. A firm that bases its actions on beliefs that are wrong does not maximize profit and might even incur an economic loss.

Dominant Firm Oligopoly

A second traditional model explains a dominant firm oligopoly, which arises when one firm—the dominant firm—has a big cost advantage over the other firms and produces a large part of the industry output. The dominant firm sets the market price and the other

FIGURE 13.12
A Dominant Firm Oligopoly

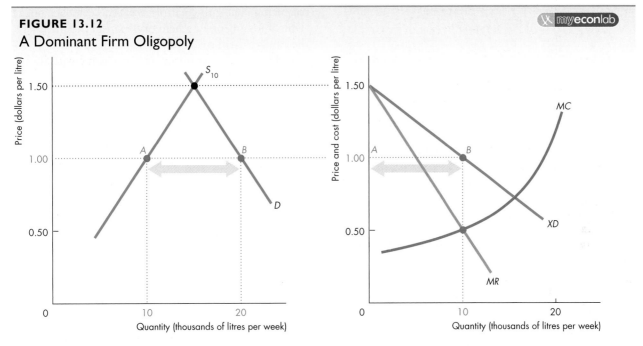

(a) Ten small firms and market demand

The market demand curve for gas in a city is *D* in part (a). There are 10 small competitive firms that together have a supply curve of S_{10}. In addition, there is 1 large firm, Big-G, shown in part (b). Big-G faces the demand curve *XD*, determined as the market demand *D* minus the supply of the 10 small firms S_{10} —the demand that is not satisfied by the small

(b) Big-G's price and output decision

firms. Big-G's marginal revenue is *MR*, and marginal cost is *MC*. Big-G sets its output to maximize profit by equating marginal cost, *MC*, and marginal revenue, *MR*. This output is 10,000 litres per week. The price at which Big-G can sell this quantity is $1 a litre. The 10 small firms take this price, and each firm sells 1,000 litres per week, point *A* in part (a).

firms are price takers. Examples of dominant firm oligopoly are a large gasoline retailer or a big video rental store that dominates its local market.

To see how a dominant firm oligopoly works, suppose that 11 firms operate gas stations in a city. Big-G is the dominant firm. Figure 13.12 shows the market for gas in this city. In part (a), the demand curve *D* tells us the total quantity of gas demanded in the city at each price. The supply curve S_{10} is the supply curve of the 10 small suppliers. Part (b) shows the situation facing Big-G. Its marginal cost curve is *MC*. Big-G faces the demand curve *XD*, and its marginal revenue curve is *MR*. The demand curve *XD* shows the excess demand not met by the 10 small firms. For example, at a price of $1 a litre, the quantity demanded is 20,000 litres, the quantity supplied by the 10 small firms is 10,000 litres, and the excess quantity demanded is 10,000 litres, measured by the distance *AB* in both parts of the figure. To maximize profit, Big-G operates like a monopoly. It sells 10,000 litres a week, where marginal revenue equals marginal

cost, for a price of $1 a litre. The 10 small firms take the price of $1 a litre. They behave just like firms in perfect competition. The quantity of gas demanded in the entire city at $1 a litre is 20,000 litres, as shown in part (a). Of this amount, Big-G sells 10,000 litres and the 10 small firms each sell 1,000 litres.

REVIEW QUIZ

1 What does the kinked demand curve model predict and why must it sometimes make a prediction that contradicts its basic assumption?

2 Do you think a market with a dominant firm is in long-run equilibrium? Explain why or why not.

 Study Plan 13.5

The traditional models don't enable us to understand all oligopoly markets and we're now going to study some newer models based on game theory.

Oligopoly Games

ECONOMISTS THINK ABOUT OLIGOPOLY AS A GAME, and to study oligopoly markets they use a set of tools called **game theory**. Game theory is a tool for studying *strategic behaviour*—behaviour that takes into account the expected behaviour of others and the recognition of mutual interdependence. Game theory was invented by John von Neumann in 1937 and extended by von Neumann and Oskar Morgenstern in 1944. Today, it is one of the major research fields in economics.

Game theory seeks to understand oligopoly as well as other forms of economic, political, social, and even biological rivalries by using a method of analysis specifically designed to understand games of all types, including the familiar games of everyday life. We will begin our study of game theory and its application to the behaviour of firms by thinking about familiar games.

What Is a Game?

What is a game? At first thought, the question seems silly. After all, there are many different games. There are ball games and parlor games, games of chance and games of skill. But what is it about all these different activities that make them games? What do all these games have in common? All games share four features:

- Rules
- Strategies
- Payoffs
- Outcome

Let's see how these common features of games apply to a game called "the prisoners' dilemma." This game, it turns out, captures some of the essential features of oligopoly, and it gives a good illustration of how game theory works and how it generates predictions.

The Prisoners' Dilemma

Art and Bob have been caught red-handed, stealing a car. Facing airtight cases, they will receive a sentence of two years each for their crime. During his interviews with the two prisoners, the Crown attorney begins to suspect that he has stumbled onto the two people who were responsible for a multimillion-dollar bank robbery some months earlier. But this is just a suspicion. The Crown attorney has no evidence on which he can convict them of the greater crime unless he can get them to confess. The district attorney decides to make the prisoners play a game with the following rules.

Rules Each prisoner (player) is placed in a separate room and cannot communicate with the other prisoner. Each is told that he is suspected of having carried out the bank robbery and that

1. If they both confess to the larger crime, each will receive a sentence of 3 years for both crimes.
2. If he alone confesses and his accomplice does not, he will receive an even shorter sentence of 1 year while his accomplice will receive a 10-year sentence.

Strategies In game theory, **strategies** are all the possible actions of each player. Art and Bob each have two possible actions:

1. Confess to the bank robbery.
2. Deny having committed the bank robbery.

Payoffs Because there are two players, each with two strategies, there are four possible outcomes:

1. Both confess.
2. Both deny.
3. Art confesses and Bob denies.
4. Bob confesses and Art denies.

Each prisoner can work out exactly what happens to him—his *payoff*—in each of these four situations. We can tabulate the four possible payoffs for each of the prisoners in what is called a payoff matrix for the game. A **payoff matrix** is a table that shows the payoffs for every possible action by each player for every possible action by each other player.

Table 13.1 shows a payoff matrix for Art and Bob. The squares show the payoffs for each prisoner—the red triangle in each square shows Art's and the blue triangle shows Bob's. If both prisoners confess (top left), each gets a prison term of 3 years. If Bob confesses but Art denies (top right), Art gets a 10-year sentence and Bob gets a 1-year sentence. If Art confesses and Bob denies (bottom left), Art gets a 1-year sentence and Bob gets a 10-year sentence. Finally, if both of them deny (bottom right), neither can be convicted of the bank robbery charge but both are sentenced for the car theft—a 2-year sentence.

Outcome The choices of both players determine the outcome of the game. To predict that outcome, we use an equilibrium idea proposed by John Nash of Princeton University (who received the Nobel Prize for Economic Science in 1994 and was the subject of the 2001 movie *A Beautiful Mind*). In **Nash equilibrium**, player *A* takes the best possible action given the action of player *B* and player *B* takes the best possible action given the action of player *A*.

In the case of the prisoners' dilemma, the Nash equilibrium occurs when Art makes his best choice given Bob's choice and when Bob makes his best choice given Art's choice.

To find the Nash equilibrium, we compare all the possible outcomes associated with each choice and eliminate those that are dominated—that are not as good as some other choice. Let's find the Nash equilibrium for the prisoners' dilemma game.

Finding the Nash Equilibrium Look at the situation from Art's point of view. If Bob confesses, Art's best action is to confess because in that case, he is sentenced to 3 years rather than 10 years. If Bob does not confess, Art's best action is still to confess because in that case he receives 1 year rather than 2 years. So Art's best action is to confess.

Now look at the situation from Bob's point of view. If Art confesses, Bob's best action is to confess because in that case, he is sentenced to 3 years rather than 10 years. If Art does not confess, Bob's best action is still to confess because in that case, he receives 1 year rather than 2 years. So Bob's best action is to confess.

Because each player's best action is to confess, each does confess, each gets a 3-year prison term, and the Crown attorney has solved the bank robbery. This is the Nash equilibrium of the game.

The Dilemma Now that you have found the solution to the prisoners' dilemma, you can better see the dilemma. The dilemma arises as each prisoner contemplates the consequences of denying. Each prisoner knows that if both of them deny, they will receive only a 2-year sentence for stealing the car. But neither has any way of knowing that his accomplice will deny. Each poses the following questions: Should I deny and rely on my accomplice to deny so that we will both get only 2 years? Or should I confess in the hope of getting just 1 year (provided that my accomplice denies) knowing that if my accomplice does confess, we will both get 3 years in

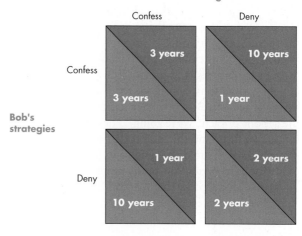

TABLE 13.1 Prisoners' Dilemma Payoff Matrix

Each square shows the payoffs for the two players, Art and Bob, for each possible pair of actions. In each square, the red triangle shows Art's payoff and the blue triangle shows Bob's. For example, if both confess, the payoffs are in the top left square. The equilibrium of the game is for both players to confess and each gets a 3-year sentence.

prison? The dilemma is resolved by finding the equilibrium of the game.

A Bad Outcome For the prisoners, the equilibrium of the game, with each confessing, is not the best outcome. If neither of them confesses, each gets only 2 years for the lesser crime. Isn't there some way in which this better outcome can be achieved? It seems that there is not, because the players cannot communicate with each other. Each player can put himself in the other player's place, and so each player can figure out that there is a best strategy for each of them. The prisoners are indeed in a dilemma. Each knows that he can serve 2 years only if he can trust the other to deny. But each prisoner also knows that it is not in the best interest of the other to deny. So each prisoner knows that he must confess, thereby delivering a bad outcome for both.

The firms in an oligopoly are in a similar situation to Art and Bob in the prisoners' dilemma game. Let's see how we can use this game to understand oligopoly.

An Oligopoly Price-Fixing Game

We can use game theory and a game like the prisoners' dilemma to understand price fixing, price wars, and other aspects of the behaviour of firms in oligopoly. We'll begin with a price-fixing game.

To understand price fixing, we're going to study the special case of duopoly—an oligopoly with two firms. Duopoly is easier to study than oligopoly with three or more firms, and it captures the essence of all oligopoly situations. Somehow, the two firms must share the market. And how they share it depends on the actions of each. We're going to describe the costs of the two firms and the market demand for the item they produce. We're then going to see how game theory helps us to predict the prices charged and the quantities produced by the two firms in a duopoly.

Cost and Demand Conditions Two firms, Trick and Gear, produce switchgears. They have identical costs. Figure 13.13(a) shows their average total cost curve (*ATC*) and marginal cost curve (*MC*). Figure 13.13(b) shows the market demand curve for switchgears (*D*). The two firms produce identical switchgears, so one firm's switchgear is a perfect substitute for the other's. So the market price of each firm's product is identical. The quantity demanded depends on that price—the higher the price, the smaller is the quantity demanded.

This industry is a natural duopoly. Two firms can produce this good at a lower cost than either one firm or three firms can. For each firm, average total cost is at its minimum when production is 3,000 units a week. And when price equals minimum average total cost, the total quantity demanded is 6,000 units a week. So two firms can just produce that quantity.

Collusion We'll suppose that Trick and Gear enter into a collusive agreement. A **collusive agreement** is an agreement between two (or more) producers to form a cartel to restrict output, raise the price, and increase profits. Such an agreement is illegal in Canada and is undertaken in secret. The strategies that firms in a cartel can pursue are to

- Comply
- Cheat

A firm that complies carries out the agreement. A firm that cheats breaks the agreement to its own benefit and to the cost of the other firm.

Because each firm has two strategies, there are four possible combinations of actions for the firms:

1. Both firms comply.
2. Both firms cheat.
3. Trick complies and Gear cheats.
4. Gear complies and Trick cheats.

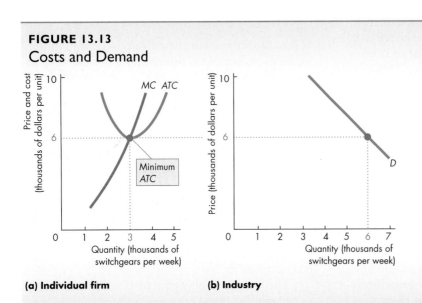

FIGURE 13.13
Costs and Demand

(a) Individual firm

(b) Industry

The average total cost curve for each firm is *ATC*, and the marginal cost curve is *MC* (part a). Minimum average total cost is $6,000 a unit, and it occurs at a production of 3,000 units a week.

Part (b) shows the market demand curve. At a price of $6,000, the quantity demanded is 6,000 units per week. The two firms can produce this output at the lowest possible average total cost. If the market had one firm, it would be profitable for another to enter. If the market had three firms, one would exit. There is room for only two firms in this industry. It is a natural duopoly.

Colluding to Maximize Profits Let's work out the payoffs to the two firms if they collude to make the maximum profit for the cartel by acting like a monopoly. The calculations that the two firms perform are the same calculations that a monopoly performs. (You can refresh your memory of these calculations by looking at Chapter 12, pp. 268–269.) The only thing that the duopolists must do beyond what a monopolist does is to agree on how much of the total output each of them will produce.

Figure 13.14 shows the price and quantity that maximize industry profit for the duopolists. Part (a) shows the situation for each firm, and part (b) shows the situation for the industry as a whole. The curve labelled MR is the industry marginal revenue curve. This marginal revenue curve is like that of a single-price monopoly (Chapter 12, p. 266). The curve labelled MC_I is the industry marginal cost curve if each firm produces the same level of output. That curve is constructed by adding together the outputs of the two firms at each level of marginal cost. That is, at each level of marginal cost, industry output is twice the output of each individual firm. Thus the curve MC_I in part (b) is twice as far to the right as the curve MC in part (a).

To maximize industry profit, the duopolists agree to restrict output to the rate that makes the industry marginal cost and marginal revenue equal. That output rate, as shown in part (b), is 4,000 units a week.

The highest price for which the 4,000 switchgears can be sold is $9,000 each. Trick and Gear agree to charge this price.

To hold the price at $9,000 a unit, production must be not exceed 4,000 units a week. So Trick and Gear must agree on production levels for each of them that total 4,000 units a week. Let's suppose that they agree to split the market equally so that each firm produces 2,000 switchgears a week. Because the firms are identical, this division is the most likely.

The average total cost (ATC) of producing 2,000 switchgears a week is $8,000, so the profit per unit is $1,000 and economic profit is $2 million (2,000 units × $1,000 per unit). The economic profit of each firm is represented by the blue rectangle in Fig. 13.14(a).

We have just described one possible outcome for a duopoly game: The two firms collude to produce the monopoly profit-maximizing output and divide that output equally between themselves. From the industry point of view, this solution is identical to a monopoly. A duopoly that operates in this way is indistinguishable from a monopoly. The economic profit that is made by a monopoly is the maximum total profit that can be made by colluding duopolists.

But with price greater than marginal cost, either firm might think of trying to increase profit by cheating on the agreement and producing more than the agreed amount. Let's see what happens if one of the firms does cheat in this way.

FIGURE 13.14
Colluding to Make Monopoly Profits

(a) Individual firm   (b) Industry

The industry marginal cost curve, MC_I in part (b), is the horizontal sum of the two firms' marginal cost curves, MC in part (a). The industry marginal revenue curve is MR. To maximize profit, the firms produce 4,000 units a week (the quantity at which marginal revenue equals marginal cost). They sell that output for $9,000 a unit. Each firm produces 2,000 units a week. Average total cost is $8,000 a unit, so each firm makes an economic profit of $2 million (blue rectangle)—2,000 units multiplied by $1,000 profit a unit.

One Firm Cheats on a Collusive Agreement To set the stage for cheating on their agreement, Trick convinces Gear that demand has decreased and that it cannot sell 2,000 units a week. Trick tells Gear that it plans to cut its price in order to sell the agreed 2,000 units each week. Because the two firms produce an identical product, Gear matches Trick's price cut but continues to produce 2,000 units a week.

In fact, there has been no decrease in demand. Trick plans to increase output, which it knows will lower the price, and Trick wants to ensure that Gear's output remains at the agreed level.

Figure 13.15 illustrates the consequences of Trick's cheating. Part (a) shows Gear (the complier); part (b) shows Trick (the cheat); and part (c) shows the industry as a whole. Suppose that Trick increases output to 3,000 units a week. If Gear sticks to the agreement to produce only 2,000 units a week, total output is 5,000 a week, and given demand in part (c), the price falls to $7,500 a unit.

Gear continues to produce 2,000 units a week at a cost of $8,000 a unit and incurs a loss of $500 a unit, or $1 million a week. This economic loss is represented by the red rectangle in part (a). Trick produces 3,000 units a week at an average total cost of $6,000 each.

With a price of $7,500, Trick makes a profit of $1,500 a unit and therefore an economic profit of $4.5 million. This economic profit is the blue rectangle in part (b).

We've now described a second possible outcome for the duopoly game: One of the firms cheats on the collusive agreement. In this case, the industry output is larger than the monopoly output and the industry price is lower than the monopoly price. The total economic profit made by the industry is also smaller than the monopoly's economic profit. Trick (the cheat) makes an economic profit of $4.5 million, and Gear (the complier) incurs an economic loss of $1 million. The industry makes an economic profit of $3.5 million. Thus the industry profit is $0.5 million less than the economic profit a monopoly would make. But the profit is distributed unevenly. Trick makes a bigger economic profit than it would under the collusive agreement, while Gear incurs an economic loss.

A similar outcome would arise if Gear cheated and Trick complied with the agreement. The industry profit and price would be the same, but in this case, Gear (the cheat) would make an economic profit of $4.5 million and Trick (the complier) would incur an economic loss of $1 million.

Let's next see what happens if both firms cheat.

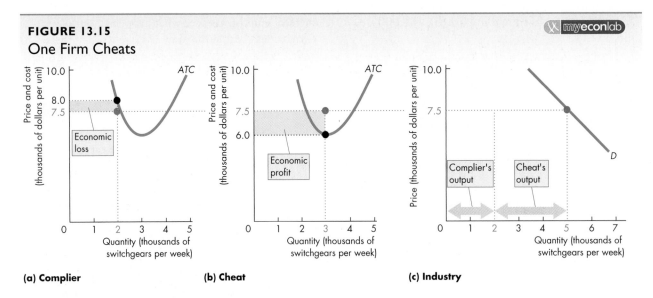

FIGURE 13.15
One Firm Cheats

(a) Complier

(b) Cheat

(c) Industry

One firm, shown in part (a), complies with the agreement and produces 2,000 units. The other firm, shown in part (b), cheats on the agreement and increases its output to 3,000 units. Given the market demand curve, shown in part (c), and with a total production of 5,000 units a week, the price falls to $7,500. At this price, the complier in part (a) incurs an economic loss of $1 million ($500 per unit × 2,000 units), shown by the red rectangle. In part (b), the cheat makes an economic profit of $4.5 million ($1,500 per unit × 3,000 units), shown by the blue rectangle.

Both Firms Cheat Suppose that both firms cheat and that each firm behaves like the cheating firm that we have just analyzed. Each tells the other that it is unable to sell its output at the going price and that it plans to cut its price. But because both firms cheat, each will propose a successively lower price. As long as price exceeds marginal cost, each firm has an incentive to increase its production—to cheat. Only when price equals marginal cost is there no further incentive to cheat. This situation arises when the price has reached $6,000. At this price, marginal cost equals price. Also, price equals minimum average total cost. At a price less than $6,000, each firm incurs an economic loss. At a price of $6,000, each firm covers all its costs and makes zero economic profit (makes normal profit). Also, at a price of $6,000, each firm wants to produce 3,000 units a week, so the industry output is 6,000 units a week. Given the demand conditions, 6,000 units can be sold at a price of $6,000 each.

Figure 13.16 illustrates the situation just described. Each firm, in part (a), produces 3,000 units a week, and its average total cost is a minimum ($6,000 per unit). The market as a whole, in part (b), operates at the point at which the market demand curve (*D*) intersects the industry marginal cost curve (*MC*ₗ). Each firm has lowered its price and increased its output to try to gain an advantage over the other firm. Each has pushed this process as far as it can without incurring an economic loss.

We have now described a third possible outcome of this duopoly game: Both firms cheat. If both firms cheat on the collusive agreement, the output of each firm is 3,000 units a week and the price is $6,000. Each firm makes zero economic profit.

The Payoff Matrix Now that we have described the strategies and payoffs in the duopoly game, we can summarize the strategies and the payoffs in the form of the game's payoff matrix. Then we can find the Nash equilibrium.

Table 13.2 sets out the payoff matrix for this game. It is constructed in the same way as the payoff matrix for the prisoners' dilemma in Table 13.1. The squares show the payoffs for the two firms—Gear and Trick. In this case, the payoffs are profits. (For the prisoners' dilemma, the payoffs were losses.)

The table shows that if both firms cheat (top left), they achieve the perfectly competitive outcome—each firm makes zero economic profit. If both firms comply (bottom right), the industry makes the monopoly profit and each firm earns an economic profit of $2 million. The top right and bottom left squares show what happens if one firm cheats while the other complies. The firm that cheats collects an economic profit of $4.5 million, and the one that complies incurs a loss of $1 million.

Nash Equilibrium in the Duopolists' Dilemma
The duopolists have a dilemma like the prisoners' dilemma. Do they comply or cheat? To answer this question, we must find the Nash equilibrium.

FIGURE 13.16
Both Firms Cheat

(a) Individual firm   **(b) Industry**

If both firms cheat by increasing production, the collusive agreement collapses. The limit to the collapse is the competitive equilibrium. Neither firm will cut its price below $6,000 (minimum average total cost) because to do so will result in losses. In part (a), each firm produces 3,000 units a week at an average total cost of $6,000. In part (b), with a total production of 6,000 units, the price falls to $6,000. Each firm now makes zero economic profit. This output and price are the ones that would prevail in a competitive industry.

TABLE 13.2   Duopoly Payoff Matrix

Gear's strategies

	Cheat	Comply
Cheat	Gear: $0 / Trick: $0	Gear: −$1.0m / Trick: +$4.5m
Comply	Gear: +$4.5m / Trick: −$1.0m	Gear: +$2m / Trick: +$2m

Trick's strategies

Each square shows the payoffs from a pair of actions. For example, if both firms comply with the collusive agreement, the payoffs are recorded in the bottom right square. The red triangle shows Gear's payoff, and the blue triangle shows Trick's. In Nash equilibrium, both firms cheat.

Look at things from Gear's point of view. Gear reasons as follows: Suppose that Trick cheats. If I comply, I will incur an economic loss of $1 million. If I also cheat, I will make zero economic profit. Zero is better than *minus* $1 million, so I'm better off if I cheat. Now suppose Trick complies. If I cheat, I will make an economic profit of $4.5 million, and if I comply, I will make an economic profit of $2 million. A $4.5 million profit is better than a $2 million profit, so I'm better off if I cheat. So regardless of whether Trick cheats or complies, it pays Gear to cheat. Cheating is Gear's best strategy.

Trick comes to the same conclusion as Gear because the two firms face an identical situation. So both firms cheat. The Nash equilibrium of the duopoly game is that both firms cheat. And although the industry has only two firms, they charge the same price and produce the same quantity as those in a competitive industry. Also, as in perfect competition, each firm makes zero economic profit.

This conclusion is not general and will not always arise. We'll see why not first by looking at some other games that are like the prisoners' dilemma. Then we'll broaden the types of games we consider.

Other Oligopoly Games

Firms in oligopoly must decide whether to mount expensive advertising campaigns; whether to modify their product; whether to make their product more reliable and more durable; whether to price discriminate and, if so, among which groups of customers and to what degree; whether to undertake a large research and development (R&D) effort aimed at lowering production costs; and whether to enter or leave an industry.

All of these choices can be analyzed as games that are similar to the one that we've just studied. Let's look at one example: an R&D game.

An R&D Game

Disposable diapers were first marketed in 1966. The two market leaders from the start of this industry have been Procter & Gamble (the maker of Pampers) and Kimberly-Clark (the maker of Huggies). Procter & Gamble has about 40 percent of the total market, and Kimberly-Clark has about 33 percent. When the disposable diaper was first introduced, it had to be cost-effective in competition with reusable, laundered diapers. A costly research and development effort resulted in the development of machines that could make disposable diapers at a low enough cost to achieve that initial competitive edge. But new firms tried to get into the business and take market share away from the two industry leaders, and the industry leaders themselves battled each other to maintain or increase their own market share.

During the early 1990s, Kimberly-Clark was the first to introduce Velcro closures. And in 1996, Procter & Gamble was the first to introduce "breathable" diapers into the North America market.

The key to success in this industry (as in any other) is to design a product that people value highly relative to the cost of producing them. The firm that creates the most highly valued product and also develops the least-cost technology for producing it gains a competitive edge, undercutting the rest of the market, increasing its market share, and increasing its profit. But the R&D that must be undertaken to achieve product improvements and cost reductions is costly. So the cost of R&D must be deducted from the profit resulting from the increased market share that lower costs achieve. If no firm does R&D, every firm can be better off, but if one firm initiates the R&D activity, all must follow.

Table 13.3 illustrates the dilemma (with hypothetical numbers) for the R&D game that Kimberly-Clark and Procter & Gamble play. Each firm has two strategies: Spend $25 million a year on R&D or spend nothing on R&D. If neither firm spends on R&D, they make a joint profit of $100 million: $30 million for Kimberly-Clark and $70 million for Procter & Gamble (bottom right of the payoff matrix). If each firm conducts R&D, market shares are maintained but each firm's profit is lower by the amount spent on R&D (top left square of the payoff matrix). If Kimberly-Clark pays for R&D but Procter & Gamble does not, Kimberly-Clark gains a large part of Procter & Gamble's market. Kimberly-Clark profits, and Procter & Gamble loses (top right square of the payoff matrix). Finally, if Procter & Gamble conducts R&D and Kimberly-Clark does not, Procter & Gamble gains market share from Kimberly-Clark, increasing its profit, while Kimberly-Clark incurs a loss (bottom left square).

TABLE 13.3   Pampers Versus Huggies: An R&D Game

If both firms undertake R&D, their payoffs are those shown in the top left square. If neither firm undertakes R&D, their payoffs are in the bottom right square. When one firm undertakes R&D and the other one does not, their payoffs are in the top right and bottom left squares. The red triangle shows Procter & Gamble's payoff, and the blue triangle shows Kimberly-Clark's. The Nash equilibrium for this game is for both firms to undertake R&D. The structure of this game is the same as that of the prisoners' dilemma.

Confronted with the payoff matrix in Table 13.3, the two firms calculate their best strategies. Kimberly-Clark reasons as follows: If Procter & Gamble does not undertake R&D, we will make $85 million if we do and $30 million if we do not; so it pays us to conduct R&D. If Procter & Gamble conducts R&D, we will lose $10 million if we don't and make $5 million if we do. Again, R&D pays off. Thus conducting R&D is the best strategy for Kimberly-Clark. It pays, regardless of Procter & Gamble's decision.

Procter & Gamble reasons similarly: If Kimberly-Clark does not undertake R&D, we will make $70 million if we follow suit and $85 million if we conduct R&D. It therefore pays to conduct R&D. If Kimberly-Clark does undertake R&D, we will make $45 million by doing the same and lose $10 million by not doing R&D. Again, it pays us to conduct R&D. So for Procter & Gamble, R&D is also the best strategy.

Because R&D is the best strategy for both players, it is the Nash equilibrium. The outcome of this game is that both firms conduct R&D. They make less profit than they would if they could collude to achieve the cooperative outcome of no R&D.

The real-world situation has more players than Kimberly-Clark and Procter & Gamble. A large number of other firms share a small portion of the market, all of them ready to eat into the market share of Procter & Gamble and Kimberly-Clark. So the R&D effort by these two firms not only serves the purpose of maintaining shares in their own battle, but also helps to keep barriers to entry high enough to preserve their joint market share.

The Disappearing Invisible Hand

All the games that we've studied are versions of the prisoners' dilemma. The essence of that game lies in the structure of its payoffs. The worst possible outcome for each player arises from cooperating when the other player cheats. The best possible outcome, for each player to cooperate, is not a Nash equilibrium because it is in neither player's *self-interest* to cooperate if the other one cooperates. It is this failure to achieve the best outcome for both players—the best *social outcome* if the two players are the entire economy—that led John Nash to claim (as he was portrayed as doing in the movie *A Beautiful Mind*) that he had challenged Adam Smith's idea that we are always guided, as if by an invisible hand, to promote the social interest when we are pursuing our self-interest.

A Game of Chicken

The Nash equilibrium for the prisoners' dilemma is called a **dominant strategy equilibrium**, which is an equilibrium in which the best strategy of each player is to cheat (deny) *regardless of the strategy of the other player*. Not all games have such an equilibrium, and one that doesn't is a game called "chicken."

In a graphic, if disturbing, version of this game, two cars race towards each other. The first driver to swerve to avoid a crash is "chicken." The payoffs are a big loss for both if no one "chickens," zero for the chicken, and a gain for the player who hangs tough.

If player 1 chickens, player 2's best strategy is to hang tough. And if player 1 hangs tough, player 2's best strategy is to chicken.

For an economic form of this game, suppose the R&D that creates a new diaper technology results in information that cannot be kept secret or patented, so both firms benefit from the R&D of either firm. The chicken in this case is the firm that does the R&D.

Table 13.4 illustrates a payoff matrix for an R&D game of chicken between Kimberly-Clark and Procter & Gamble. Each firm has two strategies: Do the R&D (and "chicken") or do not do the R&D (and hang tough).

If neither "chickens," there is no R&D and each firm earns zero additional profit. If each firm conducts R&D—each "chickens"—each firm earns $5 million (the profit from the new technology minus the cost of the research). If one of the firms does the R&D, the payoffs are $1 million for the chicken and $10 million for the one who hangs tough.

Confronted with the payoff matrix in Table 13.4, the two firms calculate their best strategies. Kimberly-Clark is better off doing R&D if Procter & Gamble does not undertake it. Procter & Gamble is better off doing R&D if Kimberly-Clark doesn't do it. There are two equilibrium outcomes: Only one firm does R&D, but we can't predict which firm it will be.

You can see that it isn't a Nash equilibrium if no firm does the R&D because one firm would then be better off doing it. And you can see that it isn't a Nash equilibrium if both firms do the R&D because then one firm would be better off not doing it.

The firms could toss a coin or use some other random device to make a decision in this game. In some circumstances, such a strategy—called a mixed strategy—is actually better for both firms than choosing any of the strategies we've considered.

TABLE 13.4   An R&D Game of Chicken

If both firms undertake R&D, their payoffs are those shown in the top left square. If neither firm undertakes R&D, their payoffs are in the bottom right square. When one firm undertakes R&D and the other one does not, their payoffs are in the top right and bottom left squares. The red triangle shows Procter & Gamble's payoff, and the blue triangle shows Kimberly-Clark's. The equilibrium for this R&D game of chicken is for only one firm to undertake R&D. We cannot tell which firm will do the R&D and which will not.

REVIEW QUIZ

1 What are the common features of all games?
2 Describe the prisoners' dilemma game and explain why the Nash equilibrium delivers a bad outcome for both players.
3 Why does a collusive agreement to restrict output and raise price create a game like the prisoners' dilemma?
4 What creates an incentive for firms in a collusive agreement to cheat and increase production?
5 What is the equilibrium strategy for each firm in a duopolists' dilemma and why do the firms not succeed in colluding to raise the price and profits?
6 Describe the payoff matrix for an R&D prisoners' dilemma and chicken game and highlight the difference between the two games.

myeconlab Study Plan 13.6

Repeated Games and Sequential Games

THE GAMES THAT WE'VE STUDIED ARE PLAYED just once. In contrast, many real-world games are played repeatedly. This feature of games turns out to enable real-world duopolists to cooperate, collude, and earn a monopoly profit.

Another feature of the game that we've studied is that the players move simultaneously. But in many real-world situations, one player moves first and then the other moves—the play is sequential rather than simultaneous. This feature of real-world games creates a large number of possible outcomes.

We're now going to examine these two aspects of strategic decision-making.

A Repeated Duopoly Game

If two firms play a game repeatedly, one firm has the opportunity to penalize the other for previous "bad" behaviour. If Gear cheats this week, perhaps Trick will cheat next week. Before Gear cheats this week, won't it consider the possibility that Trick will cheat next week? What is the equilibrium of this game?

Actually, there is more than one possibility. One is the Nash equilibrium that we analyzed on p. 306. Both players cheat, and each makes zero economic profit forever. In such a situation, it will never pay one of the players to start complying unilaterally because to do so would result in a loss for that player and a profit for the other. But a **cooperative equilibrium** in which the players make and share the monopoly profit is possible.

A cooperative equilibrium might occur if cheating is punished. There are two extremes of punishment. The smallest penalty is called "tit for tat." A *tit-for-tat strategy* is one in which a player cooperates in the current period if the other player cooperated in the previous period but cheats in the current period if the other player cheated in the previous period. The most severe form of punishment is called a trigger strategy. A *trigger strategy* is one in which a player cooperates if the other player cooperates but plays the Nash equilibrium strategy forever thereafter if the other player cheats.

In the duopoly game between Gear and Trick, a tit-for-tat strategy keeps both players cooperating and earning monopoly profits. Let's see why with an example.

Table 13.5 shows the economic profit that Trick and Gear will make over a number of periods under two alternative sequences of events: colluding and cheating with a tit-for-tat response by the other firm.

If both firms stick to the collusive agreement in period 1, each makes an economic profit of $2 million. Suppose that Trick contemplates cheating in period 1. The cheating produces a quick $4.5 million economic profit and inflicts a $1 million economic loss on Gear. But a cheat in period 1 produces a response from Gear in period 2. If Trick wants to get back into a profit-making situation, it must return to the agreement in period 2 even though it knows that Gear will punish it for cheating in period 1. So in period 2, Gear punishes Trick and Trick cooperates. Gear now makes an economic profit of $4.5 million, and Trick incurs an economic loss of $1 million. Adding up the profits over two periods of play, Trick would have made more profit by cooperating—$4 million compared with $3.5 million.

What is true for Trick is also true for Gear. Because each firm makes a larger profit by sticking with the collusive agreement, both firms do so and the monopoly price, quantity, and profit prevail.

In reality, whether a cartel works like a one-play game or a repeated game depends primarily on the

---

TABLE 13.5   Cheating with Punishment

Period of Play	Collude		Cheat with tit-for-tat	
	Trick's profit	Gear's profit	Trick's profit	Gear's profit
	(millions of dollars)		(millions of dollars)	
1	2	2	4.5	−1.0
2	2	2	−1.0	4.5
3	2	2	2.0	2.0

If duopolists repeatedly collude, each makes an economic profit of $2 million per period of play. If one player cheats in period 1, the other player plays a tit-for-tat strategy and cheats in period 2. The profit from cheating can be made for only one period and must be paid for in the next period by incurring a loss. Over two periods of play, the best that a duopolist can achieve by cheating is an economic profit of $3.5 million, compared to an economic profit of $4 million by colluding.

number of players and the ease of detecting and punishing cheating. The larger the number of players, the harder it is to maintain a cartel.

Games and Price Wars A repeated duopoly game can help us understand real-world behaviour and, in particular, price wars. Some price wars can be interpreted as the implementation of a tit-for-tat strategy. But the game is a bit more complicated than the one we've looked at because the players are uncertain about the demand for the product.

Playing a tit-for-tat strategy, firms have an incentive to stick to the monopoly price. But fluctuations in demand lead to fluctuations in the monopoly price, and sometimes, when the price changes, it might seem to one of the firms that the price has fallen because the other has cheated. In this case, a price war will break out. The price war will end only when each firm is satisfied that the other is ready to cooperate again. There will be cycles of price wars and the restoration of collusive agreements. Fluctuations in the world price of oil might be interpreted in this way.

Some price wars arise from the entry of a small number of firms into an industry that had previously been a monopoly. Although the industry has a small number of firms, the firms are in a prisoners' dilemma and they cannot impose effective penalties for price cutting. The behaviour of prices and outputs in the computer chip industry during 1995 and 1996 can be explained in this way. Until 1995, the market for Pentium chips for IBM-compatible computers was dominated by one firm, Intel Corporation, which was able to make maximum economic profit by producing the quantity of chips at which marginal cost equalled marginal revenue. The price of Intel's chips was set to ensure that the quantity demanded equalled the quantity produced. Then in 1995 and 1996, with the entry of a small number of new firms, the industry became an oligopoly. If the firms had maintained Intel's price and shared the market, together they could have made economic profits equal to Intel's profit. But the firms were in a prisoners' dilemma. So prices fell towards the competitive level.

Let's now study a sequential game. There are many such games, and the one we'll examine is among the simplest. It has an interesting implication and it will give you the flavour of this type of game. The sequential game that we'll study is an entry game in a contestable market.

A Sequential Entry Game in a Contestable Market

If two firms play a sequential game, one firm makes a decision at the first stage of the game and the other makes a decision at the second stage.

We're going to study a sequential game in a **contestable market**—a market in which firms can enter and leave so easily that firms in the market face competition from *potential* entrants. Examples of contestable markets are routes served by airlines and by barge companies that operate on the major waterways. These markets are contestable because firms could enter if an opportunity for economic profit arose and could exit with no penalty if the opportunity for economic profit disappeared.

If the Herfindahl-Hirschman Index (pp. 208–209) is used to determine the degree of competition, a contestable market appears to be uncompetitive. But a contestable market can behave as if it were perfectly competitive. To see why, let's look at an entry game for a contestable air route.

A Contestable Air Route Agile Air is the only firm operating on a particular route. Demand and cost conditions are such that there is room for only one airline to operate. Wanabe, Inc. is another airline that could offer services on the route.

We describe the structure of a sequential game by using a *game tree* like that in Fig. 13.17. At the first stage, Agile Air must set a price. Once the price is set and advertised, Agile can't change it. That is, once set, Agile's price is fixed and Agile can't react to Wanabe's entry decision. Agile can set its price at either the monopoly level or the competitive level.

At the second stage, Wanabe must decide whether to enter or to stay out. Customers have no loyalty (there are no frequent flyer programs) and they buy from the lowest-price firm. So if Wanabe enters, it sets a price just below Agile's and takes all the business.

Figure 13.17 shows the payoffs from the various decisions (Agile's in the red triangles and Wanabe's in the blue triangles).

To decide on its price, Agile's CEO reasons as follows: Suppose that Agile sets the monopoly price. If Wanabe enters, it earns 90 (think of all payoff numbers as thousands of dollars). If Wanabe stays out, it earns nothing. So Wanabe will enter. In this case Agile will lose 50.

FIGURE 13.17

Agile Versus Wanabe: A Sequential Entry Game in a Contestable Market

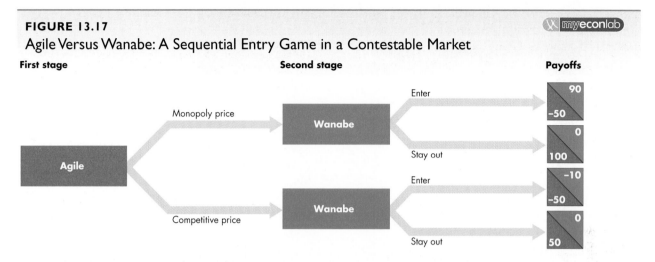

First stage **Second stage** **Payoffs**

If Agile sets the monopoly price, Wanabe makes 90 (thousand dollars) by entering and earns nothing by staying out. So if Agile sets the monopoly price, Wanabe enters.

If Agile sets the competitive price, Wanabe earns nothing if it stays out and incurs a loss if it enters. So if Agile sets the competitive price, Wanabe stays out.

Now suppose that Agile sets the competitive price. If Wanabe stays out, it earns nothing and if it enters, it loses 10, so Wanabe will stay out. In this case, Agile will earn 50.

Agile's best strategy is to set its price at the competitive level and earn 50 (normal profit). The option of earning 100 by setting the monopoly price with Wanabe staying out is not available to Agile. If Agile sets the monopoly price, Wanabe enters, undercuts Agile, and takes all the business.

In this example, Agile sets its price at the competitive level and earns normal profit. A less costly strategy, called **limit pricing**, sets the price at the highest level that inflicts a loss on the entrant. Any loss is big enough to deter entry, so it is not always necessary to set the price as low as the competitive price. In the example of Agile and Wanabe, at the competitive price, Wanabe incurs a loss of 10 if it enters. A smaller loss would still keep Wanabe out.

This game is interesting because it points to the possibility of a monopoly behaving like a competitive industry and serving the social interest without regulation. But the result is not general and depends on one crucial feature of the setup of the game: At the second stage, Agile is locked into the price set at the first stage.

If Agile could change its price in the second stage, it would want to set the monopoly price if Wanabe stayed out—100 with the monopoly price beats 50

with the competitive price. But Wanabe can figure out what Agile would do, so the price set at the first stage has no effect on Wanabe. Agile sets the monopoly price and Wanabe might either stay out or enter.

We've looked at two of the many possible repeated and sequential games, and you've seen how these types of game can provide insights into the complex forces that determine prices and profits.

◆ Monopolistic competition and oligopoly are the most common market structures that you encounter in your daily life. *Reading Between the Lines* on pp. 312–313 looks at monopolistic competition in action in China.

So far, except for a brief look at monopoly policy issues at the end of Chapter 12, we've studied unregulated market power. Your task in the next chapter is to see how Canadian competition policy influences market power.

Monopolistic Competition in China's Juice Market

WALL STREET JOURNAL, OCTOBER 13, 2003

Competition in China Erodes Profit Margins

American businessman Paul Rasch elbows his way through a crowded Carrefour supermarket to the display of Great Lakes fruit juice, the product his family's U.S. company has been selling here for a decade.

It is on sale for $2.30 a bottle, but a Chinese competitor, Huiyuan, is offering a bigger bottle at half the price. Mr. Rasch walks down an aisle teeming with dozens of fruit-juice brands, ...

Selling consumer goods in China is getting harder ... as foreign corporations face brutal competition from Chinese rivals. Veteran foreign executives now describe the mid-1990s as the golden days, when their products were novelties, consumers were impressionable, and domestic competition trailed. ...

... Great Lakes entered China in 1993 to make and sell 100% fruit juice, then a novelty. ...

China today may be the most perfectly efficient demonstration of capitalism in the world. Once a product proves popular, a business will unroll it on a national scale if it can. Rivals latch on to innovations instantly. ... The fruit-juice market took off in 2001 after three companies—Taiwan arch-rivals Tingyi Holding Corp. and Uni-President Enterprises Corp., and Coca-Cola Co.—launched fruit drinks with 10% juice content. ...

Other juice businesses piled in ... Juice and juice-drink sales hit $1.4 billion last year, a 40% surge from the year earlier ...

... In the fruit-juice market that Great Lakes pioneered, it now does $10 million in annual sales; Mr. Rasch says sales are growing 20% a year and that the business is profitable. But Tingyi, a relative latecomer to the field, now claims a 20% share of a $1 billion-plus market, while Uni-President, which holds the No. 1 spot, has an even larger business. Industry executives estimate that Huiyuan leads the pure-juice category with about $100 million in sales. ...

Essence of the Story

■ Great Lakes, a U.S. company, began selling fruit juice in China in 1993.

■ In the mid-1990s, foreign firms in China could sell products that were new to the Chinese market with little domestic competition.

■ As fruit juice became more popular, new companies, both domestic and foreign, launched new fruit drinks.

■ Now Great Lakes faces competition from dozens of brands.

■ Great Lakes now has an annual revenue of $10 million, and the business is profitable.

Economic Analysis

■ The market for fruit juice in China is an example of monopolistic competition.

■ Figure 1 shows the situation facing Great Lakes when it had little competition in the fruit-juice market in China in 1993.

■ The firm's average total cost curve is ATC_0, the marginal cost curve is MC_0, the demand curve is D_0, and the marginal revenue curve is MR_0.

■ To maximize profit, Great Lakes produces the quantity at which marginal revenue equals marginal cost. It sells 10 million bottles of fruit juice a year at a price of $3.00 a bottle.

■ The blue rectangle shows Great Lakes' economic profit.

■ Since 1993, many firms have entered the fruit-juice market in China.

■ Each firm produces a fruit juice that is slightly different from the fruit juice produced by its competitors.

■ The firms compete on quality, price, and marketing.

■ The entry of the new firms into the market decreases the demand for fruit juice from Great Lakes and makes the demand for Great Lakes fruit juice more elastic.

■ At the same time, Great Lakes' costs increase as Great Lakes increases its expenditures on advertising and marketing.

■ Figure 2 shows the situation facing Great Lakes after the entry of new firms into the market.

■ The firm's average total cost curve is ATC_1, the marginal cost curve is MC_1, the demand curve is D_1, and the marginal revenue curve is MR_1.

■ Now Great Lakes maximizes profit by selling 4.4 million bottles of fruit juice a year for a price of $2.30 a bottle.

■ Great Lakes earns zero economic profit because price is equal to average total cost.

■ Although Great Lakes earns zero economic profit, it does earn a normal profit. Normal profit is included in total cost.

Figure 1 Before entry

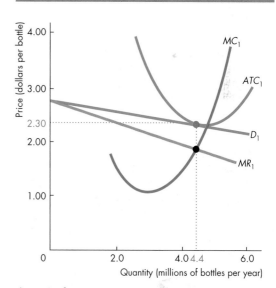

Figure 2 After entry

313

SUMMARY

KEY POINTS

What Is Monopolistic Competition?
(pp. 286–287)

- Monopolistic competition occurs when a large number of firms compete with each other on product quality, price, and marketing.

Price and Output in Monopolistic Competition (pp. 288–291)

- Each firm in monopolistic competition faces a downward-sloping demand curve and produces the quantity at which marginal revenue equals marginal cost.
- Entry and exit result in zero economic profit and excess capacity in long-run equilibrium.

Product Development and Marketing
(pp. 292–295)

- Firms in monopolistic competition innovate and develop new products.
- Advertising expenditures increase total cost, but they might lower average total cost if they increase the quantity sold by enough.
- Advertising expenditures might increase demand, but they might also decrease the demand for a firm's product by increasing competition.
- Whether monopolistic competition is inefficient depends on the value we place on product variety.

What Is Oligopoly? (pp. 296–297)

- Oligopoly is a market in which a small number of firms compete.

Two Traditional Oligopoly Models (pp. 298–299)

- If rivals match price cuts but do not match price hikes, firms face a kinked demand curve and change prices only when large cost changes occur.
- If one firm dominates a market, it acts like a monopoly and the small firms take the price as given and act like perfectly competitive firms.

Oligopoly Games (pp. 300–308)

- Oligopoly is studied by using game theory, which is a method of analyzing strategic behaviour.

- In a prisoners' dilemma game, two prisoners acting in their own self-interest harm their joint interest.
- An oligopoly (duopoly) price-fixing game is a prisoners' dilemma in which the firms might collude or cheat. The Nash equilibrium is that both firms cheat and output and price are the same as in perfect competition.
- Firms' decisions about advertising and R&D can be studied by using game theory.

Repeated Games and Sequential Games
(pp. 309–311)

- In a repeated game, a punishment strategy can produce a cooperative equilibrium in which price and output are the same as in a monopoly.
- In a sequential contestable market game, a small number of firms can behave like firms in perfect competition.

KEY FIGURES AND TABLES

KEY TERMS

PROBLEMS

Go to **myeconlab** **for solutions to odd-numbered problems and additional exercises.**

1. The shows the situation facing Lite and Kool, Inc., a producer of running shoes.

  a. What quantity does Lite and Kool produce?
  b. What does it charge?
  c. How much profit does Lite and Kool make?

2. The figure shows the situation facing The Stiff Shirt, Inc., a producer of shirts.

  a. What quantity does The Stiff Shirt produce?
  b. What does it charge?
  c. How much profit does it make?

3. A firm in monopolistic competition produces running shoes. If it spends nothing on advertising, it can sell no shoes at $100 a pair, and for each $10 cut in price, the quantity of shoes it can sell increases by 25 pairs a day, so at $20 a pair, it can sell 200 pairs a day. The firm's total fixed cost is $4,000 a day. Its average variable cost and marginal cost is a constant $20 per pair. If the firm spends $3,000 a day on advertising, it can double the quantity of shoes sold at each price.

  a. If the firm doesn't advertise, what is
    i.   The quantity of shoes produced?
    ii. The price per pair?
    iii. The firm's economic profit or loss?
  b. If the firm does advertise, what is
    i.   The quantity of shoes produced?
    ii. The price per pair?
    iii. The firm's economic profit or loss?
  c. Will the firm advertise or not? Why?

4. The firm in problem 3 has the same demand and costs as before if it does not advertise. The firm undertakes some quality improvements in its shoes that raise its marginal and average cost to $40 a pair. If the firm spends $3,000 a day on advertising with a new agency, it can double the amount that consumers are willing to pay at each quantity demanded.

  a. If the firm hires the new agency, what quantity does it produce and what price does it charge?
  b. What is the firm's economic profit or loss?
  c. What is the firm's profit in the long run?

5. A firm with a kinked demand curve experiences an increase in fixed costs. Explain how the firm's price, output, and profit change.

6. A firm with a kinked demand curve experiences an increase in variable cost. Explain how the firm's price, output, and profit change.

7. An industry with one very large firm and 100 very small firms experiences an increase in the demand for its product. Use the dominant firm model to explain the effects on the price, output, and economic profit of
  a. The large firm.
  b. The typical small firm.

8. An industry with one very large firm and 100 very small firms experiences an increase in total variable cost. Use the dominant firm model to explain the effects on the price, output, and economic profit of
  a. The large firm.
  b. The typical small firm.

9. Consider a game with two players and in which each player is asked a question. The players can answer the question honestly or lie. If both answer honestly, each receives $100. If one answers honestly and the other lies, the liar receives $500 and the honest player gets nothing. If both lie, then each receives $50.

   a. Describe this game in terms of its players, strategies, and payoffs.
   b. Construct the payoff matrix.
   c. What is the equilibrium for this game?

10. Describe the game known as the prisoners' dilemma. In describing the game,

   a. Make up a story that motivates the game.
   b. Work out a payoff matrix.
   c. Describe how the equilibrium of the game is arrived at.

11. Soapy and Suddies, Inc. are the only producers of soap powder. They collude and agree to share the market equally. If neither firm cheats, each makes $1 million profit. If either firm cheats, the cheat makes a profit of $1.5 million, while the complier incurs a loss of $0.5 million. Neither firm can police the other's actions.

   a. If the game is played once,
      i.   What is the profit of each firm if both cheat?
      ii. Describe the best strategy for each firm.
      iii. Construct the payoff matrix.
      iv. What is the equilibrium of the game?
   b. If this duopoly game can be played many times, describe some of the strategies that each firm might adopt.

12. Healthy and Energica are the only producers of a new energy drink. The firms collude and agree to share the market equally. If neither firm cheats, each firm makes $4 million profit. If either firm cheats, the cheat makes $6 million profit, while the complier incurs a loss of $1.5 million. Neither firm can police the other's actions.

   a. If the game is played once,
      i.   What is the payoff matrix?
      ii. Describe the best strategy for each firm.
      iii. What is the equilibrium of the game?
   b. If this game can be played many times, what are two strategies that could be adopted?

CRITICAL THINKING

1. Study *Reading Between the Lines* on pp. 312–313 and then answer the following questions.

   a. Why is the juice market in China an example of monopolistic competition?
   b. Why did it become harder to sell fruit juice in China during the 1990s?
   c. How do firms in the fruit-juice market in China try to earn an economic profit?
   d. Do you think the fruit-juice market in China has excess capacity? Explain why or why not.
   e. What must Paul Rasch do to keep earning an economic profit?

2. Suppose that Netscape and Microsoft each develop their own versions of an amazing new Web browser that allows advertisers to target consumers with great precision. Also, the new browser is easier and more fun to use than existing browsers. Each firm is trying to decide whether to sell the browser or to give it away. What are the likely benefits from each action? Which action is likely to occur?

3. Why do Coca-Cola and PepsiCo spend huge amounts on advertising? Do they benefit? Does the consumer benefit? Explain your answer.

WEB EXERCISES

Use the links on myeconlab **to work the following exercise.**

1. Obtain information about cell phone plans in your region of Canada.

   a. In what type of market are cell phone plans sold?
   b. Describe the main features of the cell phone plans that companies offer and classify each feature as influencing fixed cost or variable cost of the plans.
   c. Why does each cell phone company offer so many plans?
   d. Who benefits from the choice of so many plans—you the buyer of a plan or the cell phone company?
   e. Are the cell phone companies playing a game? If so, describe the game. Is it a one-shot game or a repeated game? How do you know which type of game it is?

UNDERSTANDING FIRMS AND MARKETS

Managing Change

Our economy is constantly changing. Every year, new goods appear and old ones disappear. New firms are born and old ones die. This process of change is initiated and managed by firms operating in markets. When a new product is invented, just one or two firms sell it initially. For example, when the personal computer first became available, there was an Apple or an IBM. The IBM-PC had just one operating system, DOS, made by Microsoft. One firm, Intel, made the chip that ran the IBM-PC. These are examples of industries in which the producer has market power to determine the price of the product and the quantity produced. The extreme case of a single producer that cannot be challenged by new competitors is *monopoly*, which Chapter 12 explained.

But not all industries with just one producer are monopolies. In many cases, the firm that is first to produce a new good faces severe competition from new rivals. One firm facing potential competition is the case of a *contestable market*. If demand increases and makes space for more than one firm, an industry becomes increasingly competitive. Even with just two rivals, the industry changes its face in a dramatic way. *Duopoly*—the case of just two producers—illustrates this dramatic change. The two firms must play close attention to each other's production and prices and must predict the effects of their own actions on the actions of the other firm. We call this situation one of *strategic interdependence*. As the number of rivals grows, the industry becomes an *oligopoly*, in which a small number of firms devise strategies and pay close attention to the strategies of their competitors.

With the continued arrival of new firms in an industry, the market eventually becomes competitive. Competition might be limited because each firm produces its own special version or brand of a good. This case is called *monopolistic competition* because it has elements of both monopoly and competition. Chapter 13 explored the behaviour of firms in all of these types of markets that lie between monopoly at the one extreme and perfect competition at the other.

When competition is extreme—the case that we call *perfect competition*—the market changes again in a dramatic way. Now the firm is unable to influence price. Chapter 11 explained this case.

Often, an industry that is competitive becomes less so as the bigger and more successful firms in the industry begin to swallow up the smaller firms, either by driving them out of business or by acquiring their assets. Through this process, an industry might return to oligopoly or even monopoly. You can see such a movement in the auto and banking industries today.

By studying firms and markets, we gain a deeper understanding of the forces that allocate scarce resources and begin to see the anatomy of the invisible hand.

Many economists have advanced our understanding of these forces and we'll now meet two of them. John von Neumann pioneered the idea of game theory. And Bengt Holmstrom is one of today's leading students of strategic behaviour.

317

PROBING THE IDEAS

Market Power

"Real life consists of bluffing, of little tactics of deception, of asking yourself what is the other man going to think I mean to do."

JOHN VON NEUMANN,
told to Jacob Bronowski (in a London taxi) and reported in
The Ascent of Man

THE ECONOMIST

John Von Neumann *was one of the great minds of the twentieth century. Born in Budapest, Hungary, in 1903, Johnny, as he was known, showed early mathematical brilliance. His first mathematical publication was an article that grew out of a lesson with his tutor, which he wrote at the age of 18! But it was at the age of 25, in 1928, that von Neumann published the article that began a flood of research on game theory—a flood that has still not subsided today. In that article, he proved that in a zero-sum game (like sharing a pie), there exists a best strategy for each player.*

Von Neumann invented the computer and built the first modern practical computer, and he worked on the "Manhattan Project," which developed the atomic bomb at Los Alamos, New Mexico, during World War II.

Von Neumann believed that the social sciences would progress only if they used mathematical tools. But he believed that they needed different tools from those developed from the physical sciences.

THE ISSUES

It is not surprising that firms with market power will charge higher prices than those charged by competitive firms. But how much higher?

This question has puzzled generations of economists. Adam Smith said, "The price of a monopoly is upon every occasion the highest which can be got." But he was wrong. Antoine-Augustin Cournot (see p. 148) first worked out the price a monopoly will charge. It is not the "highest which can be got" but the price that maximizes profit. Cournot's work was not appreciated until almost a century later when Joan Robinson explained how a monopoly sets its price.

Questions about monopoly became urgent and practical during the 1870s, a time when rapid technological change and falling transportation costs enabled huge monopolies to emerge in the United States. These monopolies dominated oil, steel, railroads, tobacco, and even sugar. Industrial empires grew ever larger.

The success of the nineteenth century monopolies led to the creation of our anti-combine laws—laws that limit the use of monopoly power. Those laws have been used to prevent monopolies from being set up and to break up existing monopolies. They were used in the United States during the 1960s to end a conspiracy between General Electric, Westinghouse, and other firms when they colluded to fix their prices instead of competing with each other. The laws were used during the 1980s to bring greater competition to long-distance telecommunication. But in spite of anti-combine laws, near monopolies still exist. Among the most prominent today are those in computer chips and operating systems. Like their forerunners, today's near monopolies make huge profits.

But unlike the situation in the nineteenth century, the technological change taking place today is strengthening the forces of competition. Today's information technologies are creating substitutes for services that previously had none. Direct satellite TV is competing with cable, and new phone companies are competing with the traditional phone monopolies.

THEN

Ruthless greed, exploitation of both workers and customers—these are the traditional images of monopolies and the effects of their power. These images appeared to be an accurate description during the 1880s, when monopolies stood at their peak of power and influence. One monopolist, John D. Rockefeller, Sr., built his giant Standard Oil Company, which by 1879 was refining 90 percent of the nation's oil and controlling its entire pipeline capacity.

NOW

Despite anti-combine laws that regulate monopolies, they still exist. One is the monopoly in cable television. In many cities, one firm decides which channels viewers will receive and the price they will pay. During the 1980s, with the advent of satellite technology and specialist cable program producers such as CNN and HBO, the cable companies expanded their offerings. At the same time, they steadily increased prices and their businesses became very profitable. But the very technologies that made cable television profitable are now challenging its market power. Direct satellite TV services are eroding cable's monopoly and bringing greater competition to this market.

Today, many economists who work on microeconomics use the ideas that John von Neumann pioneered. Game theory is the tool of choice. One economist who has made good use of this tool (and many other tools) is Bengt Holmstrom of MIT, whom you can meet on the following pages.

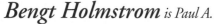

Bengt Holmstrom *is Paul A. Samuelson Professor of Economics in the department of economics and the Sloan School of Management at the Massachusetts Institute of Technology. Born in 1949 in Helsinki, Finland, he studied mathematics and physics at the University of Helsinki as an undergraduate and then worked as an operations researcher before going to Stanford University as an economics graduate student. Professor Holmstrom's research on the way firms use contracts and incentives is recognized as providing a major advance in our understanding of the mechanisms that operate inside firms. Beyond his academic research, Professor Holmstrom has provided services to a number of major corporations, including Nokia, of which he is currently a director.*

Michael Parkin and Robin Bade talked with Bengt Holmstrom about his work and the progress that economists have made in understanding firms and the markets in which they operate since the pioneering ideas about the nature of the firm by Ronald Coase.

Bengt Holmstrom

Professor Holmstrom, did you study economics as an undergraduate? What drew you to this subject?

No. I was a math and physics major as an undergraduate in Helsinki. I got into economics the way many people do through a side door from mathematics and operations research at Stanford Graduate School of Business.

How did you get interested in the economics of the firm?

I went from my undergraduate degree to work as an operations research analyst at a large conglomerate in Finland. I was hired to implement a company-wide corporate planning model. This was the early 70s, when large optimization models were expected to help firms make better long-term plans and run operations more centrally.

It didn't take me very long to realize that this was a misguided belief. The problem was that the data came from people lower down that had an apparent incentive to misrepresent the numbers. Their minds were focused on outwitting the model. My interest in incentives was entirely driven by this experience.

One of your most profound insights was to view the entire firm as an incentive system. What do you mean when you describe a firm as an incentive system? What implications follow from this view of the firm?

When people talk about incentives, they tend to think about some explicit reward system like a salesperson's commission or a stock option for an executive or something like that.

The key insight has been to understand that incentives are influenced in an enormous number of ways, indirectly and implicitly. For instance, constraints and bureaucratic rules are very important pieces of the overall incentive system. There are many different ways of getting people to do what you think they should be doing.

Sometimes the best incentive is to pay no incentive! Incentives can be terribly damaging if they are poorly designed.

The firm as an incentive system is an expression of the fact that you need to think about *all* the possible ways in which you can influence people's actions and then how you orchestrate the instruments that are available. These instruments include promotion incentives, rewards, or even just praise. The narrow view that it's just a matter of paying a bonus of some sort is very misguided.

> " *Sometimes the best incentive is to pay no incentive! Incentives can be terribly damaging if they are poorly designed.* "

Can you talk about the role of the economist as economic advisor to a firm? One view is that firms are efficient and the task of the economist is to understand why. Another view is that the economist can help firms to become efficient—for example, by devising better incentive mechanisms. Can the economist help firms to become efficient? And are there other roles for the economist as advisor to a firm?

There's a well-known paradox—and tension—in economics. Positive economics deals with figuring out what is optimal—what is the best that can be done—and then using the description of optimal behaviour as a predictive tool—as a way of explaining why things are the way they are in the world.

And yet at the same time, nothing is presumably perfect so there is room for innovation—organizational innovation and economic innovation—which leads to the economic advice you're asking about.

There are many roles an economist can play as advisor to a firm. If we really understand things better, maybe we can actually make improvements in them. If nothing else, we can understand that if the constraints change, then a system that's designed in a particular way would need to adapt itself to the new circumstances. For example, a firm might have a centralized organization that's good in one set of circumstances and then suddenly the circumstances change and innovation becomes very important, as we seem to think it is right now. Then that situation calls for changes towards organizational structures that are more suited for innovation.

So you can explain the tradeoff between central control and more flexible, innovative structures so that a firm's managers understand these forces. They then might decide to move in the direction that better achieves their objectives. Or they might realize that the reason why other firms change organizational structures may not be relevant in their case.

The economist can help people understand the variety of organizations so that they can pick the right one for the right set of circumstances. There isn't one organization that's good for everything—quite the contrary. Some activities require one kind of organization; some activities require another kind of organization. Charities, for instance, would not be well run by for-profit firms because they would run away with the money. That's an extreme example. So, non-profit organizations play a very important role in running charities.

Joint stock companies have proven to be an extremely flexible and robust form of organization both for small- and large-scale activities. Their scalability is one reason for their enormous success.

Are there any examples of serious progress that we've made in understanding which types of organizations work best in which circumstances?

I think there are lots. There's a big debate right now about airport security that's a wonderful illustration of the insight that the firm is an incentive system and an example of the possibility of having incentives that are too strong in the wrong place. One view is that profit-making companies that run the airport security checking are too oriented towards profit and too little oriented towards quality, because the quality checks come so infrequently. The standard argument is that if they make a mistake they must pay for it, so they have a strong incentive to deliver high-quality work. But if accidents happen infrequently, that sort of feedback mechanism is just too weak. This is a logical reason for moving in the direction of taking away profit-making incentives from airport security checking.

The very existence of the firm comes from the fact that it is there to remove and restructure incorrect incentives—excessively high-powered incentives that come from the market—and to get people to cooperate. In the market, it can be harder to cooperate because everyone is working for his or her own

321

benefit. This works very well if there are a lot of alternatives to choose—if there's competition. But when there is a small number of traders, or where quality is hard to assess, bringing the activity inside the firm is quite natural.

One firm, Enron, was big news during 2002. What do models of incentive systems tell us about what went wrong with Enron?

I think Enron, like most of these disaster cases, teaches that misplaced incentives lead to potentially big mistakes. It's almost tautological to say that if wrongdoing was done, it was done because the incentives weren't aligned correctly. Now, how much of it was a design flaw within Enron and how much was a flaw of the overall system, is harder to judge. There were certainly regulatory problems—energy production regulations had changed; the energy market had been opened up and arbitrage opportunities created. Some of the activities of Enron that sought to profit from this new regulatory environment were entirely legal.

Then there was financial innovation. It's an old, old idea that it would be nice to remove debts from the balance sheet of a firm to make it look better to investors. And apparently new financial instruments had been created to make off-balance sheet operations possible. Some of them were clearly questionable and perhaps some of them illegal.

But the other problem—and this is a system problem, not just an Enron problem—is that when things are going well and everybody believes that the world is moving forward, it's very hard to question something. You go further and further out on a limb, and then the limb breaks and you learn that that was too much.

> " *I don't think that a system that rules out everything that can go wrong is the right system.* "

I don't see Enron as catastrophically as most people seem to. I think that we would pay a big price if we never let anybody like Enron try. If you regulate things so that nothing like it ever could have happened, it probably would have also thrown out a lot of good innovations with it. It's part of the system to learn by having certain things like this happen.

I'm not defending Enron's actions. But I'm trying to give a different angle to the possible response. System design is different from trying to correct individual cases. I don't think that a system that rules out everything that can go wrong is the right system.

Is it important for an academic economist to have professional interests in the "real world"?

I think everybody's different. For me it has been important because I got interested in incentives through non-academic work. That's where I started, and I was just lucky that incentives happened to be a topical issue when I entered the field.

I don't think one could, in any sense, say that everybody must have real-world experience. You have to find your own sources of stimulation and discover what makes you curious and what makes you interested. For some people, that's just being exceedingly theoretical and not thinking about much else. Some are very talented that way: Other people desperately need some connection with the real world. For me, that has been very valuable.

Needless to say, the fact that we are all different is extremely important for overall progress.

What advice do you have for a student who is just starting to study economics? Do you think that economics is a good subject in which to major? What other subjects would you urge students to study alongside economics?

I'm a big believer that people do their best work and have their happiest life when they do the things that they are really interested in. With the wonderful undergraduate system that North America has, I would advise students to sample broadly and go in the direction they get most excited about. But I think there are many reasons to like economics. It spans a fascinating range of questions. At its heart, economics is about understanding social systems, current and past, and how these systems could be improved for the welfare of the human race. I'm confident that economics has contributed a great deal to the current levels of welfare in the West. And I'm optimistic that the developing world will also benefit from our intellectual progress. As an economist, you can have a really big impact, even if the results are less visible than in the natural sciences like physics. For me, it has been incredibly inspiring.

Competition Policy

CHAPTER 14

Social Interest or Special Interests?

When you consume water, electric power, cable TV, or local telephone service, you buy from a regulated monopoly. Why do we regulate the industries that produce these goods and services? How do we regulate them? Does regulation work in the interests of consumers—the public interest—or does it serve the interests of producers—special interests?

The government used its anti-combine laws to end Northern Telecom's monopoly on phone equipment and Bell Canada's monopoly on long-distance phone calls as well as the installation of phone lines. This action brought competition into all three markets. Now you can choose where to buy your phone equipment, which long-distance telephone service to use, and the company to install your phone line.

What are the anti-combine laws? How have they evolved over the years? How are they used today? Do they serve the public interest of consumers or the special interests of producers?

◆ This chapter surveys the regulation, public ownership, and anti-combine law that are designed to limit the power of firms in monopoly and oligopoly markets and to protect the interest of the consumer. You will see, in *Reading Between the Lines* at the end of the chapter, how Rogers Commuication Inc. and BCE Inc are pursuing a new natural monopoly in broadband satellite Internet service.

After studying this chapter, you will be able to

- **Explain how government arises from market failure and inequality**

- **Define regulation, public ownership, and anti-combine law and distinguish between the social interest and capture theories of regulation**

- **Explain how regulation affects prices, outputs, profits, and the distribution of the gains from trade between consumers and producers**

- **Explain how public ownership affects prices, outputs, profits, and allocative efficiency**

- **Explain how ant-combine law is used in Canada today**

The Economic Theory of Government

THE ECONOMIC THEORY OF GOVERNMENT explains the economic roles of governments, the economic choices that governments make, and the consequences of those choices.

Governments exist for two major reasons. First, they establish and maintain property rights and set the rules for the redistribution of income and wealth. Property rights are the foundation on which all market activity takes place. They replace stealing with a rule-based and law-enforced system for redistributing income and wealth.

Second, governments provide mechanisms for allocating scarce resources when the market economy results in inefficiency—a situation called **market failure**. When market failure occurs, too many of some things and too few of some other things are produced. Choices made in the pursuit of self-interest have not served the social interest. By reallocating resources, it is possible to make some people better off while making no one worse off.

In this and following chapters, we're going to study five economic problems that governments and public choices address. They are

- Monopoly and oligopoly regulation
- Externalities
- The provision of public goods
- The use of common resources
- Income redistribution

Monopoly and Oligopoly Regulation

Monopoly or oligopoly firms seek maximum profit by restricting output and keeping the price above marginal cost. For example, Microsoft has a (near) monopoly in personal computer operating systems, and the price that Microsoft is able to get for a copy of Windows vastly exceeds the marginal cost of producing it. Other practices, such as forcing consumers to buy an operating system and a Web browser in a single package might be against the social interest, but they also provide Microsoft with a bigger profit.

Governments regulate monopoly and oligopoly and enact anti-combine laws that prevent cartels and other restrictions on competition. We study these regulations and laws in the next parts of this chapter.

Externalities

When a chemical factory (legally) dumps its waste into a river and kills the fish, it imposes a cost—called an *external cost*—on the members of a fishing club who fish downstream. When a homeowner fills her garden with spring bulbs, she generates an external benefit for all the passers-by. External costs and benefits are not usually taken into account by the people whose actions create them. The chemical factory does not take the fishing club's wishes into account when it decides whether to dump waste into the river. The homeowner does not take her neighbours' views into account when she decides to fill her garden with flowers. We study externalities in Chapter 15.

The Provision of Public Goods

Some goods and services are consumed by everyone and no one can be excluded from the benefits that arise from their provision. Examples are national defence, law and order, and sewage and waste disposal services. A national defence system can't isolate individuals and refuse to protect them. Airborne diseases from untreated sewage don't favour some people and hit others. A good or service that is consumed by everyone is called a *public good*.

The market economy fails to deliver the efficient quantity of public goods because of a *free-rider problem*. Everyone tries to free ride on everyone else because the good is available to all whether they pay for it or not.

We'll provide a more thorough description of public goods and the free-rider problem in Chapter 16. We'll also study the factors that influence the scale of provision of public goods in that chapter.

The Use of Common Resources

Some resources are owned by no one and used by everyone. Examples are fish in the ocean, our lakes, and our provincial parks. Every week, hundreds of boats scoop up thousands of tonnes of fish from the Atlantic Ocean. The consequence is that the stocks of some species—Atlantic Cod is one of them—are dangerously depleted. Every summer, people trek over pathways in provincial parks and damage the natural habitat.

The market economy fails to use common resources efficiently because no one has an incentive to conserve what everyone else is free to use.

We'll describe this problem more thoroughly in Chapter 16, where we'll also review some ideas for coping with the problem.

Income Redistribution

The market economy delivers an unequal distribution of income and wealth, and income support systems and progressive income taxes influence the distribution of the gains from economic activity. You've already seen, in Chapter 6, how taxes affect markets and create deadweight losses. We'll look at the role of taxes in redistributing income in Chapter 18 after learning how factor markets operate.

Public Choice and the Political Marketplace

Replacing markets with government regulation is no simple matter. Just as there can be market failure, so also, government failure can arise. **Government failure** is a situation in which government actions result in inefficiency.

Government failure can arise because government is a complex organization made up of millions of individuals, each with his or her own economic objectives. Government policy is the outcome of the choices made by these individuals. To analyze these choices, economists have developed a *public choice theory* of the political marketplace.

Figure 14.1 shows the actors in the political marketplace. They are

- Voters
- Firms
- Politicians
- Bureaucrats

Voters Voters are consumers in the political marketplace. In the markets for goods and services, people express their preferences by their willingness to pay. In the political marketplace, they express their preferences by their votes, campaign contributions, and lobbying activity. Public choice theory assumes that voters support the policies they believe will make them better off and oppose the policies that they believe will make them worse off. It is voters' perceptions rather than reality that guide their choices.

Firms Firms are also consumers in the political marketplace. They express their preferences by their campaign contributions and lobbying activity. Public choice theory assumes that entrepreneurs support the policies that benefit their firms and oppose the policies that damage their interest. Again, it is perceptions rather than reality that guide these choices.

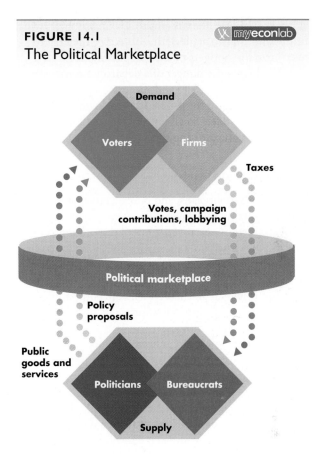

FIGURE 14.1
The Political Marketplace

Voters express their demands for policies with their votes, and voters and firms express demands by making campaign contributions and lobbying. Politicians propose policies that appeal to a majority of voters and to firms whose campaign contributions they seek. Bureaucrats try to maximize the budgets of their departments. A political equilibrium is a situation in which no group can improve its position by making a different choice.

Politicians Politicians are the entrepreneurs of the political marketplace. Public choice theory assumes that the objective of a politician is to get elected and to remain in office. Votes to a politician are like economic profit to a firm. To get enough votes, politicians propose policies that they expect will appeal to a majority of voters. But election campaigns are costly operations. So politicians also pay close attention to the demands of the firms that pay for election campaigns.

Bureaucrats Bureaucrats are the hired officials in government departments. They are the producers in the political marketplace. Public choice theory assumes that bureaucrats aim to maximize their own utility and that to achieve this objective they try to maximize the budgets of their departments.

The bigger the budget of a department, the greater is the prestige of its chief and the larger is the opportunity for promotion for people farther down the bureaucratic ladder. So all bureaucrats at all levels have an interest in maximizing the department's budget.

Political Equilibrium

Voters, firms, politicians, and bureaucrats make choices that best further their own objectives. But each group is constrained by the preferences of the other groups and by what is technologically feasible. The outcome that results from the choices of voters, firms, politicians, and bureaucrats is a **political equilibrium**, which is a situation in which all their choices are compatible and in which no group can improve its position by making a different choice.

Being in a political equilibrium is not the same thing as everyone being in agreement. Some politicians and their supporters devote resources to trying to change existing laws and regulations to their advantage. Other politicians and their supporters devote resources to opposing change. But no politician, bureaucrat, voter, or campaign contributor thinks it worthwhile to change the resources they are devoting to these activities.

REVIEW QUIZ

1 What are the two main reasons why governments exist?
2 What is market failure and what are the major sources of market failure? Can you think of some examples of market failure on the campus of your university?
3 Describe the political marketplace. Who are the demanders and who are the suppliers in the political market? How do the demanders "pay" the suppliers?

 myeconlab Study Plan 14.1

The rest of this chapter looks at the public choices that we make in regulating and controlling monopoly and oligopoly.

Monopoly and Oligopoly Regulation

GOVERNMENT INTERVENES IN MONOPOLY AND oligopoly markets to influence prices, quantities produced, and the distribution of the gains from economic activity in three main ways:

- Regulation
- Public ownership
- Anti-combine law

Regulation consists of rules administered by a government agency to influence economic activity by determining prices, product standards and types, and the conditions under which new firms may enter an industry.

Public ownership is the operation of a business as a **Crown corporation**—a corporation owned by the public and operated (in principle) in the social interest.

Anti-combine law is law that regulates and prohibits certain kinds of market behaviour, such as monopoly and monopolistic practices.

Before we describe these methods of influencing the behaviour of firms and markets, we must examine the economic theory of monopoly and oligopoly regulation, which is part of the broader public choice theory that we've just reviewed.

The Economic Theory of Regulation

In the political marketplace in which monopoly and oligopoly are regulated, there is a demand for regulation, a supply of regulation, and an equilibrium amount and type of regulation.

The Demand for Regulation People and firms demand the regulation that makes them better off and they express this demand through political activity: voting, lobbying, and making campaign contributions.

Consumers demand regulation that increases consumer surplus and firms demand regulation that increases producer surplus. The greater the number of people or firms that can benefit from a regulation, the greater is the demand for it. But numbers alone do not always translate into an effective political force because it is costly to organize for political action. A more powerful influence on the demand for regulation is the gain per person or per firm that results from it.

The Supply of Regulation Politicians supply the regulations that increase their campaign funds and that get them enough votes to achieve and maintain office. If a regulation benefits a large number of people and by enough for it to be noticed, that regulation appeals to politicians and is supplied. If a regulation benefits a large number of people but by too small an amount per person to be noticed, that regulation does not appeal to politicians and is not supplied.

If a regulation benefits a small number of people but by a large amount per person, that regulation also appeals to politicians because it helps them to get campaign funds from those who gain.

Equilibrium Regulation In political equilibrium, regulation might be in the social interest or in the self-interest of producers. The **social interest theory** of regulation is that politicians supply the regulation that achieves an efficient allocation of resources. According to this view, the political process works well and eliminates deadweight loss.

The **capture theory** of regulation is that regulation is in the self-interest of producers—a situation of government failure. The key idea of capture theory is that the cost of political organization is high and the political process will supply only those regulations that increase the surplus of small, easily identified groups that have low organization costs. Such regulations are supplied even if they impose costs on others, provided that those costs are spread thinly and widely enough that they do not decrease votes.

Political liberals tend to believe that regulation is in the social interest and that when it is not, greater efforts by politicians and bureaucrats can ensure that it is changed. Political conservatives tend to believe that most regulation is in the self-interest of producers and that no regulation is better for the social interest than the regulation that we have.

REVIEW QUIZ

1 How do consumers and producers express their demand for regulation?
2 What regulation do politicians supply?
3 Distinguish between the social interest and capture theories of regulation.

myeconlab Study Plan 14.2

Let's now look at the regulations that exist in our economy today and see how they work.

Regulation and Deregulation

THE PAST DECADE OR SO HAS SEEN DRAMATIC changes in the way in which the government has regulated the Canadian economy. We're going to examine some of these changes. To begin, we'll look at what the government regulates and also at the scope of regulation. Then we'll turn to the regulatory process itself and examine how regulators control prices and other aspects of market behaviour. Finally, we'll tackle the more difficult and controversial questions: Why does the government regulate some things but not others? Who benefits from the regulation that we have—consumers or producers?

The Scope of Regulation

Regulation in Canada touches a wide range of economic activity. Table 14.1 sets out the major federal regulatory agencies, together with a brief statement of their responsibilities. As you can see by inspecting that table, the predominant sectors subject to regulation are agriculture, energy, transport, and telecommunications.

Provincial and municipal governments also establish regulations covering a wide range of economic activity. Some of these—for example, municipal regulation of the taxicab industry—have important direct effects on the marketplace. Our analysis of the regulatory process and the effects of regulation apply with equal force to price, output, and profit regulation at these other governmental levels.

What exactly do regulatory agencies do? How do they regulate?

The Regulatory Process

Though regulatory agencies vary in size and scope and in the detailed aspects of economic life that they control, there are certain features common to all agencies.

First, the government appoints the senior bureaucrats who are the key decision makers in a regulatory agency. In addition, all agencies have a permanent bureaucracy made up of experts in the industry being regulated and who are often recruited from the regulated firms. Agencies have financial resources, voted by Parliament, to cover the costs of their operations.

TABLE 14.1   Federal Regulatory Agencies

Agency	Responsibility
Atomic Energy Control Board	Administers the Atomic Energy Control Act governing all uses of radioactive material.
Canadian Dairy Commission	Administers national dairy policy, which seeks to give producers an adequate return and keep the price to consumers low.
Canadian Radio-Television and Telecommunications Commission	Regulates all aspects of radio, television, and telecommunications.
Canadian Grain Commission	Regulates grain handling, establishes and maintains quality standards, audits grain stocks, and supervises future trading.
Canadian Wheat Board	Regulates exports of wheat and barley and domestic sales for human consumption.
National Energy Board	Regulates oil, gas, and electrical industries.
National Farm Products Marketing Council	Advises government on the establishment and operation of national agricultural marketing agencies and works with those agencies and provincial governments to promote marketing of farm products. Chicken, egg, and turkey agencies have been established under its aegis.
Canadian Transport Commission	Regulates transports under federal jurisdiction including rail, air, water, and pipeline and some interprovincial commercial motor transport.

Source: Adapted from the Statistics Canada publication *Canada Year Book*, Catalogue 11–402, 1992, pp. 543–558.

Second, each agency adopts a set of practices or operating rules for controlling prices and other aspects of economic performance. These rules and practices are based on well-defined physical and financial accounting procedures that are relatively easy to administer and to monitor.

In a regulated industry, individual firms are usually free to determine the technology that they will use in production. But they are not free to determine the prices at which they will sell their output, the quantities that they will sell, or the markets that they will serve. The regulatory agency grants certification to a company to serve a particular market with a particular line of products. The agency also determines the level and structure of prices that the company can charge. In some cases, the agency also determines the scale of output permitted.

To analyze the way in which regulation works, it is convenient to distinguish between the regulation of a natural monopoly and the regulation of cartels. Let's begin with the regulation of a natural monopoly.

Natural Monopoly

We defined *natural monopoly* in Chapter 12 (p. 264) as an industry in which one firm can supply the entire market at a lower average total cost than two or more firms can. Examples of natural monopoly include local distribution of cable television signals, electricity and gas, and urban rail services. For these activities, most of the costs are fixed and the larger the output, the lower is the monopoly's average total cost. It is much more expensive to have two or more competing sets of wires, pipes, and train lines serving every neighbourhood than it is to have a single set. (What is a natural monopoly changes over time as technology changes. With the introduction of fibre-optic cables, telephone companies and cable TV companies can compete with each other in both markets, so what was once a natural monopoly is becoming a more competitive industry. Direct satellite TV is also beginning to break the cable TV monopoly.)

Let's consider the example of cable TV. Figure 14.2 illustrates. The market demand curve for cable TV is *D*.

FIGURE 14.2

myeconlab

Natural Monopoly: Marginal Cost Pricing

A cable TV operator faces the demand curve D. The firm's marginal cost, MC, is constant at $10 per household per month. Fixed costs are large, and the average total cost curve, which includes average fixed cost, is ATC. A marginal cost pricing rule sets the price at $10 a month, with 8 million households being served. The green area is consumer surplus. The firm incurs a loss on each household, indicated by the red arrow. To remain in business, the firm must price discriminate, use a two-part tariff, or receive a subsidy.

The cable TV company's marginal cost curve is MC. That marginal cost curve is (assumed to be) horizontal at $10 per household per month—that is, the cost of providing each additional household with a month of cable programming is $10. The cable company has a heavy investment in satellite receiving dishes, cables, and control equipment and so has high fixed costs. These fixed costs are part of the company's average total cost curve, shown as ATC. The average total cost curve slopes downward because as the number of households served increases, the fixed cost is spread over a larger number of households. (If you need to refresh your memory on how the average total cost curve is calculated, take a quick look back at Chapter 10, p. 226.)

Regulation in the Social Interest How will cable TV be regulated according to the social interest theory? In social interest theory, regulation maximizes total surplus (the sum of consumer surplus and producer surplus), which occurs if marginal cost equals price. As you can see in Fig. 14.2, that outcome occurs if the price is regulated at $10 per household per month and if 8 million households are served. Such a regulation is called a **marginal cost pricing rule**. A marginal cost pricing rule sets price equal to marginal cost. It maximizes total surplus in the regulated industry.

A natural monopoly that is regulated to set price equal to marginal cost incurs an economic loss. Because its average total cost curve is falling, marginal cost is below average total cost. Because price equals marginal cost, price is below average total cost. Average total cost minus price is the loss per unit produced. It's obvious that a company that is required to use a marginal cost pricing rule will not stay in business for long. How can a company cover its costs and, at the same time, obey a marginal cost pricing rule?

One possibility is price discrimination (see Chapter 12, pp. 273–276). Another possibility is to use a two-part price (called a two-part tariff). For example, local telephone companies can charge consumers a monthly fee for being connected to the telephone system and then charge a price equal to marginal cost for each local call. A cable TV operator can charge a one-time connection fee that covers its fixed cost and then charge a monthly fee equal to marginal cost.

If a natural monopoly cannot cover its total cost from its customers, and if the government wants it to follow a marginal cost pricing rule, the government must give the firm a subsidy. In such a case, the government raises the revenue for the subsidy by taxing some other activity. But as we saw in Chapter 6, taxes themselves generate deadweight loss.

The deadweight loss that results from additional taxes must be subtracted from the efficiency gained by forcing the natural monopoly to adopt a marginal cost pricing rule.

It is possible that deadweight loss will be minimized by permitting the natural monopoly to charge a higher price than marginal cost rather than by taxing some other sector of the economy to subsidize the natural monopoly. Such a pricing arrangement is called an average cost pricing rule. An **average cost pricing rule** sets price equal to average total cost. Figure 14.3 shows the average cost pricing solution.

FIGURE 14.3   myeconlab
Natural Monopoly: Average Cost Pricing

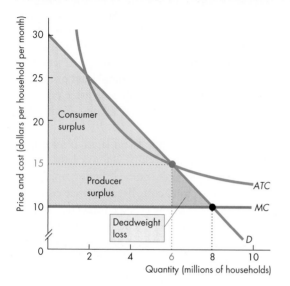

Average cost pricing sets the price equal to average total cost. The cable TV operator charges $15 a month and serves 6 million households. In this situation, the firm breaks even—average total cost equals price. Total surplus (the sum of consumer surplus and producer surplus) is reduced and a deadweight loss, shown by the grey triangle, arises.

With average cost pricing, the cable TV operator charges $15 a month and serves 6 million households. A deadweight loss arises, which is shown by the grey triangle in Fig. 14.3.

The marginal cost pricing rule and the average cost pricing rule that we've just examined are easier to state than to implement. The major obstacle to implementing them is that the regulator knows less than the regulated firm about the cost of production.

The regulator does not directly observe the firm's costs and doesn't know how hard the firm is trying to minimize cost. For this reason, regulators use one of two practical rules:

■ Rate of return regulation

■ Price cap regulation

Let's see whether these rules deliver an outcome that is in the social interest or the private interest.

Rate of Return Regulation Under **rate of return regulation**, a regulated firm must justify its price by showing that the price enables it to earn a specified target percent return on its capital. The target rate of return is determined with reference to what is normal in competitive industries. This rate of return is part of the opportunity cost of the natural monopoly and part of the firm's average total cost.

If the regulator could observe the firm's total cost and also know that the firm had minimized total cost, it would accept only a price proposal from the firm that was equivalent to average cost pricing.

The outcome would be like that in Fig. 14.3, where the regulated price is $15 a month and 6 million households are served. In this case, rate of return regulation would result in a price that favours the consumer and prevents the producer from maximizing profit. The monopoly will have failed to capture the regulator, and the outcome will be closer to that predicted by the social interest theory of regulation.

But the managers of a regulated firm might not minimize cost. And if the firm is regulated to achieve a target rate of return, the managers have an incentive to inflate costs and raise price. One way to inflate the firm's costs is to spend on inputs that are not strictly required for the production of the good. On-the-job luxury in the form of sumptuous office suites, limousines, free baseball tickets (disguised as public relations expenses), company jets, lavish international travel, and entertainment are all ways in which managers can inflate costs.

Managers also have an incentive to use more capital than the efficient amount because the more capital they use, the larger is the total return they are permitted to earn. And they have an incentive to make larger-than-required charges for depreciation and losses from bad debts.

If the cable TV operator in our example manages to persuade the regulator that its true average total cost curve is that shown as *ATC (inflated)* in Fig. 14.4, then the regulator, applying the normal rate of return principle, will accept the firm's proposed price of $20 a month. At this price, 4 million households buy cable service. So the price and quantity will be the same as those under unregulated monopoly.

Price Cap Regulation For the reason we've just examined, rate of return regulation is increasingly being replaced by price cap regulation. A **price cap regulation** is a price ceiling—a rule that specifies the highest price the firm is permitted to set. This type of

FIGURE 14.4 — myeconlab
Natural Monopoly: Inflating Cost

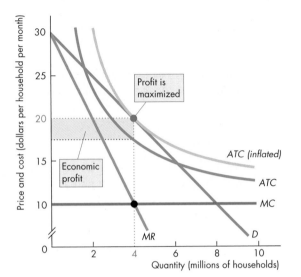

If the cable TV operator is able to inflate its costs to *ATC (inflated)* and persuade the regulator that these are genuine minimum costs of production, rate of return regulation results in a price of $20 a month—the profit-maximizing price. To the extent that the producer can inflate costs above average total cost, the price rises, output decreases, and deadweight loss increases. The profit is captured by the managers, not the shareholders (owners) of the firm.

FIGURE 14.5 — myeconlab
Price Cap Regulation of Natural Monopoly

If the cable TV operator is subject to a price cap regulation, the price cap limits the price that may be charged. At all quantities less than 6 million, the firm incurs a loss. At all quantities greater than 6 million, the firm also incurs a loss. Only at an output of 6 million can the firm break even and earn a normal rate of return. The firm has an incentive to keep costs as low as possible and to produce the quantity demanded at the price cap.

regulation gives a firm an incentive to operate efficiently and keep costs under control. Price cap regulation has become common for the electricity and telecommunications industries and is replacing rate of return regulation.

The CRTC has used price cap regulation since the mid-1990s to regulate the prices of telephone services provided by Canada's major telephone companies.

To see how a price cap works, let's suppose that the cable TV operator in our previous example is subject to this type of regulation. Figure 14.5 shows what happens.

Without regulation, the firm maximizes profit by serving 4 million households and charging a price of $20 a month. If a price cap is set at $15 a month, the firm is permitted to sell any quantity it chooses at that price or at a lower price. At 4 million house-

holds, the firm now incurs an economic loss. It can decrease the loss by *increasing* output to 6 million households. But at more than 6 million households, the firm incurs losses. So the profit-maximizing quantity is 6 million households—the same as with average cost pricing.

Notice that a price cap lowers the price and increases output. This outcome is in sharp contrast to the effect of a price ceiling in a competitive market that you studied in Chapter 6 (pp. 124–127). The reason is that in an unregulated monopoly, the equilibrium output is less than the competitive equilibrium output and the price cap regulation replicates the conditions of a competitive market.

In Fig. 14.5, the price cap delivers average cost pricing. In practice, the regulator might set the price cap too high. For this reason, price cap regulation is often combined with **earnings sharing regulation**, under which profits that rise above a target level must be shared with the firm's customers.

Social Interest or Capture in Natural Monopoly Regulation?

It is not clear whether natural monopoly regulation produces prices and quantities that more closely correspond with the predictions of capture theory or with social interest theory. But one thing is clear: Price regulation does not require natural monopolies to use the marginal cost pricing rule. If it did, most natural monopolies would make losses and receive hefty government subsidies to enable them to remain in business.

There is an exception. Many telephone companies use marginal cost pricing. They cover their total cost by charging a flat fee each month for being connected to their system and then permit each call to be made at its marginal cost—zero.

A test of whether natural monopoly regulation is in the social interest or the self-interest of the producer is to examine the rates of return earned by regulated natural monopolies. If those rates of return are significantly higher than those in the rest of the economy, then, to some degree, the regulator might have been captured by the producer. If the rates of return in the regulated monopoly industries are similar to those in the rest of the economy, then we cannot tell for sure if the regulator has been captured because we cannot know the extent to which costs have been inflated by the managers of the regulated firms. There is plenty of empirical evidence that many natural monopolies in Canada do earn higher rates of return than the economy average.

One recent striking example is cable television service; telephone service is another. The rates of return in these two industries exceed 10 percent a year, approaching double the economy average. Perhaps the most dramatic piece of evidence that regulation benefits the regulated firm is the profits of Bell Canada Enterprises (BCE), prior to deregulation of long-distance phone services. BCE is a conglomerate that produced *regulated* long-distance telephone services and *unregulated* phone equipment (Northern Telecom) and financial services (Montreal Trustco). In 1992, BCE made a total profit of $1.4 billion on total assets of $12.3 billion, a profit rate of 11.4 percent. But this total was made up of a profit for the regulated Bell Canada of $0.9 billion on assets of $7 billion—a return of 12.9 percent—and a profit for all of BCE's *unregulated* operations of $0.5 billion on assets of $5.3 billion—9.4 percent.

Until the early 1990s, long-distance telephone service was a natural monopoly, but technological advances in telecommunications have changed the situation. Today, the industry is an oligopoly. But oligopoly is also regulated. Let's examine regulation in oligopolistic industries—the regulation of cartels.

Cartel Regulation

A *cartel* is a collusive agreement among a number of firms that is designed to restrict output and achieve a higher profit for the cartel's members. Cartels are illegal in Canada and in most other countries. But international cartels can sometimes operate legally, such as the international cartel of oil producers known as OPEC (the Organization of Petroleum Exporting Countries).

Illegal cartels can arise in oligopoly industries. An oligopoly is a market structure in which a small number of firms compete with each other. We studied oligopoly (and duopoly—two firms competing for a market) in Chapter 13. There, we saw that if firms manage to collude and behave like a monopoly, they can set the same price and sell the same total quantity as a monopoly firm would. But we also discovered that in such a situation, each firm will be tempted to cheat, increasing its own output and profit at the expense of the other firms. The result of such cheating on the collusive agreement is the unravelling of the monopoly equilibrium and the emergence of a competitive outcome with zero economic profit for producers. Such an outcome benefits consumers at the expense of producers.

How is oligopoly regulated? Does regulation prevent monopoly practices or does it encourage those practices? According to the social interest theory, oligopoly is regulated to ensure a competitive outcome. According to the capture theory, oligopoly regulators are captured by the firms and the regulation enables the firms to earn economic profit and operate against the social interest.

Let's look at these two possible outcomes in the oligopoly market for trucking tomatoes from the fields in southwestern Ontario to a ketchup factory in Leamington, illustrated in Fig. 14.6. The market demand curve for trips is D. The industry marginal

FIGURE 14.6
Collusive Oligopoly

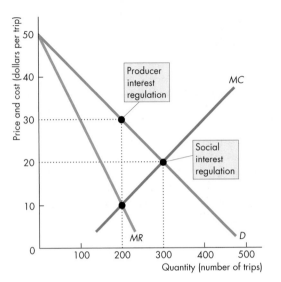

Ten trucking firms transport tomatoes from southwestern Ontario to Leamington. The demand curve is *D*, and the industry marginal cost curve is *MC*. Under competition, the *MC* curve is the industry supply curve. If the industry is competitive, the price of a trip will be $20 and 300 trips will be made each week. Producers will demand regulation that restricts entry and limits output to 200 trips a week, where industry marginal revenue (*MR*) is equal to industry marginal cost (*MC*). This regulation raises the price to $30 a trip and results in each producer making maximum profit—as if it is a monopoly.

cost curve—and the competitive supply curve—is *MC*.

If this industry is regulated in the social interest, the price will be set so that marginal benefit equals marginal cost. The price will be $20 a trip, and there will be 300 trips a week. A price cap regulation at $20 a trip could achieve this outcome.

How would this industry be regulated according to the capture theory? Regulation that is in the self-interest of the producer will maximize profit. To find the outcome in this case, we need to determine the price and quantity when marginal cost equals marginal revenue. The marginal revenue curve is *MR*. So mar-

ginal cost equals marginal revenue at 200 trips a week. The price of a trip is $30.

One way the cartel can achieve this outcome is to have regulations limit the output of each firm in the industry. If there are 10 trucking companies, an output limit of 20 trips per company ensures that the total number of trips in a week is 200. Penalties can be imposed to ensure that no single producer exceeds its output limit.

All the firms in the industry would support this type of regulation because it helps to prevent cheating and to maintain a monopoly outcome. Each firm knows that without effectively enforced production quotas, every firm has an incentive to increase output. (For each firm, price exceeds marginal cost, so a greater output brings a larger profit.) So each firm wants a method of preventing output from rising above the industry profit-maximizing level, and the quotas enforced by regulation achieve this end. With this type of cartel regulation, the regulator enables a cartel to operate legally and in its own best interest.

Social Interest or Capture in Cartel Regulation?

What does cartel regulation do in practice? Although there is disagreement about the matter, the consensus view is that regulation tends to favour the producer. Trucking and airlines (when they were regulated by the Canadian Transport Commission) and taxicabs (regulated by cities) are specific examples in which profits of producers increased as a result of regulation.

The most dramatic examples of regulation favouring the producer are in agriculture. An Economic Council of Canada study, based on the situation prevailing in the early 1980s, estimated that regulation of the egg-producing and broiler chicken industries alone transferred more than $100 million a year to just 4,600 individual producers.[1]

You can see that this situation is a good example of the predictions of capture theory. The 4,600 producers received, on the average, $22,000 a year. In the dollars of 2005, this amount becomes $53,000 a year. Contrast this large gain per producer with the loss of at the most a few pennies per dozen that the consumers of eggs paid.

[1] J.D. Forbes, R.D. Hughes, and T.K. Warley, *Economic Intervention and Regulation in Canadian Agriculture* (Ottawa: Department of Supply and Services, 1982).

The producer's self-interest was much greater than the individual consumer's and the social interest. So the producer's self-interest prevailed, even though, in aggregate, the scheme created deadweight loss.

Further evidence on cartel and oligopoly regulation can be obtained from the performance of prices and profit following deregulation. If, following deregulation, prices and profit fall, then, to some degree, the regulation must have been serving the self-interest of the producer.

In contrast, if, following deregulation, prices and profits remain constant or increase, then the regulation may be presumed to have been serving the social interest. Because there has been a substantial amount of deregulation in recent years, we can use this test of oligopoly regulation to see which of the two theories better fits the facts.

The evidence is mixed, but in the cases of the airline, trucking industries, long-distance phone calls, three main oligopolies that have been deregulated, prices fell and there was a large increase in the volume of business.

Making Predictions

Most industries have a few producers and many consumers. In these cases, public choice theory predicts that regulation will protect producers' self-interest because a small number of people stand to gain a large amount and so they will be fairly easy to organize as a cohesive lobby. Under such circumstances, politicians will be rewarded with campaign contributions rather than votes. But there are situations in which the social interest is sufficiently strong and well organized and thus able to prevail. There are also cases in which the balance switches from self-interest of producers to the social interest, as seen in the deregulation process that began in the late 1970s.

Deregulation raises some hard questions for economists seeking to understand and make predictions about regulation. Why were the transportation and telecommunications sectors deregulated? If producers gained from regulation and if the producer lobby was strong enough to achieve regulation, what happened in the 1970s to change the equilibrium to one in which the social interest prevailed? We do not have a complete answer to this question at the present time. But regulation had become so costly to voters, and the

potential benefits to them from deregulation so great, that the cost of organizing the voters' voice became a price worth paying.

One factor that increased the cost of regulation borne by voters and brought deregulation in the transportation sector was the large increase in energy prices in the 1970s. These price hikes made route regulation by the Canadian Transport Commission extremely costly and changed the balance of the political equilibrium to favour voters.

Technological change was the main factor at work in the telecommunications sector. New satellite-based, computer-controlled long-distance technologies enabled smaller producers to offer low-cost services. These producers wanted a share of Bell Canada's business—and profit.

As communications costs fall, it becomes more likely that the social interest will prevail. If this line of reasoning is correct, we will see more regulation and deregulation in the future that is in the social interest.

REVIEW QUIZ

1 What are the main regulatory agencies in Canada? What are their responsibilities?
2 Why does natural monopoly need to be regulated?
3 What pricing rule enables a natural monopoly to operate in the social interest and why is that rule difficult to implement?
4 Why is a marginal cost pricing rule difficult to implement?
5 How does rate of return regulation work and what problems does it create?
6 How does price cap regulation work and what problems is it designed to overcome?
7 How might cartels be regulated in the social interest?

myeconlab Study Plan 14.3

Let's now turn to the second method of intervention in markets: public ownership.

Public Ownership

CROWN CORPORATIONS HAVE A SIGNIFICANT AND historical presence in Canadian society. Before Confederation, Crown corporations were used for building canals and operating ports and harbours.

The establishment of the Canadian nation involved a commitment to build a railroad to link New Brunswick and Nova Scotia to central Canada. Over the years, vast distances, a sparse population, the presence of a powerful neighbour, strong and distinct national interests, and the existence of two main cultural and linguistic groups nurtured the establishment of Crown corporations.

A Crown corporation is a corporation in which the government has 100 percent ownership. There are federal and provincial Crown corporations, and they are involved in many sectors of the economy, including transportation; energy and resources; agriculture and fisheries; development and construction; government services; culture; financial intermediaries; telecommunications and broadcasting; provincial lotteries; housing; and alcoholic beverages.

Examples of Crown corporations include the Business Development Bank of Canada, the Canadian Museum of Nature, and the Ontario Lottery and Gaming Corporation.

Public ownership provides another way in which the government can influence the behaviour of a natural monopoly. And in principle, this method might achieve an efficient use of resources. But does that actually happen? What are the effects of the public ownership of a natural monopoly on the efficient use of resources? How does a publicly owned corporation actually operate?

To explore some alternative patterns of behaviour for public corporations, we'll begin by laying out the benchmark of efficiency.

Efficient Crown Corporation

One possibility is that a Crown corporation is operated in a manner that results in economic efficiency—marginal benefit equals marginal cost and the sum of producer surplus and consumer surplus is maximized.

Consider the example of a publicly owned railroad that has a natural monopoly. Figure 14.7 shows the demand for freight service and the railroad's costs.

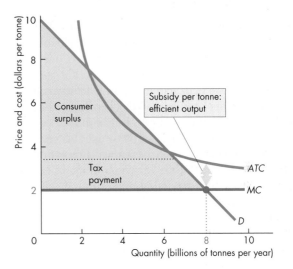

FIGURE 14.7
An Efficient Crown Corporation

This figure shows a railroad operated by a Crown corporation that produces the output at which price equals marginal cost. Its output is 8 billion tonnes a year and the price is $2 a tonne. The Crown corporation receives a subsidy that enables it to cover its total cost, and that cost is the minimum possible cost of providing the efficient quantity.

The demand curve is *D*. The marginal cost curve is *MC*. Notice that the marginal cost curve is horizontal at $2 a tonne. The railroad has a heavy investment in track, trains, and control equipment, so it has large fixed costs. These fixed costs feature in the company's average total cost curve *ATC*. The average total cost curve slopes downward because as the number of tonnes of freight carried increases, the fixed costs are spread over a larger number of tonnes.

To be efficient, a Crown corporation obeys the rule:

Produce the output at which price equals marginal cost.

In this example, that output level is 8 billion tonnes a year at a price—and marginal cost—of $2 a tonne. To be able to operate in this manner, a publicly owned railroad has to be subsidized; the subsidy on each unit of output must equal the difference between average total cost and marginal cost. And the subsidy has to be collected in a way other than through the price of the good or service produced. In other words, the subsidy has to be collected by taxation. If the government taxes each household a fixed amount, the consumer surplus will shrink to the green triangle shown in Fig. 14.7 but consumer surplus will be at its maximum.

The situation depicted in Fig. 14.7 achieves an efficient outcome because marginal benefit equals marginal cost and consumer surplus is maximized. But it is not an outcome that is necessarily compatible with the interests of the managers of the Crown corporation. Two possible models of the behaviour of managers are bureaucratic budget maximization or profit maximization. What do these alternative models predict about Crown corporation behaviour?

A Bureaucracy Model of Public Enterprise

The basic assumption of the economic theory of bureaucracy is that bureaucrats aim to maximize the budget of their bureau. The equivalent assumption for the managers of a Crown corporation is that they seek to maximize the budget of the Crown corporation. The effect of budget maximization by the managers of a Crown corporation depends on the pricing constraints under which the managers operate. We will consider two alternative cases:

- Budget maximization with marginal cost pricing
- Budget maximization at a zero price

Budget Maximization with Marginal Cost Pricing If the bureau maximizes its budget but obeys the marginal cost pricing rule, it will produce the efficient outcome. It will produce 8 billion tonnes a year and it will sell its output for $2 a tonne, as Fig. 14.8 illustrates. But the corporation will not minimize its production cost. It will inflate its costs and become inefficient. It will hire more workers than the number required to produce 8 billion tonnes a year, and its internal control mechanisms, which would ensure internal efficiency (as in a private profit-maximizing firm), will be weak. As a result, the average total cost of the corporation will rise to *ATC (inflated)*.

What determines the limit on the extent to which the corporation can inflate its costs? The answer is the

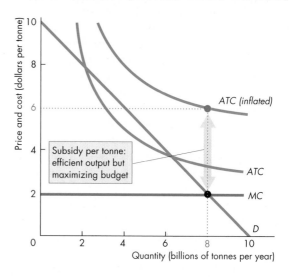

FIGURE 14.8   ⓧ myeconlab

A Bureaucratic Crown Corporation

This figure shows what happens if the managers of the Crown corporation pursue their own interest and maximize the Crown corporation's budget by padding costs. Average total cost now increases to *ATC (inflated)*. If the corporation is required to keep price equal to marginal cost, the quantity produced is efficient, but the managers divert the consumer surplus to the Crown corporation.

maximum amount that the users of the output can be made to pay through taxation. That maximum is the total consumer surplus. That maximum consumer surplus is the area beneath the demand curve and above the marginal cost curve. You can work out how big it is by using the usual formula for the area of the triangle. The height of this triangle is $8 and its base is 8 billion tonnes a year, so the consumer surplus is $32 billion a year. Spread over 8 billion tonnes, $32 billion gives a subsidy of $4 a tonne, the amount shown in Fig. 14.8. $32 billion will be the upper limit that any government—in a political democracy—can extract from the taxpayer-consumers of the product of this corporation. If the subsidy were higher, people would vote to shut down the Crown corporation because the subsidy would exceed the consumer surplus.

Budget Maximization at Zero Price What happens if a government bureau provides its goods or services free? Of course, it is improbable that a publicly owned railroad would be able to persuade politicians and taxpayers that its activities should be expanded to the point of providing its services free. But there are several examples of publicly provided goods that are indeed free. Primary and secondary education and health care are two outstanding examples. For the sake of comparison, we'll continue with our railroad, improbable though it is.

If in Fig. 14.8 the bureau increases output to the point at which the price that consumers are willing to pay for the last unit produced is zero, output rises to 10 billion tonnes a year. A deadweight loss is created because the marginal cost of production, $2 a tonne, is higher than the marginal benefit or willingness to pay, $0 per tonne. The bureau will be inefficient in its internal operations and inflate its costs. The subsidy will increase to the highest that the public will be willing to pay. The maximum subsidy will equal the consumer surplus.

A Profit-Maximizing Public Enterprise

If a public enterprise is operated in a similar way to a private natural monopoly, its managers will want to get the maximum profit available and make the largest possible contribution to the government's finances.

To maximize profit, the public enterprise would produce the quantity at which marginal revenue equals marginal cost. This outcome always involves underproduction relative to the efficient quantity unless the firm can price discriminate. A perfectly price discriminating public enterprise would produce the efficient quantity (see Chapter 12, p. 276) and it would maximize the budget of the enterprise.

Compromise Outcome

Crown corporations are unlikely to behave in exactly the way predicted by any of the three models we've considered. There will be a tendency for a public corporation to underproduce and to inflate its budget, but not to the extent shown in Fig. 14.8. There will be a tendency for consumer interest to have some influence, but not to the degree shown in Fig. 14.7. The prediction about the behaviour of a Crown corporation is that it will produce more but at a higher average total cost than a private firm would produce.

Crown Corporations in Reality

How do actual Crown corporations behave? Several studies have been directed to answering this question. One of the most fruitful ways of approaching the question is to compare public and private enterprises in which, as far as possible, other things are equal. There are two well-known and well-studied cases for which other things seemed to be fairly equal. One such comparison is of Canada's public and private railroads—Canadian National (CN) and Canadian Pacific (CP). The other is from Australia, which had two domestic airlines, one private and the other public, that flew almost identical routes at almost identical times every day. Economists studied the costs of these similar enterprises and concluded that each of the publicly owned enterprises operated with a cost structure that was significantly higher than that of the corresponding private firm. In the case of CN and CP, the estimated difference was 14 percent.[2]

Privatization

Largely because of an increasing understanding of how bureaucracies work and of the inefficiency of publicly operated enterprises, there has been a move to sell off publicly owned corporations. Since the mid-1980s, the federal government has sold a dozen companies, including Air Canada and CN.

REVIEW QUIZ
1 How might a Crown corporation operate efficiently?
2 What are the effects of budget maximization by the managers of a Crown corporation?
3 What limits the maximum budget of a Crown corporation?
Study Plan 14.4

Let's now turn to the third method of market intervention: anti-combine law.

[2] W.S.W. Caves and Lauritis Christensen, "The Relative Efficiency of Public *v.* Private Firms in a Competitive Environment: The Case of Canada's Railroads," *Journal of Political Economy* 88, 5 (September–October 1980), 958–76.

Anti-Combine Law

ANTI-COMBINE LAW GIVES POWERS TO THE courts and to government agencies to influence markets. Like regulation, anti-combine law can work in the public interest to maximize total surplus or in private interests to maximize the surpluses of particular special interest groups such as producers. We'll describe Canada's anti-combine law and then examine some recent cases.

Canada's Anti-Combine Law

Canada's anti-combine law dates from 1889. At that time, monopoly was a major political issue and people were concerned about the absence of competition in industries as diverse as sugar and groceries, biscuits and confectionery, coal, binder twine, agricultural implements, stoves, coffins, eggs, and fire insurance.

Canada's anti-combine law today is defined in the Competition Act of 1986, which is described in Table 14.6. The Act established a Competition Bureau and a Competition Tribunal. The Competition Act distinguishes between practices that are

1. Criminal
2. Noncriminal

Conspiracy to fix prices, bid-rigging, other anti-competitive price-fixing actions, and false advertising are criminal offences. The courts handle alleged offences, and the standard level of proof beyond a reasonable doubt must be established.

Mergers, abuse of a dominant market position, refusal to deal, and other actions designed to limit competition such as exclusive dealing are noncriminal offences. The Director of the Competition Bureau sends alleged violations of a noncriminal nature to the Competition Tribunal for examination.

Some Major Anti-Combine Cases

Let's see how the Competition Act has been working by looking at some recent cases. The first case we'll examine is important because it confirms the Competition Tribunal's power to enforce its orders.

Chrysler In 1986, Chrysler stopped supplying auto parts to Richard Brunet, a Montreal auto dealer. Chrysler also discouraged other dealers from supplying Brunet. The Competition Tribunal claimed that Chrysler wanted Brunet's business for itself and ordered Chrysler to resume doing business with Brunet. Chrysler did not resume sending supplies and the Tribunal cited Chrysler for contempt. Appeals against this ruling eventually reached the Supreme Court of Canada, which confirmed the Tribunal's power over contempt for its ruling. But the Tribunal subsequently dropped its contempt charge.

The second case we'll look at concerns aspartame, the sweetener in many soft drinks.

NutraSweet NutraSweet, the maker of aspartame, tried to gain a monopoly in aspartame. It did so by licensing the use of its "swirl" only on products for which it had an exclusive deal. The Competition Tribunal ruled that this action unduly limited competition and told NutraSweet that it may not enforce existing contracts, enter into new contracts in which it is the exclusive supplier, or give inducements to encourage the display of its "swirl." The result of this case was an increase in competition and a fall in the price of aspartame in Canada.

The third case we'll examine concerns a publication you use almost every day: the Yellow Pages.

Bell Canada Enterprises Two subsidiaries of Bell Canada Enterprises have a 90 percent share of the market for the publication of telephone directories in their territories. These companies tie the sale of advertising services to the sale of advertising space in the Yellow Pages. If you want to advertise in the Yellow Pages, you must buy the advertising services of one of these two companies. As a result, other advertising agencies cannot effectively compete for business in Yellow Pages advertising. The Director of the Competition Bureau applied for an order prohibiting the tied-sale practice of these two companies.

Other Anti-Competitive Agreements During 1995 and 1996, the Competition Bureau took action against several anti-competitive agreements. Among such cases were driving schools in Sherbrooke, ready-mix concrete in the Saguenay-Lac St-Jean region, real estate dealing in Calgary, the importing of Australian mandarin oranges, wire for baling pulp, and ambulance services in Alberta.

The Competition Bureau is extremely active in reviewing and, in some cases, blocking mergers. The next cases we examine fall into this category.

TABLE 14.2   Canada's Anti-Combine Law: The Competition Act, 1986

Abuse of Dominant Position

79 (1)   Where on application by the Director, the Tribunal finds that:

    (a)   one or more persons substantially or completely control, throughout Canada or any area thereof, a class or species of business,

    (b)   that person or those persons have engaged in or are engaging in a practice of anti-competitive acts, and

    (c)   the practice has had, is having or is likely to have the effect of preventing or lessening competition substantially in a market,

the Tribunal may make an order prohibiting all or any of those persons from engaging in that practice.

Mergers

92 (1)   Where on application by the Director, the Tribunal finds that a merger or proposed merger prevents or lessens, or is likely to prevent or lessen, competition substantially . . . the Tribunal may . . . [,]

in the case of a completed merger, order any party to the merger or any other person

    (i)   to dissolve the merger . . .

    (ii)   to dispose of assets and shares . . .

[or]

in the case of a proposed merger, make an order directed against any party to the proposed merger or any other person

    (i)   ordering the person . . . not to proceed with the merger

    (ii)   ordering the person not to proceed with part of the merger

Canada Packers and Labatt Canada Packers Inc. and John Labatt Ltd. proposed a merger of their flour milling operations that would have made them the biggest miller in Canada and the fifth biggest in North America. The Competition Tribunal stopped this merger, saying that the Canadian flour milling business had been run too much like a cartel and that more, not less, competition was needed.

Banks Some attempts to merge are so politically sensitive that they are decided at the highest political level. One example is the decision of the federal government to block an attempted merger by the Royal Bank and the Bank of Montreal. If Canada's two major banks eventually merge, the sanction of the federal government will be needed.

Social or Special Interest?

The intent of anti-combine law is to protect the public interest and restrain the profit-seeking and anti-competitive actions of producers. On the whole, the overall thrust of the law and its enforcement has been in line with its intent and has served the social interest. Further, if the recent cases we have examined are setting a trend, we can expect a continuation of decisions from the courts and the Competition Tribunal in future cases that serve the social interest.

REVIEW QUIZ

1 What is the Act of Parliament that provides our anti-combine law?

2 What actions violate the anti-combine law?

3 Under what circumstances is a merger unlikely to be approved?

myeconlab   Study Plan 14.5

◆ In this chapter, we've seen how the government intervenes in markets to affect prices, quantities, consumer surplus, and producer surplus. *Reading Between the Lines* on pp. 340–341 looks at a new natural monopoly in broadband Internet service.

Market Power of Broadband Providers

BLOOMBERG.COM, SEPTEMBER 16, 2005

Rogers, BCE Join to Build Canadian Broadband Net

Rogers Communications Inc. and BCE Inc., which compete for telephone and cable customers, plan to build a Canada-wide wireless broadband network together to add customers in areas including those currently without Web access.

The network will cost $200 million to build, No. 1 Canadian phone carrier BCE and Rogers, the biggest cable-television and mobile-phone company, said in a statement today. The system will be equipped to offer high-speed Internet access to more than two-thirds of Canadians in about three years.

The companies partnered on the network because both had purchased stakes in Inukshuk Internet Inc., which owns the rights to the broadband spectrum. The rivals will operate the network and compete to sell services in the 40 cities and about 50 rural and remote areas the network will cover.

. . .

"The economies of scale by a joint venture with Rogers allowed us to build one infrastructure across Canada," BCE Vice President Trevor Anderson said in an interview.

. . .

The Canadian Competition Bureau will examine the proposal to determine whether the venture requires a formal review, merger notification unit chief Daniel Campagna said in an interview. "We are aware of the matter. We have to look at whether we can actually review" the venture under Canadian law, he said.

Essence of the Story

■ BCE, Canada's biggest phone company, and Rogers Communication, the biggest cable-television company jointly own Inukshuk Internet Inc.

■ Inukshuk is building a $200 million high-speed Internet system.

■ The Inukshuk network will serve two-thirds of Canadian households and cover 40 cities and 50 rural and remote areas.

■ The Canadian Competition Bureau will examine the venture but has not yet determined whether is has the power to formally review it.

Economic Analysis

■ The cost of building a broadband Internet service is high—$200 million—and if Rogers Communication and BCE each built their own network, the cost would be double this amount.

■ The marginal cost of operating a broadband Internet service is low.

■ The marginal benefit and demand for broadband Internet services is high. Based on current prices in major cities, it is between $40 and $50 a month.

■ The combination of cost conditions and demand conditions make the market for broadband Internet service a natural monopoly.

■ Figure 1 shows this market in Canada, served by Inukshuk.

■ Inukshuk's average fixed cost curve, AFC, is based the fact that it is spending $200 million to build its network.

■ We'll assume that Inukshuk faces a real interest rate of 5 percent a year, that normal profit is another 5 percent a year, and that the system will operate for 20 years and then need replacing. These assumptions mean that Inukshuk's total fixed cost is $30 million a year—$10 million interest, $10 million normal

profit, and $10 million depreciation.

■ The AFC curve is based on this average total cost of $30 million a year.

■ We don't know Inukshuk's variable and marginal cost. But we'll assume that it is a constant $48 per customer served per year. The curve labelled AVC = MC shows this cost.

■ Adding the average fixed cost and average variable cost together give the average total cost curve, ATC.

■ We don't know how much Canadians in remote regions and cities not now served with broadband are willing to pay for this service. But we'll assume that a few are willing to pay $168 a year ($14 a month). We'll also assume that this amount decreases as shown by the demand curve D.

■ Along this demand curve, by the time 10 million customers are buying broadband service, the marginal customer is willing to pay only $48 a year, or $4 a month. (This assumption is probably too low.)

■ On the assumptions we've made, marginal revenue equals marginal cost when 5 million customers are served and the price of the service is $108 a year (or $9 a month).

Figure 1 Inukshuk cost, revenue, and profit

■ The average total cost of serving 5 million customers is $54, so this quantity maximized profit. On the assumptions made, profit is $270 million a year.

■ If the Canadian Competition Bureau could regulate this natural monopoly and force it to price at average cost, Inukshuk would serve almost 10 million customers and charge a price (on our assumptions) of about $52 a year.

You're the Voter

■ Do you think that the Canadian Competition Bureau should prevent Inukshuk from creating a natural monopoly?

■ Do you think that the Canadian Competition Bureau should permit Inukshuk to create a natural monopoly and then regulate it?

■ Do you think that the Canadian Competition Bureau should permit Inukshuk to create a natural monopoly and then let the market work without regulation?

341

SUMMARY

KEY POINTS

The Economic Theory of Government
(pp. 324–326)

- Government exists to regulate monopoly and oligopoly, cope with externalities, provide public goods, control the use of common resources, and redistribute income.
- Public choice theory explains how voters, firms, politicians, and bureaucrats interact in a political marketplace.

Monopoly and Oligopoly Regulation
(pp. 326–327)

- Government uses regulation and anti-combine law to intervene in monopoly and oligopoly markets.
- Consumers demand regulation that increases consumer surplus, and firms demand regulation that increases producer surplus.
- Equilibrium regulation might be in the social interest and eliminate deadweight loss or in the self-interest of producers who capture the regulators.

Regulation and Deregulation (pp. 327–334)

- Natural monopolies and cartels are regulated by agencies controlled by politically appointed bureaucrats and staffed by a permanent bureaucracy of experts.
- Regulated firms must comply with rules about price, product quality, and output levels.
- Regulation has not lowered the profit rates of regulated firms.

Public Ownership (pp. 335–337)

- Crown corporations are 100 percent owned by federal and provincial governments and they produce such items as broadcasting, hydroelectric power, and telecommunications.
- The economic theory of bureaucracy is that managers maximize the bureau's budget subject to political constraints.

- Crown corporations tend to be inefficient: They overproduce and their costs are too high.

Anti-Combine Law (pp. 338–339)

- Anti-combine law provides an alternative way for government to control monopoly and monopolistic practices.
- The Competition Act of 1986 sets out Canada's anti-combine law and places responsibility for enforcement with the Competition Tribunal.

KEY FIGURES AND TABLE

KEY TERMS

PROBLEMS

Go to (X) myeconlab for solutions to odd-numbered problems and additional exercises.

1. Elixir Springs, Inc., is an unregulated natural monopoly that bottles Elixir, a unique health product with no substitutes. The total fixed cost incurred by Elixir Springs is $150,000, and its marginal cost is 10¢ a bottle. The figure illustrates the demand for Elixir.

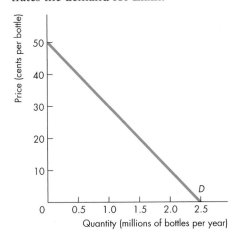

a. What is the price of a bottle of Elixir?
b. How many bottles does Elixir Springs sell?
c. Does Elixir Springs maximize total surplus or producer surplus?

2. Cascade Springs, Inc., is a natural monopoly that bottles water from a mountain spring. Its total fixed cost is $120,000, and its marginal cost is 20 cents a bottle. The figure illustrates the demand for Cascade Springs water.

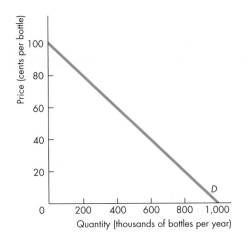

a. What is the price of Cascade Springs water?
b. How many bottles does Cascade Springs sell?
c. Does the firm maximize total surplus?

3. The government imposes a marginal cost pricing rule on Elixir Springs in problem 1.
   a. What is the price of a bottle of Elixir?
   b. How many bottles does Elixir Springs sell?
   c. What is Elixir Springs' producer surplus?
   d. What is the consumer surplus?
   e. Is the regulation in the social interest? Explain.

4. The government imposes a marginal cost pricing rule on Cascade Springs in problem 2.
   a. What is the price of Cascade Springs water?
   b. How many bottles does Cascade Springs sell?
   c. What is the economic profit?
   d. What is the consumer surplus?
   e. Is the regulation in the social interest? Explain.

5. The government imposes an average cost pricing rule on Elixir Springs in problem 1.
   a. What is the price of a bottle of Elixir?
   b. How many bottles does Elixir Springs sell?
   c. What is Elixir Springs' producer surplus?
   d. What is the consumer surplus?
   e. Is the regulation in the social interest? Explain.

6. The government imposes an average cost pricing rule on Cascade Springs in problem 2.
   a. What is the price of Cascade Springs water?
   b. How many bottles does Cascade Springs sell?
   c. What is the economic profit?
   d. What is the consumer surplus?
   e. Is the regulation in the social interest or in the private interest?

7. Two airlines share an international route. The figure shows the demand curve for trips on this route.

The figure also shows the marginal cost curve that each firm faces. This air route is regulated.

a. What is the price of a trip and what is the number of trips per day if the regulation is in the social interest?

b. What is the price of a trip and what is the number of trips per day if the regulation is in the producers' self-interest?

c. What is the deadweight loss in part (b)?

d. What do you need to know to predict whether the regulation will be in the social interest or the producers' self-interest?

8. Two phone companies offer local calls in an area. The figure shows the demand curve for calls and the marginal cost curve of each firm. These firms are regulated.

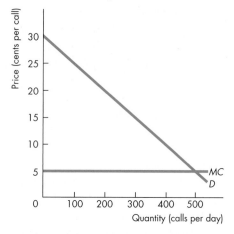

a. What is the price of a call and what is the number of calls per day if the regulation is in the social interest?

b. What is the price of a call and what is the number of calls per day if the regulation is in the producers' self-interest?

c. What is the deadweight loss in part (b)?

d. What do you need to know to predict whether the regulation will be in the social interest or the producers' self-interest?

CRITICAL THINKING

1. After you have studied *Reading Between the Lines* on pp. 340–341, answer the following questions:

   a. What do Rogers Communication and BCE plan to do in the broadband Internet market?

   b. What competition will Rogers and BCE face in this market?

   c. If Inukshuk is permitted to operate without regulation, do you expect it to maximize profit and if it does so, will the market for high-speed Internet access be efficient?

   d. How might the Canadian Competition Bureau regulate Inukshuk? And with appropriate regulation, what will be the maginitude of producer surplus, consumer surplus, and deadweight loss?

2. The government of Canada regulates the production and sale of many goods and services. For example, it regulates the prices of local phone and cable TV services, the grain prices paid to wheat and cereal farmers, and to whom they can sell the grain. The suppliers of local phone and cable TV services are monopolies, but there are many grain farmers. Why are grain farmers regulated? Is the regulation in the self-interest of grain farmers or in the social interest?

3. "Now that Canada has free trade with the United States, the government of Canada should not regulate monopolies in Canada because they are in direct competition with U.S. producers." Do you agree with this argument? If so, explain why. If not, explain why the argument is incorrect.

WEB EXERCISES

Use the links on myeconlab to work the following exercise.

1. Visit Competition Law Review. Look for cases of collusive agreement, abuse of dominant position, and mergers to restrict competition. In each case, describe the means cited as used to lessen competition.

Externalities

CHAPTER 15

Greener and Smarter

We burn huge quantities of fossil fuels—coal, natural gas, and oil—that cause acid rain and possibly global warming. We dump toxic waste into rivers, lakes, and oceans. These environmental issues are simultaneously everybody's problem and nobody's problem. How can we take account of the damage that we cause others every time we turn on our heating or air conditioning systems?

Almost every day, we hear about a new discovery—in medicine, engineering, chemistry, physics, or even economics. The advance of knowledge seems boundless. And more and more people are learning more and more of what is already known. The stock of knowledge is increasing, apparently without bound. We are getting smarter. But are we getting smarter fast enough? Are we spending enough on research and education? Do enough people remain in school for long enough? And do we work hard enough at school? Would we be better off if we spent more on research and education?

◆ In this chapter, we study the problems that arise because many of our actions create externalities. They affect other people, for ill or good, in ways that we do not usually take into account when we make our own economic choices. We study two big areas—pollution and knowledge—in which externalities are especially important. Externalities are a major source of *market failure*. When market failure occurs, we must either live with the inefficiency it creates or try to achieve greater efficiency by making *public choices*. This chapter studies these choices. We close the chapter in *Reading Between the Lines* by looking at air pollution in Ontario today.

After studying this chapter, you will be able to

- Explain how externalities arise

- Explain why negative externalities lead to inefficient overproduction and how property right, emission charges, marketable permits, and taxes can be used to achieve a more efficient outcome

- Explain why positive externalities lead to inefficient underproduction and how public provision, subsidies, vouchers, and patents can increase economic efficiency

Externalities in Our Lives

A COST OR BENEFIT THAT ARISES FROM PRODUC-
tion and falls on someone other than the producer, or
a cost or benefit that arises from consumption and
falls on someone other than the consumer is called an
externality. Let's review the range of externalities,
classify them, and look at some everyday examples.

An externality can arise from either *production* or
consumption and it can be either a **negative externality**,
which imposes an external cost, or a **positive externality**,
which provides an external benefit. So there are four
types of externalities:

- Negative production externalities
- Positive production externalities
- Negative consumption externalities
- Positive consumption externalities

Negative Production Externalities

Every weekday morning and afternoon, Highway 401
that runs across the north of Toronto slows to a crawl
as trucks and commuters compete for positions on
what looks more like an expensive parking lot than an
expressway. A similar situation occurs in every major
Canadian city from Vancouver to Halifax and every
major city around the world. Each road user imposes
a negative production externality on other road users.

Logging and the clearing of forests are the source
of another negative production externality. These
activities destroy the habitat of wildlife and influence
the amount of carbon dioxide in the atmosphere,
which has a long-term effect on temperature.
Everyone living and future generations bear these
external costs. Pollution, which we examine in the
next section, is another example of this type of
externality.

Positive Production Externalities

When Labonte Honey Inc. moves its bees into a
blueberry orchard in the Lac St-Jean area of northern
Quebec, the honeybees collect pollen and nectar
from the fruit blossoms to make the honey. At the
same time, they pollinate the blueberry flowers,
which increases the output of blueberries. Two
positive production externalities are present in this
example: Labonte Honey gets a positive production
externality from the owner of the fruit orchard, and

the fruit grower gets a positive production externality
from Labonte.

Negative Consumption Externalities

Negative consumption externalities are a source of
irritation for most of us. Smoking tobacco in a confined space creates fumes that many people find
unpleasant and that pose a health risk. So smoking in
restaurants and on airplanes generates a negative
externality. To avoid this negative externality, many
restaurants and all airlines ban smoking. But while a
smoking ban avoids a negative consumption externality for most people, it imposes a negative consumption externality on smokers who would prefer to enjoy
the consumption of tobacco while dining or taking a
plane trip.

Noisy parties and outdoor rock concerts are
other examples of negative consumption externalities.
They are also examples of the fact that a simple ban
on an activity is not a solution. Banning noisy parties
avoids the external cost on sleep-seeking neighbours,
but it results in the sleepers imposing an external cost
on the fun-seeking partygoers.

Permitting dandelions to grow in lawns, not
picking up leaves in the fall, and allowing a dog to
bark loudly or to foul a neighbour's lawn are other
sources of negative consumption externalities.

Positive Consumption Externalities

When you get a flu vaccination, you lower your
risk of getting infected this winter. And if you
avoid the flu, your neighbour who didn't get
vaccinated has a better chance of avoiding it too.
Flu vaccination generates positive consumption
externalities.

When the owner of a historic building restores it,
everyone who sees the building gets pleasure from it.
Similarly, when someone erects a spectacular house—
such as those built in Montreal's "Golden Square
Mile" in the 1800s—or another exciting structure—
such as the CN Tower or SkyDome in Toronto—an
external consumption benefit flows to everyone who
has an opportunity to view it. Education, which we
examine in this chapter, is another example of this
type of externality.

◯ myeconlab   **Study Plan 15.1**

Negative Externalities: Pollution

POLLUTION IS NOT A NEW PROBLEM AND IS NOT restricted to rich industrial countries. Preindustrial towns and cities in Europe had sewage disposal problems that created cholera epidemics and plagues that killed millions. London's air in the Middle Ages was dirtier than that of Los Angeles today. Some of the worst pollution today is found in Russia and China. Nor is the desire to find solutions to pollution new. The development in the fourteenth century of garbage and sewage disposal is an example of early attempts to tackle pollution.

Popular discussions of pollution usually pay little attention to economics. They focus on physical aspects of the problem, not on the costs and benefits. A common assumption is that if people's actions cause *any* pollution, those actions must cease. In contrast, an economic study of pollution emphasizes costs and benefits. An economist talks about the efficient amount of pollution. This emphasis on costs and benefits does not mean that economists, as citizens, do not share the same goals as others and value a healthy environment. Nor does it mean that economists have the right answers and everyone else has the wrong ones (or vice versa). The starting point for an economic analysis of pollution is the demand for a pollution-free environment.

The Demand for a Pollution-Free Environment

The demand for a pollution-free environment is greater today than it has ever been. We express this demand by joining organizations that lobby for antipollution regulations and policies. We vote for politicians who support the policies that we want to see implemented. We buy "green" products, even if we pay a bit more to do so. And we pay higher housing costs and commuting costs to live in pleasant neighbourhoods.

The demand for a pollution-free environment has grown for two main reasons. First, as our incomes increase, we demand a larger range of goods and services, and one of these "goods" is a pollution-free environment. We value clean air, unspoiled natural scenery, and wildlife, and we are willing and able to pay for them.

Second, as our knowledge of the effects of pollution grows, we are able to take measures that reduce those effects. For example, now that we know how sulphur dioxide causes acid rain and how clearing rain forests destroys natural stores of carbon dioxide, we are able, in principle, to design measures that limit these problems.

Let's look at the range of pollution problems that have been identified and the actions that create those problems.

The Sources of Pollution

Economic activity pollutes air, water, and land, and these individual areas of pollution interact through the *ecosystem*.

Air Pollution Sixty percent of our air pollution comes from road transportation and industrial processes. Only 16 percent arises from electric power generation.

A common belief is that air pollution is getting worse. In many developing countries, air pollution *is* getting worse. But air pollution in the richest country, the United States, is getting less severe for most substances. Figure 15.1 shows the trends in the concentrations of six air pollutants. Lead has been almost eliminated from our air. Sulphur dioxide, carbon monoxide, and suspended particulates have been reduced to around a half of their 1980 levels. And even the more stubborn ozone and nitrogen dioxide are at around 70 percent of their 1980 levels.

These reductions in levels of air pollution are even more impressive when they are compared with the level of economic activity. Between 1970 and 2000, total production in North America increased by 158 percent. During this same period, vehicle kilometres travelled increased by 143 percent, energy consumption increased by 45 percent, and the population increased by 36 percent. While all this economic activity was on the increase, air pollution from all sources *decreased* by 29 percent.

While the facts about the sources and trends in air pollution are not in doubt, there is disagreement about the *effects* of air pollution. The least controversial is *acid rain* caused by sulphur dioxide and nitrogen oxide emissions from coal- and oil-fired generators of electric utilities. Acid rain begins with air pollution, and it leads to water pollution and damages vegetation.

More controversial are airborne substances (suspended particulates) such as lead from leaded gasoline. Some scientists believe that in sufficiently large

FIGURE 15.1
Trends in Air Pollution

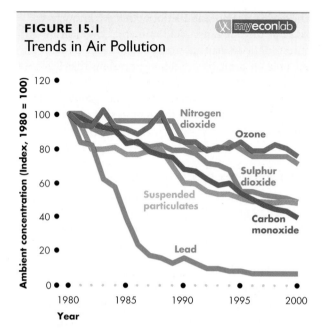

Lead has almost been eliminated from our air; concentrations of carbon monoxide, sulphur dioxide, and suspended particulates have decreased to about 50 percent of their 1980 levels; and nitrogen dioxide and ozone have fallen to about 70 percent of their 1980 levels.

Source: U.S. Environmental Protection Agency, *National Air Quality and Emissions Trends Report,* 1999 and 2000.

concentrations, these substances (189 of which have currently been identified) cause cancer and other life-threatening conditions.

Even more controversial is global warming. The United Nations' International Panel on Climate Change (IPCC), supported by many scientists, believes that the earth's temperature has increased by about 0.6 degrees Celsius over the past 100 years as a result of human generated carbon dioxide emissions. This view led to the adoption of the Kyoto Protocol by most nations, including Canada.

An alternative view is that the earth's temperature has been rising steadily since about 1500 and that human activity might be responsible for a smaller and less dramatic increase than the IPCC believes.

The data are still being debated and pored over and this controversy remains unsettled.

One air pollution problem has almost been eliminated: lead from gasoline. In part, this happened because the cost of living without leaded gasoline, it turns out, is not high. But sulphur dioxide and the so-called greenhouse gases are a much tougher prob-

lem to tackle. The major sources of these pollutants are road vehicles and electric utilities. Their alternatives are costly or have pollution problems of their own. Road vehicles can be made "greener" in a variety of ways. One is with new fuels, and some alternatives being investigated are alcohol, natural gas, propane and butane, and hydrogen. Another way of making cars and trucks "greener" is to change the chemistry of gasoline. Refiners are working on reformulations of gasoline that reduce tailpipe emissions. Similarly, electric power can be generated in cleaner ways by harnessing solar power, tidal power, or geothermal power. While technically possible, these methods are more costly than conventional carbon-fuelled generators. Another alternative is nuclear power. This method is good for air pollution but creates a potential long-term problem for land and water pollution because there is no known entirely safe method of disposing of spent nuclear fuel.

Water Pollution The largest sources of water pollution are the dumping of industrial waste and treated sewage in lakes and rivers and the runoff from fertilizers. A more dramatic source is the accidental spilling of crude oil into the oceans such as the *Exxon Valdez* spill in Alaska in 1989.

There are two main alternatives to polluting the waterways and oceans. One is the chemical processing of waste to render it inert or biodegradable. The other, in wide use for nuclear waste, is to use land sites for storage in secure containers.

Land Pollution Land pollution arises from dumping toxic waste products. Ordinary household garbage does not pose a pollution problem unless contaminants from dumped garbage seep into the water supply. This possibility increases as landfills reach capacity and less suitable landfill sites are used. It is estimated that 80 percent of existing landfills will be full by 2010. Some regions (New York, New Jersey, and other East Coast states) and some countries (Japan and the Netherlands) are seeking less costly alternatives to landfill, such as recycling and incineration. Recycling is an apparently attractive alternative, but it requires an investment in new technologies to be effective. Incineration is a high-cost alternative to landfill, and it produces air pollution. Furthermore, these alternatives are not free, and they become efficient only when the cost of using landfill is high.

Let's now turn from describing pollution to looking at the economics of pollution. We start by distinguishing between private costs and social costs.

Private Costs and Social Costs

A *private cost* of production is a cost that is borne by the producer of a good or service. *Marginal cost* is the cost of producing an *additional unit* of a good or service. So **marginal private cost** (*MC*) is the cost of producing an additional unit of a good or service that is borne by the producer of that good or service.

You've seen that an *external cost* is a cost of producing a good or service that is *not* borne by the producer but borne by other people. A **marginal external cost** is the cost of producing an additional unit of a good or service that falls on people other than the producer.

Marginal social cost (*MSC*) is the marginal cost incurred by the entire society—by the producer and by everyone else on whom the cost falls—and is the sum of marginal private cost and marginal external cost. That is,

$$MSC = MC + \text{Marginal external cost.}$$

We express costs in dollars. But we must always remember that a cost is an opportunity cost—what we give up to get something. A marginal external cost is what someone other than the producer of a good or service must give up when the producer makes one more unit of the item. Something real, such as a clean river or clean air, is given up.

Valuing an External Cost Economists use market prices to put a dollar value on the cost of pollution. For example, suppose that there are two similar rivers, one polluted and the other clean. Five hundred identical homes are built along the side of each river. The homes on the clean river rent for $2,500 a month, and those on the polluted river rent for $1,500 a month. If the pollution is the only detectable difference between the two rivers and the two locations, the rent decrease of $1,000 per month is the cost of the pollution. For the 500 homes on the polluted river, the external cost is $500,000 a month.

External Cost and Output Figure 15.2 shows an example of the relationship between output and cost in a chemical industry that pollutes. The marginal cost curve, *MC*, describes the private marginal cost borne by the firms that produce the chemical. Marginal cost increases as the quantity of chemical

produced increases. If the firms dump waste into a river, they impose an external cost that increases with the amount of the chemical produced. The marginal social cost curve, *MSC*, is the sum of marginal private cost and marginal external cost. For example, when output is 4,000 tonnes per month, marginal private cost is $100 a tonne, marginal external cost is $125 a tonne, and marginal social cost is $225 a tonne.

In Fig. 15.2, when the quantity of chemical produced increases, the amount of pollution increases and the external cost of pollution increases.

Figure 15.2 shows the relationship between the quantity of chemical produced and the amount of pollution created, but it doesn't tell us how much pollution gets created. That quantity depends on how the market for the chemical operates. First, we'll see what happens when the industry is free to pollute.

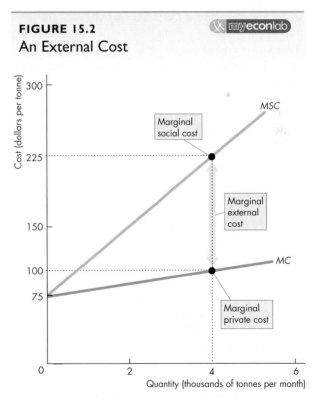

FIGURE 15.2 ⓧ myeconlab

An External Cost

The *MC* curve shows the private marginal cost borne by the factories that produce a chemical. The *MSC* curve shows the sum of marginal private cost and marginal external cost. When output is 4,000 tonnes of chemical per month, marginal private cost is $100 a tonne, marginal external cost is $125 a tonne, and marginal social cost is $225 a tonne.

Production and Pollution: How Much?

When an industry is unregulated, the amount of pollution it creates depends on the market equilibrium price and quantity of the good produced. In Fig. 15.3, the market demand curve for a pollution-creating chemical is *D*. This curve also measures the marginal social benefit, *MSB*, from the chemical. The supply curve is *S*. This curve also measures the marginal private cost, *MC*, of the producers. The supply curve is the marginal private cost curve because when firms make their production and supply decisions, they consider only the costs that they will bear. Market equilibrium occurs at a price of $100 a tonne and a quantity of 4,000 tonnes a month.

This equilibrium is inefficient. You learned in Chapter 5 that the allocation of resources is efficient when marginal social benefit equals marginal social cost. But we must count *all* the costs—private and external. So with an external cost, the allocation is efficient when marginal social benefit equals marginal *social* cost. This outcome occurs when the quantity of chemical produced is 2,000 tonnes a month. The market equilibrium overproduces and creates a deadweight loss shown by the grey triangle.

How can the people who live by the polluted river get the chemical factories to decrease their output of chemical and create less pollution? If some method can be found to achieve this outcome, everyone—the owners of the chemical factories and the residents of the riverside homes—can gain. Let's explore some solutions.

Property Rights

Sometimes it is possible to reduce the inefficiency arising from an externality by establishing a property right where one does not currently exist. **Property rights** are legally established titles to the ownership, use, and disposal of factors of production and goods and services that are enforceable in the courts.

Suppose that the chemical factories own the river and the 500 homes alongside it. The rent that people are willing to pay depends on the amount of pollution. Using the earlier example, people are willing to pay $2,500 a month to live alongside a pollution-free river but only $1,500 a month to live with the pollution created by 4,000 tonnes of chemical a month. If the factories produce this quantity of chemical, they lose $1,000 a month for each home and a total of $500,000 a month. The chemical factories are now confronted

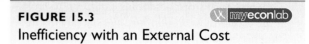

FIGURE 15.3
Inefficiency with an External Cost

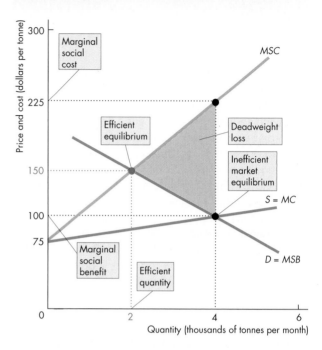

With an external cost, the market supply curve is the marginal private cost curve, *S* = *MC*. The market demand curve is the marginal social benefit curve, *D* = *MSB*. Market equilibrium at a price of $100 a tonne and 4,000 tonnes a month is inefficient because marginal social cost exceeds marginal social benefit. The efficient quantity is 2,000 tonnes a month. The grey triangle shows the deadweight loss created by the pollution externality.

with the cost of their pollution—forgone rent from the people who live by the river.

Figure 15.4 illustrates the outcome by using the same example as in Fig. 15.3. With property rights in place, the *MC* curve no longer measures all the costs that the factories face in producing the chemical. It excludes the pollution costs that they must now bear. The *MSC* curve now becomes the marginal private cost curve *MC*. All the costs fall on the factories, so the market supply curve is based on all the marginal costs and is the curve labelled *S* = *MC* = *MSC*.

The market equilibrium price is now $150 a tonne and a quantity of 2,000 tonnes a month. This outcome is efficient. The factories still produce some pollution, but it is the efficient quantity.

FIGURE 15.4

myeconlab

Property Rights Achieve an Efficient Outcome

With property rights, the marginal cost curve that excludes pollution costs shows only part of the producers' marginal cost. The marginal private cost curve includes the cost of pollution, and the supply curve is S = MC = MSC. Market equilibrium is at a price of $150 a tonne and a quantity of 2,000 tonnes a month and is efficient because marginal social cost equals marginal social benefit.

The Coase Theorem

Does it matter how property rights are assigned? Does it matter whether the polluter or the victim of the pollution owns the resource that might be polluted? Until 1960, everyone—including economists who had thought long and hard about the problem—thought that it did matter. But in 1960, Ronald Coase had a remarkable insight, now called the Coase theorem.

The **Coase theorem** is the proposition that if property rights exist, if only a small number of parties are involved, and if transactions costs are low, then private transactions are efficient. There are no externalities because the transacting parties take all the costs and benefits into account. Furthermore, it doesn't matter who has the property rights.

Application of the Coase Theorem In the example that we've just studied, the factories own the river and the homes. Suppose that instead, the residents own their homes and the river. Now the factories must pay a fee to the homeowners for the right to dump their waste. The greater the quantity of waste dumped into the river, the more the factories must pay. So again, the factories face the opportunity cost of the pollution they create. The quantity of chemical produced and the amount of waste dumped are the same whoever owns the homes and the river. If the factories own them, they bear the cost of pollution because they receive a lower income from home rents. And if the residents own the homes and the river, the factories bear the cost of pollution because they must pay a fee to the homeowners. In both cases, the factories bear the cost of their pollution and dump the efficient amount of waste into the river.

The Coase solution works only when transactions costs are low. **Transactions costs** are the opportunity costs of conducting a transaction. For example, when you buy a house, you incur a series of transactions costs. You might pay a realtor to help you find the best place and a lawyer to run checks that assure you that the seller owns the property and that after you've paid for it, the ownership has been properly transferred to you.

In the example of the homes alongside a river, the transactions costs that are incurred by a small number of chemical factories and a few homeowners might be low enough to enable them to negotiate the deals that produce an efficient outcome. But in many situations, transactions costs are so high that it would be inefficient to incur them. In these situations, the Coase solution is not available.

Suppose, for example, that everyone owns the airspace above their homes up to, say, 10 kilometres. If someone pollutes your airspace, you can charge a fee. But to collect the fee, you must identify who is polluting your airspace and persuade them to pay you. Imagine the costs of negotiating and enforcing agreements with the 300 million people who live in Canada and the United States and the several thousand factories that emit sulphur dioxide and create acid rain that falls on your property! In this situation, we use public choices to cope with externalities. But the transactions costs that block a market solution are real costs, so attempts by the government to deal with externalities offer no easy solution. Let's look at some of these attempts.

Government Actions in the Face of External Costs

The three main methods that governments use to cope with externalities are

■ Taxes
■ Emission charges
■ Marketable permits

Taxes The government can use taxes as an incentive for producers to cut back on pollution. Taxes used in this way are called **Pigovian taxes**, in honour of Arthur Cecil Pigou, the British economist who first worked out this method of dealing with externalities during the 1920s.

By setting the tax rate equal to the marginal external cost, firms can be made to behave in the same way as they would if they bore the cost of the externality directly. To see how government actions can change market outcomes in the face of externalities, let's return to the example of the chemical factories and the river.

Assume that the government has assessed the marginal external cost accurately and imposes a tax on the factories that exactly equals this cost. Figure 15.5 illustrates the effects of this tax.

The market demand curve and marginal social benefit curve, $D = MSB$, and the firms' marginal cost curve, MC, are the same as in Fig. 15.3. The pollution tax equals the marginal external cost of the pollution. We add this tax to the marginal cost to find the market supply curve. This curve is the one labelled $S = MC + tax = MSC$. This curve is the market supply curve because it tells us the quantity supplied at each price given the firms' marginal cost and the tax they must pay. This curve is also the marginal social cost curve because the pollution tax has been set equal to the marginal external cost.

Demand and supply now determine the market equilibrium price at $150 a tonne and the equilibrium quantity at 2,000 tonnes a month. At this scale of chemical production, the marginal social cost is $150 and the marginal benefit is $150, so the outcome is efficient. The firms incur a marginal cost of $88 a tonne and pay a tax of $62 a tonne. The government collects tax revenue of $124,000 a month.

Emission Charges Emission charges are an alternative to a tax for confronting a polluter with the external cost of pollution. The government sets a price per unit of pollution. The more pollution a firm creates,

FIGURE 15.5
A Pollution Tax

A pollution tax is imposed equal to the marginal external cost of pollution. The supply curve becomes the marginal private cost curve, *MC*, plus the tax: *S = MC + tax*. Market equilibrium is at a price of $150 a tonne and a quantity of 2,000 tonnes a month and is efficient because marginal social cost equals marginal social benefit. The government collects a tax revenue shown by the purple rectangle.

the more it pays in emission charges. This method of dealing with pollution externalities has been used only modestly in North America but is common in Europe where, for example, France, Germany, and the Netherlands make water polluters pay a waste disposal charge.

To work out the emission charge that achieves efficiency, the government needs a lot of information about the polluting industry that, in practice, is rarely available.

Marketable Permits Instead of taxing or imposing emission charges on polluters, each potential polluter might be assigned a permitted pollution limit. Each firm knows its own costs and benefits of pollution, and making pollution limits marketable is a clever way of using this private information that is unknown to the government. The government issues each firm a permit to emit a certain amount of pollution, and firms can buy and sell these permits. Firms that have a low marginal cost of reducing pollution sell their permits, and firms that have a high marginal cost of reducing pollution buy permits. The market in permits determines the price at which firms trade permits. And firms buy or sell permits until their marginal cost of pollution equals the market price.

This method of dealing with pollution provides an even stronger incentive than do emission charges to find technologies that pollute less because the price of a permit to pollute rises as the demand for permits increases.

A Real-World Market for Emission Permits Environment Canada has not used marketable permits but the Environmental Protection Agency (EPA) in the United States has. The EPA first implemented air quality programs following the passage of the Clean Air Act in 1970.

Trading in lead pollution permits became common during the 1980s, and this marketable permit program has been rated a success. It enabled lead to be virtually eliminated from the atmosphere of the United States (see Fig. 15.1). But this success might not easily translate to other situations because lead pollution has some special features. First, most lead pollution came from a single source: leaded gasoline. Second, lead in gasoline is easily monitored. Third, the objective of the program was clear: to eliminate lead in gasoline. The EPA is now considering using marketable permits to promote efficiency in the control of chlorofluorocarbons, the gases that are believed to damage the ozone layer.

REVIEW QUIZ

1   What is the distinction between a negative production externality and a negative consumption externality?
2   What is the distinction between private cost and social cost?
3   How does an externality prevent a competitive market from allocating resources efficiently?
4   How can an externality be eliminated by assigning property rights? How does this method of coping with an externality work?
5   How do taxes help us to cope with externalities? Can a pollution tax be used to induce firms to produce the efficient quantity of pollution?

Ⓧ myeconlab   **Study Plan 15.2**

Positive Externalities: Knowledge

KNOWLEDGE COMES FROM EDUCATION AND research. To study the economics of knowledge, we must distinguish between private and social benefits.

Private Benefits and Social Benefits

A *private benefit* is a benefit that the consumer of a good or service receives. *Marginal benefit* is the benefit from an *additional unit* of a good or service. So a **marginal private benefit** (*MB*) is the benefit from an additional unit of a good or service that the consumer of that good or service receives.

The *external benefit* from a good or service is the benefit that someone other than the consumer receives. A **marginal external benefit** is the benefit from an additional unit of a good or service that people other than the consumer enjoy.

Marginal social benefit (*MSB*) is the marginal benefit enjoyed by society—by the consumer of a good or service (marginal private benefit) plus the marginal benefit enjoyed by others (the marginal external benefit). That is,

$$MSB = MB + \text{Marginal external benefit.}$$

Figure 15.6 shows an example of the relationship between marginal private benefit, marginal external benefit, and marginal social benefit. The marginal benefit curve, *MB*, describes the marginal private benefit—such as expanded job opportunities and higher incomes—enjoyed by university graduates. Marginal private benefit decreases as the quantity of education increases.

But university graduates generate external benefits. On the average, they are better citizens. Their crime rates are lower, and they are more tolerant of the views of others. A society with a large number of university graduates can support activities such as high-quality newspapers and television channels, music, theatre, and other organized social activities.

In the example in Fig. 15.6, the marginal external benefit is $15,000 per student per year when 15 million students enroll in university. The marginal social benefit curve, *MSB*, is the sum of marginal private benefit and marginal external benefit. For example, with 15 million students, the marginal private benefit is $10,000 per student and the marginal

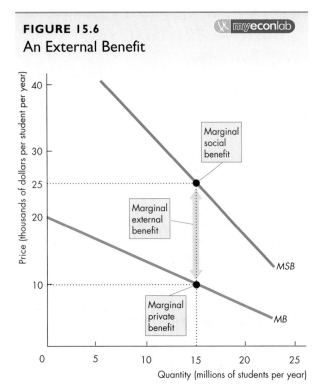

FIGURE 15.6 ⓧ **myeconlab**
An External Benefit

The *MB* curve shows the marginal private benefit enjoyed by the people who receive a university education. The *MSB* curve shows the sum of marginal private benefit and marginal external benefit. When 15 million students attend university, marginal private benefit is $10,000 per student, marginal external benefit is $15,000 per student, and marginal social benefit is $25,000 per student.

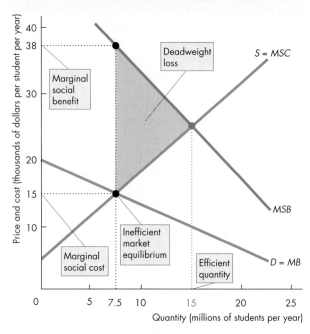

FIGURE 15.7 ⓧ **myeconlab**
Inefficiency with an External Benefit

With an external benefit, the market demand curve is the marginal private benefit curve, *D = MB*. The market supply curve is the marginal social cost curve, *S = MSC*. Market equilibrium at a tuition of $15,000 a year and 7.5 million students is inefficient. The efficient quantity is 15 million students. The grey triangle shows the deadweight loss created because too few students enroll in university.

external benefit is $15,000 per student, so the marginal social benefit is $25,000 per student.

When people make schooling decisions, they ignore its external benefits and consider only its private benefits. So if education were provided by private schools that charged full-cost tuition, we would produce too few university graduates.

Figure 15.7 illustrates the underproduction if the government left education to the private market. The market supply curve is the marginal social cost curve of the private schools, *S = MSC*. The demand curve is the marginal private benefit curve, *D = MB*. Market equilibrium occurs at a tuition of $15,000 per student per year and 7.5 million students per year. At this equilibrium, marginal social benefit is $38,000 per student, which exceeds marginal social cost by $15,000. There are too few students in university. The efficient number is 15 million, where

marginal social benefit equals marginal social cost. The grey triangle shows the deadweight loss.

Underproduction similar to that in Fig. 15.7 would occur in grade school and high school if an unregulated market produced it. When children learn basic reading, writing, and number skills, they receive the private benefit of increased earning power. But even these basic skills bring the external benefit of developing better citizens.

External benefits also arise from the discovery of new knowledge. When Isaac Newton worked out the formulas for calculating the rate of response of one variable to another—calculus—everyone was free to use his method. When a spreadsheet program called VisiCalc was invented, Lotus Corporation and Microsoft were free to copy the basic idea and create 1-2-3 and Excel. When the first shopping mall was built and found to be a successful way of arranging retailing, everyone was free to copy the idea, and malls spread like mushrooms.

Once someone has discovered how to do something, others can copy the basic idea. They do have to work to copy an idea, so they face an opportunity cost. But they do not usually have to pay a fee to the person who made the discovery to use it. When people make decisions, they ignore the external benefits and consider only the private benefits.

When people make decisions about the quantity of education or the amount of research to undertake, they balance the marginal private cost against the marginal private benefit. They ignore the external benefit. As a result, if we left education and research to unregulated market forces, we would get too little of these activities.

To get closer to producing the efficient quantity of a good or service that generates an external benefit, we make public choices, through governments, to modify the market outcome.

Government Actions in the Face of External Benefits

Four devices that governments can use to achieve a more efficient allocation of resources in the presence of external benefits are

- Public provision
- Private subsidies
- Vouchers
- Patents and copyrights

Public Provision Under **public provision**, a public authority that receives its revenue from the government produces the good or service. The education services produced by the public universities, colleges, and schools are examples of public provision.

Figure 15.8(a) shows how public provision might overcome the underproduction that arises in Fig. 15.7. Public provision cannot lower the cost of production, so marginal social cost is the same as before. Marginal

---

FIGURE 15.8   (X) myeconlab

Public Provision or Private Subsidy to Achieve an Efficient Outcome

(a) Public provision

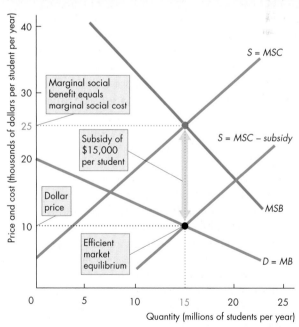

(b) Private subsidy

In part (a), marginal social benefit equals marginal social cost with 15 million students, the efficient quantity. Tuition is set at $10,000 per student, and the taxpayers cover the other $15,000 of the cost per student.

In part (b), with a subsidy of $15,000 per student, the supply curve is S = MSC – subsidy. The equilibrium price is $10,000, and the market equilibrium is efficient with 15 million students. Marginal social benefit equals marginal social cost.

private benefit and marginal external benefit are also the same as before.

The efficient quantity occurs where marginal social benefit equals marginal social cost. In Fig. 15.8(a), this quantity is 15 million students. Tuition is set to ensure that the efficient number of students enrolls. That is, tuition is set equal to the marginal private benefit at the efficient quantity. In Fig. 15.8(a), tuition is $10,000 a year. The rest of the cost of the public university is borne by the taxpayers and, in this example, is $15,000 per student per year.

Private Subsidies A **subsidy** is a payment that the government makes to private producers. By making the subsidy depend on the level of output, the government can induce private decision makers to consider external benefits when they make their choices.

Figure 15.8(b) shows how a subsidy to private universities works. In the absence of a subsidy, the market supply curve of private university education is the marginal social cost curve, $S = MSC$. If the government provides a subsidy to universities of $15,000 per student, we must subtract the subsidy from the marginal cost of education to find the supply curve. That curve is $S = MSC - subsidy$. The market demand is the marginal benefit curve, $D = MB$. The equilibrium tuition (market price) is $10,000 a year, and the equilibrium quantity is 15 million students. To educate 15 million students the marginal social cost is $25,000 a year. The marginal social benefit is also $25,000 a year. So by setting the subsidy equal to marginal external benefit, marginal social cost is equal to marginal social benefit and the outcome is efficient. The tuition and the subsidy just cover the university's costs.

Vouchers A **voucher** is a token that the government provides to households, which they can use to buy specified goods or services. Milton Friedman, recipient of the 1976 Nobel Prize for Economic Science, has long advocated vouchers as a means of providing parents with greater choice and control over the education of their children. Some people advocate them for college and university so that students can both receive financial help and exercise choice.

A school voucher allows parents to choose the school their children will attend and to use the voucher to pay part of the cost. The school cashes the vouchers to pay its bills. A voucher provided to a university student would work in a similar way. Because vouchers can be spent only on a specified item, they

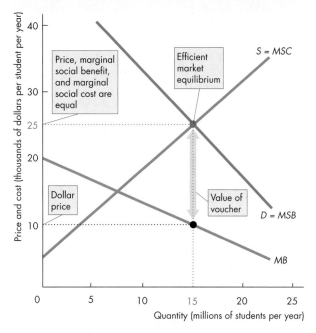

FIGURE 15.9   myeconlab

Vouchers Achieve an Efficient Outcome

With a voucher equal to marginal external benefit, buyers are willing to pay MB plus the value of the voucher, so the demand curve becomes the marginal social benefit curve, $D = MSB$. Market equilibrium is efficient with 15 million students enrolled in university because price, marginal social benefit, and marginal cost are equal. The tuition consists of the dollar price of $10,000 and the value of the voucher.

increase the willingness to pay for that item and so increase the demand for it.

Figure 15.9 shows how a voucher system works. The government provides a voucher equal to the marginal external benefit. Students use these vouchers to supplement the dollars they pay for university education. The marginal social benefit curve becomes the demand for university education, $D = MSB$. The market equilibrium occurs at a price of $25,000 per student per year, and 15 million students enrol in universities. Each student pays $10,000 tuition, and universities collect an additional $15,000 per student from the voucher.

If the government estimates the value of the external benefit correctly and makes the value of the voucher equal the marginal external benefit, the outcome from the voucher scheme is efficient. Marginal cost equals marginal social benefit, and the dead-weight loss is eliminated.

Vouchers are similar to subsidies, but their advocates say that they are more efficient than subsidies because the consumer can monitor school performance more effectively than the government can.

Patents and Copyrights Knowledge might be an exception to the principle of diminishing marginal benefit. Additional knowledge (about the right things) makes people more productive. And there seems to be no tendency for the additional productivity from additional knowledge to diminish.

For example, in just 15 years, advances in knowledge about microprocessors have given us a sequence of processor chips that has made our personal computers increasingly powerful. Each advance in knowledge about how to design and manufacture a processor chip has brought apparently ever larger increments in performance and productivity. Similarly, each advance in knowledge about how to design and build an airplane has brought apparently ever larger increments in performance: Orville and Wilbur Wright's 1903 Flyer was a one-seat plane that could hop a farmer's field. The Lockheed Constellation, designed in 1949, was an airplane that could fly 120 passengers from New York to London, but with two refueling stops in Newfoundland and Ireland. The latest version of the Airbus 340 can carry 250 people nonstop from Singapore to New York, a flight of 15,325 kilometres that takes 20 hours. Similar examples of dramatic change can be found in agriculture, biogenetics, telecommunications, engineering, entertainment, and medicine.

One reason why the stock of knowledge increases without diminishing returns is the sheer number of different techniques that can in principle be tried. Paul Romer explains this fact. "Suppose that to make a finished good, 20 different parts have to be attached to a frame, one at a time. A worker could proceed in numerical order, attaching part one first, then part two.... Or the worker could proceed in some other order, starting with part 10, then adding part seven.... With 20 parts, . . . there are [more] different sequences . . . than the total number of seconds that have elapsed since the big bang created the universe, so we can be confident that in all activities, only a very small fraction of the possible sequences have ever been tried."[1]

Think about all the processes, all the products, and all the different bits and pieces that go into each, and you can see that we have only begun to scratch around the edges of what is possible.

Because knowledge is productive and generates external benefits, it is necessary to use public policies to ensure that those who develop new ideas have incentives to encourage an efficient level of effort. The main way of providing the right incentives uses the central idea of the Coase theorem and assigns property rights—called **intellectual property rights**—to creators. The legal device for establishing intellectual property rights is the patent or copyright. A **patent** or **copyright** is a government-sanctioned exclusive right granted to the inventor of a good, service, or productive process to produce, use, and sell the invention for a given number of years. A patent enables the developer of a new idea to prevent others from benefiting freely from an invention for a limited number of years.

Although patents encourage invention and innovation, they do so at an economic cost. While a patent is in place, its holder has a monopoly. And monopoly is another source of inefficiency (which is explained in Chapter 12). But without a patent, the effort to develop new goods, services, or processes is diminished and the flow of new inventions is slowed. So the efficient outcome is a compromise that balances the benefits of more inventions against the cost of temporary monopoly in newly invented activities.

REVIEW QUIZ

1 What is special about knowledge that creates external benefits?
2 How might governments use public provision, private subsidies, and vouchers to achieve an efficient amount of education?
3 How might governments use public provision, private subsidies, vouchers, and patents and copyrights to achieve an efficient amount of research and development?

 Study Plan 15.3

◆ *Reading Between the Lines* on pp. 358–359 looks at the pollution created by generating electricity and the debate over whether the regulation of power utilities is too lax or too severe.

---

[1] Paul Romer, "Ideas and Things," in *The Future Surveyed*, supplement to *The Economist*, September 11, 1993, pp. 71–72.

The Air Pollution Debate

THE GLOBE AND MAIL, APRIL 16, 2002

Three plants spew bulk of pollutants

Three large coal-fired power plants in Southern Ontario produce 83 per cent of all the harmful air pollutants from the province's electric-power sector, according to documents obtained under the Freedom of Information Act.

In the first full look at air emissions from the province's 143 generating facilities, the coal plants— located near Toronto, Simcoe and Sarnia— stand out because they produced 24 million tonnes of contaminants that cause global warming, acid rain, smog, and heavy-metal poisoning in wildlife.

The bulk of the pollutants, tracked over an eight-month period in 2000, are carbon dioxide, sulphur dioxide and nitrogen oxides, but they also include nerve poisons, such as mercury, that are toxic to humans and wildlife even in small concentrations.

The figures also show that the province's publicly owned utility, Ontario Power Generation, is the worst polluter, producing the lion's share of the emissions, with nearly 91 per cent of the total.

The company that was the next-largest emitter, TransAlta Cogen LP, produced only 1.4 per cent.

Ontario Power is such a big polluter partly because it generates the bulk of the province's electricity, and partly because of its use of coal to carry out this task.

. . .

Reprinted with permission from *The Globe and Mail.*

Essence of the Story

■ Ontario Power Generation creates 91 percent of total emissions from Ontario's electric power producing sector.

■ Ontario Power's three largest power plants account for 83 percent of the province's air pollution.

■ These emissions include carbon dioxide, sulfur dioxide, and nitrogen oxides, as well as mercury.

Economic Analysis

■ Producing electricity brings a tradeoff between cost and air quality.

■ The cheapest fuels and technologies are dirty.

■ None of these technologies are used in Canada today. But they are used in China and Russia where air pollution is a serious problem.

■ Canada, in contrast, has achieved a high standard of air quality.

■ But is the standard high enough? Or is it too high?

■ To answer this question, we need to consider the economics of pollution from producing electricity.

■ Figure 1 shows the market demand for electricity and its marginal social benefit as the curve $D = MSB$. The curve MC shows the marginal cost of producing electricity in dirty plants.

■ With an unregulated and competitive market, the quantity produced is 6 megawatt hours.

■ Because the plants are dirty, a pollution problem arises. The curve MSC shows the marginal social cost of producing electricity.

■ The vertical distance between the MC curve and the MSC curve is the marginal external cost.

■ Taking the marginal external cost into account, we can find the efficient quantity of electricity to produce and the efficient amount of pollution.

■ In the example in Fig. 1, the efficient quantity is 4 megawatt hours. Notice that at the efficient quantity, we still have pollution, but a smaller amount than with the unregulated outcome.

■ Figure 2 shows the same demand and cost curves as Fig. 1 but focuses on the overall cost of pollution—its deadweight loss.

■ If production is cut to 4 megawatt hours, the deadweight loss disappears and we have the efficient outcome.

■ If power companies are regulated to use a more costly but cleaner technology, the MC curve shifts upward, the cost of electricity rises, the quantity produced decreases, and the deadweight loss from pollution shrinks.

Figure 1 Efficient and unregulated outcomes compared

Figure 2 Cost of pollution

■ If the additional private cost is less than the external cost of pollution, production and pollution move towards but remain above their efficient levels.

■ If the additional private cost exceeds the external cost of pollution, production and pollution move below their efficient levels.

SUMMARY

KEY POINTS

Externalities in Our Lives (p. 346)

- An externality can arise from either a production activity or a consumption activity.
- A negative externality imposes an external cost.
- A positive externality provides an external benefit.

Negative Externalities: Pollution (pp. 347–353)

- External costs are costs of production that fall on people other than the producer of a good or service. Marginal social cost equals marginal private cost plus marginal external cost.
- Producers take account only of marginal private cost and produce more than the efficient quantity when there is a marginal external cost.
- Sometimes it is possible to overcome a negative externality by assigning a property right.
- When property rights cannot be assigned, governments might overcome externalities by using taxes, emission charges, or marketable permits.

Positive Externalities: Knowledge (pp. 353–357)

- External benefits are benefits that are received by people other than the consumer of a good or service. Marginal social benefit equals marginal private benefit plus marginal external benefit.
- External benefits from education arise because better-educated people tend to be better citizens, commit fewer crimes, and support social activities.
- External benefits from research arise because once someone has worked out a basic idea, others can copy it.
- Vouchers or subsidies to schools or the provision of public education below cost can achieve a more efficient provision of education.

- Patents and copyrights create intellectual property rights and an incentive to innovate. But they do so by creating a temporary monopoly, the cost of which must be balanced against the benefit of more inventive activity.

KEY FIGURES

KEY TERMS

PROBLEMS

Go to ⓧ myeconlab for solutions to odd-numbered problems and additional exercises.

1. The table provides information about costs and benefits arising from the production of pesticide that pollutes a lake used by a trout farmer.

Total product of pesticide (tonnes per week)	Pesticide producer's MC	Marginal external cost	Marginal social benefit of pesticide
	(dollars per tonne)		
0	0	0	250
1	5	33	205
2	15	67	165
3	30	100	130
4	50	133	100
5	75	167	75
6	105	200	55
7	140	233	40

a. If no one owns the lake and there is no regulation of pollution, what is the quantity of pesticide produced and what is the marginal cost of pollution borne by the trout farmer?

b. If the trout farm owns the lake, how much pesticide is produced and what does the pesticide producer pay the farmer per tonne?

c. If the pesticide producer owns the lake, and if a pollution-free lake rents for $1,000 a week, how much pesticide is produced per week and how much rent per week does the farmer pay the factory for the use of the lake?

d. Compare the quantities of pesticide produced in your answers to (b) and (c) and explain the relationship between these quantities.

2. The table at the top of the next column provides information about the costs and benefits of steel smelting that pollutes the air of a city.

a. With no property rights in the city's air and no regulation of pollution, what is the quantity of steel produced per week and what is the marginal cost of pollution borne by the citizens?

b. If the city owns the steel plant, how much steel is produced per week and what does the city charge the steel producer per tonne?

Total product of steel (tonnes per week)	Steel producer's MC	Marginal external cost	Marginal social benefit of steel
	(dollars per tonne)		
0	0	0	1,200
10	100	15	1,100
20	200	25	1,000
30	300	50	900
40	400	100	800
50	500	200	700
60	600	300	600
70	700	400	500
80	800	500	400

c. If the steel firm owns the city, and if the residents of a pollution-free city are willing to pay $15,000 a week in property taxes, how much steel is produced per week and how much are the citizens willing to pay in property taxes to live in the polluted city?

d. Compare the quantities of steel produced in your answers to (b) and (c) and explain the relationship between these quantities.

3. Back at the pesticide plant and trout farm described in problem 1, suppose that no one owns the lake and that the government introduces a pollution tax.

a. What is the tax per tonne of pesticide produced that achieves an efficient outcome?

b. Explain the connection between your answer to (a) and the answer to problem 1.

4. Back at the steel smelter and city in problem 2, suppose that the city government introduces a pollution tax.

a. What is the tax per tonne of steel produced that will achieve an efficient outcome?

b. Explain the connection between your answer to (a) and the answer to problem 2.

5. In problem 1, suppose that no one owns the lake and that the government issues two marketable pollution permits, one to the farmer and one to the factory. Each may pollute the lake by the same amount, and the total amount of pollution is the efficient amount.

a. What is the quantity of pesticide produced?

b. What is the market price of a pollution permit? Who buys and who sells a permit?

c. What is the connection between your answer and the answers to problems 1 and 3?

6. Using the information given in problem 2, suppose that the city government issues two marketable pollution permits, one to the city government and one to the smelter. Each may pollute the air by the same amount, and the total is the efficient amount.

a. How much steel is produced?

b. What is the market price of a permit? Who buys and who sells a permit?

c. What is the connection between your answer and the answers to problems 2 and 4?

7. The marginal social cost of educating a student is $4,000 a year and is constant. The figure shows the marginal private benefit curve.

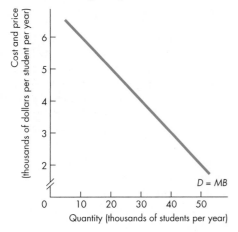

a. With no government involvement and if the schools are competitive, how many students are enrolled and what is the tuition?

b. The external benefit from education is $2,000 per student per year and is constant. If the government provides the efficient amount of education, how many school places does it offer and what is the tuition?

8. Technological advances cut the marginal social cost of educating a student to $2,000 a year. The marginal private benefit is the same as that in problem 7. The external benefit from education increases to $4,000 per student per year.

a. With no government involvement and if the schools are competitive, how many students are enrolled and what is the tuition?

b. If the government provides the efficient amount of education, how many school places does it offer and what is the tuition?

c. Compare the outcomes in problem 8 with those in problem 7. Explain the differences.

CRITICAL THINKING

1. After you have studied *Reading Between the Lines* on pp. 358–359, answer the following questions:

a. Which electric power companies create most of the air pollution in the electricity industry in Ontario?

b. What are the pros and cons of stiffening the regulations that power utilities face?

c. If a technological advance lowers the cost of producing electricity but leaves the marginal external pollution cost unchanged, would the adoption of this technology in an unregulated market increase or decrease pollution? Explain using figures like those on p. 359.

WEB EXERCISES

Use the links on myeconlab **to work the following exercises.**

1. Obtain two viewpoints on global warming and then answer these questions:

a. What are the benefits and costs of greenhouse gas emissions?

b. Do you think environmentalists are correct in the view that greenhouse gas emissions must be cut or do you think the costs of reducing greenhouse gas emissions exceed the benefits?

c. If greenhouse gas emissions are to be reduced, should firms be assigned production limits or marketable permits?

2. Visit the Canadian Wind Energy Association and read the pages on Quick Facts and Frequently Asked Questions (FAQs).

a. What sorts of positive externalities arise in the generation of electricity using wind technologies?

b. What sorts of negative externalities (external costs) arise in the generation of electricity using wind technologies?

c. Which do you think are more serious—the external costs of generating electricity from wind or from burning coal and oil?

d. Can you think of reasons why, despite the lower external costs, a campaign against the use of wind technology might be more successful than a campaign against the use of coal or oil?

Public Goods and Common Resources

CHAPTER 16

Free Riding and Overusing the Commons

Why does government provide some goods and services such as the enforcement of law and order and national defence? Why don't we let private firms produce these items and people buy the quantities that they demand in the marketplace? Is the scale of provision of these government-provided services correct? Or do governments produce either too much or too little of these items?

More and more people with ever-increasing incomes demand ever-greater quantities of most goods and services. One item that we demand more and more of is fish grown wild in the ocean. The fish stocks of the world's oceans are not owned by anyone. They are common resources and everyone is free to use them. Are our fish stocks being overused? Are we in danger of bringing extinction to some species? Must the price of fish inevitably keep rising? What can be done to conserve the world's fish stocks?

◆ These are the questions that we study in this chapter. We begin by classifying goods and resources. We then explain what determines the scale of government provision of public services. Finally, we study the tragedy of the commons. In *Reading Between the Lines* at the end of the chapter, we look at a pressing tragedy of the global commons—the problem of overuse of the world's tropical rainforests.

After studying this chapter, you will be able to

- **Distinguish among private goods, public goods, and common resources**
- **Explain how the free-rider problem arises and how the quantity of public goods is determined**
- **Explain the tragedy of the commons and its possible solutions**

Classifying Goods and Resources

WHAT'S THE DIFFERENCE BETWEEN THE TORONTO Police Department and Brink's Security; between fish in the Pacific Ocean and fish produced by a BC fish farm; and between a live Shania Twain concert and a show on network television? Each pair differs in the extent to which people can be *excluded* from them and in the extent to which one person's consumption *rivals* the consumption of others.

A good or service or a resource is **excludable** if it is possible to prevent someone from enjoying the benefits of it. Brink's security services, BC Seafood's fish, and a Shania Twain concert are examples. You must pay to consume them.

A good or service or a resource is **nonexcludable** if it is impossible (or extremely costly) to prevent someone from benefiting from it. The services of the Toronto police, fish in the Pacific Ocean, and a concert on network television are examples.

A good or service or a resource is **rival** if its use by one person decreases the quantity available for someone else. A Brink's truck can't deliver cash to two banks at the same time. A fish can be consumed only once. And one seat at a concert can hold only one person at a time. These items are rival.

A good or service or a resource is **nonrival** if its use by one person does not decrease the quantity available for someone else. The services of the Toronto police and a concert on network television are nonrival. The arrival of one more person in a neighbourhood doesn't lower the level of police protection enjoyed by the community. And no other viewer is affected when someone switches on the TV.

A Four-Fold Classification

Figure 16.1 classifies goods, services, and resources into four types.

Private Goods A **private good** is both rival and excludable. A can of Coke and a fish on East Point Seafood's farm are examples of private goods.

Public Goods A **public good** is both nonrival and nonexcludable. A public good can be consumed simultaneously by everyone, and no one can be excluded from enjoying its benefits. National defence is the best example of a public good.

FIGURE 16.1

Four-Fold Classification of Goods

	Private goods	Common resources
Rival	Food and drink Car House	Fish in ocean Atmosphere City parks
	Natural monopolies	**Public goods**
Nonrival	Internet Cable television Bridge or tunnel	National defence The law Air-traffic control
	Excludable	**Nonexcludable**

A private good is one for which consumption is rival and from which consumers can be excluded. A public good is one for which consumption is nonrival and from which it is impossible to exclude a consumer. A common resource is one that is rival but nonexcludable. And a natural monopoly is nonrival but excludable.

Common Resources A **common resource** is rival and nonexcludable. A unit of a common resource can be used only once, but no one can be prevented from using what is available. Ocean fish are a common resource. They are rival because a fish taken by one person isn't available for anyone else, and they are nonexcludable because it is difficult to prevent people from catching them.

Natural Monopolies In a natural monopoly, economies of scale exist over the entire range of output for which there is a demand (see p. 264). A special case of natural monopoly has zero marginal cost. Buyers can be excluded but the good is nonrival. The Internet and cable television are examples.

Two Problems

Public goods create a **free-rider problem**—the absence of an incentive for people to pay for what they consume. *Common resources* create the **tragedy of the commons**—the absence of incentives to prevent the overuse and depletion of a resource.

The rest of this chapter looks more closely at the free-rider problem and the tragedy of the commons and examines public choice solutions to them.

myeconlab   **Study Plan 16.1**

Public Goods and the Free-Rider Problem

SUPPOSE THAT FOR ITS DEFENCE, A COUNTRY must launch some surveillance satellites. The benefit provided by a satellite is the *value* of its services. The *value* of a *private* good is the maximum amount that a person is willing to pay for one more unit, which is shown by the person's demand curve. The *value* of a *public* good is the maximum amount that *all* the people are willing to pay for one more unit of it. To calculate the value placed on a public good, we use the concepts of total benefit and marginal benefit.

The Benefit of a Public Good

Total benefit is the dollar value that a person places on a given level of provision of a good. The greater the quantity of a good, the larger is a person's total benefit. *Marginal benefit* is the increase in total benefit that results from a one-unit increase in the quantity of a good.

Figure 16.2 shows the marginal benefit that arises from defence satellites for a society with only two people, Lisa and Max, whose marginal benefits are graphed as MB_L and MB_M, respectively, in parts (a) and (b) of the figure. The marginal benefit from a public good (like that from a private good) diminishes as the quantity of the good increases. For Lisa, the marginal benefit from the first satellite is $80 and that from the second is $60. By the time five satellites are deployed, Lisa's marginal benefit is zero. For Max, the marginal benefit from the first satellite is $50 and that from the second is $40. By the time five satellites are deployed, Max perceives only $10 worth of marginal benefit.

Part (c) shows the economy's marginal benefit curve, *MB*. The economy's marginal benefit curve for a public good is different from the market demand curve for a *private* good. To obtain the market demand curve for a private good, we sum the quantities demanded by all individuals at each price—we sum the individual demand curves *horizontally* (see Chapter 5, p. 106). But to find the economy's marginal benefit curve of a *public* good, we sum the marginal benefits of each individual at each quantity—we sum the individual marginal benefit curves *vertically*. So the curve *MB* in part (c) is the marginal benefit curve for the economy made up of Lisa and Max. Lisa's marginal benefit from

FIGURE 16.2

Benefits of a Public Good

(a) Lisa's marginal benefit

(b) Max's marginal benefit

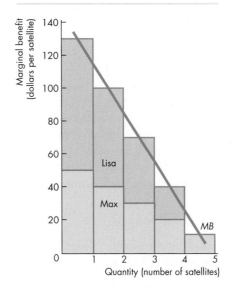

(c) Economy's marginal benefit

The marginal benefit to the economy at each quantity of the public good is the sum of the marginal benefits of all individuals. The marginal benefit curves are MB_L for Lisa, MB_M for Max, and *MB* for the economy.

each satellite gets added to Max's marginal benefit from each satellite because they *both* consume the services of each satellite.

The Efficient Quantity of a Public Good

An economy with two people would not buy any satellites—because the total benefit would fall far short of the cost. But an economy with 30 million people might. To determine the efficient quantity, we need to take the cost as well as the benefit into account.

The cost of a satellite is based on technology and the prices of the resources used to produce it (just like the cost of producing sweaters, which you studied in Chapter 10).

Figure 16.3 sets out the benefits and costs. The second and third columns of the table show the total and marginal benefits. The next two columns show the total and marginal costs of producing satellites. The final column shows net benefit. Total benefit, *TB,* and total cost, *TC,* are graphed in part (a) of the figure.

The efficient quantity is the one that maximizes *net benefit*—total benefit minus total cost—and occurs when 2 satellites are provided.

The fundamental principles of marginal analysis that you have used to explain how consumers maximize utility and how firms maximize profit can also be used to calculate the efficient scale of provision of a public good. Figure 16.3(b) shows this alternative approach. The marginal benefit curve is *MB,* and the marginal cost curve is *MC.* When marginal benefit exceeds marginal cost, net benefit increases if the quantity produced increases. When marginal cost exceeds marginal benefit, net benefit increases if the quantity produced decreases. Marginal benefit equals marginal cost with 2 satellites. So making marginal cost equal to marginal benefit maximizes net benefit and uses resources efficiently.

Private Provision by Market

We have now worked out the quantity of satellites that maximizes net benefit. Would a private firm—North Pole Protection, Inc.—deliver that quantity? It would not. To do so, it would have to collect $15 billion to cover its costs—or $500 from each of the 30 million people in the economy. But no one would have an incentive to buy his or her "share" of the satellite system. Everyone would reason as follows: The number of satellites provided by North Pole Protection, Inc., is not affected by my $500. But my

own private consumption is greater if I free ride and do not pay my share of the cost of the satellite system. If I do not pay, I enjoy the same level of security and I can buy more private goods. Therefore I will spend my $500 on other goods and free ride on the public good. This is the free-rider problem.

If everyone reasons the same way, North Pole Protection has zero revenue and so provides no satellites. Because two satellites is the efficient level, private provision is inefficient.

Public Provision by Majority Vote

Suppose that voters agree with each other on all issues except for the quantity of satellites. An equal number of voters want each level of provision from zero to five so 40 percent of voters want zero or one; 40 percent want three or four, and 20 percent want two, the efficient quantity.

There are two political parties, the Hawks represent the 40 percent who would like more than two satellites; the Doves represent the 40 percent who would like fewer than two satellites; and no party represents the 20 percent who want two satellites.

The Hawks realize that if they propose any number of satellites greater than two, the Doves can propose two and win the election. The Doves get 60 percent of the vote. Similarly, the Doves realize that if they propose any number fewer than two, the Hawks can propose two and win the election with 60 percent of the votes.

Contemplating these possible election outcomes, the Hawks realize that they cannot be too hawkish and the Doves realize that they can't be too dovish.

The only proposal that either can make that doesn't guarantee electoral defeat is two. By proposing two satellites, each party gets the support of their 40 percent plus a further 10 percent because the middle group doesn't care which party wins the election.

The result of the politicians' contemplating the alternative possible election outcomes is that each party proposes two satellites, so regardless of who wins the election, this is the quantity of satellites installed. And this quantity is efficient. It maximizes the net benefit of the voters.

Thus in this example, competition in the political marketplace results in the efficient provision of a public good. But for this outcome to occur, the median voter must want the efficient outcome, and voters must be well informed. As you will see below, voters do not always have the incentive to achieve this outcome.

FIGURE 16.3

The Efficient Quantity of a Public Good

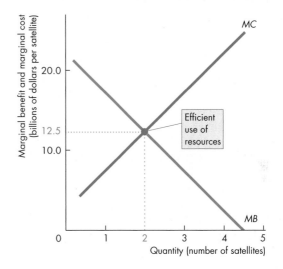

Quantity (number of satellites)	Total benefit (billions of dollars)		Marginal benefit (billions of dollars per satellite)	Total cost (billions of dollars)		Marginal cost (billions of dollars per satellite)	Net benefit (billions of dollars)
0	0			0			0
		....	20		....	5	
1	20			5			15
		....	15		....	10	
2	35			15			20
		....	10		....	15	
3	45			30			15
		....	5		....	20	
4	50			50			0
		....	0		....	25	
5	50			75			−25

Net benefit—the vertical distance between total benefit, *TB*, and total cost, *TC*—is maximized when 2 satellites are installed (part a) and where marginal benefit, *MB*, equals marginal cost, *MC* (part b). The Doves would like 1 satellite, and the Hawks would like 4. But each party recognizes that its only hope of being elected is to provide 2 satellites—the quantity that maximizes net benefit and so leaves no room for the other party to improve on.

The Principle of Minimum Differentiation In the example we've just studied, both parties propose identical policies. This tendency towards identical policies is an example of the **principle of minimum differentiation**, which is the tendency for competitors to make themselves similar to appeal to the maximum number of clients or voters. This principle not only describes the behaviour of political parties but also explains why fast-food restaurants cluster in the same block and even why new auto models have similar features. If McDonald's opens a restaurant in a new location, it is likely that Burger King will open next door to McDonald's rather than a mile down the road. If Chrysler designs a new van with a sliding door on the driver's side, most likely Ford will too.

The Role of Bureaucrats

We have analyzed the behaviour of politicians but not that of the bureaucrats who translate the choices of the politicians into programs and who control the day-to-day activities that deliver public goods. Let's now see how the economic choices of bureaucrats influence the political equilibrium.

To do so, we'll stick with the previous example. We've seen that competition between two political parties delivers the efficient quantity of satellites. But will the bureaucrats in the Department of National Defence (DND) cooperate and accept this outcome?

The bureaucrats' objective is to maximize the defence budget—see Chapter 14, pp. 325–326. With 2 satellites being provided at minimum cost, the defence budget is $15 billion (see Fig. 16.4). To increase its budget, the DND might do two things. First, it might try to persuade the politicians that 2 satellites cost more than $15 billion. As Fig. 16.4 shows, if possible, the DND would like to convince Parliament that 2 satellites cost $35 billion—the entire benefit. Second, and pressing its position even more strongly, the DND might argue for more satellites. It might press for 4 satellites and a budget of $50 billion. In this situation, total benefit and total cost are equal and net benefit is zero.

The DND wants to maximize its budget, but won't the politicians prevent it from doing so because the DND's preferred outcome costs votes? They will if voters are well informed and know what is best for them. But voters might be rationally ignorant. In this case, well-informed interest groups might enable the DND to achieve its objective.

Rational Ignorance

A principle of public choice theory is that it is rational for a voter to be ignorant about an issue unless that issue has a perceptible effect on the voter's income. **Rational ignorance** is the decision *not* to acquire information because the cost of doing so exceeds the expected benefit. For example, each voter knows that he or she can make virtually no difference to the defence policy of the government of Canada. Each voter also knows that it would take an enormous amount of time and effort to become even moderately well informed about alternative defence technologies. So voters remain relatively uninformed about the technicalities of defence issues. (Though we are using defence policy as an example, the same applies to all

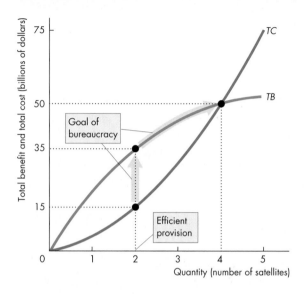

FIGURE 16.4 ⊠ myeconlab
Bureaucratic Overprovision

The goal of bureaucrats is to maximize the department's budget. A bureaucracy that maximizes the budget will seek to increase the budget until its total cost equals total benefit. Then it will use the budget to expand output and expenditure. Here, the DND tries to get $35 billion to provide 2 satellites. It would like to increase the quantity to 4 satellites with a budget of $50 billion.

aspects of government economic activity.)

All voters are consumers of national defence. But not all voters are producers of national defence. Only a small number are in this latter category. Voters who own or work for firms that produce satellites have a direct personal interest in defence because it affects their incomes. These voters have an incentive to become well informed about defence issues and to operate a political lobby aimed at furthering their own interests. In collaboration with the defence bureaucracy, these voters exert a larger influence than do the relatively uninformed voters who only consume this public good.

When the rationality of the uninformed voter and special interest groups are taken into account, the political equilibrium provides public goods in excess of the efficient quantity. So in the satellite example, 3 or 4 satellites might be installed rather than the efficient quantity, which is 2 satellites.

Two Types of Political Equilibrium

We've seen that two types of political equilibrium are possible: efficient and inefficient. These two types of political equilibrium correspond to two theories of government:

■ Social interest theory
■ Public choice theory

Social Interest Theory Social interest theory predicts that governments make choices that achieve efficiency. This outcome occurs in a perfect political system in which the median voter wants the efficient outcome and voters are fully informed about the benefits and costs of alternative policies.

Public Choice Theory Public choice theory predicts that governments make choices that result in inefficiency. This outcome occurs in political markets in which voters are rationally ignorant and base their votes only on issues that they know affect their own net benefit. Voters pay more attention to their interests as producers than their interests as consumers, and public officials also act in their own best interest. The result is *government failure* that parallels market failure.

Why Government Is Large and Grows

Now that we know how the quantity of public goods is determined, we can explain part of the reason for the growth of government. Government grows in part because the demand for some public goods increases at a faster rate than the demand for private goods. There are two possible reasons for this growth:

■ Voter preferences
■ Inefficient overprovision

Voter Preferences The growth of government can be explained by voter preferences in the following way. As voters' incomes increase (as they do in most years), the demand for many public goods increases more quickly than income. (Technically, the *income elasticity of demand* for many public goods is greater than 1—see Chapter 4, pp. 92–93.) These goods include public health, education, national defence, highways, airports, and air-traffic control systems. If politicians did not support increases in expenditures on these items, they would not get elected.

Inefficient Overprovision Inefficient overprovision might explain the *size* of government but not its *growth rate*. It (possibly) explains why government is *larger* than its efficient scale, but it does not explain why governments use an increasing proportion of total resources.

Voters Strike Back

If government grows too large relative to the value that voters place on public goods, there might be a voter backlash against government programs and a large bureaucracy. Electoral success during the 1990s at the provincial and federal levels required politicians of all parties to embrace smaller, leaner, and more efficient government. The September 11 attacks have led to a greater willingness to pay for security but have probably not lessened the desire for lean government.

Another way in which voters—and politicians—can try to counter the tendency of bureaucrats to expand their budgets is to privatize the production of public goods. Government *provision* of a public good does not automatically imply that a government-operated bureau must *produce* the good. Garbage collection (a public good) is often done by a private firm, and experiments are being conducted with private fire departments and even private prisons.

REVIEW QUIZ

1 What is the free-rider problem and why does it make the private provision of a public good inefficient?
2 Under what conditions will competition for votes among politicians result in an efficient quantity of a public good?
3 How do rationally ignorant voters and budget-maximizing bureaucrats prevent competition in the political marketplace from producing the efficient quantity of a public good? Do they result in too much or too little public provision of public goods?

myeconlab Study Plan 16.2

You've seen how public goods create a free-rider problem that would result in the underprovision of such goods. We're now going to learn about common resources and see why they result in the opposite problem—the overuse of such resources.

Common Resources

ATLANTIC OCEAN COD STOCKS HAVE BEEN declining since the 1950s, and some marine biologists fear that this species is in danger of becoming extinct in some regions. The whale population of the South Pacific and South Atlantic have been declining, and a ban on commercial whaling around Antarica is now in place to regenerate the population. Since the start of the Industrial Revolution in 1750, the concentration of carbon dioxide in the atmosphere has steadily increased. It is estimated that it is about 30 percent higher today than it was in 1750.

All these situations involve common property, and the problem that we have identified is called the tragedy of the commons.

The Tragedy of the Commons

The *tragedy of the commons* is the absence of incentives to prevent the overuse and depletion of a commonly owned resource. If no one owns a resource, no one considers the effects of her or his use of the resource on others.

The Original Tragedy of the Commons The term "tragedy of the commons" comes from fourteenth century England where areas of rough grassland surrounded villages. The commons were open to all and used for grazing cows and sheep owned by the villagers.

Because the commons were open to all, no one had an incentive to ensure that the land was not over grazed. The result was a severe overgrazing situation. Because the commons were overgrazed, the quantity of cows and sheep that they could feed kept on falling.

During the sixteenth century, the price of wool increased and England became a wool exporter to the world. Sheep farming became profitable, and sheep owners wanted to gain more effective control of the land they used. So the commons were gradually enclosed and privatized. Overgrazing ended, and land use became more efficient.

A Tragedy of the Commons Today One of today's pressing tragedies of the commons is overfishing. Several fish species have been seriously overfished, and one of them is Atlantic Cod.

To study the tragedies of the commons, we'll use the Atlantic Cod as an example.

Sustainable Production

Sustainable production is the rate of production that can be maintained indefinitely. In the case of ocean fish, the sustainable rate of production is the quantity of fish (of a given species) that can be caught each year into the indefinite future.

The production rate depends on the existing stock of fish and the number of boats that go fishing. For a given stock of fish, sending more boats to sea increases the quantity of fish caught. But sending too many boats to sea depletes the stock.

So as the number of boats increases, the quantity of fish caught increases as long as the stock is maintained. But above some crucial level, as more boats go fishing, the stock of fish decreases and the number of fish caught also decreases.

Table 16.1 provides some numbers that illustrate the relationship between the number of boats that go fishing and the quantity of fish caught. The numbers in this example are hypothetical.

TABLE 16.1	Sustainable Production: Total, Average, and Marginal Catch			
	Boats (thousands)	**Total catch** (thousands of tonnes)	**Average catch** (tonnes per boat)	**Marginal catch** (tonnes per boat)
A	0	0		
				90
B	1	90	90	
				70
C	2	160	80	
				50
D	3	210	70	
				30
E	4	240	60	
				10
F	5	250	50	
				−10
G	6	240	40	
				−30
H	7	210	30	
				−50
I	8	160	20	
				−70
J	9	90	10	
				−90
K	10	0	0	

As the number of fishing boats increases, the quantity of fish caught increases up to the maximum sustainable catch and then decreases. The average catch and marginal catch decrease as the number of boats increases.

Total Catch The total catch is the sustainable rate of production. The numbers in the first two columns of Table 16.1 show the relationship between the number of fishing boats and the total catch, and Fig. 16.5 illustrates this relationship.

You can see that as the number of boats increases from zero to 5,000, the sustainable catch increases to a maximum of 250,000 tonnes a month. As the number of boats increases above 5,000, the sustainable catch begins to decrease. By the time 10,000 boats are fishing, the fish stock is depleted to the point at which no fish can be caught.

With more than 5,000 boats, there is overfishing. Overfishing arises if the number of boats increases to the point at which the fish stock begins to fall and the remaining fish are harder to find and catch.

Average Catch The average catch is the catch per boat and equals the total catch divided by the number of boats. The numbers in the third column of Table 16.1 show the average catch.

One boat catches 100 tonnes a month. With 1,000 boats, the total catch is 90,000 tonnes and the catch per boat is 90 tonnes. With 2,000 boats, the

total catch is 160,000 tonnes, and the catch per boat 80 tonnes. As more boats take to the ocean, the catch per boat decreases. By the time 8,000 boats are fishing, each boat is catching just 20 tonnes a month.

The decreasing average catch is an example of the principle of diminishing returns.

Marginal Catch The marginal catch is the change in the total catch that occurs when one more boat joins the existing number. It is calculated as the change in the total catch divided by the increase in the number of boats. The numbers in the fourth column of Table 16.1 show the marginal catch.

For example, in rows C and D of the table, when the number of boats increases by 1,000, the catch increases by 50,000 tonnes, so the increase in the catch per boat equals 50 tonnes. In the table, we place this amount midway between the two rows because it is the marginal catch at 2,500 boats, midway between the two levels that we used to calculate it.

Notice that the marginal catch, like the average catch, decreases as the number of boats increases. Also notice that the marginal catch is always less than the average catch.

When the number of boats reaches that at which the sustainable catch is a maximum, the marginal catch is zero. At a larger number of boats, the marginal catch becomes negative—more boats decrease the total catch.

An Overfishing Equilibrium

The tragedy of the commons is that common resources are overused. Why might the fish stock be overused? Why might overfishing occur? Why isn't the maximum number of boats that take to the sea the number that maximizes the sustainable catch—5,000 in this example?

To answer this question, we need to look at the marginal cost and marginal private benefit to an individual fisher.

Suppose that the marginal cost of a fishing boat is the equivalent of 20 tonnes of fish a month. That is, to cover the opportunity cost of maintaining and operating a boat, the boat must catch 20 tonnes of fish a month. This quantity of fish also provides the boat owner with normal profit (part of the cost of operating the boat), so the boat owner is willing to go fishing.

The marginal private benefit of operating a boat is the quantity of fish the boat can catch. This quantity is

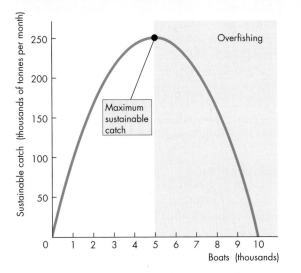

FIGURE 16.5

Sustainable Production of Fish

As the number of boats increases, the sustainable catch increases up to a maximum. Beyond that number, more boats will diminish the fish stock and the sustainable catch decreases. Overfishing occurs when the maximum sustainable catch decreases.

the average catch that we've just calculated. The average catch is the marginal private benefit because that is the quantity of fish that the boat owner gets by taking the boat to sea.

The boat owner will go fishing as long as the average catch (marginal private benefit) exceeds the marginal cost. And the boat owner will maximize profit when marginal private benefit equals marginal cost.

Figure 16.6 shows the marginal cost curve, *MC*, and the marginal private benefit curve, *MPB*. The *MPB* curve is based on the numbers for the average catch in Table 16.1.

You can see in Fig. 16.6 that with fewer than 8,000 boats, each boat catches more fish than it costs to catch them. Because boat owners can gain from fishing, the number of boats is 8,000 and there is an overfishing equilibrium.

If one boat owner stopped fishing, the overfishing would be less severe. But that boat owner would be giving up an opportunity to earn an economic profit.

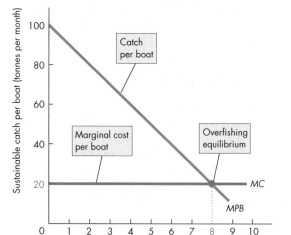

FIGURE 16.6
Why Overfishing Occurs

The average catch decreases as the number of boats increases. The average catch per boat is the marginal private benefit, *MPB*, of a boat. The marginal cost of a boat is equivalent to 20 tonnes of fish, shown by the curve *MC*. The equilibrium number of boats is 8,000—an overfishing equilibrium.

The private interest is to fish, but the social interest is to limit fishing. The quantity of fish caught by each boat decreases as additional boats are introduced. But when individual boat owners are deciding whether to fish, they ignore this decrease. They consider only the marginal *private* benefit. The result is an *inefficient* overuse of the resource.

The Efficient Use of the Commons

What is the efficient use of a common resource? It is the use of the resource that makes the marginal cost of using the resource equal to the marginal *social* benefit from its use.

Marginal Social Benefit The marginal *social* benefit of a boat is the boat's marginal catch—the increase in the total catch that results from an additional boat. The reason is that when an additional boat puts to sea, it catches the average catch but it decreases the average catch for itself and for every other boat. The social benefit is the increase in the quantity of fish caught, not the average number of fish caught.

We calculated the marginal catch in Table 16.1 and we repeat part of that table for convenience in Fig. 16.7, which also shows marginal social benefit as the *MSB* curve. Figure 16.7 also shows the marginal private benefit curve, *MPB*.

Notice that at any given number of boats, marginal social benefit is less than marginal private benefit. Each boat benefits privately from the average catch, but the addition of one more boat *decreases* the catch of every boat, and this decrease must be subtracted from the catch of the additional boat to determine the social benefit from the additional boat.

Efficient Use Figure 16.7 also shows the marginal cost curve, *MC*, and the efficient outcome. Efficiency is achieved when *MSB* equals *MC* with 4,000 boats, each catching 60 tonnes of fish a month. You can see in the table that when the number of boats increases from 3,000 to 4,000 (with 3,500 being the midpoint), marginal social benefit is 30 tonnes, which exceeds marginal cost. When the number of boats increases from 4,000 to 5,000 (with 4,500 being the midpoint), marginal social benefit is 10 tonnes, which is less than marginal cost. At 4,000 boats, marginal social benefit is 20 tonnes, which equals marginal cost.

FIGURE 16.7 ⓧ myeconlab
Efficient Use of a Common Resource

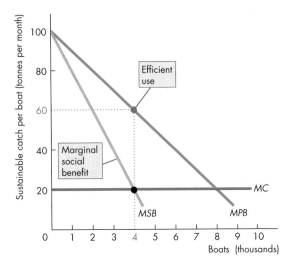

Boats (thousands)	Total catch (thousands of tonnes)	MPB (tonnes per boat)	MSB (tonnes per boat)
A 0	0		
			90
B 1	90	90	
			70
C 2	160	80	
			50
D 3	210	70	
			30
E 4	240	60	
			10
F 5	250	50	

The marginal social benefit, *MSB*, of a fishing boat is the change in total benefit that results from an additional boat. The table shows the *MSB* calculations. When the number of boats increases from 2,000 to 3,000 (from row *C* to row *D*), the total catch increases from 160,000 to 210,000 tonnes and the marginal catch and *MSB* is 50 tonnes. The figure graphs the *MSB* curve as well as the *MPB* curve. Marginal social benefit is less than marginal private benefit and decreases as the number of boats increases. The efficient quantity of boats is that at which *MSB* equals *MC* and is 4,000. The efficient use of a common resource does not overuse the resource.

Achieving an Efficient Outcome

Defining the conditions under which a common resource is used efficiently is easier than bringing those conditions about. To use a common resource efficiently, it is necessary to design an incentive mechanism that confronts the users of the resource with the marginal social consequences of their actions. The same principles apply to common resources as those that you met when you studied externalities in Chapter 15.

Three main methods might be used to achieve the efficient use of a common resource. They are

- Property rights
- Quotas
- Individual transferable quotas (ITQs)

Property Rights A common resource that no one owns and that anyone is free to use contrasts with *private property*, which is a resource that *someone* owns and has an incentive to use in the way that maximizes its value. One way of overcoming the tragedy of the commons is to remove the commons and make the resource private property. By assigning private property rights, each owner faces the same conditions as society faces. The *MSB* curve of Fig. 16.7 becomes the marginal *private* benefit curve, and the use of the resource is efficient.

The private property solution to the tragedy of the commons *is* available in some cases. It was the solution to the original tragedy of the commons in England's Middle Ages. It is also a solution that has been used to prevent the airwaves that we use to carry our cell phone messages from being overused. The right to use this space—called the frequency spectrum—has been auctioned by governments to the highest bidders, and the owner of a particular part of the spectrum is the only one permitted to use it (or license someone else to use it).

But assigning private property rights is not always feasible. It would be difficult, for example, to assign private property rights to the oceans. It would not be impossible, but the cost of enforcing private property rights over thousands of square kilometres of ocean would be high. And it would be even harder to assign and protect private property rights to the atmosphere.

In some cases, there is an emotional objection to assigning private property rights. When private property rights are too costly to assign and enforce, some form of government intervention is used, and quotas are the simplest.

Quotas You studied the effects of a quota in Chapter 6 (p. 139) and learned that a quota can drive a wedge between marginal benefit and marginal cost and create deadweight loss. But in that earlier example, the market was efficient without a quota. In the case of the use of common property, the market is inefficient and is overproducing. So a quota that limits production can bring a move towards a more efficient outcome.

Figure 16.8 shows a quota that achieves an efficient use of a common resource. A quota is set for total production at the quantity at which marginal social benefit equals marginal cost. Here, that quantity is what 4,000 boats can produce. Individual boat owners are assigned their own share of the total permitted catch. If everyone sticks to the assigned quota, the outcome is efficient.

There are two problems in implementing a quota. First, it is in everyone's self-interest to cheat and use more of a common resource than the amount based on the assigned quota. The reason is that marginal private

benefit exceeds marginal cost. So by catching more than the allocated quota, each boat owner gets a higher income. If everyone breaks the quota, overproduction returns and the tragedy of the commons remains.

Second, marginal cost is not, in general, the same for every producer. Some producers have a comparative advantage in using a resource.

Efficiency requires that producers with the lowest marginal cost are the ones that get the quotas. But the government department that allocates quotas does not possess information about individual marginal cost. Even if the government tried to get this information, producers would have an incentive to lie about their costs in order to get a bigger quota.

So a quota can work, but only if the activities of every producer can be monitored and all producers have the same marginal cost. Where producers are hard or very costly to monitor or where marginal costs vary across producers, a quota cannot achieve an efficient outcome.

Individual Transferable Quotas Where producers are hard to monitor and where marginal costs differ across producers, a more sophisticated quota system can be used. An **individual transferable quota (ITQ)** is a production limit that is assigned to an individual who is free to transfer the quota to someone else. A market in ITQs emerges, and ITQs are transferred at their market price.

Figure 16.9 shows how ITQs work. In the market for ITQs, the price is the highest price that an ITQ is worth. If the number of ITQs issued equals the efficient production level, that price will equal the amount shown in the figure. This price equals the marginal private benefit at the quota quantity minus the private marginal cost of using a boat. The price rises to this level because people who don't have a quota would be willing to pay this amount to acquire the right to fish. And people who do own a quota could sell it for this price, so to not sell it is to incur an opportunity cost. The result is that the marginal cost, which now includes the cost of the ITQ, rises from MC_0 to MC_1. The equilibrium is efficient.

Individual differences in marginal cost do not prevent an ITQ system from delivering the efficient outcome. Producers that have a low marginal cost are willing and able to pay more for a quota than are producers that have a high marginal cost. The market price of a quota will equal the marginal cost of the

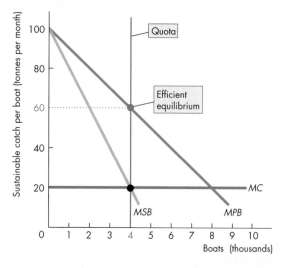

FIGURE 16.8   ⓧ myeconlab

Using a Quota to Use a Common Resource Efficiently

A quota is set at the efficient quantity, which makes the number of boats equal to the quantity at which marginal social benefit, *MSB*, equals marginal cost, *MC*. If the quota is not broken, the outcome is efficient.

FIGURE 16.9 myeconlab

Individual Transferable Quotas to Use a Common Resource Efficiently

ITQs are issued on a scale that keeps output at the efficient level. The market price of an ITQ equals the marginal private benefit minus marginal cost. Because each user of the common resource faces the opportunity cost of using the resource, self-interest achieves the social interest.

marginal producer at the efficient quantity. Producers with higher marginal costs will not produce.

Public Choice and the Political Equilibrium

You saw in the previous part of this chapter where we studied the provision of public goods that a political equilibrium might be inefficient—that there might be government failure.

This same political outcome might arise in the face of a tragedy of the commons. Defining an efficient allocation of resources and designing an ITQ system to achieve that allocation is not sufficient to ensure that the political process delivers the efficient outcome. In the case of the wild ocean fish stock, some countries have achieved an efficient political equilibrium, but not all have done so.

There is wide agreement among economists that ITQs offer the most effective tool for dealing with overfishing and achieving an efficient use of the stock of ocean fish. So a political commitment to ITQs is an

efficient outcome, and an unwillingness to use ITQs is an inefficient political outcome.

Australia and New Zealand have introduced ITQs to conserve fish stocks in the South Pacific Ocean. The evidence from these examples suggests that ITQs work well. Fishing boat operators have an incentive to cheat and produce more than the amount for which they have a quota. But such cheating seems to be relatively rare. And producers that have paid for a quota have an incentive to monitor and report on cheating by others who have not paid the market price for a quota.

So ITQs do the job they are designed to do: help to maintain fish stocks. But they also reduce the size of the fishing industry. This consequence of ITQs puts them against the self-interest of fishers.

In Canada, the opposition to ITQs has prevented this solution from being adopted. One parliamentary committee even went so far as to argue that evidence from Australia and New Zealand should not be used to justify ITQs in Canada.

In the United States the opposition to ITQs is so strong that the fishing industry managed to persuade Congress to outlaw them, a move that led to the end of attempts to introduce ITQs in the Gulf of Mexico and the Northern Pacific.

REVIEW QUIZ

1 What is the tragedy of the commons?
2 Provide two examples of the tragedy of the commons, including one from your own neighbourhood.
3 Describe the conditions under which a common resource is used efficiently.
4 Review three methods that might achieve the efficient use of a common resource and explain the obstacles to efficiency.

myeconlab **Study Plan 16.3**

◆ *Reading Between the Lines* on pp. 376–377 looks at the overuse of tropical rainforests.

The next chapter begins a new part of your study of microeconomics and examines the third big question—for whom are goods and services produced? We examine the markets for factors of production and discover how wage rates and other incomes are determined.

Rainforests: A Tragedy of the Commons

Malaysia laundering rainforest logs

Environmental campaigners in Malaysia are accusing the government of involvement in the criminal destruction of the endangered forests of Indonesia.

Their concerns come as the United Nations publishes its Global Environment Outlook report, in which it warns that 15% of the earth's land cover has now been degraded by human activity—and nearly a third of that is due to deforestation.

An investigation by the BBC has revealed that Malaysia is importing timber which has been felled illegally in nearby Indonesia, and then disguising its origin by using it for the manufacture of garden furniture or other products which are labelled as of Malaysian origin.

...

Just a few miles south of Malaysia's capital Kuala Lumpur there is a brand new port where boats with Indonesian flags are unloading the banned round logs.

And stacking them on the dockside where they will be turned into Malaysian doors or Malaysian garden furniture.

A junior manager at the Kuala Lumpur-based company Harvest, admitted that some of the timber coming in was from Indonesia and it was being stamped by the state government as an official import. ...

BBC, http://news.bbc.co.uk/2/hi/asia-pacific/2002590.stm.

Essence of the Story

■ A United Nations report says that 15 percent of the earth's land cover has been degraded by human activity, almost a third of which is due to deforestation.

■ Malaysia has been accused of importing timber felled illegally in Indonesia, disguising its origin, and using it to manufacture garden furniture or other products that are labelled as of Malaysian origin.

Economic Analysis

■ The tropical rainforests of Indonesia grow valuable hardwood timber.

■ These forests are also home to many rare species and a carbon-dioxide sink that helps to maintain the earth's atmosphere.

■ The forests are common property, but their use is subject to the laws and international agreements.

■ The private incentive to exploit these forest resources is strong.

■ And because no one owns the forests, there is no incentive to conserve the resources and use them on a sustainable basis.

■ The result is overuse, just like the overuse of the commons of England in the Middle Ages.

■ The figures illustrate the tragedy of the commons in a tropical rainforest.

■ Figure 1 shows the relationship between the sustainable production of wood from a rainforest and the number of lumber producers working the forest.

■ Figure 2 shows the marginal benefit and marginal cost of a producer and the marginal social benefit and marginal social cost.

■ The marginal cost of felling a tree incurred by a producer is assumed to be zero.

■ As a common resource, the marginal benefit received by a producer is *MB*, and *LD* producers acting in their self-interest deplete the resource. Sustainable production falls to zero.

■ As a privately owned resource, the marginal social benefit curve, *MSB*, becomes the marginal private benefit curve. Self-interest results in *LP* producers who maximize the sustainable output of the rainforest.

■ If the only benefit from the rainforest were its timber, maximum sustainable timber output would be efficient.

■ But external benefits arise from the diversity of the wildlife supported by the forest, so destroying the forest creates an external cost and marginal social cost exceeds the zero marginal private cost.

■ Production in the social interest—the efficient level of production—is achieved with *LS* producers and is less than the maximum sustainable production.

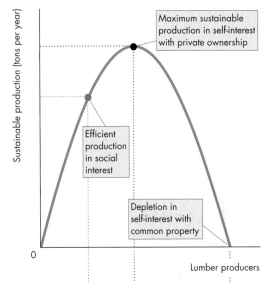

Figure 1 Rainforest timber production

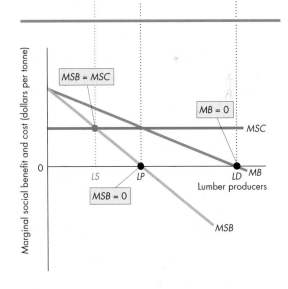

Figure 2 Marginal benefit and marginal cost

You're the Voter

■ Would you support a law that banned the importing of products made from tropical rainforests? Provide your reasons.

SUMMARY

KEY POINTS

Classifying Goods and Resources (p. 364)

- A private good is a good or service that is rival and excludable.
- A public good is a good or service that is nonrival and nonexcludable.
- A common resource is a resource that is rival but nonexcludable.

Public Goods and the Free-Rider Problem (pp. 365–369)

- A public good is a good or service that is consumed by everyone and that is *nonrival* and *nonexcludable*.
- A public good creates a *free-rider* problem: No one has an incentive to pay their share of the cost of providing a public good.
- The efficient level of provision of a public good is that at which net benefit is maximized. Equivalently, it is the level at which marginal benefit equals marginal cost.
- Competition between political parties, each of which tries to appeal to the maximum number of voters, can lead to the efficient scale of provision of a public good and to both parties proposing the same policies—the principle of minimum differentiation.
- Bureaucrats try to maximize their budgets, and if voters are rationally ignorant, producer interests might result in voting to support taxes that provide public goods in quantities that exceed those that maximize net benefit.

Common Resources (pp. 370–375)

- Common resources create the tragedy of the commons—no one has a private incentive to conserve the resources and use it at an efficient rate.
- A common resource is used to the point at which the marginal private benefit equals the marginal cost.
- A common resource might be used efficiently by creating a private property right, setting a quota, or issuing individual transferable quotas.

KEY FIGURES

KEY TERMS

PROBLEMS

Go to 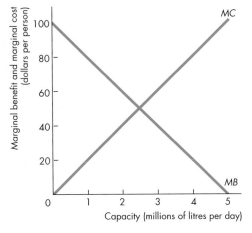 myeconlab for solutions to odd-numbered problems and additional exercises.

1. You are provided with the following information about a sewage disposal system that a city of 1 million people is considering installing.

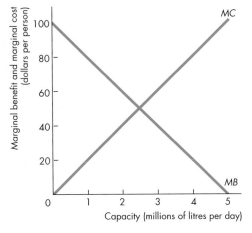

a. What is the capacity that achieves maximum net benefit?
b. How much will each person have to pay in taxes to pay for the efficient capacity level?
c. What is the political equilibrium if the median voter wants the efficient quantity and voters are well informed?
d. What is the political equilibrium if voters are rationally ignorant and bureaucrats achieve the highest attainable budget?

2. You are provided with the following information about a mosquito control program.

Quantity (square miles sprayed per day)	Marginal cost (dollars per day)	Marginal benefit (dollars per day)
0	0	0
1	1,000	5,000
2	2,000	4,000
3	3,000	3,000
4	4,000	2,000
5	5,000	1,000

a. What is the quantity of spraying that achieves maximum net benefit?
b. What is the total tax revenue needed to pay for the efficient quantity of spraying?

c. What is the political equilibrium if the median voter wants the efficient quantity and voters are well informed?
d. What is the political equilibrium if voters are rationally ignorant and bureaucrats achieve the highest attainable budget?

3. The table shows the value of cod caught in the North Atlantic Ocean by Canadian, American, and European fishing boats. It also shows the value that concerned citizens of Canada, the United States, and Europe place on the Atlantic cod stock. The marginal cost of operating a boat is $70,000 a month.

Number of boats	Value of cod caught (thousands of dollars per month)	Value placed on cod stock by concerned citizens (thousands of dollars per month)
0	0	10,000
10	2,000	9,000
20	3,500	8,000
30	4,500	7,000
40	4,800	6,000
50	5,000	5,000
60	4,800	4,000
70	4,200	3,000
80	2,400	2,000

a. What is the marginal private benefit of each fishing boat?
b. What is the marginal social cost of each fishing boat?
c. With no regulation of cod fishing, what is the equilibrium number of boats and the approximate value of cod caught?
d. Is the equilibrium in part (c) an overfishing equilibrium?
e. What is the marginal social benefit of each fishing boat?
f. What is the efficient number of boats?
g. What is the efficient value of the cod catch?
h. Do you you think that the concerned citizens of Canada, the United States, and Europe and the fishing industry will agree about how much cod should be caught?
i. If Canada, the United States, and the European Union issued ITQs to fishing boats to limit the catch to the efficient quantity, what would be the price of an ITQ?

4. The table shows the value of salmon caught in the Pacific Ocean by Canadian, American, and Japanese fishing boats. It also shows the value that concerned citizens of Canada, the United States, and Japan place on the Pacific salmon stock. The marginal cost of operating a boat is $100,000 a month.

Number of boats	Value of salmon caught (thousands of dollars per month)	Value placed on salmon stock by concerned citizens (thousands of dollars per month)
0	0	10,000
5	500	9,500
10	1,000	9,000
15	1,500	8,500
20	2,000	8,000
25	1,750	7,500
30	1,500	7,000
35	1,000	6,500
40	500	6,000

a. What is the marginal private benefit of each fishing boat?
b. What is the marginal social cost of each fishing boat?
c. With no regulation of salmon fishing, what is the equilibrium number of boats and the approximate value of salmon caught?
d. Is the equilibrium in part (c) an overfishing equilibrium?
e. What is the marginal social benefit of each fishing boat?
f. What is the efficient number of boats?
g. What is the efficient value of the salmon catch?
h. Do you think that the concerned citizens of Canada, the United States, and Japan and the fishing industry will agree about how much salmon should be caught?
i. If Canada, the United States, and Japan issued ITQs to fishing boats to limit the catch to the efficient quantity, what would be the price of an ITQ?

CRITICAL THINKING

1. After you have studied *Reading Between the Lines* on pp. 376–377, answer the following questions:
   a. What is happening in Malaysia that is contributing to the depletion of the Indonesian tropical rainforest?
   b. How would the creation of private property rights in Indonesian rainforests change the way in which the forest resources are used?
   c. Would private ownership solve all the problems of resource overuse? If not, why not?

2. Your city council is contemplating upgrading its system for controlling traffic signals. The council believes that by installing computers, it can improve the speed of the traffic flow. The bigger the computer the council buys, the better job it can do. The mayor and the other elected officials who are working on the proposal want to determine the scale of the system that will win them the most votes. The city bureaucrats want to maximize the budget. Suppose that you are an economist who is observing this public choice. Your job is to calculate the quantity of this public good that uses resources efficiently.
   a. What data would you need to reach your own conclusions?
   b. What does the public choice theory predict will be the quantity chosen?
   c. How could you, as an informed voter, attempt to influence the choice?

WEB EXERCISES

Use the links on (myeconlab) **to work the following exercises.**

1. Read the article on demand revealing processes.
   a. What is a demand revealing process and what is its purpose?
   b. Why might using a demand revealing process deliver a more efficient level of public goods than our current political system?
   c. Why might our current political system deliver a more efficient level of public goods than would a demand revealing process?

Making the Rules

Creating a system of responsible democratic government is a huge enterprise and one that can easily go wrong. Creating a constitution that makes despotic and tyrannical rule impossible is relatively easy. And we achieved such a constitution for Canada by using some sound economic ideas. We've designed a sophisticated system of incentives—of carrots and sticks—to make the government responsive to public opinion and to limit the ability of individual self-interest to gain at the expense of the social interest. But we have not managed to create a constitution that effectively blocks the ability of special interest groups to capture the consumer and producer surpluses that result from specialization and exchange.

We have created a system of government to deal with four economic problems. First, the market economy would produce too small a quantity of those public goods and services that we must consume together, such as national defence and air-traffic control. Second, the market economy enables monopoly to restrict production and charge too high a price. Third, the market economy produces too large a quantity of some goods and services, the production of which creates pollution. And fourth, the market economy generates a distribution of income and wealth that most people believe is too unequal. So we need a government to help

cope with these economic problems. But when governments get involved in the economy, people try to steer the government's actions in directions that bring personal gains at the expense of the social interest.

The three chapters in this part explained the problems with which the market has a hard time coping. Chapter 14 overviewed the entire range of problems and studied one of them, competition policy and the regulation of natural monopoly, more deeply. Chapter 15 dealt with externalities. It examined the external costs imposed by pollution and the external benefits that come from education and research. Chapter 15 described some of the ways in which externalities can be dealt with. And it explained that one way of coping with externalities is to strengthen the market and "internalize" the externalities rather than to intervene in the market. Chapter 16 studied the problems created by public goods and common resources.

Many economists have thought long and hard about the problems discussed in this part. But few have had as profound an effect on our ideas in this area as Ronald Coase, whom you can meet on the following page. You can also meet Caroline Hoxby of Harvard University, an economist whose work has shed important light on public choice issues, especially in the field of education.

Externalities and Property Rights

> "The question to be decided is: Is the value of fish lost greater or less than the value of the product which contamination of the stream makes possible?"
>
> RONALD H.
> COASE
> *The Problem of
> Social Cost*

THE ECONOMIST

Ronald Coase *(1910–), was born in England and educated at the London School of Economics, where he was deeply influenced by his teacher, Arnold Plant, and by the issues of his youth: communist central planning versus free markets. Professor Coase has lived in the United States since 1951. He first visited America as a 20-year-old on a travelling scholarship during the depths of the Great Depression. It was on this visit, and before he had completed his bachelor's degree, that he conceived the ideas that 60 years later were to earn him the 1991 Nobel Prize for Economic Science. He discovered and clarified the significance of transactions costs and property rights for the functioning of the economy. Ronald Coase has revolutionized the way we think about property rights and externalities and has opened up the growing field of law and economics.*

THE ISSUES

As knowledge accumulates, we are becoming more sensitive to environmental externalities. We are also developing more sensitive methods of dealing with them. But all the methods involve a public choice.

Urban smog, which is both unpleasant and dangerous to breathe, forms when sunlight reacts with emissions from the tailpipes of automobiles. Because of this external cost of auto exhaust, we set emission standards and tax gasoline. Emission standards increase the cost of a car, and gasoline taxes increase the cost of the marginal mile travelled. The higher costs decrease the quantity demanded of road transportation and so decrease the amount of pollution it creates. Is the value of cleaner urban air worth the higher cost of transportation? The public choices of voters, regulators, and lawmakers answer this question.

Acid rain, which imposes a cost on everyone who lives in its path, falls from sulphur-laden clouds produced by electric utility smokestacks. This external cost is being tackled with a market solution. This solution is marketable permits, the price and allocation of which are determined by the forces of supply and demand. Private choices determine the demand for pollution permits, but a public choice determines the supply.

As cars stream onto an urban freeway during the morning rush hour, the highway clogs and becomes an expensive parking lot. Each rush hour traveller imposes external costs on all the others. Today, road users bear private congestion costs but do not face a share of the external congestion costs that they create. But a market solution to this problem is now technologically feasible. It is a solution that charges road users a fee similar to a toll that varies with time of day and degree of congestion. Confronted with the social marginal cost of their actions, each road user makes a choice and the market for highway space is efficient. Here, a public choice to use a market solution leaves the final decision about the degree of congestion to private choices.

THEN

Chester Jackson, a Lake Erie fisherman, recalls that when he began fishing on the lake, boats didn't carry drinking water. Fishermen drank from the lake. Speaking after World War II, Jackson observed, "Can't do that today. Those chemicals in there would kill you." Farmers used chemicals, such as the insecticide DDT that got carried into the lake by runoff. Industrial waste and trash were also dumped in the lake in large quantities. As a result, Lake Erie became badly polluted during the 1940s and became incapable of sustaining a viable fish stock.

NOW

Today, Lake Erie supports a fishing industry, just as it did in the 1930s. No longer treated as a garbage dump for chemicals, the lake is regenerating its ecosystem. Fertilizers and insecticides are now recognized as products that have potential externalities, and their external effects are assessed by Environment Canada before new versions are put into widespread use. Dumping industrial waste into rivers and lakes is now subject to much more stringent regulations and penalties. Lake Erie's externalities have been dealt with by one of the methods available: government regulation.

Caroline Hoxby, whom you can meet on the following pages, has done much to improve our understanding of policy choices in education.

TALKING WITH

Caroline M. Hoxby *is Professor of Economics at Harvard University. Born in Cleveland, Ohio, she was an undergraduate at Harvard and a graduate student at Oxford and MIT.*

Professor Hoxby is a leading student of the economics of education. She has written many articles on this topic and has published books entitled The Economics of School Choice *and* College Choices *(both University of Chicago Press, 2003 and 2004). She is Program Director of the Economics of Education Program at the National Bureau of Economic Research, serves on several other national boards that study education issues, and has advised or provided testimony to several state legislatures and the United States Congress.*

Michael Parkin and Robin Bade talked with Caroline Hoxby about her work and the progress that economists have made in understanding how the financing and provision of education influence the quality of education and the equality of access to it.

Although this conversation deals with the experience of the United States, there are some important lessons in it for Canadians, especially Caroline Hoxby's message about public versus private schools and the ability of vouchers to achieve any desired goals.

Caroline M. Hoxby

Why did you decide to become an economist?

I've wanted to be an economist from about the age of 13. That was when I took my first class in economics (an interesting story in itself) and discovered that all of the thoughts swimming around in my head belonged to a "science" and there was an entire body of people who understood this science—a lot better than I did, anyway. I can still recall reading *The Wealth of Nations* for the first time; it was a revelation.

What drew you to study the economics of education?

We all care about education, perhaps because it is the key means by which opportunity is (or should be) extended to all in the United States. Also, nearly everyone now acknowledges that highly developed countries like the United States rely increasingly on education as the engine of economic growth. Thus, one reason I was drawn to education is its importance. However, what primarily drew me was that education issues were so clearly begging for economic analysis and that there was so little of it. I try hard to understand educational institutions and problems, but I insist on bringing economic logic to bear on educational issues.

Why is education different from fast food? Why don't we just let people buy it from private firms that are regulated to maintain quality standards analogous to the safety standards that the FDA imposes on fast-food producers?

The thing that makes education different from fast food is not that we cannot buy it from private institutions that are regulated to maintain quality standards. We do this all the time—think of private schools and colleges. What makes education different is that it is (a) an investment, not consumption, and (b) the capital markets for financing the investments work poorly when left on their own. Essentially, our country has an interest in every person investing optimally in his or her education. To make investments, however, people need funds that allow them to attend good schools and take time away from work. Children don't have these funds and cannot arrange for loans that they may or may not pay off decades later. Therefore, children depend on their families for funds, and families do not necessarily have the funds to invest optimally or the right incentives to do so. Society has a role in filling the gaps in the capital market; it fills this role by public funding of elementary and secondary education, government guaranteed loans, college savings programs, and so on. There is no particular reason, however, why government needs to actually run schools; it can provide the funding without actually providing schooling.

In one of your papers, you posed the question: Does competition among public schools benefit students or taxpayers? What are the issues, what was your answer, and how did you arrive at it?

We are all familiar with the fact that families choose public schools when they choose where to live. This traditional form is by far the most pervasive form of school choice in the United States, and few parents who exercise it would be willing to give it up. Yet, until quite recently, we did not know whether having such traditional school choice was good for students (high achievement) or taxpayers (more efficient schools). It is important to know because some people in the United States, especially poor people who live in central cities, are unable to exercise this form of school choice. Economists hypothesized that this lack of choice might be a reason why many children from poor, central city families receive such a deficient education, especially considering the dollars spent in their schools (which spend significantly more than the median school).

To investigate this hypothesis, I examined all of the metropolitan areas in the United States. They vary a great deal in the degree of traditional choice available to parents. On one extreme, there is a group of metropolitan areas with hundreds of school districts. On the other extreme, there is a group of metropolitan areas with only one school district. Most

are somewhere in between. A family in a metropolitan area with one district may have no easy way of "escaping" a badly run district administration. A family in a metropolitan area with hundreds of districts can choose among several districts that match well with its job location, housing preferences, and so on.

Looking across metropolitan areas with many districts (lots of potential competition from traditional school choice) and few districts (little potential competition), I found that areas with greater competition had substantially higher student achievement for any given level of school spending. This suggests that schools are more efficient producers of achievement when they face competition.

What do we know about the relative productivity of public and private schools?

It is somewhat difficult to say whether achievement is higher at public or private schools in the United States. The best studies use randomly assigned private school scholarships, follow the same children over time, or use "natural experiments" in which some areas accidentally end up with more private schools than others. These studies tend to find that, for the same student, private schools produce achievement that is up to 10 percent higher. However, for understanding which type of school is more productive, we actually do not need private schools to have higher achievement. For the sake of argument, let's "call it a draw" on the achievement question.

In recent studies comparing achievement in public and private schools, the public schools spent an average of $9,662 per student and the private schools spent an average of $2,427 per student. These spending numbers, combined with achievement that we will call equal, suggest that the private schools were 298 percent more productive. I would not claim that this number is precisely correct; we could think of some minor adjustments. But it is difficult not to conclude that the private schools are significantly more productive. They produce equal achievement for a fraction of the cost.

What can economists say about the alternative methods of financing education? Is there a voucher solution that could work?

385

There is definitely a voucher solution that could work because vouchers are inherently an extremely flexible policy. People often see the word "voucher" and think of, say, a $2,000 voucher being given to a small share of children. But this need not be so. Anything that we can do with public school financing we can do better with a voucher because vouchers can be specific to a student, whereas the government can never ensure that funds get to an individual student by giving those funds to his or her district.

> " *Economists should say to policy makers: "Tell me your goals; I'll design you a voucher."* "

Any well-designed voucher system will give schools an incentive to compete. However, when designing vouchers, we can also build in remedies for a variety of educational problems. Vouchers can be used to ensure that disabled children get the funding they need and the program choices they need. Compared to current school finance programs, vouchers can do a better job of ensuring that low income families have sufficient funds to invest in the child's education. Well-designed vouchers can encourage schools to make their student bodies socio-economically diverse. Economists should say to policy makers: "Tell me your goals; I'll design you a voucher."

Is there a conflict between efficiency and equity in the provision of quality education?

To raise the public funds that allow all families to invest optimally in their children's education, we have to have taxes. Taxes always create some deadweight loss, so we always create some inefficiency when we raise the funds we need to provide equitable educational opportunities. However, if the funds are used successfully and actually induce people to make optimal investments in their education, we have eliminated much more inefficiency than the taxes created. Thus, in an ideal world, there need not be a conflict between efficiency and equity.

In the real world, public funds are often raised with taxes (creating deadweight loss) and then are not successfully used. If we spend twice as much on pub-

lic schools and do not have higher achievement to show for it, then there are no efficiency gains to overwhelm the efficiency losses from taxation. In other words, to avoid a conflict between equity and efficiency, we must learn how to use public funds productively in education. This is what the economics of education is all about.

What advice do you have for a student who is just starting to study economics? Is economics a good subject in which to major? What other subjects go well alongside it? And do you have anything special to say to women who are making a career choice? What must we do to get more women in our subject?

Students who are just starting to study economics should do two things. First, learn the tools even if they seem abstruse. Once you have mastered the tools, you will be able to "see the forest for the trees." As long as you don't master the tools, you will be in the trees and will find it hard to think about economic problems. Second, think about economic problems! The real world is a great moving textbook of economics, once you have the tools to analyze it.

Economics is a great subject in which to major because it trains you for life, for many careers, and for the thinking that you would need in a leadership position. I think that it is the best training for a future career in business, the law, or policy making. Don't forget non-profits: every year, non-profit organizations try to hire people with economics skills who are also interested in charitable schemes.

Math and statistics courses are complementary to economics because they make it easier for a student to master the tools quickly. Economics goes well with many studies in the arts and sciences, too. It all depends on what you want to use economics for. If you want to do health policy-making, take economics along with pre-medical courses. If you want to be a policy maker in the performing arts, take economics along with music.

I wish that there were more women in economics: Our field loses far too many talented minds. Also, women who need to understand economics for their careers are sometimes without it. To aspiring women economists, I can only say to hang in there. Mastering economics is empowering. You will never have to worry about your opinion not being taken seriously if you are a good economist.

Demand and Supply in Factor Markets

Many Happy Returns

It may not be your birthday, and even if it is, chances are you are spending most of it working. But at the end of the week or month (or, if you're devoting all your time to university, when you graduate), you will receive the *returns* from your labour. Those returns vary a lot. Ed Jones, who spends his days in a small container suspended from the top of Toronto's high-rise buildings cleaning windows, makes a happy return of $12 an hour. Roy Halladay, a Blue Jays pitcher, makes a very happy return of $10.5 million for playing around 80 baseball games. Some differences in earnings might seem surprising. For example, your university football coach might earn much more than your economics professor. Why aren't *all* jobs well paid?

Most of us have little trouble spending our pay. But most of us do manage to save some of what we earn. What determines the amount of saving that people do and the returns they make on that saving?

Some people earn their income by supplying natural resources such as oil. What determines the price of a natural resource?

◆ In this chapter, we study the markets for factors of production—labour, capital, natural resources—and learn how their prices and people's incomes are determined. And we'll see in *Reading Between the Lines* at the end of the chapter how Atlantic storms in the summer of 2005 influenced the price of oil.

After studying this chapter, you will be able to

- ■ **Explain how a market for a factor of production works**

- ■ **Explain how firms' demand for labour and households' supply of labour determine the wage rate and employment**

- ■ **Explain how firms choose the quantity of capital to use**

- ■ **Explain how natural resource prices are determined in competitive resource markets**

- ■ **Explain the concept of economic rent and distinguish between economic rent and opportunity cost**

Factor Prices and Incomes

GOODS AND SERVICES ARE PRODUCED USING THE four *factors of production—labour, capital, land,* and *entrepreneurship.* We defined these factors of production in Chapter 1, pp. 3–4. Incomes are determined by the quantities of the factors used and by *factor prices.* The factor prices are the *wage* rate earned by labour, the *interest* rate earned by capital, the *rental* rate earned by land, and the *normal* profit rate earned by entrepreneurship.

In addition to the four factor incomes, a residual income *economic profit* (or *economic loss*) is earned (or borne) by the firm's owners, who might be the entrepreneur or the stockholders.

Factors of production, like goods and services, are traded in markets. Some factor markets are competitive and behave similarly to competitive markets for goods and services. Other factor markets have monopoly elements. Our focus in this chapter is on competitive factor markets but an appendix (pp. 413–418) examines monopoly elements in labour markets. Demand and supply is the main tool used to understand a competitive factor market.

Firms demand factors of production and households supply them. The quantity demanded of a factor of production is the quantity that firms plan to hire during a given time period and at a given factor price. The law of demand applies to factors of production just as it does to goods and services. The lower the factor price, other things remaining the same, the greater is the quantity demanded of that factor.

The demand for a factor of production is called a **derived demand** because it is *derived* from the demand for the goods and services produced by the factor.

The quantity supplied of a factor of production also depends on its price. With a possible exception that you'll see later in this chapter, the law of supply applies to factors of production. The higher the price of a factor, other things remaining the same, the greater is the quantity supplied of that factor.

Figure 17.1 shows a factor market. The demand curve for the factor is the curve labelled *D,* and the supply curve of the factor is the curve labelled *S.* The equilibrium factor price is *PF,* and the equilibrium quantity is *QF.* The income earned by the factor is its price multiplied by the quantity used. In Fig. 17.1, the factor income equals the area of the blue rectangle.

A change in demand or supply changes the equilibrium price, quantity, and income. An increase in

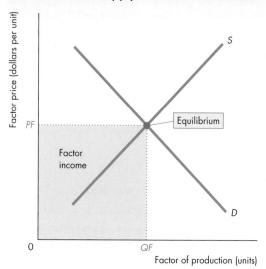

FIGURE 17.1 myeconlab

Demand and Supply in a Factor Market

The demand curve for a factor of production (*D*) slopes downward, and the supply curve (*S*) slopes upward. Where the demand and supply curves intersect, the factor price (*PF*) and the quantity of the factor used (*QF*) are determined. The factor income is the product of the factor price and the quantity of the factor, as represented by the blue rectangle.

demand shifts the demand curve rightward and increases income. An increase in supply shifts the supply curve rightward and income might increase, decrease, or remain constant depending on the elasticity of demand for the factor. If demand is elastic, income rises; if demand is inelastic, income falls; and if demand is unit elastic, income remains constant (see Chapter 4, p. 88).

REVIEW QUIZ

1 Why do we call the demand for a factor of production a *derived demand*? From what is it derived?

2 Why does an increase in the supply of a factor of production have an ambiguous effect on the factor's income?

myeconlab **Study Plan 17.1**

The rest of this chapter explores the influences on the demand for and supply of factors of production. We begin with the market for labour.

Labour Markets

FOR MOST OF US, THE LABOUR MARKET IS OUR only source of income. And in recent years, many people have had a tough time. But over the years, both wages and the quantity of labour have moved steadily upward. Figure 17.2(a) shows the record since 1975. Using 1997 dollars to remove the effects of inflation, the real wage rate (measured as total compensation per hour of work) increased by about 20 percent, from $16 in 1975 to more than $19 in 2004. Over the same period, the quantity of labour employed increased by 60 percent, from 18 billion hours in 1975 to 29 billion hours in 2004.

Figure 17.2(b) shows why these trends occurred. The demand for labour increased from LD_{75} to LD_{04}, and this increase was much larger than the increase in the supply of labour from LS_{75} to LS_{04}.

A lot of diversity lies behind the average wage rate and the aggregate quantity of labour. During the 1980s and 1990s, some wage rates grew much more rapidly than the average and others fell. To understand the trends in the labour market, we must probe the forces that influence the demand for labour and the supply of labour. This chapter studies these forces. We begin on the demand side of the labour market.

The Demand for Labour

The demand for labour is a derived demand. A **derived demand** is a demand for a factor of production that is derived from the demand for the goods and services produced by that factor of production. The derived demand for labour (and for the other factors demanded by firms) is driven by the firm's objective, which is to maximize profit.

You learned in Chapters 11, 12, and 13 that a profit-maximizing firm produces the output at which marginal cost equals marginal revenue. This principle holds true for all firms regardless of whether they operate in perfect competition, monopolistic competition, oligopoly, or monopoly.

A firm that maximizes profit hires the quantity of labour that can produce the profit-maximizing output. What is that quantity of labour? And how does the quantity of labour used change as the real wage rate changes? We can answer these questions by comparing the *marginal revenue* earned by hiring one more worker with the *marginal cost* of that worker. Let's look first at the marginal revenue side of this comparison.

FIGURE 17.2

Canadian Labour Market Trends

(a) Labour and wage rate

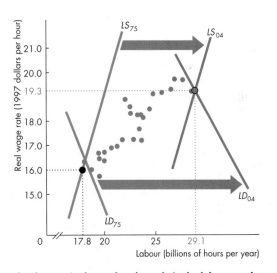

(b) Changes in demand and supply in the labour market

Between 1975 and 2004, the real wage rate increased by 20 percent and the quantity of labour employed increased by 60 percent. Part (a) shows these increases. Each dot in part (b) shows the real wage rate and the quantity of labour in each year from 1975 to 2004. Part (b) also shows the changes in demand and supply that generated these trends. The demand for labour increased from LD_{75} to LD_{04}, and the supply of labour increased from LS_{75} to LS_{04}. Demand increased by more than supply increased, so both the real wage rate and the quantity of labour employed increased.

Source of data: Statistics Canada, CANSIM Tables 282–0002, 282–0022, and 380–0001.

Marginal Revenue Product

The change in total revenue that results from employing one more unit of labour is called the **marginal revenue product** of labour. Table 17.1 shows you how to calculate marginal revenue product for a firm in perfect competition.

The first two columns show the total product schedule for Max's Wash 'n' Wax car wash service. The numbers tell us how the number of car washes per hour varies as the quantity of labour varies. The third column shows the *marginal product of labour*—the change in total product that results from a one-unit increase in the quantity of labour employed. (Look back at p. 221 for a quick refresher.)

The car wash market in which Max operates is perfectly competitive, and he can sell as many washes as he chooses at $4 a wash, the (assumed) market price. So Max's *marginal revenue* is $4 a wash.

Given this information, we can now calculate *marginal revenue product* (the fourth column). It equals marginal product multiplied by marginal revenue. For example, the marginal product of hiring a second worker is 4 car washes, and because marginal revenue is $4 a wash, the marginal revenue product of the second worker is $16 (4 washes at $4 each).

The last two columns of Table 17.1 show an alternative way of calculating the marginal revenue product of labour. Total revenue is equal to total product multiplied by price. For example, 2 workers produce 9 washes per hour and generate a total revenue of $36 (9 washes at $4 each). One worker produce 5 washes per hour and generates a total revenue of $20 (5 washes at $4 each). Marginal revenue product, in the sixth column, is the change in total revenue from hiring one more worker. When the second worker is hired, total revenue increases from $20 to $36, an increase of $16. So the marginal revenue product of the second worker is $16, which agrees with our previous calculation.

Diminishing Marginal Revenue Product As the quantity of labour increases, marginal revenue product diminishes. For a firm in perfect competition, marginal revenue product diminishes because marginal product diminishes. For a monopoly (or in monopolistic competition or oligopoly), marginal revenue product diminishes for a second reason. When more labour is hired and total product increases, the firm must cut its price to sell the extra product. So marginal product *and* marginal revenue decrease, both of which bring decreasing marginal revenue product.

TABLE 17.1   Marginal Revenue Product at Max's Wash 'n' Wax

	Quantity of labour (L) (workers)	Total product (TP) (car washes per hour)	Marginal product (MP = ΔTP/ΔL) (washes per worker)	Marginal revenue product (MRP = MR × MP) (dollars per worker)	Total revenue (TR = P × TP) (dollars)	Marginal revenue product (MRP = ΔTR/ΔL) (dollars per worker)
A	0	0		20	0	
			 5			 20
B	1	5		16	20	
			 4			 16
C	2	9		12	36	
			 3			 12
D	3	12		8	48	
			 2			 8
E	4	14		4	56	
			 1			 4
F	5	15			60	

The car wash market is perfectly competitive, and the price is $4 a wash, so marginal revenue is $4 a wash. Marginal revenue product equals marginal product (column 3) multiplied by marginal revenue. For example, the marginal product of the second worker is 4 washes and marginal revenue is $4 a wash, so the marginal revenue product of the second

worker (in column 4) is $16. Alternatively, if Max hires 1 worker (row B), total product is 5 washes an hour and total revenue is $20 (column 5). If he hires 2 workers (row C), total product is 9 washes an hour and total revenue is $36. By hiring the second worker, total revenue rises by $16— the marginal revenue product of labour is $16.

The Labour Demand Curve

Figure 17.3 shows how the labour demand curve is derived from the marginal revenue product curve. The *marginal revenue product curve* graphs the marginal revenue product of a factor at each quantity of the factor hired. Figure 17.3(a) illustrates the marginal revenue product curve for workers employed by Max. The horizontal axis measures the number of workers that Max hires, and the vertical axis measures the marginal revenue product of labour. The blue bars show the marginal revenue product of labour as Max employs more workers. These bars correspond to the numbers in Table 17.1. The curve labelled *MRP* is Max's marginal revenue product curve.

A firm's marginal revenue product curve is also its demand for labour curve. Figure 17.3(b) shows Max's demand for labour curve (*D*). The horizontal axis measures the number of workers hired—the same as in Fig. 17.3(a). The vertical axis measures the wage rate in dollars per hour. In Fig. 17.3(a), when Max increases the quantity of labour employed from 2 workers an hour to 3 workers an hour, his marginal revenue product is $12 an hour. In Fig. 17.3(b), at a wage rate of $12 an hour, Max hires 3 workers.

The marginal revenue product curve is also the demand for labour curve because the firm hires the profit-maximizing quantity of labour. If the wage rate is *less* than marginal revenue product, the firm can increase its profit by employing one more worker. Conversely, if the wage rate is *greater* than marginal revenue product, the firm can increase its profit by employing one fewer worker. But if the wage rate *equals* marginal revenue product, then the firm cannot increase its profit by changing the number of workers it employs. The firm is making the maximum possible profit. Thus the quantity of labour demanded by the firm is such that the wage rate equals the marginal revenue product of labour.

The demand for labour curve slopes downward: The lower the wage rate, other things remaining the same, the more workers a firm hires. Why? Because the demand curve is also the marginal revenue product curve and marginal revenue product diminishes as the quantity of labour employed increases.

When we studied firms' output decisions, we discovered that a condition for maximum profit is that marginal revenue equals marginal cost. We've now discovered another condition for maximum profit: Marginal revenue product of a factor equals the factor's price. Let's study the connection between these two conditions.

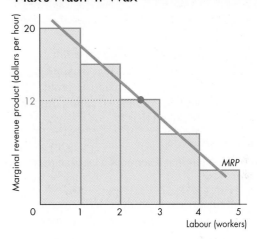

FIGURE 17.3   ⓧ myeconlab

The Demand for Labour at Max's Wash 'n' Wax

(a) Marginal revenue product

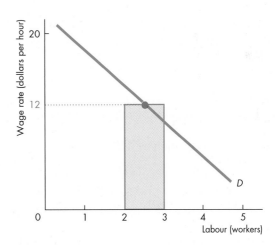

(b) Demand for labour

Max's Wash 'n' Wax operates in a perfectly competitive car wash market and can sell any quantity of washes at $4 a wash. The blue bars in part (a) represent the firm's marginal revenue product of labour. They are based on the numbers in Table 17.1. The orange line is the firm's marginal revenue product of labour curve. Part (b) shows Max's demand for labour curve. This curve is identical to Max's marginal revenue product curve. Max demands the quantity of labour that makes the wage rate equal to the marginal revenue product of labour. The demand for labour curve slopes downward because marginal revenue product diminishes as the quantity of labour employed increases.

Equivalence of Two Conditions for Profit Maximization

Profit is maximized when, at the quantity of labour hired, *marginal revenue product* equals the wage rate and when, at the output produced, *marginal revenue* equals *marginal cost*.

These two conditions for maximum profit are equivalent. The quantity of labour that maximizes profit produces the output that maximizes profit.

To see the equivalence of the two conditions for maximum profit, first recall that

Marginal revenue product = Marginal revenue × Marginal product.

If we call marginal revenue product *MRP*, marginal revenue *MR*, and marginal product *MP*, we have

$$MRP = MR \times MP.$$

If we call the wage rate *W*, the first condition for maximum profit is

$$MRP = W.$$

But $MRP = MR \times MP$, so

$$MR \times MP = W.$$

This equation tells us that when profit is maximized, marginal revenue multiplied by marginal product equals the wage rate.

Divide the last equation by *MP* to obtain

$$MR = W \div MP.$$

This equation states that when profit is maximized, marginal revenue equals the wage rate divided by the marginal product of labour.

The wage rate divided by the marginal product of labour equals marginal cost. It costs the firm *W* to hire one more hour of labour. But the labour produces *MP* units of output. So the cost of producing one of those units of output, which is marginal cost, is *W* divided by *MP*.

If we call marginal cost *MC*, then

$$MR = MC,$$

which is the second condition for maximum profit.

Because the first condition for maximum profit implies the second condition, these two conditions are equivalent. Table 17.2 summarizes the calculations you've just done and shows the equivalence of the two conditions for maximum profit.

TABLE 17.2   Two Conditions for Maximum Profit

Symbols

Marginal product	**MP**
Marginal revenue	**MR**
Marginal cost	**MC**
Marginal revenue product	**MRP**
Wage rate	**W**

Two Conditions for Maximum Profit

1. **MR = MC**   2.   **MRP = W**

Equivalence of Conditions

The two conditions for maximum profit are that marginal revenue (*MR*) equals marginal cost (*MC*) and that marginal revenue product (*MRP*) equals the wage rate (*W*). These two conditions are equivalent because marginal revenue product (*MRP*) equals marginal revenue (*MR*) multiplied by marginal product (*MP*) and the wage rate (*W*) equals marginal cost (*MC*) multiplied by marginal product (*MP*).

Max's Numbers   Check the numbers for Max's Wash 'n' Wax and confirm that the conditions you've just examined work. Max's profit-maximizing labour decision is to hire 3 workers if the wage rate is $12 an hour. When Max hires 3 workers, marginal product is 3 washes. Max sells the 3 washes for a marginal revenue of $4 a wash. So marginal revenue product is 3 washes multiplied by $4 a wash, which equals $12 per hour. At a wage rate of $12 an hour, Max is maximizing profit.

Equivalently, Max's marginal cost is $12 an hour divided by 3 washes per hour, which equals $4 per wash. At a marginal revenue of $4 a wash, Max is maximizing profit.

You've discovered that the law of demand applies for labour just as it does for goods and services. Other things remaining the same, the lower the wage rate (the price of labour), the greater is the quantity of labour demanded.

Let's now see what changes the demand for labour and shifts the demand for labour curve.

Changes in the Demand for Labour

The demand for labour depends on three factors:

1. The price of the firm's output
2. Other factor prices
3. Production technology

The Price of the Firm's Output The higher the price of the firm's output, the greater is its demand for labour. The price of output affects the demand for labour through its influence on marginal revenue product. A higher price for the firm's output increases marginal revenue, which, in turn, increases the marginal revenue product of labour. A change in the price of a firm's output leads to a shift in the firm's demand for labour curve. If the price of the firm's output increases, the demand for labour increases and the demand for labour curve shifts rightward.

Other Factor Prices If the price of some other factor of production changes, the demand for labour changes, but only in the *long run* when all factors of production can be varied. The effect of a change in some other factor price depends on whether that factor is a *substitute* for or a *complement* of labour. Computers are substitutes for telephone operators but complements of word processor operators. So if computers become less costly to use, the demand for telephone operators decreases but the demand for word processor operators increases.

Production Technology An advance in technology that changes the marginal product of labour changes

the demand for labour. There is a general belief that advances in technology destroy jobs and therefore decrease the demand for labour. In fact, the opposite is true. Advances in technology destroy *some* jobs and create others. But the number of jobs created exceeds the number destroyed.

New technologies are substitutes for some types of labour and complements of other kinds. For example, the electronic telephone exchange is a substitute for telephone operators, so the arrival of this new technology has decreased the demand for telephone operators. This same new technology is a complement of systems managers, programmers, and electronic engineers. So its arrival has increased the demand for these types of labour.

Again, these effects on the demand for labour are long-run effects that occur when a firm adjusts all its resources and incorporates new technologies into its production process.

Table 17.3 summarizes the influences on a firm's demand for labour.

TABLE 17.3   A Firm's Demand for Labour

The Law of Demand

(Movements along the demand curve for labour)

The quantity of labour demanded by a firm

Decreases if:	Increases if:
■ The wage rate increases	■ The wage rate decreases

Changes in Demand

(Shifts in the demand curve for labour)

A firm's demand for labour

Decreases if:	Increases if:
■ The firm's output price decreases	■ The firm's output price increases
■ The price of a substitute for the factor falls	■ The price of a substitute for the factor rises
■ The price of a complement of the factor rises	■ The price of a complement of the factor falls
■ A new technology decreases the marginal product of labour	■ A new technology increases the marginal product of labour

Market Demand

So far, we've studied the demand for labour by an individual firm. The market demand for labour is the total demand by all firms. The market demand for labour curve is derived (like the market demand curve for any good or service) by adding together the quantities demanded by all firms at each wage rate. Because each firm's demand for labour curve slopes downward, so does the market demand curve.

Elasticity of Demand for Labour

The elasticity of demand for labour measures the responsiveness of the quantity of labour demanded to the wage rate. This elasticity is important because it tells us how labour income changes when the supply of labour changes. An increase in supply (other things remaining the same) brings a lower wage rate. If demand is inelastic, it also brings lower labour income. But if demand is elastic, an increase in supply brings a lower wage rate and an increase in labour income. And if the demand for labour is unit elastic, a change in supply leaves labour income unchanged.

The demand for labour is less elastic in the short run, when only the quantity of labour can be varied, than in the long run, when the quantities of labour and other factors of production can be varied. The elasticity of demand for labour depends on

- The labour intensity of the production process
- The elasticity of demand for the product
- The substitutability of capital for labour

Labour Intensity A labour-intensive production process is one that uses a lot of labour and little capital. Home building is an example. The greater the degree of labour intensity, the more elastic is the demand for labour. To see why, first suppose that wages are 90 percent of total cost. A 10 percent increase in the wage rate increases total cost by 9 percent. Firms will be sensitive to such a large change in total cost, so if the wage rate increases, firms will decrease the quantity of labour demanded by a relatively large amount. But if wages are 10 percent of total cost, a 10 percent increase in the wage rate increases total cost by only 1 percent. Firms will be less sensitive to this increase in cost, so if the wage rate increases in this case, firms will decrease the quantity of labour demanded by a relatively small amount.

The Elasticity of Demand for the Product The greater the elasticity of demand for the good, the larger is the elasticity of demand for the labour used to produce it. An increase in the wage rate increases the marginal cost of producing the good and decreases the supply of it. The decrease in the supply of the good increases the price of the good and decreases the quantity demanded of the good and the quantities of the factors of production used to produce it. The greater the elasticity of demand for the good, the larger is the decrease in the quantity demanded of the good and so the larger is the decrease in the quantities of the factors of production used to produce it.

The Substitutability of Capital for Labour The more easily capital can be used instead of labour in production, the more elastic is the long-run demand for labour. For example, it is easy to use robots rather than assembly-line workers in car factories and grape-picking machines rather than labour in vineyards. So the demand for these types of labour is elastic. At the other extreme, it is difficult (though possible) to substitute computers for newspaper reporters, bank loan officers, and teachers. So the demand for these types of labour is inelastic.

Let's now turn from the demand side of the labour market to the supply side and examine the decisions that people make about how to allocate time between working and other activities.

The Supply of Labour

People can allocate their time to two broad activities: labour supply and leisure. (Leisure is a catch-all term. It includes all activities other than supplying labour.) For most people, leisure is more enjoyable than supplying labour. We'll look at the labour supply decision of Jill, who is like most people. She enjoys her leisure time, and she would be pleased if she didn't have to spend her weekends working a supermarket checkout line.

But Jill has chosen to work weekends. The reason is that she is offered a wage rate that exceeds her *reservation wage*. Jill's reservation wage is the lowest wage at which she is willing to supply labour. If the wage rate exceeds her reservation wage, she supplies some labour. But how much labour does she supply? The quantity of labour that Jill supplies depends on the wage rate.

Substitution Effect Other things remaining the same, the higher the wage rate Jill is offered, at least over a range, the greater is the quantity of labour that she supplies. The reason is that Jill's wage rate is her *opportunity cost of leisure*. If she quits work an hour early to catch a movie, the cost of that extra hour of leisure is the wage rate that Jill forgoes. The higher the wage rate, the less willing Jill is to forgo the income and take the extra leisure time. This tendency for a higher wage rate to induce Jill to work longer hours is a *substitution effect*.

But there is also an *income effect* that works in the opposite direction to the substitution effect.

Income Effect The higher Jill's wage rate, the higher is her income. A higher income, other things remaining the same, induces Jill to increase her demand for most goods. Leisure is one of those goods. Because an increase in income creates an increase in the demand for leisure, it also creates a decrease in the quantity of labour supplied.

Backward-Bending Supply of Labour Curve As the wage rate rises, the substitution effect brings an increase in the quantity of labour supplied while the income effect brings a decrease in the quantity of labour supplied. At low wage rates, the substitution effect is larger than the income effect, so as the wage rate rises, people supply more labour. But as the wage rate continues to rise, the income effect eventually becomes larger than the substitution effect and the quantity of labour supplied decreases. The labour supply curve is *backward bending*.

Figure 17.4(a) shows the labour supply curves for Jill, Jack, and Kelly. Each labour supply curve is backward bending, but the three people have different reservation wage rates.

Market Supply The market supply of labour curve is the sum of the individual supply curves. Figure 17.4(b) shows the market supply curve (S_M) derived from the supply curves of Jill, Jack, and Kelly (S_A, S_B, and S_C, respectively) in Fig. 17.4(a). At a wage rate of less than $1 an hour, no one supplies any labour. At a wage rate of $1 an hour, Jill works but Jack and Kelly don't. As the wage rate increases and reaches $7 an hour, all three of them are working. The market supply curve S_M eventually bends backward, but it has a long upward-sloping section.

Changes in the Supply of Labour The supply of labour changes when influences other than the wage rate change. The key factors that change the supply of labour and that over the years have increased it are

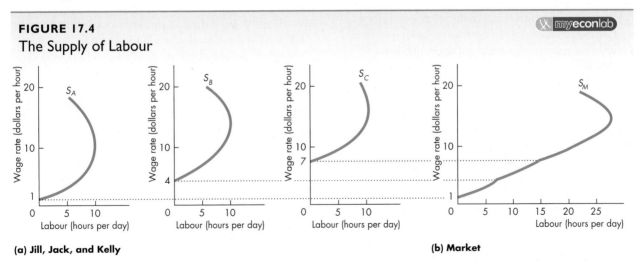

FIGURE 17.4

The Supply of Labour

(a) Jill, Jack, and Kelly

(b) Market

Part (a) shows the labour supply curves of Jill (S_A), Jack (S_B), and Kelly (S_C). Each person has a reservation wage below which she or he will supply no labour. As the wage rises, the quantity of labour supplied increases to a maximum. If the wage continues to rise, the quantity of labour supplied begins to decrease. Each person's supply curve eventually bends backward.

Part (b) shows how, by adding the quantities of labour supplied by each person at each wage rate, we derive the market supply curve of labour (S_M). The market supply curve has a long upward-sloping region before it bends backward.

1. Adult population
2. Technology in the home

An increase in the adult population increases the supply of labour. So does a technological change in home production (of meals, laundry services, and cleaning services). These factors that increase the supply of labour shift the labour supply curve rightward.

Let's now build on what we've learned about the demand for labour and the supply of labour and study labour market equilibrium and the trends in wage rates and employment.

Labour Market Equilibrium

Wages and employment are determined by equilibrium in the labour market, as you saw in Fig. 17.1. Over the years, the equilibrium wage rate and employment level have both increased. You can now explain why.

Trends in the Demand for Labour The demand for labour has *increased* because of advances in production technology, and the demand for labour curve has shifted steadily rightward.

Many people are surprised that advances in production technology *increase* the demand for labour. They see new technologies *destroying jobs*, not creating them. Downsizing has become a catchword as the use of computers has eliminated millions of "good" jobs, even those of managers. So how can it be that technological change *creates* jobs and increases the demand for labour?

Technological change destroys some jobs and creates others. But it creates more jobs than it destroys, and *on the average*, the new jobs pay more than the old ones did. But to benefit from the advances in technology, people must acquire new skills and change their jobs. For example, during the past 20 years, the demand for typists has fallen almost to zero. But the demand for people who can type (on a computer rather than a typewriter) and do other tasks as well has increased. And the output of these people is worth more than that of a typist. So the demand for people with typing (and other) skills has increased.

Trends in the Supply of Labour The supply of labour has increased because of growth in the adult population and technological change in home production. The mechanization of home production of fast-food preparation services (the freezer and the microwave oven) and laundry services (the automatic

washer and dryer and wrinkle-free fabrics) has decreased the time spent on activities that once were full-time jobs and have led to a large increase in the supply of labour. As a result, the supply labour curve has shifted steadily rightward, but at a slower pace than the shift in the demand curve.

Trends in Equilibrium Because advances in production technology have increased demand by more than population growth and technological change in home production have increased supply, both wage rates and employment have increased. But not everyone has shared in the increased prosperity that comes from higher wage rates. Some groups have been left behind, and some have even seen their wage rates fall. Why?

Two key reasons can be identified. First, advances in production technology affect the marginal productivity of different groups in different ways. High-skilled computer-literate workers have benefited from the information revolution while low-skilled workers have suffered. The demand for the services of the first group has increased, and the demand for the services of the second group has decreased. (Draw a supply and demand graph, and you will see that these changes widen the wage difference between the two groups.) Second, international competition has lowered the marginal revenue product of low-skilled workers and so has decreased the demand for their labour. We look further at skill differences and at trends in the distribution of income in Chapter 18.

REVIEW QUIZ

1 What links the quantity that a firm produces and the quantity of labour it employs?

2 What is the distinction between marginal revenue product and marginal revenue? Provide an example that illustrates the distinction.

3 When a firm's marginal revenue product equals the wage rate, marginal revenue also equals marginal cost. Why? Provide a numerical example different from that in the text.

4 What determines the amount of labour that households plan to supply?

5 Describe and explain the trends in wage rates and employment.

(X) myeconlab **Study Plan 17.2**

Capital Markets

CAPITAL MARKETS ARE THE CHANNELS THROUGH which firms obtain *financial* resources to buy *physical* capital resources. These financial resources come from saving. The "price of capital," which adjusts to make the quantity of capital supplied equal to the quantity demanded, is the interest rate.

For most of us, capital markets are where we make our biggest-ticket transactions. We borrow in a capital market to buy a home. And we lend in capital markets to build up a fund on which to live when we retire. Do the rates of return in capital markets increase as wage rates do?

Figure 17.5(a) answers this question by showing the record from 1975 to 2004. Measuring interest rates as *real* interest rates, which means that we subtract the loss in the value of money from inflation, returns have fluctuated. They ranged from close to zero in the late 1970s to a bit more than 10 percent in 1984. Over the same period, the quantity of capital employed increased steadily. In 2004, it stood at $4.6 trillion, twice its 1975 level.

Figure 17.5(b) shows why these trends occurred. Demand increased from KD_{75} to KD_{04}, and this increase was similar to the increase in supply from KS_{75} to KS_{04}. The interest rate in 2004 was almost identical to that of 1975.

To understand the trends in the capital market, we must again probe the forces of demand and supply. Many of the ideas you've already met in your study of the labour market apply to the capital market as well. But there are some special features of capital. Its main special feature is that in the capital market, people must compare *present* costs with *future* benefits. Let's discover how people make these comparisons by studying the demand for capital.

The Demand for Capital

A firm's demand for *financial* capital stems from its demand for *physical* capital, and the amount that a firm plans to borrow in a given time period is determined by its planned investment—purchases of new capital. This decision is driven by the firm's attempt to maximize profit.

As a firm increases the quantity of capital employed, other things remaining the same, the marginal revenue product of capital eventually diminishes. To maximize profit, a firm increases its plant size and

FIGURE 17.5

Canadian Capital Market Trends

(a) Capital stock and interest rate

(b) Changes in demand and supply in the capital market

The real interest rate (the interest rate adjusted for inflation) fluctuated between close to zero and 10 percent a year between 1975 and 2004. During the same period, the quantity of capital approximately doubled. Part (a) shows these trends. Part (b) shows the changes in the demand for and supply of capital that generated the trends. The demand for capital increased from KD_{75} to KD_{04}, and the supply of capital increased from KS_{75} to KS_{04}.

Sources of data: Statistics Canada, CANSIM Tables 378–0004 and 176–0043.

uses more capital if the marginal revenue product of capital exceeds the price of capital. But the marginal revenue product comes in the future, and capital must be paid for in the present. So the firm must convert *future* marginal revenue products into a *present value* so that it can be compared with the price of the new equipment. To make this conversion, we use the technique of discounting.

Discounting and Present Value

Discounting is converting a future amount of money to a present value. And the **present value** of a future amount of money is the amount that, if invested today, will grow to be as large as that future amount when the interest that it will earn is taken into account.

The easiest way to understand discounting and present value is to begin with the relationship between an amount invested today, the interest that it earns, and the amount that it will grow to in the future. The future amount is equal to the present amount (present value) plus the interest it will accumulate in the future. That is,

$$\text{Future amount} = \text{Present value} + \text{Interest income.}$$

The interest income is equal to the present value multiplied by the interest rate, r, so

$$\text{Future amount} = \text{Present value} + (r \times \text{Present value})$$

or

$$\text{Future amount} = \text{Present value} \times (1 + r).$$

If you have $100 today and the interest rate is 10 percent a year ($r = 0.1$), one year from today you will have $110—the original $100 plus $10 interest. Check that the above formula delivers that answer: $100 \times 1.1 = \$110$.

The formula that we have just used calculates a future amount one year from today from the present value and an interest rate. To calculate the present value, we just work backward. Instead of multiplying the present value by $(1 + r)$, we divide the future amount by $(1 + r)$. That is,

$$\text{Present value} = \frac{\text{Future value}}{(1 + r)}.$$

You can use this formula to calculate present value. This calculation of present value is called discounting.

Let's check that we can use the present value formula by calculating the present value of $110 one year from now when the interest rate is 10 percent a year. You'll be able to guess that the answer is $100 because we just calculated that $100 invested today at 10 percent a year becomes $110 in one year. So it follows immediately that $100 is the present value of $110 in one year's time. But let's use the formula. Putting the numbers into the above formula, we have

$$\text{Present value} = \frac{\$110}{(1 + 0.1)}$$

$$= \frac{\$110}{1.1} = \$100.$$

Calculating the present value of an amount of money one year from now is the easiest case. But we can also calculate the present value of an amount any number of years in the future. As an example, let's see how we calculate the present value of an amount of money that will be available two years from now.

Suppose that you invest $100 today for two years at an interest rate of 10 percent a year. The money will earn $10 in the first year, which means that by the end of the first year, you will have $110. If the interest of $10 is invested, then the interest earned in the second year will be a further $10 on the original $100 plus $1 on the $10 interest. Thus the total interest earned in the second year will be $11. The total interest earned overall will be $21 ($10 in the first year and $11 in the second year). After two years, you will have $121. From the definition of present value, you can see that $100 is the present value of $121 two years hence. That is, $100 is the present amount that, if invested at an interest rate of 10 percent a year, will grow to $121 two years from now.

To calculate the present value of an amount of money two years in the future, we use the formula:

$$\text{Present value} = \frac{\substack{\text{Amount of money} \\ \text{two years in future}}}{(1 + r)^2}.$$

Use this formula to calculate the present value of $121 two years from now at an interest rate of 10 percent a year. With these numbers, the formula gives

$$\text{Present value} = \frac{\$121}{(1 + 0.1)^2}$$

$$= \frac{\$121}{(1.1)^2}$$

$$= \frac{\$121}{1.21}$$

$$= \$100.$$

We can calculate the present value of an amount of money n years in the future by using a formula similar to the one we've already used. The general formula is

$$\text{Present value} = \frac{\text{Amount of money } n \text{ years in future}}{(1 + r)^n}.$$

For example, if the interest rate is 10 percent a year, $100 to be received 10 years from now has a present value of $38.55. That is, if $38.55 is invested today at 10 percent a year it accumulates to $100 in 10 years.

You've seen how to calculate the present value of an amount of money one year in the future, two years in the future, and n years in the future. Most practical applications of present value calculate the present value of a sequence of future amounts of money that spread over several years. To calculate the present value of a sequence of amounts over several years, we use the formula you have learned and apply it to each year. We then sum the present values for each year to find the present value of the sequence of amounts.

For example, suppose that a firm expects to receive $100 a year for each of the next five years. And suppose that the interest rate is 10 percent per year (0.1 per year). The present value of these five payments of $100 each is calculated by using the following formula

$$PV = \frac{\$100}{1.1} + \frac{\$100}{1.1^2} + \frac{\$100}{1.1^3} + \frac{\$100}{1.1^4} + \frac{\$100}{1.1^5},$$

which equals

$$PV = \$90.91 + \$82.64 + \$75.13 + \$68.30 + \$62.09$$

$$= \$379.07.$$

You can see that the firm receives $500 over five years. But because the money arrives in the future, it is not worth $500 today. Its present value is only $379.07. And the farther in the future the money arrives, the smaller is its present value. The $100 received one year in the future is worth $90.91 today. And the $100 received five years in the future is worth only $62.09 today.

Let's now see how a firm uses the concept of present value to achieve an efficient use of capital.

The Present Value of a Computer We'll see how a firm decides how much capital to buy by calculating the present value of a new computer.

Tina runs Taxfile, Inc., a firm that sells advice to taxpayers. Tina is considering buying a new computer that costs $2,000. The computer has a life of two years, after which it will be worthless. If Tina buys the computer, she will pay $2,000 now and she expects to generate business that will bring in an additional $1,150 at the end of each of the next two years.

To calculate the present value, PV, of the marginal revenue product of a new computer, Tina calculates

$$PV = \frac{MRP_1}{(1 + r)} + \frac{MRP_2}{(1 + r)^2}.$$

Here, MRP_1 is the marginal revenue product received by Tina at the end of the first year. MRP_1 is converted to a present value by dividing it by $(1 + r)$. The term MRP_2 is the marginal revenue product received at the end of the second year. It is converted to a present value by dividing it by $(1 + r)^2$.

If Tina can borrow or lend at an interest rate of 4 percent a year, the present value of her marginal revenue product is given by

$$PV = \frac{\$1,150}{(1 + 0.04)} + \frac{\$1,150}{(1 + 0.04)^2}$$

$$PV = \$1,106 + \$1,063$$

$$PV = \$2,169.$$

The present value (PV) of $1,150 one year in the future is $1,150 divided by 1.04 (4 percent as a proportion is 0.04). The present value of $1,150 two years in the future is $1,150 divided by $(1.04)^2$. Tina works out those two present values and then adds them to get the present value of the future flow of marginal revenue product, which is $2,169.

Parts (a) and (b) of Table 17.4 summarize the data and the calculations we've just made. Review these calculations and make sure you understand them.

TABLE 17.4   Net Present Value of an Investment—Taxfile, Inc.

(a) Data

Price of computer	$2,000
Life of computer	2 years
Marginal revenue product	$1,150 at end of each year
Interest rate	4% a year

(b) Present value of the flow of marginal revenue product

$$PV = \frac{MRP_1}{(1 + r)} + \frac{MRP_2}{(1 + r)^2}$$

$$= \frac{\$1,150}{1.04} + \frac{\$1,150}{(1.04)^2}$$

$$= \$1,106 + \$1,063$$

$$= \$2,169$$

(c) Net present value of investment

NPV = PV of marginal revenue product − Price of computer

$$= \$2,169 - \$2,000$$

$$= \$169$$

Tina's Decision to Buy Tina decides whether to buy the computer by comparing the present value of its future flow of marginal revenue product with its purchase price. She makes this comparison by calculating the net present value (*NPV*) of the computer. **Net present value** is the present value of the future flow of marginal revenue product generated by the capital minus the price of the capital. If the net present value is positive, the firm buys additional capital. If the net present value is negative, the firm does not buy additional capital. Table 17.4(c) shows the calculation of Tina's net present value of a computer. The net present value is $169—greater than zero—so Tina buys the computer.

Tina can buy any number of computers that cost $2,000 and have a life of two years. But like all other factors of production, capital is subject to diminishing marginal returns. The greater the amount of capital employed, the smaller is its marginal revenue product. So if Tina buys a second computer or a third one, she

gets successively smaller marginal revenue products from the additional machines.

Table 17.5(a) sets out Tina's marginal revenue products for one, two, and three computers. The marginal revenue product of one computer (the case just reviewed) is $1,150 a year. The marginal revenue product of a second computer is $1,100 a year, and the marginal revenue product of a third computer is $1,050 a year. Table 17.5(b) shows the calculations of the present values of the marginal revenue products of the first, second, and third computers.

You've seen that with an interest rate of 4 percent a year, the net present value of one computer is posi-

---

TABLE 17.5   Taxfile's Investment Decision

(a) Data

Price of computer	$2,000
Life of computer	2 years
Marginal revenue product:	
Using 1 computer	$1,150 a year
Using 2 computers	$1,100 a year
Using 3 computers	$1,050 a year

(b) Present value of the flow of marginal revenue product

If r = 0.04 (4% a year):

Using 1 computer $PV = \dfrac{\$1,150}{1.04} + \dfrac{\$1,150}{(1.04)^2} = \$2,169$

Using 2 computers $PV = \dfrac{\$1,100}{1.04} + \dfrac{\$1,100}{(1.04)^2} = \$2,075$

Using 3 computers $PV = \dfrac{\$1,050}{1.04} + \dfrac{\$1,050}{(1.04)^2} = \$1,980$

If r = 0.08 (8% a year):

Using 1 computer $PV = \dfrac{\$1,150}{1.08} + \dfrac{\$1,150}{(1.08)^2} = \$2,051$

Using 2 computers $PV = \dfrac{\$1,100}{1.08} + \dfrac{\$1,100}{(1.08)^2} = \$1,962$

If r = 0.12 (12% a year):

Using 1 computer $PV = \dfrac{\$1,150}{1.12} + \dfrac{\$1,150}{(1.12)^2} = \$1,944$

tive. At an interest rate of 4 percent a year, the present value of the marginal revenue product of a second computer is $2,075, which exceeds its price by $75. So Tina buys a second computer. But at an interest rate of 4 percent a year, the present value of the marginal revenue product of a third computer is $1,980, which is $20 less than the price of the computer. So Tina does not buy a third computer.

A Change in the Interest Rate We've seen that at an interest rate of 4 percent a year, Tina buys two computers. Suppose that the interest rate is 8 percent a year. In this case, the present value of the first computer is $2,051 (see Table 17.5(b)), so Tina still buys one machine because it has a positive net present value. But at an interest rate of 8 percent a year, the present value of the second computer is $1,962, which is less than $2,000, the price of the computer. So at this interest rate, Tina buys only one computer.

Suppose that the interest rate is even higher, 12 percent a year. In this case, the present value of the marginal revenue product of one computer is $1,944 (see Table 17.5(b)). At this interest rate, Tina buys no computers.

These calculations trace Taxfile's demand schedule for capital, which shows the value of computers demanded by Taxfile at each interest rate. Other things remaining the same, as the interest rate rises, the quantity of capital demanded decreases. The higher the interest rate, the smaller is the quantity of *physical* capital demanded. But to finance the purchase of *physical* capital, firms demand *financial* capital. So the higher the interest rate, the smaller is the quantity of *financial* capital demanded.

Demand Curve for Capital

A firm's demand curve for capital shows the relationship between the quantity of financial capital demanded by the firm and the interest rate, other things remaining the same. Figure 17.6(a) shows Tina's demand curve for capital and the four points on it that we've just found. If Tina can buy other capital items so that her demand for capital is divisible into one-dollar units (not restricted to jumping in $2,000 units, her demand curve for capital would look like the entire blue curve in Fig. 17.6(a).

Figure 17.6(b) shows the market demand curve for capital, *KD*, which is the horizontal sum of the demand curves of each firm. In the figure, the quantity of capital demanded in the entire capital market is $1,500 billion when the interest rate is 6 percent a year.

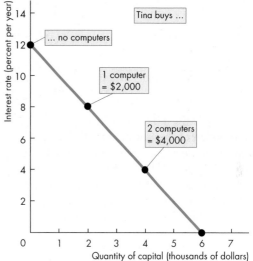

FIGURE 17.6
A Firm's Demand and the Market Demand for Capital

(a) Tina's demand curve for capital

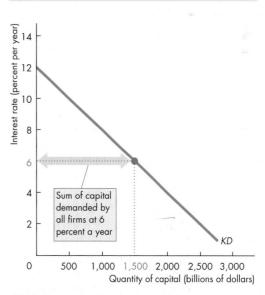

(b) Market demand curve for capital

For each firm, the lower the interest rate, the greater is the quantity of capital demanded. The market demand curve is the (horizontal) sum of the firms' demand curves.

You've seen how the demand for capital is determined. Let's now look at the supply side of the capital market.

The Supply of Capital

The quantity of financial capital supplied results from people's saving decisions. The main factors that determine saving are

- Income
- Expected future income
- Interest rate

Let's see how these factors influence Aaron's saving decisions.

Income Saving is the act of converting *current* income into *future* consumption. When Aaron's income increases, he plans to consume more both now and in the future. But to increase *future* consumption, Aaron must save today. So, other things remaining the same, the higher Aaron's income, the more he saves. The relationship between saving and income is remarkably stable.

Expected Future Income If Aaron's current income is high and his expected future income is low, he will have a high level of saving. But if Aaron's current income is low and his expected future income is high, he will have a low (perhaps even negative) level of saving.

Students have low current incomes compared with expected future incomes so they tend to consume more than they earn. In middle age, most people are earning more than they expect to earn when they retire. So they save for their retirement years.

Interest Rate A dollar saved today grows into a dollar plus interest tomorrow. The higher the interest rate, the greater is the amount that a dollar saved today becomes in the future. Thus the higher the interest rate, the greater is the opportunity cost of current consumption. With a higher opportunity cost of current consumption, Aaron cuts his current consumption and increases his saving.

Supply Curve of Capital

The supply curve of capital shows the relationship between the quantity of financial capital supplied and the interest rate, other things remaining the same. The curve KS_0 in Fig. 17.7 is a supply curve of capital. An increase in the interest rate brings an increase in the quantity of capital supplied and a movement along the supply curve.

Let's now use what we've learned about the demand for and supply of capital and see how the interest rate is determined.

The Interest Rate

Saving plans and investment plans are coordinated through capital markets, and the real interest rate adjusts to make these plans compatible.

Figure 17.7 shows the capital market. The demand for capital is KD_0, and the supply of capital is KS_0. The equilibrium real interest rate is 6 percent a year, and the quantity of capital—the amount of investment by firms and saving by households—is $1,500 billion.

If the interest rate exceeded 6 percent a year, the quantity of capital supplied would exceed the quantity of capital demanded and the interest rate would fall. The interest rate would keep falling until the capital surplus was eliminated.

If the interest rate were less than 6 percent a year, the quantity of capital demanded would exceed the quantity of capital supplied and the interest rate would rise. The interest rate would keep rising until the capital shortage was eliminated.

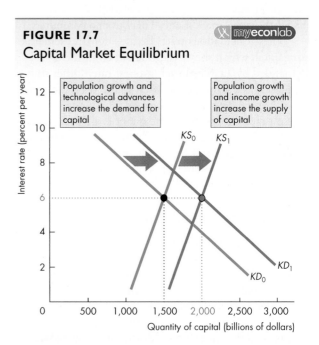

FIGURE 17.7
Capital Market Equilibrium

Initially, the demand for capital is KD_0 and the supply of capital is KS_0. The equilibrium interest rate is 6 percent a year, and the quantity of capital is $1,500 billion. Over time, the demand and supply of capital increase to KD_1 and KS_1. The quantity of capital increases, but the interest rate is constant. The demand and supply of capital are influenced by common and related factors.

Changes in Demand and Supply

Over time, both the demand for capital and the supply of capital increase. The demand curve shifts rightward to KD_1, and the supply curve shifts to KS_1. Both curves shift because the same or related forces influence them. Population growth increases both demand and supply. Technological advances increase demand and bring higher incomes, which in turn increase supply. Because both demand and supply increase over time, the quantity of capital increases but the real interest rate remains constant.

In reality, the real interest rate fluctuates, as you can see in Fig. 17.5(a). The reason is that the demand for capital and the supply of capital do not change in lockstep. Sometimes rapid technological change brings an increase in the demand for capital *before* it brings the higher incomes that increase the supply of capital. When this sequence of events occurs, the real interest rate rises. The first half of the 1980s was such a time, as you can see in Fig. 17.5(a).

At other times, the demand for capital grows slowly or even decreases temporarily. Supply outgrows demand and the real interest rate falls. Figure 17.5(a) shows that the mid-1970s and the period from 1984 through 1991 were two such periods.

REVIEW QUIZ

1 What is the distinction between *physical* capital and *financial* capital and what is the capital market?

2 What is discounting and how is it used to calculate a present value? When might you want to calculate a present value to make a decision?

3 How does a firm compare the future marginal revenue product of capital with the current price of capital?

4 What are the main influences on a firm's demand for capital?

5 What are the main influences on the supply of capital?

6 What have been the main changes in the interest rate and how can we explain those changes by using the demand for and supply of capital?

X myeconlab Study Plan 17.3

The lessons that we've just learned about capital markets can be used to understand the prices of nonrenewable natural resources. Let's see how.

Natural Resource Markets

NATURAL RESOURCES, OR WHAT ECONOMISTS CALL *land*, fall into two categories:

■ Renewable
■ Nonrenewable

Renewable natural resources are natural resources that are repeatedly replenished by nature. Examples are land (in its everyday sense), rivers, lakes, rain, and sunshine.

Nonrenewable natural resources are natural resources that nature does not replenish. Once used, they are no longer available. Examples are coal, natural gas, and oil—the so-called hydrocarbon fuels.

The demand for natural resources as inputs into production is based on the same principle of marginal revenue product as the demand for labour (and the demand for capital). But the supply of natural resources is special. Let's look first at the supply of renewable natural resources.

The Supply of a Renewable Natural Resource

The quantity of land and other renewable natural resources is fixed. The quantity supplied cannot be changed by individual decisions. People can vary the amount of land they own. But when one person buys some land, another person sells it. The aggregate quantity of land supplied of any particular type and in any particular location is fixed, regardless of the decisions of any individual. This fact means that the supply of each particular piece of land is perfectly inelastic. Figure 17.8 illustrates such a supply. Regardless of the rent available, the quantity of land supplied on Toronto's Yorkville is a fixed number of square metres.

Because the supply of land is fixed regardless of its price, price is determined by demand. The greater the demand for a specific piece of land, the higher is its price.

Expensive land can be, and is, used more intensively than inexpensive land. For example, high-rise buildings enable land to be used more intensively. However, to use land more intensively, it has to be combined with another factor of production: capital. An increase in the amount of capital per block of land does not change the supply of land itself.

FIGURE 17.8
The Supply of Land

The supply of a given piece of land is perfectly inelastic. No matter what the rent, no more land than the quantity that exists can be supplied.

Although the supply of each type of land is fixed and its supply is perfectly inelastic, each individual firm, operating in competitive land markets, faces an elastic supply of land. For example, Bloor Street in Toronto has a fixed amount of land, but Chapters, the bookstore, could rent some space from The Bay, the department store. Each firm can rent the quantity of land that it demands at the going rent, as determined in the marketplace. Thus, provided that land markets are competitive, firms are price takers in these markets, just as they are in the markets for other productive resources.

The Supply of a Nonrenewable Natural Resource

The *stock* of a natural resource is the quantity in existence at a given time. This quantity is fixed and is independent of the price of the resource. The *known* stock of a natural resource is the quantity that has been discovered. This quantity increases over time because advances in technology enable ever less accessible sources to be discovered. Both of these *stock* concepts influence the price of a nonrenewable natural resource. But the influence is indirect. The direct influence on

price is the rate at which the resource is supplied for use in production—called the *flow* supply.

The flow supply of a nonrenewable natural resource is *perfectly elastic* at a price that equals the present value of the expected price next period.

To see why, think about the economic choices of Saudi Arabia, a country that possesses a large inventory of oil. Saudi Arabia can sell an additional billion barrels of oil right now and use the income it receives to buy U.S. bonds. Or it can keep the billion barrels in the ground and sell them next year. If it sells the oil and buys bonds, it earns the interest rate on the bonds. If it keeps the oil and sells it next year, it earns the amount of the price increase or loses the amount of the price decrease between now and next year.

If Saudi Arabia expects the price of oil to rise next year by a percentage that equals the current interest rate, the price that it expects next year equals $(1 + r)$ multiplied by this year's price. For example, if this year's price is $40 a barrel and the interest rate is 5 percent a year ($r = 0.5$), then next year's expected price is $1.05 \times \$40$, which equals $42 a barrel.

With the price expected to rise to $42 a barrel next year, Saudi Arabia is indifferent between selling now for $40 and not selling now but waiting until next year and selling for $42. Saudi Arabia expects to make the same return either way. So at $40 a barrel, Saudi Arabia will sell whatever quantity is demanded.

But if Saudi Arabia expects the price to rise next year by a percentage that exceeds the current interest rate, then Saudi Arabia expects to make a bigger return by hanging onto the oil than by selling the oil and buying bonds. So it keeps the oil and sells none. And if Saudi Arabia expects the price to rise next year by a percentage that is less than the current interest rate, the bond gives a bigger return than the oil, so Saudi Arabia sells as much oil as it can.

Recall the idea of discounting and present value. The minimum price at which Saudi Arabia is willing to sell oil is the present value of the expected future price. At this price, it will sell as much oil as buyers demand. So its supply is perfectly elastic.

Price and the Hotelling Principle

Figure 17.9 shows the equilibrium in a natural resource market. Because supply is perfectly elastic at the present value of next period's expected price, the actual price of the natural resource equals the present value of next period's expected price. Also, because the current price is the present value of the expected

FIGURE 17.9
A Nonrenewable Natural Resource Market

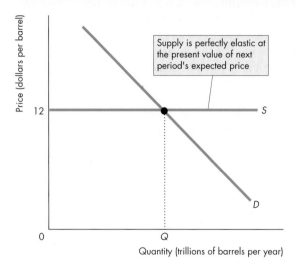

The supply of a nonrenewable natural resource is perfectly elastic at the *present value* of next period's expected price. The demand for a nonrenewable natural resource is determined by its marginal revenue product. The price is determined by supply and equals the *present value* of next period's expected price.

FIGURE 17.10
Falling Resource Prices

The prices of metals (here a price index that measures the average of the prices of aluminum, copper, iron ore, lead, manganese, nickel, silver, tin, and zinc) have tended to fall over time, not rise as predicted by the Hotelling Principle. The reason is that unanticipated advances in technology have decreased the cost of extracting resources and greatly increased the exploitable known reserves.

Source of data: International Financial Statistics (various issues), Washington, DC: International Monetary Fund.

future price, the price of the resource is expected to rise at a rate equal to the interest rate.

The proposition that the price of a resource is expected to rise at a rate equal to the interest rate is called the *Hotelling Principle*. It was first realized by Harold Hotelling, a mathematician and economist at Columbia University. But as Fig. 17.10 shows, *actual* prices do not follow the path *predicted* by the Hotelling Principle. Why do the prices of nonrenewable natural resources sometimes fall rather than follow their expected path and increase over time?

The key reason is that the future is unpredictable. Expected technological change is reflected in the price of a natural resource. But a previously unexpected new technology that leads to the discovery or the more efficient use of a nonrenewable natural resource causes its price to fall. Over the years, as technology has advanced, we have become more efficient in our use of nonrenewable natural resources. And we haven't just become more efficient. We've become more efficient than we expected to.

REVIEW QUIZ

1   Why is the supply of a *renewable* natural resource such as land perfectly inelastic?
2   At what price is the flow supply of a nonrenewable natural resource perfectly elastic and why?
3   Why is the price of a nonrenewable natural resource expected to rise at a rate equal to the interest rate?
4   Why do the prices of nonrenewable resources not follow the path predicted by the Hotelling Principle?

Study Plan 17.4

People supply resources to earn an income. But some people earn enormous incomes. Are such incomes necessary to induce people to work and supply other resources? Let's now answer this question.

Income, Economic Rent, and Opportunity Cost

YOU'VE NOW SEEN HOW FACTOR PRICES ARE determined by the interaction of demand and supply. And you've seen that demand is determined by marginal productivity and supply is determined by the resources available and by people's choices about their use. The interaction of demand and supply in factor markets determines who receives a large income and who receives a small income.

Large and Small Incomes

A major-league baseball player earns $12 million a year because he has a high marginal revenue product—reflected in the demand for his services—and the supply of people with the combination of talents needed for this kind of job is small—reflected in the supply. Equilibrium occurs at a high wage rate and a small quantity employed.

People who work at fast-food restaurants earn a low wage rate because they have a low marginal revenue product—reflected in the demand for their services—and many people are able and willing to supply their labour for these jobs. Equilibrium occurs at a low wage rate and a large quantity employed.

If the demand for baseball players increases, their incomes increase by a large amount and the number of baseball players barely changes. If the demand for fast-food workers increases, the number of people doing these jobs increases by a large amount and the wage rate barely changes.

Another difference between a major-league baseball player and a fast-food worker is that if the baseball player were hit with a pay cut, he would probably still supply his services, but if a fast-food worker were hit with a pay cut, he would probably quit. This difference arises from the distinction between economic rent and opportunity cost.

Economic Rent and Opportunity Cost

The total income of a factor of production is made up of its economic rent and its opportunity cost. **Economic rent** is the income received by the owner of a factor of production over and above the amount required to induce that owner to offer the factor for use. Any factor of production can receive an economic rent. The income required to induce the supply of a factor of production is the opportunity cost of using the factor—the value of the factor in its next best use.

Figure 17.11(a) illustrates the way in which a factor income has an economic rent and opportunity cost component. The figure shows the market for a factor of production. It could be *any* factor of production—labour, capital, or land—but we'll suppose that it is labour. The demand curve is D, and the supply curve is S. The wage rate is W, and the quantity employed is C. The income earned is the sum of the yellow and green areas. The yellow area below the supply curve measures opportunity cost, and the green area above the supply curve but below the factor price measures economic rent.

To see why the area below the supply curve measures opportunity cost, recall that a supply curve can be interpreted in two different ways. It shows the quantity supplied at a given price, and it shows the minimum price at which a given quantity is willingly supplied. If suppliers receive only the minimum amount required to induce them to supply each unit of the factor, they will be paid a different price for each unit. The prices will trace the supply curve, and the income received will be entirely opportunity cost—the yellow area in Fig. 17.11(a).

The concept of economic rent is similar to the concept of producer surplus that you met in Chapter 5. Economic rent is the price a person receives for the use of a factor minus the minimum price at which a given quantity of the factor is willingly supplied. Economic rent is *not* the same thing as the "rent" that a farmer pays for the use of some land or the "rent" that you pay for your apartment. Everyday "rent" is a price paid for the services of land or a building. *Economic rent* is a component of the income received by any factor of production.

The portion of the factor income that consists of economic rent depends on the elasticity of the supply of the factor. When the supply of a factor is perfectly inelastic, its entire income is economic rent. Most of the income received by Garth Brooks and Pearl Jam is economic rent. Also, a large part of the income of a major-league baseball player is economic rent. When the supply of a factor of production is perfectly elastic, none of its income is economic rent. Most of the income of a babysitter is opportunity cost. In general, when supply is neither perfectly elastic nor perfectly

FIGURE 17.11

Economic Rent and Opportunity Cost

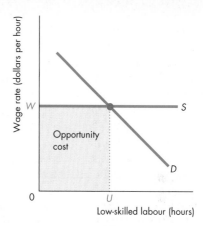

(a) General case

(b) All economic rent

(c) All opportunity cost

When the supply curve of a factor slopes upward—the general case—as in part (a), part of the factor income is economic rent (the green area) and part is opportunity cost (the yellow area). When the supply of a factor is perfectly

inelastic (the supply curve is vertical), as in part (b), the entire factor income is economic rent. When the supply of the factor is perfectly elastic, as in part (c), the factor's entire income is opportunity cost.

inelastic, like that illustrated in Fig. 17.11(a), some part of the factor income is economic rent and the other part is opportunity cost.

Figures 17.11(b) and 17.11(c) show the other two possibilities. Part (b) shows the market for a particular parcel of land in Vancouver. The quantity of land is fixed in size at L square metres. So the supply curve of the land is vertical—perfectly inelastic. No matter what the rent on the land is, there is no way of increasing the quantity that can be supplied. Suppose that the demand curve in Fig. 17.11(b) shows the marginal revenue product of this block of land. Then it commands a rent of R. The entire income accruing to the owner of the land is the green area in the figure. This income is *economic rent*.

Figure 17.11(c) shows the market for a factor of production that is in perfectly elastic supply. An example of such a market might be that for low-skilled labour in a poor country such as India or China. In those countries, large amounts of labour flock to the cities and are available for work at the going wage rate (in this case, W). In these situations, the supply of labour is almost perfectly elastic. The entire income earned by these workers is opportunity cost. They receive no economic rent.

1 Why does a major-league baseball player earn a larger income than a babysitter?

2 What is the distinction between an economic rent and an opportunity cost?

3 Is the income that the Toronto Blue Jays pay to Roy Halliday an economic rent or compensation for his opportunity cost?

4 Is a Big Mac more expensive in Toronto than in Sudbury because land rents are higher in Toronto, or are land rents higher in Toronto because people in Toronto are willing to pay more for a Big Mac?

myeconlab **Study Plan 17.5**

◆ *Reading Between the Lines* on pp. 408–409 looks at the market for crude oil and the impact of hurricanes on that market.

The next chapter looks at how the market economy distributes income and explains the trends in the distribution of income. The chapter also looks at the efforts by governments to redistribute income and modify the market outcome.

A Resource Market in Action

GLOBEANDMAIL.COM, SEPTEMBER 21, 2005

Rita fuels oil's rise

Oil prices climbed Wednesday as Hurricane Rita gathered force and approached the Gulf of Mexico, threatening to disrupt production in an area still reeling from the damage inflicted by Katrina.

In the U.S., the National Hurricane Centre said Rita has become a Category 4 storm, and could strengthen further in the coming hours. In a new release, it called Rita an "extremely dangerous hurricane" and warned that it could reach Category 5, the top of the hurricane scale. ...

The news inflamed fears that the storm could damage coastal Texas and Louisiana by week's end. A slew of energy companies, including Exxon Mobil Corp., Chevron Corp. and ConocoPhillips, have evacuated workers from platforms in the Gulf.

In its weekly update, the Energy Department said crude stockpiles fell by 322,000 barrels to 308.1 million in the week ended Sept. 16. Analysts were expecting a rise of 1 million barrels.

Gasoline inventories, however, rose by 3.5 million barrels to 195 million while distillate fuel, a category that includes heating oil and diesel, rose 820,000 barrels to 134 million.

Crude oil for November delivery rose 60 cents to $66.80 a barrel on the New York Mercantile Exchange Wednesday. ...

The U.S. Minerals Management Service said Tuesday that 136 platforms — mostly in the New Orleans area — remain unstaffed from both Katrina and Rita. That is 53 more than Monday.

The industry has lost production of more than 26 million barrels of oil since Aug. 26, when companies first evacuated for Katrina — about 4.7 per cent of the Gulf's yearly oil output, the agency said. ...

Reprinted with permission from *The Globe and Mail.*

Essence of the Story

■ Hurricane Katrina in the U.S oil producing Gulf region cut oil production by 26 million barrels between August 26 and September 21—a cut of 4.7 percent of the region's annual output.

■ On September 21, a second major hurricane, Rita, was expected to bring even more damage, and cut production even more.

■ Energy stockplies fell by 322,000 barrels to 308.1 million barrels in just one week.

■ As Rita continued to build, the price of crude oil rose 60 cents to $66.80 a barrel.

Economic Analysis

- August and September 2005 were months of unusual hurricane activity in the Atlantic Ocean.

- Hurricane Katrina (August 24 to 29) wiped out New Orleans and decreased U.S. crude oil production by almost 1 million barrels per day.

- Hurricane Rita (September 18 to 23) devastated the Texas coast and took yet more oil production off line.

- The world oil price reacted to these events in a way that is consistent with the theory of resource price determination that you've studied in this chapter.

- Figure 1 shows the daily price of crude oil from August 1 through September 21.

- Before Katrina, the price was $65 a barrel. At its peak after Katrina, the price had risen to $68 a barrel.

- Figure 2 shows why this price rise occurred.

- The decrease in production in the U.S. gulf region of 0.9 million barrels a day meant that the oil market must allocate a smaller total output among competing uses.

- The demand for oil, D, is inelastic. In the figure, the elasticity of demand is 0.24.

- The price at which the new smaller quantity is demanded is $68 a barrel.

- Anticipating this equilibrium price, rational traders stand ready to buy into inventory or sell from inventory, so the market supply curve is perfectly elastic at this price. The supply curve shifts from S_0 before Katrina to S_1 after Katrina.

- Even before Rita hit, the price increased in anticipation of a further decrease in the capacity to produce crude oil.

- Figure 3 puts the events of the summer of 2005 in a longer perspective.

- The real price of crude oil in 2005 was high by historical standards. But it was not at a record high.

- That occurred in 1979, when the Organization of Petroleum Exporting Countries, OPEC, cut production by a staggering 8 million barrels a day—approaching 10 times the cut that resulted from the 2005 hurricanes.

- The words you're reading were written on September 22, 2005. At that date, it seemed unlikely that the price of oil would remain above $60 a barrel into 2006. But you now know whether this prediction was correct.

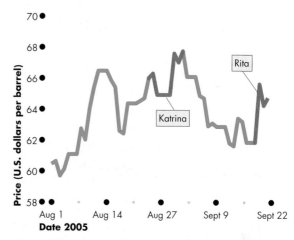

Figure 1 The price of oil in August and September 2005

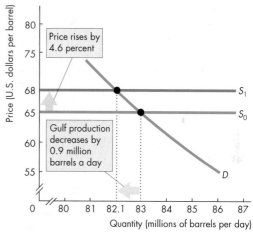

Figure 2 The world market for crude oil after Katrina

Figure 3 A hundred years of the real price of oil

Sources of data: See page C–1.

SUMMARY

KEY POINTS

Factor Prices and Incomes (p. 388)

- An increase in the demand for a factor of production increases the factor's price and total income; a decrease in the demand for a factor of production decreases its price and total income.
- An increase in the supply of a factor of production increases the quantity used but decreases its price and might increase or decrease its total income depending on whether demand is elastic or inelastic.

Labour Markets (pp. 389–396)

- The demand for labour is determined by the marginal revenue product of labour.
- The demand for labour increases if the price of the firm's output rises or if an advance in production technology increases marginal product.
- The elasticity of demand for labour depends on the labour intensity of production, the elasticity of demand for the product, and the ease with which labour can be substituted for capital.
- The quantity of labour supplied increases as the real wage rate increases, but at high wage rates, the supply curve eventually bends backward.
- The supply of labour increases as the adult population increases and with technological change in home production.
- Wage rates increase because demand for labour increases by more than the supply for labour.

Capital Markets (pp. 397–403)

- To make an investment decision, a firm compares the *present value* of the marginal revenue product of capital with the price of capital.
- The higher the interest rate, the greater is the amount of saving and the quantity of capital supplied.
- Capital market equilibrium determines the real interest rate.
- Common and related factors influence both demand and supply so the interest rate fluctuates but doesn't rise or fall over time.

Natural Resource Markets (pp. 403–405)

- The demand for natural resources is determined by marginal revenue product.
- The supply of land is inelastic.
- The supply of nonrenewable natural resources is perfectly elastic at a price equal to the present value of the expected future price.
- The price of nonrenewable natural resources is expected to rise at a rate equal to the interest rate but fluctuates and sometimes falls.

Income, Economic Rent, and Opportunity Cost (pp. 406–407)

- Economic rent is the income received by the owner of a factor of production over and above the amount needed to induce the owner to supply the factor for use.
- The rest of a factor's income is an opportunity cost.
- When the supply of a factor is perfectly inelastic, its entire income is made up of economic rent, and when supply is perfectly elastic, the entire income is made up of opportunity cost.

KEY FIGURES AND TABLES

KEY TERMS

PROBLEMS

Go to **myeconlab** for solutions to odd-numbered problems and additional exercises.

1. The figure illustrates the market for blueberry pickers.

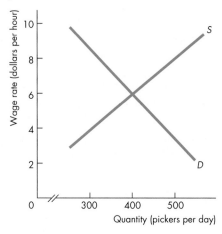

What is the wage rate paid to blueberry pickers, how many blueberry pickers get hired, and what is the total income received by pickers?

2. In problem 1, if the demand for blueberry pickers decreases by 100 a day, what is the new wage rate paid to the pickers, how many pickers get laid off, and what is the total income paid to pickers?

3. In Wanda's fish shop, students can pack the following amounts of fish in an hour:

Number of students	Quantity of fish (kilograms)
1	20
2	50
3	90
4	120
5	145
6	165
7	180
8	190

Wanda can sell her fish for 50¢ a kilogram, and the wage rate of packers is $7.50 an hour.

a. Calculate the marginal product of the students and draw the marginal product curve.

b. Calculate the marginal revenue product and draw the marginal revenue product curve.

c. Find Wanda's demand for labour curve.

d. How many students does Wanda employ?

4. In Larry's gourmet ice cream factory, workers can produce the following quantities in a day:

Number of workers	Quantity of ice cream (batches)
1	4
2	10
3	18
4	24
5	29
6	33
7	36
8	38

Larry can sell ice cream for $25 a batch, and the wage rate of his workers is $100 a day.

a. Calculate the marginal product of the workers and draw the marginal product curve.

b. Calculate the marginal revenue product of the workers and draw the marginal revenue product curve.

c. Find Larry's demand for labour curve.

d. How much ice cream does Larry sell?

5. Back at Wanda's fish shop described in problem 3, the price of fish falls to 33.33¢ a kilogram but fish packers' wages remain at $7.50 an hour.

a. What happens to the students' marginal product?

b. What happens to Wanda's marginal revenue product?

c. What happens to her demand for labour curve?

d. What happens to the number of students that she employs?

6. Back at Larry's ice cream making plant described in problem 4, the price of ice cream falls to $20 a batch but the wage rate remains at $100 a day.

a. What happens to the workers' marginal product?

b. What happens to Larry's marginal revenue product?

c. What happens to his demand for labour curve?

d. What happens to the number of workers that he employs?

7. Back at Wanda's fish shop described in problem 3, packers' wages increase to $10 an hour but the price of fish remains at 50¢ a kilogram.
   a. What happens to marginal revenue product?
   b. What happens to Wanda's demand for labour curve?
   c. How many students does Wanda employ?

8. Back at Larry's ice cream factory described in problem 4, the wage rate rises to $125 a day but the price of ice cream remains at $25 a batch.
   a. What happens to marginal revenue product?
   b. What happens to Larry's demand for labour curve?
   c. How many workers does Larry employ?

9. Using the information provided in problem 3, calculate Wanda's marginal revenue, marginal cost, and marginal revenue product. Show that when Wanda is making maximum profit, marginal cost equals marginal revenue and marginal revenue product equals the wage rate.

10. Using the information provided in problem 4, calculate Larry's marginal revenue, marginal cost, and marginal revenue product. Show that when Larry is making maximum profit, marginal cost equals marginal revenue and marginal revenue product equals the wage rate.

11. Greg has found an oil well in his backyard. A geologist estimates that a total of 10 million barrels can be pumped for a pumping cost of $2 a barrel. The price of oil is $40 a barrel. How much oil does Greg sell each year? If you can't predict how much he will sell, what extra information would you need to be able to do so?

12. Orley has a wine cellar in which he keeps choice wines from around the world. What does Orley expect to happen to the prices of the wines he keeps in his cellar? Explain your answer. How does Orley decide which wine to drink and when to drink it?

13. Draw a graph to illustrate the situation in problem 1. Show on the graph the blueberry pickers':
   a. Economic rent.
   b. Opportunity cost.

14. Draw a graph to illustrate the situation in problem 2. Show on the graph the blueberry pickers':
   a. Economic rent.
   b. Opportunity cost.

CRITICAL THINKING

1. Study *Reading Between the Lines* on pp. 408–409 and answer the following questions:
   a. What determines the price of a natural resource such as crude oil?
   b. How did hurricane Katrina affect the price of oil in August and September 2005?
   c. What was the elasticity of demand implied by the price and quantity changes that occurred in the crude oil market following hurricane Katrina?
   d. How has the price of oil moved over the past 100 years? Do the movements confirm or contradict the Hotelling Principle?
   e. Do you expect the price of oil to keep rising? Explain why or why not.

2. "We are running out of natural resources and must take urgent action to conserve our precious reserves." "There is no shortage of resources that the market cannot cope with." Debate these two views. List the pros and cons for each.

3. Why do we keep finding new reserves of oil? Why don't we do a once-and-for-all big survey that catalogues the earth's entire inventory of natural resources?

WEB EXERCISES

Use the links on myeconlab to work the following exercise.

1. Read the article on prize money in the tennis grand slams.
   a. Do women get the same pay as men in professional tennis?
   b. Why might men earn more than women in tennis?
   c. What is the case for equal pay for men and women tennis players?
   d. Can you think of other sports in which there is either equality or a big disparity between the earnings of men and women? How would you explain the rewards in this sport?

APPENDIX

Labour Unions

After studying this appendix you will be able to

- Explain why union workers earn more than nonunion workers
- Explain how a labour market works in a monopsony
- Explain the effects of a minimum wage law in a monopsony

Market Power in the Labour Market

JUST AS A MONOPOLY PRODUCER CAN RESTRICT output and raise price, so a monopoly resource owner can restrict supply and raise the price of the resource.

Labour unions are the main source of market power in the labour market. A **labour union** is an organized group of workers that aims to increase wages and influence other job conditions.

Traditionally, a union was formed by a group of workers who had similar skills but who worked for firms in different industries and regions—for example, the union of electrical workers. The industrial union was created when workers in mass-production industries unionized. These workers had a variety of skills but they worked in the same industry. Today, most unions have members who work in different industries and have a wide range of skills. For example, the members of the United Steelworkers union work in steel mills, factories, bakeries, and offices.

Most unions are members of the Canadian Labour Congress, which was created in 1956 with the merger of the Labour Council of Canada (founded in 1883) and the Canadian Congress of Labour (founded in 1940).

Around one-third of workers are members of a union. Some of these unions are small, but industrial unions are large. Union organization is based on a subdivision known as the *local*. The local can be organized as a closed shop, a union shop, or an open shop. A *closed shop* is an arrangement in which the firm can hire only union members. Most closed shops are in the construction industry. A *union shop* is an arrangement in which the firm can hire workers who are not union members, but new workers must join the union, usually at the end of their probationary period. Union shops are common in manufacturing industries and the public sector. An *open shop* is an arrangement in which no employee is required to join the union or pay union dues. There is no restriction on who can work in the "shop." A compromise between the union shop and the open shop is the **Rand Formula**: a requirement that all workers represented by a union must pay union dues, whether they join the union or not.

Unions negotiate with employers or their representatives in a process called *collective bargaining*. The main weapons available to the union and the employer in collective bargaining are the strike and the lockout. A *strike* is a group decision by the workers to refuse to work under prevailing conditions. A *lockout* is a firm's refusal to operate its plant and employ its workers. Each party uses the threat of a strike or a lockout to try to get an agreement in its own favour. Sometimes, when the two parties in the collective bargaining process cannot agree on the wage rate or other conditions of employment, they agree to submit their disagreement to binding arbitration. *Binding arbitration* is a process in which a third party—an arbitrator—determines wages and other employment conditions on behalf of the negotiating parties.

Although they are not labour unions in a legal sense, professional associations act in ways similar to labour unions. A *professional association* is an organized group of professional workers such as lawyers or physicians (for example, the Ontario Medical Association). Professional associations control entry into the professions and license practitioners, ensuring the adherence to minimum standards of competence. But they also influence the compensation and other labour market conditions of their members.

Union Objectives and Constraints

A union has three broad objectives that it strives to achieve for its members:

1. To increase compensation
2. To improve working conditions
3. To expand job opportunities

Each of these objectives contains a series of more detailed goals. For example, in seeking to increase members' compensation, a union operates on a variety of fronts: wage rates, fringe benefits, retirement pay, and such things as vacation allowances. In seeking to improve working conditions, a union is concerned with occupational health and safety as well as the environmental quality of the workplace. In seeking to expand job opportunities, a union tries to get greater job security for existing union members and to find ways of creating additional jobs for them.

A union's ability to pursue its objectives is restricted by two sets of constraints—one on the supply side of the labour market and the other on the demand side. On the supply side, the union's activities are limited by how well it can restrict nonunion workers from offering their labour in the same market as union labour. The larger the fraction of the work force controlled by the union, the more effective the union can be in this regard. It is difficult for unions to operate in markets where there is an abundant supply of willing nonunion labour. For example, the market for part-time checkout clerks is very tough for a union to organize because of the enormous rate of turnover of participants in that market. At the other extreme, unions in the construction industry can better pursue their goals because they can influence the number of people who can obtain skills as electricians, plasterers, and carpenters. The professional associations of dentists and physicians are best able to restrict the supply of dentists and physicians. These groups control the number of qualified workers by controlling either the examinations that new entrants must pass or entrance into professional degree programs.

On the demand side of the labour market, the union faces a tradeoff that arises from firms' profit-maximizing decisions. Because labour demand curves slope downward, anything a union does that increases the wage rate or other employment costs decreases the quantity of labour demanded.

Let's see how unions operate in competitive labour markets.

A Union in a Competitive Labour Market

When a union operates in an otherwise competitive labour market, it seeks to increase wages and other compensation and to limit employment reductions by increasing demand for the labour of its members.

That is, the union tries to take actions that shift the demand curve for its members' labour rightward.

Figure A17.1 illustrates a competitive labour market that a union enters. The demand curve is D_C, and the supply curve is S_C. Before the union enters the market, the wage rate is $7 an hour and 100 hours of labour are employed.

Now suppose that a union is formed to organize the workers in this market. The union can attempt to increase wages in this market in two ways. It can try to restrict the supply of labour, or it can try to stimulate the demand for labour. First, look at what happens if the union has sufficient control over the supply of labour to be able to restrict that supply artificially below its competitive level—to S_U. If that is all the union is able to do, employment falls to 85 hours of labour and the wage rate rises to $8 an hour. The

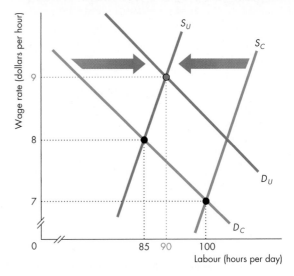

FIGURE A17.1   myeconlab
Union in a Competitive Labour Market

In a competitive labour market, the demand curve is D_C and the supply curve is S_C. Competitive equilibrium occurs at a wage rate of $7 an hour with 100 hours employed. By restricting employment below the competitive level, the union shifts the supply of labour to S_U. If the union can do no more than that, the wage rate will increase to $8 an hour but employment will fall to 85 hours. If the union can increase the demand for labour and shift the demand curve to D_U, then it can increase the wage rate still higher, to $9 an hour, and achieve employment of 90 hours.

union simply picks its preferred position along the demand curve that defines the tradeoff it faces between employment and the wage rate.

You can see that if the union can only restrict the supply of labour, it raises the wage rate but decreases the number of jobs available. Because of this outcome, unions try to increase the demand for labour and shift the demand curve rightward. Let's see what they might do to achieve this outcome.

How Unions Try to Change the Demand for Labour

Unless a union can take actions that change the demand for the labour that it represents, it has to accept the fact that a higher wage rate can be obtained only at the price of lower employment.

The union tries to operate on the demand for labour in two ways. First, it tries to make the demand for union labour inelastic. Second, it tries to increase the demand for union labour. Making the demand for labour less elastic does not eliminate the tradeoff between employment and the wage rate. But it does make the tradeoff less unfavourable. If a union can make the demand for labour less elastic, it can increase the wage rate at a lower cost in terms of lost employment opportunities. But if the union can increase the demand for labour, it might even be able to increase both the wage rate and the employment opportunities of its members. Some of the methods used by the unions to change the demand for the labour of its members are to

- Increase the marginal product of union members
- Encourage import restrictions
- Support minimum wage laws
- Support immigration restrictions
- Increase demand for the good produced

Unions try to increase the marginal product of their members, which in turn increases the demand for their labour, by organizing and sponsoring training schemes, by encouraging apprenticeship and other on-the-job training activities, and by professional certification.

One of the best examples of import restrictions is the support by the Canadian Auto Workers union (CAW) for import restrictions on foreign cars.

Unions support minimum wage laws to increase the cost of employing low-skilled labour. An increase in the wage rate of low-skilled labour leads to a decrease in the quantity demanded of low-skilled labour and to an increase in demand for high-skilled union labour, a substitute for low-skilled labour.

Restrictive immigration laws decrease the supply of low-skilled workers and increase their wage rate. As a result, the demand for high-skilled union labour increases.

Because the demand for labour is a derived demand, an increase in the demand for the good produced by union labour increases the demand for union labour. The garment workers' union urging us to buy union-made clothes and the CAW asking us to buy only North American cars made by union workers are examples of attempts by unions to increase the demand for union labour.

Figure A17.1 illustrates the effects of an increase in the demand for the labour of a union's members. If the union can increase the demand for labour to D_U, it can achieve an even bigger increase in the wage rate with a smaller fall in employment. By maintaining the restricted labour supply at S_U, the union increases the wage rate to $9 an hour and achieves an employment level of 90 hours of labour.

Because a union restricts the supply of labour in the market in which it operates, its actions increase the supply of labour in nonunion markets. Workers who can't get union jobs must look elsewhere for work. This increase in the supply of labour in nonunion markets lowers the wage rate in those markets and further widens the union–nonunion differential.

The Scale of Union–Nonunion Wage Differentials

We have seen that unions can influence the wage rate by restricting the supply of labour and increasing the demand for labour. How much of a difference to wage rates do unions make in practice?

Union wage rates are, on the average, 30 percent higher than nonunion wage rates. In mining and financial services, union and nonunion wages are similar. In services, manufacturing, and transportation, the differential is between 11 and 19 percent. In wholesale and retail trades, the differential is 28 percent, and in construction, it is 65 percent.

But these union–nonunion wage differentials don't give a true measure of the effects of unions. In some industries, union wages are higher than nonunion wages because union members do jobs that involve greater skill. Even without a union, those workers would receive a higher wage. To calculate the effects of unions, we have to examine the wages of unionized and nonunionized workers who do nearly identical work. The evidence suggests that after allowing for skill differentials, the union–nonunion wage differential lies between 10 percent and 25 percent. For example, airline pilots who belong to the Air Line Pilots' Association earn about 25 percent more than nonunion pilots with the same skill.

Let's now look at monopsony.

Monopsony

A MARKET IN WHICH THERE IS A SINGLE BUYER IS called **monopsony**. This market type is unusual, but it does exist. With the growth of large-scale production over the last century, large manufacturing plants such as coal mines, steel and textile mills, and car manufacturers became the major employer in some regions, and in some places a single firm employed almost all the labour. Today, the provincial health insurance plans are the major employers of health-care professionals. These employers have market power. In monopsony, the employer determines the wage rate and pays the lowest wage at which it can attract the labour it plans to hire. A monopsony makes a bigger profit than a group of firms that compete with each other for their labour. Let's find out how a monopsony achieves this outcome.

Like all firms, a monopsony has a downward-sloping marginal revenue product curve, which is *MRP* in Fig. A17.2. This curve tells us the extra revenue the monopsony receives by selling the output produced by an extra hour of labour. The labour supply curve is *S*. This curve tells us how many hours are supplied at each wage rate. It also tells us the minimum wage for which a given quantity of labour is willing to work.

A monopsony recognizes that to hire more labour, it must pay a higher wage; equivalently, by hiring less labour, it can pay a lower wage. Because a monopsony controls the wage rate, the marginal cost of labour exceeds the wage rate. The marginal cost of labour is shown by the curve *MCL*. The relationship between the marginal cost of labour curve and the supply curve is similar to the relationship between the marginal cost and average cost curves that you studied in Chapter 10. The supply curve is like the average cost of labour curve. In Fig. A17.2, the firm can hire 49 hours of labour for a wage rate of just below $4.90 an hour.

The firm's total labour cost is $240. But suppose that the firm hires 50 hours of labour. It can hire the 50th hour of labour for $5 an hour. The total cost of labour is now $250 an hour. So hiring the 50th hour of labour increases the total cost of labour from $240 to $250, which is a $10 increase. The marginal cost of labour is $10 an hour. The curve *MCL* shows the $10 marginal cost of hiring the 50th hour of labour.

To calculate the profit-maximizing quantity of labour to hire, the firm sets the marginal cost of labour equal to the marginal revenue product of labour. That is, the firm wants the cost of the last worker hired to equal the extra total revenue brought in. In Fig. A17.2, this outcome occurs when the monopsony employs 50 hours of labour. What is the wage rate that the monopsony pays? To hire 50 hours of labour, the firm must pay $5 an hour, as shown by the supply of labour curve. So each worker is paid $5 an hour. But the marginal revenue product of labour is $10 an hour, which means that the firm makes an economic profit of $5 on the last hour of labour that it hires. Compare this outcome with that in a competitive labour market. If

FIGURE A17.2
A Monopsony Labour Market

A monopsony is a market structure in which there is a single buyer. A monopsony in the labour market has the marginal revenue product curve *MRP* and faces a labour supply curve *S*. The marginal cost of labour curve is *MCL*. Making the marginal cost of labour equal to marginal revenue product maximizes profit. The monopsony hires 50 hours of labour and pays the lowest wage for which that labour will work, which is $5 an hour.

the labour market shown in Fig. A17.2 were competitive, equilibrium would occur at the point of intersection of the demand curve and the supply curve. The wage rate would be $7.50 an hour, and 75 hours of labour a day would be employed. So compared with a competitive labour market, a monopsony decreases both the wage rate and employment.

The ability of a monopsony to cut the wage rate and employment to increase its profit depends on the elasticity of labour supply. If the supply of labour is highly elastic, a monopsony has little power to cut the wage rate and employment to boost its profit.

Monopsony Tendencies

Today, monopsony is rare. Workers can commute long distances to a job, so most people have more than one potential employer. But firms that are dominant employers in isolated communities do face an upward-sloping supply of labour curve and so have a marginal cost of labour that exceeds the wage rate. But in such situations, there is also, usually, a union. Let's see how unions and monopsonies interact.

Monopsony and a Union

In Chapter 12, we discovered that in monopoly, a firm can determine the market price. We've now seen that in monopsony—a market with a single buyer—the buyer can determine the price. Suppose that a union operates in a monopsony labour market. A union is like a monopoly. If the union (monopoly seller) faces a monopsony buyer, the situation is called **bilateral monopoly**. In bilateral monopoly, the wage rate is determined by bargaining.

In Fig. A17.2, if the monopsony is free to determine the wage rate and the level of employment, it hires 50 hours of labour for a wage rate of $5 an hour. But suppose that a union represents the workers. The union agrees to maintain employment at 50 hours but seeks the highest wage rate that the employer can be forced to pay. That wage rate is $10 an hour—the wage rate that equals the marginal revenue product of labour. The union might not be able to get the wage rate up to $10 an hour. But it won't accept $5 an hour. The monopsony firm and the union bargain over the wage rate, and the result is an outcome between $10 an hour and $5 an hour.

The outcome of the bargaining depends on the costs that each party can inflict on the other as a result of a failure to agree on the wage rate. The firm can shut down the plant and lock out its workers, and the

workers can shut down the plant by striking. Each party knows the other's strength and knows what it will lose if it does not agree to the other's demands. If the two parties are equally strong and they realize it, they will split the gap between $5 and $10 and agree to a wage rate of $7.50 an hour. If one party is stronger than the other—and both parties know that—the agreed wage will favour the stronger party. Usually, an agreement is reached without a strike or a lockout. The threat is usually enough to bring the bargaining parties to an agreement. When a strike or lockout does occur, it is usually because one party has misjudged the costs each party can inflict on the other.

Minimum wage laws have interesting effects in monopsony labour markets. Let's study these effects.

Monopsony and the Minimum Wage

In a competitive labour market, a minimum wage that exceeds the equilibrium wage decreases employment (see Chapter 6, p. 130). In a monopsony labour market, a minimum wage can *increase* both the wage rate and employment. Let's see how.

Figure A17.3 shows a monopsony labour market in which the wage rate is $5 an hour and 50 hours of labour are employed. A minimum wage law is passed that requires employers to pay at least $7.50 an hour.

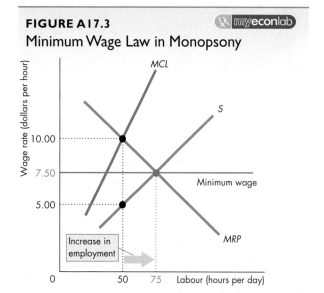

FIGURE A17.3 myeconlab

Minimum Wage Law in Monopsony

In a monopsony labour market, the wage rate is $5 an hour and 50 hours are hired. If a minimum wage law increases the wage rate to $7.50 an hour, employment increases to 75 hours.

The monopsony in Fig. A17.3 now faces a perfectly elastic supply of labour at $7.50 an hour up to 75 hours. Above 75 hours, a wage above $7.50 an hour must be paid to hire additional hours of labour. Because the wage rate is a fixed $7.50 an hour up to 75 hours, the marginal cost of labour is also constant at $7.50 up to 75 hours. Beyond 75 hours, the marginal cost of labour rises above $7.50 an hour. To maximize profit, the monopsony sets the marginal cost of labour equal to the marginal revenue product of labour. That is, the monopsony hires 75 hours of labour at $7.50 an hour. The minimum wage law has made the supply of labour perfectly elastic and made the marginal cost of labour the same as the wage rate up to 75 hours. The law has not affected the supply of labour curve or the marginal cost of labour at employment levels above 75 hours. The minimum wage law has succeeded in raising the wage rate by $2.50 an hour and increasing the amount of labour employed by 25 hours.

SUMMARY

KEY POINTS

Market Power in the Labour Market
(pp. 413–416)

■ In a competitive labour market, a union obtains a higher wage rate only at the expense of lower employment but it tries to influence the demand for labour.

■ Union workers earn 10 to 25 percent more than comparable nonunion workers.

Monopsony (pp. 416–418)

■ A monopsony employs less labour and pays a wage rate below that in a competitive labour market.

■ In bilateral monopoly, the wage rate is determined by bargaining.

■ In monopsony, a minimum wage law can raise the wage rate and increase employment.

KEY TERMS

Bilateral monopoly, 417
Labour union, 413
Monopsony, 416
Rand Formula, 413

PROBLEMS

Go to   myeconlab   for solutions to odd-numbered problems and additional exercises.

1. A monopsony gold-mining firm operates in an isolated part of the Amazon basin. The table shows the firm's labour supply schedule (columns 1 and 2) and total product schedule (columns 2 and 3). The price of gold is $1.40 a grain.

Wage rate (dollars per day)	Number of workers	Quantity produced (grains per day)
5	0	0
6	1	10
7	2	25
8	3	45
9	4	60
10	5	70
11	6	75

a. What wage rate does the company pay?
b. How many workers does the gold mine hire?
c. What is the value of marginal product at the quantity of labour employed?

2. A monopsony logging firm operates in an isolated part of the Yukon. The table shows the firm's labour supply schedule (columns 1 and 2) and total product schedule (columns 2 and 3). The price of logs is $2 a tonne.

Wage rate (dollars per day)	Number of workers	Quantity produced (tonnes per day)
5	0	0
6	1	9
7	2	17
8	3	24
9	4	30
10	5	35
11	6	39
12	7	42

a. What wage rate does the company pay?
b. How many workers does the company hire?
c. What is the value of marginal product at the quantity of labour employed?

Economic Inequality

CHAPTER 18

Rags and Riches

Ken Thomson's family fortune, Canada's largest, is estimated at more than $22 billion. The poorest of Canada's richest 100 families is worth a mere $336 million.

In stark contrast to these richest Canadians are the poorest, who can be seen any evening on the park benches of our major cities and in the hostels of the Salvation Army. Here are men and women who have no visible wealth other than their clothes and a few meagre possessions.

Most Canadians are not as poor as those who seek help from the Salvation Army, but there is a large amount of relative poverty in our nation. One in ten families has an income that is so low that it spends close to half of it on rent.

Why are some people exceedingly rich, while others are very poor?

In this chapter, we study economic inequality—its extent, its sources, and the things governments do to make it less extreme. We begin by looking at some facts about economic inequality in Canada today. We end, in *Reading Between the Lines*, by looking at the changing gap between the rich and the poor and the changing scale of redistribution in Canada.

After studying this chapter, you will be able to

- Describe the inequality in income and wealth and the trends in inequality in Canada

- Explain the features of the labour market that contribute to economic inequality

- Describe the methods and scale of government income redistribution

419

Measuring Economic Inequality

STATISTICS CANADA PROVIDES MEASURES OF economic inequality based on three definitions of income: market income, total income, and after-tax income. **Market income** equals the wages, interest, rent, and profit earned in factor markets before paying income taxes. **Total income** equals *market income* plus cash payments to households by governments. **After-tax income** equals *total income* minus tax payments by households to governments.

The Distribution of After-Tax Income

Figure 18.1 shows the distribution of annual after-tax income across all households in Canada in 2003. Note that the *x*-axis measures income and the *y*-axis measures the percentage of households.

The most common household income, called the *mode* income, was received by the 8.2 percent of the households whose income fell between $15,000 and $19,999.

The income that separated the households into two equal groups, called the *median* income, was $39,700. One-half of Canadian households had an income greater than this amount, and the other half had an income less than this amount. The average household income in 2003, called the *mean* income, was $48,400.

You can see in Fig. 18.1 that the mode income is less than the median income, and the median income is less than the mean income. This feature of the distribution of income tells us that there are more households with low incomes than with high incomes. And some of the high incomes are very high.

The income distribution in Fig. 18.1 is called a *positively skewed* distribution, which means that it has a long tail of high values. This distribution's shape contrasts with a *bell-shaped* distribution like that of people's heights. In a bell-shaped distribution, the mean, median, and mode are all equal.

Another way of looking at the distribution of income is to measure the percentage of after-tax income received by each given percentage of households. Data are reported for five groups—called quintiles or one-fifth shares—each consisting of 20 percent of households.

FIGURE 18.1

The Distribution of Income in Canada in 2003

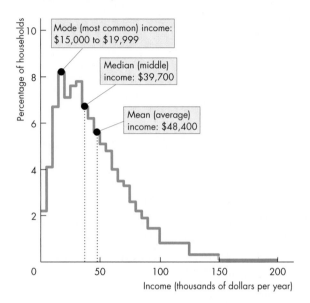

Mode (most common) income: $15,000 to $19,999

Median (middle) income: $39,700

Mean (average) income: $48,400

The distribution of income is positively skewed. The mode (most common) income is less than the median (middle) income, which in turn is less than the mean (average) income. A very small percentage of households earn incomes in the range above $150,000 up to several million dollars a year—this part of the distribution is off the scale of this figure.

Source of data: Income Statistics Division, Statistics Canada, Table 202–0601.

Figure 18.2 shows the distribution of after-tax income based on these shares in 2003. The poorest 20 percent of households received 5 percent of after-tax income; the second-poorest 20 percent received 10.8 percent of after-tax income; the middle 20 percent received 16.5 percent of after-tax income; the second-highest 20 percent received 24.1 percent of after-tax income; and the highest 20 percent received 43.6 percent of after-tax income.

The distribution of after-tax income in Fig. 18.1 and the quintile shares in Fig. 18.2 tell us that income is distributed unequally. But we need a way of comparing the distribution of income in different periods and using different measures. A neat graphical tool called the Lorenz curve enables us to make such comparisons.

FIGURE 18.2

Canadian Quintile Shares

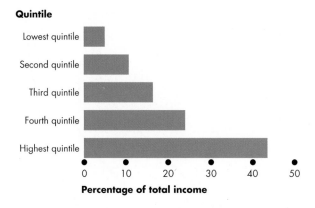

Households	Income (percentage of total income)
Lowest 20 percent	5.0
Second-lowest 20 percent	10.8
Middle 20 percent	16.5
Second-highest 20 percent	24.1
Highest 20 percent	43.6

All households are ranked from those with the lowest income to those with the highest income and then divided into 5 equal groups. Each group is called a quintile (or a one-fifth of the households). The bar chart shows that the distribution of after-tax income in Canada is unequal.

Source of data: Income Statistics Division, Statistics Canada, Table 202–0604.

FIGURE 18.3

The Income Lorenz Curve

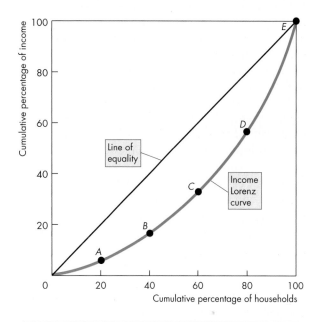

	Households		Income	
	Percentage	Cumulative percentage	Percentage	Cumulative percentage
A	Lowest 20	20	5.0	5.0
B	Second-lowest 20	40	10.8	15.8
C	Middle 20	60	16.5	32.3
D	Second-highest 20	80	24.1	56.4
E	Highest 20	100	43.6	100.0

The cumulative percentage of income is graphed against the cumulative percentage of households. Points A through E on the Lorenz curve correspond to the rows of the table. If incomes were distributed equally, each 20 percent of households would receive 20 percent of income and the Lorenz curve would fall along the line of equality. The Lorenz curve shows that income is unequally distributed.

Source of data: Income Statistics Division, Statistics Canada, Table 202–0604.

The Income Lorenz Curve

The income **Lorenz curve** graphs the cumulative percentage of income against the cumulative percentage of households. Figure 18.3 shows the income Lorenz curve using the quintile shares from Fig. 18.2. The table shows the percentage of income in each quintile group. For example, row *A* tells us that the lowest quintile of households receives 5 percent of after-tax income. The table also shows the *cumulative* percentages of households and income. For example, row *B* tells us that the lowest two quintiles (lowest 40 percent) of households receive 15.8 percent of after-tax

income (5 percent for the lowest quintile and 10.8 percent for the second-lowest). The income Lorenz curve graphs the cumulative income shares against the cumulative household percentages.

If income were distributed equally across all the households, each quintile would receive 20 percent of after-tax income and the cumulative percentages of income received by the cumulative percentages of households would fall along the straight line labelled "Line of equality" in Fig. 18.3. The actual distribution of income is shown by the curve labelled "Income Lorenz curve." The closer the Lorenz curve is to the line of equality, the more equal is the distribution.

The Distribution of Wealth

The distribution of wealth provides another way of measuring economic inequality. A household's wealth is the value of the things that it owns at a *point in time*. In contrast, income is the amount that the household receives over a given *period of time*.

Figure 18.4 shows the Lorenz curve for wealth in Canada in 1999. Median household wealth in that year was $64,000. Wealth is extremely unequally distributed, and for this reason, the data are grouped by unequal groups of households. The poorest 40 percent of households owns only 1.1 percent of total wealth (row *A'* in the table). The next poorest 10 percent owns only 2.8 percent of total wealth (row *B'*) and the next poorest 10 percent owns only 4.7 percent of total wealth (row *C'*). So the poorest 60 percent of households owns only 8.6 percent of total wealth. At the other end of the wealth distribution, the wealthiest 10 percent of households owns 55.6 percent of total wealth (row *G'*).

Figure 18.4 shows the income Lorenz curve (from Fig. 18.2) alongside the wealth Lorenz curve. You can see that the Lorenz curve for wealth is much farther away from the line of equality than the Lorenz curve for income is, which means that the distribution of wealth is much more unequal than the distribution of income.

Wealth Versus Income

We've seen that wealth is much more unequally distributed than income. Which distribution provides the better description of the degree of inequality? To answer this question, we need to think about the connection between wealth and income.

Wealth is a stock of assets, and income is the flow of earnings that results from the stock of wealth. Suppose that Kate owns assets worth $1 million—has a wealth of $1 million. If the rate of return on assets is

FIGURE 18.4

Lorenz Curves for Income and Wealth

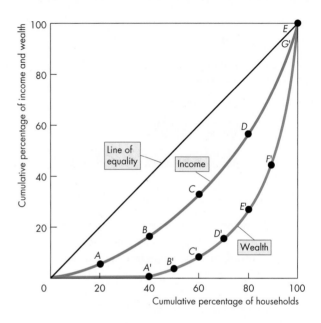

	Households		Wealth	
	Percentage	**Cumulative percentage**	**Percentage**	**Cumulative percentage**
A'	Lowest 40	40	1.1	1.1
B'	Next 10	50	2.8	3.9
C'	Next 10	60	4.7	8.6
D'	Next 10	70	7.4	16.0
E'	Next 10	80	11.0	27.0
F'	Next 10	90	17.4	44.4
G'	Next 10	100	55.6	100.0

The cumulative percentage of wealth is graphed against the cumulative percentage of households. Points *A'* through *G'* on the Lorenz curve for wealth correspond to the rows of the table. By comparing the Lorenz curves for income and wealth, we can see that wealth is distributed much more unequally than income.

Source of data: Income Statistics Division, Statistics Canada, Table 202–0604 and Catalogue 75–202–XIE.

5 percent a year, then she receives an income of $50,000 a year from those assets. We can describe Kate's economic condition by using either her wealth of $1 million or her income of $50,000 a year. When the rate of return is 5 percent a year, $1 million of wealth equals $50,000 of income in perpetuity. Wealth and income are just different ways of looking at the same thing.

But in Fig. 18.4, the distribution of wealth is more unequal than the distribution of income. Why? It is because the wealth data do not include the value of human capital, while the income data measure income from all forms of wealth, including human capital.

Table 18.1 illustrates the consequence of omitting human capital from the wealth data. Lee has twice the wealth and twice the income of Peter. But Lee's human capital is less than Peter's—$200,000 compared with $499,000. And Lee's income from human capital of $10,000 is less than Peter's income from human capital of $24,950. Lee's nonhuman capital is larger than Peter's—$800,000 compared with $1,000. And Lee's income from nonhuman capital of $40,000 is larger than Peter's income from nonhuman capital of $50.

When Lee and Peter are surveyed by Statistics Canada in a national wealth and income survey, their incomes are recorded as $50,000 and $25,000, respectively, which implies that Lee is twice as well off as Peter. And their tangible assets are recorded as $800,000 and $1,000, respectively, which implies that Lee is 800 times as wealthy as Peter.

Because the national survey of wealth excludes human capital, the income distribution is a more accurate measure of economic inequality than the wealth distribution.

Annual or Lifetime Income and Wealth?

A typical household's income changes over time. It starts out low, grows to a peak when the household's workers reach retirement age, and then falls after retirement. Also, a typical household's wealth changes over time. Like income, wealth starts out low, grows to a peak at the point of retirement, and falls after retirement.

Suppose we look at three households that have identical lifetime incomes. One household is young, one is middle-aged, and one is retired. The middle-aged household has the highest income and wealth, the retired household has the lowest, and the young household falls in the middle. The distributions of annual income and wealth in a given year are unequal, but the

TABLE 18.1   Capital, Wealth, and Income

	Lee		Peter	
	Wealth	**Income**	**Wealth**	**Income**
Human capital	$200,000	$10,000	$499,000	$24,950
Other capital	800,000	40,000	1,000	50
Total	$1,000,000	$50,000	$500,000	$25,000

When wealth is measured to include the value of human capital as well as other forms of capital, the distribution of income and the distribution of wealth display the same degree of inequality.

distributions of lifetime income and wealth are equal. So some of the inequality in annual income arises because different households are at different stages in the life cycle. But we can see *trends* in the income distribution using annual income data.

Trends in Inequality

Figure 18.5 shows how the distribution of income has changed between 1980 and 2003. The trends are

■ The share of total income received by the richest 20 percent of households has increased from 40 percent in 1980 to 43.7 percent in 2003.

■ The share of total income received by the poorest 20 percent of households has remained constant at 5 percent.

■ The shares of total income received by the other three groups have decreased, and the share of the third (the middle) 20 percent of households has decreased most from 18.3 percent in 1980 to 16.5 percent in 2003.

No one knows for sure why these trends have occurred, and a large amount of research has been done to try to explain them.

The most likely explanation is one that we'll explore and explain in the next section: Higher-income groups have gained and lower-income groups have lost because the technological change of the past few decades has increased the productivity of higher skilled workers and decreased the productivity of lower-skilled workers. Increased international mobility and competition is another possible explanation.

FIGURE 18.5

Trends in the Distribution of Income

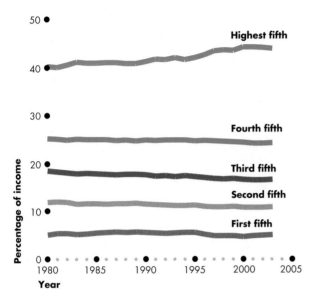

The distribution of income in Canada became more unequal in the 1980s and 1990s. The percentage of total income earned by the highest fifth increased the most, and the third (middle) fifth lost the most.

Source of data: Income Statistics Division, Statistics Canada, Table 202–0604.

Poverty

Families at the low end of the income distribution are so poor that they are considered to be living in poverty. **Poverty** is a state in which a family's income is too low to be able to buy the quantities of food, shelter, and clothing that are deemed necessary. Poverty is a relative concept. Millions of people in Africa and Asia survive on less than $400 a year.

In Canada, poverty is measured in terms of a low-income cutoff. The **low-income cutoff** is the income level, determined separately for different types of families (for example, single persons, couples, one parent), that is selected such that families with incomes below that limit normally spend 55 percent or more of their income on food, shelter, and clothing.

How much poverty (defined as incomes below the low-income cutoff) is there in Canada, and is the problem getting worse or better? Figure 18.6 answers this question.

FIGURE 18.6

The Poverty Rate

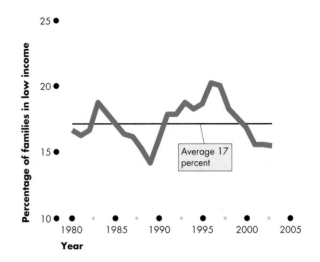

The incidence of poverty in Canada has fluctuated between 14 and 20 percent of families. On the average, 17 percent of families have incomes below the low-income cutoff.

Source of data: Income Statistics Division, Statistics Canada, Table 202–0804.

The incidence of poverty has fluctuated between a low of 14 percent in 1989 and a high of 20 percent in 1996 and 1997. But there has been no trend in poverty and on the average, 17 percent of Canadian families have incomes below the low-income cutoff.

Who Are the Poor?

The lowest incomes are earned by people who scratch out a living doing seasonal work on farms. But the poorest Canadians are people who earn nothing and rely on handouts to survive. The incidence of poverty varies systematically depending on family characteristics and six characteristics stand out:

- Source of income
- Household type
- Age of householder
- Number of children
- Education
- Labour force status

Source of Income Not surprisingly, a household that earns its income either by working or from investments is unlikely to be poor and a household that receives its income in the form of a transfer payment from the government is more likely to be poor.

Household Type Households with two parents present are unlikely to be poor. The most likely to be poor are households with a single female parent, almost 50 percent of whom live in poverty.

Age of Householder The youngest and the oldest households have lower incomes and a greater incidence of poverty than middle-aged households.

Number of Children On the average, the greater the number of children in a household, the smaller is the income per person. And the greater the number of children, the more likely is the household to be living below the poverty level.

Education Education makes a huge difference to a household's income and to the risk of poverty. A person who has not completed high school earns a fraction of a high school graduate's earnings and has the highest poverty risk. University graduates and those with a post-graduate or professional degree have the lowest risk of poverty.

Labour Force Status Households that are in the labour force, even if unemployed, tend to have higher incomes than those not in the labour force—either because they've retired or because they have become discouraged by a persistent failure to find a suitable job.

How Long Does Poverty Last?

Most poverty is temporary and short-lived. Figure 18.7 shows the numbers: 75 percent of those in poverty remain in that state for less than a year and another 8 percent of those in poverty remain so for 1 year. Poverty rates for people who are in that state for 2 years or more are very low.

Given that the average poverty rate is 17 percent of families, you can see that around 2 percent of Canadian families experience poverty that persists for more than 2 years.

The duration of poverty, like its level, depends on household characteristics, and education is the key

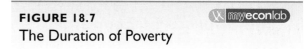

FIGURE 18.7
The Duration of Poverty

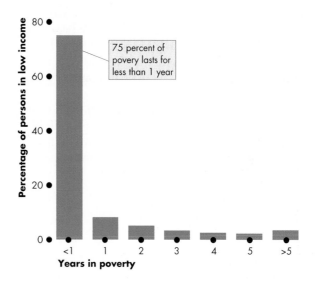

75 percent of poverty lasts for less than 1 year

Most people in poverty do not remain in that state for long. The poverty rate falls off as the duration of poverty increases. Poverty spells that last for 4 and 5 years are extremely rare. But poverty spells that last for 1 year are quite common.

Source of data: Income Statistics Division, Statistics Canada, Table 202–0807.

characteristic. The least well educated tend to be those who experience the most persistent poverty.

REVIEW QUIZ

1 Which is distributed more unequally: income or wealth? Why? Which is the better measure?

2 Has the distribution of income become more equal or more unequal? The share of which quintile has changed most?

3 What are the main characteristics of people who earn large incomes and small incomes?

4 What is poverty and how does its incidence vary over time and across households?

myeconlab **Study Plan 18.1**

The Sources of Economic Inequality

WE'VE DESCRIBED ECONOMIC INEQUALITY IN Canada. Our task now is to explain it. We began this task in Chapter 17 by learning about the forces that influence demand and supply in the markets for labour, capital, and land. We're now going to deepen our understanding of these forces.

Inequality arises from unequal labour market outcomes and from unequal ownership of capital. We'll begin by looking at labour markets and two of their features that contribute to differences in incomes:

- Human capital
- Discrimination

Human Capital

A clerk in a law firm earns less than a tenth of the amount earned by the lawyer he assists. An operating room assistant earns less than a tenth of the amount earned by the surgeon with whom she works. A bank teller earns less than a tenth of the amount earned by the bank's CEO. These differences in earnings arise from differences in human capital. We can explain these differences by using a model of competitive labour markets.

We'll study a model economy with two levels of human capital, which we'll call high-skilled labour and low-skilled labour. The low-skilled labour might represent the law clerk, the operating room assistant, or the bank teller, and the high-skilled labour might represent the lawyer, the surgeon, or the bank's CEO. We'll first look at the demand side of the markets for these two types of labour.

The Demand for High-Skilled and Low-Skilled Labour High-skilled workers can perform tasks that low-skilled labour would perform badly or perhaps could not perform at all. Imagine an untrained person doing open-heart surgery. High-skilled labour has a higher marginal revenue product than low-skilled labour. As we learned in Chapter 14, a firm's demand for labour curve is the same as the marginal revenue product of labour curve.

Figure 18.8(a) shows the demand curves for high-skilled and low-skilled labour. The demand curve for high-skilled labour is D_H, and that for low-skilled labour is D_L. At any given level of employment, firms

are willing to pay a higher wage rate to a high-skilled worker than to a low-skilled worker. The gap between the two wage rates measures the marginal revenue product of skill. For example, at an employment level of 2,000 hours, firms are willing to pay $12.50 for a high-skilled worker and only $5 for a low-skilled worker, a difference of $7.50 an hour. Thus the marginal revenue product of skill is $7.50 an hour.

The Supply of High-Skilled and Low-Skilled Labour High-skilled labour has more human capital than low-skilled labour, and human capital is costly to acquire. The opportunity cost of acquiring human capital includes actual expenditures on such things as tuition and room and board and also costs in the form of lost or reduced earnings while the skill is being acquired. When a person goes to school full-time, that cost is the total earnings forgone. But some people acquire skills on the job—on-the-job training. Usually, a worker undergoing on-the-job training is paid a lower wage than one doing a comparable job but not undergoing training. In such a case, the cost of acquiring the skill is the difference between the wage paid to a person not being trained and that paid to a person being trained.

The position of the supply curve of high-skilled labour reflects the cost of acquiring human capital. Figure 18.8(b) shows two supply curves: one for high-skilled labour and the other for low-skilled labour. The supply curve for high-skilled labour is S_H, and that for low-skilled labour is S_L.

The high-skilled labour supply curve lies above the low-skilled labour supply curve. The vertical distance between the two supply curves is the compensation that high-skilled labour requires for the cost of acquiring the skill. For example, suppose that the quantity of low-skilled labour supplied is 2,000 hours at a wage rate of $5 an hour. This wage rate compensates the low-skilled workers mainly for their time on the job. Consider next the supply of high-skilled labour. To induce 2,000 hours of high-skilled labour to be supplied, firms must pay a wage rate of $8.50 an hour. This wage rate for high-skilled labour is higher than that for low-skilled labour because high-skilled workers must be compensated not only for the time on the job but also for the time and other costs of acquiring the skill.

Wage Rates of High-Skilled and Low-Skilled Labour To work out the wage rates of high-skilled and low-skilled labour, we have to bring together the effects of skill on the demand for and supply of labour.

FIGURE 18.8
Skill Differentials

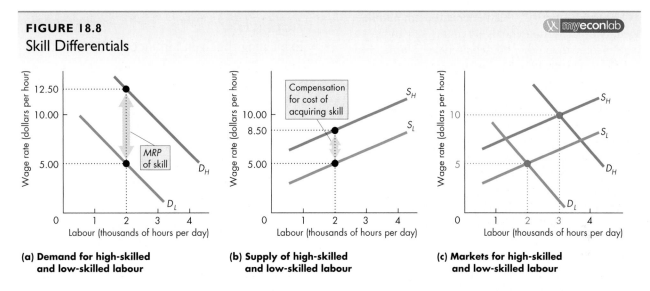

(a) Demand for high-skilled and low-skilled labour

(b) Supply of high-skilled and low-skilled labour

(c) Markets for high-skilled and low-skilled labour

Part (a) illustrates the marginal revenue product of skill. Low-skilled workers have a marginal revenue product that gives rise to the demand curve D_L. High-skilled workers have a higher marginal revenue product than low-skilled labour, so the demand curve for high-skilled labour, D_H, lies to the right of D_L. The vertical distance between these two curves is the marginal revenue product of the skill.

Part (b) shows the effects of the cost of acquiring skills on the supply of labour. The supply curve of low-skilled

labour is S_L. The supply curve of high-skilled labour is S_H. The vertical distance between these two curves is the required compensation for the cost of acquiring a skill.

Part (c) shows the equilibrium employment and the wage differential. Low-skilled workers earn $5 an hour, and 2,000 hours of low-skilled labour are employed. High-skilled workers earn $10 an hour, and 3,000 hours of high-skilled labour are employed. The wage rate for high-skilled labour always exceeds that for low-skilled labour.

Figure 18.8(c) shows the demand curves and the supply curves for high-skilled and low-skilled labour. These curves are the same as those plotted in parts (a) and (b). Equilibrium occurs in the market for low-skilled labour where the supply and demand curves for low-skilled labour intersect. The equilibrium wage rate is $5 an hour, and the quantity of low-skilled labour employed is 2,000 hours. Equilibrium in the market for high-skilled labour occurs where the supply and demand curves for high-skilled labour intersect. The equilibrium wage rate is $10 an hour, and the quantity of high-skilled labour employed is 3,000 hours.

As you can see in part (c), the equilibrium wage rate of high-skilled labour is higher than that of low-skilled labour. There are two reasons why this occurs: First, high-skilled labour has a higher marginal revenue product than low-skilled labour, so at a given wage rate, the quantity of high-skilled labour demanded exceeds that of low-skilled labour. Second, skills are costly to acquire, so at a given wage rate, the quantity of high-skilled labour supplied is less than that of low-skilled labour. The wage differential (in this case, $5 an

hour) depends on both the marginal revenue product of the skill and the cost of acquiring it. The higher the marginal revenue product of the skill, the larger is the vertical distance between the demand curves. The more costly it is to acquire a skill, the larger is the vertical distance between the supply curves. The higher the marginal revenue product of the skill and the more costly it is to acquire, the larger is the wage differential between high-skilled and low-skilled labour.

Do Education and Training Pay? Rates of return on high school and college education have been estimated to be in the range of 5 to 10 percent a year after allowing for inflation, which suggests that a university or college degree is a better investment than almost any other that a person can undertake.

Inequality Explained by Human Capital Differences Human capital differences help to explain some of the inequality that we've described. They also help to explain some of the trends in the distribution of income that occurred during the past 20 years.

You saw on p. 425 that better educated, middle-aged, two-parent households are more likely to have a high income than other household types. Human capital differences are correlated with these household characteristics. Education contributes directly to human capital. Age contributes indirectly to human capital because older workers have more experience than younger workers. Human capital differences can also explain a small part of the inequality associated with sex. A larger proportion of men than women have completed a college or university degree. These differences in education levels have disappeared in the current generation and for the population as a whole they are becoming smaller. But they have not yet been eliminated.

Interruptions to a career reduce the effectiveness of job experience in contributing to human capital. Historically, job interruptions have been more common for women than for men because women's careers have been interrupted for bearing and raising children. This factor is a possible source of lower wages, on the average, for women. Although maternity leave and day-care facilities are making career interruptions for women less common, job interruptions remain a problem for many women.

Trends in Inequality Explained by Human Capital Trends You saw in Fig. 18.5 that high-income households have earned an increasing share of after-tax income while low-income households have earned a decreasing share. Human capital differences are a possible explanation for this trend, and Fig. 18.9 illustrates this explanation. The supply of low-skilled labour (part a) and that of high-skilled labour (part b) are S, and initially, the demand in each market is D_0. The low-skilled wage rate is $5 an hour, and the high-skilled wage rate is $10 an hour.

Information technologies such as computers and laser scanners are *substitutes* for low-skilled labour: They perform tasks that previously were performed by low-skilled labour. The introduction of these technologies has decreased the demand for low-skilled labour (part a), decreased the number of low-skilled jobs, and lowered the wage rate of low-skilled workers.

These same technologies require high-skilled labour to design, program, and run them. High-skilled labour and the information technologies are *complements*. So the introduction of these technologies has increased the demand for high-skilled labour (part b), increased the number of high-skilled jobs, and raised the wage rate of high-skilled workers.

FIGURE 18.9 myeconlab

Explaining the Trend in Income Distribution

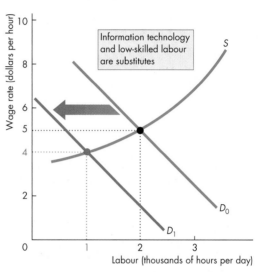

(a) A decrease in demand for low-skilled labour

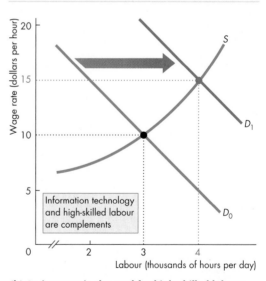

(b) An increase in demand for high-skilled labour

Low-skilled labour in part (a) and information technologies are substitutes. When these technologies were introduced, the demand for low-skilled labour decreased and the quantity of this type of labour and its wage rate decreased. High-skilled labour in part (b) and information technologies are complements. When these technologies were introduced, the demand for high-skilled labour increased and the quantity of this type of labour and its wage rate increased.

Discrimination

Human capital differences can explain some of the economic inequality that we observe. But it can't explain all of it. Discrimination is another possible source of inequality.

Suppose that females and males have identical abilities as investment advisors. Figure 18.10 shows the supply curves of females, S_F (in part a), and of males, S_M (in part b). The marginal revenue product of investment advisors shown by the two curves labelled MRP in parts (a) and (b) is the same for both groups.

If everyone is free of sex-based prejudice, the market determines a wage rate of $40,000 a year for investment advisors. But if the customers are prejudiced against women, this prejudice is reflected in the wage rate and employment.

Suppose that the perceived marginal revenue product of the females, when discriminated against, is MRP_{DA}. Suppose that the perceived marginal revenue product for males, the group discriminated in favour of, is MRP_{DF}. With these MRP curves, females earn $20,000 a year and only 1,000 females work as investment advisors. Males earn $60,000 a year, and 3,000 of them work as investment advisors.

Counteracting Forces Economists disagree about whether prejudice actually causes wage differentials, and one line of reasoning implies that it does not. In the example you've just studied, customers who buy from men pay a higher service charge for investment advice than do the customers who buy from women. This price difference acts as an incentive to encourage people who are prejudiced to buy from the people against whom they are prejudiced. This force could be strong enough to eliminate the effects of discrimination altogether.

Suppose, as is true in manufacturing, that a firm's customers never meet its workers. If such a firm discriminates against women (or against visible minorities), it can't compete with firms who hire these groups because its costs are higher than those of the unprejudiced firms. Only firms that do not discriminate survive in a competitive industry.

Whether because of discrimination or for some other reason, women on average do earn lower incomes than men. Another possible source of women's lower wage rates arises from differences in the relative degree of specialization of women and men.

FIGURE 18.10   [X] myeconlab
Discrimination

(a) Women

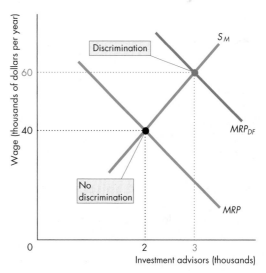

(b) Men

With no discrimination, the wage rate is $40,000 a year and 2,000 of each group are hired. With discrimination against women, the marginal revenue product curve in part (a) is MRP_{DA} and that in part (b) is MRP_{DF}. The wage rate for women falls to $20,000 a year, and only 1,000 are employed. The wage rate for men rises to $60,000 a year, and 3,000 are employed.

Differences in the Degree of Specialization
Couples must choose how to allocate their time between working for a wage and doing jobs in the home, such as cooking, cleaning, shopping, organizing vacations, and, most important, bearing and raising children. Let's look at the choices of Bob and Sue.

Bob might specialize in earning an income and Sue in taking care of the home. Or Sue might specialize in earning an income and Bob in taking care of the home. Or both of them might earn an income and share home production jobs.

The allocation they choose depends on their preferences and on the earning potential of each of them. The choice of an increasing number of households is for each person to diversify between earning an income and doing some home chores. But in most households, Bob will specialize in earning an income and Sue will both earn an income and bear a larger share of the task of running the home. With this allocation, Bob will probably earn more than Sue. If Sue devotes time and effort to ensuring Bob's mental and physical well-being, the quality of Bob's market labour will be higher than it would be if he were diversified. If the roles were reversed, Sue would be able to supply market labour that earns more than Bob.

To test whether the degree of specialization accounts for earnings differences between the sexes, economists have compared the incomes of men and women who never married. They have found that, on the average, with equal amounts of human capital, the wages of these two groups are the same.

We've examined some sources of inequality in the labour market. Let's now look at the way inequality arises from unequal ownership of capital.

Unequal Ownership of Capital

You've seen that inequality in wealth (excluding human capital) is much greater than inequality in income. This inequality arises from saving and transfers of wealth from one generation to the next.

The higher a household's income, the more that household tends to save and pass on to the next generation. Saving is not always a source of increased inequality. If a household saves to redistribute an uneven income over its life cycle and enable consumption to fluctuate less than income, saving decreases inequality. If a lucky generation that has a high income saves a large part of that income and leaves capital to a succeeding generation that is unlucky, this act of saving also decreases the degree of inequality. But two fea-

tures of intergenerational transfers of wealth lead to increased inequality: People can't inherit debt, and marriage tends to concentrate wealth.

Can't Inherit Debt Although a person may die in debt—with negative wealth—a debt can't be forced onto the next generation of a family. So inheritance only adds to a future generation's wealth; inheritance cannot decrease wealth.

Most people inherit nothing or a very small amount. A few people inherit an enormous fortune. As a result, intergenerational transfers make the distribution of income persistently more unequal than the distribution of ability and job skills. A household that is poor in one generation is more likely to be poor in the next. A household that is wealthy in one generation is more likely to be wealthy in the next. And marriage reinforces this tendency.

Marriage and Wealth Concentration People tend to marry within their own socioeconomic class—a phenomenon called *assortative mating*. In everyday language, "like attracts like." Although there is a good deal of folklore that "opposites attract," perhaps such Cinderella tales appeal to us because they are so rare in reality. Wealthy people seek wealthy partners.

Because of assortative mating, wealth becomes more concentrated in a small number of families and the distribution of wealth becomes more unequal.

REVIEW QUIZ

1 What role does human capital play in accounting for income inequality?
2 What role might discrimination play in accounting for income inequality?
3 What are the possible reasons for income inequality by sex and race?
4 What are the possible reasons for income inequality by age group?
5 Does inherited wealth make the distribution of income less equal or more equal?
6 Why does wealth inequality persist across generations?

myeconlab Study Plan 18.2

Next, we're going to see how taxes and government programs redistribute income and decrease the degree of economic inequality.

Income Redistribution

THE THREE MAIN WAYS IN WHICH GOVERNMENTS in Canada redistribute income are

- Income taxes
- Income maintenance programs
- Subsidized services

Income Taxes

Income taxes may be progressive, regressive, or proportional. A **progressive income tax** is one that taxes income at an average rate that increases with the level of income. The **average tax rate** is the percentage of income paid in taxes. A **regressive income tax** is one that taxes income at an average rate that decreases with the level of income. A **proportional income tax** (also called a *flat-rate income tax*) is one that taxes income at a constant rate, regardless of the level of income.

The income tax rates that apply in Canada are composed of two parts: federal and provincial taxes. The highest income tax rates are in Quebec and the lowest are in Alberta. There is variety in the detailed tax arrangements in the individual provinces but the tax system, at both the federal and provincial levels, is progressive.

The poorest Canadians pay no income tax. Even those who earn $30,000 a year pay a very low rate of income tax. Those whose incomes are $50,000 a year pay about 21 percent of their income in income taxes; those whose incomes are $100,000 a year pay about 28 percent in income tax; and as incomes increase, the average tax rate increases to 45 percent or higher.

Income Maintenance Programs

Three main types of programs redistribute income by making direct payments (in cash, services, or vouchers) to people in the lower part of the income distribution. They are

- Social security programs
- Employment Insurance program
- Welfare programs

Social Security Programs Four programs—Old Age Security (OAS), Guaranteed Income Supplement (GIS), the Allowance (for spouses of low-income OAS pensioners), and the Allowance for the Survivor (AS)—ensure a minimum level of income for senior citizens. Cash payments to retired or disabled workers or their surviving spouses are paid for by compulsory payroll taxes on both employers and employees. In 2005, the maximum OAS was $476.97 a month, the maximum GIS for a single person was $566.87, the maximum Allowance was $846.21, and the maximum AS was $934.24.

Employment Insurance Program To provide an income to unemployed workers, the federal government has established an unemployment compensation program. The Employment Insurance program is funded by employee and employer contributions, and after a qualifying period the worker is entitled to receive a benefit if he or she becomes unemployed. In 2005, the maximum unemployment benefit was $413 a week or 55 percent of gross weekly earnings over the previous 20 weeks.

Welfare Programs Other welfare programs provide income maintenance for families and persons. They are

1. Canada Assistance Plan, a plan shared equally by the federal and provincial governments that gives financial assistance to families and individuals who are in need, regardless of the cause; the assistance includes food, shelter, fuel, utilities, family supplies, items required to carry on a trade, certain welfare services, and health and social services
2. Family Supplement and Canada Child Tax Benefit programs, designed to help families who have inadequate financial support
3. Canada/Quebec Pension Plans, funded equally by employee and employer contributions, provide retirement benefits, survivor benefits, disability benefits, and death benefits
4. Workers' Compensation, a provincial program funded by employers, designed to provide financial assistance as well as medical care and rehabilitation of workers injured at work

Subsidized Services

A great deal of redistribution takes place in Canada through the provision of subsidized services, which is the provision of goods and services by the government at prices below the cost of production. The taxpayers who consume these goods and services receive a transfer in kind from the taxpayers who do not consume them. The two most important areas in which this form of redistribution takes place are education—both kindergarten through Grade 12 and college and university—and health care.

Canadian students enrolled in the universities in Ontario pay annual tuition fees of around $5,000. The cost of one year's education at one of these universities is about $20,000. Thus families with a member enrolled in these institutions receive a benefit from the government of about $15,000 a year. Those with several college or university students receive proportionately higher benefits.

Government provision of health care to all residents has brought high-quality and high-cost health care to millions of people who earn too little to buy such services themselves. As a result, this program has contributed to reducing inequality.

The Scale of Income Redistribution

To determine the scale of income redistribution, we need to compare the distribution of *market income* with the distribution of *after-tax income*. The data available on benefits exclude the value of subsidized services (such as the value of university education and health care services), so the resulting distribution might understate the total amount of redistribution from the rich to the poor.

Figure 18.11 shows the scale of redistribution based on the calculations just described. In part (a), the blue Lorenz curve describes the market distribution of income and the green Lorenz curve shows the distribution of income after all taxes and benefits. (The Lorenz curve based on *total income*—market income plus transfer payments from governments—lies between these two curves.)

The distribution after taxes and benefits is much less unequal than the market distribution. In 2003, the lowest 20 percent of households received only 1.1 percent of market income but 5 percent of after-tax income. The highest 20 percent of households received 51.6 percent of market income but only 43.7 percent of after-tax income.

Figure 18.11(b) highlights the percentage of total income redistributed among the five groups. The share of total income received by the lowest three quintiles (60 percent) of households increased. The share of total income received by the fourth quintile fell slightly. And the share of total income received by the highest quintile fell by almost 8 percent of total income.

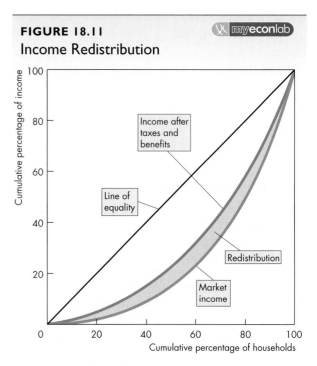

FIGURE 18.11
Income Redistribution

(a) Income distribution before and after redistribution

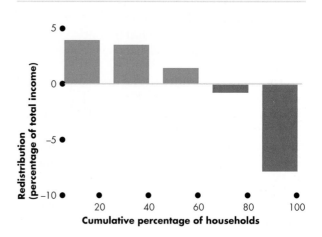

(b) The scale of redistribution

Redistribution reduces the degree of inequality that the market generates. In 2003, the 20 percent of households with the lowest incomes received net benefits that increased their share from 1.1 percent of market income to 5 percent of income after redistribution. The 20 percent of households with the highest incomes paid taxes that decreased their share from 51.6 percent of market income to 43.7 percent of income after redistribution.

Source of data: Income Statistics Division, Statistics Canada, Table 202–0701.

The Big Tradeoff

The redistribution of income creates what has been called the **big tradeoff**, a tradeoff between equity and efficiency. The big tradeoff arises because redistribution uses scarce resources and weakens incentives.

A dollar collected from a rich person does not translate into a dollar received by a poor person. Some of the dollar collected gets used up in the process of redistribution. Tax-collecting agencies such as the Canada Revenue Agency and welfare-administering agencies (as well as tax accountants and lawyers) use skilled labour, computers, and other scarce resources to do their work. The bigger the scale of redistribution, the greater is the opportunity cost of administering it.

But the cost of collecting taxes and making welfare payments is a small part of the total cost of redistribution. A bigger cost arises from the inefficiency—deadweight loss—of taxes and benefits. Greater equality can be achieved only by taxing productive activities such as work and saving. Taxing people's income from their work and saving lowers the after-tax income they receive. This lower after-tax income makes them work and save less, which in turn results in smaller output and less consumption not only for the rich who pay the taxes but also for the poor who receive the benefits.

It is not only taxpayers who face weaker incentives to work. Benefit recipients also face weaker incentives. In fact, under the welfare arrangements that prevail in Canada today, the weakest incentives to work are those faced by households that benefit most from welfare. When a welfare recipient gets a job, benefits are withdrawn and eligibility for support is withdrawn. In effect, these households face a marginal tax rate of more than 100 percent on their earnings. This arrangement locks poor households in a welfare trap.

So the scale and methods of income redistribution must pay close attention to the incentive effects of taxes and benefits.

A Major Welfare Challenge The poorest people in Canada are women who have not completed high school, have a child (or children), and live without a partner. But all single mothers present a major welfare challenge. First, their numbers are large. There are approximately one million single mothers in Canada today. Second, their economic plight and the economic prospects for their children are serious.

Janet Peterson and her four children aged 3 to 13 are one example. Janet has a serious physical disability.

She receives a social assistance cheque each month for $1,286, or $15,432 a year. The low-income cutoff for a family of five is $30,910. So Janet and her children live in severe poverty. She spends $625 a month on rent, $400 on food, and the rest on gas, hydro, the phone, and transportation. To provide Janet Peterson (and the other million single mothers) with an income that matches the low-income cutoff would cost more than $10 billion a year.

Janet Peterson has a physical disability that makes it unlikely that she could work. Many other single mothers are in this situation. But this is not the typical case. Most single mothers are physically fit and are capable of working. And some of them are well educated and therefore can earn a high wage rate. Even those single mothers who have not completed high school are capable of either attending school or getting a job.

For physically fit single mothers, the long-term solution to their problem is education and on-the-job training—acquiring human capital. The short-term solution is welfare. But welfare must be designed to minimize the disincentive to pursue the long-term goal. This is the challenge in designing an adequate welfare program.

REVIEW QUIZ

1 How do governments in Canada redistribute income?
2 How large is the scale of redistribution in Canada?
3 What is one of the major welfare challenges today and how is it being tackled in Canada?

 Study Plan 18.3

We've examined economic inequality in Canada, and we've seen how inequality arises. And we've seen that inequality has increased since 1980. *Reading Between the Lines* on pp. 434–435 looks at Canada's changing inequality and redistribution through taxes.

You've now completed your study of microeconomics. You've seen how markets work and do a remarkable job of reconciling self-interest and the social interest. You've also seen that in situations in which market failure occurs government action might improve the allocation of resources. But you've seen too that failure can occur in the political marketplace.

Changing Inequality and Redistribution

CALGARY HERALD, 23 APRIL 2005

Rich Canadians pay half of all federal income tax

More than half the taxes the federal government collected in 2002 came from the top 10 per cent of the country's income earners, according to a study released Friday by Statistics Canada.

People in the highest income bracket saw the smallest drop in their effective tax rate between 1990 and 2002, a time when rates fell for all Canadians, the study said. Moreover, the share of federal income taxes paid by this group of high-income earners rose in the decade covered by the report.

By comparison, the share of federal taxes paid by people in the bottom half of Canada's tax scale diminished significantly, the study showed. ...

"We do know that top income tax rates in this country are still high, they're among the highest in the world, particularly if you combine them with provincial rates," said Derek Burleton, senior economist with TD Bank Financial Group. ...

Jim Stanford, an economist with the Canadian Auto Workers, looked at the study results differently, suggesting they painted only a partial picture of the economic well-being of low-income earners and pointing to the last decade as a time of growing income inequality.

The tax cuts implemented in this period favoured the rich more than the poor, Stanford said, though he acknowledged that measures such as the child tax credit helped low-income earners.

"The progressivity of the system has actually diminished somewhat since 1990," he added.

"Some people who support a progressive system could say (such a system) is good, but the actual driving force is a regressive force, namely that pre-tax income is becoming more unequal."

The impact of taxes such as the GST, not considered in the study, hit low-income earners harder than they did richer Canadians, Stanford said.

"If you were to measure the total taxes—not just income taxes—paid by the lower-income people, it wouldn't look as positive as this study which focused only on the income tax," he said.

"The overall tax burden borne by lower-income people is much higher than just their share of income taxes."

Reprinted by permission of Joe Paraskevas.

Essence of the Story

■ A Statistics Canada report says that more than 50 percent of federal income tax came from the country's top 10 percent of earners.

■ The share of income tax paid by the bottom 50 percent of earners decreased.

■ Jim Stanford of the Canadian Auto Workers says the study is misleading and that the tax cuts of the 1990s favoured the rich.

■ Also, says Stanford, taking account of the GST further favours the rich against the poor.

■ The overall burden of the tax system borne by lower income groups is much larger than the report says.

Economic Analysis

■ In this chapter, we described the degree of income redistribution by examining the Lorenz curve for after-tax income with that for market income.

■ We analyzed the shift in the Lorenz curve that arises from taxes and benefits by calculating the percentage of total income that is transferred across the quintiles.

■ We made this comparison for 2003 only and didn't examine how redistribution has changed.

■ The news article compares 1990 and 2002. We will do some further analysis and compare 1990 and 2003.

■ Figure 1 shows the quintile shares of after-tax income in 1990 and 2003. The blue bars show the data for 1990 and the red bars for 2003.

■ You can see that the share of after-tax income received by the highest quintile increased while the shares of the other four quintiles decreased—after-tax income inequality increased.

■ Was the amount of redistribution from taxes and benefits responsible for this increase in inequality?

■ Figure 2 answers this question and shows that it was not.

■ Figure 2 shows the percentage of total after-tax income transferred across the quintiles in 1990 (blue bars) and 2003 (red bars).

■ You can see that the highest quintile paid a larger percentage of its income to the lower quintiles.

■ But you can also see that the fourth quintile paid less and the third (middle) quintile received more. The two lowest quintiles received less.

■ So the changes in taxes and benefits hurt the richest and the poorest Canadians and benefitted the middle income and upper middle income groups.

■ This change in redistribution is consistent with the idea that the political process favours the median voter—the voter needed to gain a majority in an election.

■ Jim Stanford of the Canadian Auto Workers says that taking account of the GST would change the picture and show that the poorer Canadians pay a much bigger share of taxes.

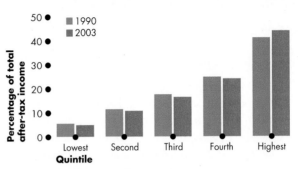

Figure 1 Quintile shares of after-tax income

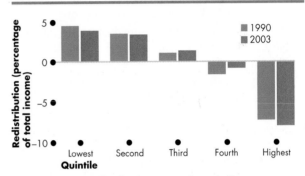

Figure 2 Income redistribution across the quintiles

■ He is correct in saying that the GST makes a difference to the calculation of who pays the taxes and how much redistribution comes from the tax system.

■ But the GST doesn't change the picture radically because the higher quintiles also pay most of the GST.

■ Remember that the GST is a flat percentage of expenditure on items covered by the tax. Some of the items on which the lower quintiles spend a large proportion of their incomes are exempt from the GST. So the higher quintiles, who spend much more than the lower quintiles, end up paying the bulk of the GST.

■ Whether the tax system in Canada redistributes too much or too little is a difficult question and one that will always be on the political agenda.

435

SUMMARY

KEY POINTS

Measuring Economic Inequality (pp. 420–425)

- In 2003, the mode after-tax income was in the range between $15,000 and $19,999 a year, the median after-tax income was $39,700, and the mean after-tax income was $48,400.
- The income distribution is positively skewed.
- The poorest 20 percent of households received 5 percent of total income, and the wealthiest 20 percent received 43.6 percent of total income.
- Wealth is distributed more unequally than income because the wealth data exclude the value of human capital.
- Since 1980, the share of income received by the richest 20 percent of households has increased, the share of the poorest 20 percent has remained constant, and the shares of income received by the other three groups of households have decreased.
- Source of income, household type, age of householder, number of children, education, and labour market status all influence household income.

The Sources of Economic Inequality (pp. 426–430)

- Inequality arises from differences in human capital.
- Inequality might arise from discrimination.
- Inequality between men and women might arise from differences in the degree of specialization.
- Intergenerational transfers of wealth lead to increased inequality because people can't inherit debt, and assortative mating tends to concentrate wealth.

Income Redistribution (pp. 431–433)

- Governments redistribute income through progressive income taxes, income maintenance programs, and subsidized services.
- Redistribution increases the share of total income received by the lowest three quintiles (60 percent) of households and decreases the share of total income received by the highest quintile. The share of the fourth quintile falls slightly.

- Because the redistribution of income weakens incentives, it creates a tradeoff between equity and efficiency.
- Effective redistribution seeks to support the long-term solution to low income, which is education and job training—acquiring human capital.

KEY FIGURES

Figure 18.1   The Distribution of Income in Canada in 2003, 420
Figure 18.4   Lorenz Curves for Income and Wealth, 422
Figure 18.5   Trends in the Distribution of Income, 424
Figure 18.6   The Poverty Rate, 424
Figure 18.8   Skill Differentials, 427
Figure 18.9   Explaining the Trend in Income Distribution, 428
Figure 18.10 Descrimination, 429
Figure 18.11 Income Redistribution, 432

KEY TERMS

After-tax income, 420
Average tax rate, 431
Big tradeoff, 433
Lorenz curve, 421
Low-income cutoff, 424
Market income, 420
Poverty, 424
Progressive income tax, 431
Proportional income tax, 431
Regressive income tax, 431
Total income, 420

PROBLEMS

Go to (X myeconlab) for solutions to odd-numbered problems and additional exercises.

1. The table shows income shares in the United States in 2000.

Households	Income (percent of total)
Lowest 20 percent	4.8
Second-lowest 20 percent	10.5
Third-lowest 20 percent	15.8
Fourth-lowest 20 percent	22.8
Highest 20 percent	46.1

a. Draw a Lorenz curve for the United States in 2000 and compare it with that for Canada in 2003 shown in Fig. 18.3.

b. Was Canadian income distributed more equally or less equally than that in the United States?

c. Can you think of some reasons for the differences in the distribution of income in Canada and the United States?

2. The table shows income shares in Sweden in 1992.

Households	Income (percent of total)
Lowest 20 percent	6.7
Second-lowest 20 percent	12.2
Third-lowest 20 percent	17.6
Fourth-lowest 20 percent	24.5
Highest 20 percent	39.0

a. Draw the Lorenz curve for income in Sweden in 1992.

b. Was income distributed more equally or less equally in Canada in 2003 than in Sweden in 1992?

c. Use the information provided in problem 1 on the distribution of income in the United States in 2000. Was income distributed more equally or less equally in the United States in 2000 than in Sweden in 1992?

d. Can you think of some reasons for the differences in the distribution of income in Canada and Sweden?

3. The following figure shows the demand for and supply of low-skilled labour.

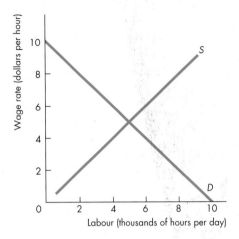

High-skilled workers have twice the marginal revenue product of low-skilled workers. (The marginal revenue product at each employment level is twice the marginal revenue product of a low-skilled worker.) But the cost of acquiring the skill adds $2 an hour to the wage that must be offered to attract high-skilled labour. What is

a. The wage rate of low-skilled labour?

b. The quantity of low-skilled labour employed?

c. The wage rate of high-skilled labour?

d. The quantity of high-skilled labour employed?

4. The following figure shows the demand for and supply of low-skilled labour.

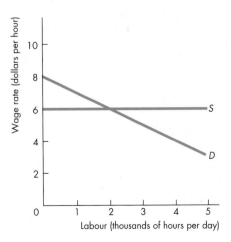

The marginal revenue product of a high-skilled worker is $10 an hour greater than that of a low-skilled worker. (The marginal revenue product at each employment level is $10 greater than that of a low-skilled worker.) The cost of acquiring the skill adds $6 an hour to the wage that must be offered to attract high-skilled labour.

a. What is the wage rate of low-skilled labour?

b. What is the quantity of low-skilled labour employed?

c. What is the wage rate of high-skilled labour?

d. What is the quantity of high-skilled labour employed?

e. Why does the wage rate of a high-skilled worker exceed that of a low-skilled worker by exactly the cost of acquiring the skill?

5. The table shows the distribution of market income in Canada in 2003.

Households	Market income (percent of total)
Lowest 20 percent	1.1
Second-lowest 20 percent	7.3
Third-lowest 20 percent	15.1
Fourth-lowest 20 percent	24.9
Highest 20 percent	51.6

a. What is market income?

b. Draw the Lorenz curve for the distribution of market income.

c. Compare the distribution of market income with the distribution of after-tax income shown in Fig. 18.3. Which distribution is more unequal and why?

6. Use the information provided in problem 5 and in Fig. 18.3.

a. What is the percentage of market income that is redistributed from the highest income group?

b. What are the percentages of market income that are redistributed to the lower income groups?

c. Describe the effects of increasing the amount of income redistribution in Canada to the point at which the lowest income group receives 15 percent of after-tax income and the highest income group receives 30 percent of after-tax income.

CRITICAL THINKING

1. Study *Reading Between the Lines* on pp. 434–435 and then

a. Describe the main facts about the changes in the distribution of after-tax income in Canada.

b. Describe the main facts about changes in the distribution of the burden of the federal income tax reported in the news article.

c. Why might it be argued that the rich pay too much tax?

d. Why might it be argued that the rich pay too little tax?

e. What policy issues are raised by the news article?

f. How do you think the tax system and the welfare system should be changed to influence the distribution of after-tax income in Canada today?

WEB EXERCISES

Use the links on **myeconlab** to work the following exercises.

1. Obtain data on income distribution among major league baseball players. Then

a. Describe the main facts about the income distribution of major league players.

b. Compare the income distribution of these players with the income distribution of Canada.

c. Which is more unequal?

d. What is the problem with inequality?

2. Download the World Bank's Deininger and Squire Data Set on income distribution in a large number of countries.

a. Which country in the data set has the most unequal distribution?

b. Which country in the data set has the most equal distribution?

c. Can you think of reasons that might explain the differences in income distribution in the two countries you've identified?

UNDERSTANDING FACTOR MARKETS

For Whom?

During the past 40 years, the rich have been getting richer at a faster pace than the poor. This trend is new. From the end of World War II until 1965, the poor got richer at a faster pace than the rich and the gap between rich and poor narrowed a bit. What are the forces that generate these trends? The answer to this question is the forces of demand and supply in factor markets. These forces determine wages, interest rates, and the prices of land and natural resources. These forces also determine people's incomes.

The three categories of resources are human, capital, and natural. Human resources include labour, human capital, and entrepreneurship. The income of labour and human capital depends on wage rates and employment levels, which are determined in labour markets. The income from capital depends on interest rates and the amount of capital, which are determined in capital markets. The income from natural resources depends on prices and quantities that are determined in natural resource markets. Only the return to entrepreneurship is not determined directly in a market. That return is normal profit plus economic profit, and it depends on how successful each entrepreneur is in the business that he or she runs.

The chapters in this part study the forces at play in factor markets and explain how those forces have led to changes in the distribution of income.

The overview of all the factor markets in Chapter 17 explained how the demand for factors of production results from the profit-maximizing decisions of firms. You studied these decisions from a different angle in Chapters 9–13, where you learned how firms choose their profit-maximizing output and price. Chapter 17 explained how a firm's profit-maximizing decisions determine its demand for productive factors. It also explained how factor supply decisions are made and how equilibrium in factor markets determines factor prices and the incomes of owners of factors of production.

Some of the biggest incomes earned by superstars are a surplus that we call *economic rent.*

Chapter 17 used labour resources and the labour market as its main example. But it also looked at some special features of capital markets and natural resource markets.

Chapter 18 studied the distribution of income. This chapter took you right back to the fundamentals of economics and answered one of the big economic questions: Who gets to consume the goods and services that are produced?

Many outstanding economists have advanced our understanding of factor markets and the role they play in helping to resolve the conflict between the demands of humans and the resources available. One of them is Thomas Robert Malthus, whom you can meet on the following page. You can also enjoy the insights of Janet Currie, a Canadian professor of economics at UCLA and a prominent contemporary labour economist.

PROBING THE IDEAS

Running Out of Resources

> *"The passion between the sexes has appeared in every age to be so nearly the same, that it may always be considered, in algebraic language, as a given quantity."*
>
> THOMAS
> ROBERT
> MALTHUS
> *An Essay on the Principle of Population*

THE ECONOMIST

Thomas Robert Malthus

(1766–1834), an English clergyman and economist, was an extremely influential social scientist. In his best-selling Essay on the Principle of Population, *published in 1798, he predicted that population growth would outstrip food production and said that wars, famine, and disease were inevitable unless population growth was held in check by what he called "moral restraint." By "moral restraint," he meant marrying at a late age and living a celibate life. He married at the age of 38 a wife of 27, marriage ages that he recommended for others. Malthus's ideas were regarded as too radical in their day. And they led Thomas Carlyle, a contemporary thinker, to dub economics the "dismal science." But the ideas of Malthus had a profound influence on Charles Darwin, who got the key idea that led him to the theory of natural selection from reading the* Essay on the Principle of Population. *And David Ricardo and the classical economists were strongly influenced by Malthus's ideas.*

THE ISSUES

Is there a limit to economic growth, or can we expand production and population without effective limit? Thomas Malthus gave one of the most influential answers to these questions in 1798. He reasoned that population, unchecked, would grow at a geometric rate—1, 2, 4, 8, 16 . . . —while the food supply would grow at an arithmetic rate—1, 2, 3, 4, 5. . . . To prevent the population from outstripping the available food supply, there would be periodic wars, famines, and plagues. In Malthus's view, only what he called moral restraint could prevent such periodic disasters.

As industrialization proceeded through the nineteenth century, Malthus's idea came to be applied to all natural resources, especially those that are exhaustible.

Modern-day Malthusians believe that his basic idea is correct and that it applies not only to food but also to every natural resource. In time, these prophets of doom believe, we will be reduced to the subsistence level that Malthus predicted. He was a few centuries out in his predictions but not dead wrong.

One modern-day Malthusian is ecologist Paul Ehrlich, who believes that we are sitting on a "population bomb." Governments must, says Ehrlich, limit both population growth and the resources that may be used each year.

In 1931, Harold Hotelling developed a theory of natural resources with different predictions from those of Malthus. The Hotelling Principle is that the relative price of an exhaustible natural resource will steadily rise, bringing a decline in the quantity used and an increase in the use of substitute resources.

Julian Simon (who died in 1998) challenged both the Malthusian gloom and the Hotelling Principle. He believed that people are the "ultimate resource" and predicted

440

that an increasing population lessens the pressure on natural resources. A bigger population provides a larger number of resourceful people who can work out more efficient ways of using scarce resources. As these solutions are found, the prices of exhaustible resources actually fall. To demonstrate his point, in 1980, Simon bet Ehrlich that the prices of five metals—copper, chrome, nickel, tin, and tungsten—would fall during the 1980s. Simon won the bet!

THEN

No matter whether it is agricultural land, an exhaustible natural resource, or the space in the centre of Winnipeg and no matter whether it is 2006 or, as shown here, 1913, there is a limit to what is available, and we persistently push against that limit. Economists see urban congestion as a consequence of the value of doing business in the city centre relative to the cost. They see the price mechanism, bringing ever-higher rents and prices of raw materials, as the means of allocating and rationing scarce natural resources. Malthusians, in contrast, explain congestion as the consequence of population pressure, and they see population control as the solution.

NOW

In Tokyo, the pressure on space is so great that in some residential neighbourhoods, a parking space costs $1,700 a month. To economize on this expensive space—and to lower the cost of car ownership and hence boost the sale of new cars—Honda, Nissan, and Toyota, three of Japan's big car producers, have developed a parking machine that enables two cars to occupy the space of one. The most basic of these machines costs a mere $10,000—less than six months' parking fees.

Malthus developed his ideas about population growth in a world in which women played a limited role in the economy. Malthus did not consider the opportunity cost of women's time a factor to be considered in predicting trends in the birth rate and population growth. But today, the opportunity cost of women's time is a crucial factor because women play an expanded role in the labour force. One woman who has made significant contributions to our knowledge of labour markets is Janet Currie of UCLA. You can meet Professor Currie on the following pages.

Janet Currie is a professor of economics at the University of California, Los Angeles. Born in 1960 in Kingston, Canada, she attended the University of Toronto, where she received her B.A. and M.A. in economics before moving to Princeton University, where she completed her Ph.D. in 1988. Professor Currie's research examines a wide range of public programs —medical, nutritional, educational, and housing—on (mainly) poor families. She has provided valuable assessments of the short-term and long-term effects of the Head Start program (enriched pre-school for children in poor households) and Medicaid (government provided health insurance for poor mothers and their children).

Michael Parkin and Robin Bade talked with Janet Currie about her work and the progress that economists have made in understanding how public policies can influence the distribution of income and economic well-being as well as the supply of labour and human capital.

Professor Currie, what attracted you to economics?

I was attracted to economics because it addresses questions of broad human interest (such as poverty and inequality) with intellectual rigour. Some may view the economic paradigm as restrictive (does everyone really maximize utility all the time?), but it provides a set of tools that yield powerful predictions about human behaviour, and it can be tested. For example, the "Law of Demand" (people consume less of a good when the price goes up) can be adopted to think about why many eligible people do not participate in social programs that might benefit them.

Why are there still relatively few women in our field?

Like other scientific careers, that of an economist requires an initial investment in mathematical skills. Mathematics is the language of science, and it is difficult to become a scientist if you don't speak the language. Undergraduate programs in economics may be partially to blame for not preparing students adequately for graduate work in the field. Many programs are aimed more at preparing students for careers in law or business. While this may be what the majority of undergraduate economics students want, we should also serve those who may go on to study economics in graduate school.

Difficulties in combining work and family are also an issue, but economics is not unique in requiring women to devote a lot of time to their careers at precisely the point when traditionally women would spend most time with their families. However, supports such as maternity leave and child care are improving, and making it easier for younger women to "do it all."

Could you briefly describe Head Start and summarize your main conclusions about its effects?

Head Start is a preschool program for disadvantaged three- to five-year-old children. In a series of studies comparing Head Start children to siblings who did not attend, I find evidence of lasting effects of Head Start in terms of schooling attainment and reductions in criminal activity. These findings are important because, while everyone would like to believe that investments in children pay off, there was little prior evidence of longer-term effects of Head Start.

You asked in a recent paper "Are public housing projects good for kids?" What's the answer?

The title of this paper is intentionally provocative. Given all the negative publicity about some housing projects, most people assume that public housing must be bad for children. However, the key question is not whether kids in public housing do worse than other kids (they do) but whether they do better than they would have done in the absence of the program. For example, without the program, some children might have become homeless or had to move many times. It turns out that on average, public housing programs do improve the housing available to poor families and have some positive effects in terms of schooling attainments.

In another paper, published in 1998, you summarized what we know and need to know about the effects of welfare programs on children. What, in a nutshell, do we know? What do we still need to know? And how would we set about finding the needed answers?

One striking conclusion from this review of welfare programs is that the available evidence suggests that in-kind programs are more effective than traditional welfare programs, which give cash to parents. This might account for the growing proportion of aid to poor families that is given in the form of specific in-kind benefits (e.g., Head Start, medical insurance, housing assistance). However, the evidence is far from complete. We need a lot more information about effects of programs on children, since antipoverty programs are often justified in terms of their possible beneficial effects on children. We also need more information about longer-term effects of programs. For example, does it matter at what age the benefits are received?

In terms of how to find out what we need to know, I am a big supporter of social experiments, since a real random-assignment, treatment-control design provides more convincing answers than most statistical studies. On the other hand, it isn't possible to mount an experiment for every question. Much more could be done with existing data if more of it was made available to researchers, and if governments were more willing to allow linkages of different data sources.

What are some of the social experiments that have provided convincing answers? And how could economists do better work if governments were more willing to allow linkages of different data sources?

The great thing about a well-designed experiment is that anyone can understand the results. For example, in a drug trial, we randomly assign people to a treatment group that gets the drug and to a control group that gets a placebo. Because of the random assignment, the two groups are the same on average, so that any *ex poste* differences in how they do can be attributed to the treatment.

> " *The great thing about a well-designed experiment is that anyone can understand the results.* "

Social experiments like the "Moving to Opportunity" project also rely on random assignment. In this experiment, the treatment consisted of giving a voucher to families in public housing projects that allowed the families to move into a low-poverty neighbourhood and gave them some assistance in relocating. The initial results indicate that the experiment had an effect on youth crime, as well as on criminal victimization. So far, there are no positive effects on schooling attainment or parental employment, but it is possible that these will emerge in the followup that is currently being conducted.

Another interesting experiment involves Early Head Start, a program that extends Head Start benefits to infants and toddlers. This program has demonstrated short-term effects of the program on cognitive test scores. Again, it will be necessary to do some long-term followup in order to see whether these benefits are retained.

The downside of experiments is that they are very expensive, relative to a statistical study, and cannot be used to answer questions other than those they were designed to address. Some of my work on the effects of Medicaid expansions provides an example of what can be done by linking various types of data. The U.S. government collects a good deal of survey data about health insurance and health-care utilization. Because my co-author, Jon Gruber, was working in Washington, we were able to get state identifiers so that we could link information about Medicaid income cut-offs in each state to the individual-level records. This enabled us to ask how changing the income cutoffs affected health-care utilization. In recent years, the government has been unwilling to release geographic identifiers, so that it is not possible to do a similar study of more recent health insurance expansions.

A few years ago, you stuck out your neck on the never-to-end minimum wage issue. What, according to your work, is the effect of the minimum wage on youth employment?

We found compelling evidence that youths affected by minimum wage legislation were less likely to be employed than those who were not (because they had wages either above or below the affected group). There are some obvious methodological flaws with some of the work arguing that minimum wages actually increase employment (such as failures to properly control for increases in demand, which might be driving increases in employment even at the higher minimum wages). However, much of the work (my own included) ignores an important question, which is whether we actually want to increase employment among youths. If higher minimum wages reduced employment but increased schooling, perhaps this would be a good outcome.

You've studied the effects of restrictions on the use of public funds for abortion. What did you discover?

Many people have argued that restrictions on abortion may cause more unwanted children to be born and hence worsen infant and child outcomes. The basic idea of my paper was that if this were true, then one ought to be able to see the effect in the distribution of birthweights. That is, if children who would have been aborted are more likely to be of low birthweight (because their mothers did not take care of themselves), then one should see more low birthweight infants in areas that adopt abortion restrictions. We did not, however, find this effect. In hindsight, it is not obvious that children who are born as a result of abortion restrictions ought to be less healthy than average, since the majority of women seeking abortions are young and non-poor.

> " *. . . economists are increasingly contributing to debate (and frequently having the last word) on questions that used to be considered far outside their scope.* "

What advice do you have for a student who is just starting to study economics? Do you think that economics is a good subject in which to major? What other subjects would you urge students to study alongside economics?

I have never regretted choosing economics as a major. Economics gives one the tools to study a vast array of social issues in a rigorous manner. Not surprisingly, economists are increasingly contributing to debate (and frequently having the last word) on questions that used to be considered far outside their scope. Economic concepts such as "opportunity cost," "selection bias," and "cost-benefit analysis" are central to the discussion of a vast array of policy issues.

Students who want to leave open the option of graduate work in economics should make sure they take enough mathematics courses to get them through a good graduate program.

Trading with the World

Silk Routes and Sucking Sounds

Since ancient times, people have expanded their trading as far as technology allowed. Marco Polo opened up the silk route between Europe and China in the thirteenth century. Today, container ships laden with cars and electronics and Boeing 747s stuffed with farm-fresh foods ply sea and air routes, carrying billions of dollars' worth of goods. Why do people go to such great lengths to trade with those in other nations?

In 1994, Canada entered into a free trade agreement with the United States and Mexico—the North American Free Trade Agreement, or NAFTA. Some people predicted a "giant sucking sound" as jobs were transferred from high-wage Michigan and Ontario to low-wage Mexico. Can we compete with a country that pays its workers a fraction of Canadian wages? Are there any industries, besides perhaps the software and movie industries, in which we have an advantage?

Canada exports lumber to the United States for home building. But U.S. lumber producers say that Canadian producers receive an unfair subsidy from their government, so the United States has imposed a tariff on Canadian lumber imports. Do tariffs benefit the importing country? We examine this question in *Reading Between the Lines*.

◆ In this chapter, we're going to learn about international trade and discover how *all* nations can gain from trading with other nations. We'll discover that all nations can compete, no matter how high their wages. We'll also explain why, despite the fact that international trade brings benefits to all, governments restrict trade.

After studying this chapter, you will be able to

■ Describe the trends and patterns in international trade

■ Explain comparative advantage and explain why all countries can gain from international trade

■ Explain the effects of international trade restrictions

■ Explain the arguments for trade restrictions and why they are flawed

■ Describe a country's balance of payments accounts and explain what determines the current account balance

■ Describe the North American Free Trade Agreement

Patterns and Trends in International Trade

THE GOODS AND SERVICES THAT WE BUY FROM people in other countries are called **imports**. The goods and services that we sell to people in other countries are called **exports**. What are the most important things that we import and export? Most people would probably guess that a rich nation such as Canada imports raw materials and exports manufactured goods. Although that is one feature of Canadian international trade, it is not its most important feature. The vast bulk of our exports *and* imports is manufactured goods. We sell foreigners earth-moving equipment, airplanes, telecommunications equipment, and scientific equipment. We buy televisions, DVDs, blue jeans, and T-shirts from foreigners. Also, we are a major exporter of agricultural products and raw materials. We also import and export a huge volume of services.

Trade in Goods

Of the goods that we trade, manufactured goods account for 74 percent of our exports and 84 percent of our imports. Industrial materials (raw materials and semimanufactured items) account for 44 percent of our exports and 28 percent of our imports, and agricultural products account for only 7 percent of our exports and 5 percent of our imports. Our largest individual export and import items are capital goods and automobiles.

But goods account for only 87 percent of our exports and 83 percent of our imports. The rest of our international trade is in services.

Trade in Services

You may be wondering how a country can "export" and "import" services. Here are some examples.

If you take a vacation in France and travel there on an Air France flight from Montreal, you import transportation services from France. The money you spend in France on hotel bills and restaurant meals is also classified as the import of services. Similarly, the money spent by a French student on vacation in Canada is a Canadian export of services to France.

When we import TV sets from South Korea, the owner of the ship that transports them might be Greek and the company that insures them might be British. The payments that we make for the transportation and insurance are Canadian imports of services. Similarly, when a Canadian shipping company transports timber from British Columbia to Tokyo, the transportation cost is a Canadian export of a service to Japan. Our international trade in these types of services is large and growing.

Geographical Patterns of International Trade

Canada has trading links with every part of the world, but the United States is our biggest trading partner. In 2004, 82 percent of our exports went to the United States and 69 percent of our imports came from the United States. Our trade with the European Union is also large—6 percent of our exports and 10 percent of our imports in 2004. Other trading partners include the countries of Latin America and Japan. But our trade with Japan is only 2 percent of exports and 3 percent of imports.

Trends in the Volume of Trade

In 1978, we exported 25 percent of total output and imported 25 percent of the goods and services that we bought. In 2004, we exported 44 percent of total output and imported 39 percent of the goods and services that we bought.

On the export side, capital goods, automobiles, food, and raw materials have remained large items and held a roughly constant share of total exports. But the composition of imports has changed. Food and raw material imports have fallen steadily. Imports of fuel increased during the 1970s but decreased during the 1980s. Imports of machinery have grown and today approach 30 percent of total imports.

Net Exports and International Borrowing

The value of exports minus the value of imports is called **net exports**. In 2004, Canadian net exports were $54 billion. Our exports were $54 billion more than our imports. When we export more than we import, as we did in 2004, we lend to foreigners or buy some of their assets. When we import more than we export, we borrow from foreigners or sell some of our assets to them.

myeconlab   Study Plan 32.1

The Gains from International Trade

THE FUNDAMENTAL FORCE THAT GENERATES international trade is *comparative advantage*. And the basis of comparative advantage is divergent *opportunity costs*. You met these ideas in Chapter 2, when we learned about comparative advantages and the gains from specialization and trade between Liz and Joe.

Joe specializes in producing just one good, but most nations, like Liz, do not go to the extreme of specializing in a single good and importing everything else. Like Liz and Joe, nations can increase the consumption of all goods if they redirect their scarce resources towards the production of those goods and services in which they have a comparative advantage.

To see how this outcome occurs, we'll apply the same basic ideas that we learned in the case of Liz and Joe to trade among nations. We'll begin by recalling how we can use the production possibilities frontier to measure opportunity cost. Then we'll see how divergent opportunity costs bring comparative advantage and how by moving resources to increase production of the good in which each country has a comparative advantage countries can gain from international trade, just as Liz and Joe did.

Opportunity Cost in Farmland

Farmland (a fictitious country) can produce grain and cars at any point inside or along its production possibilities frontier, *PPF*, shown in Fig. 32.1. (We're holding constant the output of all the other goods that Farmland produces.) The Farmers (the people of Farmland) are consuming all the grain and cars that they produce, and they are operating at point *A* in the figure. That is, Farmland is producing and consuming 15 million tonnes of grain and 8 million cars each year. What is the opportunity cost of a car in Farmland?

We can answer that question by calculating the slope of the production possibilities frontier at point *A*. The magnitude of the slope of the frontier measures the opportunity cost of one good in terms of the other. To measure the slope of the frontier at point *A*, place a straight line tangential to the frontier at point *A* and calculate the slope of that straight line. Recall that the formula for the slope of a line is the change in the value of the variable measured on the *y*-axis divided by the change in the value of the variable

measured on the *x*-axis as we move along the line. Here, the variable measured on the *y*-axis is millions of tonnes of grain, and the variable measured on the *x*-axis is millions of cars. So the slope is the change in the number of tonnes of grain divided by the change in the number of cars.

As you can see from the red triangle at point *A* in the figure, if the number of cars produced increases by 2 million, grain production decreases by 18 million tonnes. So the magnitude of the slope is 18 million divided by 2 million, which equals 9. That is, to get 1 more car, the people of Farmland must give up 9 tonnes of grain. So the opportunity cost of 1 car is 9 tonnes of grain. Equivalently, 9 tonnes of grain cost 1 car. For the people of Farmland, these opportunity costs are the prices they face. The price of a car is 9 tonnes of grain, and the price of 9 tonnes of grain is 1 car.

FIGURE 32.1
Opportunity Cost in Farmland

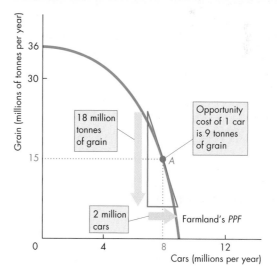

Farmland produces and consumes 15 million tonnes of grain and 8 million cars a year. That is, it produces and consumes at point *A* on its production possibilities frontier. Opportunity cost is equal to the magnitude of the slope of the production possibilities frontier. The red triangle tells us that at point *A*, 18 million tonnes of grain must be forgone to get 2 million cars. That is, at point *A*, 2 million cars cost 18 million tonnes of grain. Equivalently, 1 car costs 9 tonnes of grain or 9 tonnes of grain cost 1 car.

Opportunity Cost in Mobilia

Figure 32.2 shows the production possibilities frontier of Mobilia (another fictitious country). Like the Farmers, the Mobilians consume all the grain and cars that they produce. Mobilia consumes 18 million tonnes of grain a year and 4 million cars, at point A'.

Let's calculate the opportunity costs in Mobilia. At point A', the opportunity cost of a car is equal to the magnitude of the slope of the red line tangential to the production possibilities frontier, *PPF*. You can see from the red triangle that the magnitude of the slope of Mobilia's production possibilities frontier is 6 million tonnes of grain divided by 6 million cars, which equals 1 tonne of grain per car. To get 1 more car, the Mobilians must give up 1 tonne of grain. So the opportunity cost of 1 car is 1 tonne of grain, or equivalently, the opportunity cost of 1 tonne of grain is 1 car. These are the prices faced in Mobilia.

Comparative Advantage

Cars are cheaper in Mobilia than in Farmland. One car costs 9 tonnes of grain in Farmland but only

FIGURE 32.2
Opportunity Cost in Mobilia

Mobilia produces and consumes 18 million tonnes of grain and 4 million cars a year. That is, it produces and consumes at point A' on its production possibilities frontier. Opportunity cost is equal to the magnitude of the slope of the production possibilities frontier. The red triangle tells us that at point A', 6 million tonnes of grain must be forgone to get 6 million cars. That is, at point A', 6 million cars cost 6 million tonnes of grain. Equivalently, 1 car costs 1 tonne of grain or 1 tonne of grain costs 1 car.

1 tonne of grain in Mobilia. But grain is cheaper in Farmland than in Mobilia—9 tonnes of grain cost only 1 car in Farmland, while that same amount of grain costs 9 cars in Mobilia.

Mobilia has a comparative advantage in car production. Farmland has a comparative advantage in grain production. A country has a comparative advantage in producing a good if it can produce that good at a lower opportunity cost than any other country. Let's see how opportunity cost differences and comparative advantage generate gains from international trade.

The Gains from Trade: Cheaper to Buy Than to Produce

If Mobilia bought grain for what it costs Farmland to produce it, then Mobilia could buy 9 tonnes of grain for 1 car. That is much lower than the cost of growing grain in Mobilia, for there it costs 9 cars to produce 9 tonnes of grain. If the Mobilians can buy grain at the low Farmland price, they will reap some gains.

If the Farmers can buy cars for what it costs Mobilia to produce them, they will be able to obtain a car for 1 tonne of grain. Because it costs 9 tonnes of grain to produce a car in Farmland, the Farmers would gain from such an opportunity.

In this situation, it makes sense for Mobilians to buy their grain from Farmers and for Farmers to buy their cars from Mobilians. But at what price will Farmland and Mobilia engage in mutually beneficial international trade?

The Terms of Trade

The quantity of grain that Farmland must pay Mobilia for a car is Farmland's **terms of trade** with Mobilia. Because Canada exports and imports many different goods and services, we measure the terms of trade in the real world as an index number that averages the terms of trade over all the items we trade.

The forces of international supply and demand determine the terms of trade. Figure 32.3 illustrates these forces in the Farmland–Mobilia international car market. The quantity of cars *traded internationally* is measured on the *x*-axis. On the *y*-axis, we measure the price of a car. This price is expressed as the *terms of trade*: tonnes of grain per car. If no international trade takes place, the price of a car in Farmland is 9 tonnes of grain, its opportunity cost, indicated by

FIGURE 32.3

International Trade in Cars

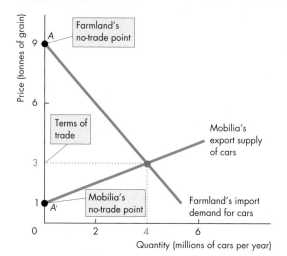

Farmland's import demand curve for cars is downward sloping, and Mobilia's export supply curve of cars is upward sloping. Without international trade, the price of a car is 9 tonnes of grain in Farmland (point A) and 1 tonne of grain in Mobilia (point A').

With free international trade, the price (terms of trade) is determined where the export supply curve intersects the import demand curve: 3 tonnes of grain per car. At that price, 4 million cars a year are imported by Farmland and exported by Mobilia. The value of grain exported by Farmland and imported by Mobilia is 12 million tonnes a year, the quantity required to pay for the cars imported.

point *A* in the figure. Again, if no trade takes place, the price of a car in Mobilia is 1 tonne of grain, its opportunity cost, indicated by point *A'* in the figure. The no-trade points *A* and *A'* in Fig. 32.3 correspond to the points identified by those same letters in Figs. 32.1 and 32.2. The lower the price of a car (terms of trade), the greater is the quantity of cars that the Farmers are willing to import from the Mobilians. This fact is illustrated by the downward-sloping curve, which shows Farmland's import demand for cars.

The Mobilians respond in the opposite direction. The higher the price of a car (terms of trade), the greater is the quantity of cars that Mobilians are willing to export to Farmers. This fact is reflected in Mobilia's export supply of cars—the upward-sloping line in Fig. 32.3.

The international market in cars determines the equilibrium terms of trade (price) and quantity traded. This equilibrium occurs where the import demand curve intersects the export supply curve. In this case, the equilibrium terms of trade are 3 tonnes of grain per car. Mobilia exports and Farmland imports 4 million cars a year. Notice that the terms of trade are lower than the initial price in Farmland but higher than the initial price in Mobilia.

Balanced Trade

The number of cars exported by Mobilia—4 million a year—is exactly equal to the number of cars imported by Farmland. How does Farmland pay for its cars? The answer is by exporting grain. How much grain does Farmland export? You can find the answer by noticing that for 1 car, Farmland must pay 3 tonnes of grain. So for 4 million cars, Farmland pays 12 million tonnes of grain. Farmland's exports of grain are 12 million tonnes a year, and Mobilia imports this same quantity of grain.

Mobilia is exchanging 4 million cars for 12 million tonnes of grain each year, and Farmland is doing the opposite: exchanging 12 million tonnes of grain for 4 million cars. Trade is balanced between these two countries. The value received from exports equals the value paid out for imports.

Changes in Production and Consumption

We've seen that international trade makes it possible for Farmers to buy cars at a lower price than they can produce them and sell their grain for a higher price. International trade also enables Mobilians to sell their cars for a higher price and buy grain for a lower price. Both countries gain. How is it possible for *both* countries to gain? What are the changes in production and consumption that accompany these gains?

An economy that does not trade with other economies has identical production and consumption possibilities. Without trade, the economy can consume only what it produces. But with international trade, an economy can consume different quantities of goods from those that it produces. The production possibilities frontier describes the limit of what a country can produce, but it does not describe the limits to what it can consume. Figure 32.4 will help you to see the distinction between production possibilities and consumption possibilities when a country trades with other countries.

FIGURE 32.4
Expanding Consumption Possibilities

(a) Farmland

(b) Mobilia

With no international trade, the Farmers produce and consume at point *A* and the opportunity cost of a car is 9 tonnes of grain (the slope of the black line in part a). Also, with no international trade, the Mobilians produce and consume at point *A'* and the opportunity cost of 1 tonne of grain is 1 car (the slope of the black line in part b).

    Goods can be exchanged internationally at a price of 3 tonnes of grain for 1 car along the red line in each part of the figure. In part (a), Farmland decreases its production of cars and increases its production of grain, moving from

A to *B*. It exports grain and imports cars, and it consumes at point *C*. The Farmers have more of both cars and grain than they would if they produced all their own consumption goods—at point *A*. In part (b), Mobilia increases car production and decreases grain production, moving from *A'* to *B'*. Mobilia exports cars and imports grain, and it consumes at point *C'*. The Mobilians have more of both cars and grain than they would if they produced all their own consumption goods—at point *A'*.

First of all, notice that the figure has two parts: part (a) for Farmland and part (b) for Mobilia. The production possibilities frontiers that you saw in Figs. 32.1 and 32.2 are reproduced here. The slopes of the two black lines in the figure represent the opportunity costs in the two countries when there is no international trade. Farmland produces and consumes at point *A*, and Mobilia produces and consumes at *A'*. Cars cost 9 tonnes of grain in Farmland and 1 tonne of grain in Mobilia.

Consumption Possibilities The red line in each part of Fig. 32.4 shows the country's consumption possibilities with international trade. These two red

lines have the same slope, and the magnitude of that slope is the opportunity cost of a car in terms of grain on the world market: 3 tonnes per car. The *slope* of the consumption possibilities line is common to both countries because its magnitude equals the *world* price. But the position of a country's consumption possibilities line depends on the country's production possibilities. A country cannot produce outside its production possibilities curve, so its consumption possibilities curve touches its production possibilities curve. Farmland could choose to consume at point *B* with no international trade or, with international trade, at any point on its red consumption possibilities line.

Free Trade Equilibrium With international trade, the producers of cars in Mobilia can get a higher price for their output. As a result, they increase car production. At the same time, grain producers in Mobilia get a lower price for their grain, and so they reduce grain production. Producers in Mobilia adjust their output by moving along their production possibilities frontier until the opportunity cost in Mobilia equals the world price (the opportunity cost in the world market). This situation arises when Mobilia is producing at point B' in Fig. 32.4(b).

But the Mobilians do not consume at point B'. That is, they do not increase their consumption of cars and decrease their consumption of grain. Instead, they sell some of their car production to Farmland in exchange for some of Farmland's grain. They trade internationally. But to see how that works out, we first need to check in with Farmland to see what's happening there.

In Farmland, producers of cars now get a lower price and producers of grain get a higher price. As a consequence, producers in Farmland decrease car production and increase grain production. They adjust their outputs by moving along the production possibilities frontier until the opportunity cost of a car in terms of grain equals the world price (the opportunity cost on the world market). They move to point B in part (a). But the Farmers do not consume at point B. Instead, they trade some of their additional grain production for the now cheaper cars from Mobilia.

The figure shows us the quantities consumed in the two countries. We saw in Fig. 32.3 that Mobilia exports 4 million cars a year and Farmland imports those cars. We also saw that Farmland exports 12 million tonnes of grain a year and Mobilia imports that grain. So Farmland's consumption of grain is 12 million tonnes a year less than it produces, and its consumption of cars is 4 million a year more than it produces. Farmland consumes at point C in Fig. 32.4(a).

Similarly, we know that Mobilia consumes 12 million tonnes of grain more than it produces and 4 million cars fewer than it produces. Mobilia consumes at point C' in Fig. 32.4(b).

Calculating the Gains from Trade

You can now literally see the gains from trade in Fig. 32.4. Without trade, Farmers produce and consume at A (part a)—a point on Farmland's production possibilities frontier. With international trade, Farmers

consume at point C in part (a)—a point *outside* the production possibilities frontier. At point C, Farmers are consuming 3 million tonnes of grain a year and 1 million cars a year more than before. These increases in consumption of both cars and grain, beyond the limits of the production possibilities frontier, are the Farmers' gains from international trade.

Mobilians also gain. Without trade, they consume at point A' in part (b)—a point on Mobilia's production possibilities frontier. With international trade, they consume at point C'—a point outside their production possibilities frontier. With international trade, Mobilia consumes 3 million tonnes of grain a year and 1 million cars a year more than it would without trade. These are the gains from international trade for Mobilia.

Gains for Both Countries

Trade between the Farmers and the Mobilians does not create a winner and a loser. Both countries gain. Farmers selling grain and Mobilians selling cars face an increased demand for their products because the net demand by foreigners is added to domestic demand. With an increase in demand, the price rises.

Farmers buying cars and Mobilians buying grain face an increased supply of these products because the net foreign supply is added to domestic supply. With an increase in supply, the price falls.

Gains from Trade in Reality

The gains from trade that we have just studied between Farmland and Mobilia in grain and cars occur in a model economy—in a world economy that we have imagined. But these same phenomena occur every day in the real global economy.

Comparative Advantage in the Global Economy
We buy TVs and DVD players from Korea, machinery from Europe, and fashion goods from Hong Kong. In exchange, we sell machinery, grain and lumber, airplanes, computers, and financial services. All this international trade is generated by comparative advantage, just like the international trade between Farmland and Mobilia in our model economy. All international trade arises from comparative advantage, even when trade is in similar goods such as tools and machines. At first thought, it seems puzzling that countries exchange manufactured goods. Why doesn't each developed country produce all the manufactured goods its citizens want to buy?

Trade in Similar Goods Why does Canada produce airplanes for export at the same time that Air Canada and our other airlines buy airplanes from the United States and Europe? Wouldn't it make more sense to produce all the airplanes that Air Canada and other Canadian airlines want to buy here in Canada? After all, we have access to the best technology available for producing planes. Aerospace workers in Canada are surely as productive as their fellow workers in the United States and Europe. So why does Canada have a comparative advantage in some types of airplanes and the United States and Europe in others?

Diversity of Taste and Economies of Scale The first part of the answer is that buyers have a large diversity of wants. Let's stick with the example of airplanes. Some airline operators sell time-share services in small executive jets, some airlines fly short routes in sparsely populated areas, some fly short routes in densely populated areas, some serve long-haul intercontinental routes that have heavy traffic, some serve long-haul intercontinental routes that have light traffic, some carry people and some specialize in cargo.

Because they face such highly varied markets, the airlines and other firms that offer air transportation services look for the types of airplanes that most closely match their wants. The large diversity in the characteristics of air transportation services means that airlines are willing to pay more for an airplane that matches their needs than they would be willing to pay for a single one-type-all-purpose airplane.

The second part of the answer to the puzzle is economies of scale—the tendency for the average cost to be lower, the larger the scale of production. In such situations, larger and larger production runs lead to ever lower average costs. Production of many goods, including airplanes, involves economies of scale. For example, if Bombardier makes only a handful of planes of a particular type and design, it must use production techniques that are much more labour-intensive and much less automated than those employed to make a hundred planes of a particular model. With short production runs and labour-intensive production techniques, costs are high. With very large production runs and automated assembly lines, production costs are much lower. But to obtain lower costs, the automated assembly lines have to produce a large number of planes.

It is the combination of diversity of wants and economies of scale that determines opportunity cost, produces comparative advantages, and generates such a large amount of international trade in similar commodities. With international trade, each airplane maker has the whole world market to serve. Each producer can specialize in a limited range of products and then sell its output to the entire world market.

This arrangement enables large production runs on the most popular planes to achieve economies of scale and low production costs.

The situation in the market for airplanes is also present in many other industries, especially those producing specialized equipment and parts. For example, Canada exports illustration software but imports database software, exports telecommunications systems but imports PCs, exports specialized video equipment but imports DVD players. International trade in similar but slightly different manufactured products is profitable.

REVIEW QUIZ

1 What is the fundamental source of the gains from international trade?

2 In what circumstances can countries gain from international trade?

3 What determines the goods and services that a country will export?

4 What determines the goods and services that a country will import?

5 What is comparative advantage and what role does it play in determining the amount and type of international trade that occurs?

6 How can it be that all countries gain from international trade and that there are no losers?

7 Provide some examples of comparative advantage in today's world.

8 Why does Canada both export and import automobiles?

myeconlab **Study Plan 32.2**

You've now seen how free trade brings gains for all countries. But trade is not free in our world. We'll now take a brief look at the history of trade restrictions and work out their effects. We'll see that free trade brings the greatest possible benefits and that international trade restrictions are costly.

International Trade Restrictions

GOVERNMENTS RESTRICT INTERNATIONAL TRADE to protect domestic industries from foreign competition by using two main tools:

1. Tariffs
2. Nontariff barriers

A **tariff** is a tax that is imposed by the importing country when an imported good crosses its international boundary. A **nontariff barrier** is any action other than a tariff that restricts international trade. Examples of nontariff barriers are quantitative restrictions and licensing regulations limiting imports. First, let's look at tariffs.

The History of Tariffs

The Canadian economy has always been protected by a tariff. Figure 32.5 shows the history of that tariff, from Confederation through 2004. The figure shows tariffs as a percentage of total imports—the average tariff rate. As you can see, the average tariff rate climbed from the early 1870s to exceed 20 percent by the late 1880s. The rate fluctuated but gradually decreased through the early 1920s. It increased again

during the Great Depression years of the early 1930s. During these years, most countries increased their tariff rates in what became a "beggar-thy-neighbour" policy. The average tariff then decreased through the late 1930s and continued its decrease throughout the years after World War II. Today, the average tariff rate is less than 1 percent.

The reduction in tariffs after World War II followed the signing in 1947 of the **General Agreement on Tariffs and Trade** (GATT). From its formation, GATT organized a series of "rounds" of negotiations that resulted in a steady process of tariff reduction. One of these, the Kennedy Round that began in the early 1960s, resulted in large tariff cuts starting in 1967. Another, the Tokyo Round, resulted in further tariff cuts in 1979. The final round, the Uruguay Round, started in 1986 and was completed in 1994.

The Uruguay Round was the most ambitious and comprehensive of the rounds and led to the creation of the **World Trade Organization** (WTO). Membership of the WTO brings greater obligations for countries to observe the GATT rules. Canada signed the Uruguay Round agreements, and Parliament ratified them in 1994.

In 2005, the WTO embarked on the Doha Round, which aimed to further liberalize world trade. But at the end of 2005, this round was stalled by disagreement on U.S. and E.U. agricultural subsidies.

FIGURE 32.5
Canadian Tariffs: 1867–2004

Canadian tariffs were in place before Confederation. Tariffs increased sharply in the 1870s and remained high until the 1930s. Since the establishment of the GATT in 1947, tariffs have steadily declined in a series of negotiating rounds, the most significant of which are identified in the figure. Tariffs are now as low as they have ever been.

Sources of data: Statistics Canada, *Historial Statistics of Canada,* Series G485, CANSIM Tables 380–0002 and 380–0034.

In addition to the agreements under the GATT and the WTO, Canada is a party to the **North American Free Trade Agreement** (NAFTA), which became effective on January 1, 1994, and under which barriers to international trade among the United States, Canada, and Mexico will be virtually eliminated after a 15-year phasing-in period.

In other parts of the world, trade barriers have virtually been eliminated among the member countries of the European Union, which has created the largest unified tariff-free market in the world. In 1994, discussions among the Asia-Pacific Economic Cooperation (APEC) led to an agreement in principle to work towards a free-trade area that embraces China, all the economies of East Asia and the South Pacific, and the United States and Canada. These countries include the fastest-growing economies and hold the promise of heralding a global free-trade area.

The effort to achieve freer trade underlines the fact that trade in some goods is still subject to a high tariff. Textiles and footwear are among the goods that face the highest tariffs, and rates on these items average more than 10 percent. Some individual items face a tariff much higher than the average. For example, when you buy a pair of blue jeans for $20, you pay about $5 more than you would if there were no tariffs on textiles. Other goods that are protected by tariffs are agricultural products, energy and chemicals, minerals, and metals. The meat, cheese, milk, and eggs that you consume cost significantly more because of protection than they would with free international trade.

The temptation for governments to impose tariffs is a strong one. First, tariffs provide revenue to the government. Second, they enable the government to satisfy special interest groups in import-competing industries. But, as we'll see, free international trade brings enormous benefits that are reduced when tariffs are imposed. Let's see how.

How Tariffs Work

To see how tariffs work, let's return to the example of trade between Farmland and Mobilia. Figure 32.6 shows the international market for cars in which these two countries are the only traders. The volume of trade and the price of a car are determined at the point of intersection of Mobilia's export supply curve of cars and Farmland's import demand curve for cars.

In Fig. 32.6, these two countries trade cars and grain in exactly the same way that we saw in Fig. 32.3.

FIGURE 32.6
The Effects of a Tariff

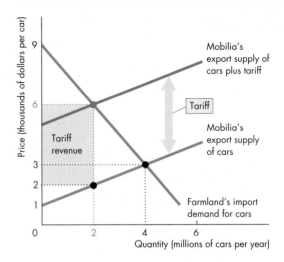

Farmland imposes a tariff on car imports from Mobilia. The tariff increases the price that Farmers have to pay for cars. It shifts the supply curve of cars in Farmland leftward. The vertical distance between the original supply curve and the new one is the amount of the tariff, $4,000 per car. The price of a car in Farmland increases, and the quantity of cars imported decreases. The government of Farmland collects a tariff revenue of $4,000 per car—a total of $8 billion on the 2 million cars imported. Farmland's exports of grain decrease because Mobilia now has a lower income from its exports of cars.

Mobilia exports cars, and Farmland exports grain. The volume of car imports into Farmland is 4 million a year, and the world market price of a car is 3 tonnes of grain. Figure 32.6 expresses prices in dollars rather than in units of grain and is based on a money price of grain of $1,000 a tonne. With grain costing $1,000 a tonne, the money price of a car is $3,000.

Now suppose that the government of Farmland, perhaps under pressure from car producers, decides to impose a tariff on imported cars. In particular, suppose that a tariff of $4,000 per car is imposed. (This is a huge tariff, but the car producers of Farmland are pretty fed up with competition from Mobilia.) What happens?

■ The supply of cars in Farmland decreases.

■ The price of a car in Farmland rises.

■ The quantity of cars imported by Farmland decreases.

■ The government of Farmland collects the tariff revenue.

■ Resource use is inefficient.

■ The *value* of exports changes by the same amount as the *value* of imports, and trade remains balanced.

Change in the Supply of Cars Farmland cannot buy cars at Mobilia's export supply price. It must pay that price plus the $4,000 tariff. So the supply curve in Farmland shifts leftward. The new supply curve is that labelled "Mobilia's export supply of cars plus tariff." The vertical distance between Mobilia's original export supply curve and the new supply curve is the tariff of $4,000 a car.

Rise in Price of a Car A new equilibrium occurs where the new supply curve intersects Farmland's import demand curve for cars. That equilibrium is at a price of $6,000 a car, up from $3,000 with free trade.

Fall in Imports Car imports fall from 4 million to 2 million cars a year. At the higher price of $6,000 a car, domestic car producers increase their production. Domestic grain production decreases as resources are moved into the expanding car industry.

Tariff Revenue Total expenditure on imported cars by the Farmers is $6,000 a car multiplied by the 2 million cars imported ($12 billion). But not all of that money goes to the Mobilians. They receive $2,000 a car, or $4 billion for the 2 million cars. The difference—$4,000 a car, or a total of $8 billion for the 2 million cars—is collected by the government of Farmland as tariff revenue.

Inefficiency The people of Farmland are willing to pay $6,000 for the marginal car imported. But the opportunity cost of that car is $2,000. So there is a gain from trading an extra car. In fact, there are gains—willingness to pay exceeds opportunity cost—all the way up to 4 million cars a year. Only when 4 million cars are being traded is the maximum price that a Farmer is willing to pay equal to the minimum price that is acceptable to a Mobilian. Restricting trade reduces the gains from trade.

Trade Remains Balanced With free trade, Farmland was paying $3,000 a car and buying 4 million cars a year from Mobilia. The total amount paid to Mobilia for imports was $12 billion a year. With a tariff, Farmland's imports have been cut to 2 million cars a year and the price paid to Mobilia has also been cut to only $2,000 a car. The total amount paid to Mobilia for imports has been cut to $4 billion a year. Doesn't this fact mean that Farmland now has a balance of trade surplus? It does not.

The price of a car in Mobilia has fallen. But the price of grain remains at $1 a tonne. So the relative price of a car has fallen, and the relative price of grain has increased. With free trade, the Mobilians could buy 3,000 tonnes of grain for the price of one car. Now they can buy only 2,000 tonnes for the price of a car. With a higher relative price of grain, the quantity demanded by the Mobilians decreases and Mobilia imports less grain. But because Mobilia imports less grain, Farmland exports less grain. In fact, Farmland's grain industry suffers from two sources. First, there is a decrease in the quantity of grain sold to Mobilia. Second, there is increased competition for inputs from the now-expanded car industry. The tariff leads to a contraction in the scale of the grain industry in Farmland.

It seems paradoxical at first that a country imposing a tariff on cars hurts its own export industry, lowering its exports of grain. It may help to think of it this way: Mobilians buy grain with the money they make from exporting cars to Farmland. If they export fewer cars, they cannot afford to buy as much grain. In fact, in the absence of any international borrowing and lending, Mobilia must cut its imports of grain by exactly the same amount as the loss in revenue from its export of cars. Grain imports into Mobilia are cut back to a value of $4 billion, the amount that can be paid for by the new lower revenue from Mobilia's car exports. Trade is still balanced. The tariff cuts imports and exports by the same amount. The tariff has no effect on the *balance* of trade, but it reduces the *volume* of trade.

The result that we have just derived is perhaps one of the most misunderstood aspects of international economics. On countless occasions, politicians and others call for tariffs to lower a balance of trade deficit or argue that lowering tariffs will create a balance of trade deficit. The balance of international trade is not caused by a lack of competitiveness. Its cause lies in a nation's saving as you'll see later in this chapter (on pp. 774–775).

Nontariff Barriers

The two main forms of nontariff barriers are

1. Quotas
2. Voluntary export restraints

A **quota** is a quantitative restriction on the import of a particular good, which specifies the maximum amount of the good that may be imported in a given period of time. A **voluntary export restraint** (VER) is an agreement between two governments in which the government of the exporting country agrees to restrain the volume of its own exports.

Quotas are especially prominent in agriculture. Voluntary export restraints are used to regulate trade between Japan and Canada.

How Quotas and VERs Work

To see how a quota works, suppose that Farmland imposes a quota that restricts its car imports to 2 million cars a year. Figure 32.7 shows the effects of this action. The quota is shown by the vertical red line at 2 million cars a year. Because it is illegal to exceed the quota, car importers buy only that quantity from Mobilia, for which they pay $2,000 a car. But because the import supply of cars is restricted to 2 million cars a year, people are willing to pay $6,000 per car. This is the price of a car in Farmland.

The value of imports falls to $4 billion, exactly the same as in the case of the tariff in Fig. 32.6. So with lower incomes from car exports and with a higher relative price of grain, Mobilians cut back on their imports of grain in exactly the same way that they did under a tariff.

The key difference between a quota and a tariff lies in who collects the gap between the import supply price and the domestic price. In the case of a tariff, it is the government of the importing country. In the case of a quota, it goes to the person who has the right to import under the import quota regulations.

A VER is like a quota arrangement in which quotas are allocated to each exporting country. The effects of a VER are similar to those of a quota but differ from them in that the gap between the domestic price and the export price is captured not by domestic importers but by the foreign exporter. The government of the exporting country has to establish procedures for allocating the restricted volume of exports among its producers.

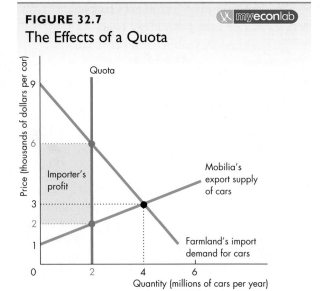

FIGURE 32.7   ⓧ myeconlab

The Effects of a Quota

Farmland imposes a quota of 2 million cars a year on car imports from Mobilia. That quantity appears as the vertical line labelled Quota. Because the quantity of cars supplied by Mobilia is restricted to 2 million, the price of a car in Farmland increases to $6,000. Importing cars is profitable because Mobilia is willing to supply cars at $2,000 each. There is competition for import quotas.

REVIEW QUIZ

1 What are the tools that a country can use to restrict international trade?
2 What do international trade restrictions do to the gains from international trade?
3 Which is best for a country: restricted trade, no trade, or free trade? Why?
4 What does a tariff on imports do to the volume of imports and the volume of exports?
5 In the absence of international borrowing and lending, how do tariffs and other international trade restrictions influence the total value of imports and exports and the balance of trade— the value of exports minus the value of imports?

ⓧ myeconlab   **Study Plan 32.3**

We're now going to look at some commonly heard arguments for restricting international trade and see why they are almost never correct.

The Case Against Protection

FOR AS LONG AS NATIONS AND INTERNATIONAL trade have existed, people have debated whether a country is better off with free international trade or with protection from foreign competition. The debate continues, but for most economists, a verdict has been delivered and is the one you have just seen. Free trade promotes prosperity for all; protection is inefficient. We've seen the most powerful case for free trade in the example of how Farmland and Mobilia both benefit from their comparative advantage. But there is a broader range of issues in the free trade versus protection debate. Let's review these issues.

Three arguments for restricting international trade are

- The employment argument
- The infant-industry argument
- The dumping argument

Let's look at each in turn.

The Employment Argument

The argument that protection saves jobs goes as follows: When we buy shoes from Brazil or shirts from Taiwan, Canadian workers in these industries lose their jobs. With no earnings and poor prospects, these workers become a drain on welfare and spend less, causing a ripple effect of further job losses. The proposed solution to this problem is to ban imports of cheap foreign goods and protect Canadian jobs. This argument for protection does not withstand scrutiny for three reasons.

First, free trade does cost some jobs, but it also creates other jobs. It brings about a global rationalization of labour and allocates labour resources to their highest-valued activities. Because of international trade in textiles, tens of thousands of workers in Canada have lost their jobs because textile mills and other factories have closed. But tens of thousands of workers in other countries have gotten jobs because textile mills have opened there. And tens of thousands of Canadian workers have gotten better-paying jobs than those of textile workers because other export industries have expanded and created more jobs than have been destroyed.

Second, imports create jobs. They create jobs for retailers that sell imported goods and firms that service those goods. They also create jobs by creating incomes in the rest of the world, some of which are spent on imports of Canadian-made goods and services.

Although protection does save particular jobs, it does so at inordinate cost. A striking example of the cost of quotas is that of the quotas on the import of textiles. Quotas imposed under an international agreement called the Multifibre Arrangement (which ended in 2005) protected textile jobs, especially in the United States. The U.S. International Trade Commission (ITC) estimated that because of quotas, 72,000 jobs existed in textiles that would otherwise have disappeared and the annual clothing expenditure in the United States was $US 15.9 billion or $U.S. 160 per family higher than it will be with free trade. Equivalently, the ITC estimated that each textile job saved cost $US 221,000 a year.

The Infant-Industry Argument

The so-called **infant-industry argument** for protection is that it is necessary to protect a new industry to enable it to grow into a mature industry that can compete in world markets. The argument is based on the idea of *dynamic comparative advantage*, which can arise from learning-by-doing (see Chapter 2).

Learning-by-doing is a powerful engine of productivity growth, and comparative advantage does evolve and change because of on-the-job experience. But these facts do not justify protection.

First, the infant-industry argument is valid only if the benefits of learning-by-doing *not only* accrue to the owners and workers of the firms in the infant industry but also *spill over* to other industries and parts of the economy. For example, there are huge productivity gains from learning-by-doing in the manufacture of aircraft. But almost all of these gains benefit the stockholders and workers of Bombardier. Because the people making the decisions, bearing the risk, and doing the work are the ones who benefit, they take the dynamic gains into account when they decide on the scale of their activities. In this case, almost no benefits spill over to other parts of the economy, so there is no need for government assistance to achieve an efficient outcome.

Second, even if the case is made for protecting an infant industry, it is more efficient to do so by subsidizing the firms in the industry, with the subsidy paid out of taxes.

The Dumping Argument

Dumping occurs when a foreign firm sells its exports at a price below its cost of production. Dumping might be used by a firm that wants to gain a global monopoly. In this case, the foreign firm sells its output at a price below its cost to drive domestic firms out of business. When the domestic firms have gone, the foreign firm takes advantage of its monopoly position and charges a higher price for its product. Dumping is usually regarded as a justification for temporary countervailing tariffs.

But there are powerful reasons to resist the dumping argument for protection. First, it is virtually impossible to detect dumping because it is hard to determine a firm's costs. As a result, the test for dumping is whether a firm's export price is below its domestic price. But this test is a weak one because it can be rational for a firm to charge a low price in markets in which the quantity demanded is highly sensitive to price and a higher price in a market in which demand is less price-sensitive.

Second, it is hard to think of a good that is produced by a natural *global* monopoly. So even if all the domestic firms were driven out of business in some industry, it would always be possible to find several and usually many alternative foreign sources of supply and to buy at prices determined in competitive markets.

Third, if a good or service were a truly global natural monopoly, the best way of dealing with it would be by regulation—just as in the case of domestic monopolies. Such regulation would require international cooperation.

The three arguments for protection that we've just examined have an element of credibility. The counterarguments are in general stronger, however, so these arguments do not make the case for protection. But they are not the only arguments that you might encounter. There are many other newer arguments against globalization and for protection. The most common of them are that protection

- Maintains national security
- Allows us to compete with cheap foreign labour
- Brings diversity and stability
- Penalizes lax environmental standards
- Protects national culture
- Prevents rich countries from exploiting developing countries

Maintains National Security

The national security argument for protection is that a country must protect industries that produce defence equipment and armaments and industries on which the defence industries rely for their raw materials and other intermediate inputs. This argument for protection does not withstand close scrutiny.

First, it is an argument for international isolation, for in a time of war, there is no industry that does not contribute to national defence. Second, if the case is made for boosting the output of a strategic industry, it is more efficient to achieve this outcome with a subsidy to the firms in the industry that is financed out of taxes. Such a subsidy would keep the industry operating at the scale judged appropriate, and free international trade would keep the prices faced by consumers at their world market levels.

Allows Us to Compete with Cheap Foreign Labour

With the removal of tariffs in Canadian trade with Mexico, people said we would hear a "giant sucking sound" as jobs rushed to Mexico. Let's see what's wrong with this view.

The labour cost of a unit of output equals the wage rate divided by labour productivity. For example, if a Canadian auto worker earns $30 an hour and produces 15 units of output an hour, the average labour cost of a unit of output is $2. If a Mexican auto assembly worker earns $3 an hour and produces 1 unit of output an hour, the average labour cost of a unit of output is $3. Other things remaining the same, the higher a worker's productivity, the higher is the worker's wage rate. High-wage workers have high productivity. Low-wage workers have low productivity.

Although high-wage Canadian workers are more productive, on the average, than low-wage Mexican workers, there are differences across industries. Canadian labour is relatively more productive in some activities than in others. For example, the productivity of Canadian workers in producing financial services and telephone systems is relatively higher than their productivity in the production of metals and some standardized machine parts. The activities in which Canadian workers are relatively more productive than their Mexican counterparts are those in which Canada has a *comparative advantage*. By engaging in free trade, increasing our production and exports of the goods and services in which we have a comparative advantage and decreasing our production and increasing our imports of the goods and services in which our trading partners have a comparative advantage, we can make ourselves and the citizens of other countries better off.

Brings Diversity and Stability

A diversified investment portfolio is less risky than one that has all the eggs in one basket. The same is true for an economy's production. A diversified economy fluctuates less than an economy that produces only one or two goods.

But big, rich, diversified economies such as those of Canada, the United States, Japan, and Europe do not have this type of stability problem. Even a country such as Saudi Arabia that produces only one good (in this case, oil) can benefit from specializing in the activity at which it has a comparative advantage and then investing in a wide range of other countries to bring greater stability to its income and consumption.

Penalizes Lax Environmental Standards

Another argument for protection is that many poorer countries, such as Mexico, do not have the same environmental policies that we have and, because they are willing to pollute and we are not, we cannot compete with them without tariffs. So if they want free trade with the richer and "greener" countries, they must clean up their environments to our standards.

This argument for trade restrictions is not entirely convincing. A poor country is less able than a rich one to devote resources to achieving high environmental standards. So if free trade helps a poor country to become richer, it will also help that country to develop the means to improve its environment.

But there probably is a case for using the negotiation of free trade agreements such as NAFTA to hold member countries to higher environmental standards. There is an especially large payoff from using such bargaining to try to avoid irreversible damage to resources such as tropical rainforests.

Protects National Culture

The national culture argument is that free trade in books, magazines, movies, and television programs means U.S. domination and the end of local culture. So, the reasoning continues, it is necessary to protect domestic "culture" industries from free

international trade to ensure the survival of a national cultural identity.

Protection of these industries is common and takes the form of nontariff barriers. For example, local content regulations on radio and television broadcasting and in magazines is often required.

The cultural identity argument for protection has no merit. Writers, publishers, and broadcasters want to limit foreign competition so that they can earn larger economic profits. But many of the creators of so-called American cultural products are not Americans but the talented citizens of other countries, ensuring the survival of their national cultural identities in Hollywood! Also, if national culture is in danger, it isn't clear that preventing competition is the best way of restoring it to health. Competition among cultures might be a source of strength.

Prevents Rich Countries from Exploiting Developing Countries

Wage rates in some developing countries are indeed very low. Do we, by trading with these countries, exploit them and their workers?

By trading with developing countries, we increase the demand for the goods that these countries produce and, more significantly, we increase the demand for their labour. When the demand for labour in developing countries increases, the wage rate also increases. So, rather than exploiting people in developing countries, international trade improves their opportunities and increases their incomes.

We have reviewed five arguments in favour of protection and seen that they all have flaws and leave the case for free international trade a strong one.

Why Is International Trade Restricted?

Why, despite all the arguments against protection, is trade restricted? There are two key reasons:

- Tariff revenue
- Rent seeking

Tariff Revenue Government revenue is costly to collect. In the developed countries such as Canada, a well-organized tax collection system is in place that can generate billions of dollars of income tax and sales tax revenues. This tax collection system is made possible by the fact that most economic transactions are done by firms that must keep properly audited financial records. Without such records, the revenue collection agencies (for example, Canada Revenue Agency) would be severely hampered in the work. Even with audited financial accounts, some proportion of potential tax revenue is lost. Nonetheless, for the industrialized countries, income taxes and sales taxes are the major sources of revenue and the tariff plays a very small role.

But governments in developing countries have a difficult time collecting taxes from their citizens. Much economic activity takes place in an informal economy with few financial records. So only a small amount of revenue is collected from income taxes and sales taxes in these countries. The one area in which economic transactions are well recorded and audited is in international trade. So this activity is an attractive base for tax collection in these countries and is used much more extensively than in the developed countries.

Rent Seeking   Rent seeking is the major reason why international trade is restricted. Rent seeking is lobbying and other political activity that seeks to capture the gains from trade. Free trade increases consumption possibilities *on the average*, but not everyone shares in the gain and some people even lose. Free trade brings benefits to some and imposes costs on others, with total benefits exceeding total costs. It is the uneven distribution of costs and benefits that is the principal source of impediment to achieving more liberal international trade.

Think about our example of trade in cars and grain between Farmland and Mobilia. In Farmland, the benefits from free trade accrue to all the producers of grain and to those producers of cars who would not have to bear the costs of adjusting to a smaller car industry. Those costs are transition costs, not permanent costs. The costs of moving to free trade are borne by those car producers and their employees who have to become grain producers.

The number of people who gain will, in general, be enormous in comparison with the number who lose. The gain per person will therefore be rather small. But the loss per person to those who bear the loss will be large. Because the losses that fall on those who bear them are large, it pays those people to incur considerable expense to lobby against free trade. On the other hand, it does not pay those who gain to organize to achieve free trade. The gain from trade for any one individual is too small for that individual to spend much time or money on a political organization whose goal is to achieve free trade.

Winners—free traders—and losers–anti-free traders—each in pursuit of their self-interest, weigh benefits against costs and choose their best actions. But because only the anti-free traders have enough at stake, they will do more political lobbying than the free traders.

Compensating Losers

If, in total, the gains from free international trade exceed the losses, why don't those who stand to gain from free trade offer to compensate those who stand to lose so that everyone votes for free trade?

The main answer is that there are serious obstacles to providing direct and correctly calculated compensation. First, the cost of identifying the losers from free trade and of estimating the value of their losses would be enormous.

Second, it would never be clear whether a person who has fallen on hard times is suffering because of free trade or for other reasons, perhaps reasons that are largely under the control of the individual. Third, some people who look like losers at one point in time may, in fact, end up gaining. The young auto worker that loses her job in Windsor and becomes a computer assembly worker in Ottawa resents the loss of work and the need to move. But a year or two later, looking back on events, she counts herself fortunate. She has made a move that has increased her income and given her greater job security.

Despite the absence of explicit compensation, those who lose from a change in protection do receive some compensation. But compensation is not restricted to the losers from changes in trade policy. In Canada (and in all the other rich industrial countries) elaborate schemes are in place to ensure that people who suffer from economic change receive help during their transition to new activities.

Two major forms of compensation in Canada arise from interprovincial fiscal transfers and employment insurance. Interprovincial fiscal transfers result in tax dollars collected in the rich and expanding regions of the country being spent in the

When the United States and Canada negotiated the Canada–U.S. Free Trade Agreement (the predecessor of NAFTA), U.S. President Ronald Reagan (hand outstretched on the right) and Prime Minister Brian Mulroney (maple-leafed figure on the left), were able to go only as far as their national self-interested rent seekers would allow them to go in dismantling tariffs and other barriers to free trade between the world's two largest trading partners.

Cartoon by Alan King, *The Ottawa Citizen*, Canwest News Service. Reprinted by permission of Alan King/*The Ottawa Citizen*.

poorer regions. Employment insurance provides compensation for workers who lose their jobs regardless of the reason for the job loss. Jobs lost because of changes in international protection are included among those for which benefits are paid.

But because we do not explicitly compensate the losers from free international trade, protectionism remains a popular and permanent feature of our national economic and political life.

Protection to Avoid a Trade Deficit

In our review of the arguments for protection, we did not consider the idea of limiting imports to help a country to achieve an international trade surplus or avoid a deficit. But this argument is sometimes heard.

Today, Canada has a surplus in its international trade. But many countries have deficits and the United States is the largest deficit nation. Some people say that because China floods the United States with cheap goods, China is a major source of the U.S. deficit. So limiting imports from China is justified as a way of limiting the deficit. In the next section, you will see what determines a country's international trade balance and why a deficit doesn't justify protection.

REVIEW QUIZ

1 Can we save jobs, develop new industries, or restrain foreign monopoly by restricting international trade?

2 Can trade protection help to achieve national security goals, or better protect the environmental and national culture?

3 What is the main argument against international trade restrictions?

4 What are the two main reasons for imposing tariffs on imports?

5 What type of country benefits most from the revenue from tariffs? Provide some examples of such countries.

6 If international trade restrictions are costly, why do we use them? Why don't the people who gain from trade organize a political force that is strong enough to ensure that their interests are protected?

7 Why don't we have free trade and compensate the people who lose from it?

myeconlab **Study Plan 32.4**

The Balance of International Payments

SO FAR IN THIS CHAPTER, WE'VE LOOKED AT balanced trade between countries. We're now going to see what makes trade unbalanced—why countries have international deficits and surpluses. When a country has an international deficit, it must borrow from the rest of the world. And when a country has an international surplus, it must lend to the rest of the world. Let's look at the scale of Canada's international trading and borrowing and lending and at the way in which we keep our records of these transactions. These records are called the balance of payments accounts.

Balance of Payments Accounts

A country's *balance of payments accounts* record its international trading, borrowing, and lending. There are in fact three balance of payments accounts:

1. Current account
2. Capital account
3. Official settlements account

The *current account* records payments for imports of goods and services from abroad, receipts from exports of goods and services sold abroad, net interest paid abroad, and net transfers (such as foreign aid payments). The *current account balance* equals exports minus imports, net interest payments, and net transfers. The *capital account* records foreign investment in Canada minus Canadian investment abroad. The *official settlements account* records the change in official Canadian reserves. *Official Canadian reserves* are the government's holdings of foreign currency. If Canadian official reserves increase, the official settlements account balance is *negative*. The reason is that holding foreign money is like investing abroad. Canadian investment abroad is a minus item in the capital account and in the official settlements account. (By the same reasoning, if official Canadian reserves decrease, the official settlements account balance is *positive*.)

The sum of the balances on the three accounts always equals zero. That is, to pay for a current account deficit, we must either borrow more from abroad than we lend abroad or use our official reserves to cover the shortfall.

Table 32.1 shows the Canadian balance of payments accounts in 2004. Items in the current account and capital account that provide foreign currency to Canada have a plus sign; items that cost Canada foreign currency have a minus sign. The table shows that in 2004, exports plus net transfers exceeded imports plus net interest payments and the current account had a surplus of $29 billion.

What do we do with our current account surplus? We lend it to the rest of the world. The capital account tells us by how much. We borrowed $62 billion (foreign investment in Canada) but made loans of $88 billion (Canadian investment abroad). Thus our net foreign lending was $26 billion. A statistical discrepancy arises because of illegal and hidden transactions, which in 2004 was –$6 billion.

The sum of our current account balance, capital account balance and statistical discrepancy is the change in our official reserves. In 2004, reserves decreased because our current account balance of $29 billion plus the capital account balance of –$26 billion and the statistical discrepancy of –$6 billion was –$3 billion. When our reserves decrease, we record

TABLE 32.1   Canadian Balance of Payments Accounts in 2004

Current account	Billions of dollars
Imports of goods and services	–437
Exports of goods and services	+491
Net interest payments	–50
Net transfers	+25
Current account balance	+29

Capital account	
Foreign investment in Canada	+62
Canadian investment abroad	–88
Capital account balance	–26
Statistical discrepancy	–6

Official settlements account	
Official settlements account balance	+3

Source: Statistics Canada, CANSIM tables 376–0001 and 376–0002.

the official settlements balance as a positive number. Why? Because a decrease in our reserves is like borrowing from the rest of the world.

The numbers in Table 34.1 give a snapshot of the balance of payments accounts in 2004. Figure 32.8 puts that snapshot into perspective by showing the balance of payments between 1984 and 2004. Because the economy grows and the price level rises, changes in the dollar value of the balance of payments do not convey much information. To remove the influences of growth and inflation, Fig. 32.8 shows the balance of payments as a percentage of nominal GDP.

As you can see, the capital account balance is almost a mirror image of the current account balance. The official settlements balance is very small in comparison with the balances of these other two accounts. A large current account deficit (and capital account surplus) emerged during the 1980s but declined after 1993. By 1996 we had a small surplus and after two more years of deficit, the early 2000s saw an increasing current account surplus.

You can understand the balance of payments and the way the accounts are linked together if you think about the income and expenditure, borrowing and lending, and bank account of an individual.

Individual Analogy Joanne's income from her job in 2005 was $25,000 and she has $10,000 worth of investments that earned her an interest income of $1,000 in that year. Joanne's current account shows an income of $26,000. Joanne spent $18,000 on consumption goods and services. She also bought a new house, which cost her $60,000. So Joanne's total expenditure was $78,000. Her income minus her expenditure is –$52,000 ($26,000 minus $78,000). This amount is Joanne's current account deficit.

To cover her $52,000 deficit, Joanne has to use the money that she has in the bank or take a loan. Joanne took a mortgage of $50,000 to help buy her house so her capital account surplus was $50,000. With a current account deficit of $52,000 and a capital account surplus of $50,000, Joanne is still $2,000 short. She got that $2,000 from her bank account. Her cash holdings decreased by $2,000.

Joanne's income from work is like a country's income from exports. Her income from investments is like a country's interest income from foreigners. Her purchases of goods and services, are like a country's imports. Joanne's mortgage—borrowing from someone else—is like a country's borrowing from the rest of the world. The change in her bank account is like the change in the country's official reserves.

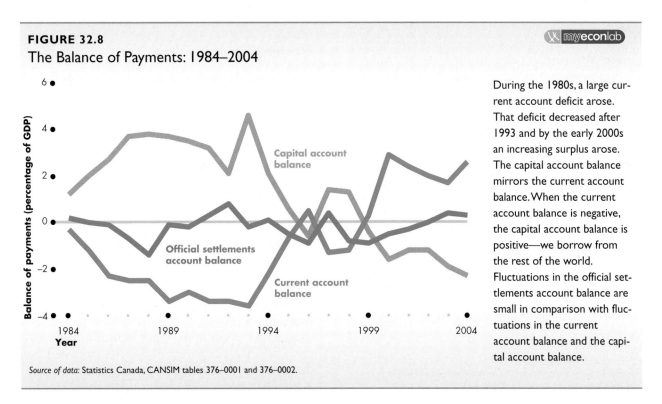

FIGURE 32.8

The Balance of Payments: 1984–2004

During the 1980s, a large current account deficit arose. That deficit decreased after 1993 and by the early 2000s an increasing surplus arose. The capital account balance mirrors the current account balance. When the current account balance is negative, the capital account balance is positive—we borrow from the rest of the world. Fluctuations in the official settlements account balance are small in comparison with fluctuations in the current account balance and the capital account balance.

Source of data: Statistics Canada, CANSIM tables 376–0001 and 376–0002.

Borrowers and Lenders, Debtors and Creditors

A country that has a current account deficit and that borrows more from the rest of the world than it lends to it is called a *net borrower*. Similarly, a *net lender* is a country that lends more to the rest of the world than it borrows from it.

From 1999 through 2004, Canada was a net lender. But most years, Canada has been a net borrower. And most countries are net borrowers.

A net borrower might be going deeper into debt or might simply be reducing its net assets held in the rest of the world. The total stock of foreign investment determines whether a country is a debtor or creditor. A *debtor nation* is a country that during its entire history has borrowed more from the rest of the world than it has lent to it. It has a stock of outstanding debt to the rest of the world that exceeds the stock of its own claims on the rest of the world. A *creditor nation* is a country that has invested more in the rest of the world than other countries have invested in it.

Canada is a debtor nation. Should we be concerned that Canada is a net borrower and debtor nation? The answer to this question depends on what we do with the funds that we borrow. If borrowing finances investment that in turn generates economic growth and higher income, borrowing is not a problem. If borrowing finances consumption, then higher interest payments are being incurred, and as a consequence, consumption will eventually have to be reduced. In this case, the more the borrowing and the longer it goes on, the greater is the reduction in consumption that will eventually be necessary.

Current Account Balance

The current account balance (in Table 32.1) is the sum of exports minus imports, net interest income, and net transfers. Exports minus imports equals net exports and fluctuations in net exports are the main source of fluctuations in the current account balance.

You are about to discover that net exports do not depend on our competitiveness in international markets. Instead, they depend on the government budget and private saving and investment. To see how, look at Table 32.2[1].

---

[1]If you've studied macroeconomics, you learned about the National Income Accounts in Chapter 20.

TABLE 32.2   Net Exports, the Government Budget, Saving, and Investment

	Symbols and equations	Canada in 2004 (billions of dollars)
(a) Variables		
Exports*	X	493
Imports*	M	438
Government expenditures	G	282
Net taxes	NT	302
Investment	I	234
Saving	S	269
(b) Balances		
Net exports	$X - M$	$493 - 438 = 55$
Government sector	$NT - G$	$302 - 282 = 20$
Private sector	$S - I$	$269 - 234 = 35$
(c) Relationship among balances		
National accounts	$Y = C + I + G + X - M$	
	$= C + S + NT$	
Rearranging:	$X - M = S - I + NT - G$	
Net exports	$X - M$	55
Equals:		
Government sector	$NT - G$	20
Plus		
Private sector	$S - I$	35

Source of data: Statistics Canada, CANSIM tables 380–0002 and 380–0022.

* The national income accounts' measures of exports and imports are different from the balance of payments' accounts measures by small amounts.

Part (a) lists the national income variables that we need, with their symbols. Part (b) defines three balances. We've just defined net exports. The *government sector balance* is equal to net taxes minus government expenditures on goods and services. If that number is positive, the government sector has a surplus that is lent to the other sectors; if that number is negative, the government sector has a deficit that must be financed by borrowing from the other sectors. The government sector balance is the sum of the balances of the federal, provincial, and municipal governments. The *private sector balance* is equal to saving minus investment. If saving exceeds investment, a private sector has a surplus and it is lent to other sectors. If investment exceeds saving, borrowing from other sectors finances a private sector deficit.

Part (b) shows the values of these balances for Canada in 2004. Net exports were a surplus of $55 billion. The government sector had a surplus of $20 billion. And the private sector had a surplus of $35 billion.

Part (c) shows the relationship among the three balances. From the national income accounts, we know that real GDP (Y) is the sum of consumption expenditure (C), investment (I), government expenditures (G), and net exports ($X - M$). It also equals the sum of consumption expenditure (C), saving (S), and net taxes (NT). Rearranging these equations tells us that net exports ($X - M$) is the sum of the government sector surplus ($NT - G$) and the private sector surplus ($S - I$). In Canada in 2004, the government sector had a surplus of $20 billion and the private sector had a surplus of $35 billion. The government sector surplus plus the private sector surplus equals net exports of $55 billion.

The Twin Deficits

You've seen that net exports equals the sum of the government surplus and the private surplus. And net exports plus debt interest (and other small transfers) equals the current account balance. What is the relationship over time between the current account balance and the government budget balance? How do these balances fluctuate over time? Figure 32.9 answers this question. It shows the government budget (the red line) and the current account balance (the blue line).

You can see that, with an important exception during the early 1980s, there is a tendency for the current account to go into a deeper deficit when the government budget goes into a deeper deficit. Because of the tendency for the government budget deficit and the current account deficit to move in the same direction they have been called the *twin deficits*.

Why are the two deficits linked? They are linked because capital is highly mobile in today's world. If the Canadian government increases expenditures or lowers taxes, total spending in Canada rises. But with the economy at or near full employment, the extra

FIGURE 32.9
The Twin Deficits

The current account balance and the government budget balance move in similar ways and look like twin deficits. But this relationship broke down during the early 1980s when the private sector surplus swelled.

Source of data: Statistics Canada, CANSIM tables 376–0001 and 380–0007.

goods and services demanded are sucked in from the rest of the world. Imports increase. Capital flows in to pay for those imports. Saving and investment don't change. This relationship broke down during the early 1980s because Canada was in recession and investment decreased relative to saving.

REVIEW QUIZ

1 What types of transactions do we record in the balance of payments accounts?
2 What transactions does the current account record? What transactions does the capital account record? What transactions does the official settlements account record?
3 What determines the current account balance?

myeconlab Study Plan 32.5

The North American Free Trade Agreement

THE NORTH AMERICAN FREE TRADE AGGREEMENT came into effect on January 1, 1994. It was the outgrowth of an earlier Canada–United States Free Trade Agreement, which was signed in 1988 and came into effect on January 1, 1989. Both agreements were struck only after years of intense negotiations and, on the Canadian side of the border, an intense political debate. First, let's look at the terms of the Canada–United States Free Trade Agreement and at the progress made in achieving freer trade between two of the world's largest trading partners.

The Terms of the Canada–United States Agreement

The main terms of the Canada–United States Free Trade Agreement are:

- Tariffs to be phased out through 1999
- Nontariff barriers to be reduced
- Free trade in energy products, with energy resource sharing in times of national shortage
- More freedom of trade in services
- Future negotiations to eliminate subsidies
- Creation of dispute-settling mechanisms

Removal of Tariffs Scheduled tariff cuts began on January 1, 1989 and were completed on January 1, 1998. But tariff protection remains in place and an atmosphere of tension prevails in many areas. Agriculture remains effectively protected with new tariffs that have replaced old quotas. And a series of *countervailing duties* has been introduced to offset the effects of domestic subsidies. Further, several *antidumping duties* have also been introduced in cases in which it is alleged that products are being exported at a price below the cost of production.

Nontariff Barriers Nontariff barriers such as government procurement policies of buying local products are removed by the agreement. Subsequent to entering into the free trade agreement, Canada and the United States took on additional obligations as members of the WTO that require the removal of agricultural quotas. Many agricultural quotas have been removed but they have been replaced with tar-

iffs. So despite the free trade agreement, we remain a long way from achieving free trade in agricultural products.

Energy Products Free trade in energy products existed before the free trade agreement but the agreement ratified the intent to maintain that arrangement. The agreement that scarce energy resources will be shared in times of national shortage became a controversial one. In effect, what the energy sharing clause amounts to is an agreement that governments will not intervene in energy markets to prevent firms from selling their energy to the other country.

Trade in Services International trade in services has expanded more quickly than trade in manufactured goods in recent years. The free trade agreement, recognizing this factor and seeking to facilitate further expansion of trade in services between the United States and Canada, incorporates two principles: the *right of establishment* and *national treatment*. The right of establishment means that American firms have the right to set up branches in Canada and Canadian firms have the right to set up operations in the United States. National treatment means that each country will treat the goods and firms and investors of the other country as if they were operating within its own borders.

Future Negotiations on Subsidies In both the United States and Canada, there are many subsidies, especially on agricultural products. The presence of subsidies causes problems and makes it legitimate under the agreement for the country importing subsidized goods to impose countervailing duties. As we have just noted, several such duties have been imposed.

Dispute-Settling Mechanisms The Free Trade Agreement included two dispute-settling mechanisms: one to settle disputes relating to all aspects of the agreement, and the other to deal with applications of countervailing duties and antidumping laws in either country. For example, the United States has applied for and received permission to impose countervailing duties on Canadian exports of durum wheat, lumber products, poultry, and live hogs. In each case, the United States accuses Canada of subsidizing these industries unfairly so that Canadian exports are cheaper than the prices at which U.S. producers can supply these goods.

The Extension of the Agreement: NAFTA

The North American Free Trade Agreement (NAFTA) is an agreement among Canada, the United States, and Mexico that has six objectives. They are to

1. Eliminate trade barriers
2. Promote conditions of fair competition
3. Increase investment opportunities
4. Protect intellectual property rights
5. Create an effective dispute resolution mechanism
6. Establish a framework for the expansion of the agreement to include other nations in the hemisphere

Effects of the Free Trade Agreement

Working out the effects of an agreement as complex as NAFTA is difficult, and there is no general consensus on what the effects have been. The theory that you have studied in this chapter predicts that the removal of tariffs will produce an increase in the *volume* of international trade. That is, the theory predicts that Canadians will increasingly specialize in those activities at which they have a comparative advantage and Mexicans and Americans will specialize in a different range of activities and that the three countries will exchange a larger volume of goods and services.

As predicted, trade among the three countries has increased. During the first five years of NAFTA, Canada's trade with the United States increased by 80 percent and Canada's trade with Mexico doubled.

The trade expansion that followed the entry of Mexico in 1995 was especially dramatic. Mexico's exports increased by 31 percent (in U.S. dollar value) in 1995 and by 21 percent in 1996, compared with increases that averaged less than 15 percent a year during the two years before the agreement. But trade expansion with Mexico has not been in one direction. Mexico's imports also increased following the agreement by 23 percent in both 1996 and 1997.

During the 1990s, Canada's exports expanded from less than 30 percent of total production to 36 percent, and Canada's imports have increased from 27 percent to 34 percent of total expenditure.

Canada greatly increased its exports of advertising services, office and telecommunications equipment, paper, and transportation services. And its imports of meat and dairy products, communications services, clothing, furniture, and processed foods and beverages also increased by a large percentage.

These huge changes in exports and imports brought gains from increased specialization and exchange. But they also brought a heavy toll of adjustment. Thousands of jobs were lost in the declining sectors and new jobs were created in the expanding sectors. The amount of job destruction in the years following the free trade agreement was historically high and the unemployment rate rose for three successive years. Only during the Great Depression did the rate of job destruction exceed that of the late 1980s and early 1990s. To what extent a high rate of labour market turnover was caused by the free trade agreement is unclear and controversial. But the net outcome of NAFTA appears to be strongly positive. More than a million new Canadian jobs were created between 1994 and 1999.

REVIEW QUIZ

1 Describe the main features of the Canada–U.S. Free Trade Agreement of 1988.
2 What effect has NAFTA had on nontariff barriers?
3 What effect has NAFTA had on trade in services?
4 How has the volume of trade among Canada, the United States, and Mexico changed during the period since NAFTA was established?

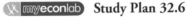 **Study Plan 32.6**

◆ You've now seen how free international trade enables all nations to gain from trade. By producing goods in which we have a comparative advantage and trading some of our production for that of others, we expand our consumption possibilities. Placing impediments on that trade decreases the gains from trade. By opening our country up to free international trade, the market for the things that we sell expands and their relative prices rise. The market for the things that we buy also expands, and their relative prices fall.

Reading Between the Lines on pp. 778–779 looks at the softwood lumber dispute between the United States and Canada. This dispute provides a clear example of the economic cost of restricting international trade.

Tariffs in Action: Lumber

TELEGRAPH–JOURNAL, OCTOBER 20, 2005

Retaliation in softwood lumber dispute not advised

Retaliating against the United States over its refusal to accept legal defeat in the softwood lumber dispute would hurt Canada more than the Americans, a Canadian forest industry spokesman says.

Instead, Canada should get more active in U.S. politics by advancing the interests of the mass of American homeowners and other lumber consumers against a small group of protectionist corporations, Carl Grenier, general manager of the Free Trade Lumber Council, said Wednesday.

"Sabre-rattling makes some people feel good, especially when it's against the U.S.," Mr. Grenier, whose group represents companies accounting for about 40 per cent of Canadian lumber shipments to America, told the Economic Club of Toronto. ...

A better approach is to "transform what has been a fight between U.S. producers and Canadian producers of softwood lumber into a fight between U.S. producers and consumers."

And although it might seem attractive to find new markets for Canadian exports—especially oil and gas for which "other customers are lining up at the pump"—Mr. Grenier noted that the North American Free Trade Agreement originated from the failure of the Trudeau government's 1970s Third Option strategy of trade diversification.

"For the foreseeable future, most of our trade eggs will stay firmly in the U.S. basket."...

Reprinted with permission from The Canadian Press.

Essence of the Story

■ It is not in Canada's interest to retaliate against the United States for the U.S. tariff on softwood imports from Canada.

■ Instead, Canada should appeal to the self-interest of American homeowners and other lumber consumers.

■ While it might seem attractive to find new markets for Canadian oil and gas exports, we must remember that NAFTA had its origin in the failure to diversify trade when Pierre Trudeau was prime minister.

■ The reality is that our trading future is with the United States.

Economic Analysis

■ The United States has imposed a 27 percent tariff on imports of Canadian lumber.

■ The tariff damages Canada, but it also damages the United States.

■ Figure 1 shows the U.S. market for lumber.

■ The demand curve of U.S. buyers of lumber is D.

■ There are two supply curves: the supply curve of the Canadian producers, S_C, and the supply curve of U.S. producers, S_{US}. We'll assume that Canada can supply any quantity at a price of $100 per load.

■ With no tariff, the quantity of lumber bought in the United States is QC_0. Of this amount, QP_0 is produced in the United States and the rest is imported from Canada, as shown by the arrow in Fig. 1.

■ Now the United States puts a 27 percent tariff on the import of lumber. Canadian lumber is now supplied to the U.S. market at the original supply price, $100, plus the tariff, $27, so the supply curve of lumber from Canada shifts to become S_C + *tariff*.

■ With the tariff, the quantity of lumber bought in the United States is QC_1. Of this amount, QP_1 is produced in the United States and the rest is imported from Canada, as shown by the arrow in Fig. 1.

■ The tariff decreases U.S. consumption and imports and increases U.S. production.

■ Figure 2 shows the winners and the losers in the United States.

■ The winners include U.S lumber producers, who gain additional producer surplus, which is shown by the blue area in Fig. 2.

■ Another winner is the U.S. government, which collects additional revenue, shown by the purple area in Fig. 2.

■ The sum of the blue, purple, and grey areas is the loss of consumer surplus that results from the tariff.

■ A deadweight loss arises—the decrease in consumer surplus exceeds the increase in producer surplus plus the tariff revenue—regardless of whether Canadian lumber producers receive a subsidy.

Figure 1 Tariffs and imports

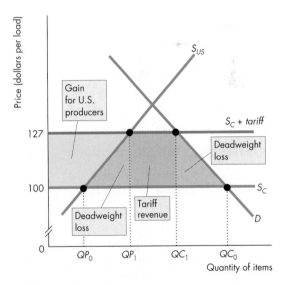

Figure 2 Winners and losers

SUMMARY

KEY POINTS

Patterns and Trends in International Trade
(p. 756)

- Large flows of trade take place between countries, most of which is in manufactured goods exchanged among rich industrialized countries.
- The volume of Canadian international trade is about 40 percent of total production.

The Gains from International Trade (pp. 757–762)

- When opportunity costs diverge, comparative advantage brings gains from trade.
- By increasing its production of goods in which it has a comparative advantage and then trading some of the increased output, a country can consume at points outside its production possibilities frontier.
- In the absence of international borrowing and lending, trade is balanced as prices adjust to reflect the international supply of and demand for goods.
- The world price balances the production and consumption plans of the trading parties. At the equilibrium price, trade is balanced.

International Trade Restrictions (pp. 763–766)

- Countries restrict international trade by imposing tariffs and nontariff barriers, such as quotas and VERS.
- International trade restrictions raise the domestic price of imported goods, lower the volume of imports, and reduce the total value of imports and exports by the same amount.

The Case Against Protection (pp. 767–771)

- Arguments that protection is necessary to save jobs, to protect infant industries, and to prevent dumping are weak.
- Arguments that protection is necessary for national security, allows us to compete with cheap foreign labour, makes the economy diversified and stable, penalizes lax environmental standards, protects national culture, and prevents exploitation of developing countries are flawed.

- Trade is restricted because tariffs raise government revenue and because protection brings a small loss to a large number of people and a large gain per person to a small number of people.

The Balance of International Payments
(pp. 772–775)

- A country's international transactions are recorded in its balance of payments accounts.
- The net exports surplus is equal to the government sector surplus plus the private sector surplus.

The North American Free Trade Agreement
(pp. 776–777)

- NAFTA is an agreement among Canada, the United States, and Mexico, which began in 1994 and grew from a previous Canada–U.S. agreement.
- Under NAFTA, trade has expanded more rapidly than before the agreement.

KEY FIGURES AND TABLE

KEY TERMS

PROBLEMS

Go to **myeconlab** for solutions to odd-numbered problems and additional exercises.

1. The table provides information about Virtual Reality's production possibilities.

TV sets (per day)		Computers (per day)
0	and	36
10	and	35
20	and	33
30	and	30
40	and	26
50	and	21
60	and	15
70	and	8
80	and	0

   a. Calculate Virtual Reality's opportunity cost of a TV set when it produces 10 sets a day.
   b. Calculate Virtual Reality's opportunity cost of a TV set when it produces 40 sets a day.
   c. Calculate Virtual Reality's opportunity cost of a TV set when it produces 70 sets a day.
   d. Using the answers to parts (a), (b), and (c), sketch the relationship between the opportunity cost of a TV set and the quantity of TV sets produced in Virtual Reality.

2. The table provides information about Vital Sign's production possibilities.

TV sets (per day)		Computers (per day)
0	and	18.0
10	and	17.5
20	and	16.5
30	and	15.0
40	and	13.0
50	and	10.5
60	and	7.5
70	and	4.0
80	and	0

   a. Calculate Vital Sign's opportunity cost of a TV set when it produces 10 sets a day.
   b. Calculate Vital Sign's opportunity cost of a TV set when it produces 40 sets a day.
   c. Calculate Vital Sign's opportunity cost of a TV set when it produces 70 sets a day.

   d. Using the answers to parts (a), (b), and (c), sketch the relationship between the opportunity cost of a TV set and the quantity of TV sets produced in Vital Sign.

3. Suppose that with no international trade, Virtual Reality in problem 1 produces and consumes 10 TV sets a day and Vital Sign in problem 2 produces and consumes 60 TV sets a day. Now suppose that the two countries begin to trade with each other.
   a. Which country exports TV sets?
   b. What adjustments are made to the amount of each good produced by each country?
   c. What adjustments are made to the amount of each good consumed by each country?
   d. What can you say about the terms of trade (the price of a TV set expressed as computers per TV set) under free trade?

4. Suppose that with no international trade, Virtual Reality in problem 1 produces and consumes 50 TV sets a day and Vital Sign in problem 2 produces and consumes 20 TV sets a day. Now suppose that the two countries begin to trade with each other.
   a. Which country exports TV sets?
   b. What adjustments are made to the amount of each good produced by each country?
   c. What adjustments are made to the amount of each good consumed by each country?
   d. What can you say about the terms of trade (the price of a TV set expressed as computers per TV set) under free trade?

5. Compare the total quantities of each good produced in problems 1 and 2 with the total quantities of each good produced in problems 3 and 4.
   a. Does free trade increase or decrease the total quantities of TV sets and computers produced in each case? Why?
   b. What happens to the price of a TV set in Virtual Reality in each case? Why does it rise in one case and fall in the other?
   c. What happens to the price of a computer in Vital Sign in each case? Why does it rise in one case and fall in the other?

6. Compare the international trade in problem 3 with that in problem 4.
   a. Why does Virtual Reality export TV sets in one case and import them in the other case?
   b. Do the TV producers or the computer producers gain in each case?
   c. Do consumers gain in each case?

7. The figure depicts the world market for soybeans. With free trade, what is the world price of soybeans, the quantities exported and imported, and the balance of trade?

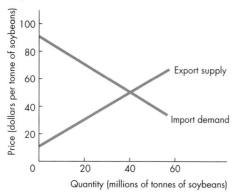

8. If in problem 7, a tariff of $20 per tonne is imposed on imported soybean, what is the world price of soybeans, the quantity of soybean imports, the price in the importing country, and the tariff revenue?

9. The Silecon, whose currency is the grain, conducted the following transactions in 2002:

Item	Billions of grains
Net exports of goods and services	250
Borrowing from the rest of the world	–60
Lending to the rest of the world	200
Change in official reserves	–10

What are the current account, capital account, and official settlements balances?

10. Spin, whose currency is the wheel, conducted the following transactions in 2002:

Item	Billions of wheels
Net exports of goods and services	20
Borrowing from the rest of the world	4
Lending to the rest of the world	24
Change in official reserves	0

What are the current account, capital account, and official settlements balances?

CRITICAL THINKING

1. Study *Reading Between the Lines* on pp. 778–779 and then answer the following questions:
   a. Why did the United States impose a tariff on lumber imports from Canada?
   b. What are the effects of the tariff on lumber?
   c. Who are the winners and who are the losers from the tariff on lumber?
   d. Modify the figures on page 779 to show the effects of a Canadian subsidy to lumber producers on the consumer surplus, producer surplus, and deadweight loss in the United States.

WEB EXERCISES

Use the links on ⓧ myeconlab to work the following exercises.

1. Visit the Web site of the World Trade Organization and obtain information about the latest round of trade talks on freeing trade in agricultural products.
   a. What is the argument for ending agricultural subsidies in rich countries?
   b. Why is the European Union so opposed to dismantling farm subsidies?
   c. Why do you think Australia and New Zealand have ended farm subsidies?
   d. What is Canada's position of farm subsidies ? What accounts for Canada's position?
2. Obtain information to write a NAFTA report card on agriculture. Then answer the following questions:
   a. What does NAFTA seek to achieve in agriculture trade?
   b. What has NAFTA achieved to date?
   c. What are the obstacles to greater gains for North American trade in agricultural products?
   d. Would you vote to maintain NAFTA? Why or why not?
   e. Would you vote to expand NAFTA to include other countries? Why or why not?

It's a Small World

The scale of international trade, borrowing, and lending, both in absolute dollar terms and as a percentage of total world production expands every year. One country, Singapore, imports and exports goods and services in a volume that exceeds its total production. The world's largest nation, China, returned to the international economic stage during the 1980s and is now a major producer of manufactured goods.

International economic activity is large because today's economic world is small and because communication is so incredibly fast. But today's world is not a new world. From the beginning of recorded history, people have traded over large and steadily increasing distances. The great Western civilizations of Greece and Rome traded not only around the Mediterranean but also into the Gulf of Arabia. The great Eastern civilizations traded around the Indian Ocean. By the Middle Ages, the East and the West were trading routinely overland on routes pioneered by Venetian traders and explorers such as Marco Polo. When, in 1497, Vasco da Gama opened a sea route between the Atlantic and Indian Oceans around Africa, a new trade between East and West began, which brought tumbling prices of Eastern goods in Western markets.

The European discovery of America and the subsequent opening up of Atlantic trade continued the process of steady globalization. So, the developments of the 1990s, amazing though many of them are, represent a continuation of an ongoing expansion of human horizons.

Chapter 32 studied the interaction of nations in today's global economy. It described and explained international trade in goods and services. In this chapter, you came face to face with one of the biggest policy issues of all ages, free trade versus protection and the globalization debate.

You saw how protection from competition brings big benefits to a few and small losses to the many. The total gains from protection are dwarfed by the total losses, but because the losses are spread thinly and the gains thickly, protectionism always has its supporters and political backers.

Chapter 32 also explained a country's balance of payments accounts and the poorly understood fact that the size of a nation's international deficit depends not on how efficient it is, but on how much its citizens save relative to how much they invest. Nations with low saving rates, everything else being the same, have international deficits.

This chapter also described Free Trade Agreement between Canada and the United States and the huge expansion in trade between the three countries of NAFTA: Canada, the United States, and Mexico.

The global economy is big news these days. And it has always attracted attention. On the next page, you can meet the economist who first understood comparative advantage, David Ricardo. And you can meet one of Canada's leading international economists, Dan Trefler of the University of Toronto.

Gains from International Trade

THE ECONOMIST

David Ricardo *(1772–1832) was a highly successful 27-year-old stockbroker when he stumbled on a copy of Adam Smith's* Wealth of Nations *(see p. 54) on a weekend visit to the country. He was immediately hooked and went on to become the most celebrated economist of his age and one of the all-time great economists. One of his many contributions was to develop the principle of comparative advantage, the foundation on which the modern theory of international trade is built. The example he used to illustrate this principle was the trade between England and Portugal in cloth and wine.*

The World Trade Organization (WTO) and its predecessor, General Agreement on Tariffs and Trade, were established as a reaction against the devastation wrought by beggar-thy-neighbour tariffs imposed during the 1930s. But the WTO and the goals that it pursues are also triumphs for the logic first worked out by Smith and Ricardo.

THE ISSUES

Until the mid-eighteenth century, it was generally believed that the purpose of international trade was to keep exports greater than imports and pile up gold. If gold was accumulated, it was believed, the nation would prosper; if gold was lost through an international deficit, the nation would be drained of money and impoverished. These beliefs are called *mercantilism*, and the *mercantilists* were pamphleteers who advocated with missionary fervor the pursuit of an international surplus. If exports did not exceed imports, the mercantilists wanted imports restricted.

In the 1740s, David Hume explained that as the quantity of money (gold) changes, so also does the price level, and the nation's *real* wealth is unaffected. In the 1770s, Adam Smith argued that import restrictions would lower the gains from specialization and make a nation poorer. Thirty years later, David Ricardo proved the law of comparative advantage and demonstrated the superiority of free trade. Mercantilism was intellectually bankrupt but remained politically powerful.

Gradually, through the nineteenth century, the mercantilist influence waned and North America and Western Europe prospered in an environment of increasingly free international trade. But despite remarkable advances in economic understanding, mercantilism never quite died. It had a brief and devastating revival in the 1920s and 1930s when tariff hikes brought about the collapse of international trade and accentuated the Great Depression. It subsided again after World War II with the establishment of the General Agreement on Tariffs and Trade (GATT).

But mercantilism lingers on. The often-expressed view that the United States should restrict Chinese imports and reduce its deficit with China and the fear that NAFTA will bring economic ruin to Canada are modern manifestations of mercantilism. It would be interesting to have David Hume, Adam Smith, and David Ricardo commenting on these views. But we know what they would say—the same things that they said to the eighteenth-century mercantilists. And they would still be right today.

THEN

In the eighteenth century, when mercantilists and economists were debating the pros and cons of free international exchange, the transportation technology that was available limited the gains from international trade. Sailing ships with tiny cargo holds took close to a month to cross the Atlantic Ocean. But the potential gains were large, and so was the incentive to cut shipping costs. By the 1850s, the clipper ship had been developed, cutting the journey from Boston to Liverpool to only $12\frac{1}{4}$ days. Half a century later, 10,000-ton steamships were sailing between North America and England in just 4 days. As sailing times and costs declined, the gains from international trade increased and the volume of trade expanded.

NOW

The container ship has revolutionized international trade and contributed to its continued expansion. Today, most goods cross the oceans in containers—metal boxes—packed into and piled on top of ships like this one. Container technology has cut the cost of ocean shipping by economizing on handling and by making cargoes harder to steal, thereby lowering insurance costs. It is unlikely that there would be much international trade in goods such as television sets and DVD players without this technology. High-value and perishable cargoes such as flowers and fresh foods, as well as urgent courier packages, travel by air. Every day, dozens of cargo-laden 747s fly between every major North American city and to destinations across the Atlantic and Pacific oceans.

Dan Trefler, whom you can meet on the following pages, is one of Canada's the most distinguished international trade economists. He has contributed to our understanding of the effects of international trade and trade policy on economic growth and development and today's global trading arrangements.

TALKING WITH

Dan Trefler is the J. Douglas and Ruth Grant Canada Research Chair in Competitiveness and Prosperity at the University of Toronto's Rotman School of Management. Born in Toronto, he was an undergraduate at the University of Toronto and a graduate student at Cambridge University and the University of California, Los Angeles.

Professor Trefler is a Research Fellow at the Canadian Institute for Advanced Research and a Research Associate at the National Bureau of Economic Research. He also serves on the Ontario Task Force on Competitiveness, Productivity, and Economic Progress. He was the winner of the Canadian Economics Association's Rae Award for Excellence in Research and is a co-editor of the Journal of International Economics. Professor Trefler's research is broad but focuses on policy levers for promoting Canadian competitiveness.

Dan Trefler

Michael Parkin and Robin Bade talked with Dan Trefler about his work and the light that it sheds on international trade issues such as offshoring and NAFTA.

Dan, what attracted you to economics?

Throughout my life, including when I was a teenager, I've been interested in how social systems work and what makes some societies so much more successful than others.

Economics offers one of several perspectives on that question. What is so nice about the economic perspective is that it tries to combine a whole bunch of nifty theories about what makes a society successful with evidence-based data-driven analysis that is often lacking in other approaches.

So why is it that Africa has done so poorly over the years? We often use very vague terms like colonial heritage or poor institutions, but if you gave me a large-scale database to analyze the problem, I'd be like a pig at the trough, delighted to really think about it.

Why did you decide to focus on international economics?

In part, because of a profound interest in development economics, which is so tightly linked to international trade. But more specifically, as a young man just starting out in economics, the hot topic of the day was the 1988 General Election which was fought on the issue of should Canada have a free trade agreement with the United States, after more than 100 years of protectionism.

Who has had the greatest influence on your development as an economist?

Again, as a teenager I was thinking about society in political science and sociological terms until I read a book by Che Guevara (now back in fashion), who said that if you really want to understand society you have to understand economics. The best place to think about that is to be doing things like reading the *Wall Street Journal*, and from there it was downhill. I was completely entranced by the economic approach.

Why should Canadians care about international trade?

Because it is where little things make a big difference. I think most of us would like to think that we have solutions to all of society's problems, which are magic bullets. In fact, the way to make Canada an even greater place is to make it even a little bit more productive, say 10 to15 percent more productive. Even a 10 percent increase in our productivity would generate for us upwards of $100 billion in revenue to play with. With $100 billion, think of what you could do. You could, if you're a new conservative, eliminate all corporate taxes, which would cost maybe about $25 billion. If you were very left leaning, you could pour huge amounts of money into single moms, natives, immigrants, and male high school dropouts—the four poorest groups in our country.

> " *Little things make a big difference. ... Even a 10 percent increase in our productivity would generate for us upwards of $100 billion in revenue to play with. ... Interntional trade is one of the biggest drivers of productivity.* "

You would have plenty of money left to drive an agenda for children if you were so inclined; lots of money left for redistributing to our have-not provinces like Newfoundland. You could run every single one of these things that I've mentioned at a cadillac level of service or delivery with $100 billion.

So worrying about productivity is really worrying about how we're going to feed our social agenda. And then that's where trade comes in. International trade is one of the biggest drivers of productivity, and it does so in two ways. First, it pressures our companies to become more innovative than they ever have been; and second, it supports our companies by providing them with the possibility of accessing larger markets, say like the U.S. market or the Chinese market.

So I think about international trade as a way of pressuring firms to be more competitive and in supporting them in entering the foreign markets.

Let's talk about the aspect of international economic activity that scares most people: offshoring. First, is it really new, or has it been around a long time? Or, what is new about it?

You know I read recently in the back of a news magazine an advertisement saying "offshore your personal life." They provided dating services for people!

We hear a lot of hype around offshoring. There are two aspects of it that are new. One is that the pace at which we are seeing manufacturing rise in low-wage countries like China is really breathtaking. That's both wonderful and scary. It's wonderful for these poor countries, which are suddenly finding themselves to be more affluent. It's a little scary for Canadian workers in the manufacturing sector.

The other aspect that is really fundamentally new and we've never seen it before is the tradability of services. The idea that somebody sitting in, say, Bangalore, India, is providing services to us is truly remarkable. And it speaks to the word "globalization" in a way that I think no other statement does. Nothing like that has ever been seen in history.

How big is the offshoring of services?

The Bangalore example turned out to be the exception to the rule. First of all, offshoring is not that large. There are different ways of doing the accounting, but if you think about offshoring of services, which is not all of offshoring, it accounts for only about 10 percent of our international trade. It's a small amount though it is growing fast and that's why people are so interested in it.

The second aspect of offshoring of services is that 85 percent of it goes to other rich countries, like the United States, so only a small portion of it is with countries like India. But that is changing rapidly. So right now, it's not important. Where we'll be in the future, that's another question.

What are the effects of offshoring on unemployment and wages?

The unemployment rate fluctuates for reasons that have very little to do with international trade. That is very obvious if you just plot the data.

787

Offshoring does have an impact on wages, but much less of an impact than people think. There is a small group of people out there, maybe less than 5 percent of the population, who has been hammered by international trade, seeing their jobs displaced and wages absolutely collapse under the weight to Chinese competition. That is the exception.

The interesting thing about offshoring of services is what impact it will have on wages because now we're seeing international trade affecting the wages of the very skilled. That is something new. That is not something we've ever seen before. It is too early to say for sure what the impacts are but the early research suggests that it will have a very large impact on wages and a moderate impact on employment.

Let's now turn to another big source of discussion and concern: NAFTA. What is the latest tally on its benefits and costs?

NAFTA was my teething grounds in economics—I spent years and years studying it. There are many aspects of it that interest people. Let's start with the narrowest and simplest and that is its affect on employment, wages, and productivity. NAFTA has had a large effect on displacing workers. That is, the shipping of workers from low value-added activities, activities that were once protected, into higher value-added activities. Some workers were definitely displaced. And it hurts if you're unemployed for six months, looking for a new job. That's a big hit.

There's been absolutely no affect of the free trade agreement on wages, which to me was a big surprise since I was expecting that we would be competing with labour from south of the Mason-Dixon Line in the United States.

The surprise has been the huge impact on productivity and that impact has been upward of 6 percent for manufacturing as a whole, which is a very, very large number. The idea that a single government policy like liberalizing trade could have such a big impact on productivity is to me remarkable and a testament to what government can do when it puts its mind to it.

> " *The surprise has been the huge impact [of NAFTA] on productivity ... upward of 6 percent for manufacturing as a whole.* "

> " *Become informed so you know exactly why you're demonstrating.* "

Now there is also a larger issue about what is sometimes called the "Trade and ..." agenda, which deals with things like the environment and sovereignty issues where we retain our rights over water and so on. Those have turned out so far to be a non-issue.

What advice do you have for a student who is just starting to study economics? Is economics a good subject in which to major?

Economics works extremely well with the social sciences. It works with sociology, it works with political science, and it's starting to work with areas that are more surprising, which is psychology and the natural sciences; we're getting an increased insight in that area. What advice do I have? It would be to read a lot. Becoming knowledgeable is the best way to have fun.

What would you suggest students read?

Read books, read books. People all around you are writing books that are acceptable to very general audiences. Go out and read some books on neuroscience and economics, or sociology and economics, or political science. If you're interested in economic development, read books about the new institutionalism. If you're interested in international trade, read Helpman's *The Mystery of Economic Growth* or Jared Diamond's *Guns, Germs, and Steel*. Or if you're interested in something more historical, read David S. Landes, *The Wealth and Poverty of Nations*.

What can a student do to make a difference?

When it comes to international trade, it's very important to know that you have a huge impact through activism, that you can do it through going out there and demonstrating on the lines every time there is an international trade agreement. But it's important to become informed so that you know exactly why you're out there demonstrating.

You can also make a difference through consumer activism—that is things like eco-labelling, insisting on it or making the effort to try to find out where the goods that you use are produced, or even something simple like going to Second Cup or Starbucks and saying "what you're doing for fair trade in coffee is not nearly enough, you could do a lot more."

GLOSSARY

Absolute advantage A person has an absolute advantage if that person is more productive than another person. (p. 42)

After-tax income Total income minus tax payments by households to governments. (p. 420)

Allocative efficiency A situation in which we cannot produce more of any good without giving up some of another good that we *value more highly*. (p. 39)

Anti-combine law A law that regulates and prohibits certain kinds of market behaviour, such as monopoly and monopolistic practices. (p. 326)

Average cost pricing rule A rule that sets price to cover cost including normal profit, which means setting the price equal to average total cost. (pp. 279, 329)

Average fixed cost Total fixed cost per unit of output. (p. 226)

Average product The average product of a factor of production. It equals total product divided by the quantity of the factor employed. (p. 221)

Average tax rate The percentage of income that is paid in tax. (p. 431)

Average total cost Total cost per unit of output. (p. 226)

Average variable cost Total variable cost per unit of output. (p. 226)

Barriers to entry Legal or natural constraints that protect a firm from potential competitors. (p. 264)

Big tradeoff The conflict between equity and efficiency. (pp. 10, 115, 433)

Bilateral monopoly A situation in which a single seller (a monopoly) faces a single buyer (a monopsony). (p. 417)

Black market An illegal trading arrangement in which the price exceeds the legally imposed price ceiling. (p. 126)

Budget line The limits to a household's consumption choices. (p. 172)

Capital The tools, equipment, buildings, and other constructions that businesses now use to produce goods and services. (p. 4)

Capital accumulation The growth of capital resources, which includes human capital. (p. 40)

Capture theory A theory of regulation that states that the regulations are supplied to satisfy the demand of producers to maximize producer surplus—to maximize economic profit. (p. 327)

Cartel A group of firms that has entered into a collusive agreement to restrict output and increase prices and profits. (p. 297)

Ceteris paribus Other things being equal—all other relevant things remaining the same. (p. 13)

Change in demand A change in buyers' plans that occurs when some influence on those plans other than the price of the good changes. It is illustrated by a shift of the demand curve. (p. 62)

Change in supply A change in sellers' plans that occurs when some influence on those plans other than the price of the good changes. It is illustrated by a shift of the supply curve. (p. 67)

Change in the quantity demanded A change in buyers' plans that occurs when the price of a good changes but all other influences on buyers' plans remain unchanged. It is illustrated by a movement along the demand curve. (p. 65)

Change in the quantity supplied A change in sellers' plans that occurs when the price of a good changes but all other influences on sellers' plans remain unchanged. It is illustrated by a movement along the supply curve. (p. 68)

Coase theorem The proposition that if property rights exist, if only a small number of parties are involved, and transactions costs are low, then private transactions are efficient. (p. 351)

Collusive agreement An agreement between two (or more) producers to restrict output, raise the price, and increase profits. (p. 302)

Command system A method of organizing production that uses a managerial hierarchy—resources are allocated by order (command) of someone in authority. (pp. 104, 203)

Common resource A resource that is rival and nonexcludable. (p. 364)

Comparative advantage A person or country has a comparative advantage in an activity if that person or country can perform the activity at a lower opportunity cost than anyone else or any other country. (p. 42)

Competitive market A market that has many buyers and many sellers, so no single buyer or seller can influence the price. (p. 60)

Complement A good that is used in conjunction with another good. (p. 63)

Constant returns to scale Features of a firm's technology that lead to constant long-run average cost as output increases. When constant returns to scale are present, the *LRAC* curve is horizontal. (p. 233)

Consumer equilibrium A situation in which a consumer has allocated all his or her available income in the way that, given the prices of goods and services, maximizes his or her total utility. (p. 158)

Consumer surplus The value of a good minus the price paid for it, summed over the quantity bought. (p. 107)

Contestable market A market in which firms can enter and leave so easily that firms in the market face competition from potential entrants. (p. 310)

Cooperative equilibrium The outcome of a game in which the players make and share the monopoly profit. (p. 309)

Copyright A government-sanctioned exclusive right granted to the inventor of a good, service, or productive process to produce, use, and sell the invention for a given number of years. (p. 357)

Cross elasticity of demand The responsiveness of the demand for a good to a change in the price of a substitute or complement, other things remaining the same. It is calculated as the percentage change in the quantity demanded of the good divided by the percentage change in the price of the substitute or complement. (p. 91)

Cross-section graph A graph that shows the values of an economic variable for different groups in a population at a point in time. (p. 18)

Crown Corporation A publicly owned firm in Canada. (p. 326)

Deadweight loss A measure of inefficiency. It is equal to the decrease in consumer surplus and producer surplus that results from an inefficient level of production. (p. 111)

Demand The relationship between the quantity of a good that consumers plan to buy and the price of the good when all other influences on buyers' plans remain the same. It is described by a demand schedule and illustrated by a demand curve. (p. 61)

Demand curve A curve that shows the relationship between the quantity demanded of a good and its price when all other influences on consumers' planned purchases remain the same. (p. 62)

Derived demand Demand for a factor of production, which is derived from the demand for the goods and services produced by that factor. (p. 388)

Diminishing marginal rate of substitution The general tendency for a person to be willing to give up less of good *y* to get one more unit of good *x*, and at the same time remain indifferent, as the quantity of good *x* increases. (p. 176)

Diminishing marginal returns The tendency for the marginal product of an additional unit of a factor of production to be less than the marginal product of the previous unit of the factor. (p. 223)

Diminishing marginal utility The decrease in marginal utility as the quantity consumed increases. (p. 156)

Direct relationship A relationship between two variables that move in the same direction. (p. 20)

Discounting The conversion of a future amount of money to its present value. (p. 398)

Diseconomies of scale Features of a firm's technology that lead to rising long-run average cost as output increases. (p. 232)

Dominant strategy equilibrium A Nash equilibrium in which the best strategy for each player is to cheat (deny) regardless of the strategy of the other player. (p. 308)

Dumping The sale by a foreign firm of exports at a lower price than the cost of production. (p. 768)

Duopoly A market structure in which two producers of a good or service compete. (p. 296)

Dynamic comparative advantage A comparative advantage that a person or country possesses as a result of having specialized in a particular activity and then, as a result of learning-by-doing, having become the producer with the lowest opportunity cost. (p. 45)

Earnings sharing regulation A regulation that if a firm's profits rise above a target level, they must be shared with the firm's customers. (p. 332)

Economic depreciation The change in the market value of capital over a given period. (p. 198)

Economic efficiency A situation that occurs when the firm produces a given output at the least cost. (p. 201)

Economic growth The expansion of production possibilities that results from capital accumulation and technological change. (p. 40)

Economic model A description of some aspect of the economic world that includes only those features of the world that are needed for the purpose at hand. (p. 12)

Economic profit A firm's total revenue minus its opportunity cost. (p. 199)

Economic rent The income received by the owner of a factor of production over and above the amount required to induce that owner to offer the factor for use. (p. 406)

Economics The social science that studies the choices that we make as we cope with *scarcity* and the *incentives* that influence and reconcile those choices. (p. 2)

Economic theory A generalization that summarizes what we think we understand about the economic choices that people make and the performance of industries and entire economies. (p. 12)

Economies of scale Features of a firm's technology that lead to a falling long-run average cost as output increases. (pp. 213, 232)

Economies of scope Decreases in average total cost that occur when a firm uses specialized resources to produce a range of goods and services. (p. 213)

Elastic demand Demand with a price elasticity greater than 1; other things remaining the same, the percentage change in the quantity demanded exceeds the percentage change in price. (p. 87)

Elasticity of supply The responsiveness of the quantity supplied of a good to a change in its price, other things remaining the same. (p. 94)

Entrepreneurship The human resource that organizes the other three factors of production: labour, land, and capital. (p. 4)

Equilibrium price The price at which the quantity demanded equals the quantity supplied. (p. 70)

Equilibrium quantity The quantity bought and sold at the equilibrium price. (p. 70)

Excludable A good or service or a resource is excludable if it is possible to prevent someone from enjoying the benefit of it. (p. 364)

Exports The goods and services that we sell to people in other countries. (p. 756)

External diseconomies Factors outside the control of a firm that raise the firm's costs as the industry produces a larger output. (p. 253)

External economies Factors beyond the control of a firm that lower the firm's costs as the industry produces a larger output. (p. 253)

Externality A cost or a benefit that arises from production and falls on someone other than the producer, or a cost or a benefit that arises from consumption and falls on someone other than the consumer. (p. 346)

Factors of production The resources used to produce goods and services. (p. 3)

Farm marketing board A regulatory agency that intervenes in an agricultural market to stabilize the price of an agricultural product. (p. 138)

Firm An economic unit that hires factors of production and organizes those factors to produce and sell goods and services. (pp. 45, 198)

Four-firm concentration ratio A measure of market power that is calculated as the percentage of the value of sales accounted for by the four largest firms in an industry. (p. 208)

Free-rider problem The absence of an incentive for people to pay for what they consume. (p. 364)

Game theory A tool that economists use to analyze strategic behaviour—behaviour that takes into account the expected behaviour of others and the recognition of mutual interdependence. (p. 300)

General Agreement on Tariffs and Trade An international agreement signed in 1947 to reduce tariffs on international trade. (p. 763)

Goods and services All the objects that people value and produce to satisfy their wants. (p. 3)

Government failure A situation in which government actions result in inefficiency. (p. 325)

Herfindahl–Hirschman Index A measure of market power that is calculated as the square of the market share of each firm (as a percentage) summed over the largest 50 firms (or over all firms if there are fewer than 50) in a market. (p. 208)

Human capital The knowledge and skill that people obtain from education, on-the-job training, and work experience. (p. 3)

Implicit rental rate The firm's opportunity cost of using its own capital. (p. 198)

Imports The goods and services that we buy from people in other countries. (p. 756)

Incentive A reward that encourages or a penalty that discourages an action. (p. 2)

Incentive system A method of organizing production that uses a market-like mechanism inside the firm. (p. 203)

Income effect The effect of a change in income on consumption, other things remaining the same. (p. 180)

Income elasticity of demand The responsiveness of demand to a change in income, other things remaining the same. It is calculated as the percentage change in the quantity demanded divided by the percentage change in income. (p. 92)

Indifference curve A line that shows combinations of goods among which a consumer is indifferent. (p. 175)

Individual transferable quota (ITQ) A production limit that is assigned to an individual who is free to transfer the quota to someone else. (p. 374)

Inelastic demand A demand with a price elasticity between 0 and 1; the percentage change in the quantity demanded is less than the percentage change in price. (p. 87)

Infant-industry argument The argument that it is necessary to protect a new industry to enable it to grow into a mature industry that can compete in world markets. (p. 767)

Inferior good A good for which demand decreases as income increases. (p. 64)

Intellectual property rights Property rights for discoveries owned by the creators of knowledge. (p. 357)

Interest The income that capital earns. (p. 4)

Inverse relationship A relationship between variables that move in opposite directions. (p. 21)

Labour The work time and work effort that people devote to producing goods and services. (p. 3)

Labour union An organized group of workers whose purpose is to increase wages and to influence other job conditions. (p. 413)

Land All the gifts of nature that we use to produce goods and services. (p. 3)

Law of demand Other things remaining the same, the higher the price of a good, the smaller is the quantity demanded of it. (p. 61)

Law of diminishing returns As a firm uses more of a variable input, with a given quantity of other inputs (fixed inputs), the marginal product of the variable input eventually diminishes. (p. 223)

Law of supply Other things remaining the same, the higher the price of a good, the greater is the quantity supplied of it. (p. 66)

Learning-by-doing People become more productive in an activity (learn) just by repeatedly producing a particular good or service (doing). (p. 45)

Legal monopoly A market structure in which there is one firm and entry is restricted by the granting of a public franchise, government licence, patent, or copyright. (p. 264)

Limit pricing The practice of setting the price at the highest level that inflicts a loss on an entrant. (p. 311)

Linear relationship A relationship between two variables that is illustrated by a straight line. (p. 20)

Living wage An hourly wage rate that enables a person who works a 40-hour work week to rent adequate housing for not more than 30 percent of the amount earned. (p. 131)

Long run A period of time in which the quantities of all resources can be varied. (p. 220)

Long-run average cost curve The relationship between the lowest attainable average total cost and output when both plant size and labour are varied. (p. 231)

Long-run industry supply curve A curve that shows how the quantity supplied by an industry varies as the market price varies after all the possible adjustments have been made, including changes in plant size and the number of firms in the industry. (p. 253)

Lorenz curve A curve that graphs the cumulative percentage of income or wealth against the cumulative percentage of households. (p. 421)

Low-income cutoff The income level, determined separately for different types of families (for example, single persons, couples, one parent) that is selected such that families with incomes below that limit normally spend 55 percent or more of their income on food, shelter, and clothing. (p. 424)

Macroeconomics The study of the performance of the national economy and the global economy. (p. 2)

Margin When a choice is changed by a small amount or by a little at a time, the choice is made at the margin. (p. 11)

Marginal benefit The benefit that a person receives from consuming one more unit of a good or service. It is measured as the maximum amount that a person is willing to pay for one more unit of the good or service. (pp. 11, 38)

Marginal benefit curve A curve that shows the relationship between the marginal benefit of a good and the quantity of that good consumed. (p. 38)

Marginal cost The opportunity cost of producing one more unit of a good or service. It is the best alternative forgone. It is calculated as the increase in total cost divided by the increase in output. (pp. 11, 37, 226)

Marginal cost pricing rule A rule that sets the price of a good or service equal to the marginal cost of producing it. (pp. 278, 329)

Marginal external benefit The benefit from an additional unit of a good or service that people other than the consumer enjoy. (p. 353)

Marginal external cost The cost of producing an additional unit of a good or service that falls on people other than the producer. (p. 349)

Marginal private benefit The benefit from an additional unit of a good or service that the consumer of that good or service receives. (p. 353)

Marginal private cost The cost of producing an additional unit of a good or service that is borne by the producer of that good or service. (p. 349)

Marginal product The increase in total product that results from a one-unit increase in the variable input, with all other inputs remaining the same. It is calculated as the increase in total product divided by the increase in the variable input employed, when the quantities of all other inputs are constant. (p. 221)

Marginal rate of substitution The rate at which a person will give up good y (the good measured on the y-axis) to get an additional unit of good x (the good measured on the x-axis) and at the same time remain

Payoff matrix A table that shows the payoffs for every possible action by each player for every possible action by each other player. (p. 300)

Perfect competition A market in which there are many firms each selling an identical product; there are many buyers; there are no restrictions on entry into the industry; firms in the industry have no advantage over potential new entrants; and firms and buyers are well informed about the price of each firm's product. (pp. 207, 240)

Perfectly elastic demand Demand with an infinite price elasticity; the quantity demanded changes by an infinitely large percentage in response to a tiny price change. (p. 87)

Perfectly inelastic demand Demand with a price elasticity of zero; the quantity demanded remains constant when the price changes. (p. 86)

Perfect price discrimination Price discrimination that extracts the entire consumer surplus. (p. 275)

Pigovian taxes Taxes that are used as an incentive for producers to cut back on an activity that creates an external cost. (p. 352)

Political equilibrium The outcome that results from the choices of voters, firms, politicians, and bureaucrats. (p. 326)

Positive externality An externality that arises from either production or consumption and that provides an external benefit. (p. 346)

Positive relationship A relationship between two variables that move in the same direction. (p. 20)

Poverty A state in which a household's income is too low to be able to buy the quantities of food, shelter, and clothing that are deemed necessary. (p. 424)

Preferences A description of a person's likes and dislikes. (p. 38)

Present value The amount of money that, if invested today, will grow to be as large as a given future amount when the interest that it will earn is taken into account. (p. 398)

Price cap regulation A regulation that specifies the highest price that the firm is permitted to set. (p. 330)

Price ceiling A regulation that makes it illegal to charge a price higher than a specified level. (p. 125)

Price discrimination The practice of selling different units of a good or service for different prices or of charging one customer different prices for different quantities bought. (p. 265)

Price effect The effect of a change in the price on the quantity of a good consumed, other things remaining the same. (p. 179)

Price elasticity of demand A units-free measure of the responsiveness of the quantity demanded of a good to a change in its price, when all other influences on buyers' plans remain the same. (p. 84)

Price floor A regulation that makes it illegal to charge a price lower than a specified level. (p. 130)

Price taker A firm that cannot influence the price of the good or service it produces. (p. 240)

Principal–agent problem The problem of devising compensation rules that induce an agent to act in the best interest of a principal. (p. 204)

Principle of minimum differentiation The tendency for competitors to make themselves identical as they try to appeal to the maximum number of clients or voters. (p. 367)

Private good A good or service that is both rival and excludable. (p. 364)

Producer surplus The price of a good minus the opportunity cost of producing it, summed over the quantity sold. (p. 109)

Product differentiation Making a product slightly different from the product of a competing firm. (pp. 207, 286)

Production efficiency A situation in which the economy cannot produce more of one good without producing less of some other good. (p. 35)

Production possibilities frontier The boundary between the combinations of goods and services that can be produced and the combinations that cannot. (p. 34)

Production quota An upper limit to the quantity of a good that may be produced in a specified period. (p. 139)

Profit The income earned by entrepreneurship. (p. 4)

Progressive income tax A tax on income at an average rate that increases with the level of income. (p. 431)

Property rights Social arrangements that govern the ownership, use, and disposal of resources or factors of production, goods, and services that are enforceable in the courts. (pp. 46, 350)

Proportional income tax A tax on income at a constant average rate, regardless of the level of income. (p. 431)

Public good A good or service that is both nonrival and nonexcludable—it can be consumed simultaneously by everyone and from which no one can be excluded. (p. 364)

Public provision The production of a good or service by a public authority that receives its revenue from the government. (p. 355)

Quantity demanded The amount of a good or service that consumers plan to buy during a given time period at a particular price. (p. 61)

Quantity supplied The amount of a good or service that producers plan to sell during a given time period at a particular price. (p. 66)

Quota A quantitative restriction on the import of a particular good, which specifies the maximum

indifferent (remain on the same indifference curve). (p. 176)

Marginal revenue The change in total revenue that results from a one-unit increase in the quantity sold. It is calculated as the change in total revenue divided by the change in quantity sold. (p. 240)

Marginal revenue product The change in total revenue that results from employing one more unit of a factor of production (labour) while the quantity of all other factors remains the same. It is calculated as the increase in total revenue divided by the increase in the quantity of the factor (labour). (p. 390)

Marginal social benefit The marginal benefit enjoyed by society—by the consumer of a good or service (marginal private benefit) plus the marginal benefit enjoyed by others (marginal external benefit). (p. 353)

Marginal social cost The marginal cost incurred by the entire society—by the producer and by everyone else on whom the cost falls— and is the sum of marginal private cost and marginal external cost. (p. 349)

Marginal utility The change in total utility resulting from a one-unit increase in the quantity of a good consumed. (p. 156)

Marginal utility per dollar The marginal utility from a good divided by its price. (p. 158)

Market Any arrangement that enables buyers and sellers to get information and to do business with each other. (p. 46)

Market failure A state in which the market does not allocate resources efficiently. (p. 324)

Market income The wages, interest, rent, and profit earned in factor markets and before paying income taxes. (p. 420)

Market power The ability to influence the market, and in particular the market price, by influencing the total quantity offered for sale. (p. 264)

Microeconomics The study of the choices that individuals and businesses make, the way these choices interact, and the influence governments exert on them. (p. 2)

Minimum efficient scale The smallest quantity of output at which the long-run average cost curve reaches its lowest level. (p. 233)

Minimum wage A regulation that makes the hiring of labour below a specified wage rate illegal. (p. 130)

Money Any commodity or token that is generally acceptable as the means of payment. (p. 46)

Money price The number of dollars that must be given up in exchange for a good or service. (p. 60)

Monopolistic competition A market structure in which a large number of firms compete by making similar but slightly different products. (pp. 207, 286)

Monopoly A market structure in which there is one firm, which produces a good or service that has no close substitutes and in which the firm is protected from competition by a barrier preventing the entry of new firms. (pp. 207, 264)

Monopsony A market in which there is a single buyer. (p. 416)

Nash equilibrium The outcome of a game that occurs when player A takes the best possible action given the action of player B and player B takes the best possible action given the action of player A. (p. 301)

Natural monopoly A monopoly that occurs when one firm can supply the entire market at a lower price than two or more firms can. (p. 264)

Negative externality An externality that arises from either production or consumption and that imposes an external cost. (p. 346)

Negative relationship A relationship between variables that move in opposite directions. (p. 21)

Net exports The value of exports minus the value of imports. (p. 756)

Net present value The present value of the future flow of marginal revenue product generated by capital minus the cost of the capital. (p. 400)

Nonexcludable A good or service or a resource is nonexcludable if it is impossible (or extremely costly) to prevent someone from benefiting from it. (p. 364)

Nonrenewable natural resources Natural resources that can be used only once and that cannot be replaced once they have been used. (p. 403)

Nonrival A good or service or a resource is nonrival if its use by one person does not decrease the quantity available for someone else. (p. 364)

Nontariff barrier Any action other than a tariff that restricts international trade. (p. 763)

Normal good A good for which demand increases as income increases. (p. 64)

Normal profit The expected return for supplying entrepreneurial ability. (p. 199)

North American Free Trade Agreement An agreement, which became effective on January 1, 1994, to eliminate all barriers to international trade between the United States, Canada, and Mexico after a 15-year phasing-in period. (p. 764)

Oligopoly A market structure in which a small number of firms compete. (pp. 207, 296)

Opportunity cost The highest-valued alternative that we give up to get something. (p. 10)

Patent A government-sanctioned exclusive right granted to the inventor of a good, service, or productive process to produce, use, and sell the invention for a given number of years. (p. 357) amount that can be imported in a given time period. (p. 766)

Rand Formula A requirement that all workers represented by a union must pay union dues, whether they join the union or not. (p. 413)

Rate of return regulation A regulation that requires the firm to justify its price by showing that the price enables it to earn a specified target percent return on its capital. (p. 330)

Rational ignorance The decision not to acquire information because the cost of doing so exceeds the expected benefit. (p. 368)

Real income A household's income expressed as a quantity of goods that the household can afford to buy. (p. 173)

Regressive income tax A tax on income at an average rate that decreases with the level of income. (p. 431)

Regulation Rules administered by a government agency to influence economic activity by determining price, product standards and types, and conditions under which a new firm may enter an industry. (p. 326)

Relative price The ratio of the price of one good or service to the price of another good or service. A relative price is an opportunity cost. (pp. 60, 154, 173)

Renewable natural resources Natural resources that can be used repeatedly without depleting what is available for future use. (p. 403)

Rent The income that land earns. (p. 4)

Rent ceiling A regulation that makes it illegal to charge a rent higher than a specified level. (p. 125)

Rent seeking Any attempt to capture a consumer surplus, a producer surplus, or an economic profit. (p. 272)

Rival A good or service or a resource is rival if its use by one person decreases the quantity available for someone else. (p. 364)

Scarcity The state in which the resources available are insufficient to satisfy people's wants. (p. 2)

Scatter diagram A diagram that plots the value of one variable against the value of another. (p. 19)

Search activity The time spent looking for someone with whom to do business. (p. 126)

Self-interest The choices that you think are best for you. (p. 5)

Short run The short run in microeconomics has two meanings. For the firm, it is the period of time in which the quantity of at least one input is fixed and the quantities of the other inputs can be varied. The fixed input is usually capital—that is, the firm has a given plant size. For the industry, the short run is the period of time in which each firm has a given plant size and the number of firms in the industry is fixed. (p. 220)

Short-run industry supply curve A curve that shows the quantity supplied by the industry at each price when the plant size of each firm and the number of firms in the industry remain the same. (p. 247)

Shutdown point The output and price at which the firm just covers its total variable cost. In the short run, the firm is indifferent between producing the profit-maximizing output and shutting down temporarily. (p. 246)

Signal An action taken by an informed person (or firm) to send a message to uninformed people. (p. 294)

Single-price monopoly A monopoly that must sell each unit of its output for the same price to all its customers. (p. 265)

Slope The change in the value of the variable measured on the y-axis divided by the change in the value of the variable measured on the x-axis. (p. 24)

Social interest Choices that are the best for society as a whole. (p. 5)

Social interest theory A theory that politicians supply the regulation that achieves an efficient allocation of resources. (p. 327)

Strategies All the possible actions of each player in a game. (p. 300)

Subsidy A payment that the government makes to private producers. (pp. 138, 356)

Substitute A good that can be used in place of another good. (p. 63)

Substitution effect The effect of a change in price of a good or service on the quantity bought when the consumer (hypothetically) remains indifferent between the original and the new consumption situations—that is, the consumer remains on the same indifference curve. (p. 181)

Sunk cost The past cost of buying a plant that has no resale value. (p. 220)

Supply The relationship between the quantity of a good that producers plan to sell and the price of the good when all other influences on producers' plans remain the same. It is described by a supply schedule and illustrated by a supply curve. (p. 66)

Supply curve A curve that shows the relationship between the quantity supplied and the price of a good when all other influences on producers' planned sales remain the same. (p. 66)

Symmetry principle A requirement that people in similar situations be treated similarly. (p. 116)

Tariff A tax that is imposed by the importing country when an imported good crosses its international boundary. (p. 763)

Tax incidence The division of the burden of the tax between the buyer and the seller. (p. 132)

Technological change The development of new goods and of better ways of producing goods and services. (p. 40)

Technological efficiency A situation that occurs when the firm produces a given output by using the least amount of inputs. (p. 201)

Technology Any method of producing a good or service. (p. 200)

Terms of trade The quantity of goods and services that a country exports to pay for its imports of goods and services. (p. 758)

Time-series graph A graph that measures time (for example, months or years) on the *x*-axis and the variable or variables in which we are interested on the *y*-axis. (p. 18)

Total cost The cost of all the productive resources that a firm uses. (p. 225)

Total fixed cost The cost of the firm's fixed inputs. (p. 225)

Total income Market income plus cash payments to households by governments. (p. 420)

Total product The total output produced by a firm in a given period of time. (p. 221)

Total revenue The value of a firm's sales. It is calculated as the price of the good multiplied by the quantity sold. (pp. 88, 240)

Total revenue test A method of estimating the price elasticity of demand by observing the change in total revenue that results from a change in the price, when all other influences on the quantity sold remain the same. (p. 88)

Total utility The total benefit that a person gets from the consumption of goods and services. (p. 156)

Total variable cost The cost of all the firm's variable inputs. (p. 225)

Tradeoff A constraint that involves giving up one thing to get something else. (p. 9)

Transactions costs The costs that arise from finding someone with whom to do business, of reaching an agreement about the price and other aspects of the exchange, and of ensuring that the terms of the agreement are fulfilled. The opportunity costs of conducting a transaction. (pp. 113, 212, 351)

Trend The general tendency for a variable to move in one direction. (p. 18)

Unit elastic demand Demand with a price elasticity of 1; the percentage change in the quantity demanded equals the percentage change in price. (p. 86)

Utilitarianism A principle that states that we should strive to achieve "the greatest happiness for the greatest number of people." (p. 114)

Utility The benefit or satisfaction that a person gets from the consumption of a good or service. (p. 156)

Voluntary export restraint An agreement between two governments in which the government of the exporting country agrees to restrain the volume of its own exports. (p. 766)

Voucher A token that the government provides to households, which they can use to buy specified goods and services. (p. 356)

Wages The income that labour earns. (p. 4)

World Trade Organization An international organization that places greater obligations on its member countries to observe the GATT rules. (p. 763)

INDEX

Note: Key terms and the pages on which they are defined are bolded. References to "*f*" denote a figure and "*t*" denote a table.